MW00782369

ODE

TO

KIRIHITO

PART ONE

OSAMU TEZUKA

VERTICAL.

TRANSLATION—CAMELLIA NIEH
PRODUCTION—HIROKO MIZUNO
SHINOBU SATO

PUBLISHED BY VERTICAL, INC., NEW YORK.

ORIGINALLY SERIALIZED IN JAPANESE AS *KIRIHITO SANKA*
IN *BIGGU KOMIKKU*, SHOGAKUKAN, 1970-71.

ISBN 978-1-934287-97-2

MANUFACTURED IN THE UNITED STATES OF AMERICA

SECOND EDITION

THIS IS A WORK OF FICTION.
THE ARTWORK OF THE ORIGINAL HAS BEEN PRODUCED AS A MIRROR-IMAGE
IN ORDER TO CONFORM WITH THE ENGLISH LANGUAGE.

VERTICAL, INC.
1185 AVENUE OF THE AMERICAS 32ND FLOOR
NEW YORK, NY 10036
WWW.VERTICAL-INC.COM

CONTENTS

ODE TO KIRIHITO

CHAPTER 1

ROOM 66

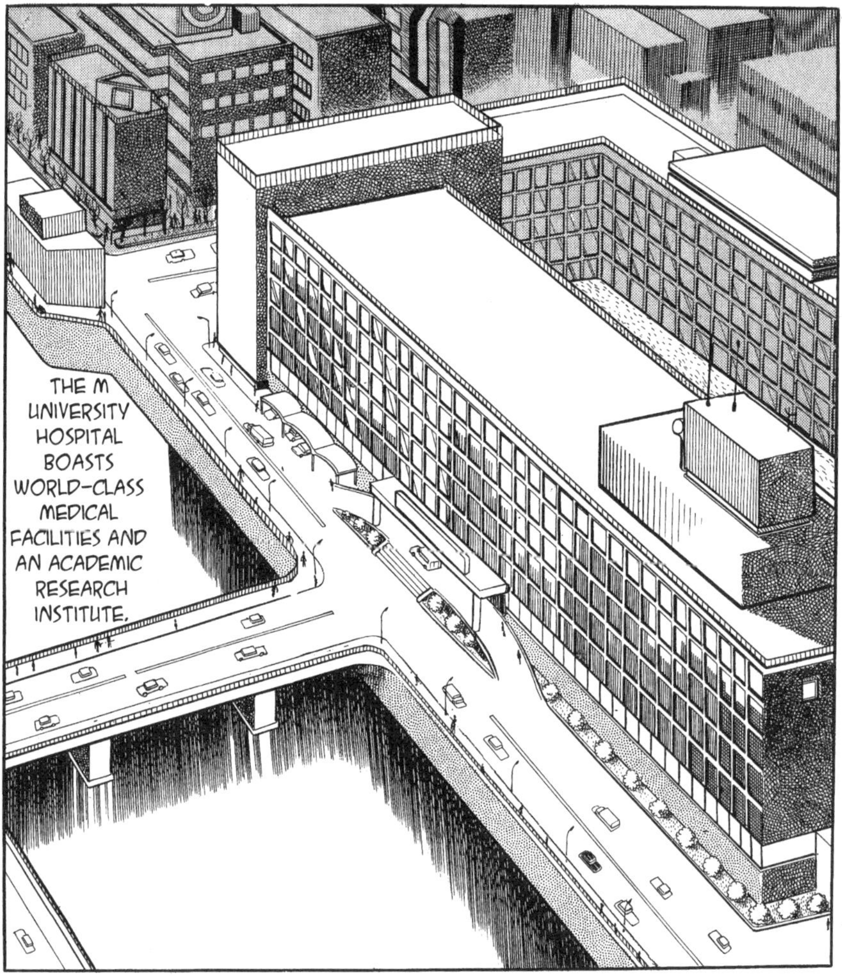
THE M UNIVERSITY HOSPITAL BOASTS WORLD-CLASS MEDICAL FACILITIES AND AN ACADEMIC RESEARCH INSTITUTE.

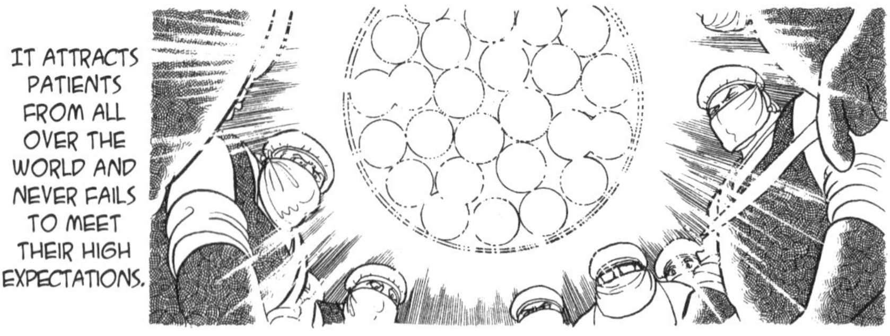
IT ATTRACTS PATIENTS FROM ALL OVER THE WORLD AND NEVER FAILS TO MEET THEIR HIGH EXPECTATIONS.

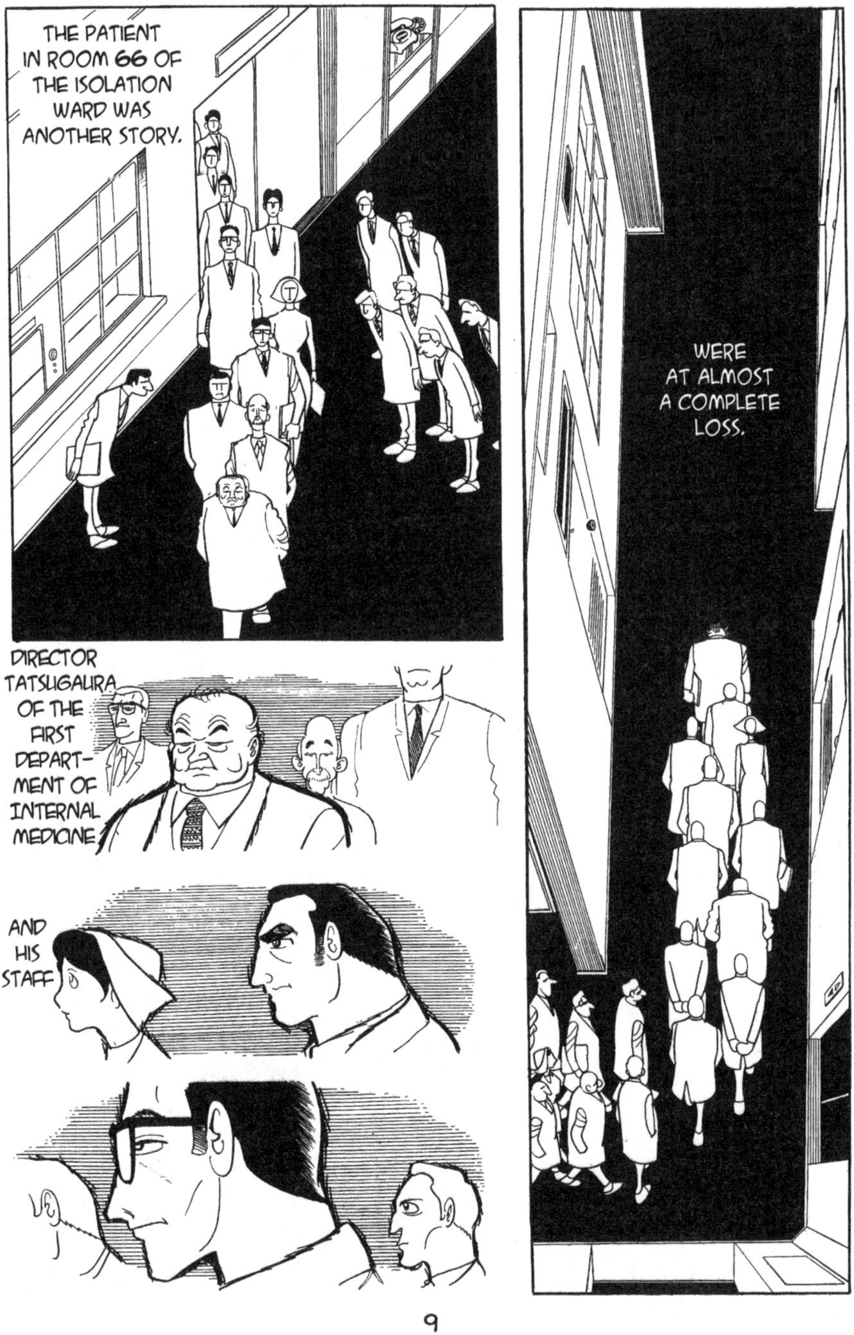
THE PATIENT IN ROOM 66 OF THE ISOLATION WARD WAS ANOTHER STORY.
DIRECTOR TATSUGAURA OF THE FIRST DEPARTMENT OF INTERNAL MEDICINE
AND HIS STAFF
WERE AT ALMOST A COMPLETE LOSS.

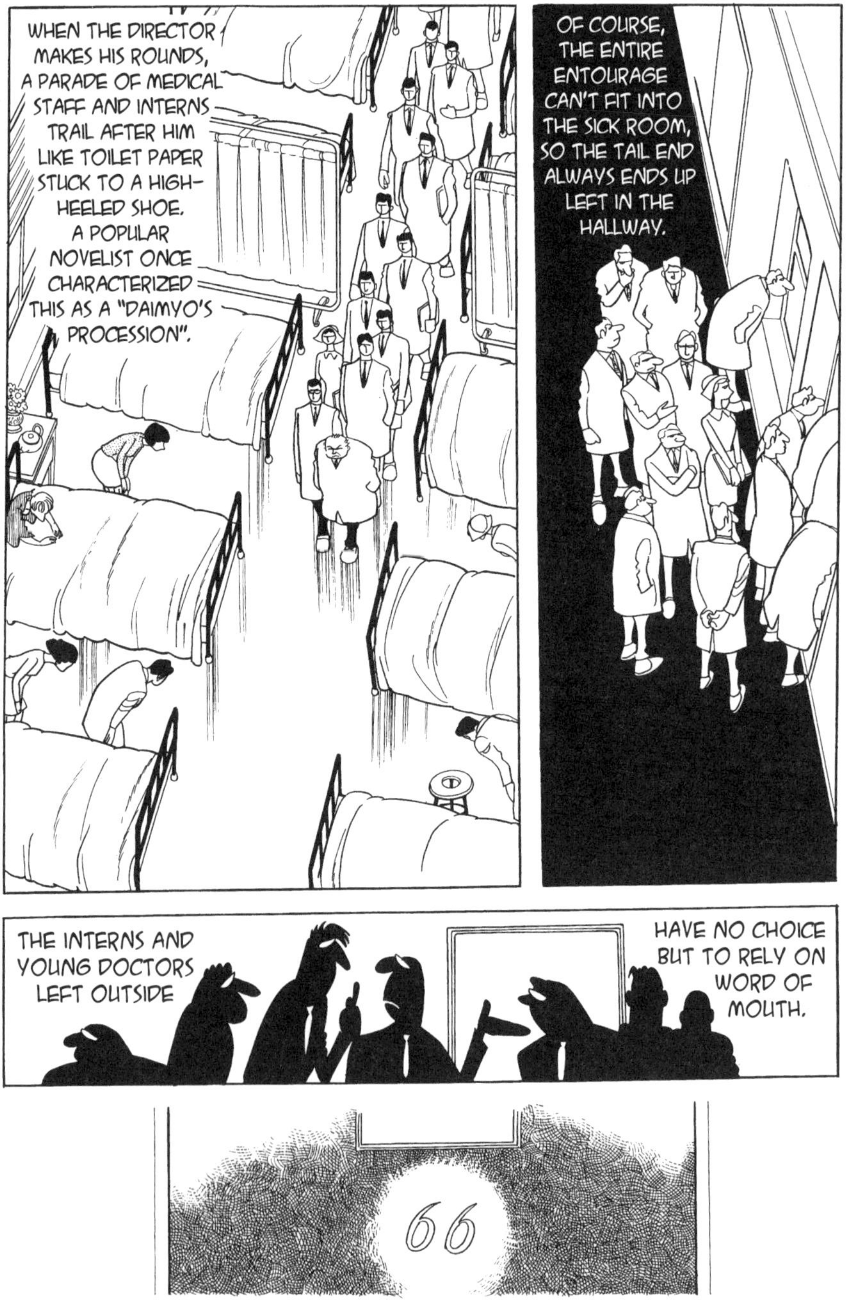
WHEN THE DIRECTOR MAKES HIS ROUNDS, A PARADE OF MEDICAL STAFF AND INTERNS TRAIL AFTER HIM LIKE TOILET PAPER STUCK TO A HIGH-HEELED SHOE. A POPULAR NOVELIST ONCE CHARACTERIZED THIS AS A "DAIMYO'S PROCESSION".
OF COURSE, THE ENTIRE ENTOURAGE CAN'T FIT INTO THE SICK ROOM, SO THE TAIL END ALWAYS ENDS UP LEFT IN THE HALLWAY.
THE INTERNS AND YOUNG DOCTORS LEFT OUTSIDE
HAVE NO CHOICE BUT TO RELY ON WORD OF MOUTH.
66

ZIP
SNAP
X-RAY
YES, SIR!
HMM...

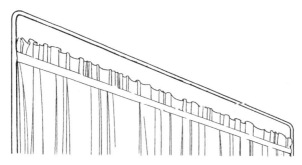

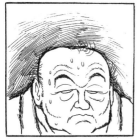

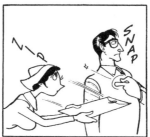

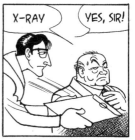

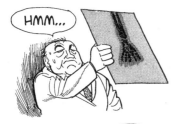

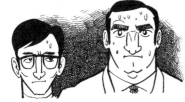

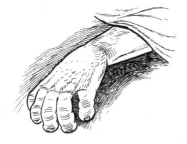

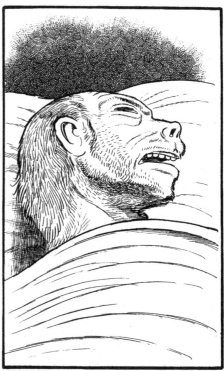

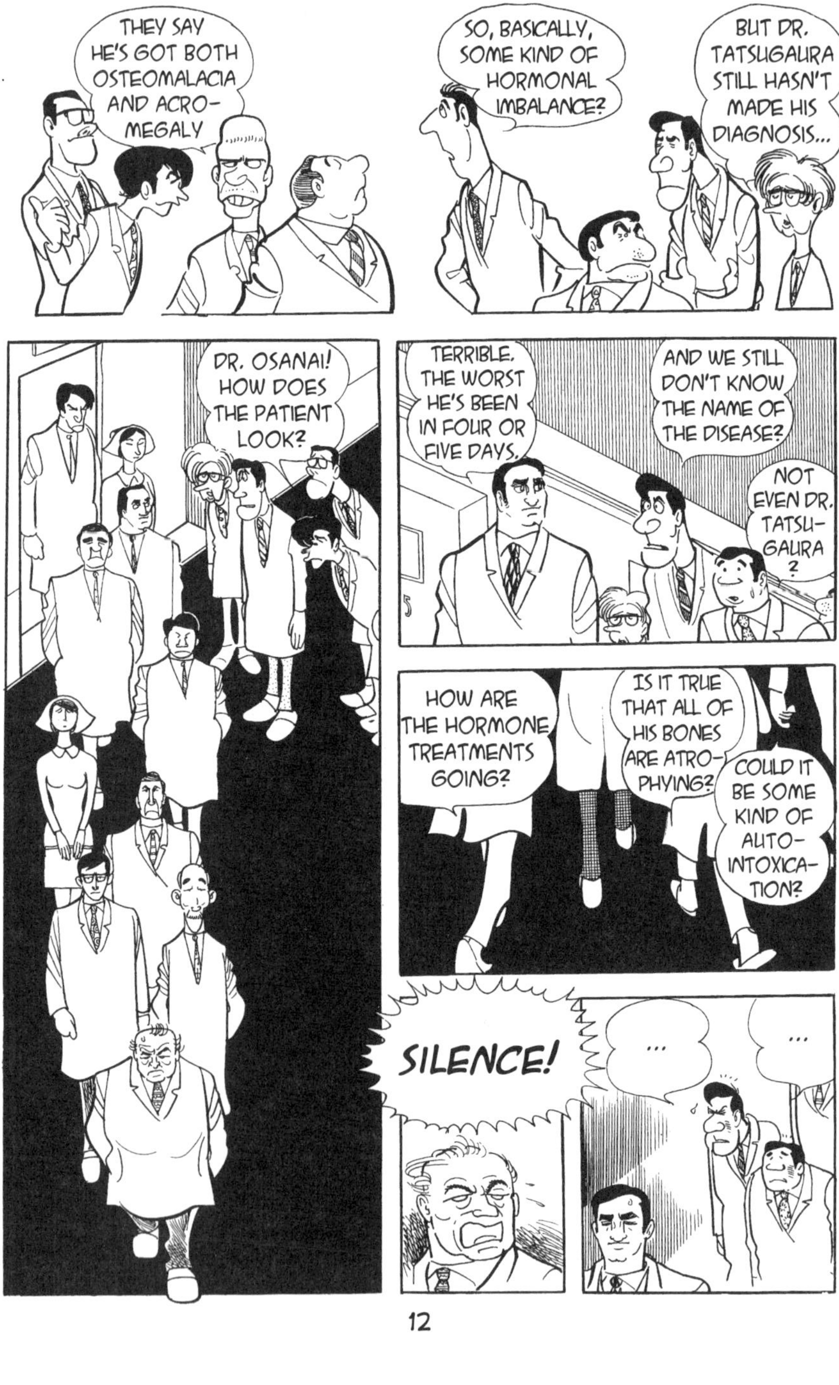
THEY SAY HE'S GOT BOTH OSTEOMALACIA AND ACRO-MEGALY
SO, BASICALLY, SOME KIND OF HORMONAL IMBALANCE?
BUT DR. TATSUGAURA STILL HASN'T MADE HIS DIAGNOSIS...
DR. OSANAI! HOW DOES THE PATIENT LOOK?
TERRIBLE. THE WORST HE'S BEEN IN FOUR OR FIVE DAYS.
AND WE STILL DON'T KNOW THE NAME OF THE DISEASE?
NOT EVEN DR. TATSU-GAURA?
HOW ARE THE HORMONE TREATMENTS GOING?
IS IT TRUE THAT ALL OF HIS BONES ARE ATRO-PHYING?
COULD IT BE SOME KIND OF AUTO-INTOXICA-TION?
SILENCE!
...
...

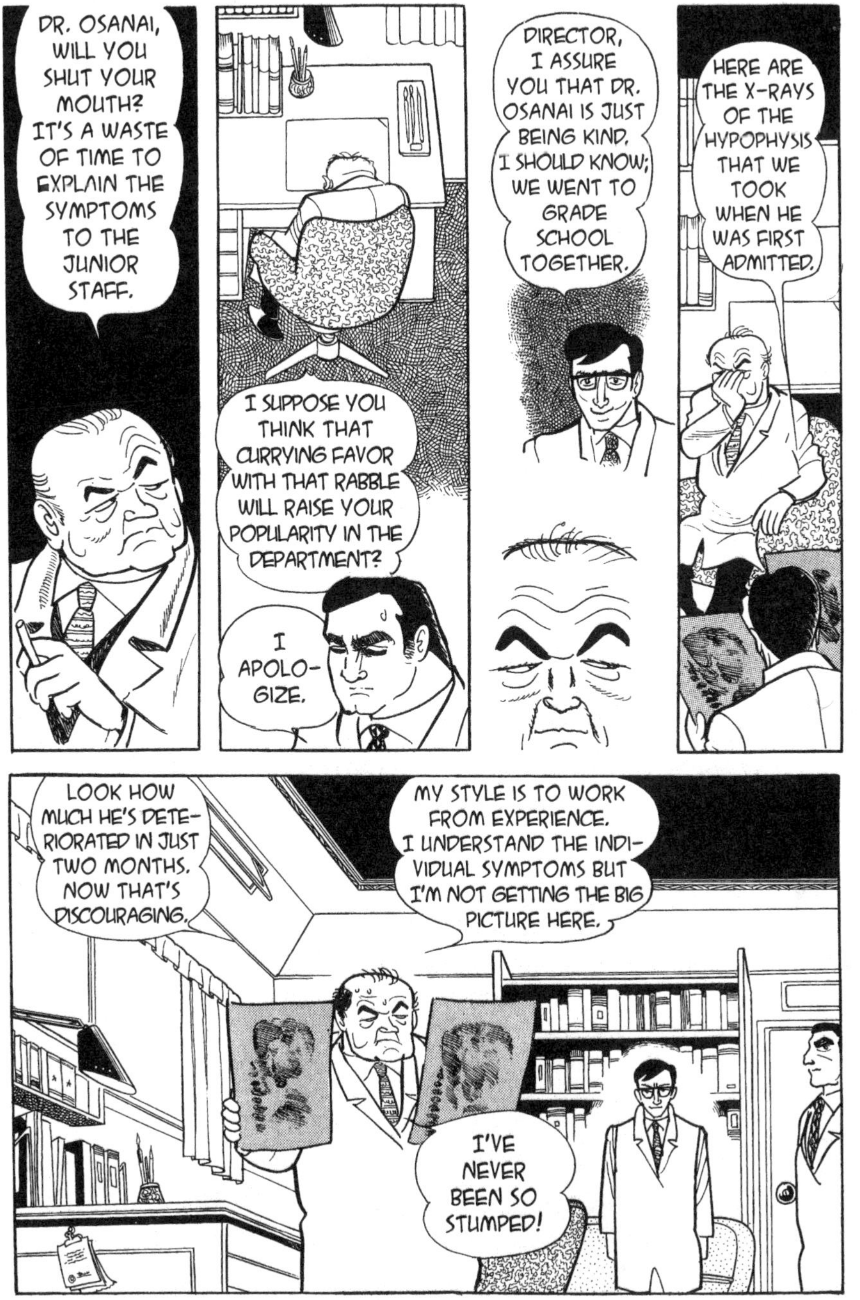

DR. OSANAI, WILL YOU SHUT YOUR MOUTH? IT'S A WASTE OF TIME TO EXPLAIN THE SYMPTOMS TO THE JUNIOR STAFF.
I SUPPOSE YOU THINK THAT CURRYING FAVOR WITH THAT RABBLE WILL RAISE YOUR POPULARITY IN THE DEPARTMENT?
I APOLO-GIZE.
DIRECTOR, I ASSURE YOU THAT DR. OSANAI IS JUST BEING KIND. I SHOULD KNOW; WE WENT TO GRADE SCHOOL TOGETHER.
HERE ARE THE X-RAYS OF THE HYPOPHYSIS THAT WE TOOK WHEN HE WAS FIRST ADMITTED.
LOOK HOW MUCH HE'S DETE-RIORATED IN JUST TWO MONTHS. NOW THAT'S DISCOURAGING.
MY STYLE IS TO WORK FROM EXPERIENCE. I UNDERSTAND THE INDI-VIDUAL SYMPTOMS BUT I'M NOT GETTING THE BIG PICTURE HERE.
I'VE NEVER BEEN SO STUMPED!

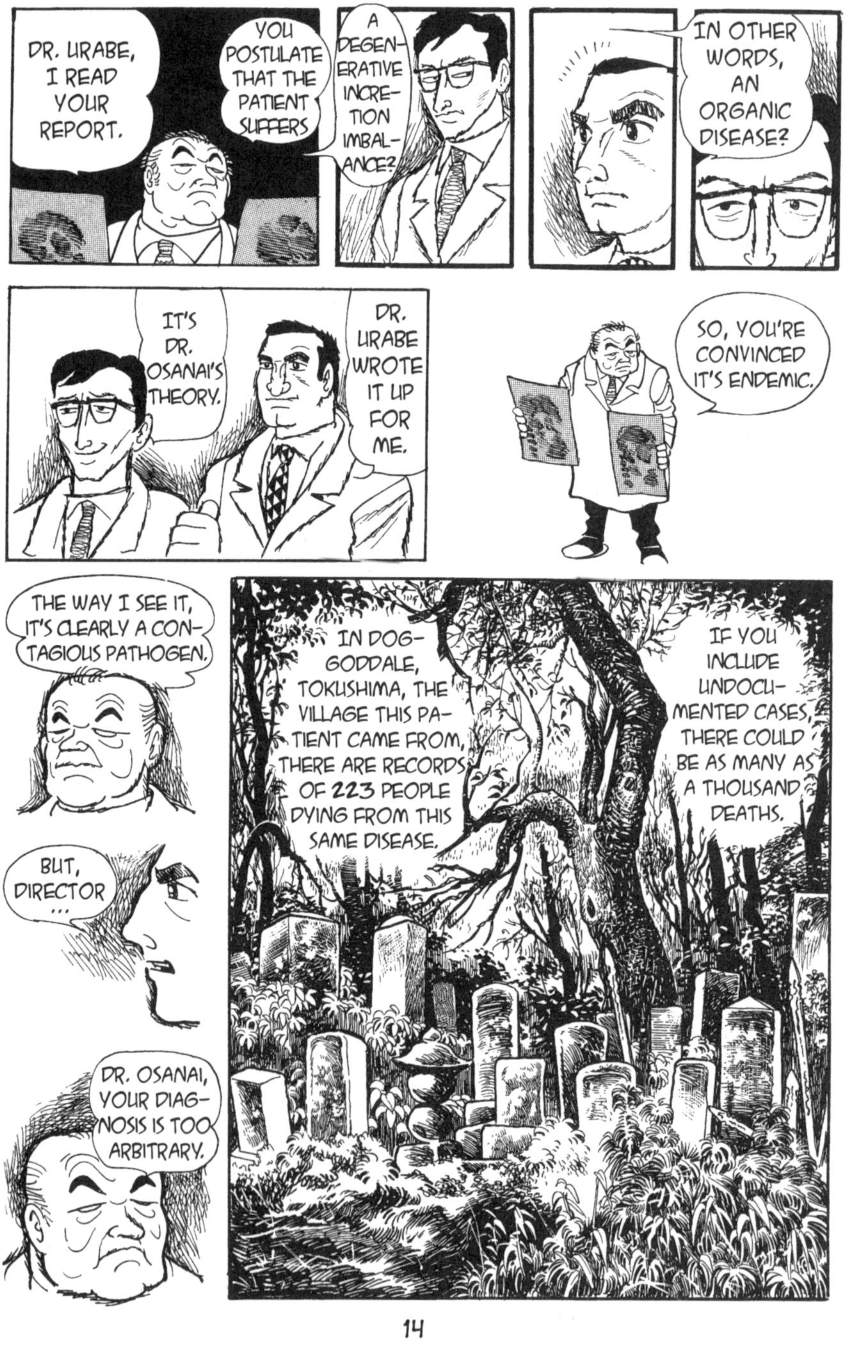
DR. URABE, I READ YOUR REPORT.
YOU POSTULATE THAT THE PATIENT SUFFERS
A DEGENERATIVE INCRETION IMBALANCE?
IN OTHER WORDS, AN ORGANIC DISEASE?
IT'S DR. OSANAI'S THEORY.
DR. URABE WROTE IT UP FOR ME.
SO, YOU'RE CONVINCED IT'S ENDEMIC.
THE WAY I SEE IT, IT'S CLEARLY A CONTAGIOUS PATHOGEN.
BUT, DIRECTOR ...
DR. OSANAI, YOUR DIAGNOSIS IS TOO ARBITRARY.
IN DOGGODDALE, TOKUSHIMA, THE VILLAGE THIS PATIENT CAME FROM, THERE ARE RECORDS OF 223 PEOPLE DYING FROM THIS SAME DISEASE.
IF YOU INCLUDE UNDOCUMENTED CASES, THERE COULD BE AS MANY AS A THOUSAND DEATHS.

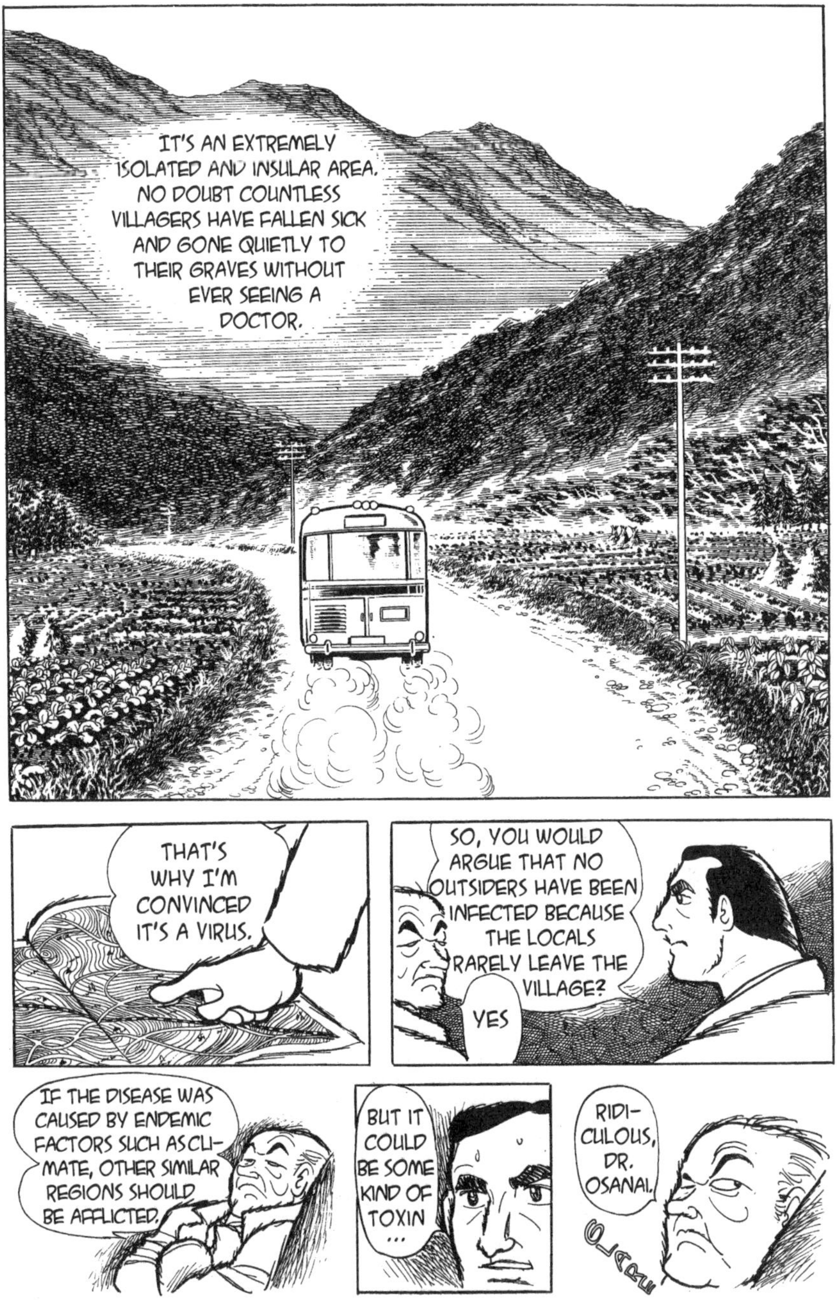
IT'S AN EXTREMELY ISOLATED AND INSULAR AREA. NO DOUBT COUNTLESS VILLAGERS HAVE FALLEN SICK AND GONE QUIETLY TO THEIR GRAVES WITHOUT EVER SEEING A DOCTOR.
THAT'S WHY I'M CONVINCED IT'S A VIRUS.
SO, YOU WOULD ARGUE THAT NO OUTSIDERS HAVE BEEN INFECTED BECAUSE THE LOCALS RARELY LEAVE THE VILLAGE?
YES
IF THE DISEASE WAS CAUSED BY ENDEMIC FACTORS SUCH AS CLI-MATE, OTHER SIMILAR REGIONS SHOULD BE AFFLICTED.
BUT IT COULD BE SOME KIND OF TOXIN ...
RIDI-CULOUS, DR. OSANAI.

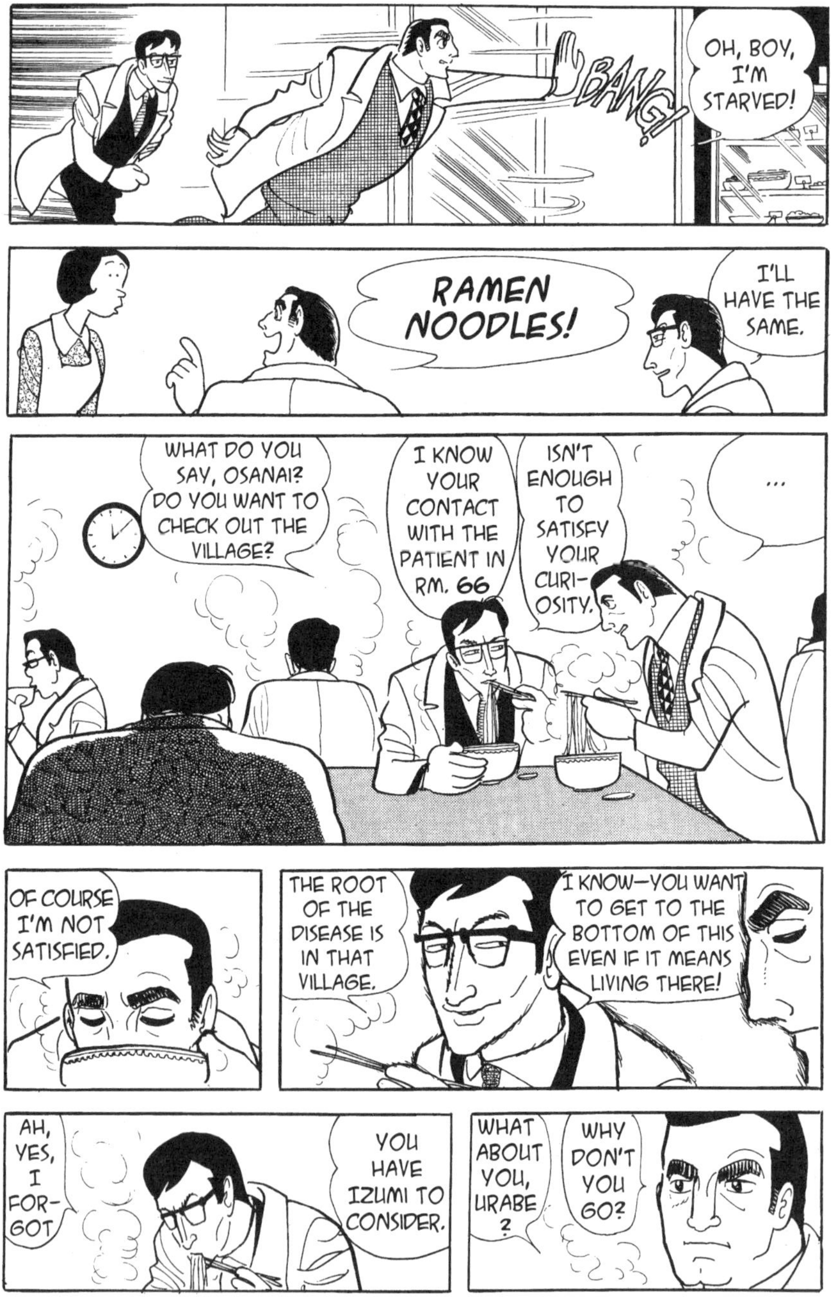
BANG!
OH, BOY, I'M STARVED!
RAMEN NOODLES!
I'LL HAVE THE SAME.
WHAT DO YOU SAY, OSANAI? DO YOU WANT TO CHECK OUT THE VILLAGE?
I KNOW YOUR CONTACT WITH THE PATIENT IN RM. 66
ISN'T ENOUGH TO SATISFY YOUR CURI-OSITY.
...
OF COURSE I'M NOT SATISFIED.
THE ROOT OF THE DISEASE IS IN THAT VILLAGE.
I KNOW—YOU WANT TO GET TO THE BOTTOM OF THIS EVEN IF IT MEANS LIVING THERE!
AH, YES, I FOR-GOT
YOU HAVE IZUMI TO CONSIDER.
WHAT ABOUT YOU, URABE ?
WHY DON'T YOU GO?

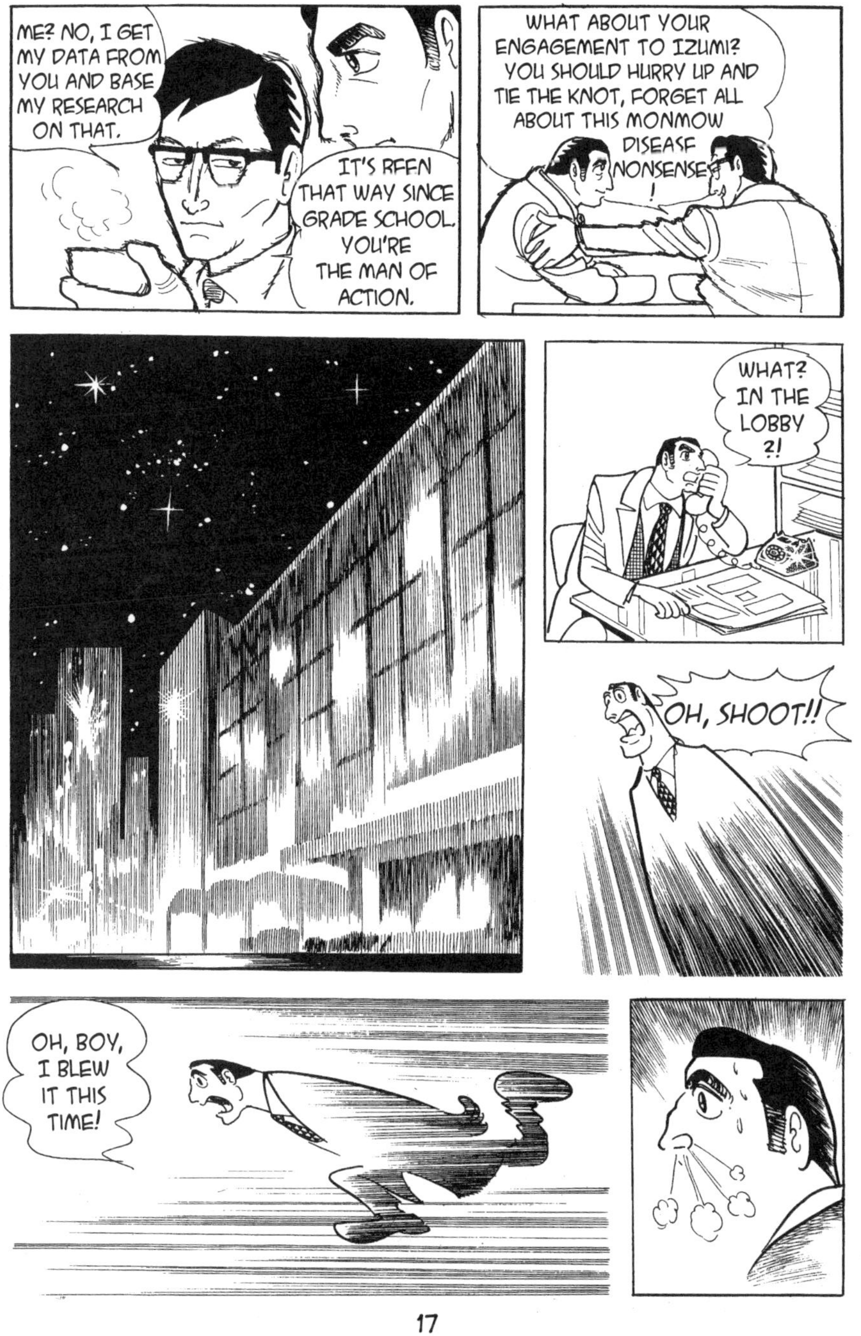

ME? NO, I GET MY DATA FROM YOU AND BASE MY RESEARCH ON THAT.
IT'S BEEN THAT WAY SINCE GRADE SCHOOL. YOU'RE THE MAN OF ACTION.
WHAT ABOUT YOUR ENGAGEMENT TO IZUMI? YOU SHOULD HURRY UP AND TIE THE KNOT, FORGET ALL ABOUT THIS MONMOW DISEASE NONSENSE!
WHAT? IN THE LOBBY?!
OH, SHOOT!!
OH, BOY, I BLEW IT THIS TIME!

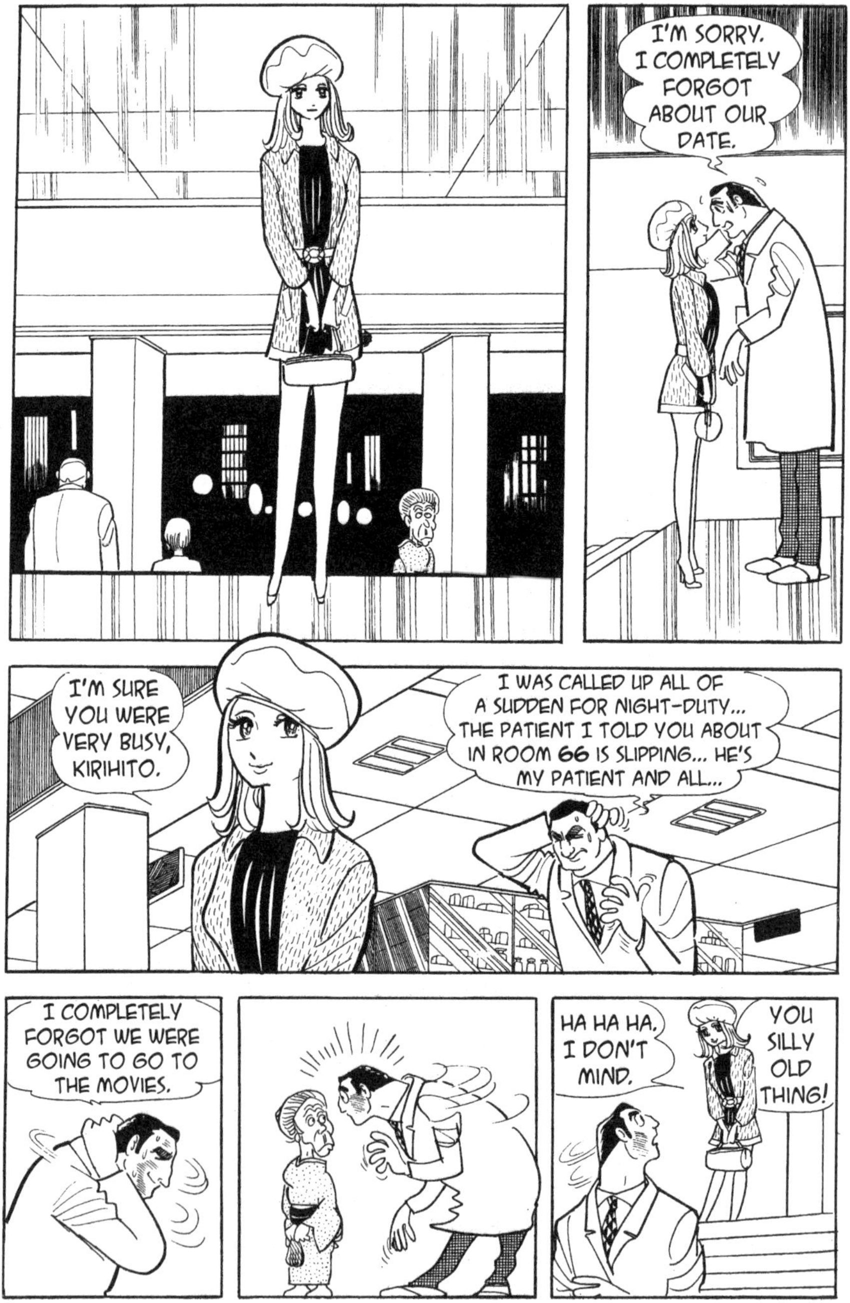

I'M SORRY. I COMPLETELY FORGOT ABOUT OUR DATE.
I'M SURE YOU WERE VERY BUSY, KIRIHITO.
I WAS CALLED UP ALL OF A SUDDEN FOR NIGHT-DUTY... THE PATIENT I TOLD YOU ABOUT IN ROOM 66 IS SLIPPING... HE'S MY PATIENT AND ALL...
I COMPLETELY FORGOT WE WERE GOING TO GO TO THE MOVIES.
HA HA HA. I DON'T MIND.
YOU SILLY OLD THING!

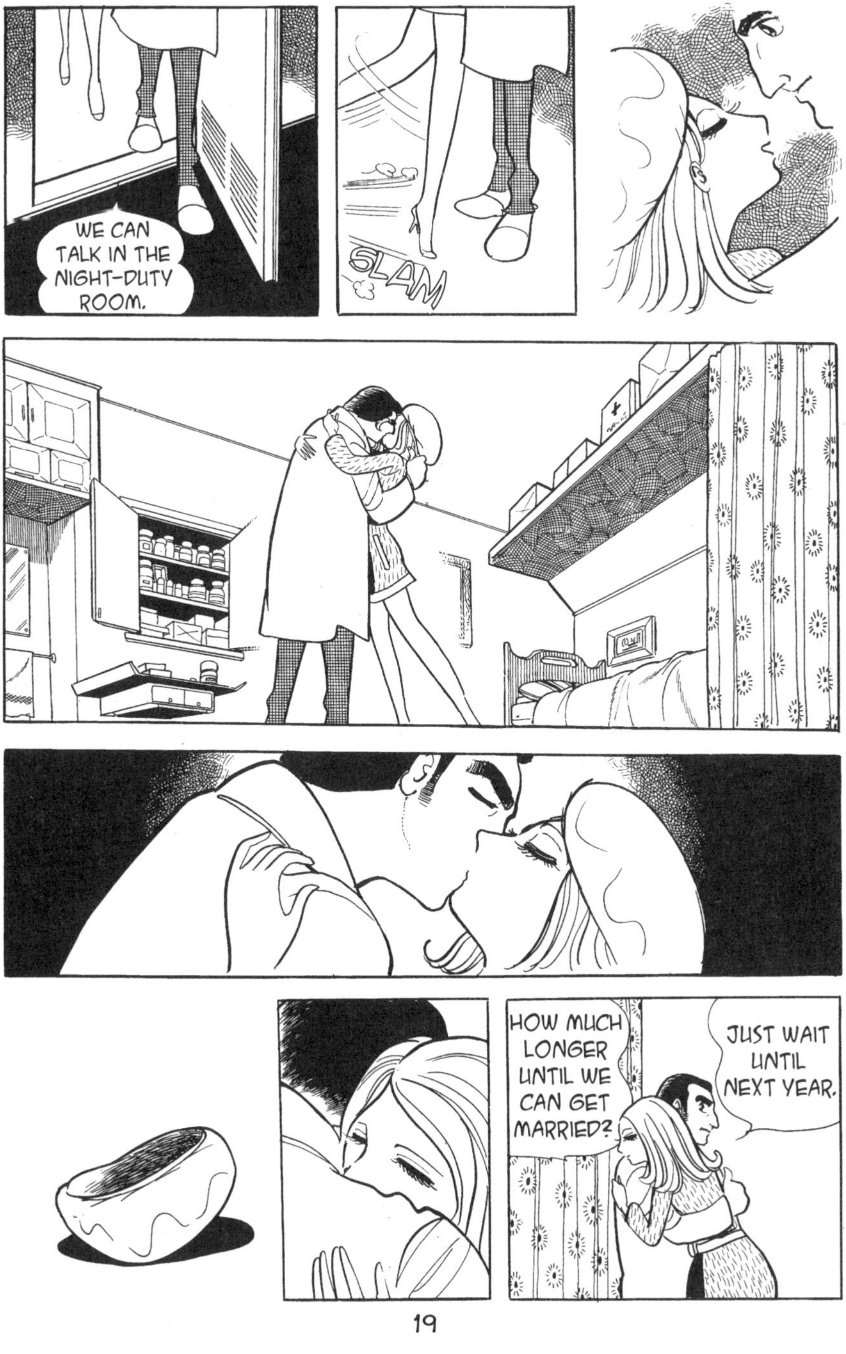
WE CAN TALK IN THE NIGHT-DUTY ROOM.
SLAM
HOW MUCH LONGER UNTIL WE CAN GET MARRIED?
JUST WAIT UNTIL NEXT YEAR.

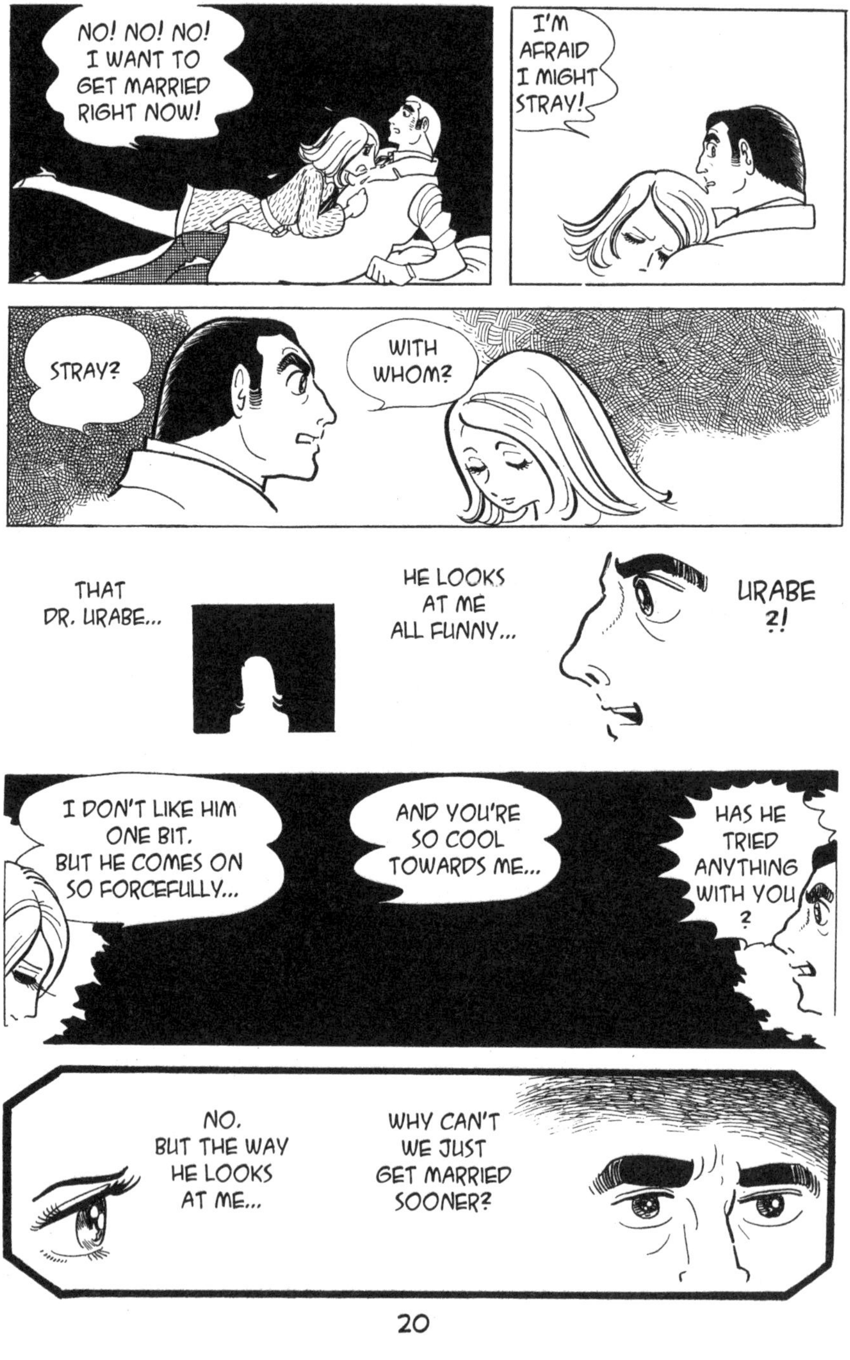
NO! NO! NO! I WANT TO GET MARRIED RIGHT NOW!
I'M AFRAID I MIGHT STRAY!
STRAY?
WITH WHOM?
THAT DR. URABE...
HE LOOKS AT ME ALL FUNNY...
URABE ?!
I DON'T LIKE HIM ONE BIT. BUT HE COMES ON SO FORCEFULLY...
AND YOU'RE SO COOL TOWARDS ME...
HAS HE TRIED ANYTHING WITH YOU ?
NO. BUT THE WAY HE LOOKS AT ME...
WHY CAN'T WE JUST GET MARRIED SOONER?

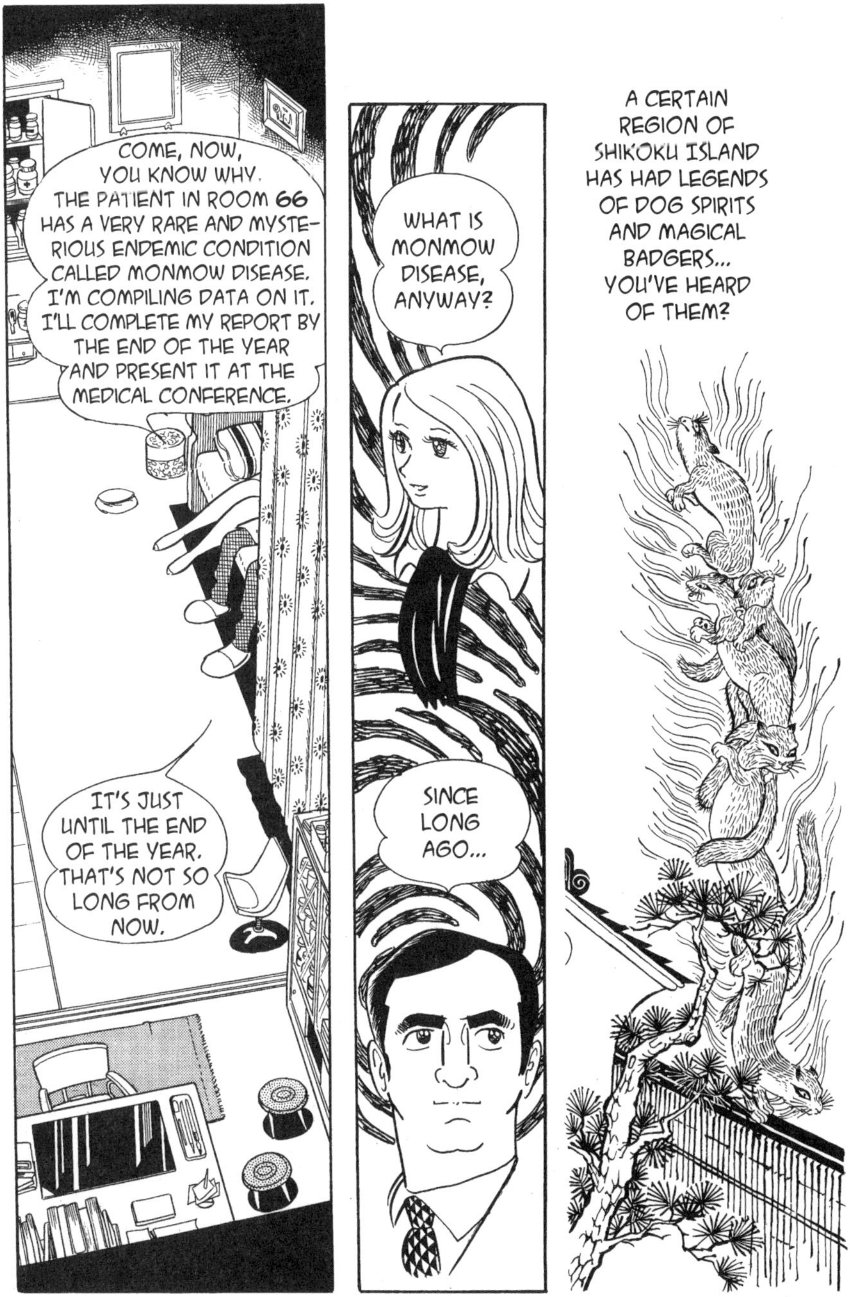
COME, NOW, YOU KNOW WHY. THE PATIENT IN ROOM 66 HAS A VERY RARE AND MYSTERIOUS ENDEMIC CONDITION CALLED MONMOW DISEASE. I'M COMPILING DATA ON IT. I'LL COMPLETE MY REPORT BY THE END OF THE YEAR AND PRESENT IT AT THE MEDICAL CONFERENCE.
IT'S JUST UNTIL THE END OF THE YEAR. THAT'S NOT SO LONG FROM NOW.
WHAT IS MONMOW DISEASE, ANYWAY?
SINCE LONG AGO...
A CERTAIN REGION OF SHIKOKU ISLAND HAS HAD LEGENDS OF DOG SPIRITS AND MAGICAL BADGERS... YOU'VE HEARD OF THEM?

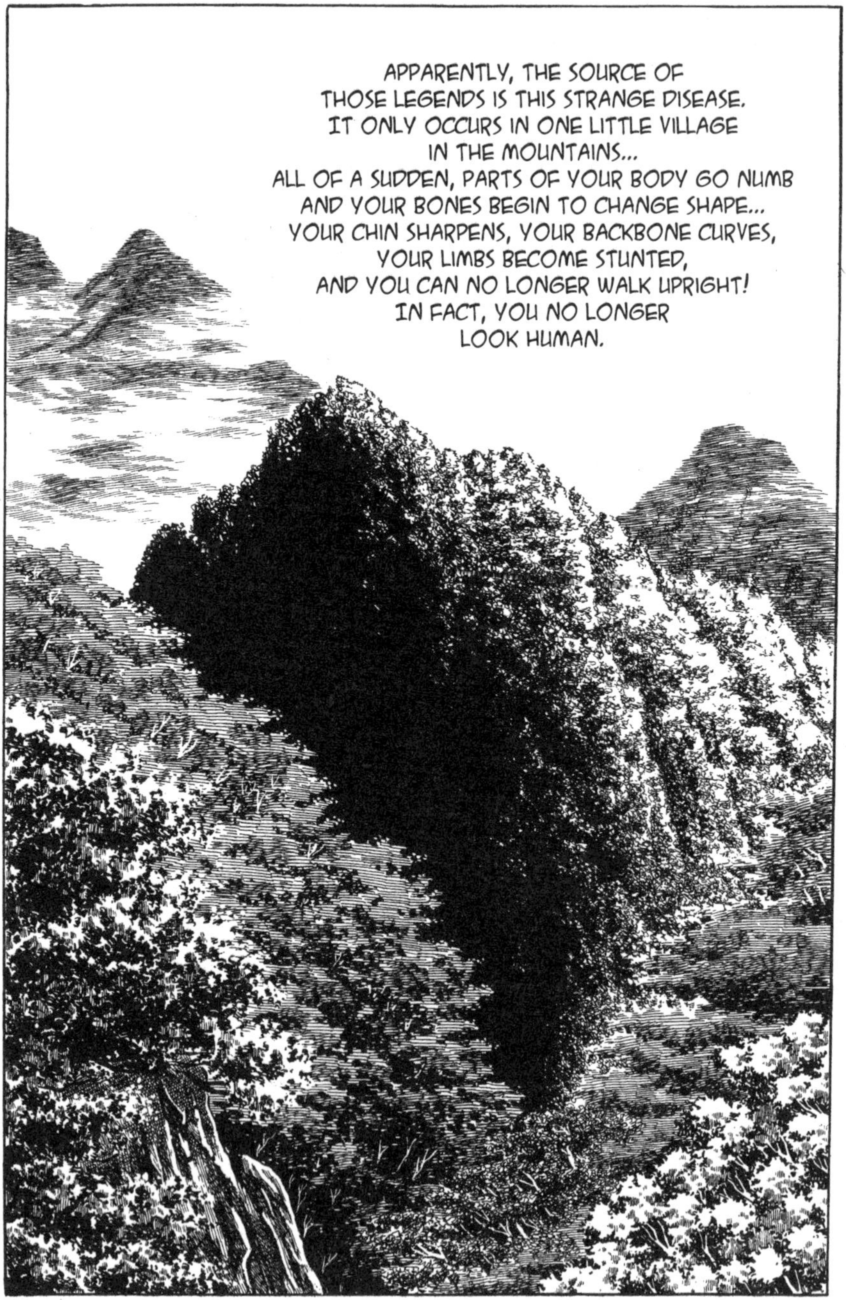
APPARENTLY, THE SOURCE OF THOSE LEGENDS IS THIS STRANGE DISEASE. IT ONLY OCCURS IN ONE LITTLE VILLAGE IN THE MOUNTAINS... ALL OF A SUDDEN, PARTS OF YOUR BODY GO NUMB AND YOUR BONES BEGIN TO CHANGE SHAPE... YOUR CHIN SHARPENS, YOUR BACKBONE CURVES, YOUR LIMBS BECOME STUNTED, AND YOU CAN NO LONGER WALK UPRIGHT! IN FACT, YOU NO LONGER LOOK HUMAN.

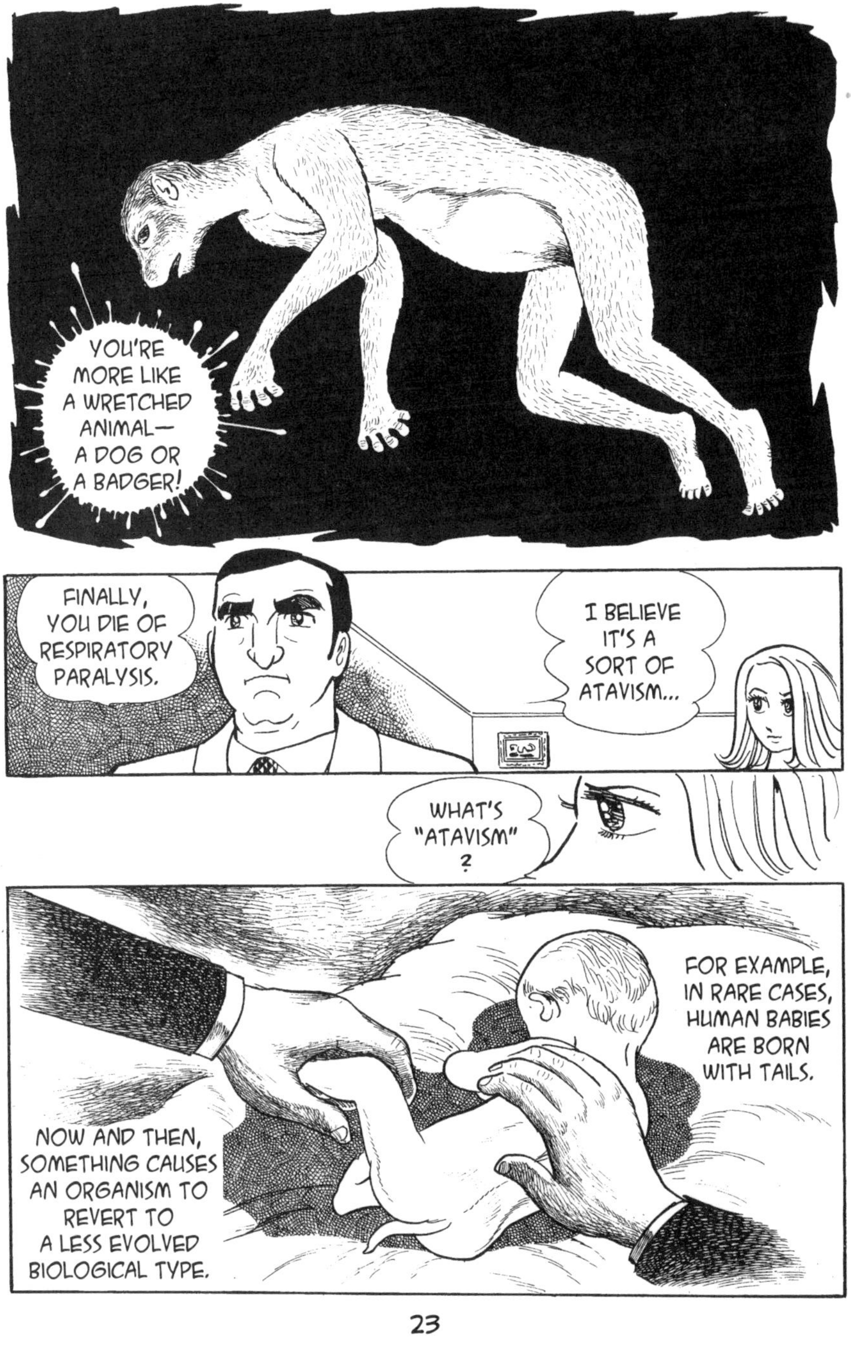
YOU'RE MORE LIKE A WRETCHED ANIMAL— A DOG OR A BADGER!
FINALLY, YOU DIE OF RESPIRATORY PARALYSIS.
I BELIEVE IT'S A SORT OF ATAVISM...
WHAT'S "ATAVISM" ?
FOR EXAMPLE, IN RARE CASES, HUMAN BABIES ARE BORN WITH TAILS.
NOW AND THEN, SOMETHING CAUSES AN ORGANISM TO REVERT TO A LESS EVOLVED BIOLOGICAL TYPE.

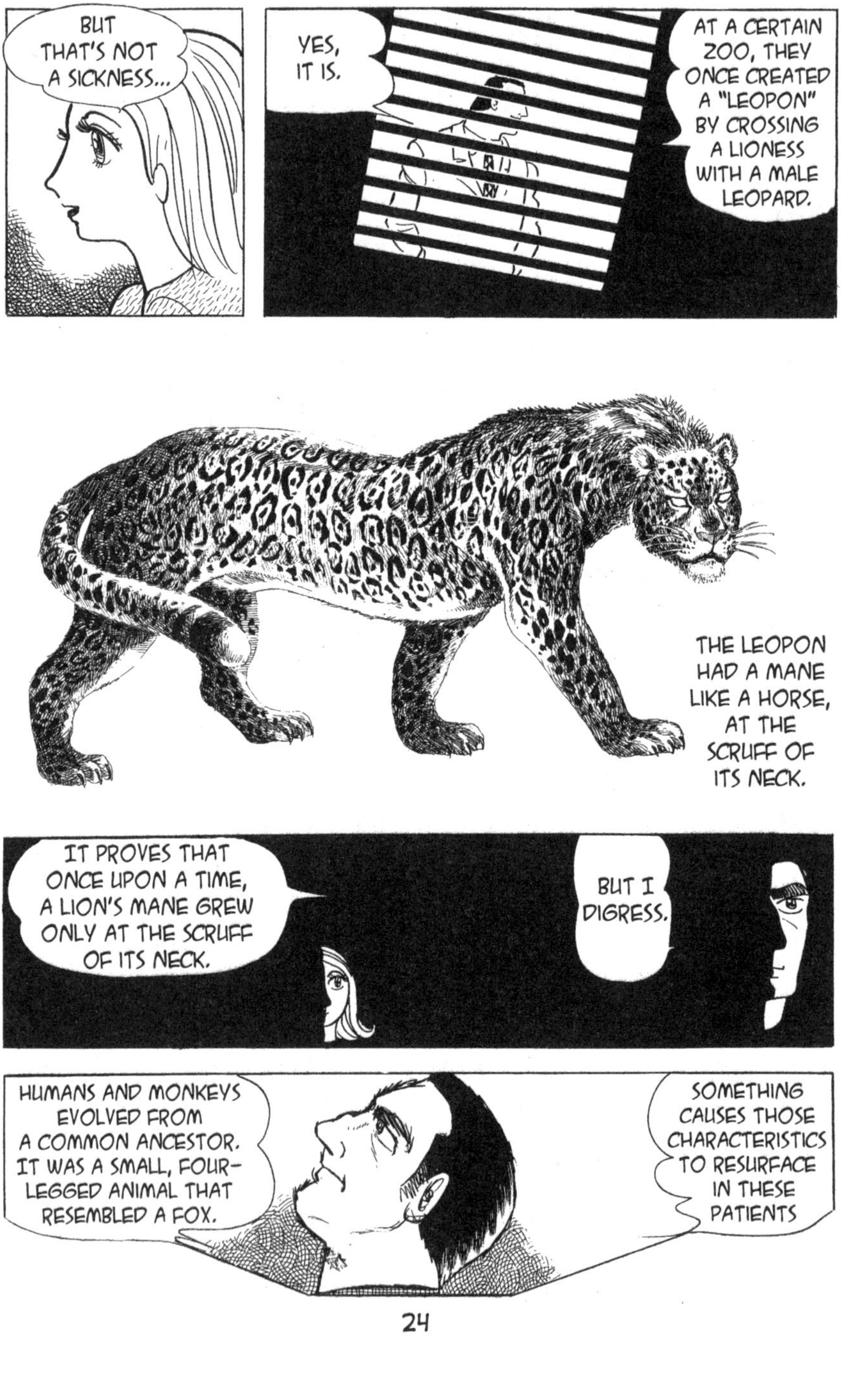
BUT THAT'S NOT A SICKNESS...
YES, IT IS.
AT A CERTAIN ZOO, THEY ONCE CREATED A "LEOPON" BY CROSSING A LIONESS WITH A MALE LEOPARD.
THE LEOPON HAD A MANE LIKE A HORSE, AT THE SCRUFF OF ITS NECK.
IT PROVES THAT ONCE UPON A TIME, A LION'S MANE GREW ONLY AT THE SCRUFF OF ITS NECK.
BUT I DIGRESS.
HUMANS AND MONKEYS EVOLVED FROM A COMMON ANCESTOR. IT WAS A SMALL, FOUR-LEGGED ANIMAL THAT RESEMBLED A FOX.
SOMETHING CAUSES THOSE CHARACTERISTICS TO RESURFACE IN THESE PATIENTS

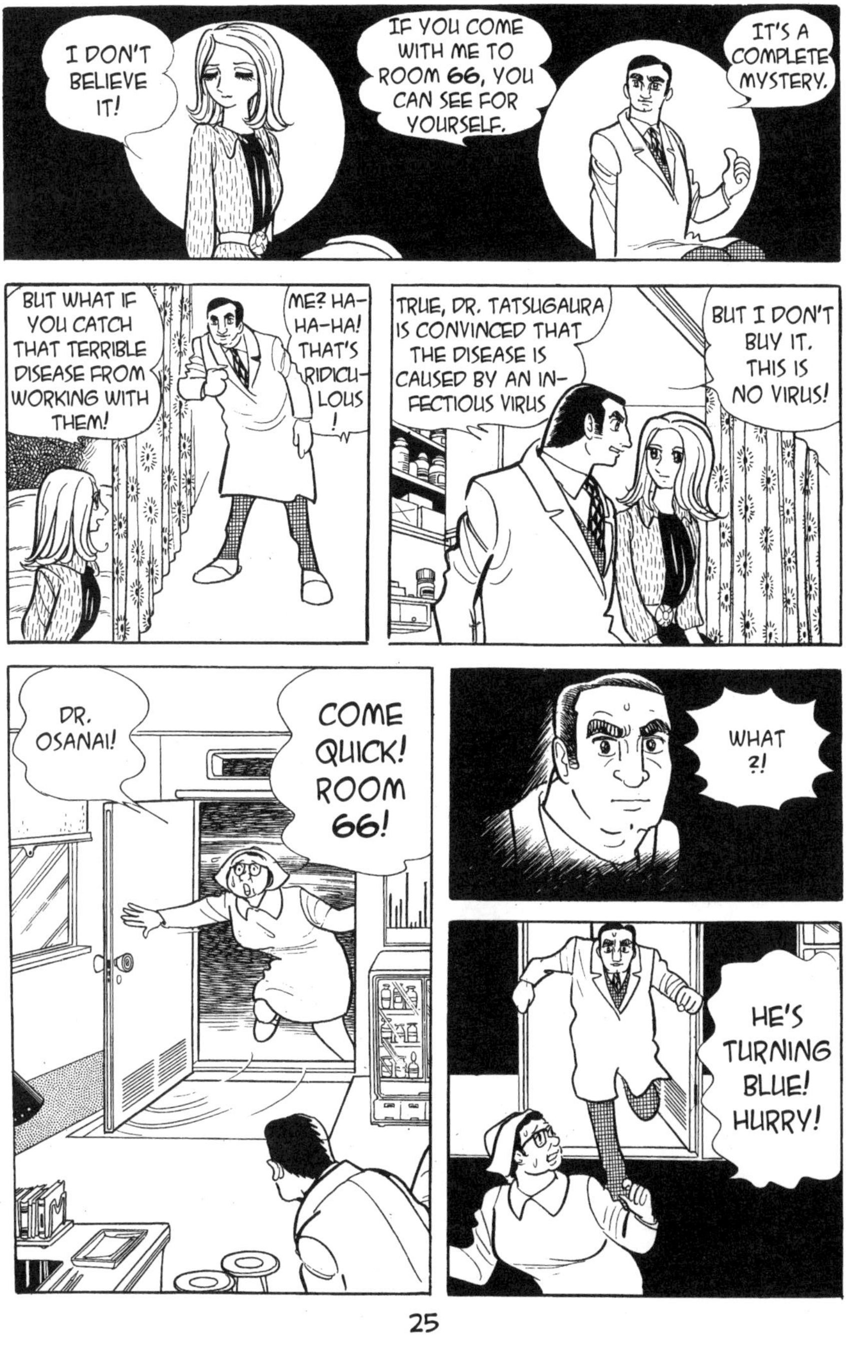
I DON'T BELIEVE IT!
IF YOU COME WITH ME TO ROOM 66, YOU CAN SEE FOR YOURSELF.
IT'S A COMPLETE MYSTERY.
BUT WHAT IF YOU CATCH THAT TERRIBLE DISEASE FROM WORKING WITH THEM!
ME? HA-HA-HA! THAT'S RIDICU-LOUS!
TRUE, DR. TATSUGAURA IS CONVINCED THAT THE DISEASE IS CAUSED BY AN IN-FECTIOUS VIRUS
BUT I DON'T BUY IT. THIS IS NO VIRUS!
DR. OSANAI!
COME QUICK! ROOM 66!
WHAT?!
HE'S TURNING BLUE! HURRY!

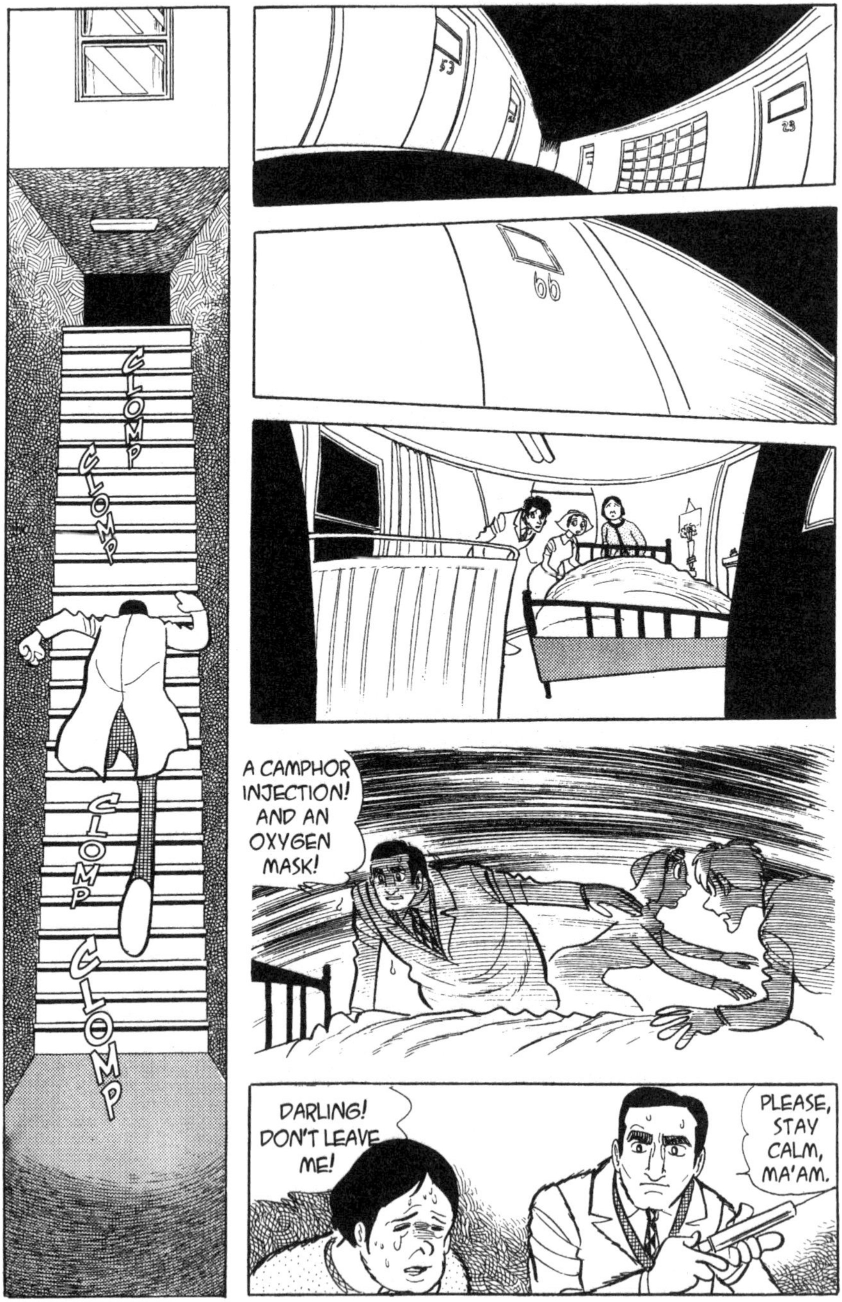
CLOMP
CLOMP
CLOMP
CLOMP
A CAMPHOR INJECTION! AND AN OXYGEN MASK!
DARLING! DON'T LEAVE ME!
PLEASE, STAY CALM, MA'AM.

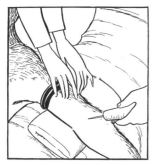
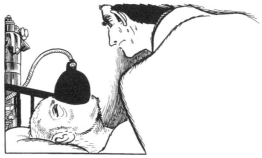

PULSE 70 AND ARRHYTHMIC. D.P. 65.

YOU DIDN'T SEE THIS COMING?!

I'M SORRY, DR. OSANAI. IT WAS SO SUDDEN!

THE CRITICAL THING IS TO KEEP HIM ALIVE.

MY REPU-TATION IS AT STAKE!

PLEASE SAVE HIM, DOCTOR.

DON'T WORRY. I PROMISE THAT WE'LL GET TO THE BOTTOM OF THIS.

27

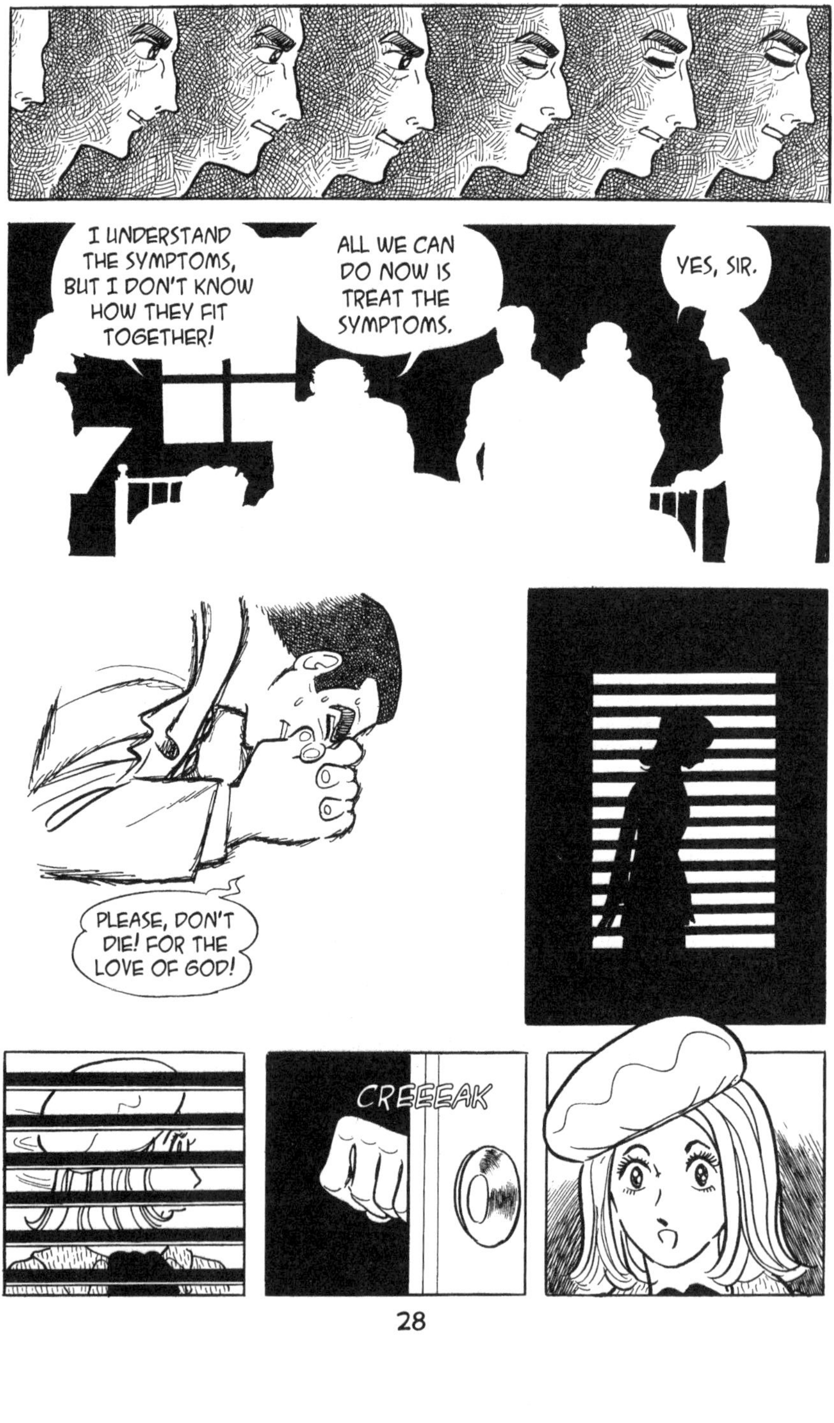
I UNDERSTAND THE SYMPTOMS, BUT I DON'T KNOW HOW THEY FIT TOGETHER!
ALL WE CAN DO NOW IS TREAT THE SYMPTOMS.
YES, SIR.
PLEASE, DON'T DIE! FOR THE LOVE OF GOD!
CREEEAK

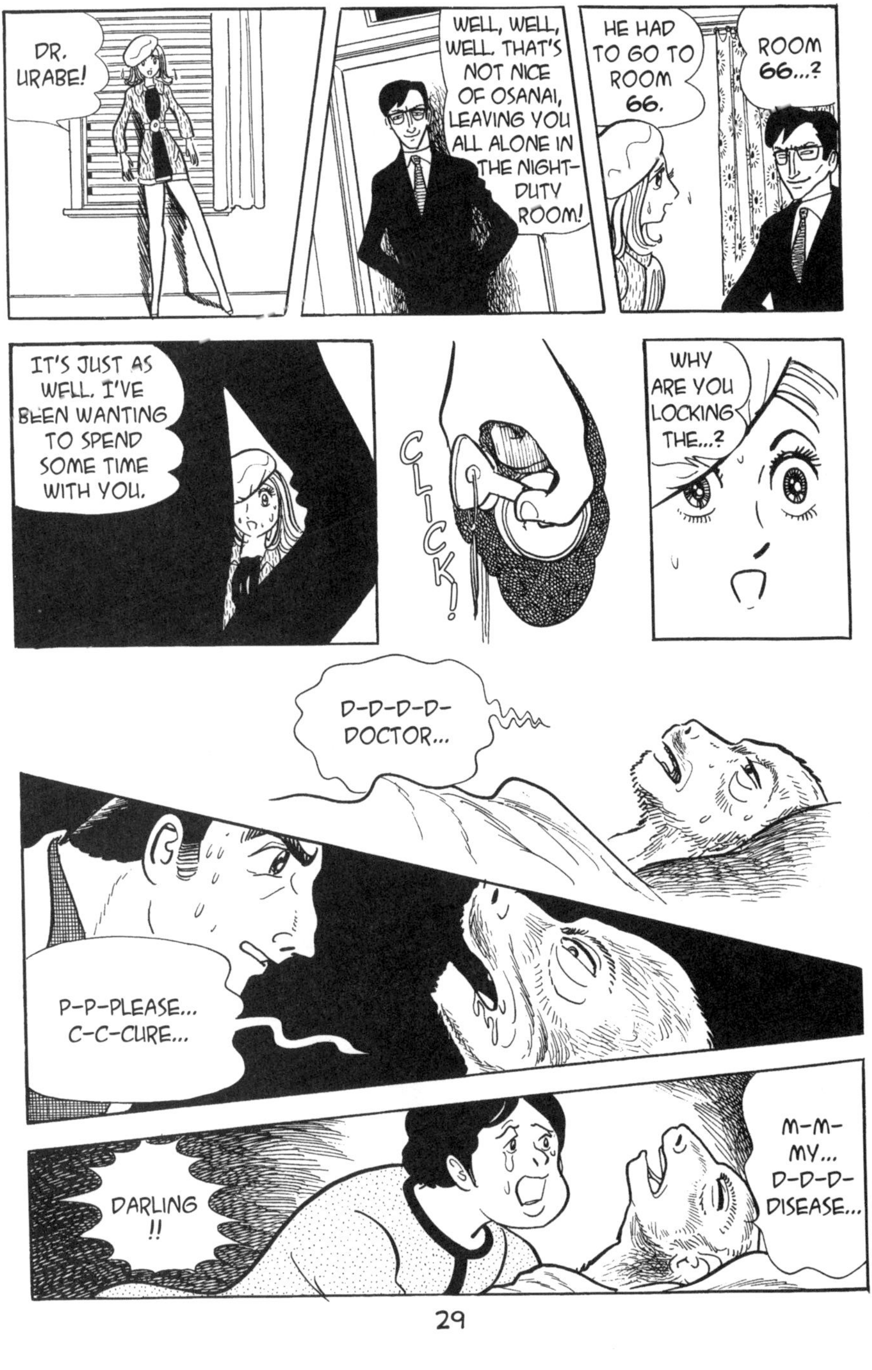
DR. URABE!
WELL, WELL, WELL. THAT'S NOT NICE OF OSANAI, LEAVING YOU ALL ALONE IN THE NIGHT-DUTY ROOM!
HE HAD TO GO TO ROOM 66.
ROOM 66...?
IT'S JUST AS WELL. I'VE BEEN WANTING TO SPEND SOME TIME WITH YOU.
CLICK!
WHY ARE YOU LOCKING THE...?
D-D-D-D-DOCTOR...
P-P-PLEASE... C-C-CURE...
M-M-MY... D-D-D-DISEASE...
DARLING !!

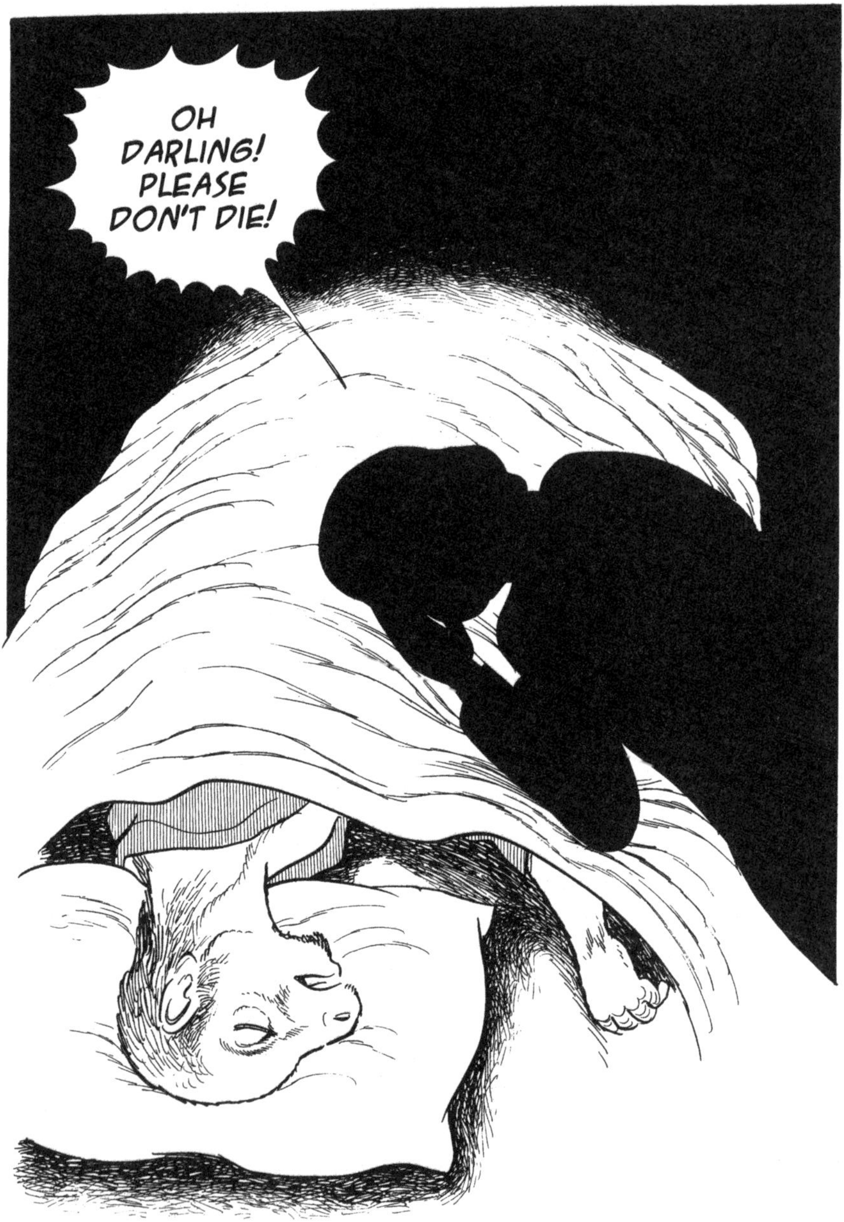
OH DARLING! PLEASE DON'T DIE!

EEEEEEEEK!
...
FOR-GIVE ME...

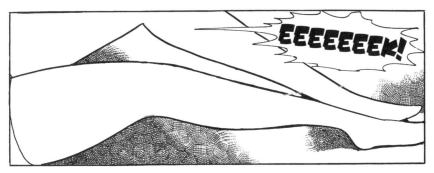

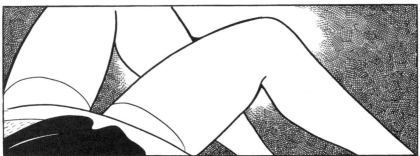

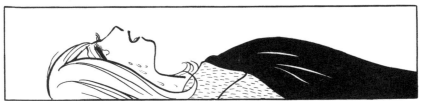

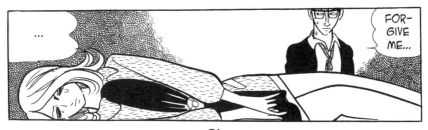

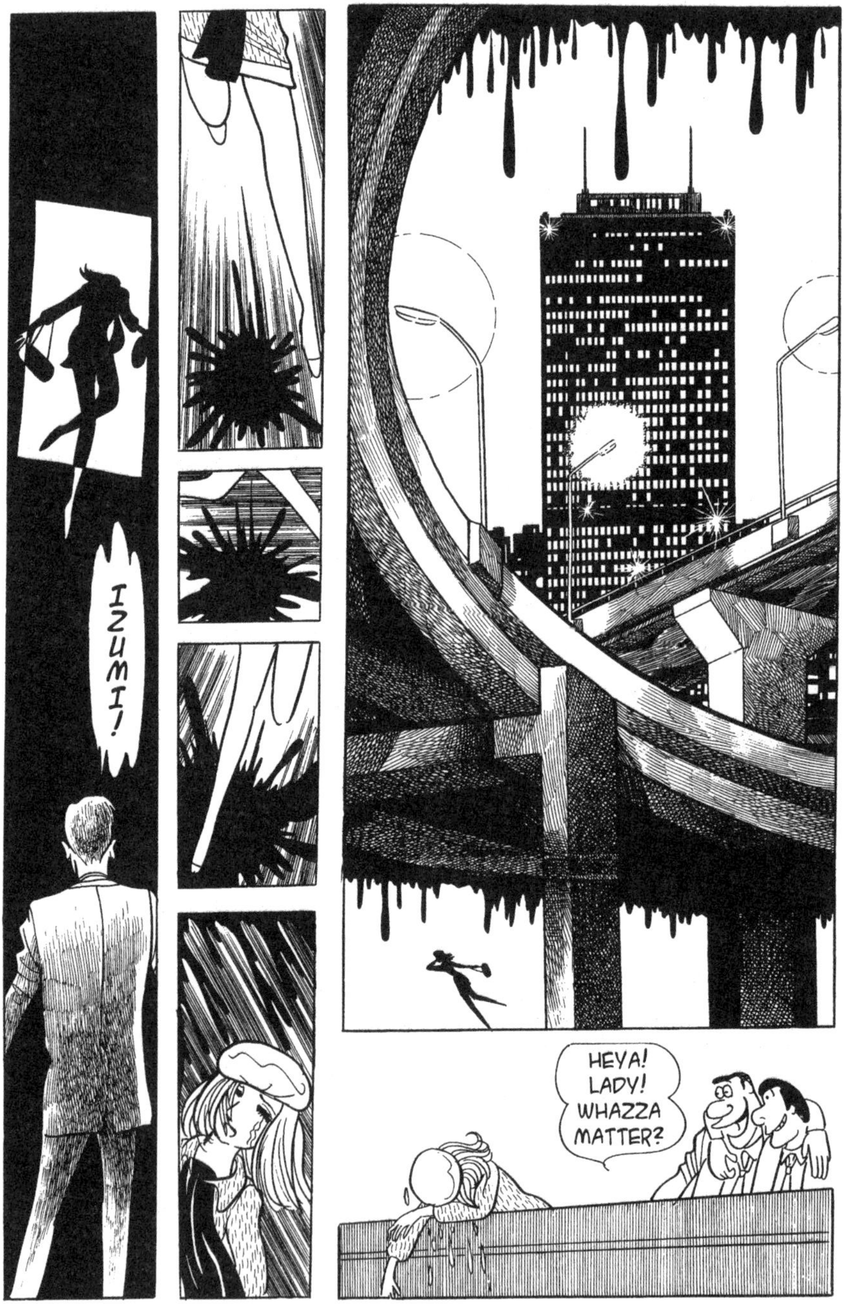
IZUMI!
HEYA! LADY! WHAZZA MATTER?

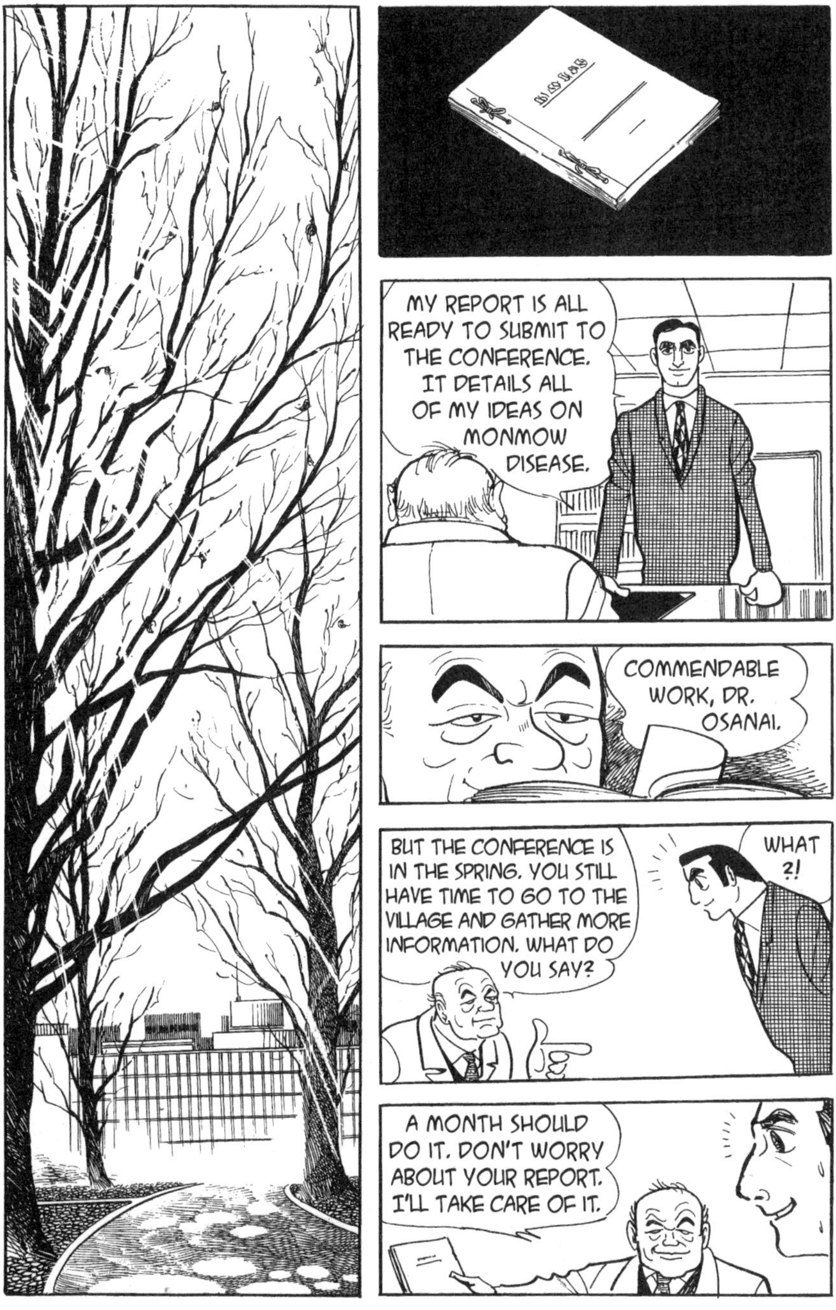
MY REPORT IS ALL READY TO SUBMIT TO THE CONFERENCE. IT DETAILS ALL OF MY IDEAS ON MONMOW DISEASE.
COMMENDABLE WORK, DR. OSANAI.
BUT THE CONFERENCE IS IN THE SPRING. YOU STILL HAVE TIME TO GO TO THE VILLAGE AND GATHER MORE INFORMATION. WHAT DO YOU SAY?
WHAT ?!
A MONTH SHOULD DO IT. DON'T WORRY ABOUT YOUR REPORT. I'LL TAKE CARE OF IT.

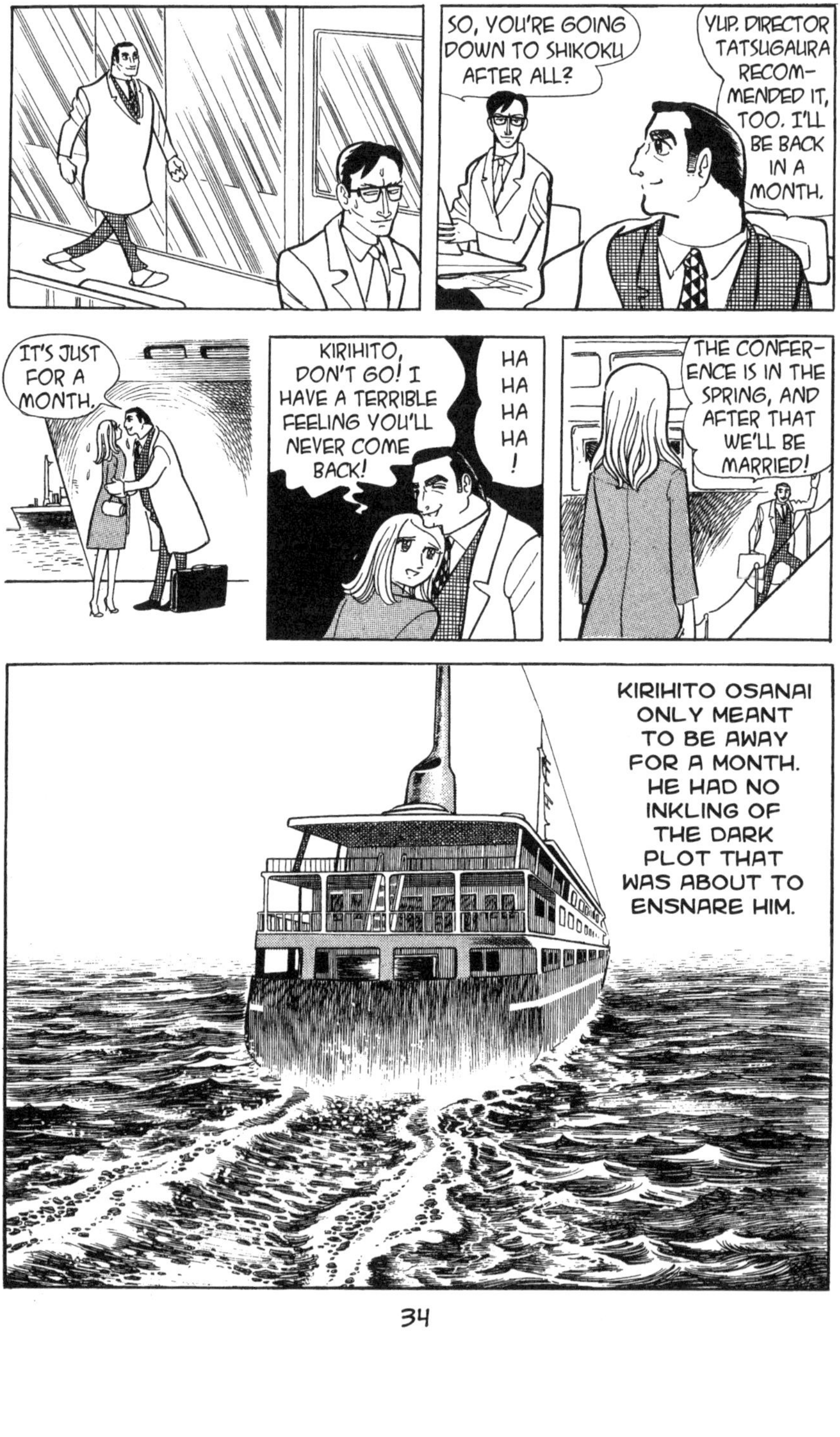
SO, YOU'RE GOING DOWN TO SHIKOKU AFTER ALL?
YUP. DIRECTOR TATSUGAURA RECOMMENDED IT, TOO. I'LL BE BACK IN A MONTH.
IT'S JUST FOR A MONTH.
KIRIHITO, DON'T GO! I HAVE A TERRIBLE FEELING YOU'LL NEVER COME BACK!
HA HA HA HA!
THE CONFERENCE IS IN THE SPRING, AND AFTER THAT WE'LL BE MARRIED!
KIRIHITO OSANAI ONLY MEANT TO BE AWAY FOR A MONTH. HE HAD NO INKLING OF THE DARK PLOT THAT WAS ABOUT TO ENSNARE HIM.

CHAPTER 2

DEAD END

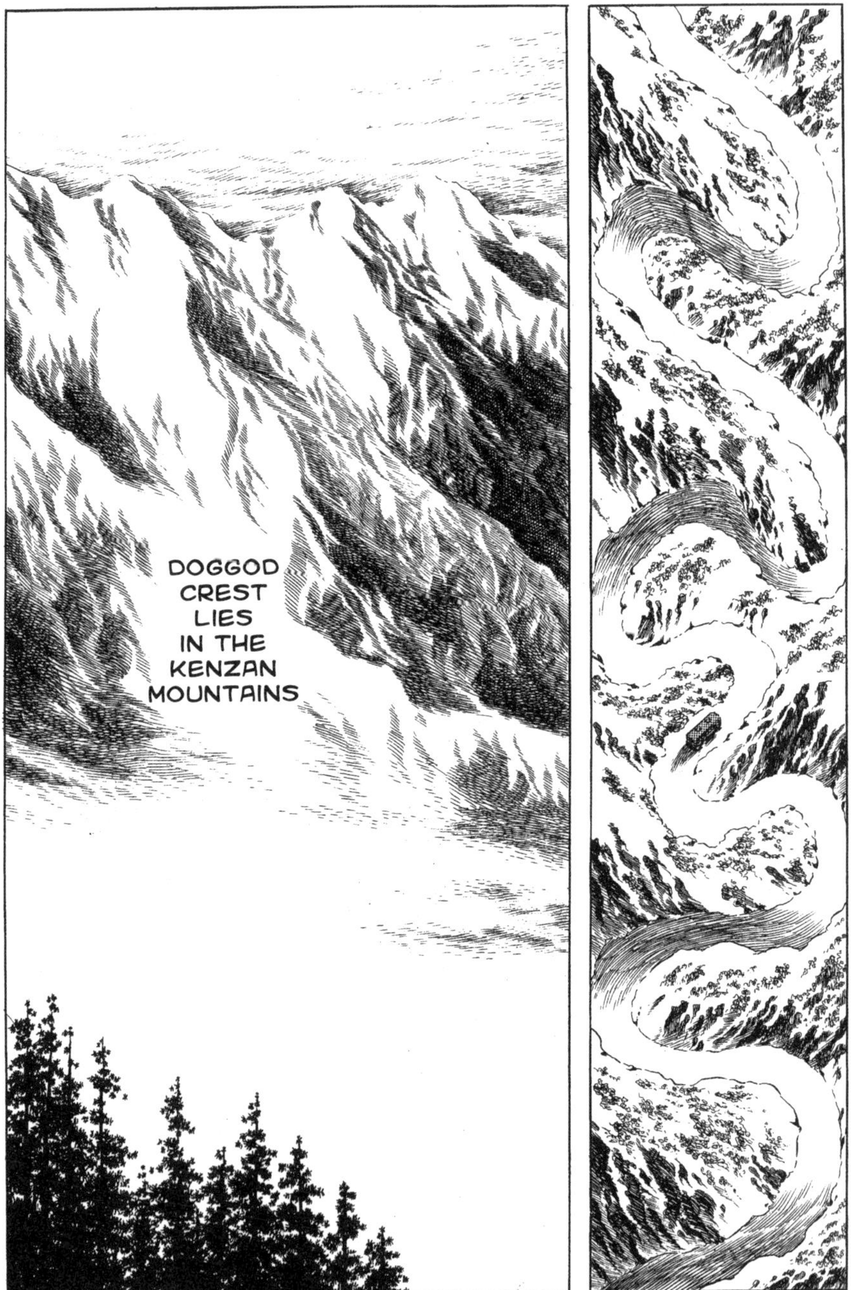
DOGGOD CREST LIES IN THE KENZAN MOUNTAINS

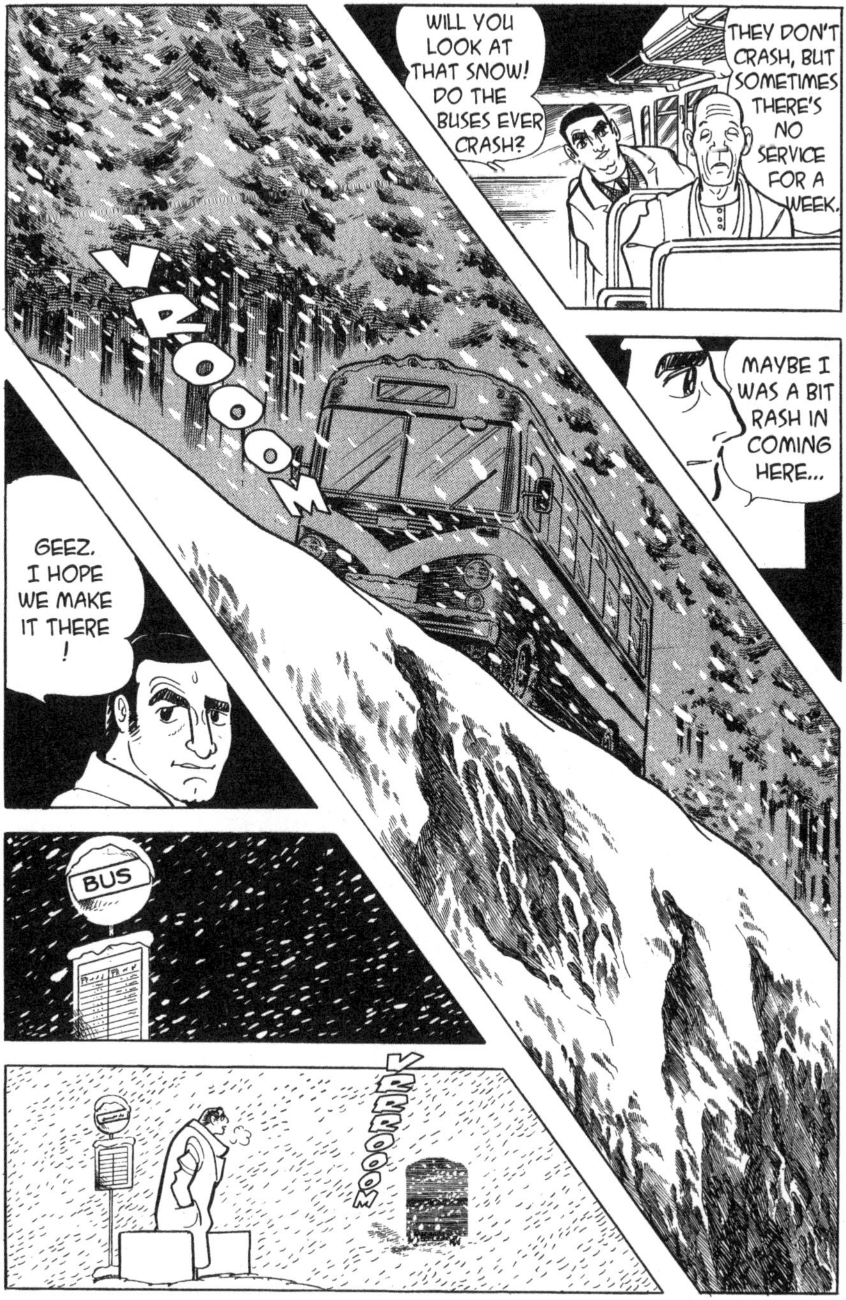
WILL YOU LOOK AT THAT SNOW! DO THE BUSES EVER CRASH?
THEY DON'T CRASH, BUT SOMETIMES THERE'S NO SERVICE FOR A WEEK.
VROOOOM
MAYBE I WAS A BIT RASH IN COMING HERE...
GEEZ. I HOPE WE MAKE IT THERE!
BUS
VRRROOOOM

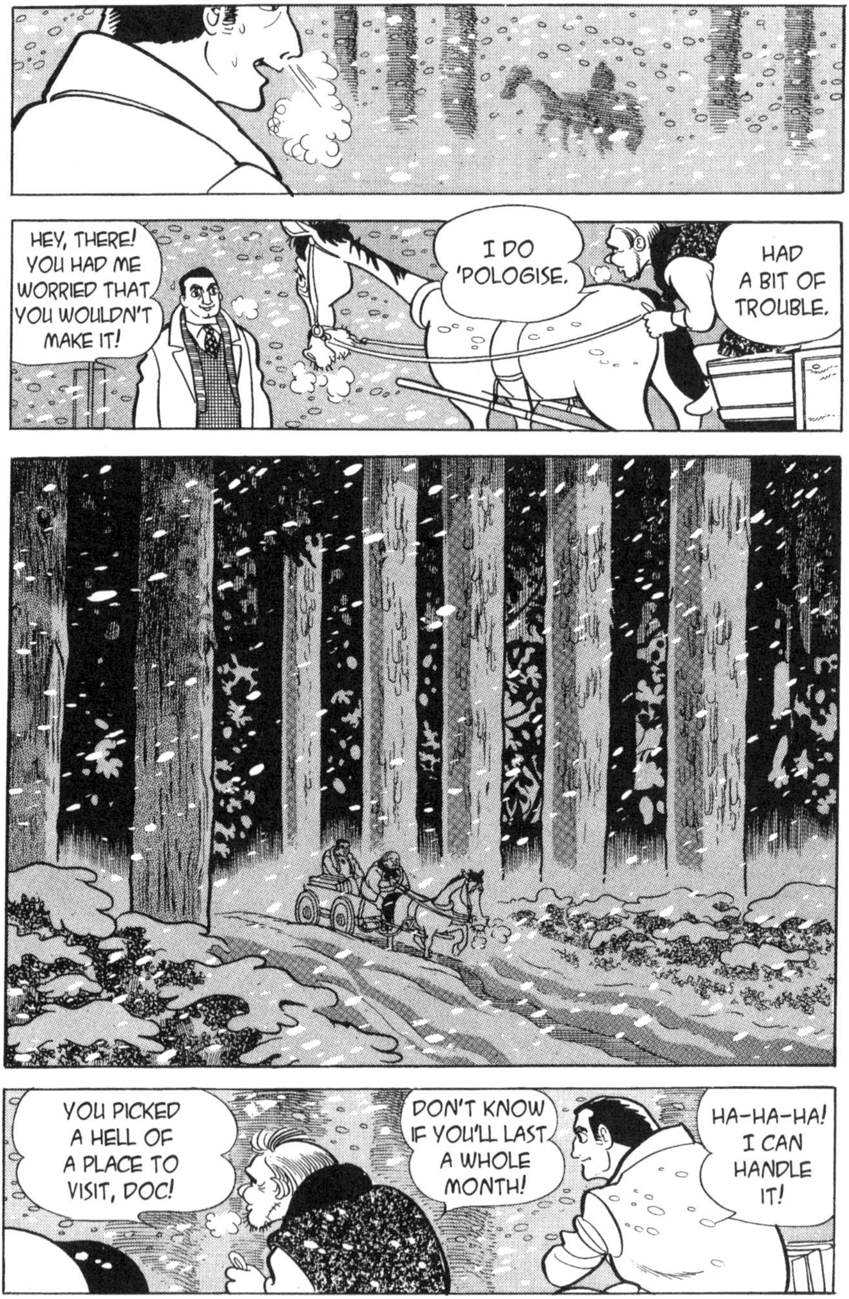
HEY, THERE! YOU HAD ME WORRIED THAT YOU WOULDN'T MAKE IT!
I DO 'POLOGISE.
HAD A BIT OF TROUBLE.
YOU PICKED A HELL OF A PLACE TO VISIT, DOC!
DON'T KNOW IF YOU'LL LAST A WHOLE MONTH!
HA-HA-HA! I CAN HANDLE IT!

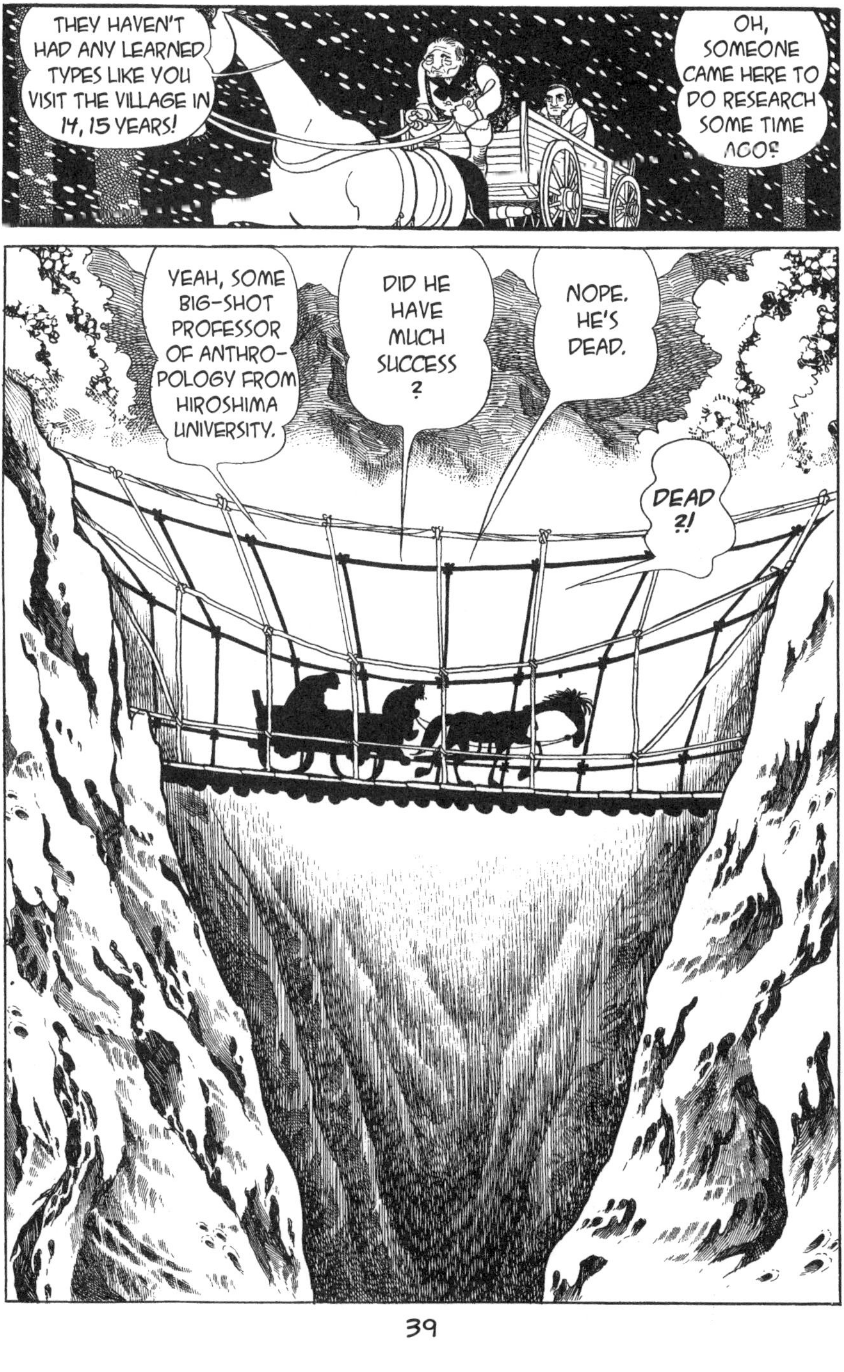
THEY HAVEN'T HAD ANY LEARNED TYPES LIKE YOU VISIT THE VILLAGE IN 14, 15 YEARS!
OH, SOMEONE CAME HERE TO DO RESEARCH SOME TIME AGO?
YEAH, SOME BIG-SHOT PROFESSOR OF ANTHRO-POLOGY FROM HIROSHIMA UNIVERSITY.
DID HE HAVE MUCH SUCCESS?
NOPE. HE'S DEAD.
DEAD?!

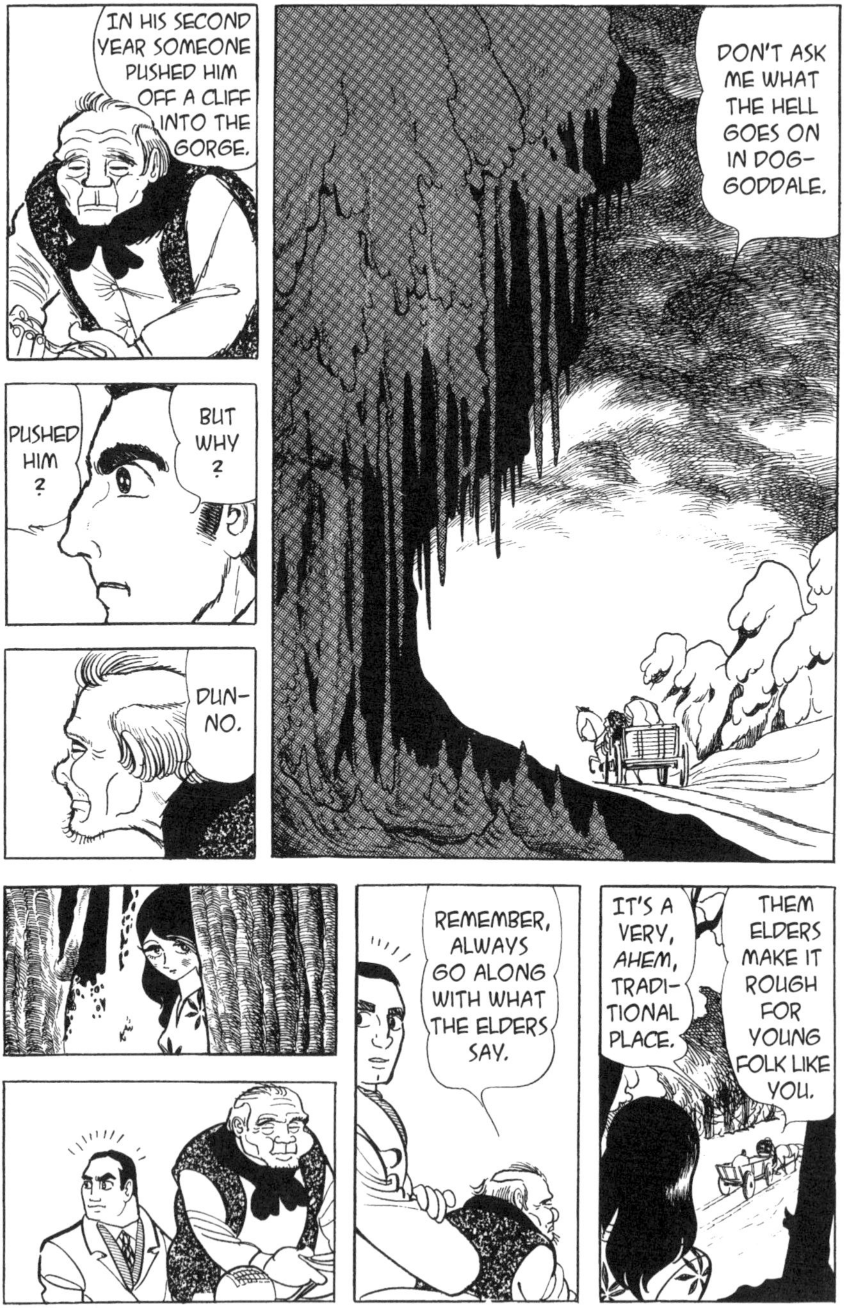
IN HIS SECOND YEAR SOMEONE PUSHED HIM OFF A CLIFF INTO THE GORGE.
PUSHED HIM?
BUT WHY?
DUN-NO.
DON'T ASK ME WHAT THE HELL GOES ON IN DOG-GODDALE.
REMEMBER, ALWAYS GO ALONG WITH WHAT THE ELDERS SAY.
IT'S A VERY, AHEM, TRADI-TIONAL PLACE.
THEM ELDERS MAKE IT ROUGH FOR YOUNG FOLK LIKE YOU.

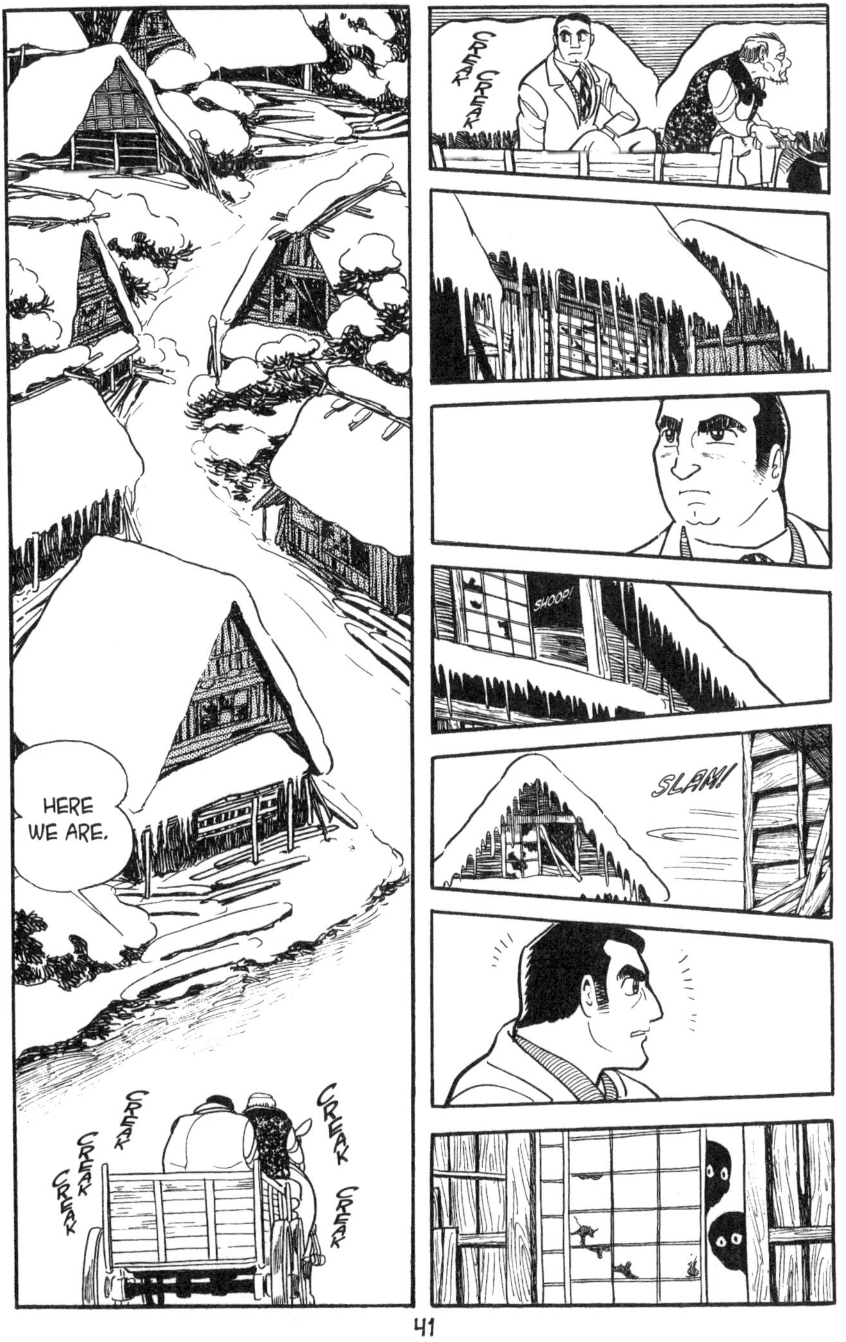
HERE WE ARE.
CREAK CREAK CREAK
CREAK CREAK
CREAK CREAK
SHOOP!
SLAM!

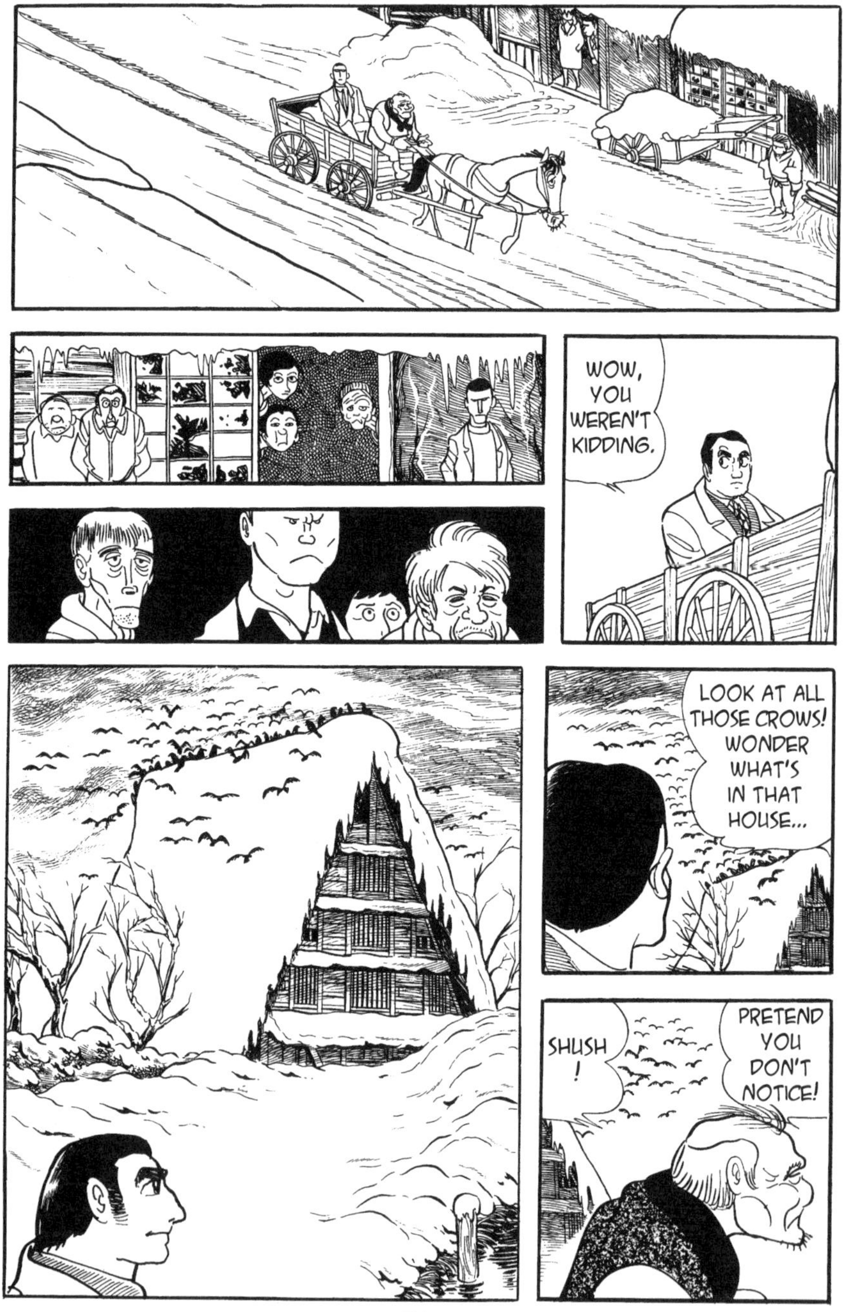
WOW, YOU WEREN'T KIDDING.
LOOK AT ALL THOSE CROWS! WONDER WHAT'S IN THAT HOUSE...
PRETEND YOU DON'T NOTICE!
SHUSH!

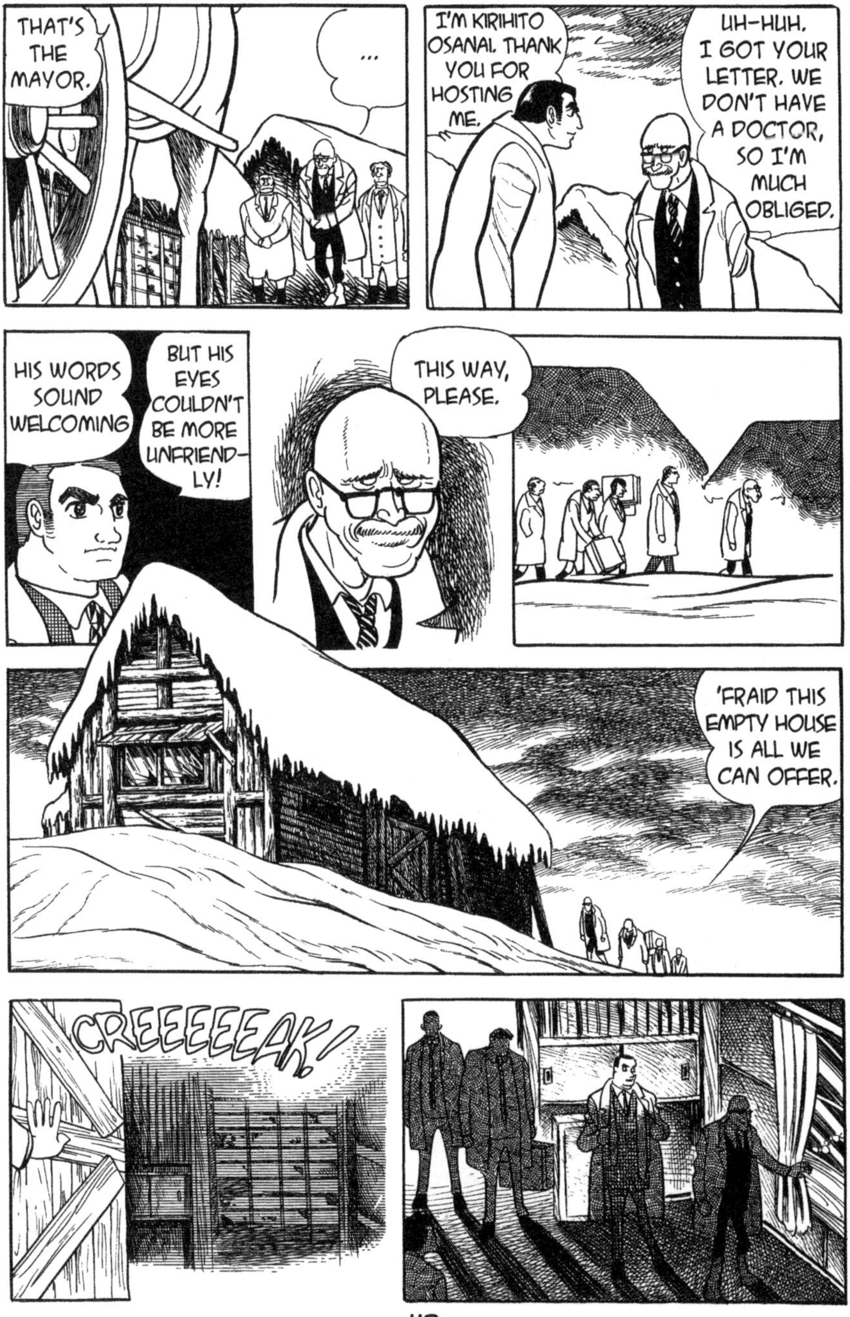

THAT'S THE MAYOR.
...
I'M KIRIHITO OSANAI. THANK YOU FOR HOSTING ME.
UH-HUH. I GOT YOUR LETTER. WE DON'T HAVE A DOCTOR, SO I'M MUCH OBLIGED.
HIS WORDS SOUND WELCOMING
BUT HIS EYES COULDN'T BE MORE UNFRIEND-LY!
THIS WAY, PLEASE.
'FRAID THIS EMPTY HOUSE IS ALL WE CAN OFFER.
CREEEEEEAK!

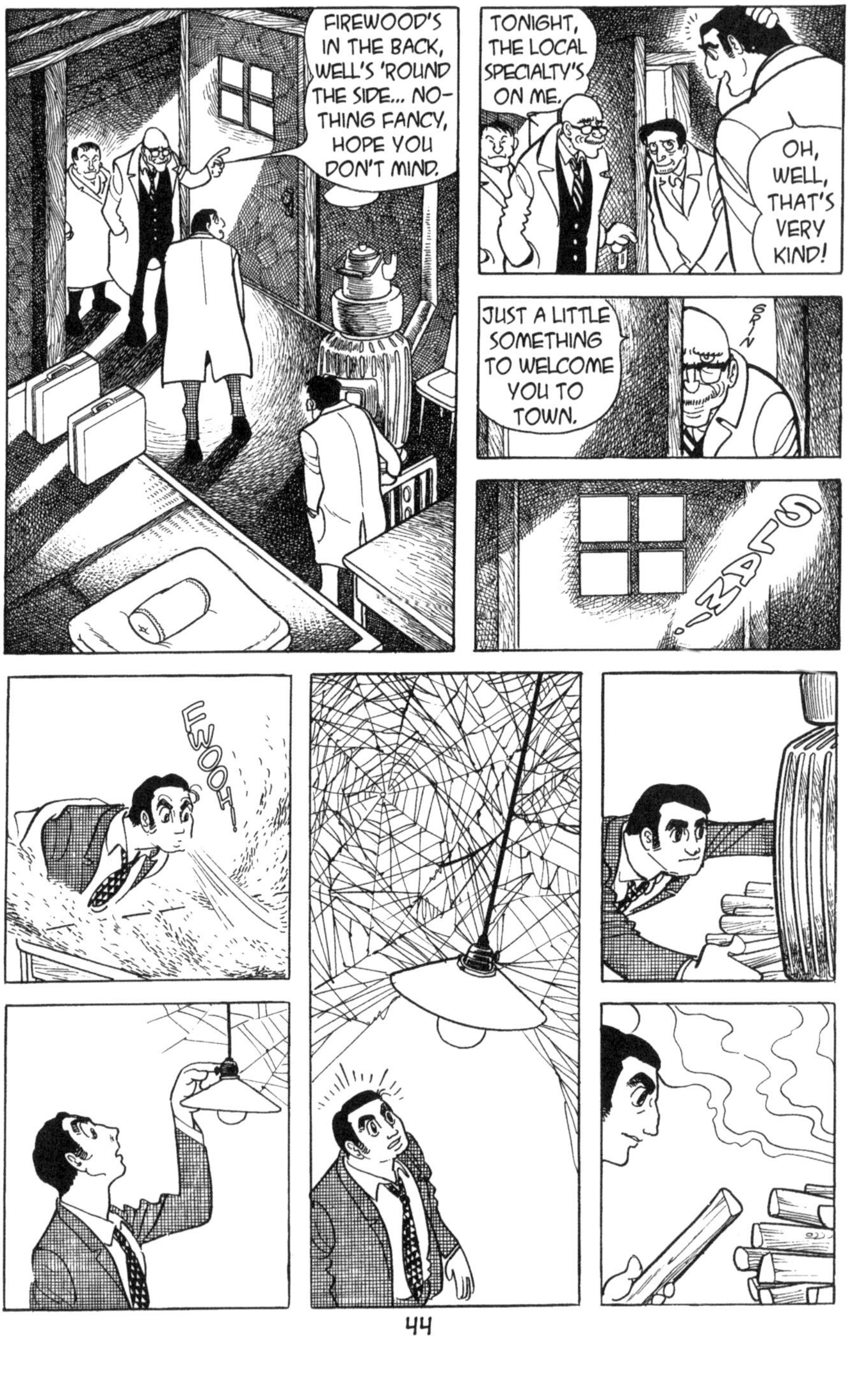
FIREWOOD'S IN THE BACK, WELL'S 'ROUND THE SIDE... NOTHING FANCY, HOPE YOU DON'T MIND.
TONIGHT, THE LOCAL SPECIALTY'S ON ME.
OH, WELL, THAT'S VERY KIND!
JUST A LITTLE SOMETHING TO WELCOME YOU TO TOWN.
GRIN
SLAM!
FWOOH!

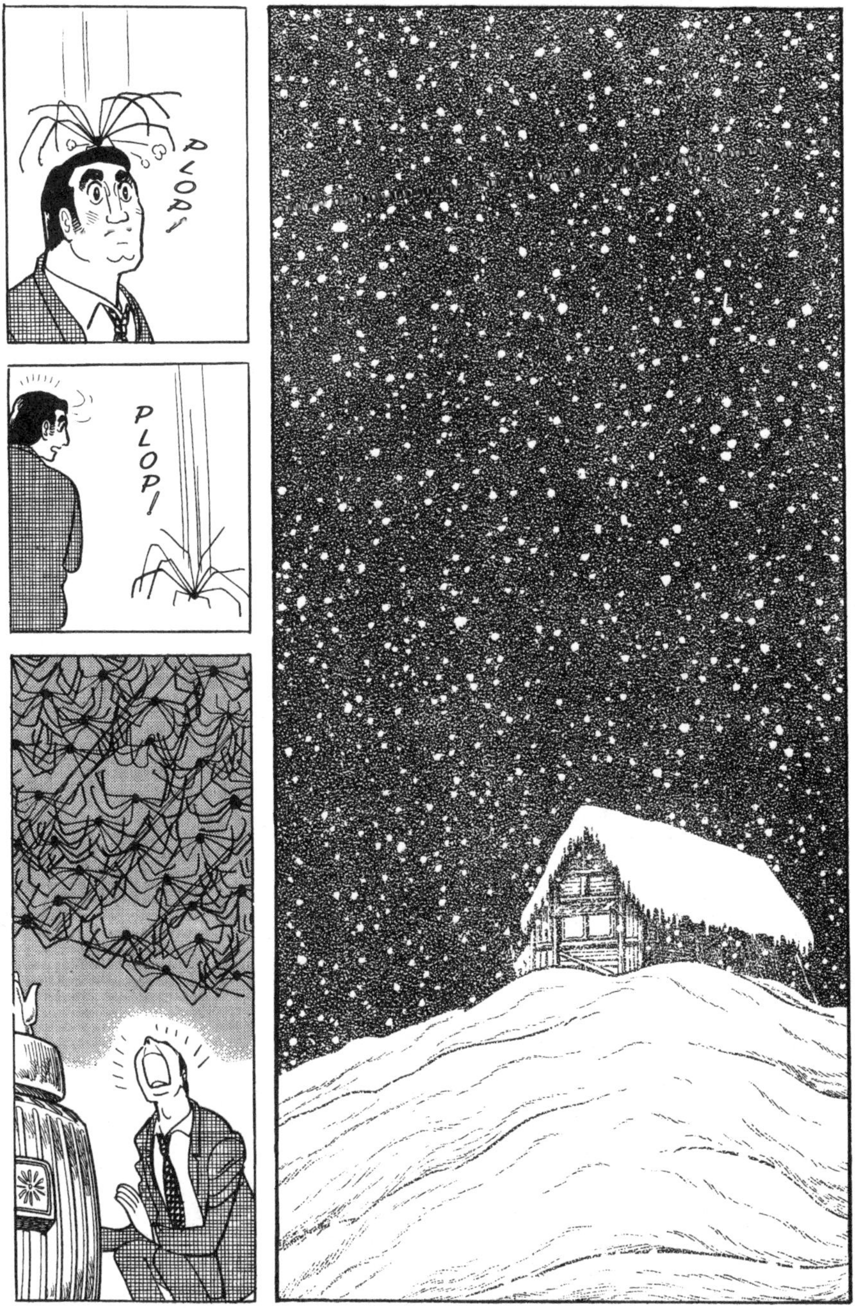
PLOP!
PLOP!

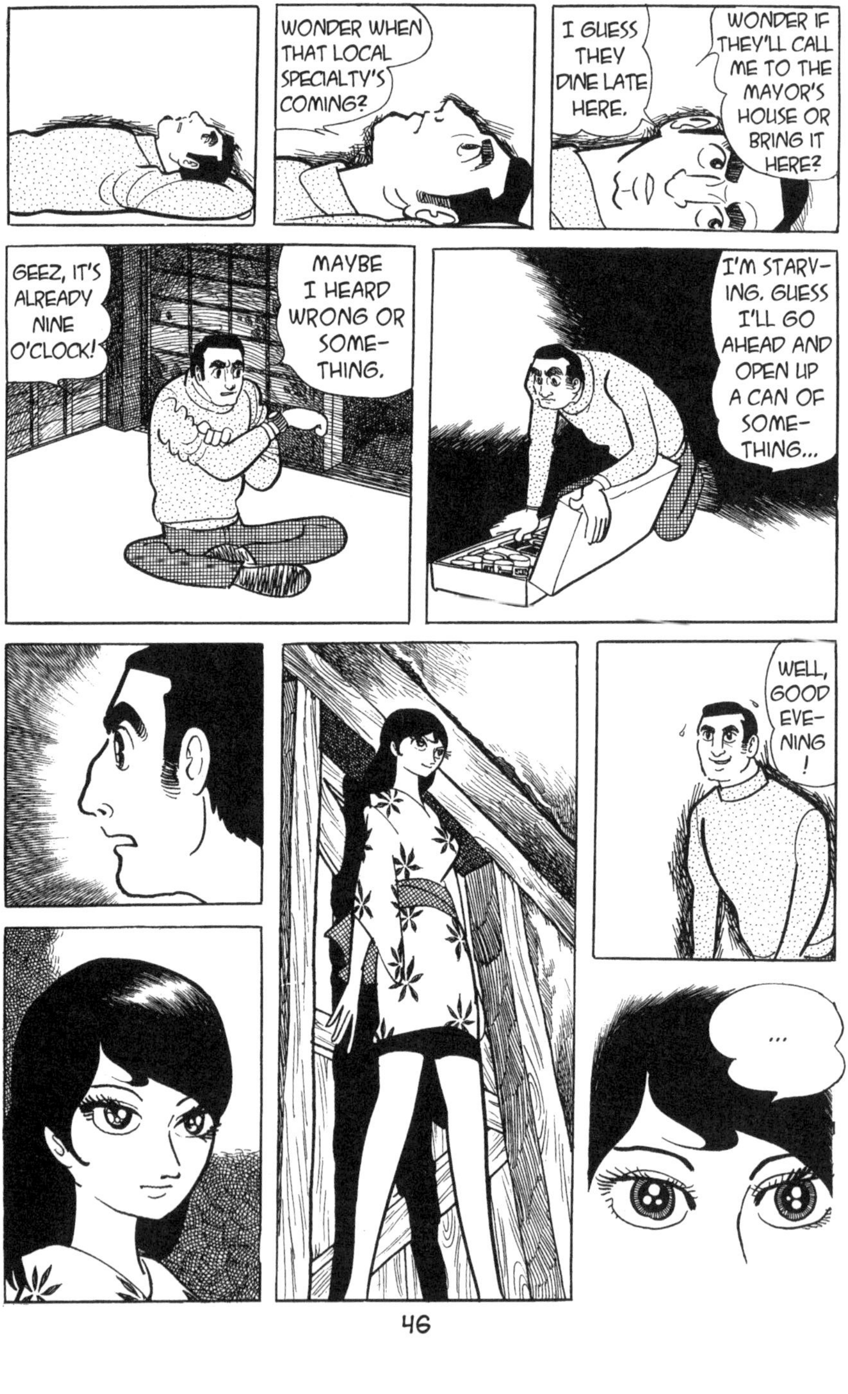
WONDER WHEN THAT LOCAL SPECIALTY'S COMING?
I GUESS THEY DINE LATE HERE.
WONDER IF THEY'LL CALL ME TO THE MAYOR'S HOUSE OR BRING IT HERE?
GEEZ, IT'S ALREADY NINE O'CLOCK!
MAYBE I HEARD WRONG OR SOME-THING.
I'M STARV-ING. GUESS I'LL GO AHEAD AND OPEN UP A CAN OF SOME-THING...
WELL, GOOD EVE-NING!
...

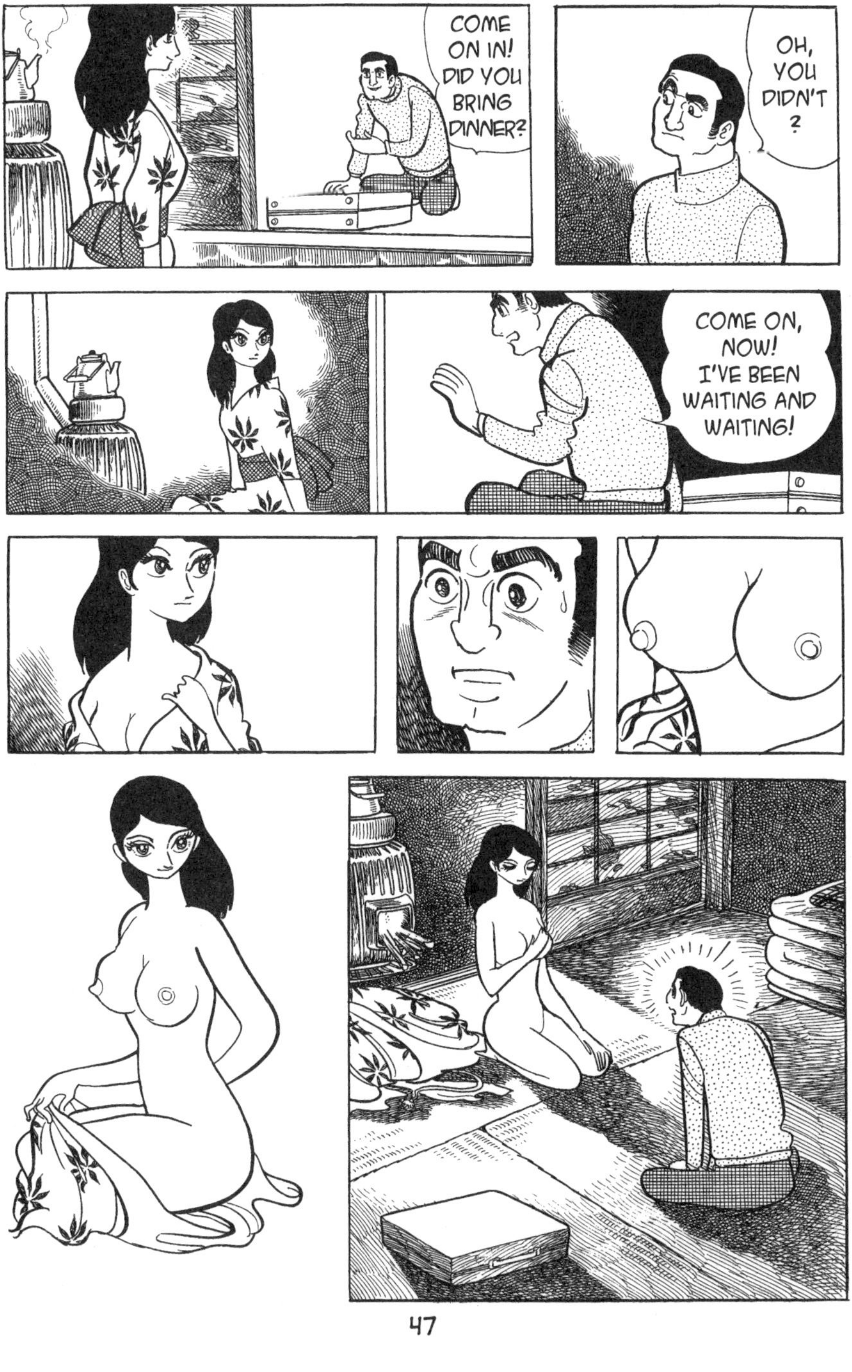
COME ON IN! DID YOU BRING DINNER?
OH, YOU DIDN'T ?
COME ON, NOW! I'VE BEEN WAITING AND WAITING!

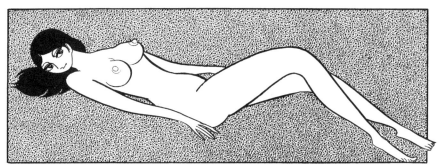

HUH?!

ARE YOU OUT OF YOUR MIND?

I GET IT. IN SOME REGIONS, THEY EXPRESS HOSPITALITY THIS WAY. ARE YOU THE...?

PUT YOUR CLOTHES BACK ON. I'M REALLY NOT IN THE MOOD.

I'M COLD ...

THEN HURRY UP AND GET DRESSED! HEY! WHAT ARE YOU DOING?

I'M COLD.

48

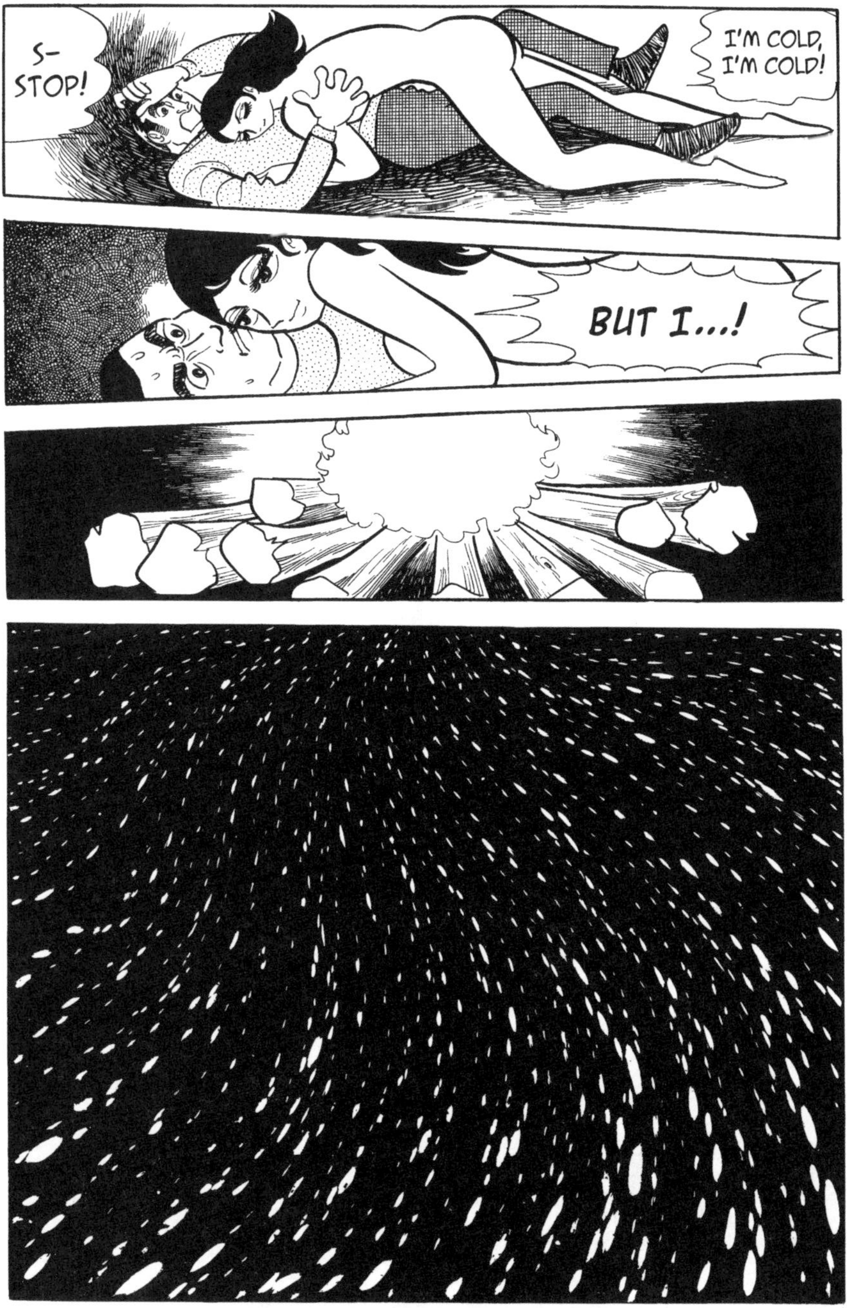
I'M COLD, I'M COLD!
S-STOP!
BUT I...!

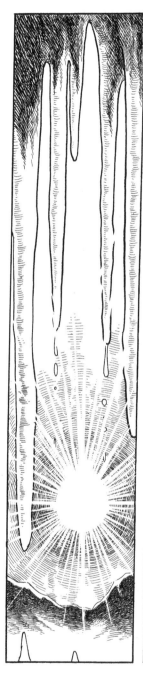

YOU REALLY SHOULDN'T HAVE DONE THAT.

IF WORSE CAME TO WORST... WE'D BOTH BE IN A REAL BIND.

HEY, THE SNOW'S STOPPED!

IT'S COLD, BUT THE FRESH AIR FEELS GOOD!

WHAT'S YOUR NAME?

TAZU

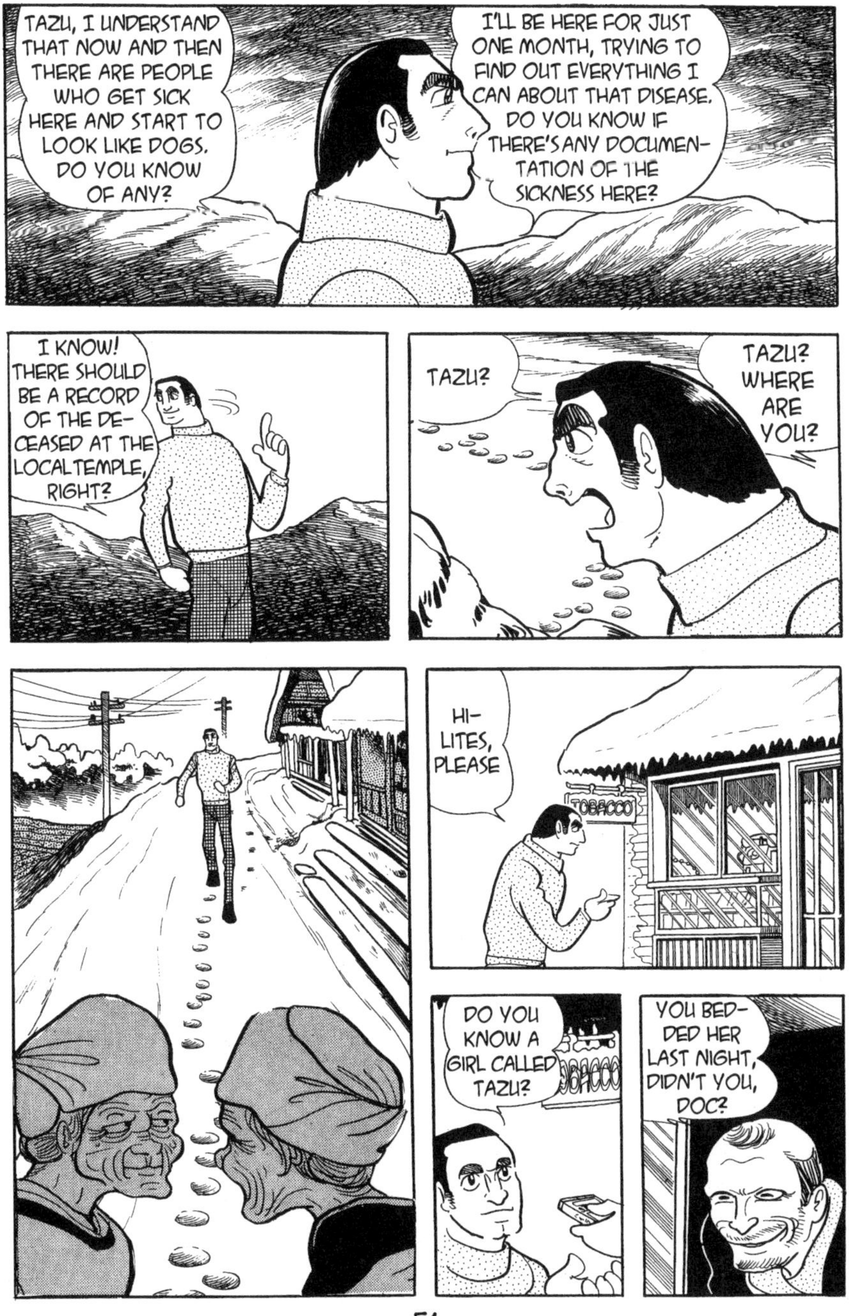
TAZU, I UNDERSTAND THAT NOW AND THEN THERE ARE PEOPLE WHO GET SICK HERE AND START TO LOOK LIKE DOGS. DO YOU KNOW OF ANY?
I'LL BE HERE FOR JUST ONE MONTH, TRYING TO FIND OUT EVERYTHING I CAN ABOUT THAT DISEASE. DO YOU KNOW IF THERE'S ANY DOCUMENTATION OF THE SICKNESS HERE?
I KNOW! THERE SHOULD BE A RECORD OF THE DECEASED AT THE LOCAL TEMPLE, RIGHT?
TAZU?
TAZU? WHERE ARE YOU?
HI-LITES, PLEASE
TOBACCO
DO YOU KNOW A GIRL CALLED TAZU?
YOU BEDDED HER LAST NIGHT, DIDN'T YOU, DOC?

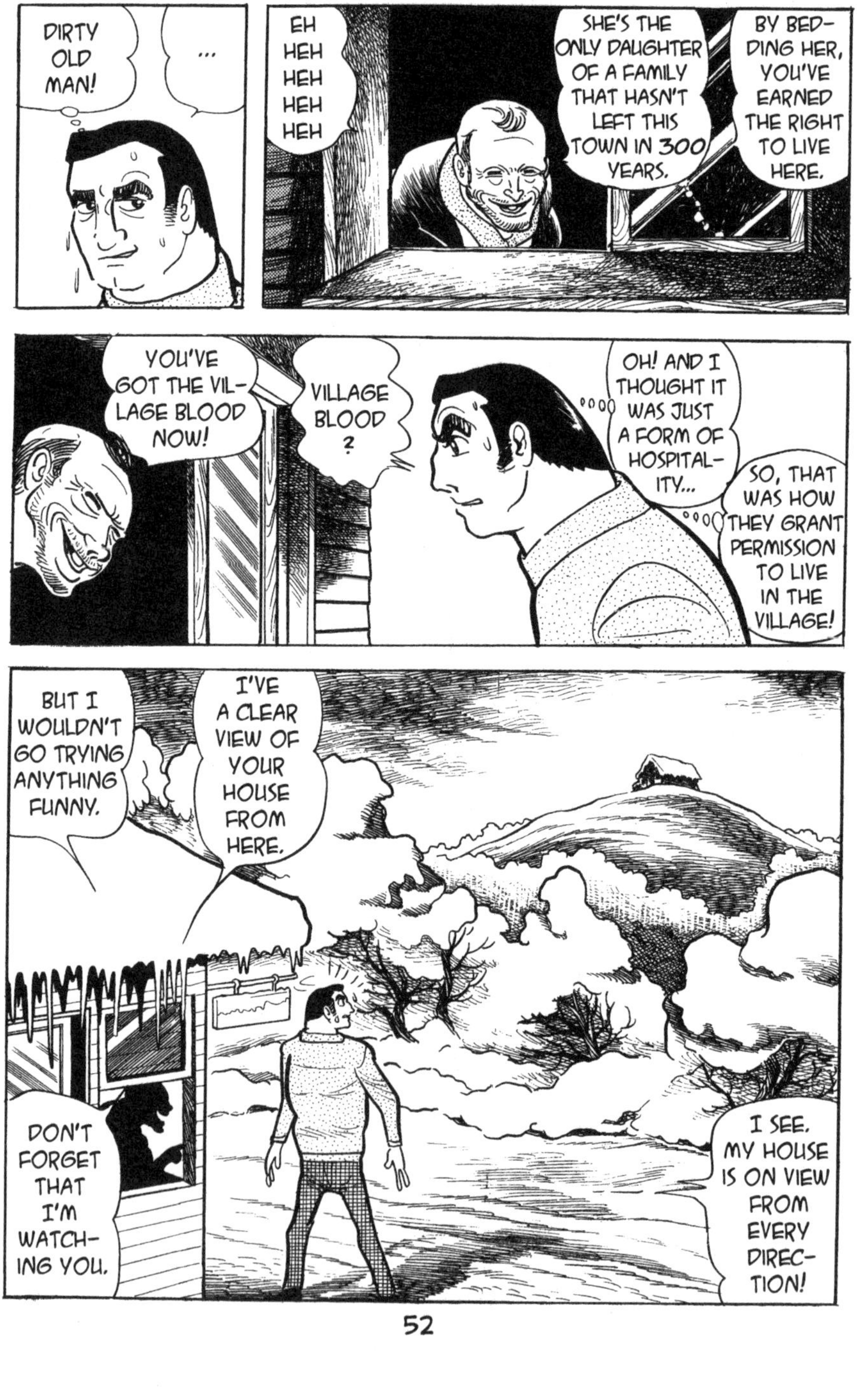
DIRTY OLD MAN!
...
EH HEH HEH HEH HEH
SHE'S THE ONLY DAUGHTER OF A FAMILY THAT HASN'T LEFT THIS TOWN IN 300 YEARS.
BY BEDDING HER, YOU'VE EARNED THE RIGHT TO LIVE HERE.
YOU'VE GOT THE VILLAGE BLOOD NOW!
VILLAGE BLOOD?
OH! AND I THOUGHT IT WAS JUST A FORM OF HOSPITALITY...
SO, THAT WAS HOW THEY GRANT PERMISSION TO LIVE IN THE VILLAGE!
BUT I WOULDN'T GO TRYING ANYTHING FUNNY.
I'VE A CLEAR VIEW OF YOUR HOUSE FROM HERE.
DON'T FORGET THAT I'M WATCHING YOU.
I SEE. MY HOUSE IS ON VIEW FROM EVERY DIRECTION!

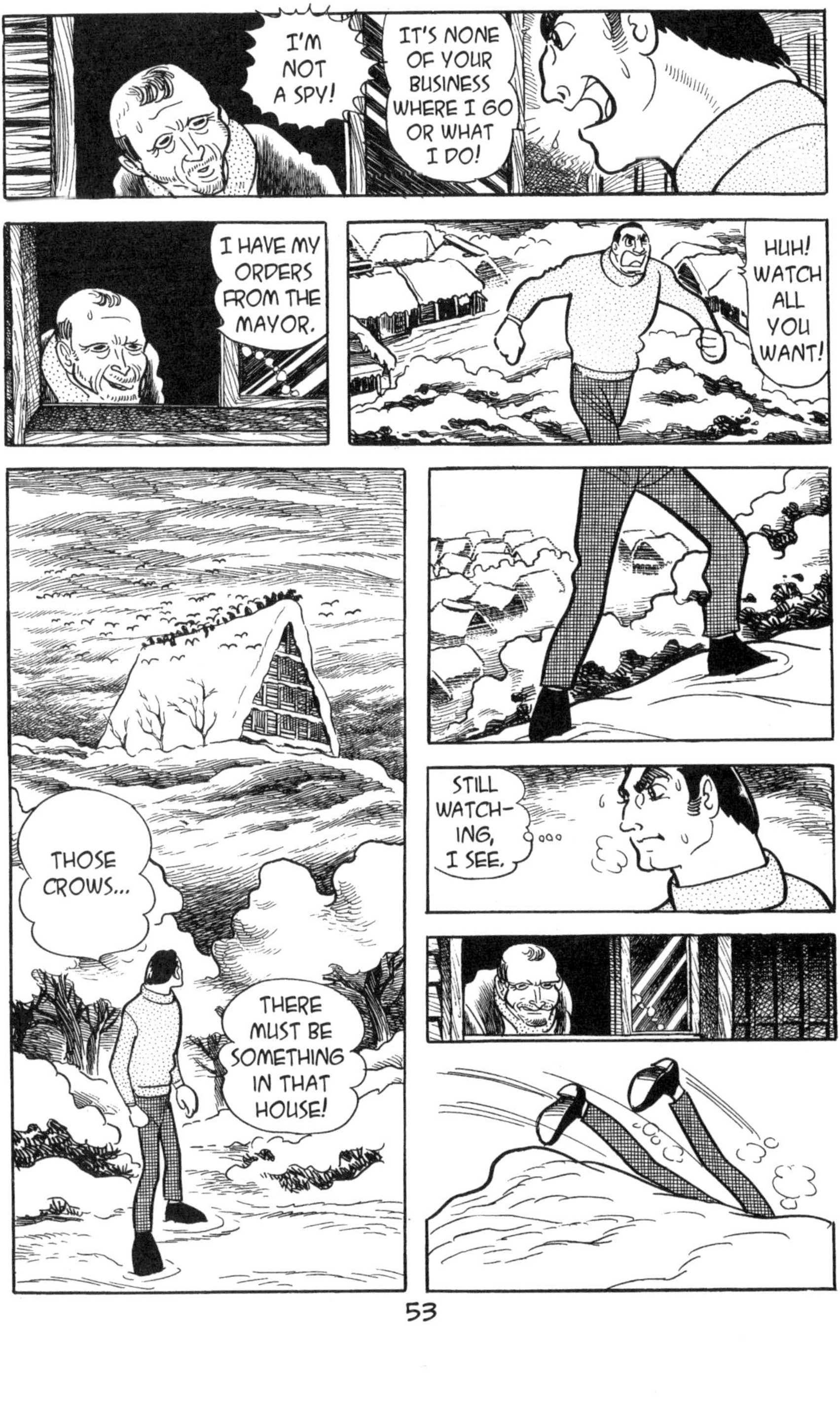

I'M NOT A SPY!
IT'S NONE OF YOUR BUSINESS WHERE I GO OR WHAT I DO!
I HAVE MY ORDERS FROM THE MAYOR.
HUH! WATCH ALL YOU WANT!
STILL WATCHING, I SEE.
THOSE CROWS...
THERE MUST BE SOMETHING IN THAT HOUSE!

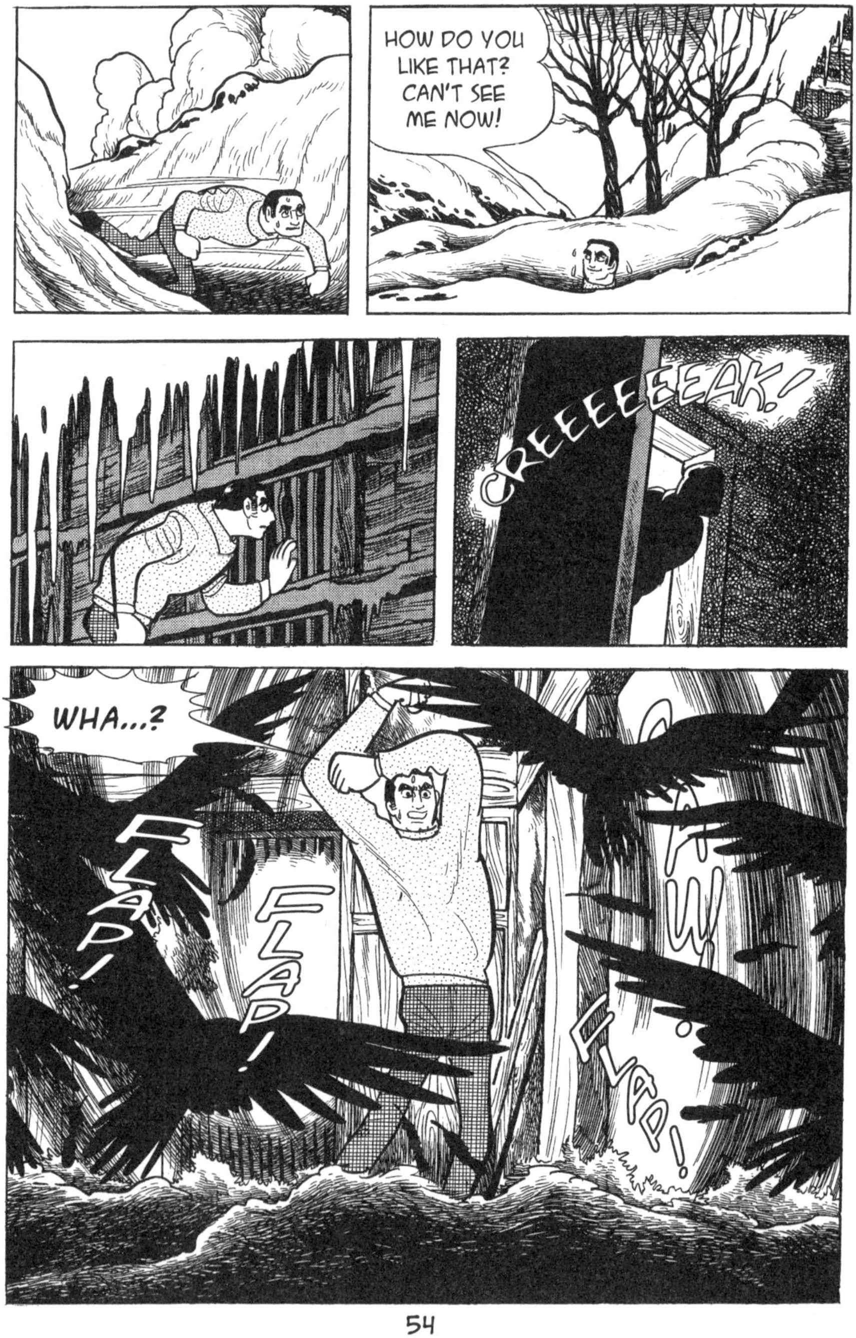
HOW DO YOU LIKE THAT? CAN'T SEE ME NOW!
CREEEEEEEAK!
WHA...?
FLAP!
FLAP!
FLAP!
FLAP!

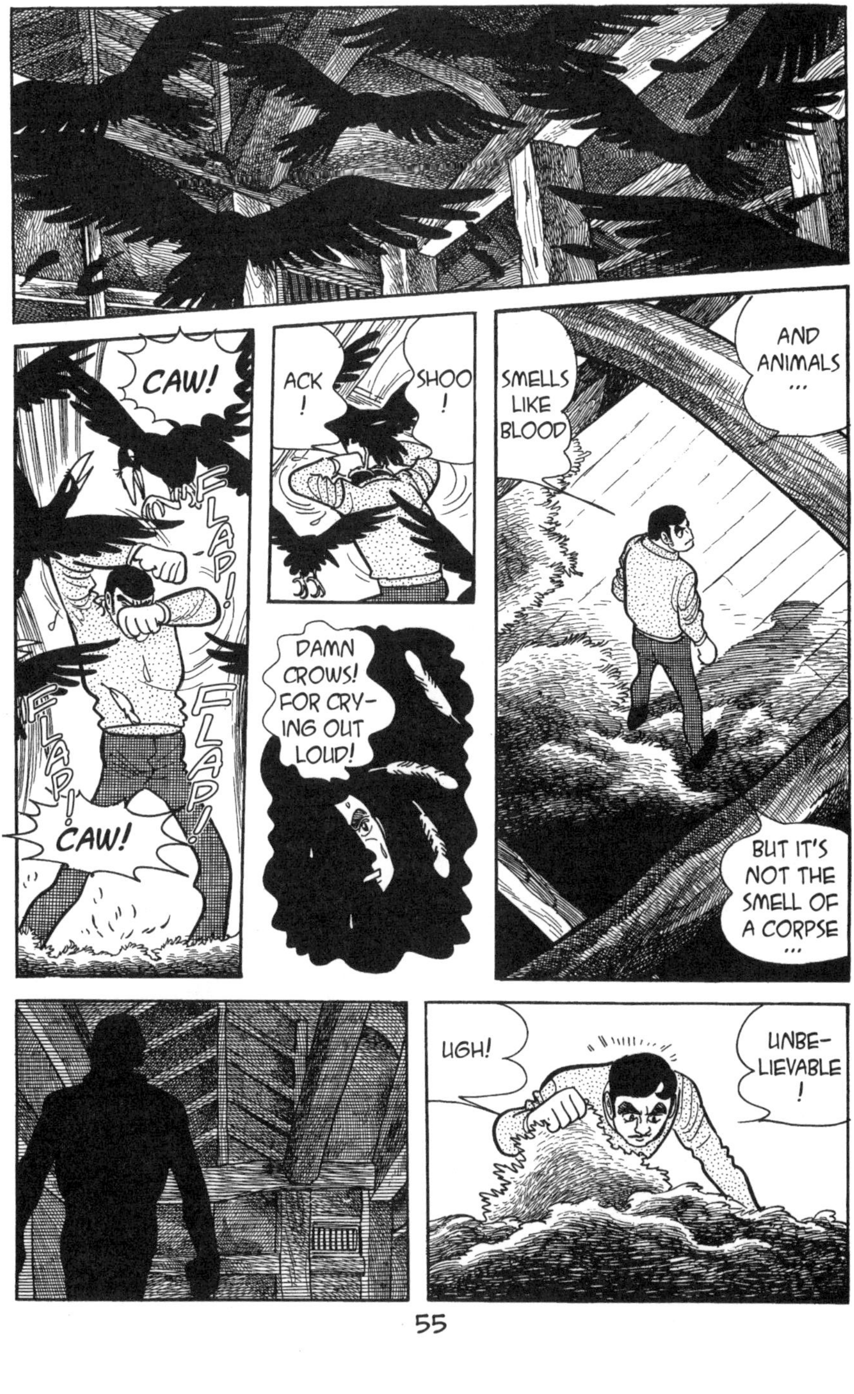
CAW!
FLAP!
FLAP!
FLAP!
CAW!
SHOO!
ACK!
DAMN CROWS! FOR CRYING OUT LOUD!
AND ANIMALS ...
SMELLS LIKE BLOOD
BUT IT'S NOT THE SMELL OF A CORPSE ...
UNBELIEVABLE!
UGH!

 WHAT ARE ALL THESE DEAD DOGS AND CHICKENS DOING HERE?

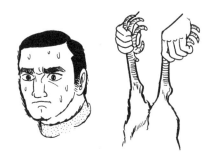

 THIS ISN'T JUST THE WORK OF CROWS.

SOMETHING ELSE HAS BEEN EATING THESE ANIMALS.

 DOESN'T LOOK LIKE ANYONE'S USED THIS FIRE PIT IN A WHILE.

 SO, NOBODY'S LIVED HERE IN A LONG TIME.

WHAT ARE FRESH ANIMAL CARCASSES DOING IN AN ABANDONED HOUSE?

 IT MAY BE COLD OUT HERE, BUT I'LL GET TO THE BOTTOM OF THIS!

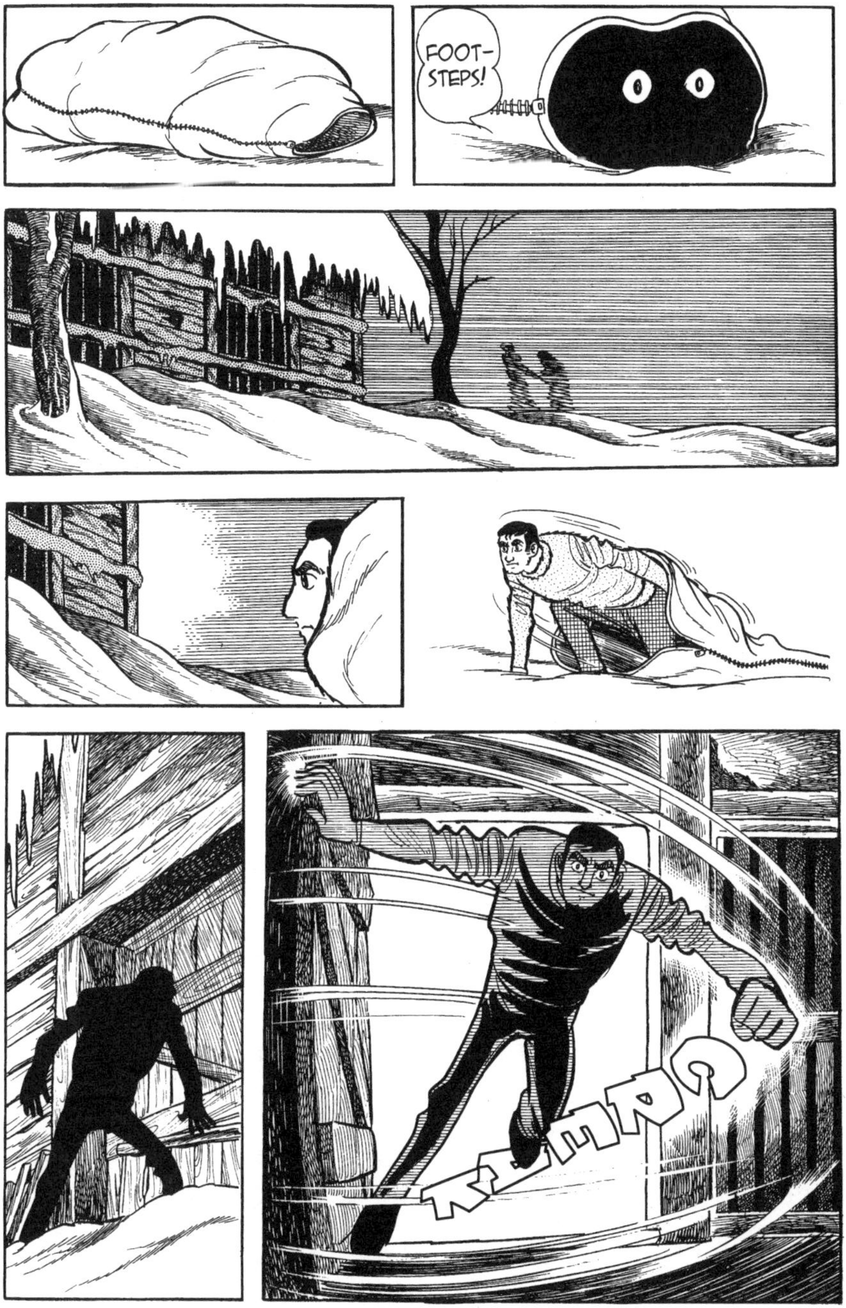
FOOT-STEPS!

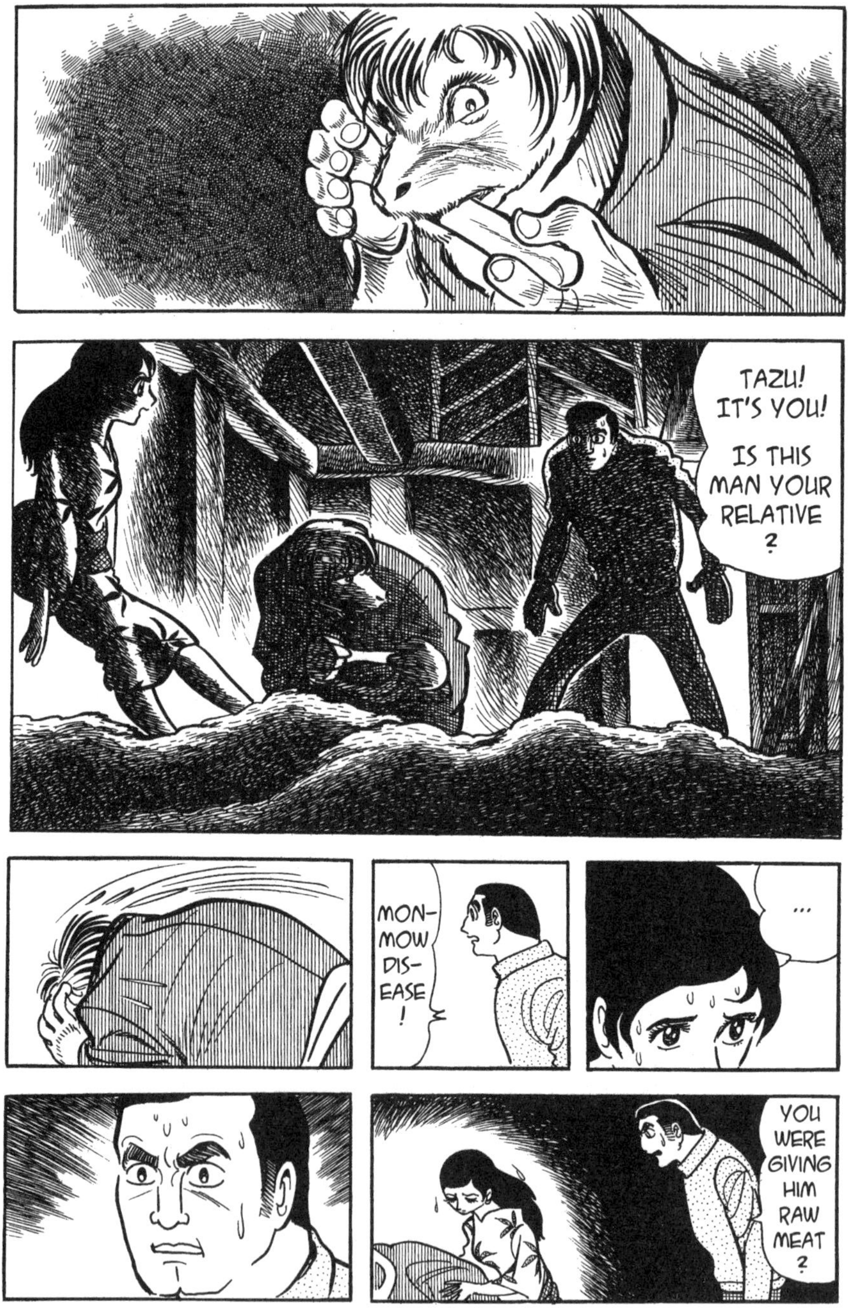
TAZU! IT'S YOU!
IS THIS MAN YOUR RELATIVE?
MON-MOW DIS-EASE!
...
YOU WERE GIVING HIM RAW MEAT?

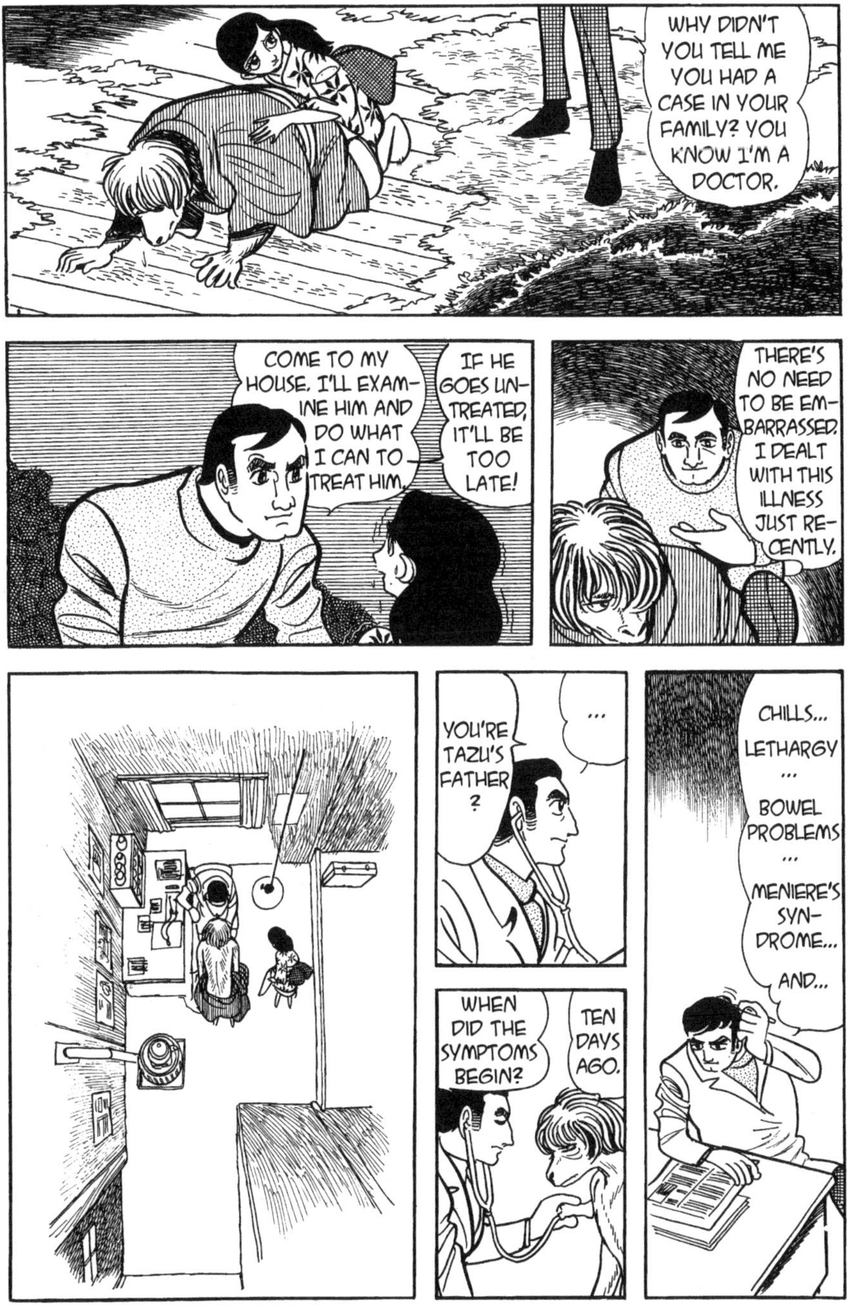
WHY DIDN'T YOU TELL ME YOU HAD A CASE IN YOUR FAMILY? YOU KNOW I'M A DOCTOR.
COME TO MY HOUSE. I'LL EXAMINE HIM AND DO WHAT I CAN TO TREAT HIM.
IF HE GOES UNTREATED, IT'LL BE TOO LATE!
THERE'S NO NEED TO BE EMBARRASSED. I DEALT WITH THIS ILLNESS JUST RECENTLY.
YOU'RE TAZU'S FATHER?
...
WHEN DID THE SYMPTOMS BEGIN?
TEN DAYS AGO.
CHILLS... LETHARGY ... BOWEL PROBLEMS ... MENIERE'S SYNDROME... AND...

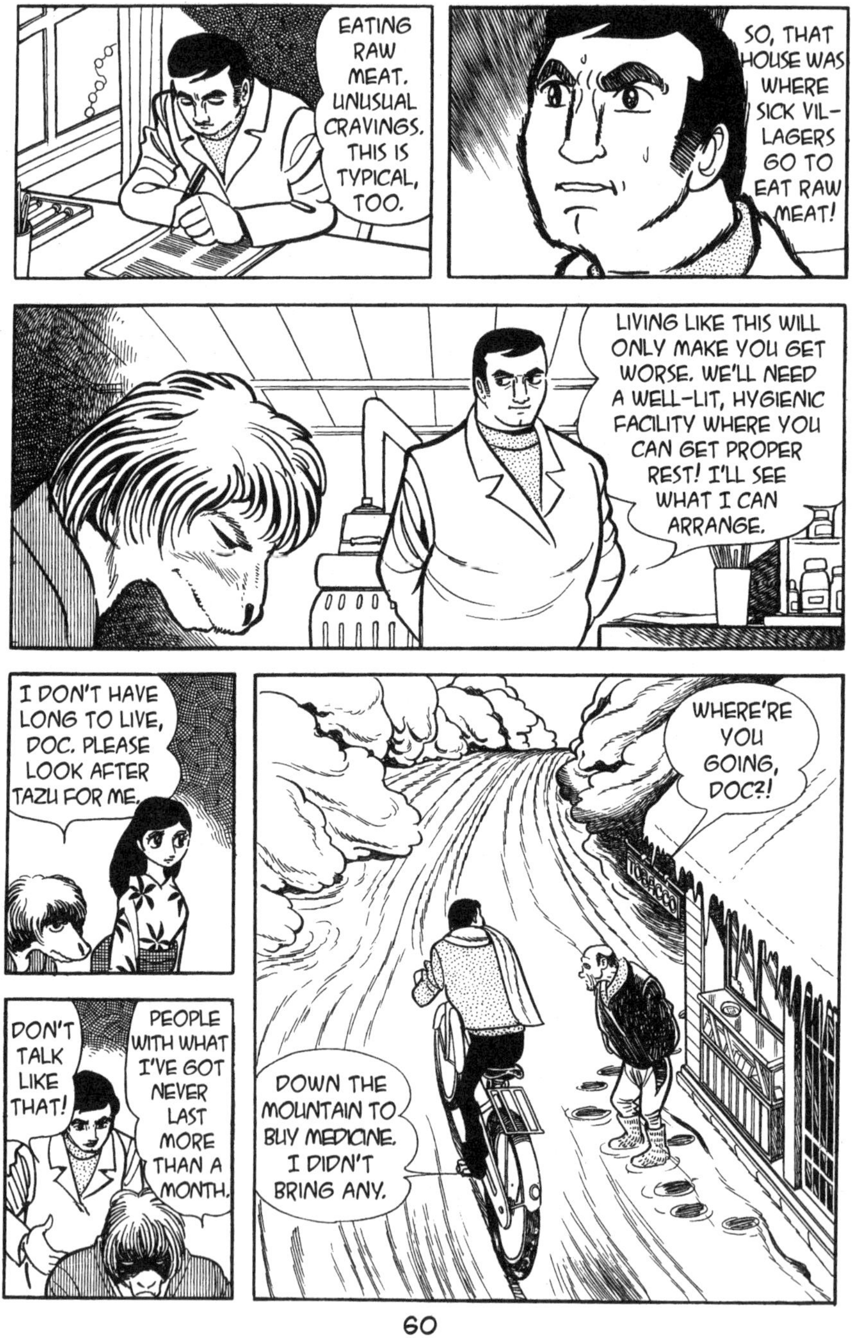
EATING RAW MEAT. UNUSUAL CRAVINGS. THIS IS TYPICAL, TOO.
SO, THAT HOUSE WAS WHERE SICK VIL-LAGERS GO TO EAT RAW MEAT!
LIVING LIKE THIS WILL ONLY MAKE YOU GET WORSE. WE'LL NEED A WELL-LIT, HYGIENIC FACILITY WHERE YOU CAN GET PROPER REST! I'LL SEE WHAT I CAN ARRANGE.
I DON'T HAVE LONG TO LIVE, DOC. PLEASE LOOK AFTER TAZU FOR ME.
DON'T TALK LIKE THAT!
PEOPLE WITH WHAT I'VE GOT NEVER LAST MORE THAN A MONTH.
WHERE'RE YOU GOING, DOC?!
DOWN THE MOUNTAIN TO BUY MEDICINE. I DIDN'T BRING ANY.
TOBACCO

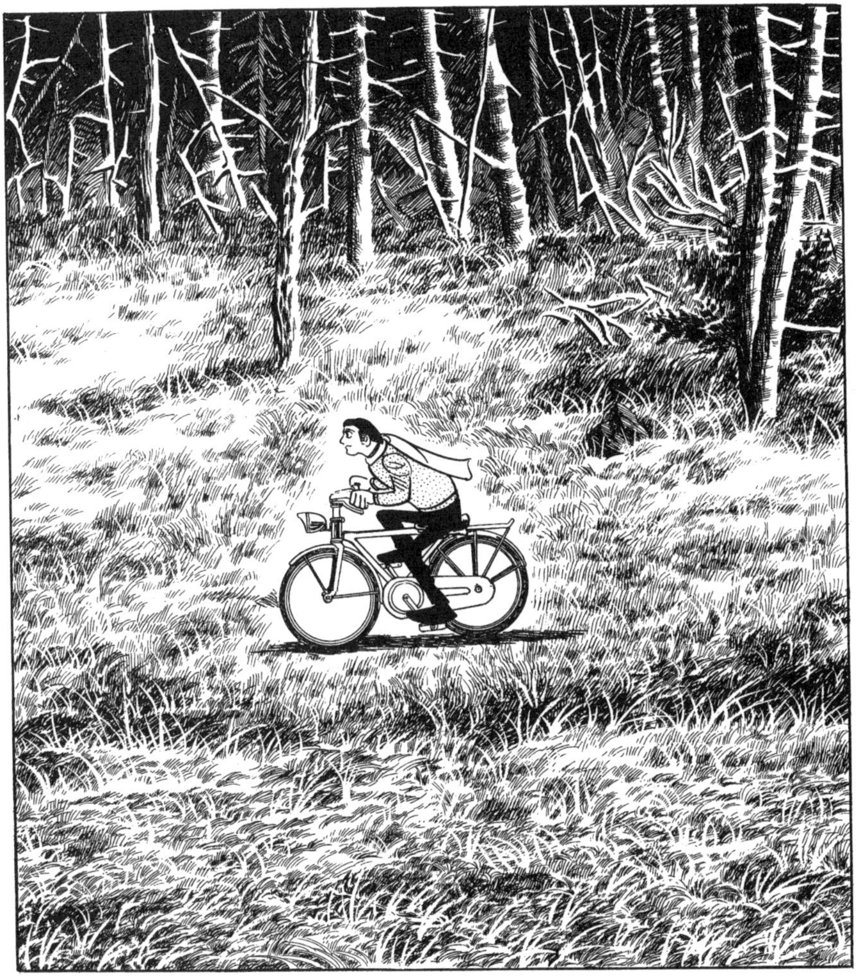

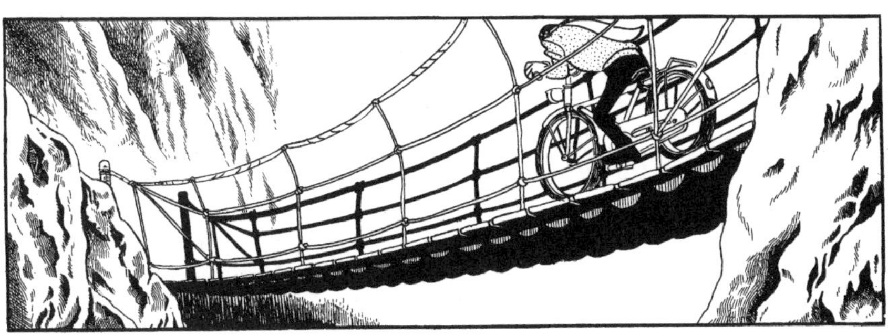

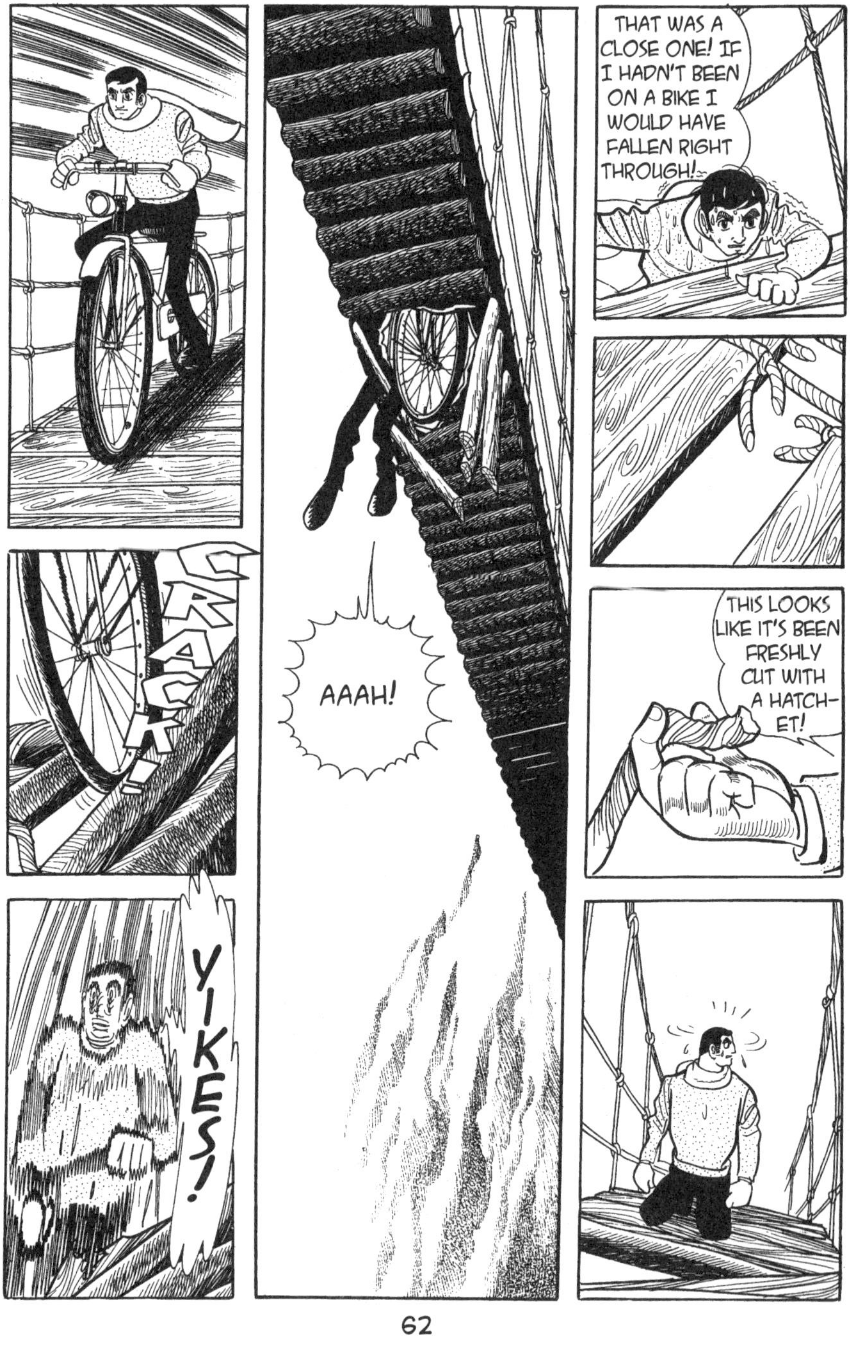
CRACK!
YIKES!
AAAH!
THAT WAS A CLOSE ONE! IF I HADN'T BEEN ON A BIKE I WOULD HAVE FALLEN RIGHT THROUGH!
THIS LOOKS LIKE IT'S BEEN FRESHLY CUT WITH A HATCHET!

HUH ?!

WHAT DO YOU THINK YOU'RE ...?!

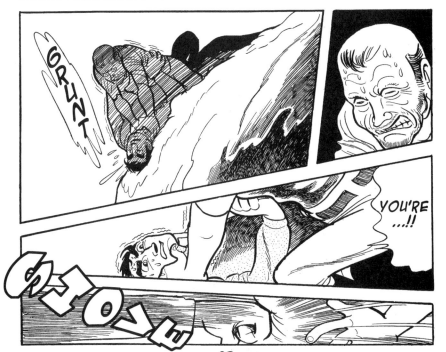

GRUNT

YOU'RE ...!!

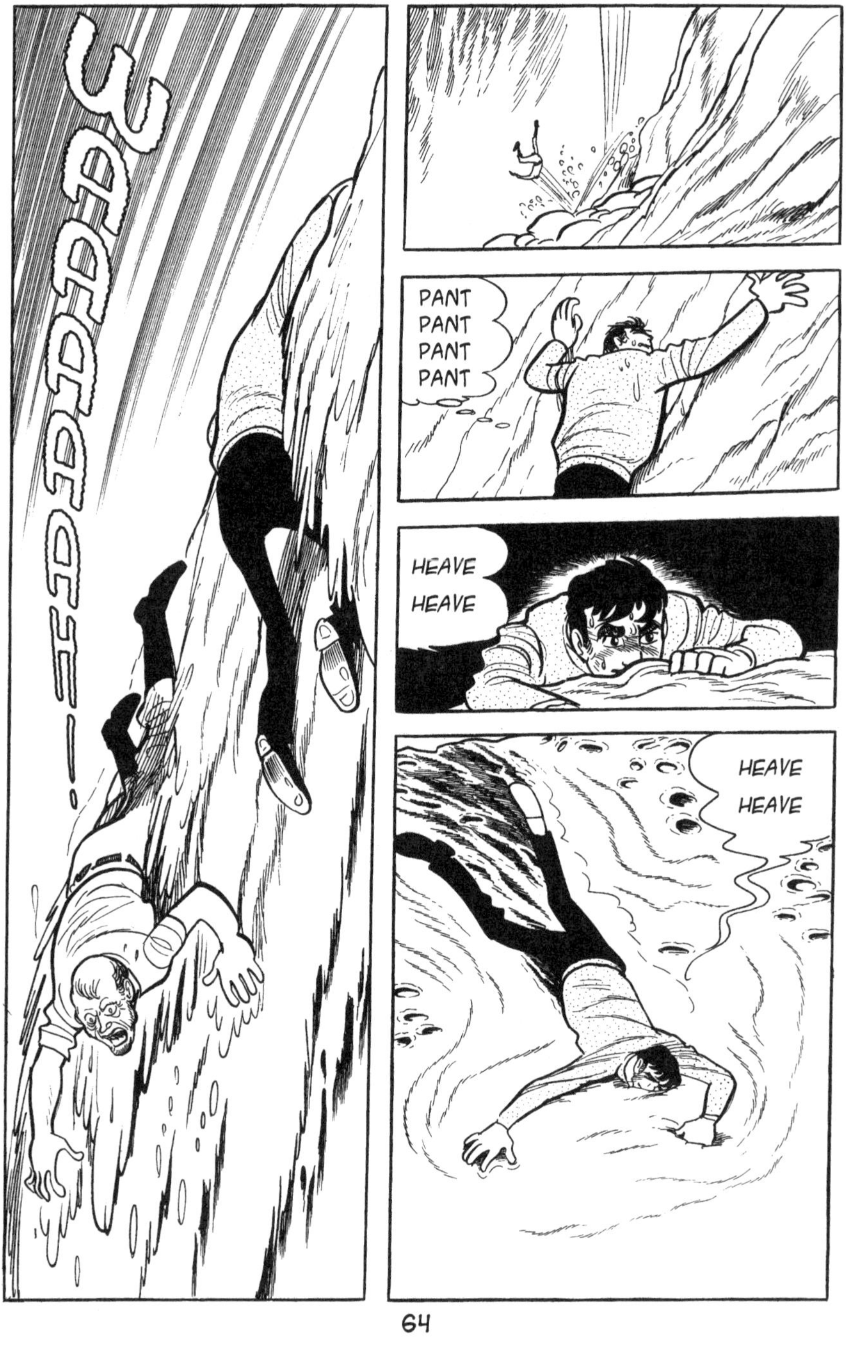
ZAAAAAASH—!
PANT PANT PANT PANT
HEAVE HEAVE
HEAVE HEAVE

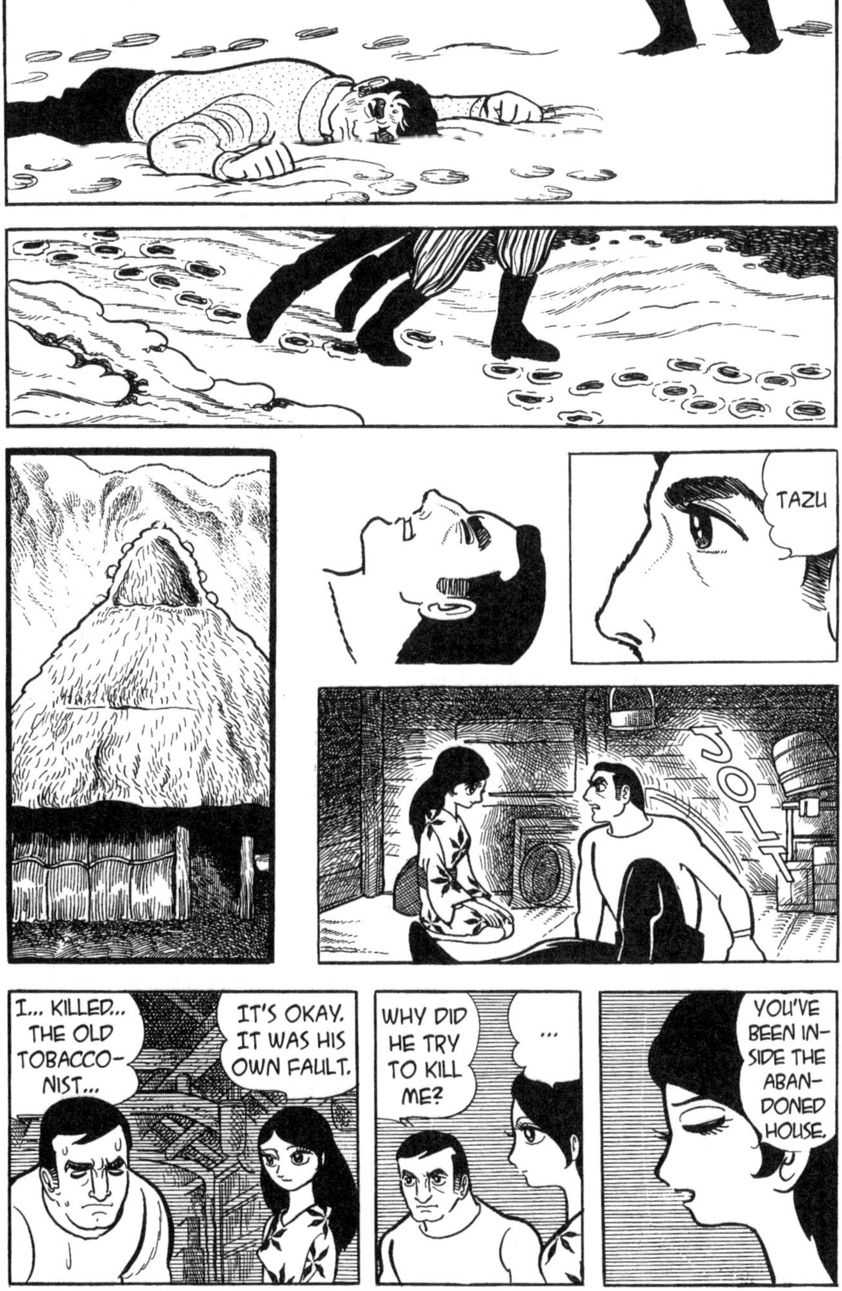
TAZU
JOLT
I... KILLED... THE OLD TOBACCONIST...
IT'S OKAY. IT WAS HIS OWN FAULT.
WHY DID HE TRY TO KILL ME?
...
YOU'VE BEEN INSIDE THE ABANDONED HOUSE.

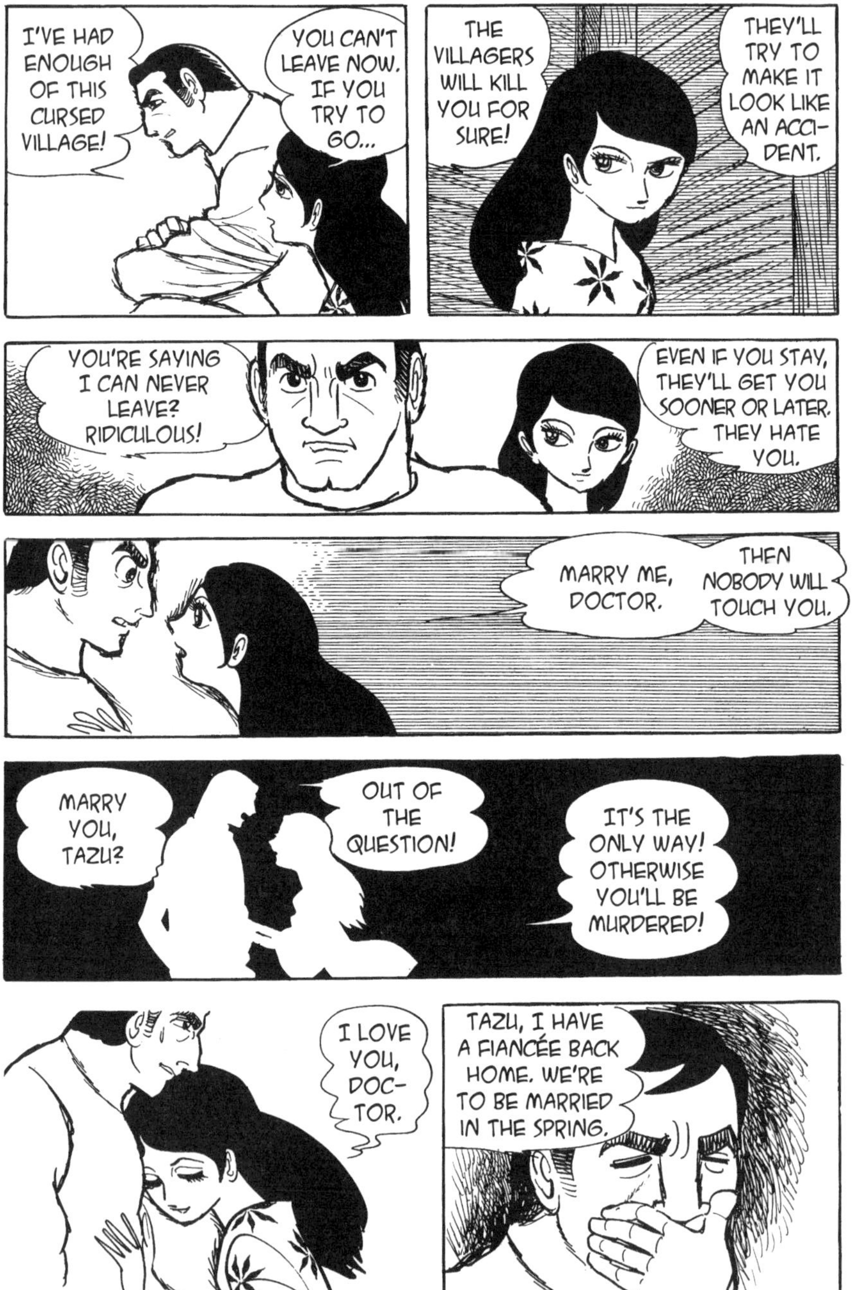
I'VE HAD ENOUGH OF THIS CURSED VILLAGE!
YOU CAN'T LEAVE NOW. IF YOU TRY TO GO...
THE VILLAGERS WILL KILL YOU FOR SURE!
THEY'LL TRY TO MAKE IT LOOK LIKE AN ACCI-DENT.
YOU'RE SAYING I CAN NEVER LEAVE? RIDICULOUS!
EVEN IF YOU STAY, THEY'LL GET YOU SOONER OR LATER. THEY HATE YOU.
MARRY ME, DOCTOR.
THEN NOBODY WILL TOUCH YOU.
MARRY YOU, TAZU?
OUT OF THE QUESTION!
IT'S THE ONLY WAY! OTHERWISE YOU'LL BE MURDERED!
I LOVE YOU, DOC-TOR.
TAZU, I HAVE A FIANCÉE BACK HOME. WE'RE TO BE MARRIED IN THE SPRING.

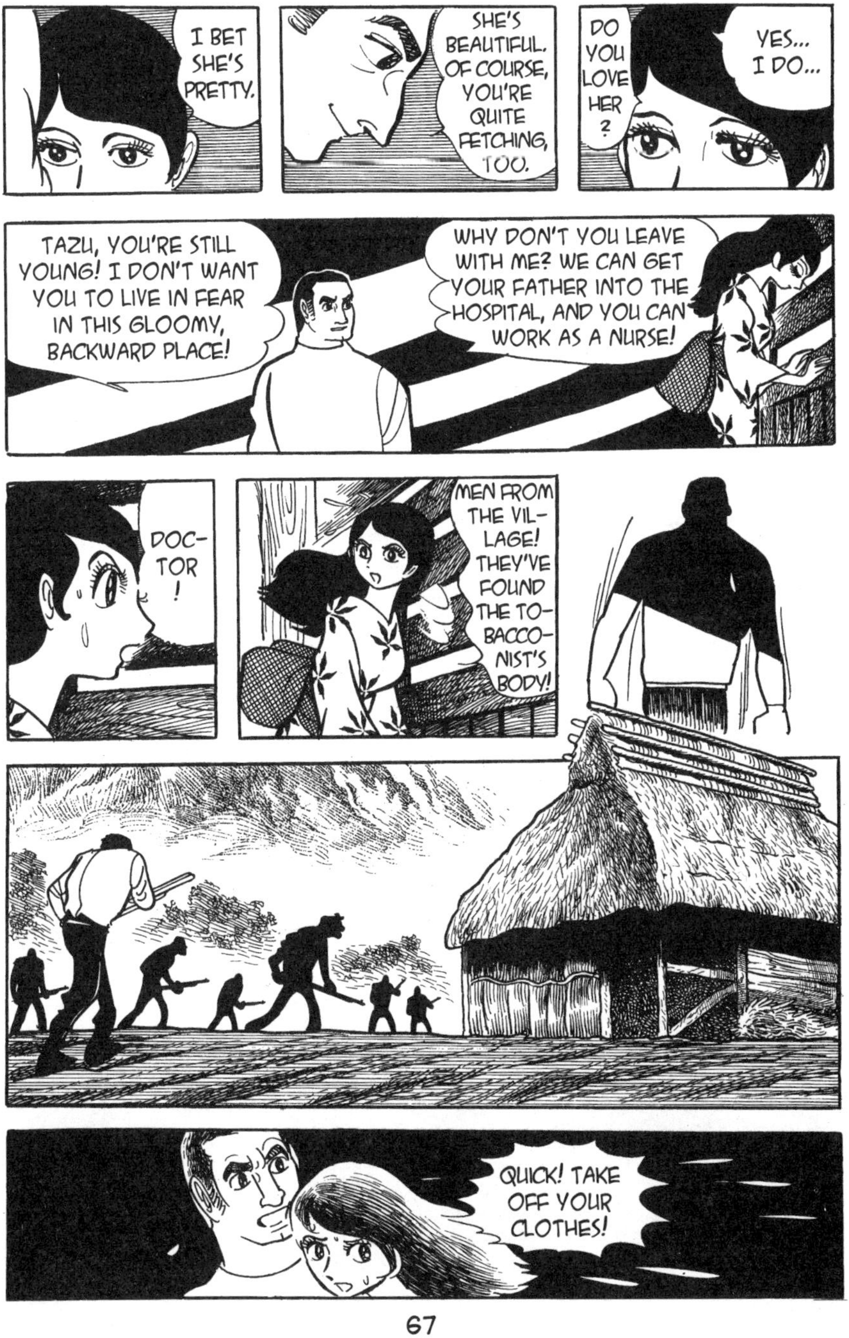
I BET SHE'S PRETTY.
SHE'S BEAUTIFUL. OF COURSE, YOU'RE QUITE FETCHING, TOO.
DO YOU LOVE HER?
YES... I DO...
TAZU, YOU'RE STILL YOUNG! I DON'T WANT YOU TO LIVE IN FEAR IN THIS GLOOMY, BACKWARD PLACE!
WHY DON'T YOU LEAVE WITH ME? WE CAN GET YOUR FATHER INTO THE HOSPITAL, AND YOU CAN WORK AS A NURSE!
DOC-TOR!
MEN FROM THE VIL-LAGE! THEY'VE FOUND THE TO-BACCO-NIST'S BODY!
QUICK! TAKE OFF YOUR CLOTHES!

TAKE THEM OFF !
...
...

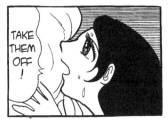

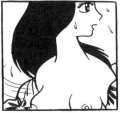

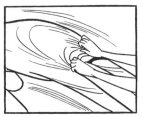

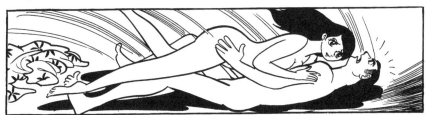

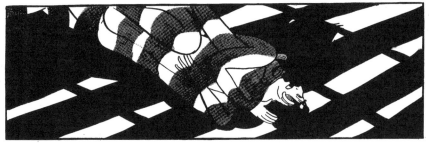

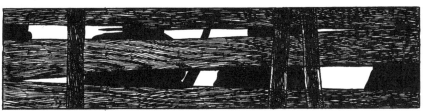

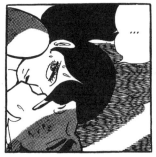

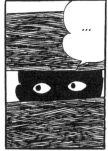

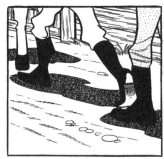

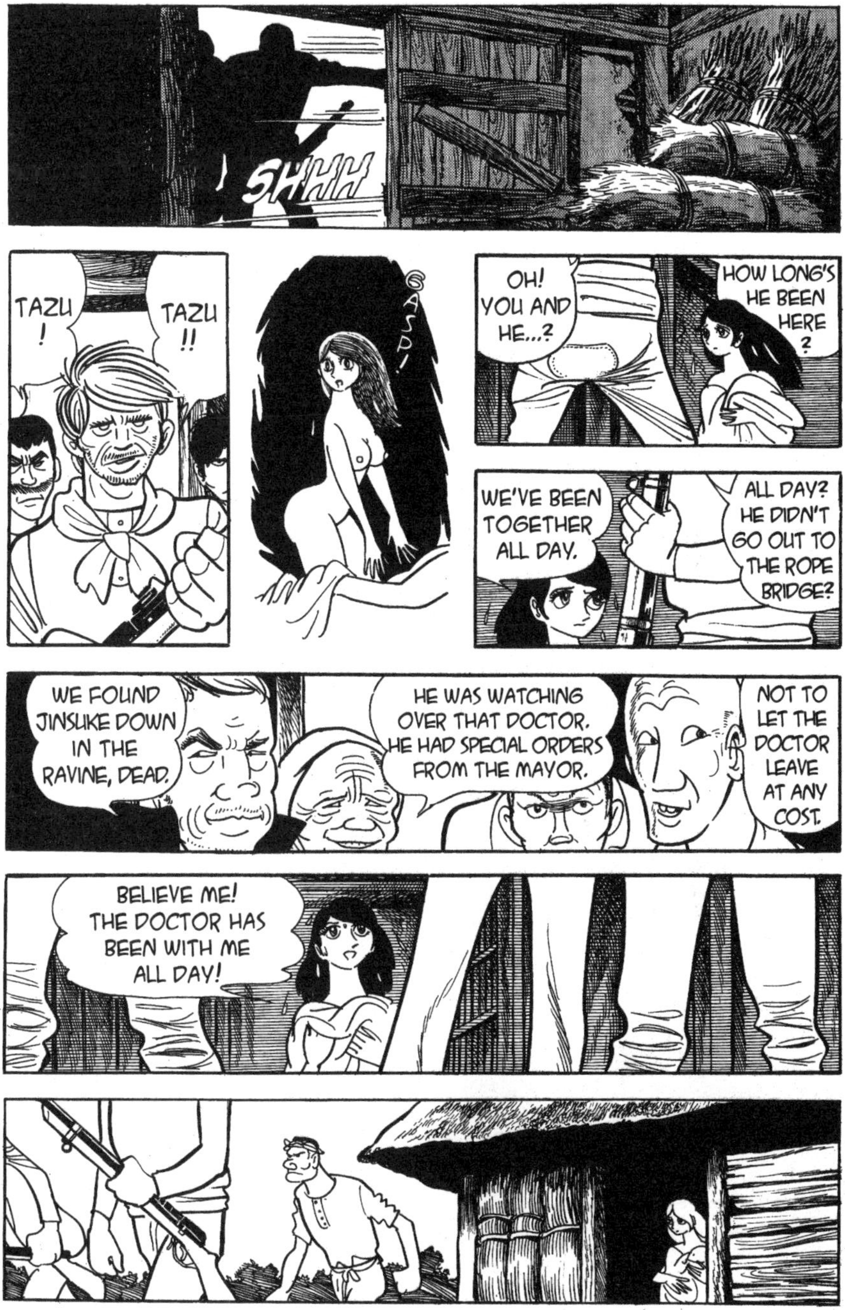
SHHH
TAZU!
TAZU!!
GASP!
OH! YOU AND HE...?
HOW LONG'S HE BEEN HERE?
WE'VE BEEN TOGETHER ALL DAY.
ALL DAY? HE DIDN'T GO OUT TO THE ROPE BRIDGE?
WE FOUND JINSUKE DOWN IN THE RAVINE, DEAD.
HE WAS WATCHING OVER THAT DOCTOR. HE HAD SPECIAL ORDERS FROM THE MAYOR.
NOT TO LET THE DOCTOR LEAVE AT ANY COST.
BELIEVE ME! THE DOCTOR HAS BEEN WITH ME ALL DAY!

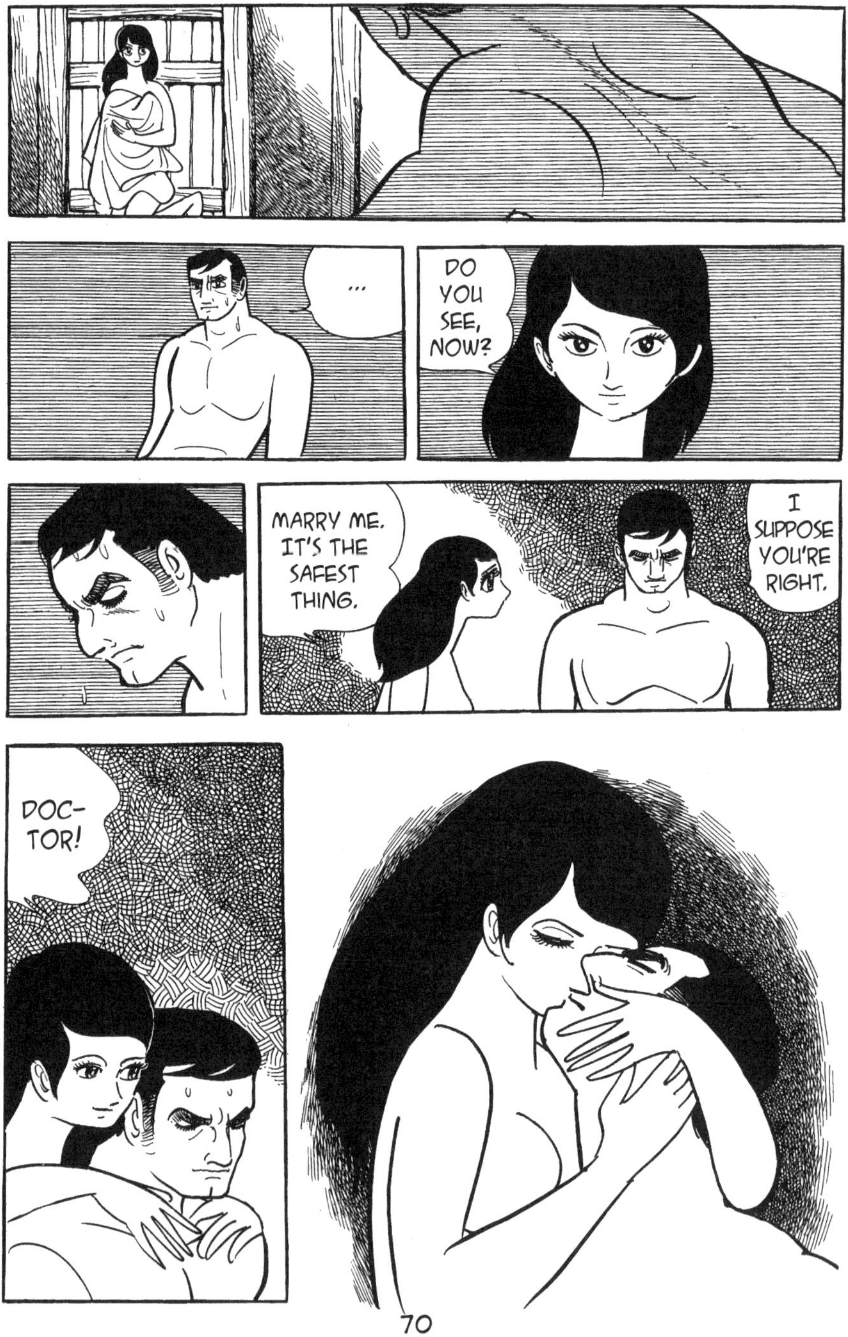
...
DO YOU SEE, NOW?
MARRY ME. IT'S THE SAFEST THING.
I SUPPOSE YOU'RE RIGHT.
DOC-TOR!

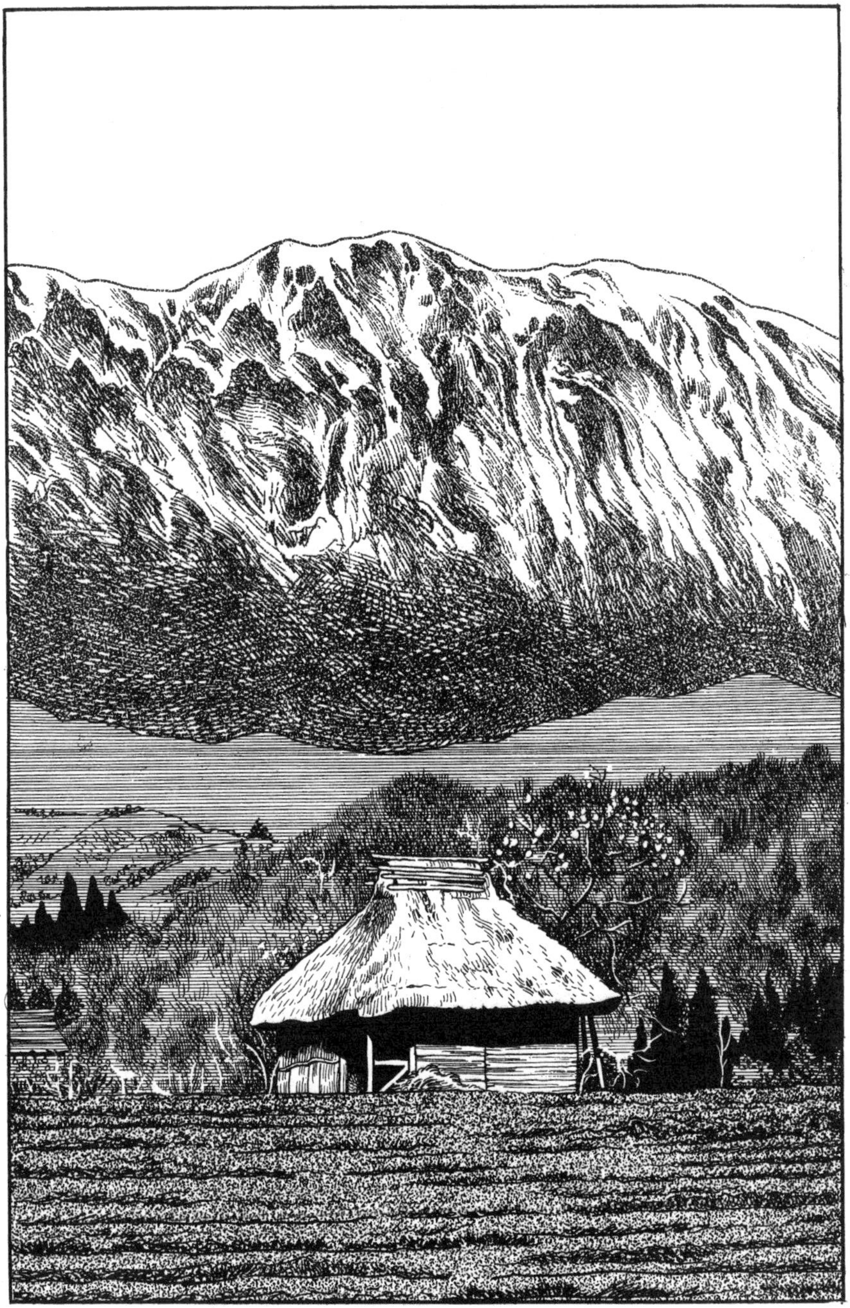

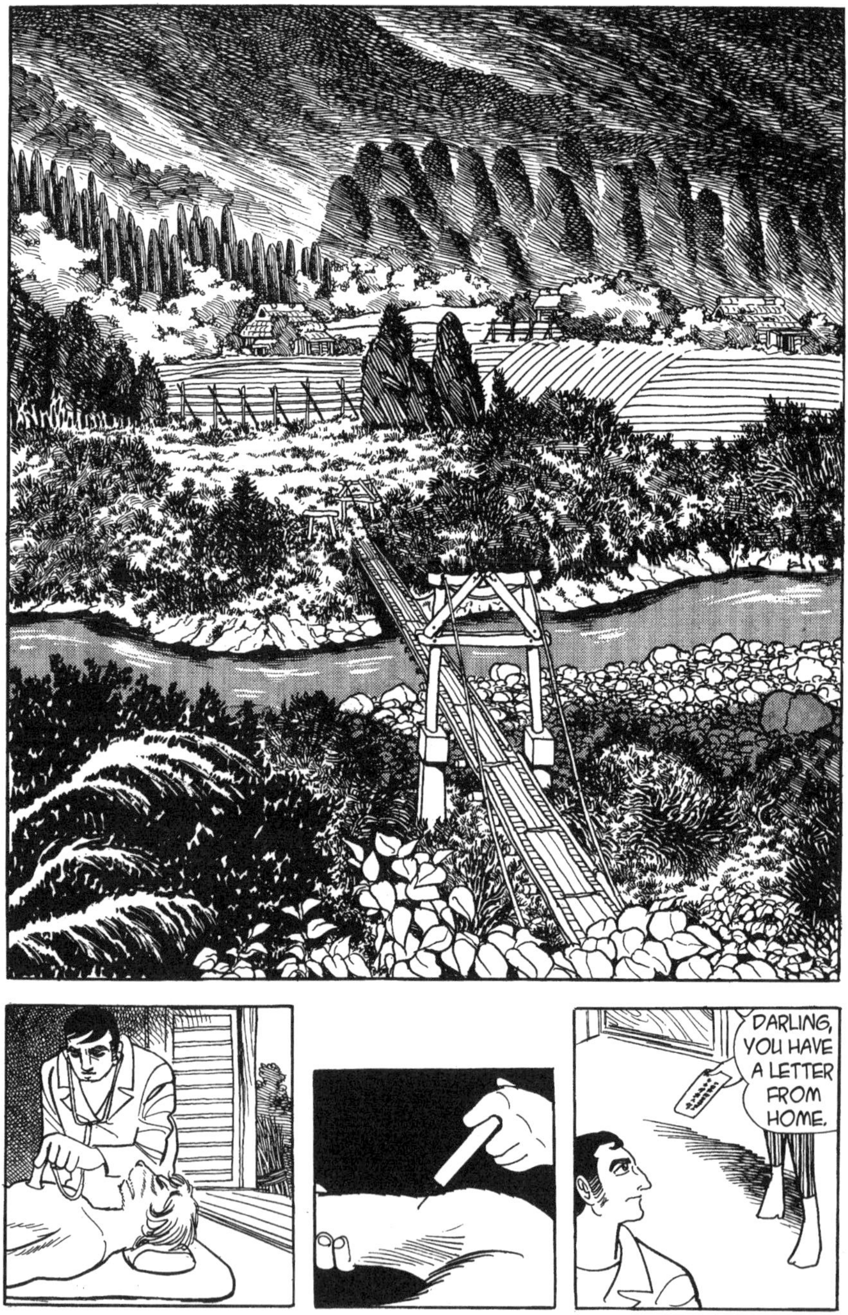
DARLING, YOU HAVE A LETTER FROM HOME.

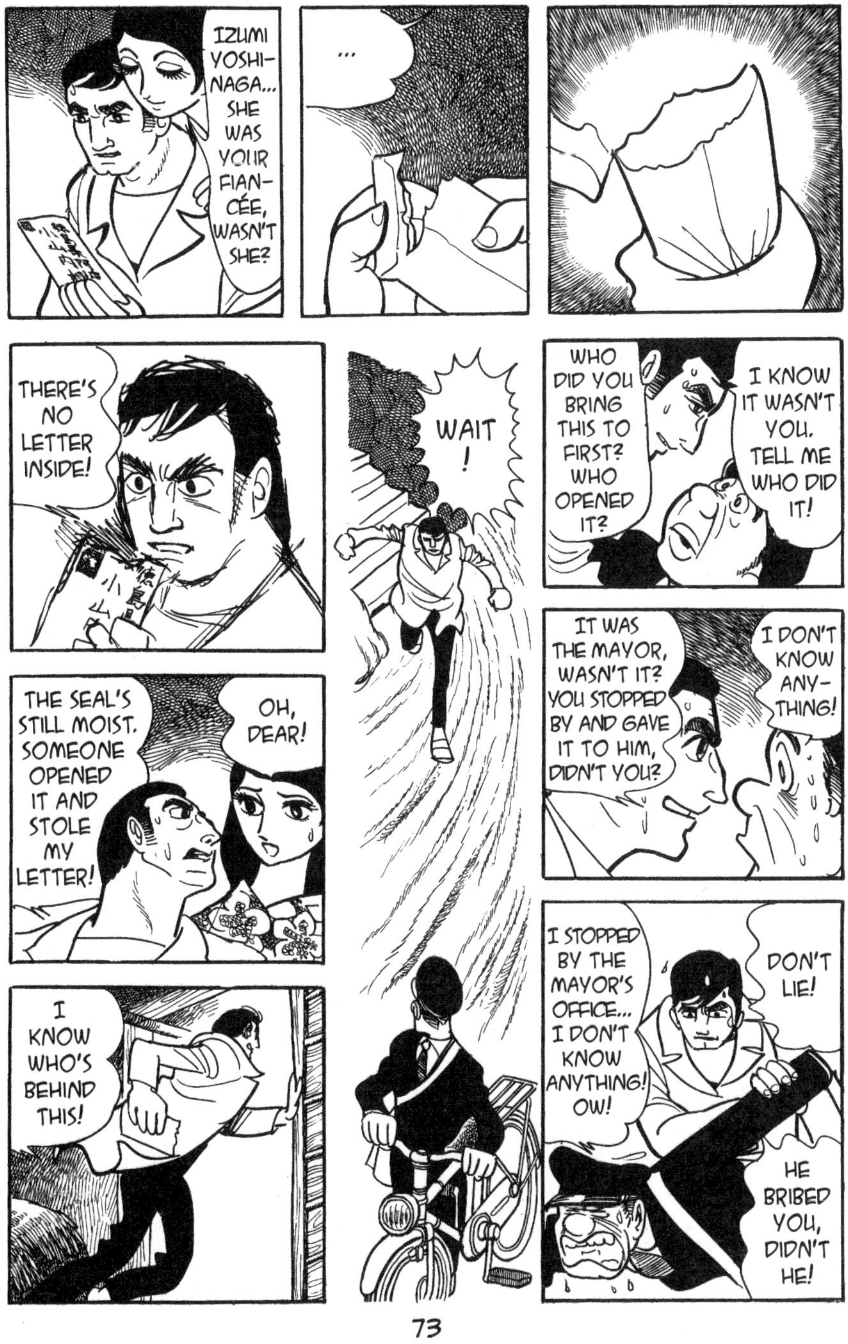
IZUMI YOSHINAGA... SHE WAS YOUR FIANCÉE, WASN'T SHE?
...
THERE'S NO LETTER INSIDE!
THE SEAL'S STILL MOIST. SOMEONE OPENED IT AND STOLE MY LETTER!
OH, DEAR!
I KNOW WHO'S BEHIND THIS!
WAIT!
WHO DID YOU BRING THIS TO FIRST? WHO OPENED IT?
I KNOW IT WASN'T YOU. TELL ME WHO DID IT!
IT WAS THE MAYOR, WASN'T IT? YOU STOPPED BY AND GAVE IT TO HIM, DIDN'T YOU?
I DON'T KNOW ANYTHING!
I STOPPED BY THE MAYOR'S OFFICE... I DON'T KNOW ANYTHING! OW!
DON'T LIE!
HE BRIBED YOU, DIDN'T HE!

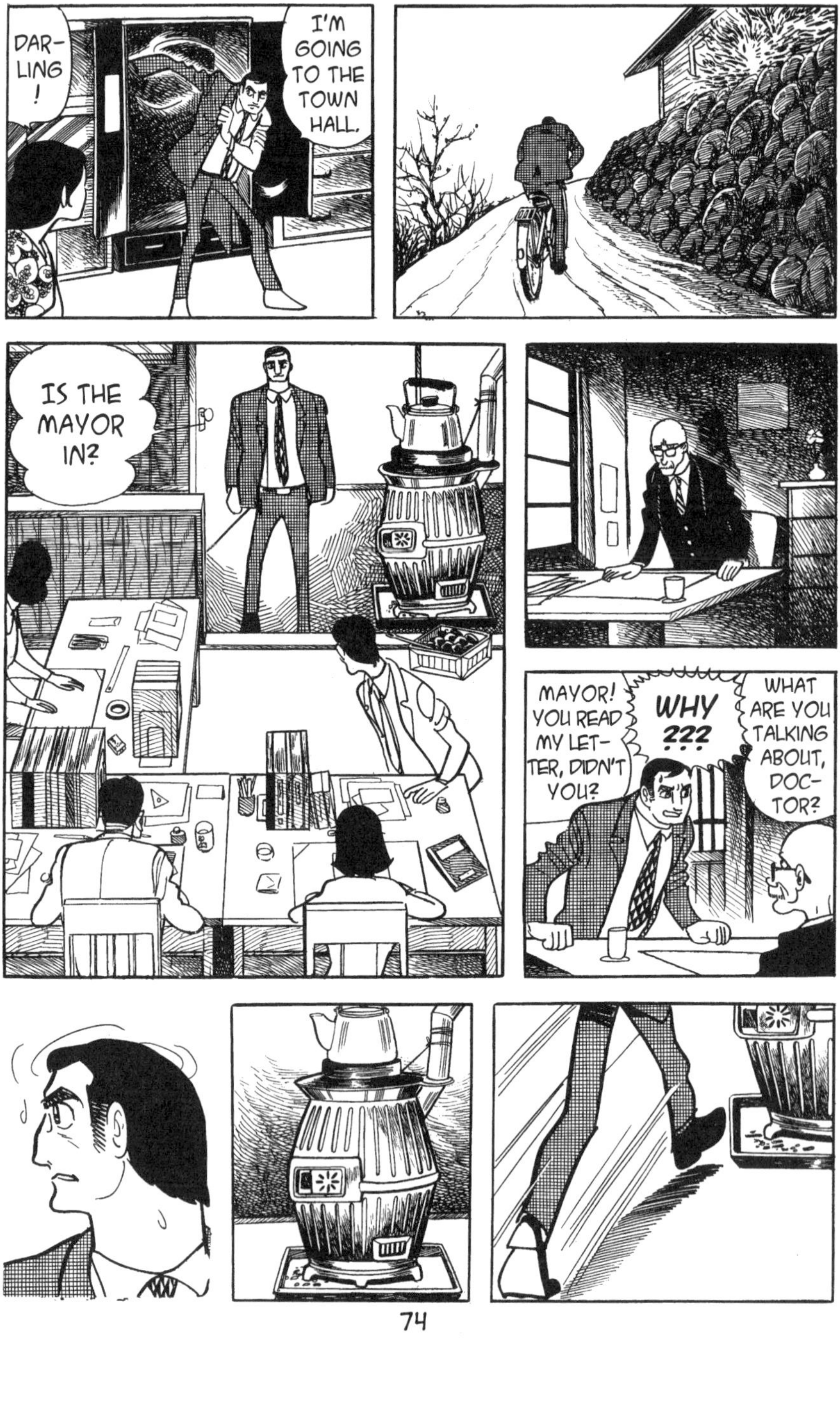
DARLING!
I'M GOING TO THE TOWN HALL.
IS THE MAYOR IN?
MAYOR! YOU READ MY LETTER, DIDN'T YOU?
WHY ???
WHAT ARE YOU TALKING ABOUT, DOCTOR?

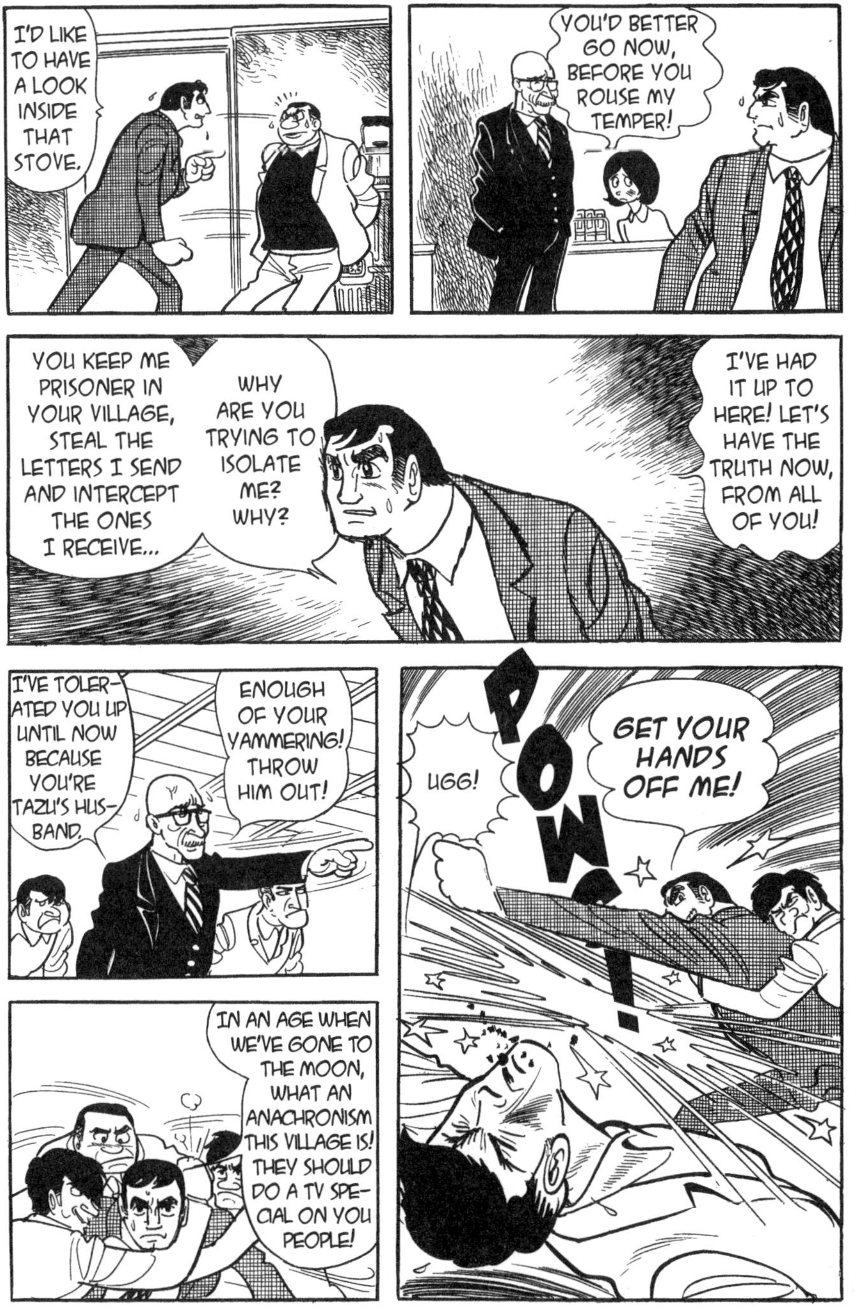
I'D LIKE TO HAVE A LOOK INSIDE THAT STOVE.
YOU'D BETTER GO NOW, BEFORE YOU ROUSE MY TEMPER!
YOU KEEP ME PRISONER IN YOUR VILLAGE, STEAL THE LETTERS I SEND AND INTERCEPT THE ONES I RECEIVE...
WHY ARE YOU TRYING TO ISOLATE ME? WHY?
I'VE HAD IT UP TO HERE! LET'S HAVE THE TRUTH NOW, FROM ALL OF YOU!
I'VE TOLERATED YOU UP UNTIL NOW BECAUSE YOU'RE TAZU'S HUSBAND.
ENOUGH OF YOUR YAMMERING! THROW HIM OUT!
IN AN AGE WHEN WE'VE GONE TO THE MOON, WHAT AN ANACHRONISM THIS VILLAGE IS! THEY SHOULD DO A TV SPECIAL ON YOU PEOPLE!
POW!
UGG!
GET YOUR HANDS OFF ME!

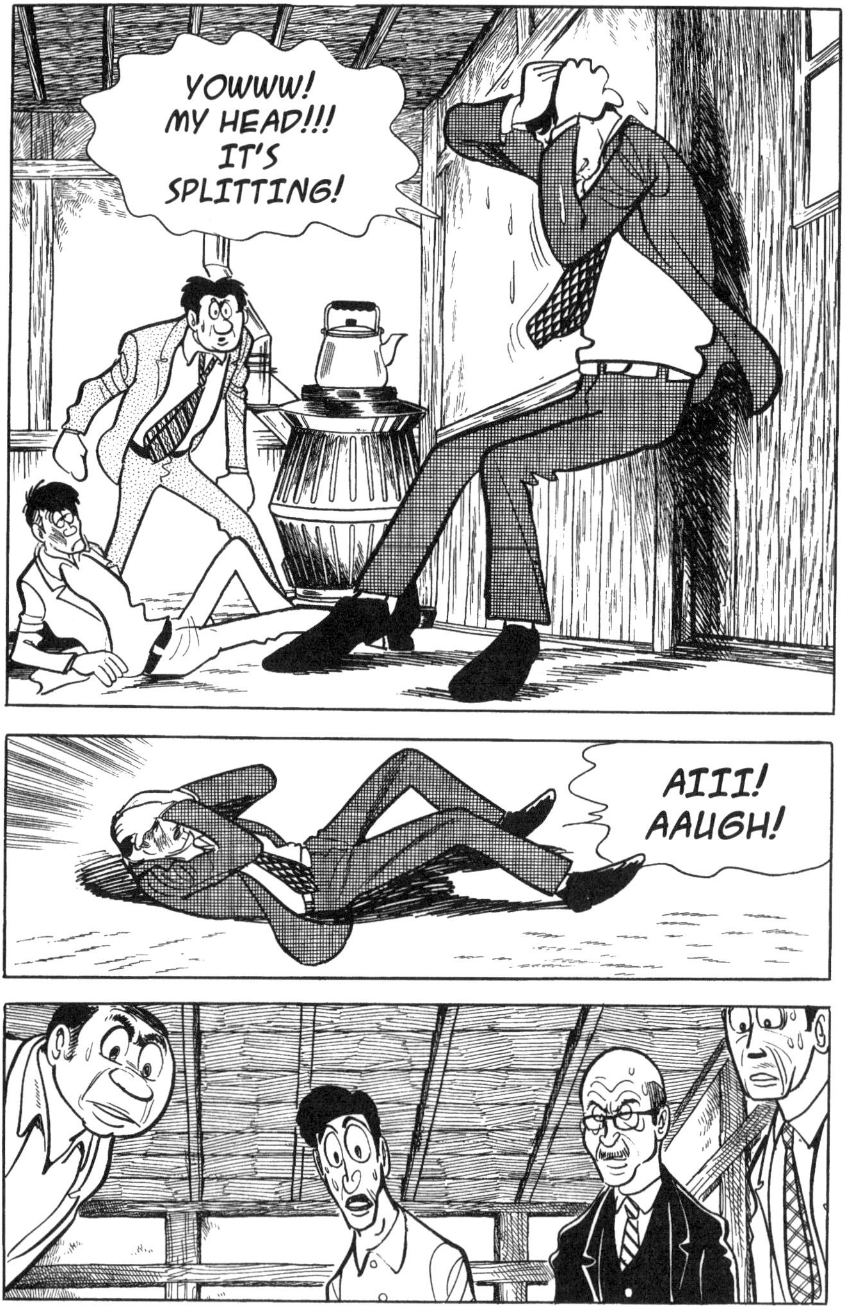
YOWWW! MY HEAD!!! IT'S SPLITTING!
AIII! AAUGH!

CHAPTER 3

THE FIRST
SYMPTOMS

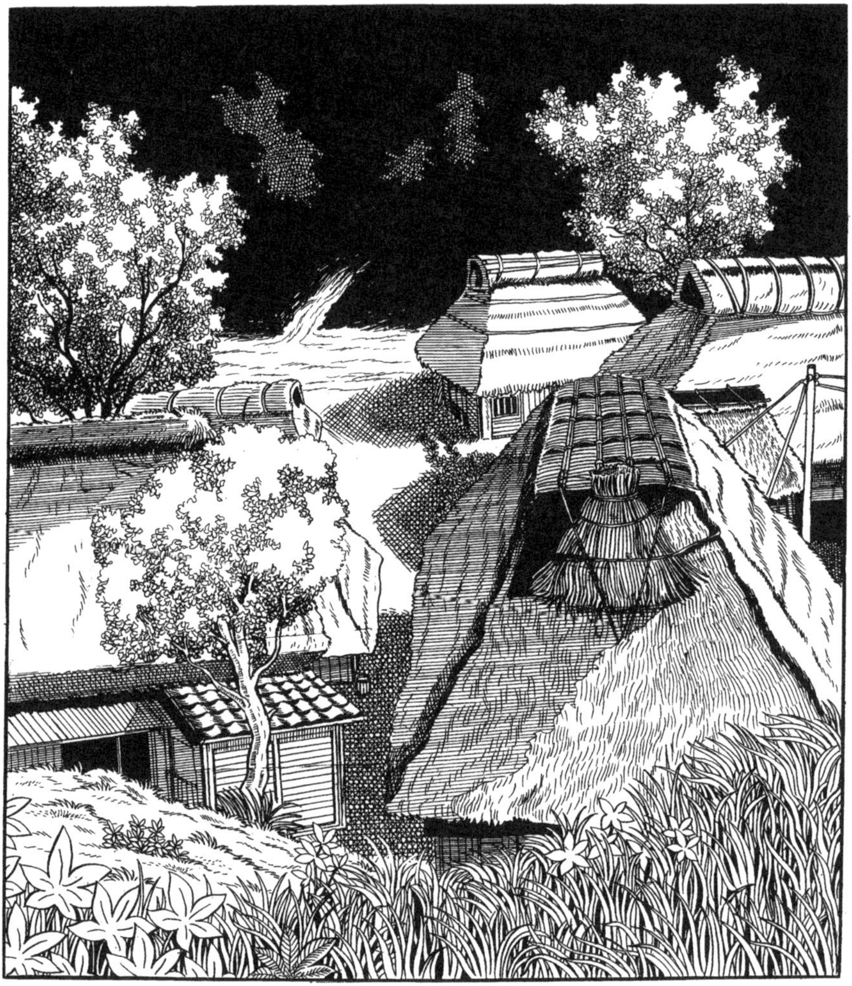

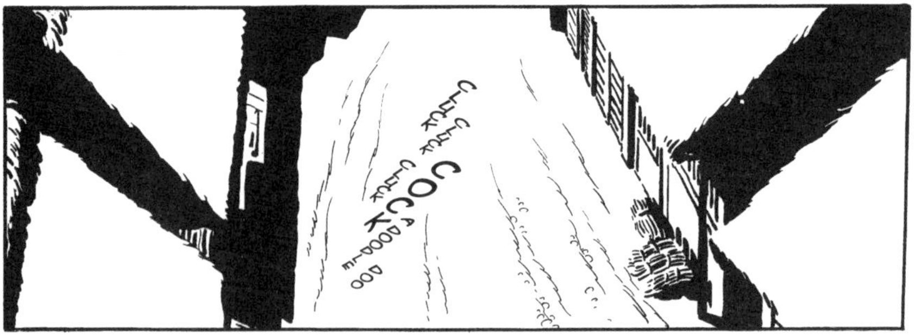
CLUCK CLUCK
CLUCK
COCK A DOODLE DOO
DOODLE DOO

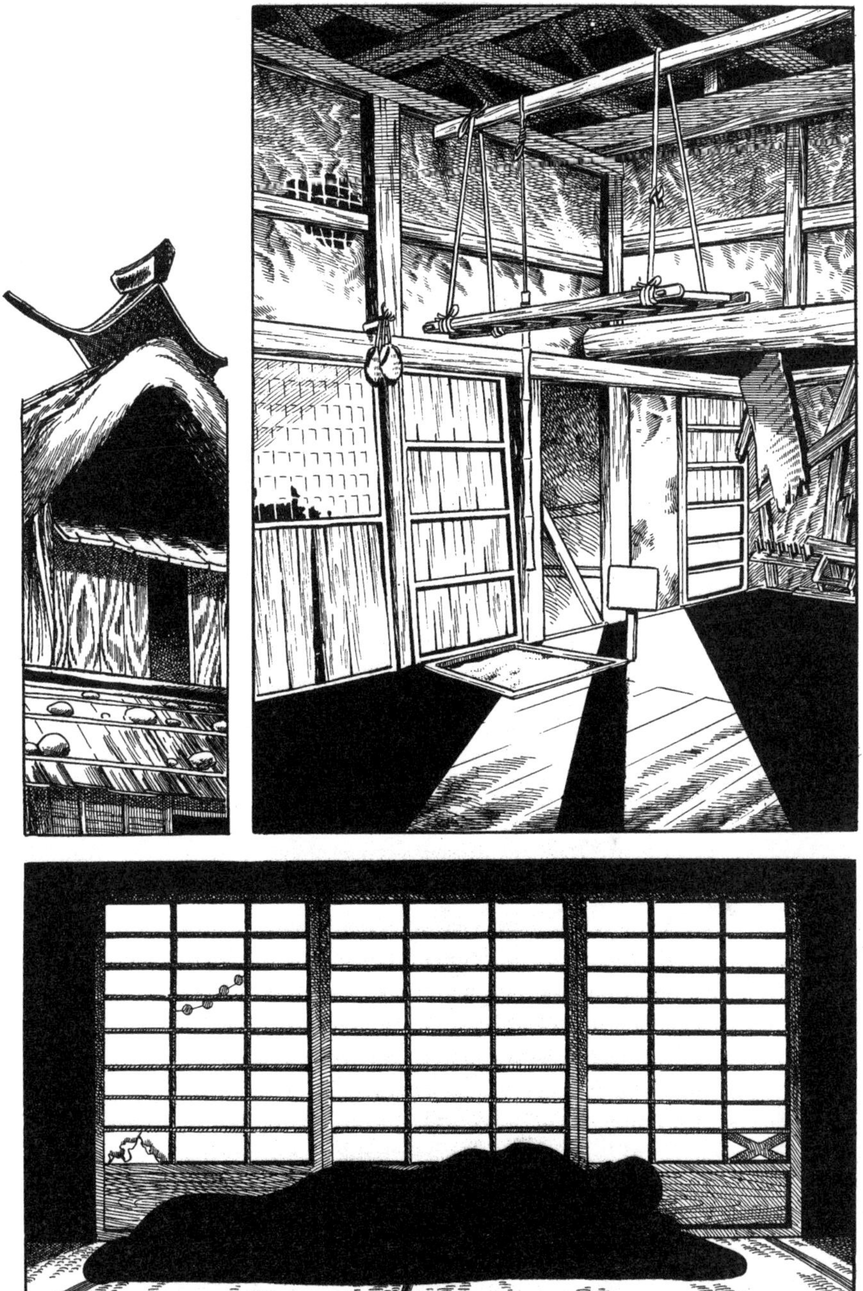

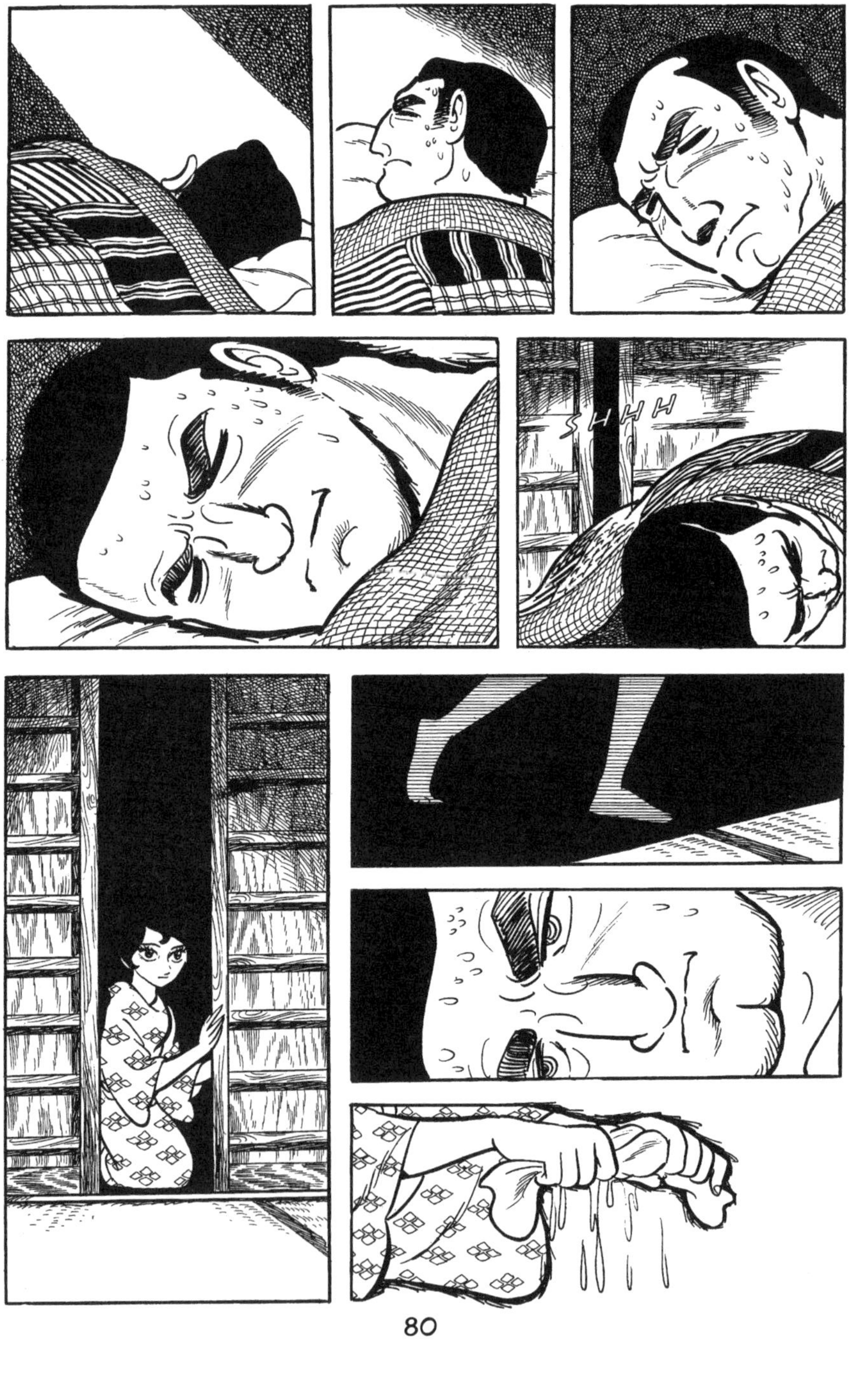
SHHH

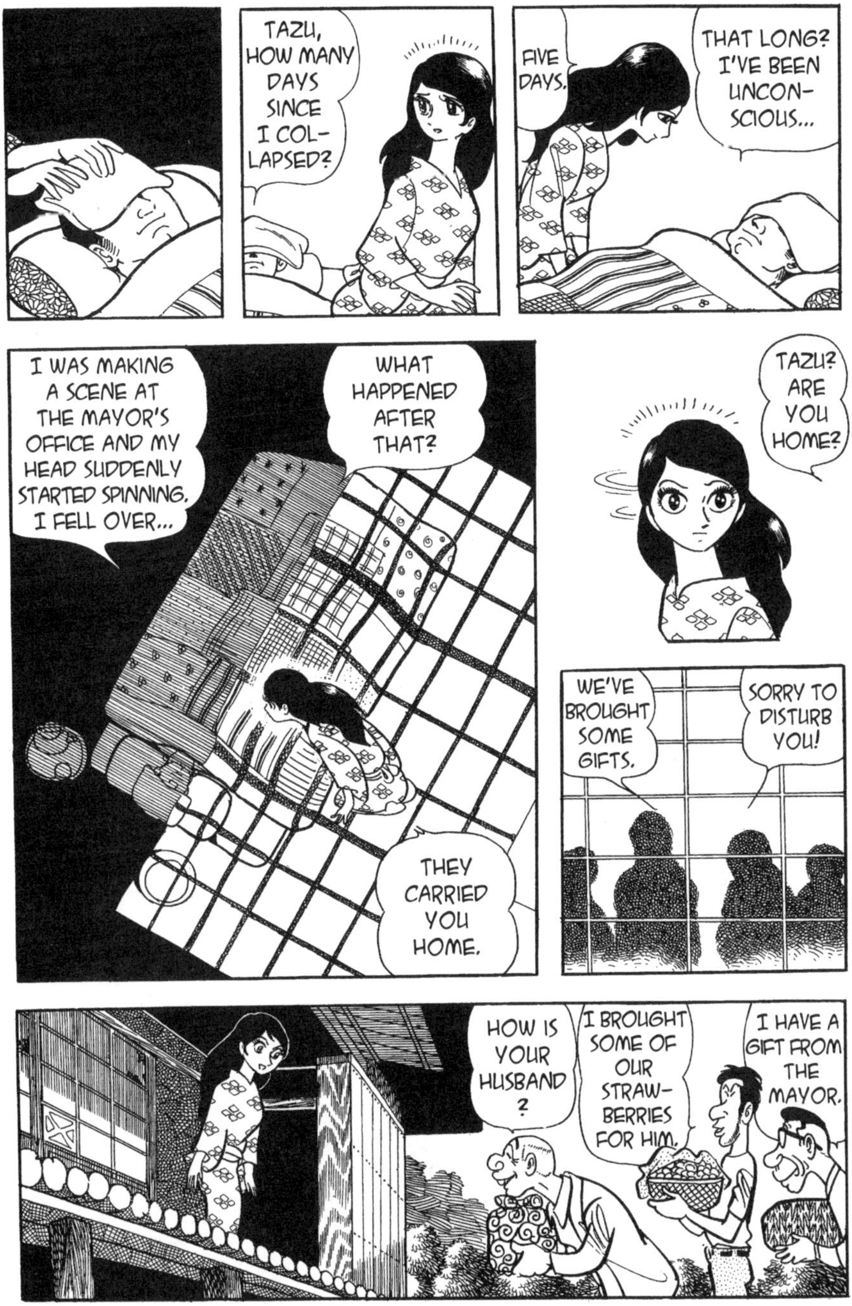
TAZU, HOW MANY DAYS SINCE I COL-LAPSED?
FIVE DAYS.
THAT LONG? I'VE BEEN UNCON-SCIOUS...
I WAS MAKING A SCENE AT THE MAYOR'S OFFICE AND MY HEAD SUDDENLY STARTED SPINNING. I FELL OVER...
WHAT HAPPENED AFTER THAT?
THEY CARRIED YOU HOME.
TAZU? ARE YOU HOME?
SORRY TO DISTURB YOU!
WE'VE BROUGHT SOME GIFTS.
HOW IS YOUR HUSBAND ?
I BROUGHT SOME OF OUR STRAW-BERRIES FOR HIM.
I HAVE A GIFT FROM THE MAYOR.

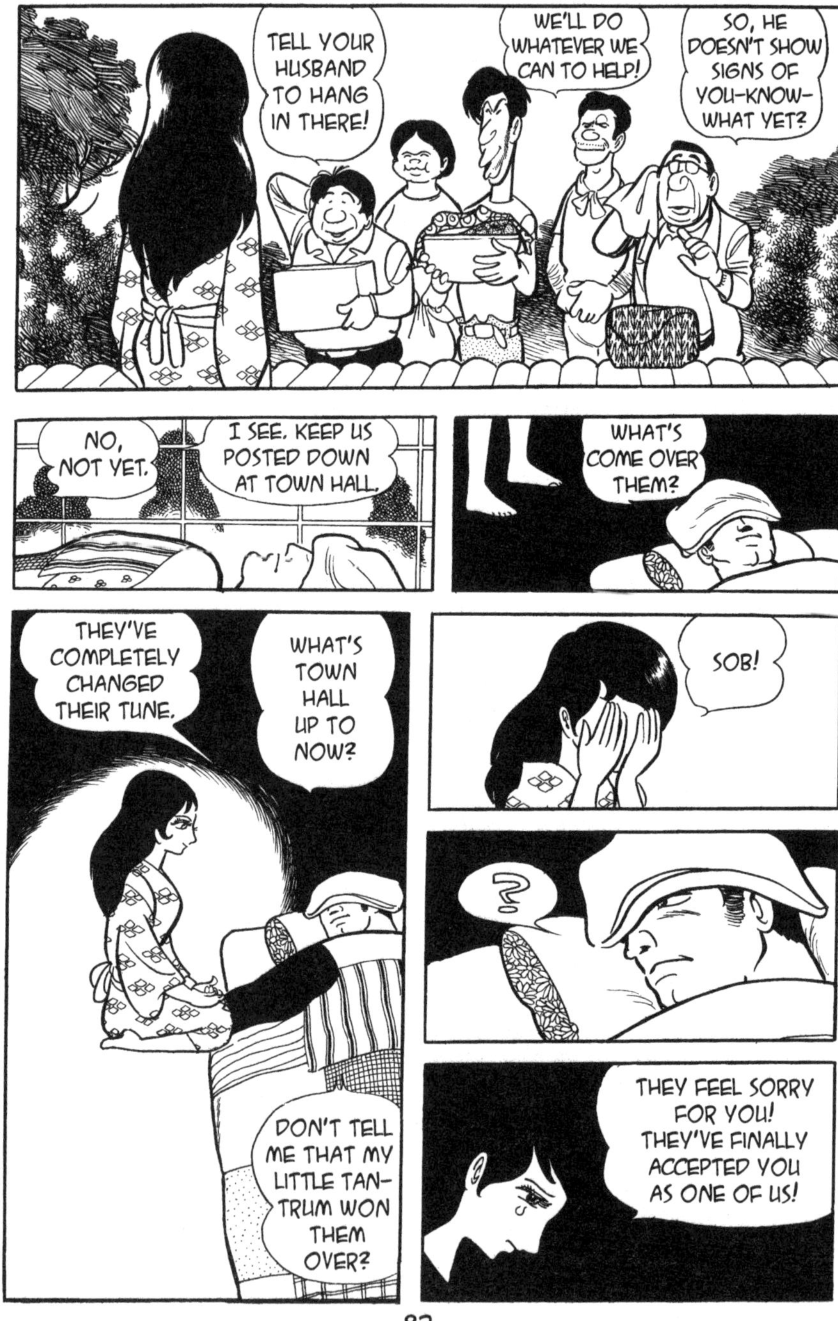
TELL YOUR HUSBAND TO HANG IN THERE!
WE'LL DO WHATEVER WE CAN TO HELP!
SO, HE DOESN'T SHOW SIGNS OF YOU-KNOW-WHAT YET?
NO, NOT YET.
I SEE. KEEP US POSTED DOWN AT TOWN HALL.
WHAT'S COME OVER THEM?
THEY'VE COMPLETELY CHANGED THEIR TUNE.
WHAT'S TOWN HALL UP TO NOW?
SOB!
?
DON'T TELL ME THAT MY LITTLE TAN-TRUM WON THEM OVER?
THEY FEEL SORRY FOR YOU! THEY'VE FINALLY ACCEPTED YOU AS ONE OF US!

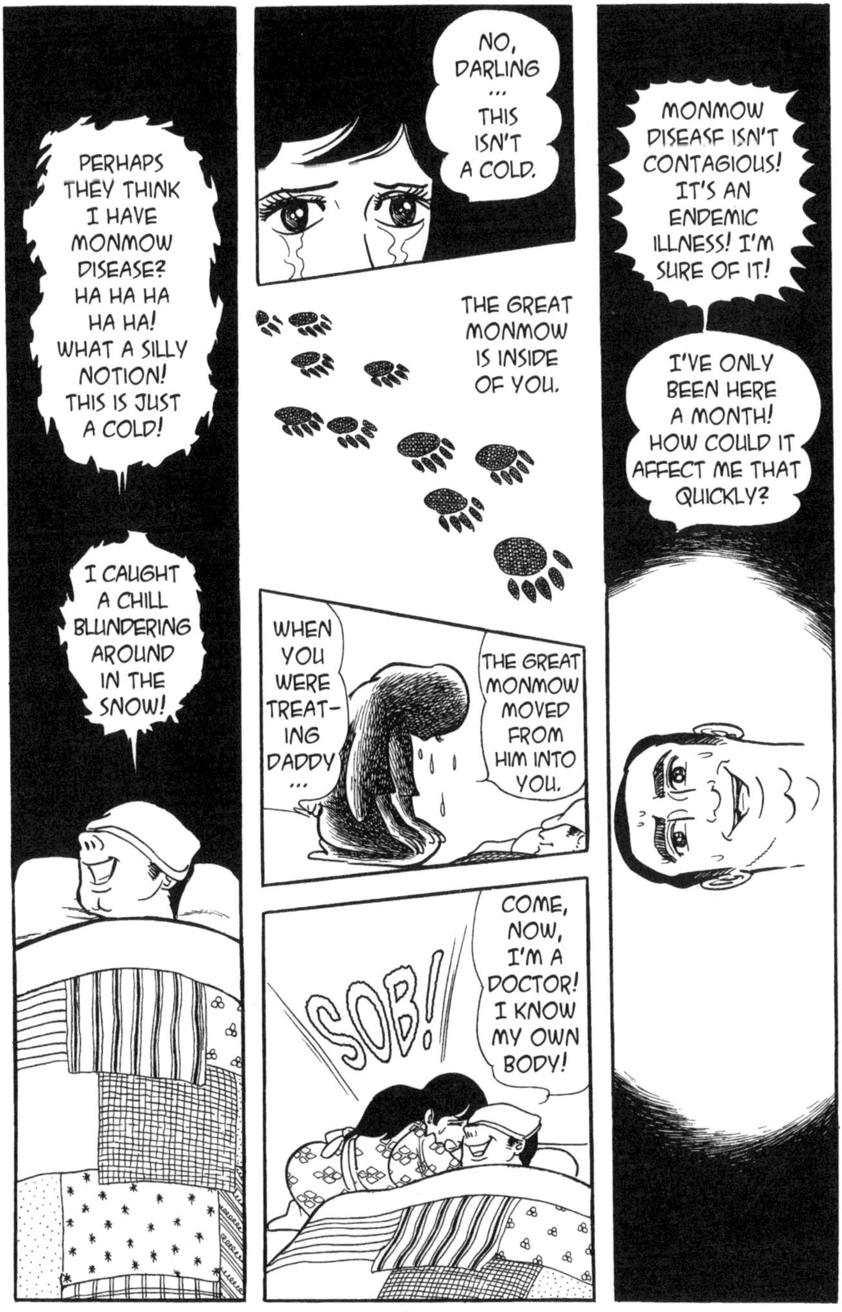
NO, DARLING ... THIS ISN'T A COLD.
PERHAPS THEY THINK I HAVE MONMOW DISEASE? HA HA HA HA HA! WHAT A SILLY NOTION! THIS IS JUST A COLD!
I CAUGHT A CHILL BLUNDERING AROUND IN THE SNOW!
MONMOW DISEASF ISN'T CONTAGIOUS! IT'S AN ENDEMIC ILLNESS! I'M SURE OF IT!
I'VE ONLY BEEN HERE A MONTH! HOW COULD IT AFFECT ME THAT QUICKLY?
THE GREAT MONMOW IS INSIDE OF YOU.
WHEN YOU WERE TREATING DADDY ...
THE GREAT MONMOW MOVED FROM HIM INTO YOU.
COME, NOW, I'M A DOCTOR! I KNOW MY OWN BODY!
SOB!

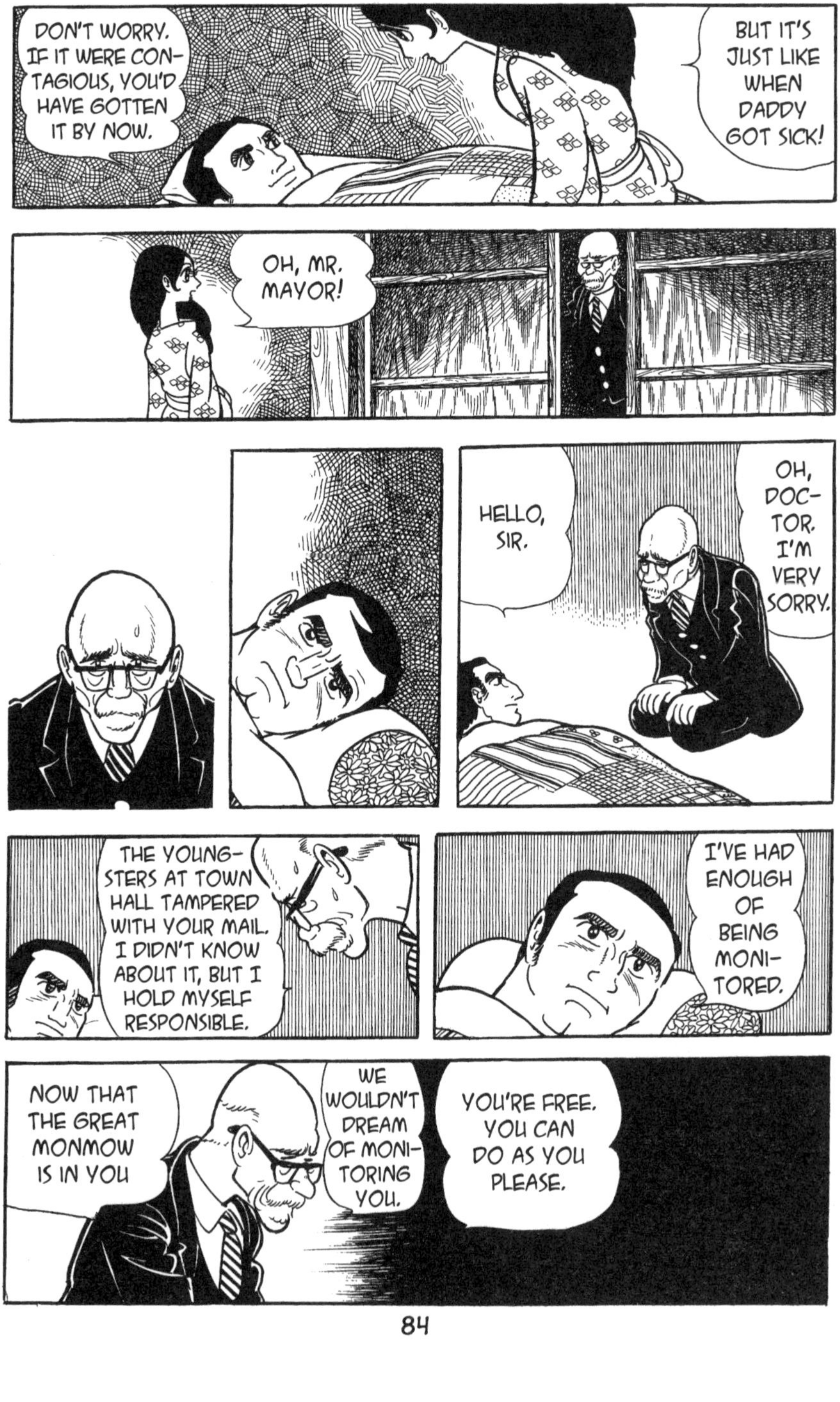
DON'T WORRY. IF IT WERE CONTAGIOUS, YOU'D HAVE GOTTEN IT BY NOW.
BUT IT'S JUST LIKE WHEN DADDY GOT SICK!
OH, MR. MAYOR!
OH, DOCTOR. I'M VERY SORRY.
HELLO, SIR.
THE YOUNGSTERS AT TOWN HALL TAMPERED WITH YOUR MAIL. I DIDN'T KNOW ABOUT IT, BUT I HOLD MYSELF RESPONSIBLE.
I'VE HAD ENOUGH OF BEING MONITORED.
NOW THAT THE GREAT MONMOW IS IN YOU
WE WOULDN'T DREAM OF MONITORING YOU.
YOU'RE FREE. YOU CAN DO AS YOU PLEASE.

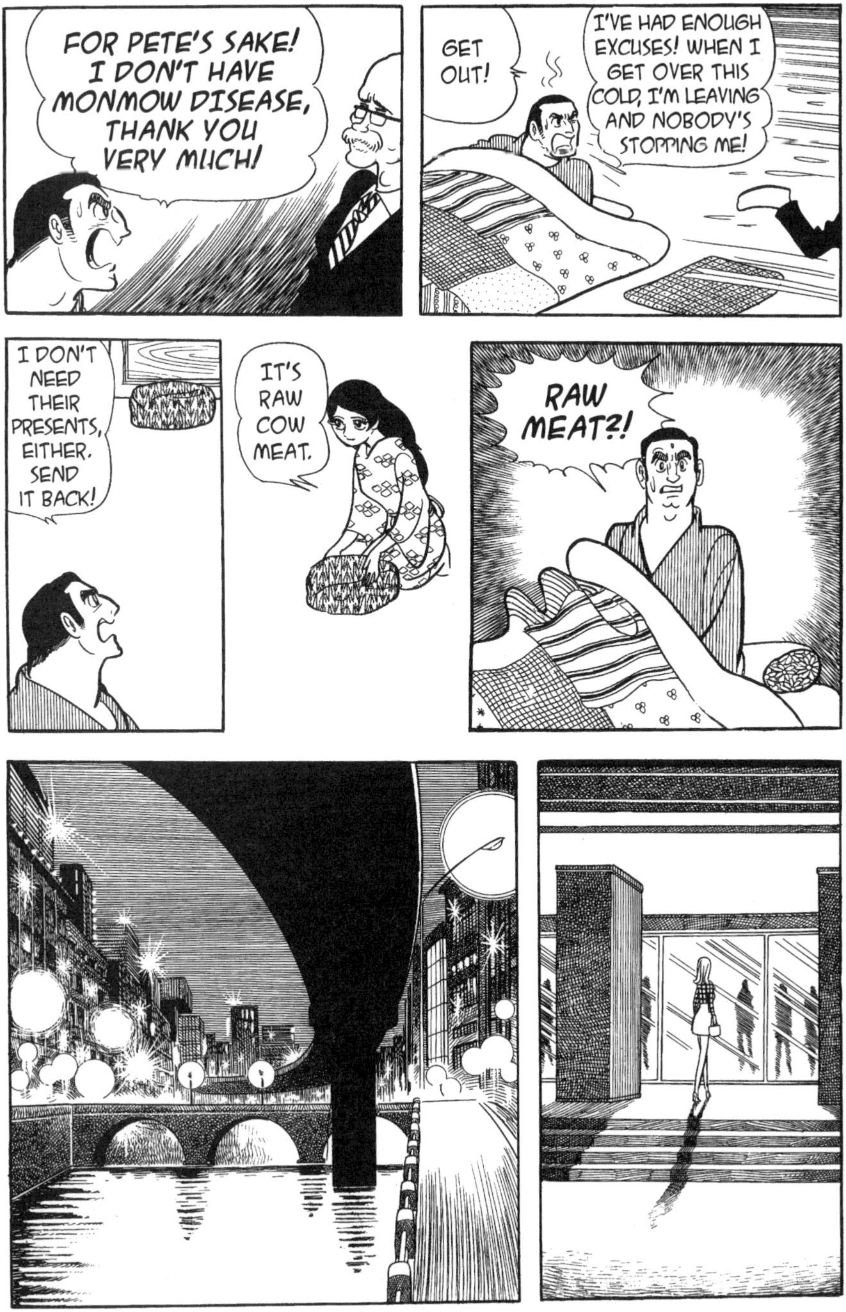
FOR PETE'S SAKE! I DON'T HAVE MONMOW DISEASE, THANK YOU VERY MUCH!
GET OUT!
I'VE HAD ENOUGH EXCUSES! WHEN I GET OVER THIS COLD, I'M LEAVING AND NOBODY'S STOPPING ME!
I DON'T NEED THEIR PRESENTS, EITHER. SEND IT BACK!
IT'S RAW COW MEAT.
RAW MEAT?!

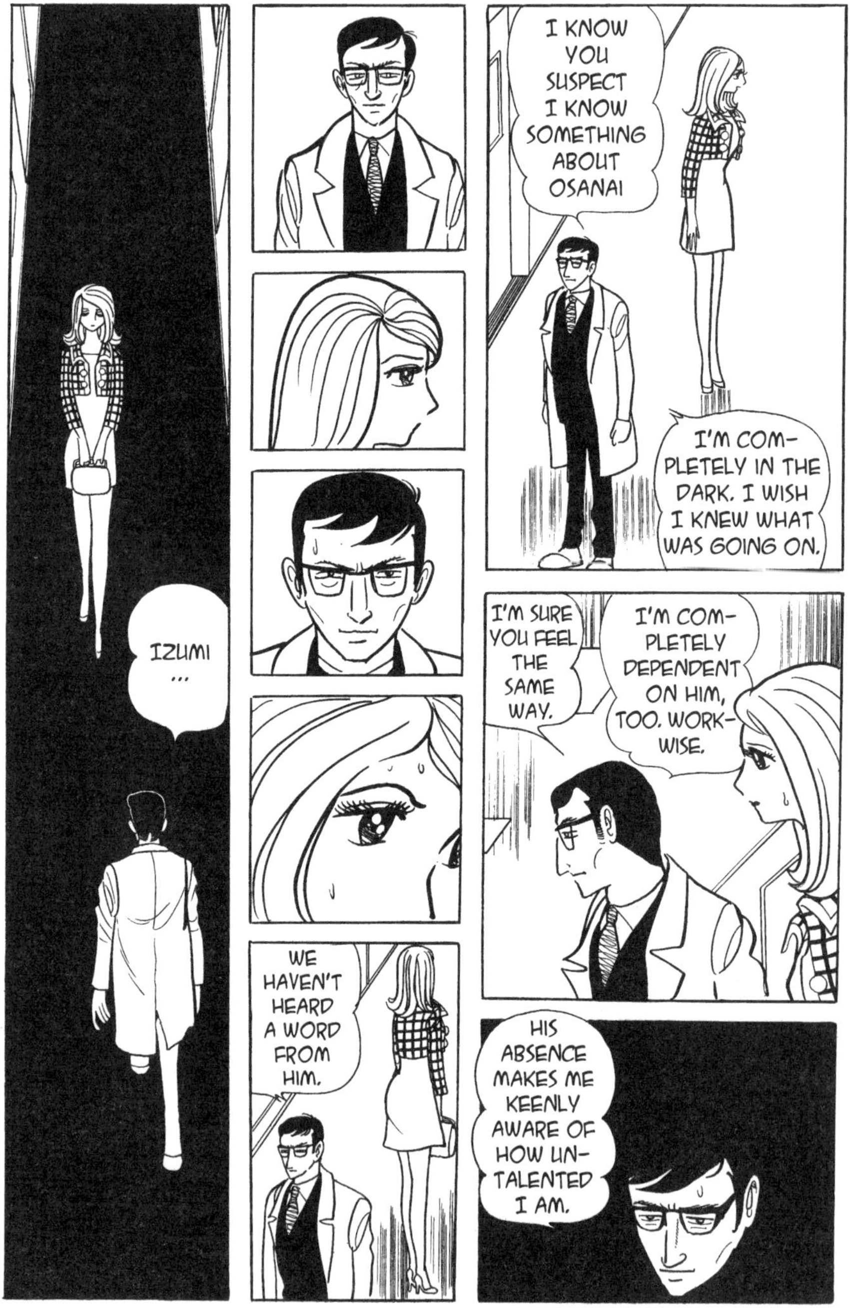
IZUMI ...
WE HAVEN'T HEARD A WORD FROM HIM.
I KNOW YOU SUSPECT I KNOW SOMETHING ABOUT OSANAI
I'M COM-PLETELY IN THE DARK. I WISH I KNEW WHAT WAS GOING ON.
I'M SURE YOU FEEL THE SAME WAY.
I'M COM-PLETELY DEPENDENT ON HIM, TOO. WORK-WISE.
HIS ABSENCE MAKES ME KEENLY AWARE OF HOW UN-TALENTED I AM.

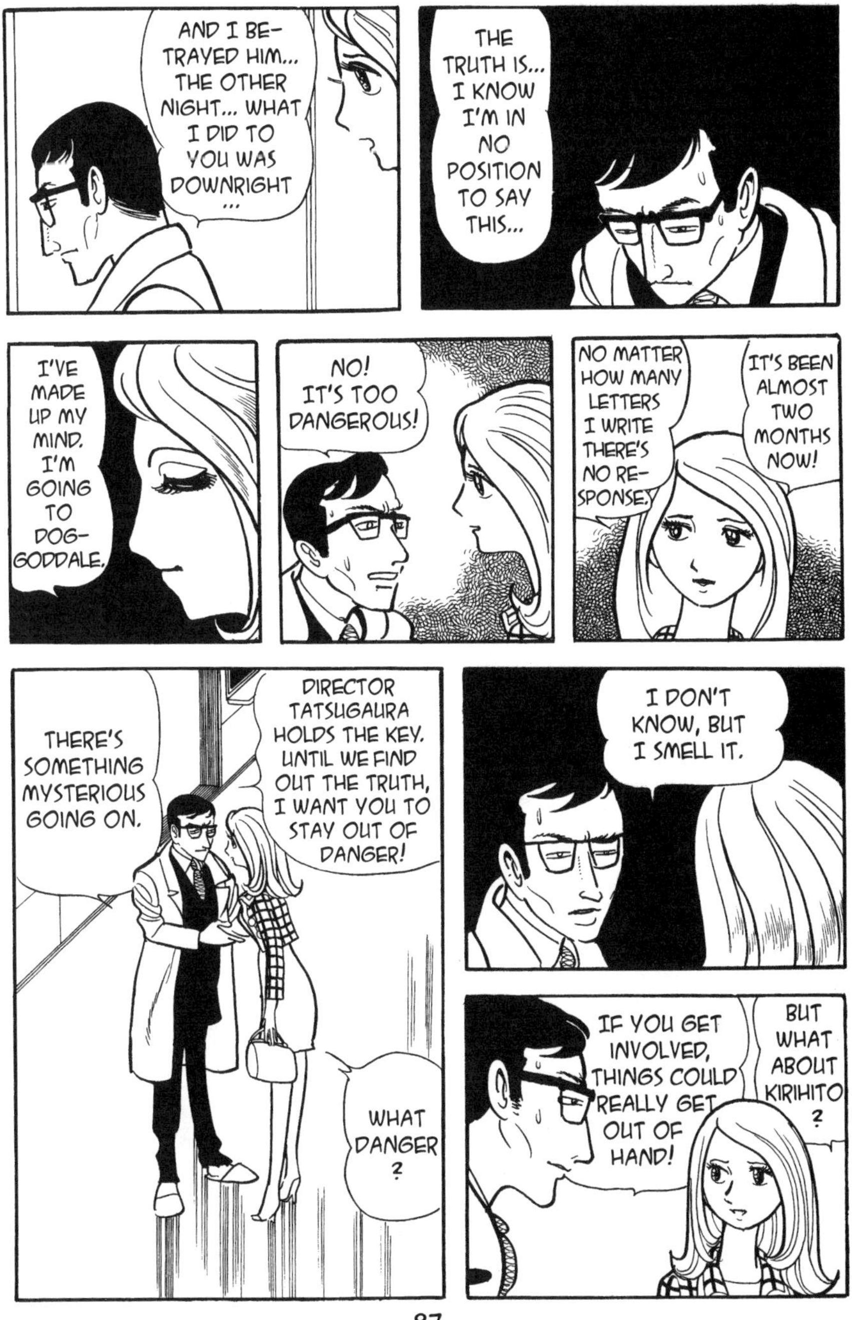
AND I BE-TRAYED HIM... THE OTHER NIGHT... WHAT I DID TO YOU WAS DOWNRIGHT ...
THE TRUTH IS... I KNOW I'M IN NO POSITION TO SAY THIS...
I'VE MADE UP MY MIND. I'M GOING TO DOG-GODDALE.
NO! IT'S TOO DANGEROUS!
NO MATTER HOW MANY LETTERS I WRITE THERE'S NO RE-SPONSE.
IT'S BEEN ALMOST TWO MONTHS NOW!
THERE'S SOMETHING MYSTERIOUS GOING ON.
DIRECTOR TATSUGAURA HOLDS THE KEY. UNTIL WE FIND OUT THE TRUTH, I WANT YOU TO STAY OUT OF DANGER!
WHAT DANGER?
I DON'T KNOW, BUT I SMELL IT.
IF YOU GET INVOLVED, THINGS COULD REALLY GET OUT OF HAND!
BUT WHAT ABOUT KIRIHITO?

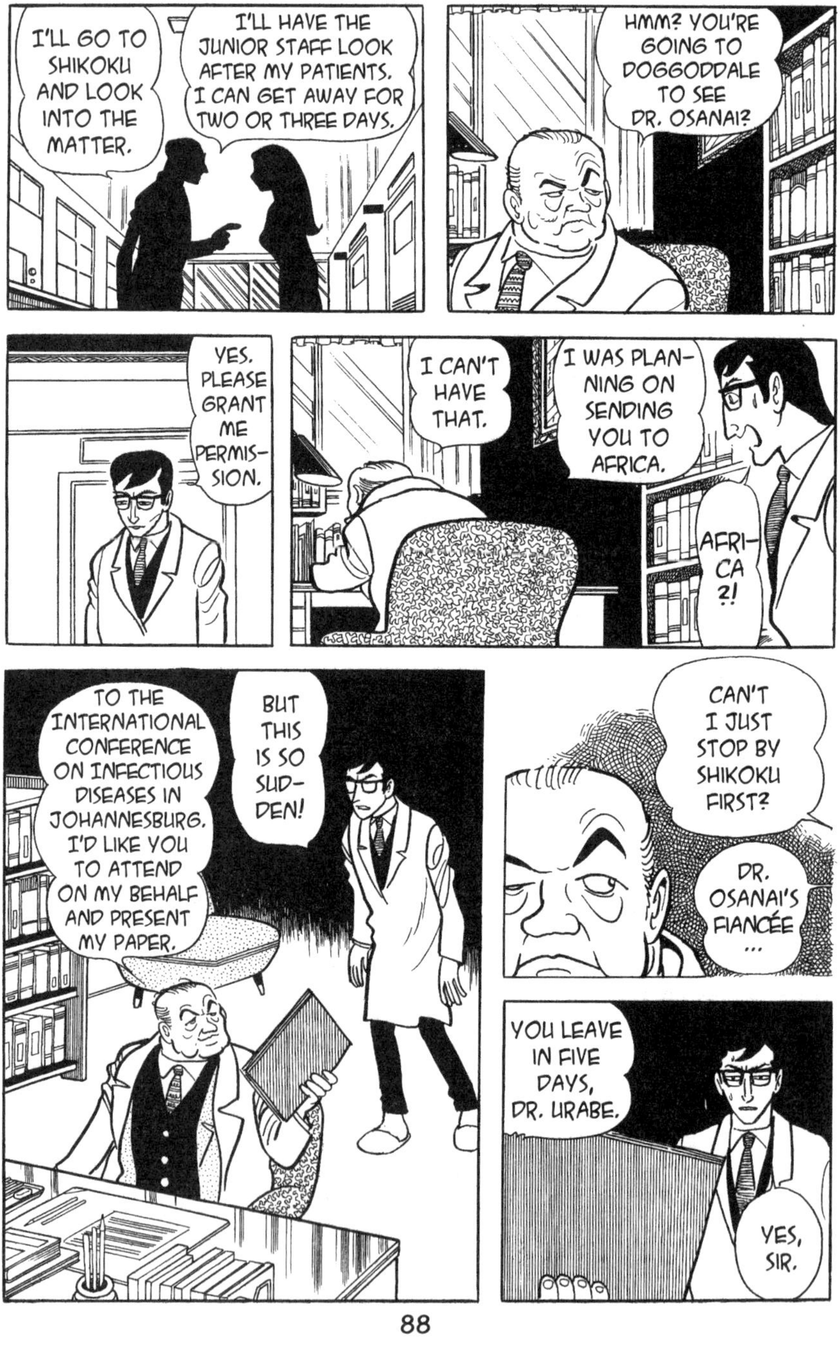
I'LL GO TO SHIKOKU AND LOOK INTO THE MATTER.
I'LL HAVE THE JUNIOR STAFF LOOK AFTER MY PATIENTS. I CAN GET AWAY FOR TWO OR THREE DAYS.
HMM? YOU'RE GOING TO DOGGODDALE TO SEE DR. OSANAI?
YES. PLEASE GRANT ME PERMIS-SION.
I CAN'T HAVE THAT.
I WAS PLAN-NING ON SENDING YOU TO AFRICA.
AFRI-CA ?!
TO THE INTERNATIONAL CONFERENCE ON INFECTIOUS DISEASES IN JOHANNESBURG. I'D LIKE YOU TO ATTEND ON MY BEHALF AND PRESENT MY PAPER.
BUT THIS IS SO SUD-DEN!
CAN'T I JUST STOP BY SHIKOKU FIRST?
DR. OSANAI'S FIANCÉE ...
YOU LEAVE IN FIVE DAYS, DR. URABE.
YES, SIR.

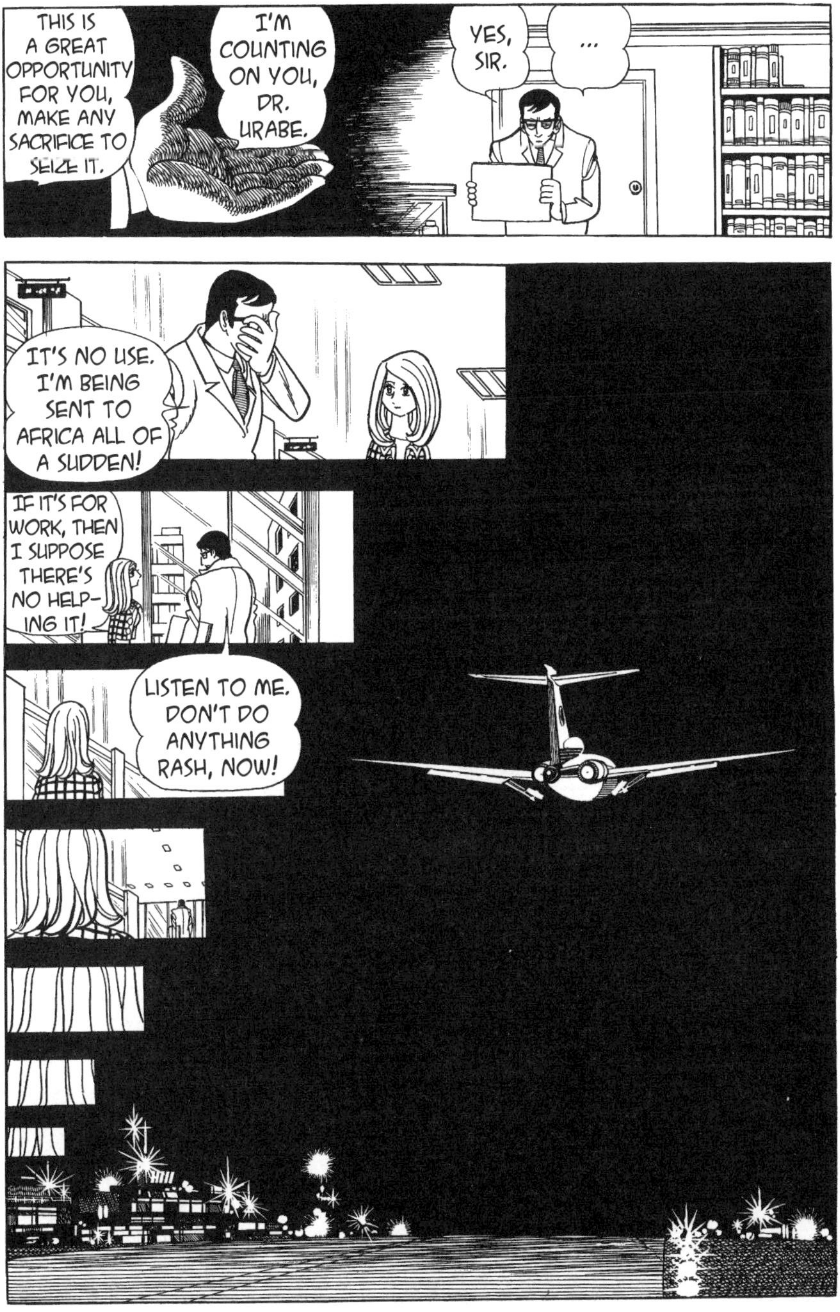
THIS IS A GREAT OPPORTUNITY FOR YOU, MAKE ANY SACRIFICE TO SEIZE IT.
I'M COUNTING ON YOU, DR. URABE.
YES, SIR.
...
IT'S NO USE. I'M BEING SENT TO AFRICA ALL OF A SUDDEN!
IF IT'S FOR WORK, THEN I SUPPOSE THERE'S NO HELPING IT!
LISTEN TO ME. DON'T DO ANYTHING RASH, NOW!

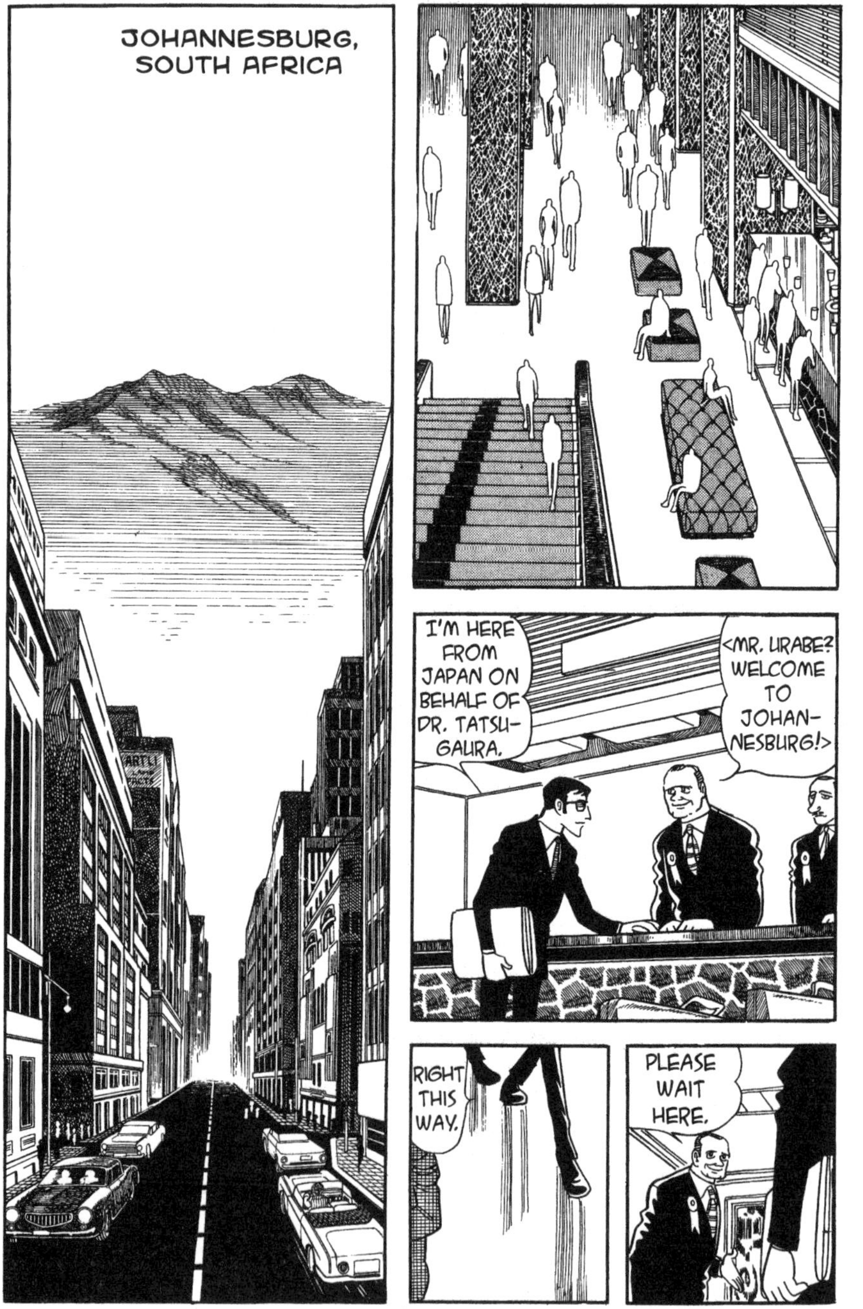
JOHANNESBURG, SOUTH AFRICA
I'M HERE FROM JAPAN ON BEHALF OF DR. TATSU-GAURA.
<MR. URABE? WELCOME TO JOHAN-NESBURG!>
RIGHT THIS WAY.
PLEASE WAIT HERE.

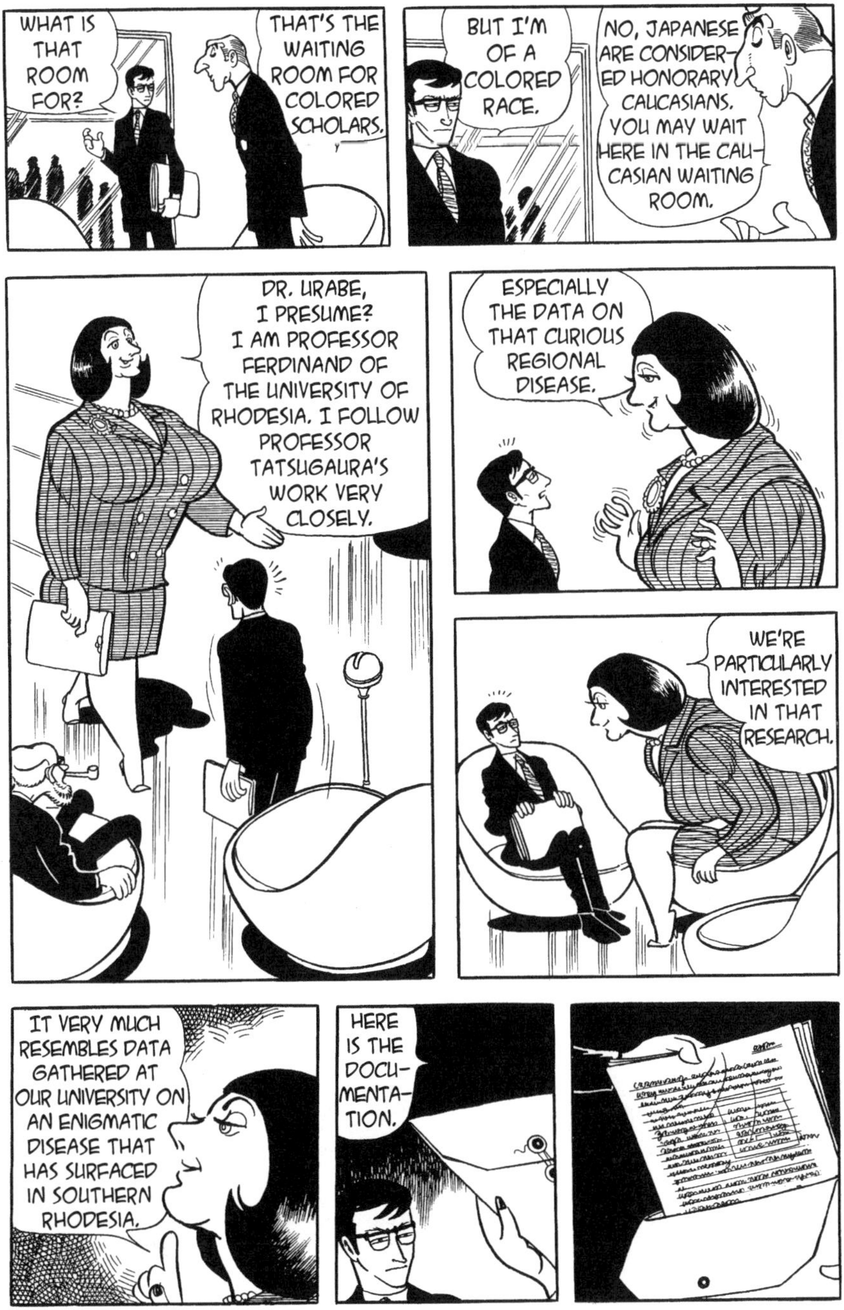

WHAT IS THAT ROOM FOR?
THAT'S THE WAITING ROOM FOR COLORED SCHOLARS.
BUT I'M OF A COLORED RACE.
NO, JAPANESE ARE CONSIDERED HONORARY CAUCASIANS. YOU MAY WAIT HERE IN THE CAUCASIAN WAITING ROOM.
DR. URABE, I PRESUME? I AM PROFESSOR FERDINAND OF THE UNIVERSITY OF RHODESIA. I FOLLOW PROFESSOR TATSUGAURA'S WORK VERY CLOSELY.
ESPECIALLY THE DATA ON THAT CURIOUS REGIONAL DISEASE.
WE'RE PARTICULARLY INTERESTED IN THAT RESEARCH.
IT VERY MUCH RESEMBLES DATA GATHERED AT OUR UNIVERSITY ON AN ENIGMATIC DISEASE THAT HAS SURFACED IN SOUTHERN RHODESIA.
HERE IS THE DOCUMENTATION.

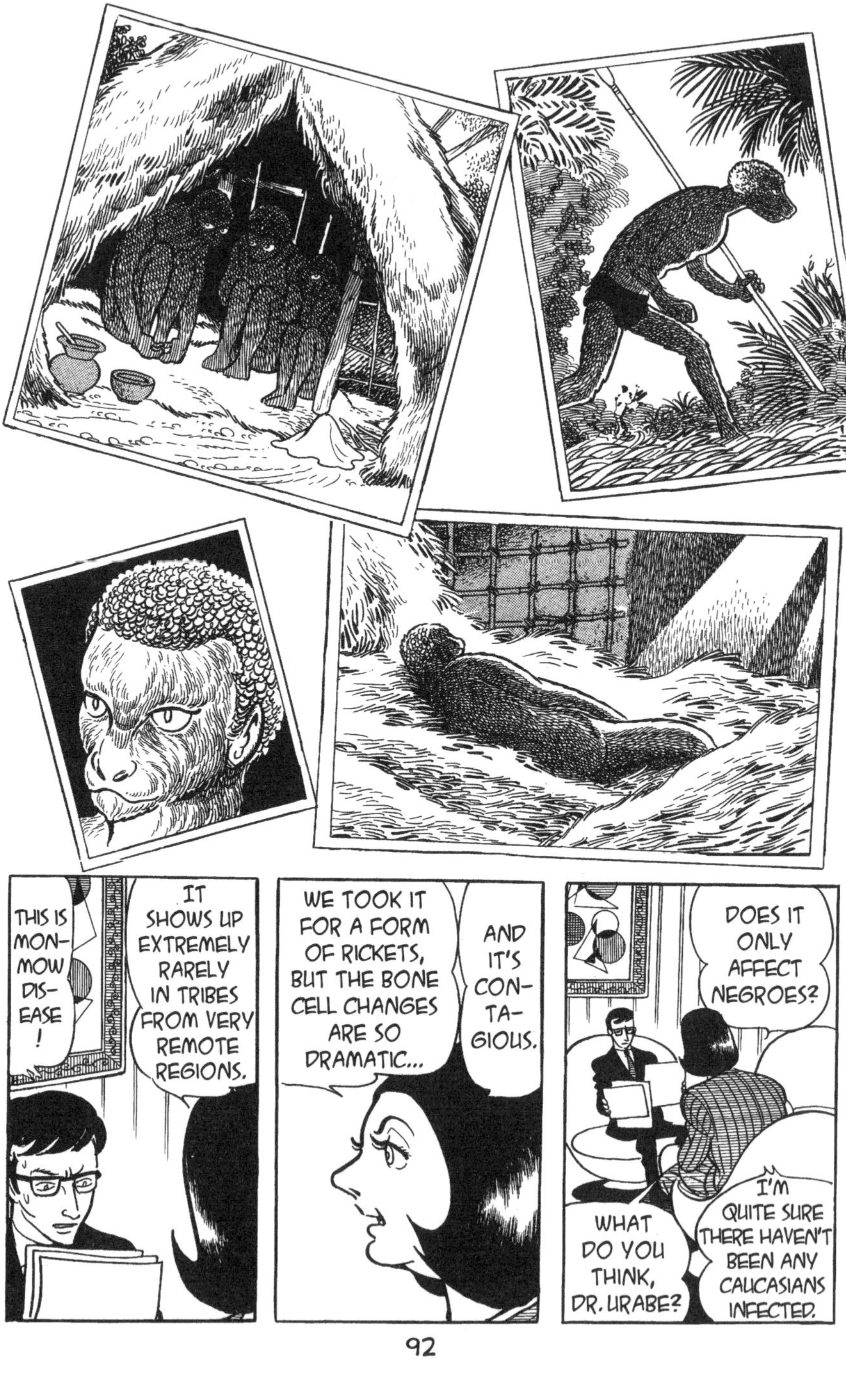
THIS IS MON-MOW DIS-EASE!
IT SHOWS UP EXTREMELY RARELY IN TRIBES FROM VERY REMOTE REGIONS.
WE TOOK IT FOR A FORM OF RICKETS, BUT THE BONE CELL CHANGES ARE SO DRAMATIC...
AND IT'S CON-TA-GIOUS.
DOES IT ONLY AFFECT NEGROES?
WHAT DO YOU THINK, DR. URABE?
I'M QUITE SURE THERE HAVEN'T BEEN ANY CAUCASIANS INFECTED.

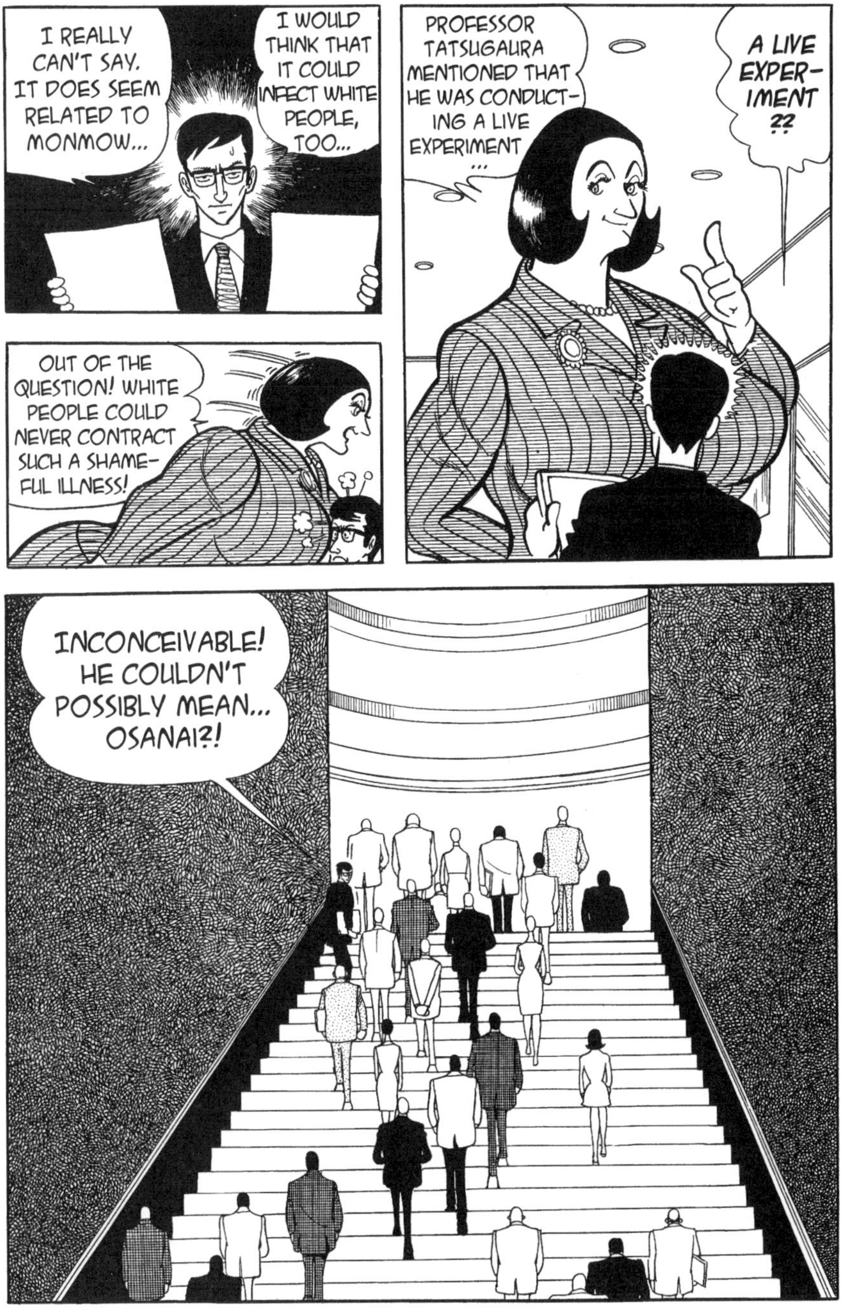

I REALLY CAN'T SAY. IT DOES SEEM RELATED TO MONMOW...
I WOULD THINK THAT IT COULD INFECT WHITE PEOPLE, TOO...
PROFESSOR TATSUGAURA MENTIONED THAT HE WAS CONDUCTING A LIVE EXPERIMENT ...
A LIVE EXPERIMENT ⁇
OUT OF THE QUESTION! WHITE PEOPLE COULD NEVER CONTRACT SUCH A SHAMEFUL ILLNESS!
INCONCEIVABLE! HE COULDN'T POSSIBLY MEAN... OSANAI?!

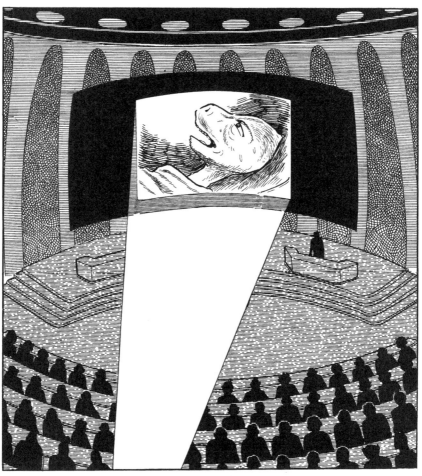

IN JAPAN, MONMOW DISEASE HAS ALREADY CLAIMED MORE THAN 200 LIVES.

THE OTHER DAY, ONE OF THESE PATIENTS DIED AT OUR HOSPITAL.

...

HOW HORRIBLE!

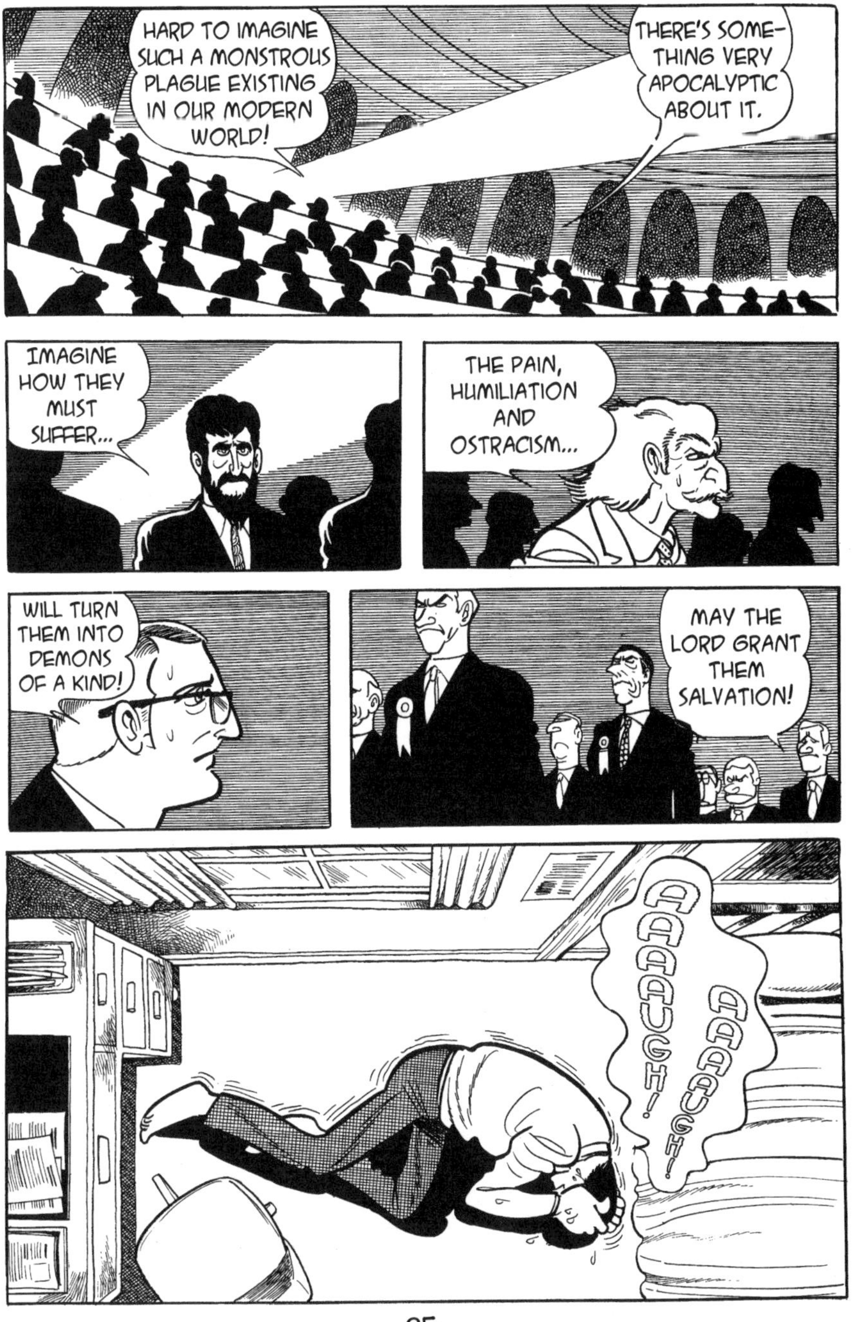
HARD TO IMAGINE SUCH A MONSTROUS PLAGUE EXISTING IN OUR MODERN WORLD!
THERE'S SOME-THING VERY APOCALYPTIC ABOUT IT.
IMAGINE HOW THEY MUST SUFFER...
THE PAIN, HUMILIATION AND OSTRACISM...
WILL TURN THEM INTO DEMONS OF A KIND!
MAY THE LORD GRANT THEM SALVATION!
AAAAAUGH!
AAAAAUGH!

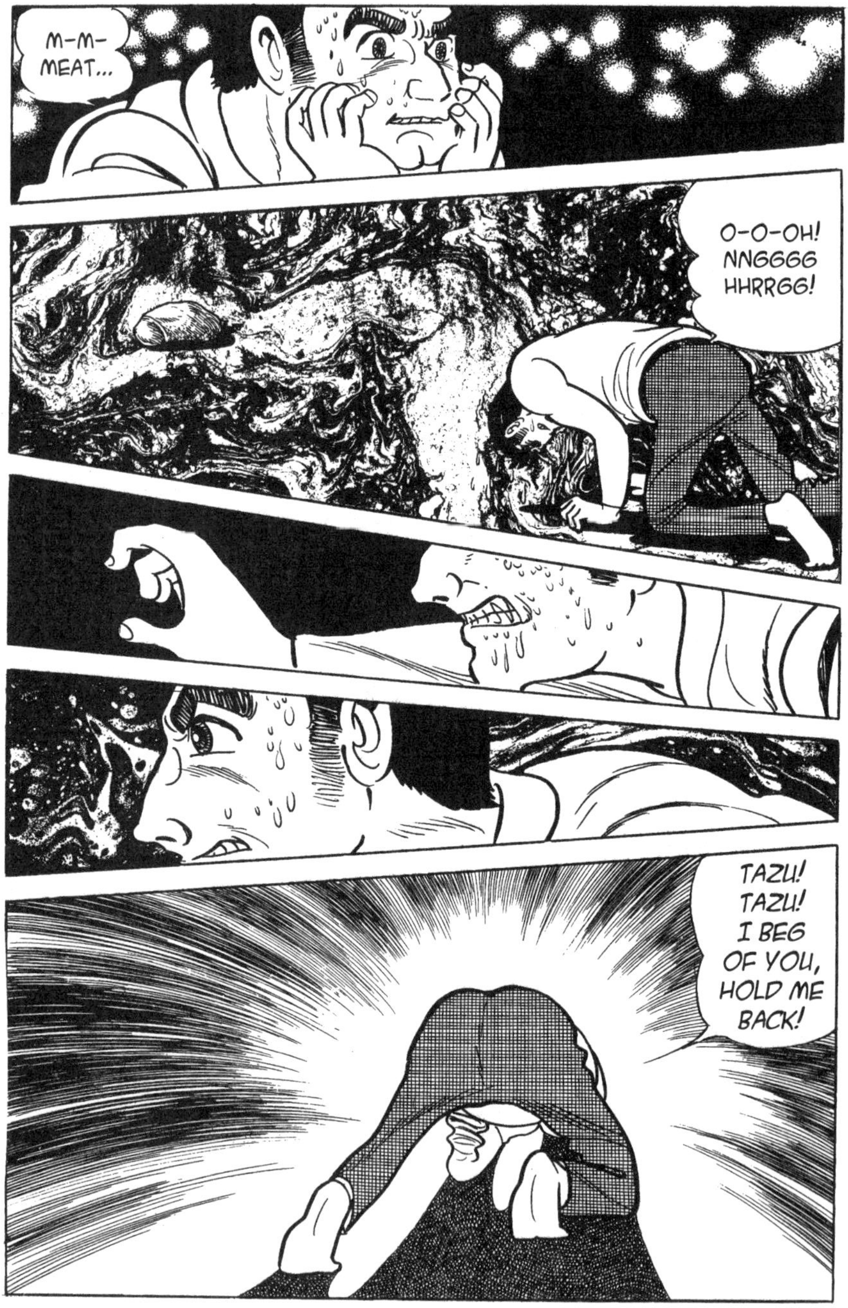
M-M-MEAT...
O-O-OH! NNGGGG HHRRGG!
TAZU! TAZU! I BEG OF YOU, HOLD ME BACK!

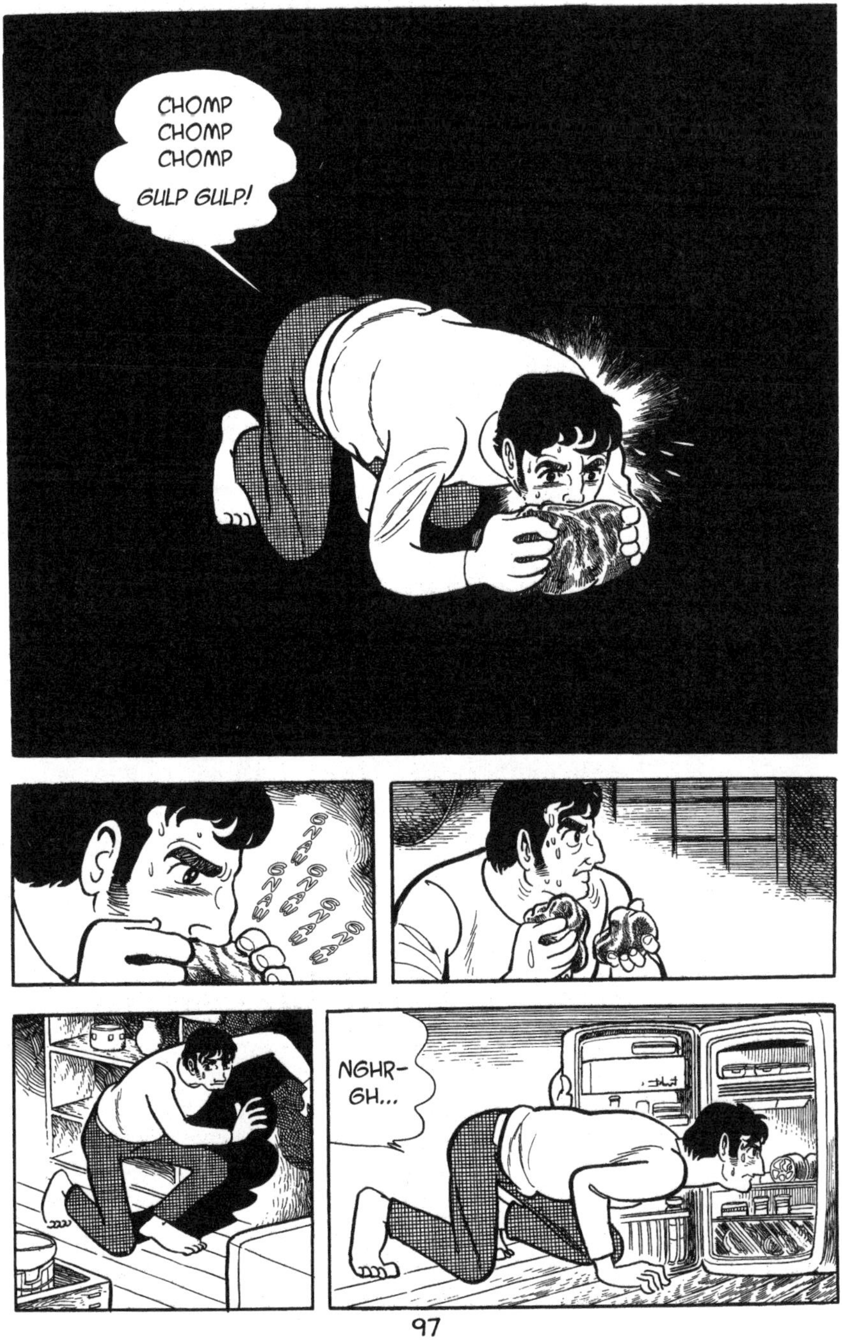
CHOMP CHOMP CHOMP
GULP GULP!
GNAW GNAW GNAW GNAW GNAW
NGHR-GH...

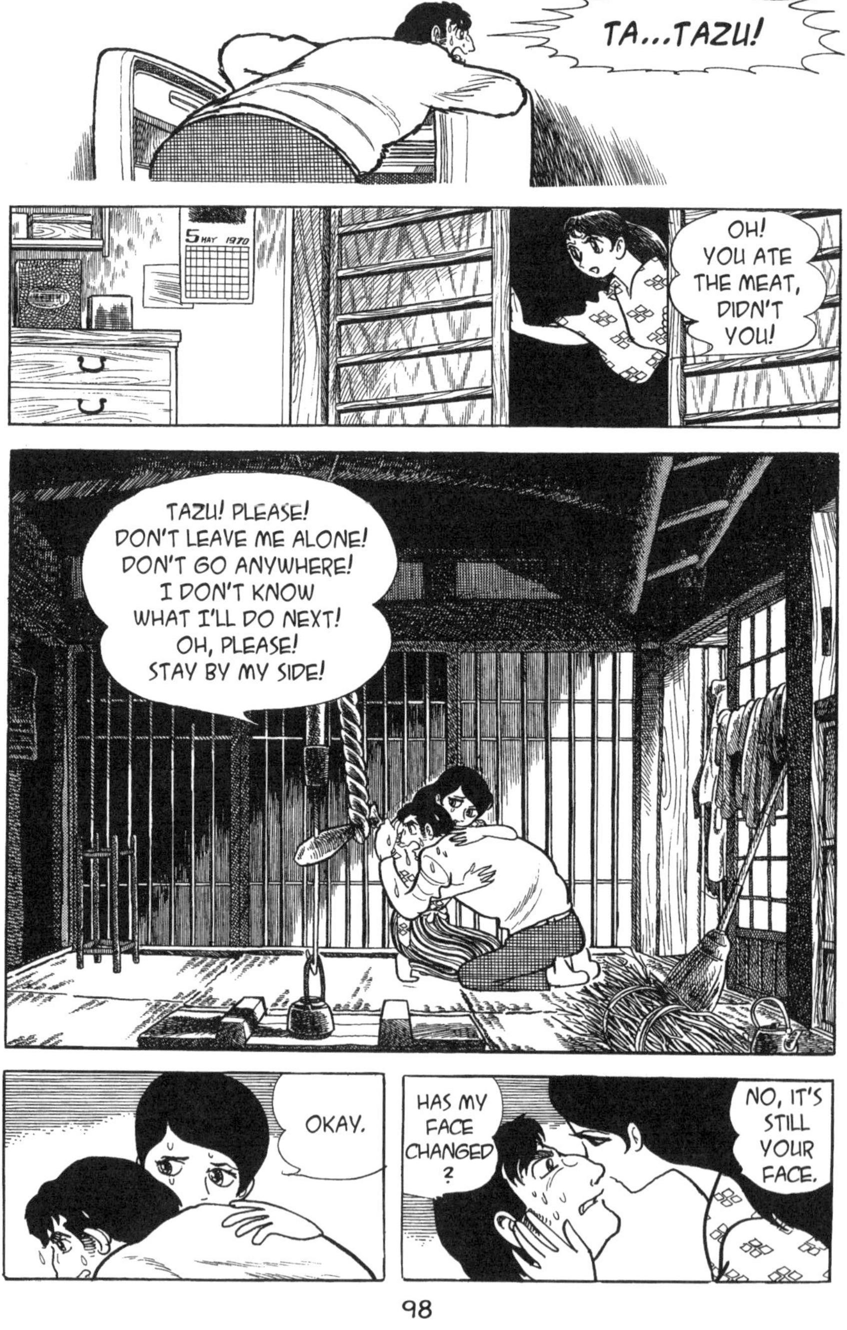
TA...TAZU!
5 MAY 1970
OH! YOU ATE THE MEAT, DIDN'T YOU!
TAZU! PLEASE! DON'T LEAVE ME ALONE! DON'T GO ANYWHERE! I DON'T KNOW WHAT I'LL DO NEXT! OH, PLEASE! STAY BY MY SIDE!
OKAY.
HAS MY FACE CHANGED?
NO, IT'S STILL YOUR FACE.

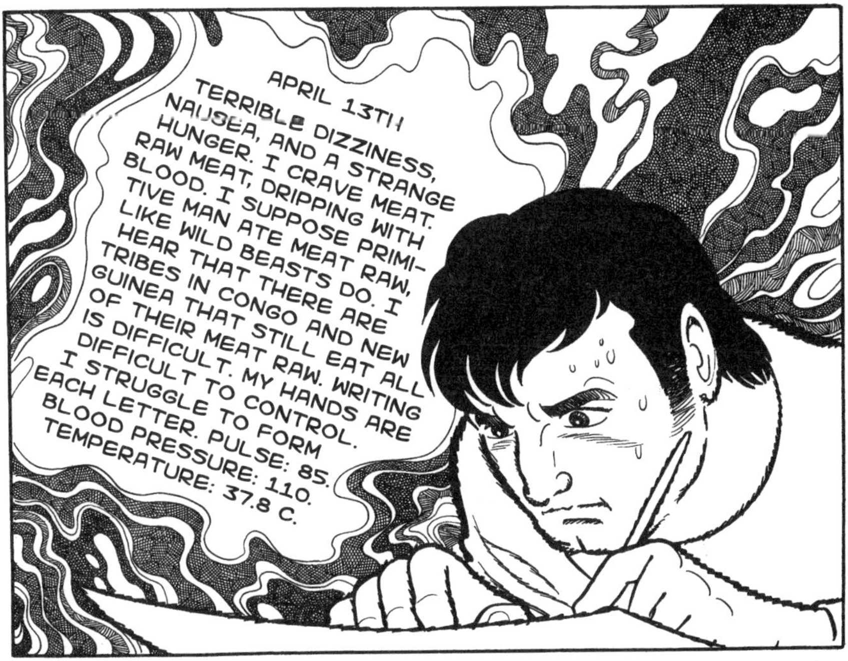
APRIL 13TH
TERRIBLE DIZZINESS, NAUSEA, AND A STRANGE HUNGER. I CRAVE MEAT. RAW MEAT, DRIPPING WITH BLOOD. I SUPPOSE PRIMITIVE MAN ATE MEAT RAW, LIKE WILD BEASTS DO. I HEAR THAT THERE ARE TRIBES IN CONGO AND NEW GUINEA THAT STILL EAT ALL OF THEIR MEAT RAW. WRITING IS DIFFICULT. MY HANDS ARE DIFFICULT TO CONTROL. I STRUGGLE TO FORM EACH LETTER. PULSE: 85. BLOOD PRESSURE: 110. TEMPERATURE: 37.8 C.

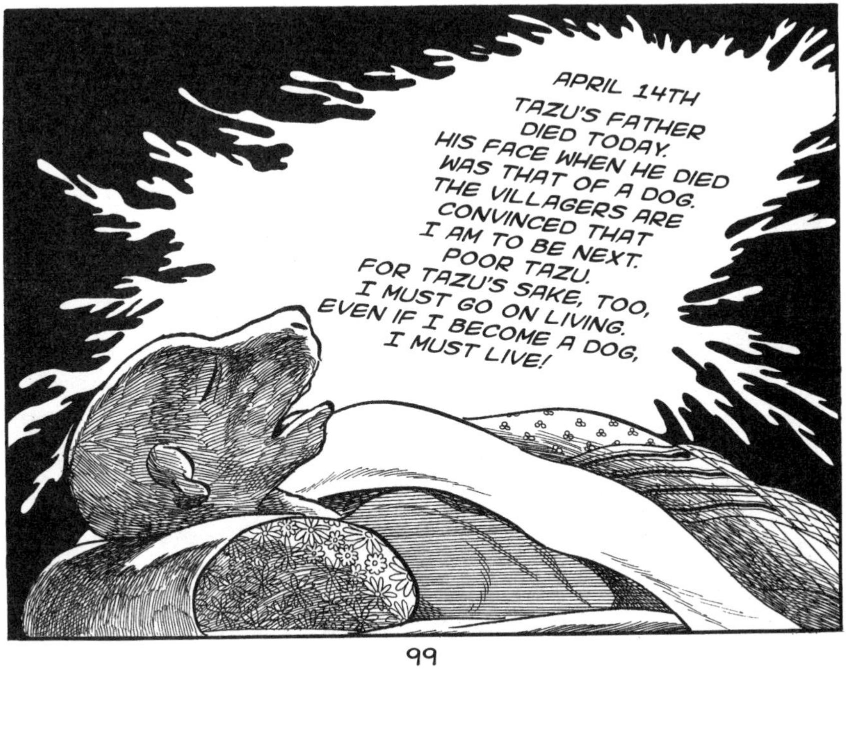
APRIL 14TH
TAZU'S FATHER DIED TODAY. HIS FACE WHEN HE DIED WAS THAT OF A DOG. THE VILLAGERS ARE CONVINCED THAT I AM TO BE NEXT. POOR TAZU. FOR TAZU'S SAKE, TOO, I MUST GO ON LIVING. EVEN IF I BECOME A DOG, I MUST LIVE!

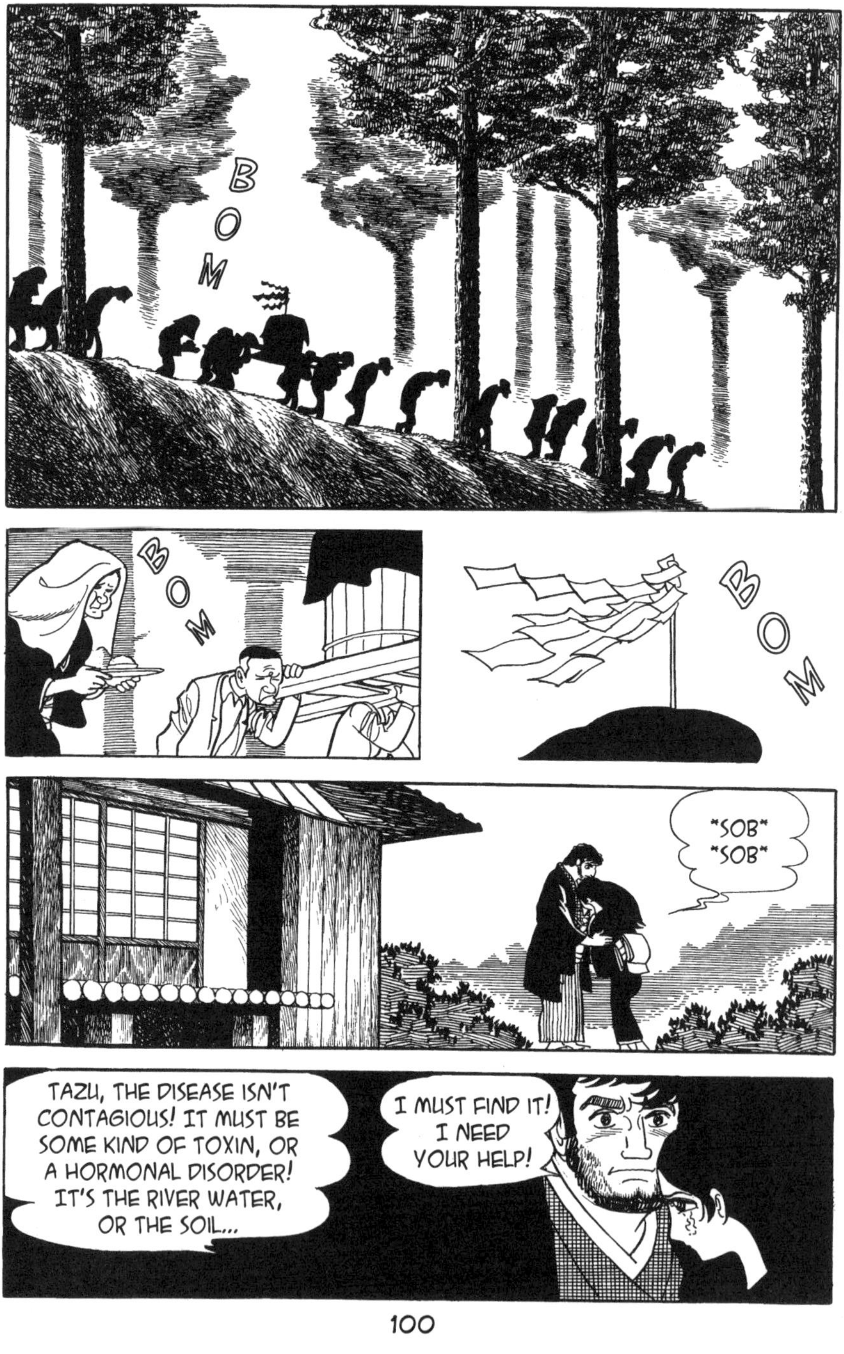
BOM
BOM
BOM
SOB
SOB
TAZU, THE DISEASE ISN'T CONTAGIOUS! IT MUST BE SOME KIND OF TOXIN, OR A HORMONAL DISORDER! IT'S THE RIVER WATER, OR THE SOIL...
I MUST FIND IT! I NEED YOUR HELP!

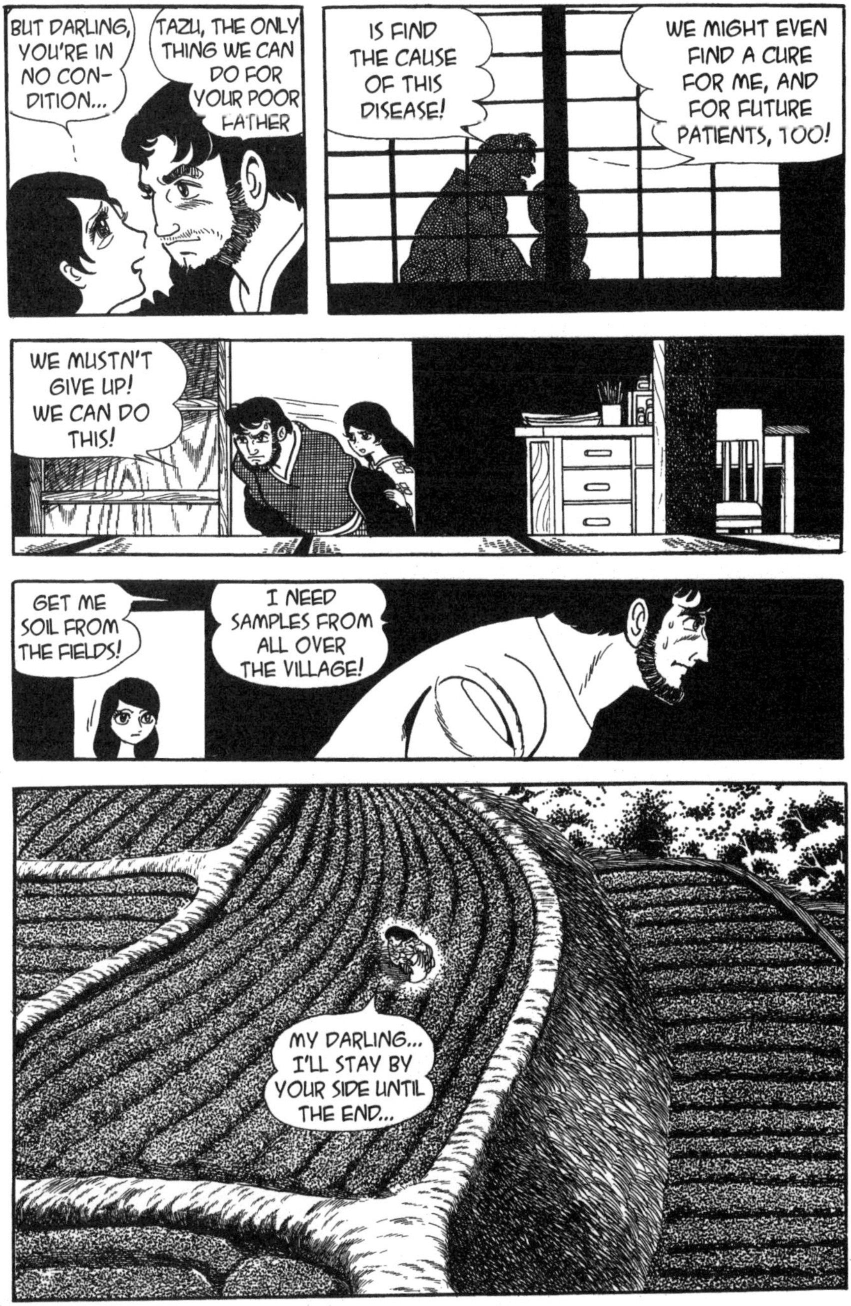
BUT DARLING, YOU'RE IN NO CON-DITION...
TAZU, THE ONLY THING WE CAN DO FOR YOUR POOR FATHER
IS FIND THE CAUSE OF THIS DISEASE!
WE MIGHT EVEN FIND A CURE FOR ME, AND FOR FUTURE PATIENTS, TOO!
WE MUSTN'T GIVE UP! WE CAN DO THIS!
GET ME SOIL FROM THE FIELDS!
I NEED SAMPLES FROM ALL OVER THE VILLAGE!
MY DARLING... I'LL STAY BY YOUR SIDE UNTIL THE END...

CHAPTER 4

COLLAPSE

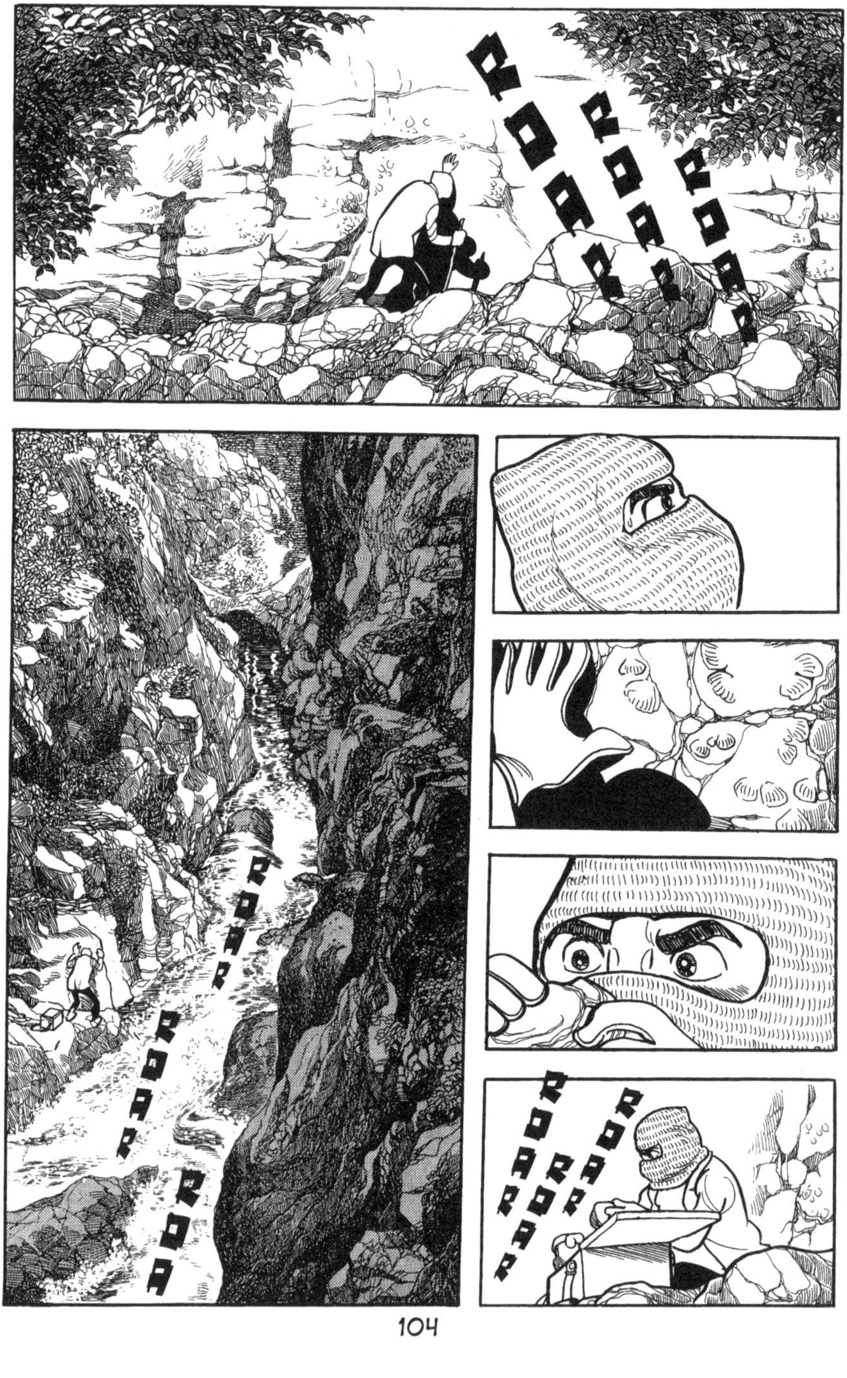
ROAR
ROAR
ROAR
ROAR
ROAR
ROA
ROAR
ROAR
ROAR

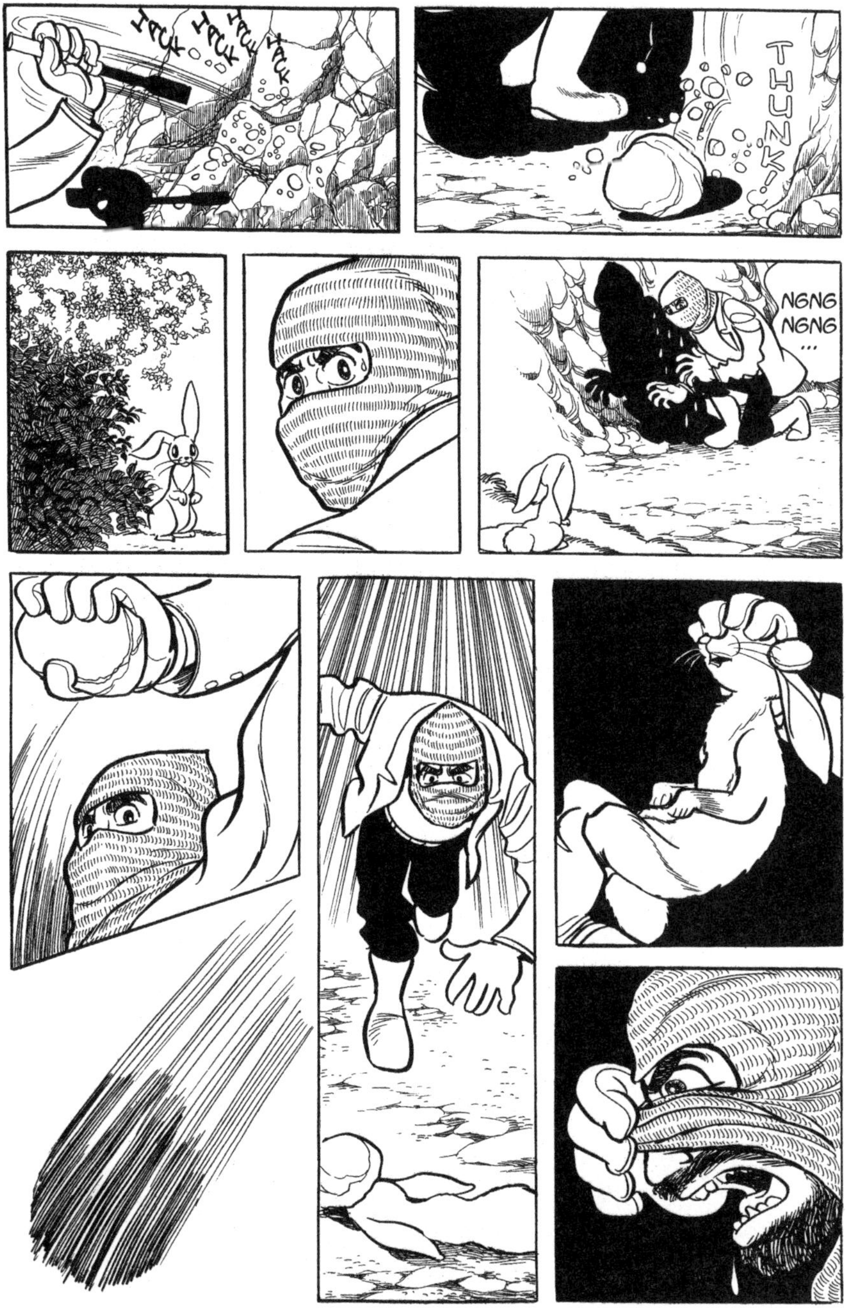
HACK HACK HACK HACK
THUNK!
NGNG NGNG ...

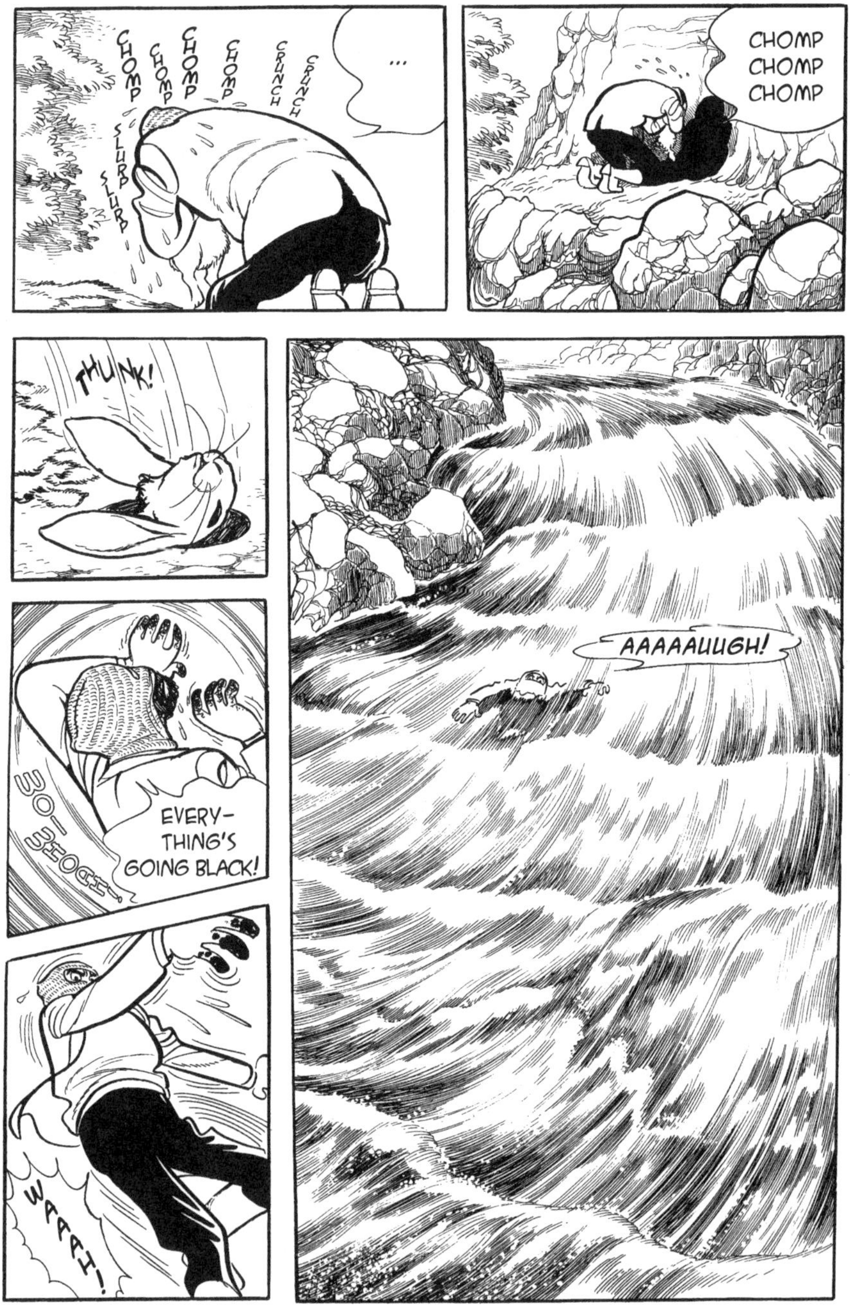
CHOMP
CHOMP
CHOMP
CHOMP
CRUNCH
CRUNCH
SLURP
SLURP
...
CHOMP
CHOMP
CHOMP
THUNK!
EVERY-
THING'S
GOING BLACK!
WAAAH!
AAAAAUUGH!

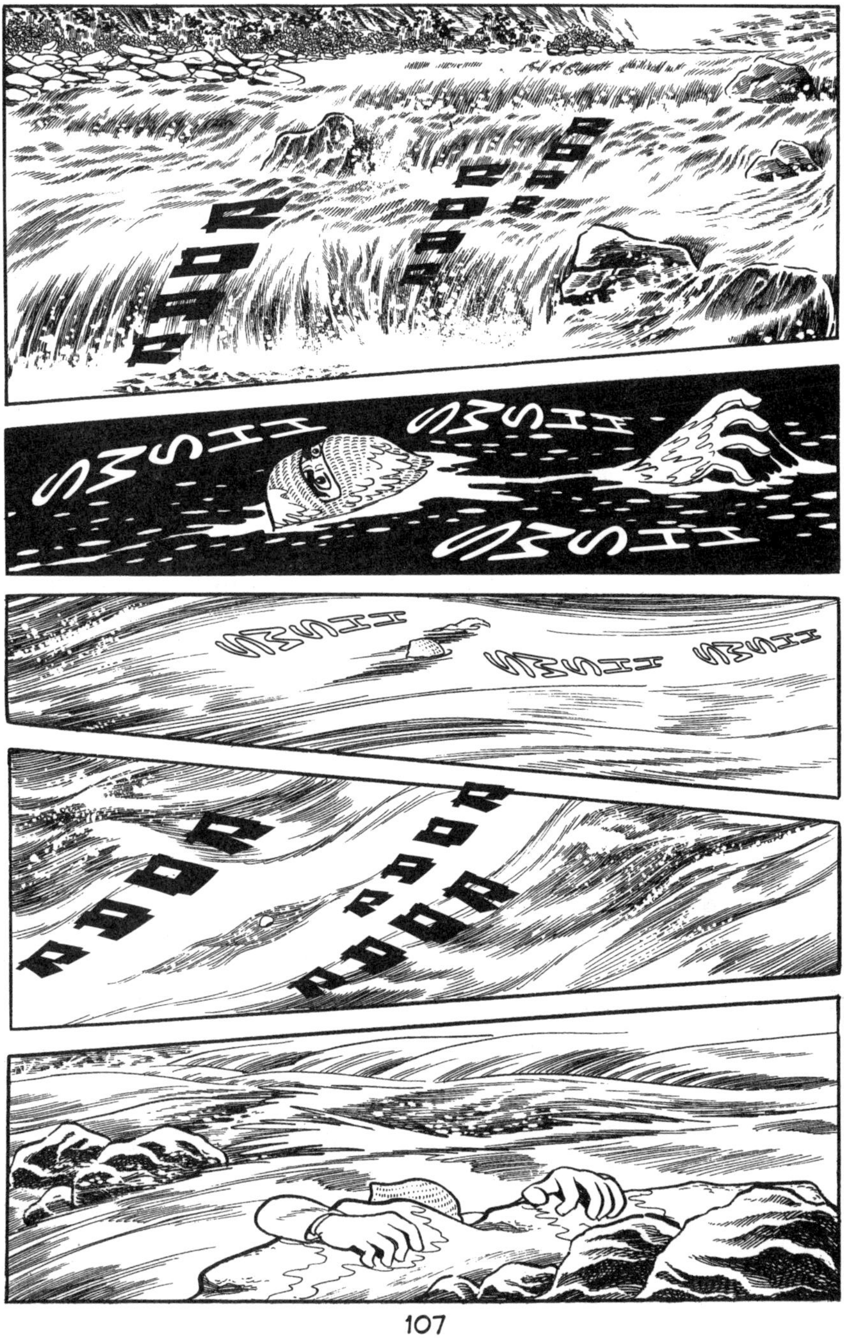

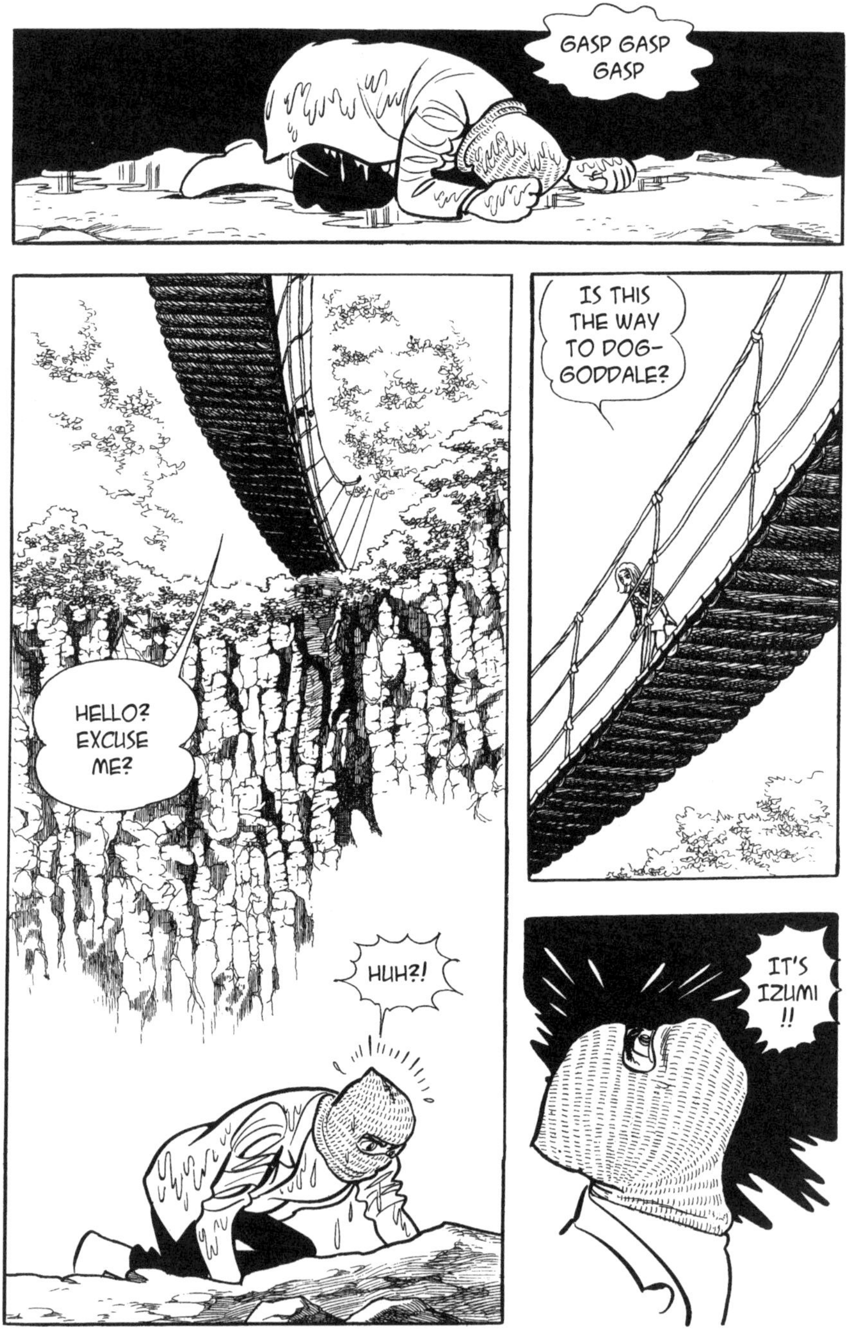
GASP GASP GASP
HELLO? EXCUSE ME?
IS THIS THE WAY TO DOG-GODDALE?
HUH?!
IT'S IZUMI !!

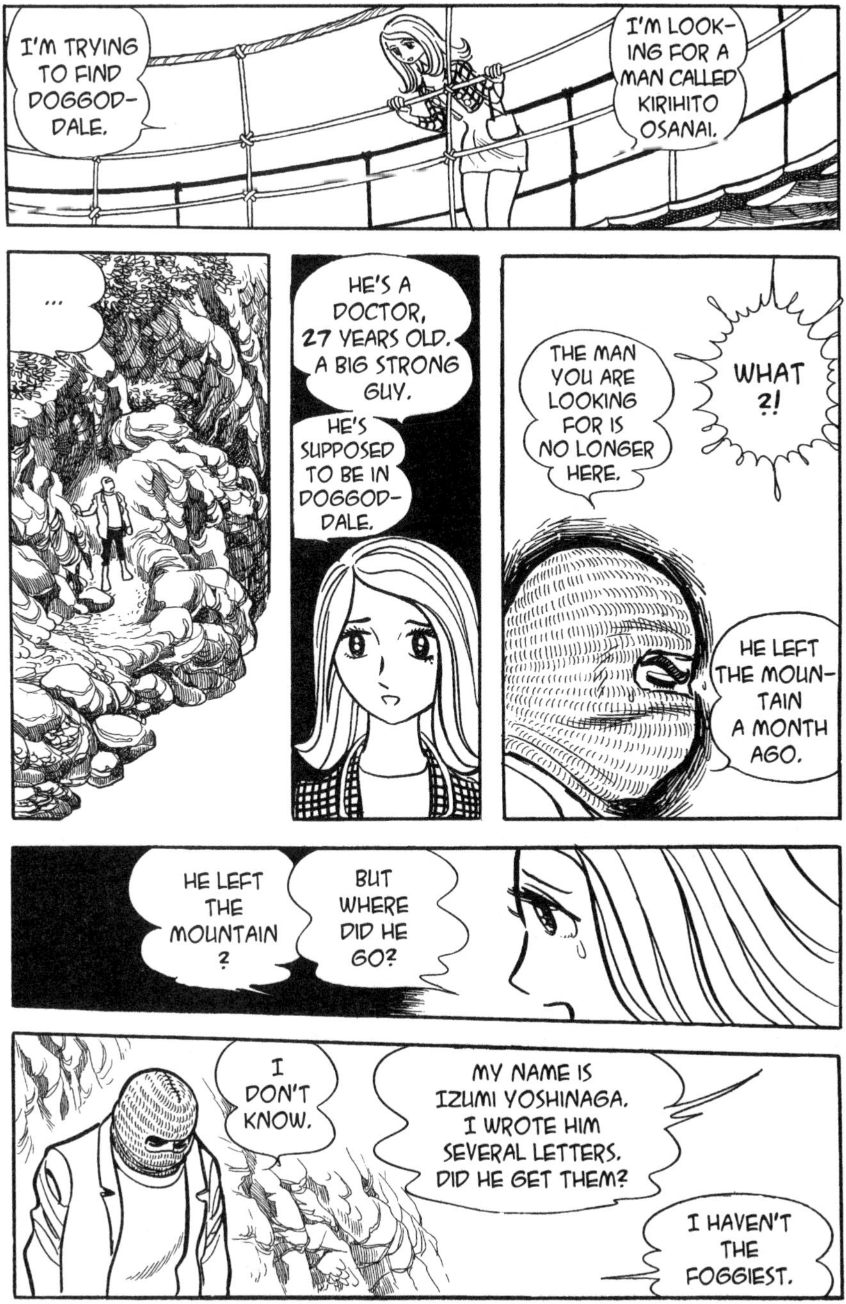
I'M TRYING TO FIND DOGGOD-DALE.
I'M LOOKING FOR A MAN CALLED KIRIHITO OSANAI.
...
HE'S A DOCTOR, 27 YEARS OLD. A BIG STRONG GUY.
HE'S SUPPOSED TO BE IN DOGGOD-DALE.
THE MAN YOU ARE LOOKING FOR IS NO LONGER HERE.
WHAT ?!
HE LEFT THE MOUNTAIN A MONTH AGO.
HE LEFT THE MOUNTAIN ?
BUT WHERE DID HE GO?
I DON'T KNOW.
MY NAME IS IZUMI YOSHINAGA. I WROTE HIM SEVERAL LETTERS. DID HE GET THEM?
I HAVEN'T THE FOGGIEST.

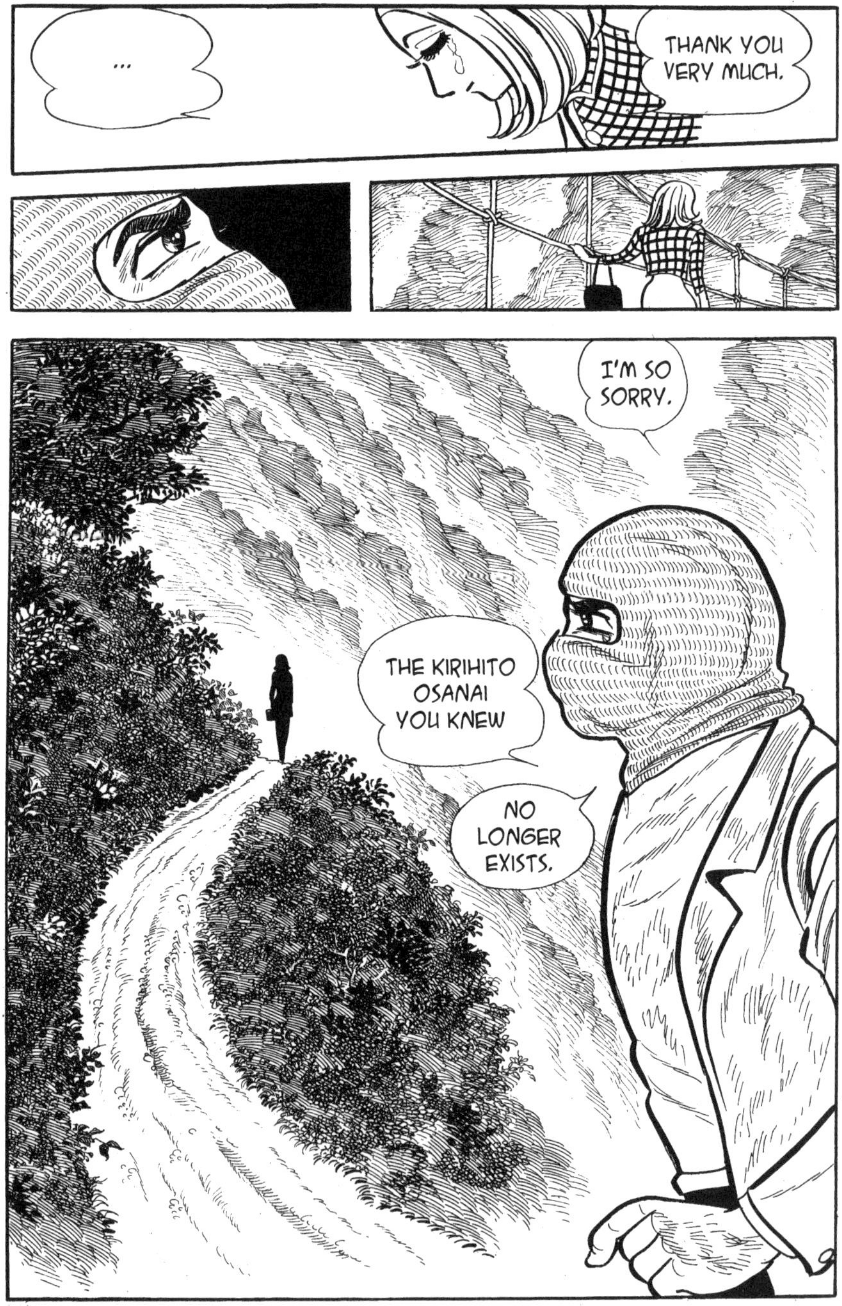
...
THANK YOU VERY MUCH.
I'M SO SORRY.
THE KIRIHITO OSANAI YOU KNEW
NO LONGER EXISTS.

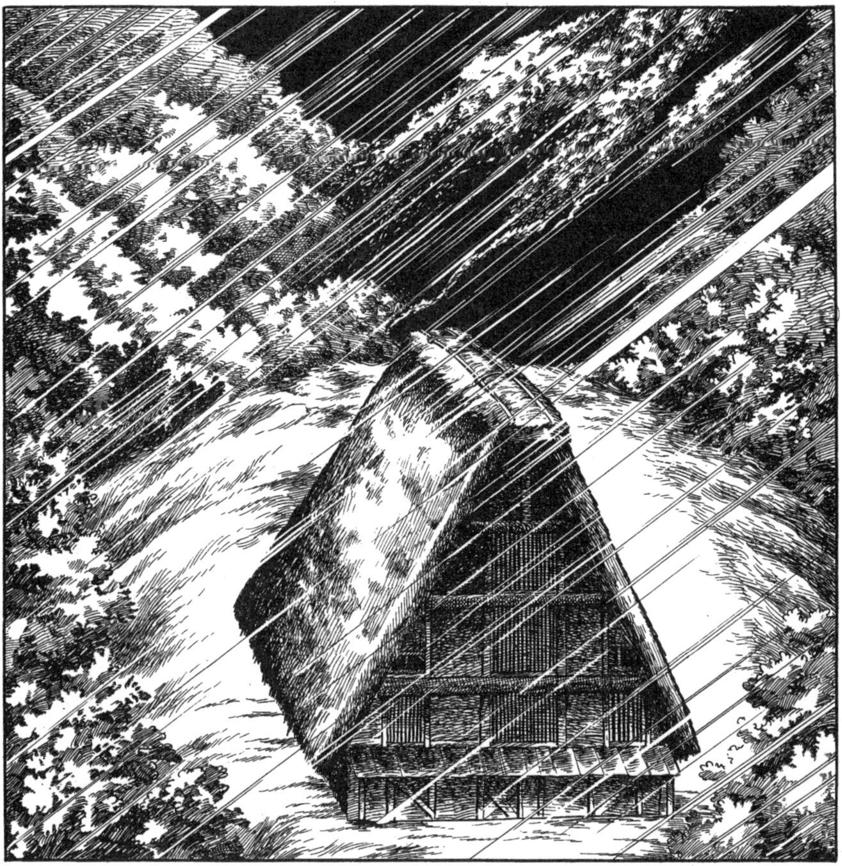

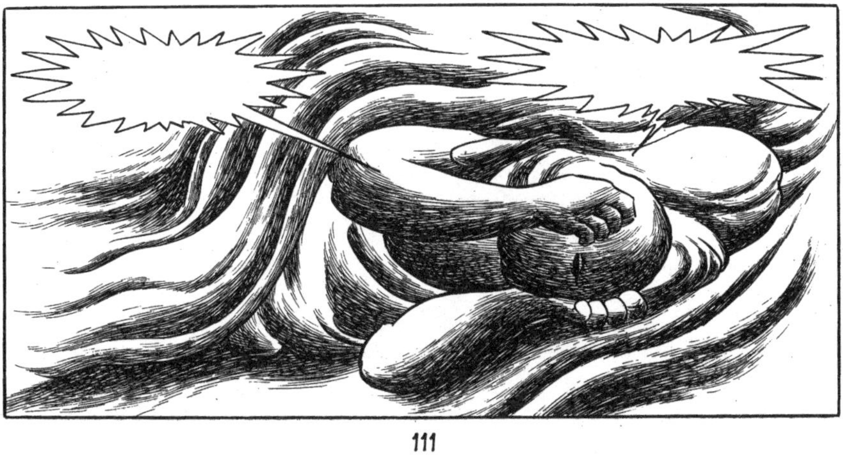

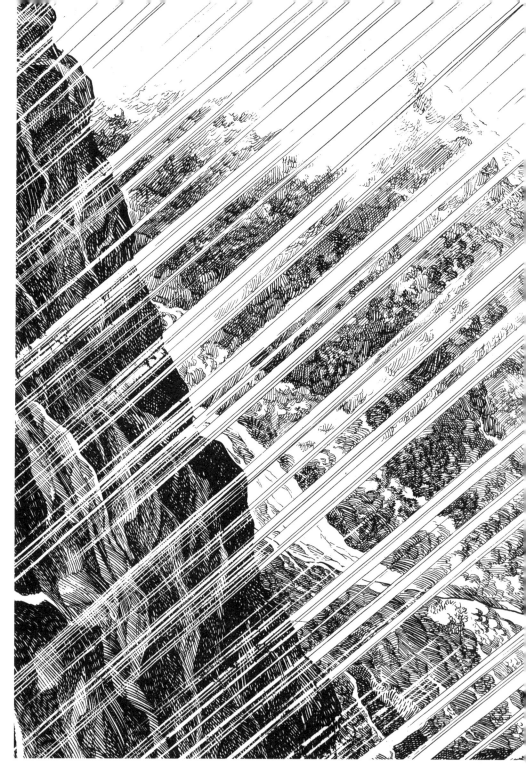

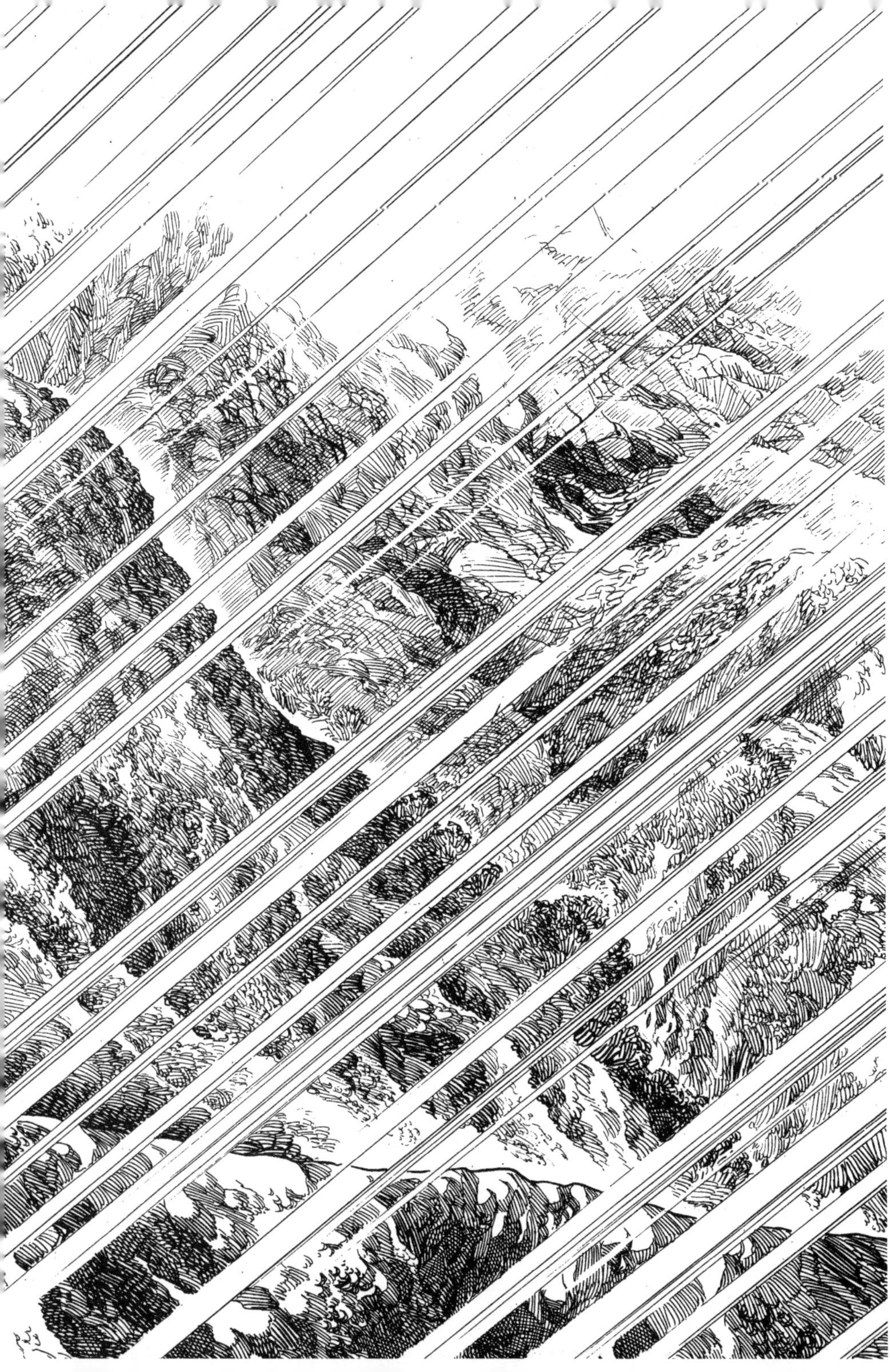

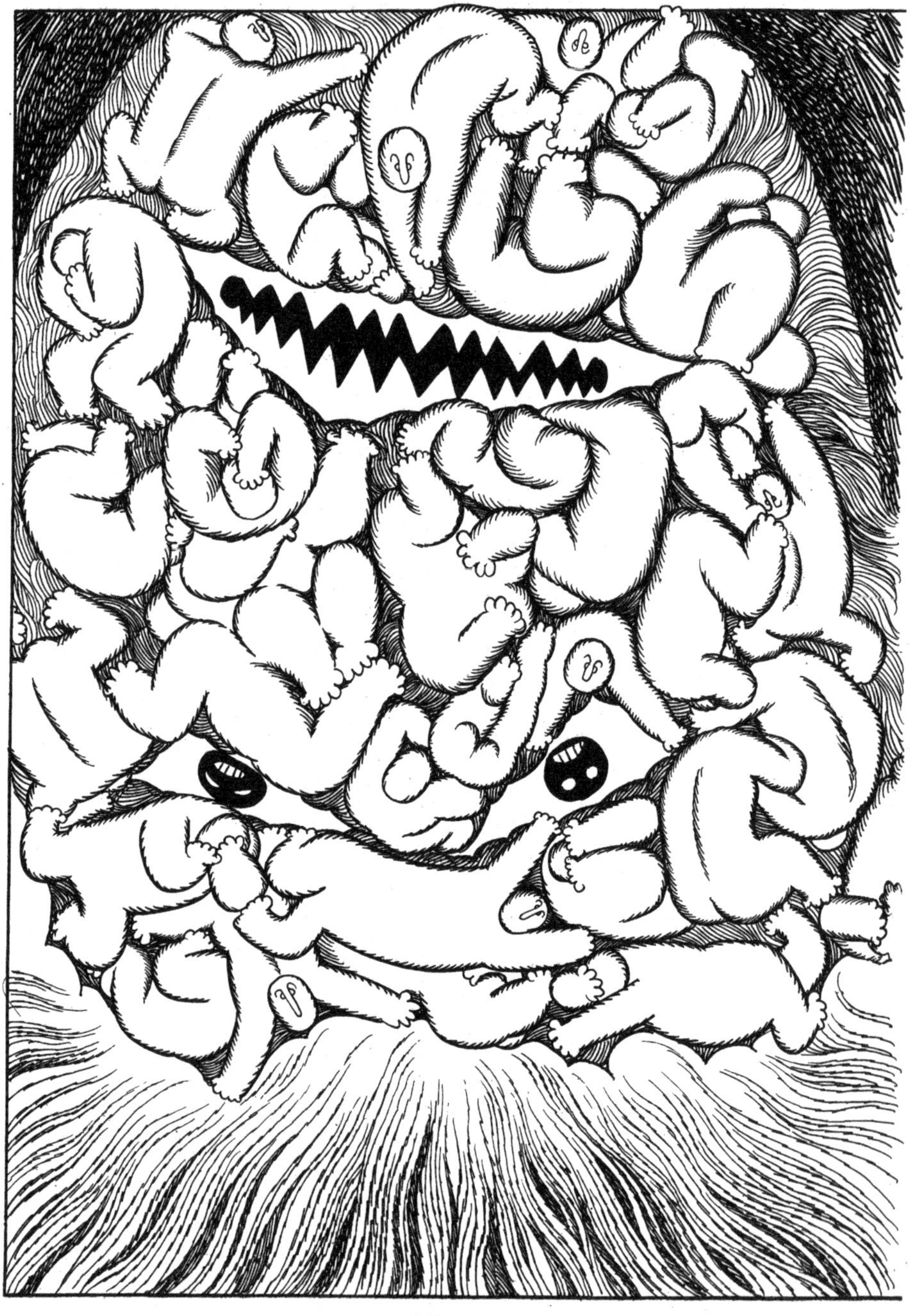

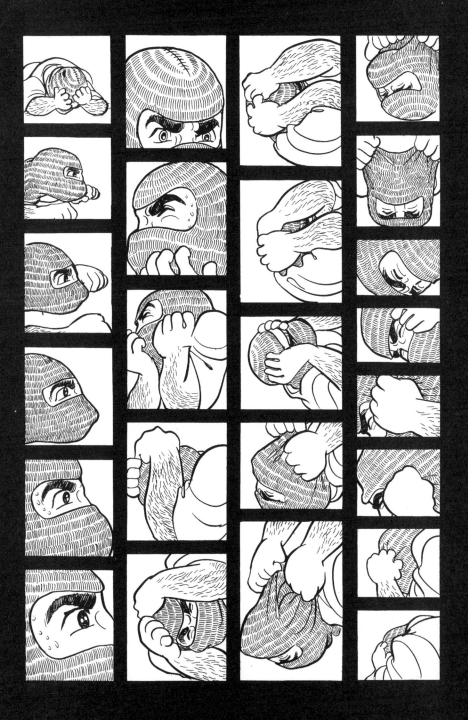

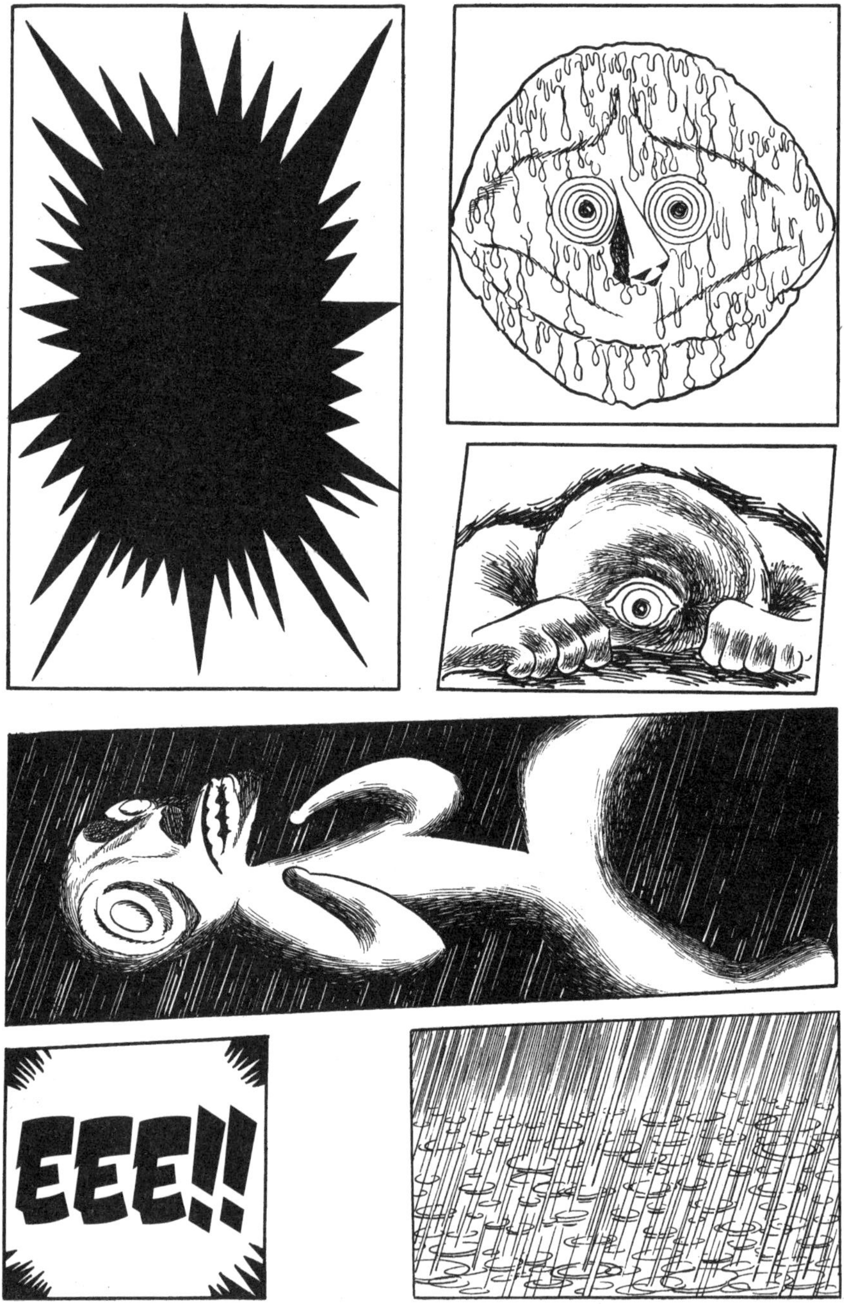
EEE!!

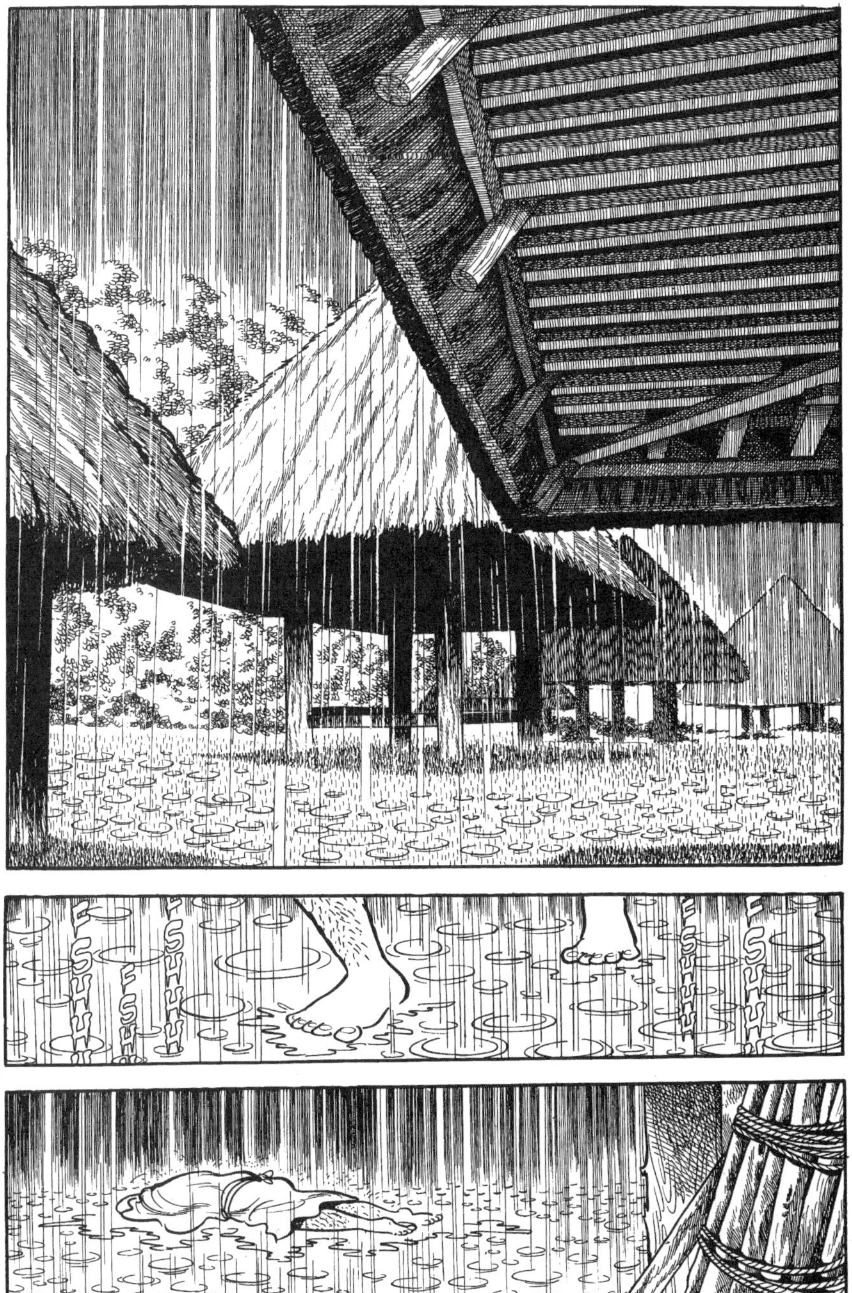
FSHHHH
FSHHH
FSHHHH
FSHHHH
FSHHHH

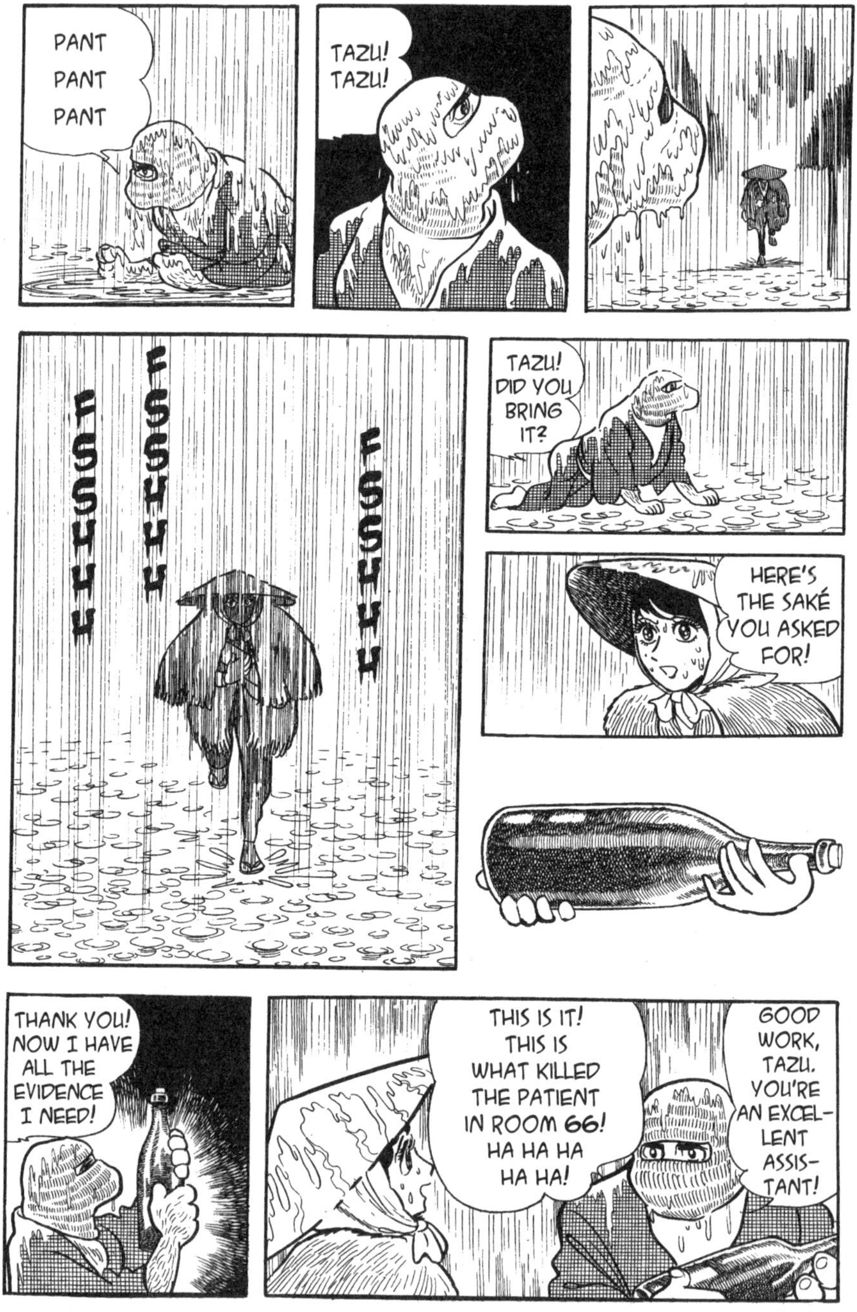
PANT
PANT
PANT
TAZU! TAZU!
FSSHUUU
FSSHUUU
FSSHUUU
TAZU! DID YOU BRING IT?
HERE'S THE SAKÉ YOU ASKED FOR!
THANK YOU! NOW I HAVE ALL THE EVIDENCE I NEED!
GOOD WORK, TAZU. YOU'RE AN EXCEL-LENT ASSIS-TANT!
THIS IS IT! THIS IS WHAT KILLED THE PATIENT IN ROOM 66! HA HA HA HA HA!

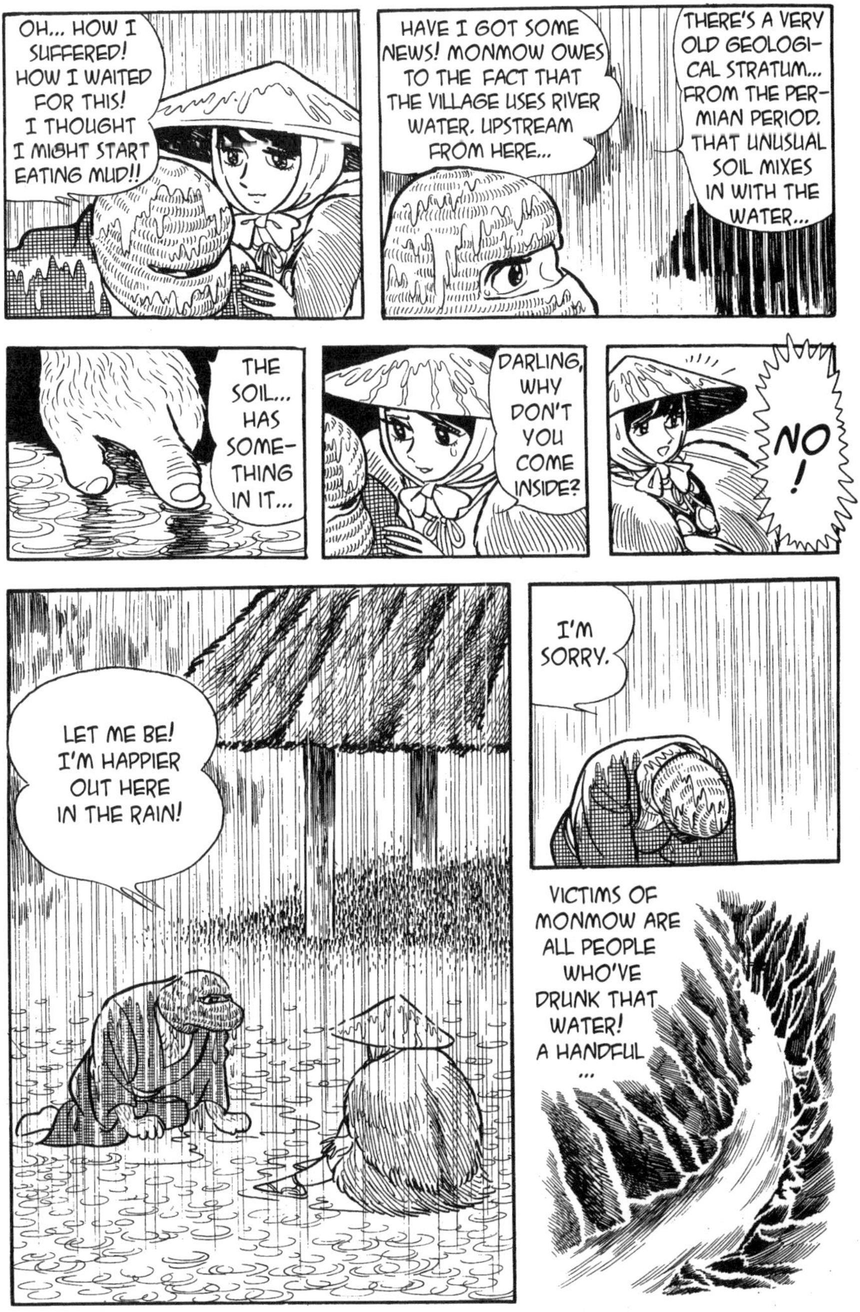
OH... HOW I SUFFERED! HOW I WAITED FOR THIS! I THOUGHT I MIGHT START EATING MUD!!
HAVE I GOT SOME NEWS! MONMOW OWES TO THE FACT THAT THE VILLAGE USES RIVER WATER. UPSTREAM FROM HERE...
THERE'S A VERY OLD GEOLOGICAL STRATUM... FROM THE PERMIAN PERIOD. THAT UNUSUAL SOIL MIXES IN WITH THE WATER...
THE SOIL... HAS SOMETHING IN IT...
DARLING, WHY DON'T YOU COME INSIDE?
NO!
LET ME BE! I'M HAPPIER OUT HERE IN THE RAIN!
I'M SORRY.
VICTIMS OF MONMOW ARE ALL PEOPLE WHO'VE DRUNK THAT WATER! A HANDFUL ...

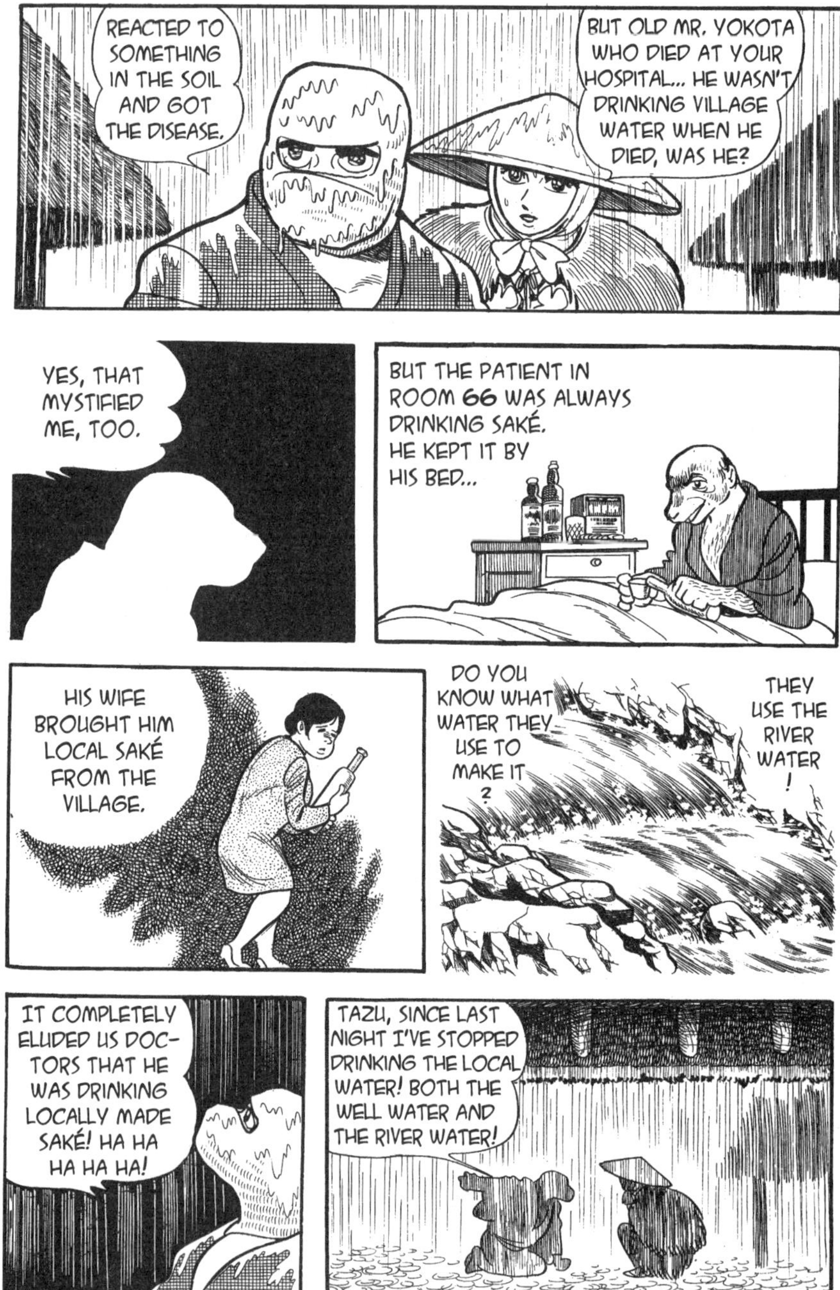
REACTED TO SOMETHING IN THE SOIL AND GOT THE DISEASE.
BUT OLD MR. YOKOTA WHO DIED AT YOUR HOSPITAL... HE WASN'T DRINKING VILLAGE WATER WHEN HE DIED, WAS HE?
YES, THAT MYSTIFIED ME, TOO.
BUT THE PATIENT IN ROOM 66 WAS ALWAYS DRINKING SAKÉ. HE KEPT IT BY HIS BED...
HIS WIFE BROUGHT HIM LOCAL SAKÉ FROM THE VILLAGE.
DO YOU KNOW WHAT WATER THEY USE TO MAKE IT ?
THEY USE THE RIVER WATER !
IT COMPLETELY ELUDED US DOCTORS THAT HE WAS DRINKING LOCALLY MADE SAKÉ! HA HA HA HA HA!
TAZU, SINCE LAST NIGHT I'VE STOPPED DRINKING THE LOCAL WATER! BOTH THE WELL WATER AND THE RIVER WATER!

WILL THAT MAKE YOU BETTER?

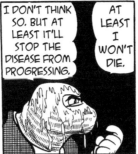

I DON'T THINK SO. BUT AT LEAST IT'LL STOP THE DISEASE FROM PROGRESSING. AT LEAST I WON'T DIE.

DOCTOR! HOW ARE YOU FEELING?

121

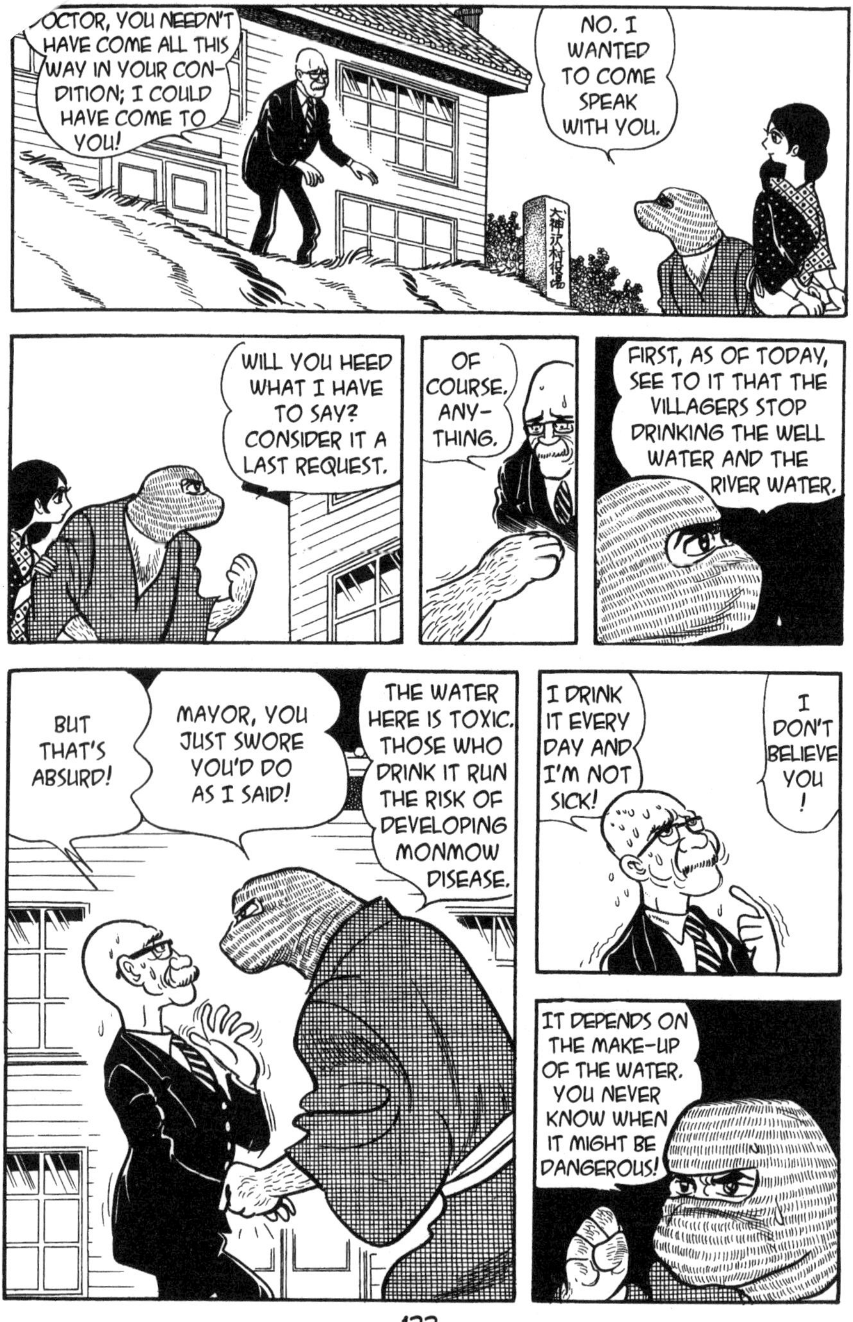
DOCTOR, YOU NEEDN'T HAVE COME ALL THIS WAY IN YOUR CON-DITION; I COULD HAVE COME TO YOU!
NO. I WANTED TO COME SPEAK WITH YOU.
大神沢村役場
WILL YOU HEED WHAT I HAVE TO SAY? CONSIDER IT A LAST REQUEST.
OF COURSE. ANY-THING.
FIRST, AS OF TODAY, SEE TO IT THAT THE VILLAGERS STOP DRINKING THE WELL WATER AND THE RIVER WATER.
BUT THAT'S ABSURD!
MAYOR, YOU JUST SWORE YOU'D DO AS I SAID!
THE WATER HERE IS TOXIC. THOSE WHO DRINK IT RUN THE RISK OF DEVELOPING MONMOW DISEASE.
I DRINK IT EVERY DAY AND I'M NOT SICK!
I DON'T BELIEVE YOU!
IT DEPENDS ON THE MAKE-UP OF THE WATER. YOU NEVER KNOW WHEN IT MIGHT BE DANGEROUS!

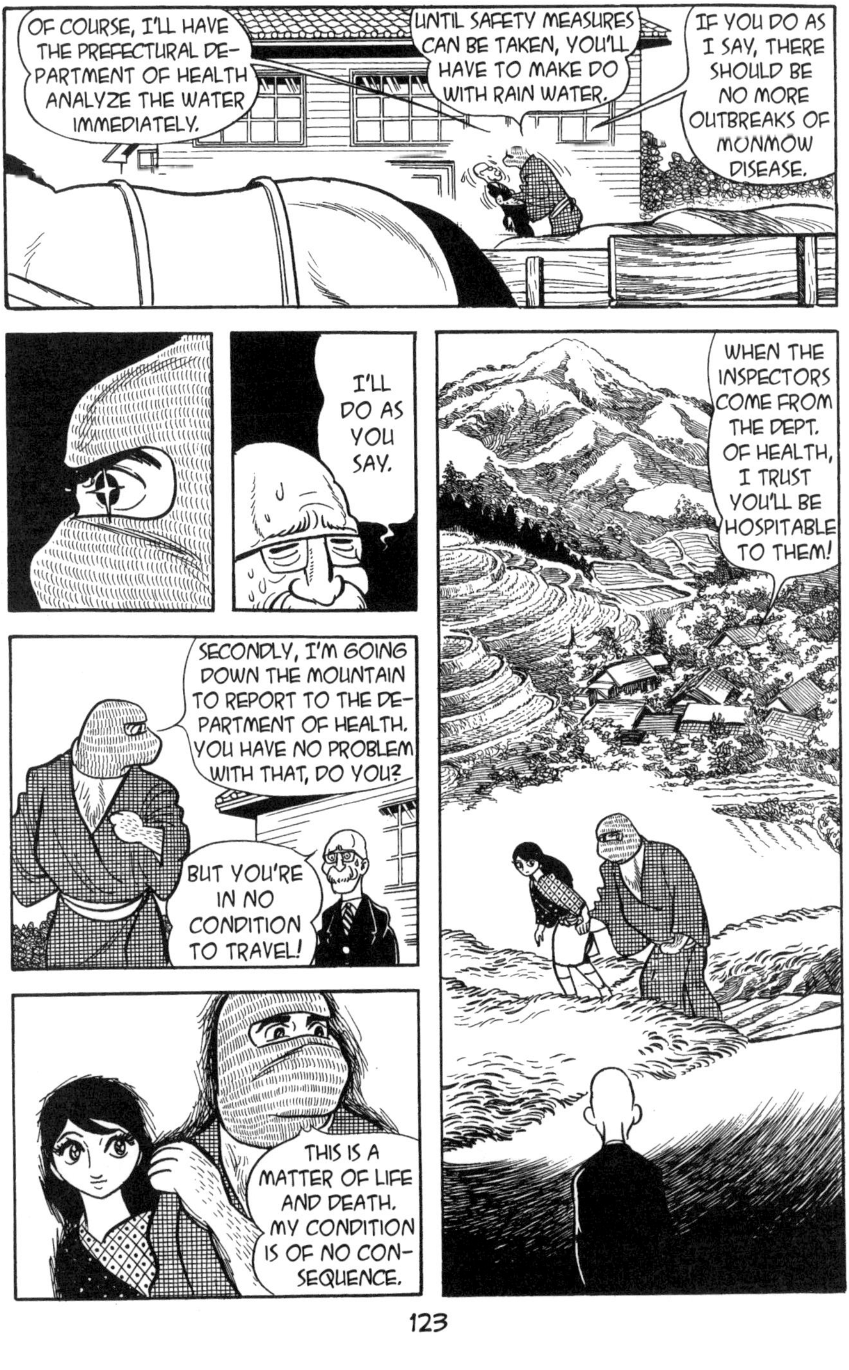
OF COURSE, I'LL HAVE THE PREFECTURAL DE-PARTMENT OF HEALTH ANALYZE THE WATER IMMEDIATELY.
UNTIL SAFETY MEASURES CAN BE TAKEN, YOU'LL HAVE TO MAKE DO WITH RAIN WATER.
IF YOU DO AS I SAY, THERE SHOULD BE NO MORE OUTBREAKS OF MONMOW DISEASE.
I'LL DO AS YOU SAY.
WHEN THE INSPECTORS COME FROM THE DEPT. OF HEALTH, I TRUST YOU'LL BE HOSPITABLE TO THEM!
SECONDLY, I'M GOING DOWN THE MOUNTAIN TO REPORT TO THE DE-PARTMENT OF HEALTH. YOU HAVE NO PROBLEM WITH THAT, DO YOU?
BUT YOU'RE IN NO CONDITION TO TRAVEL!
THIS IS A MATTER OF LIFE AND DEATH. MY CONDITION IS OF NO CON-SEQUENCE.

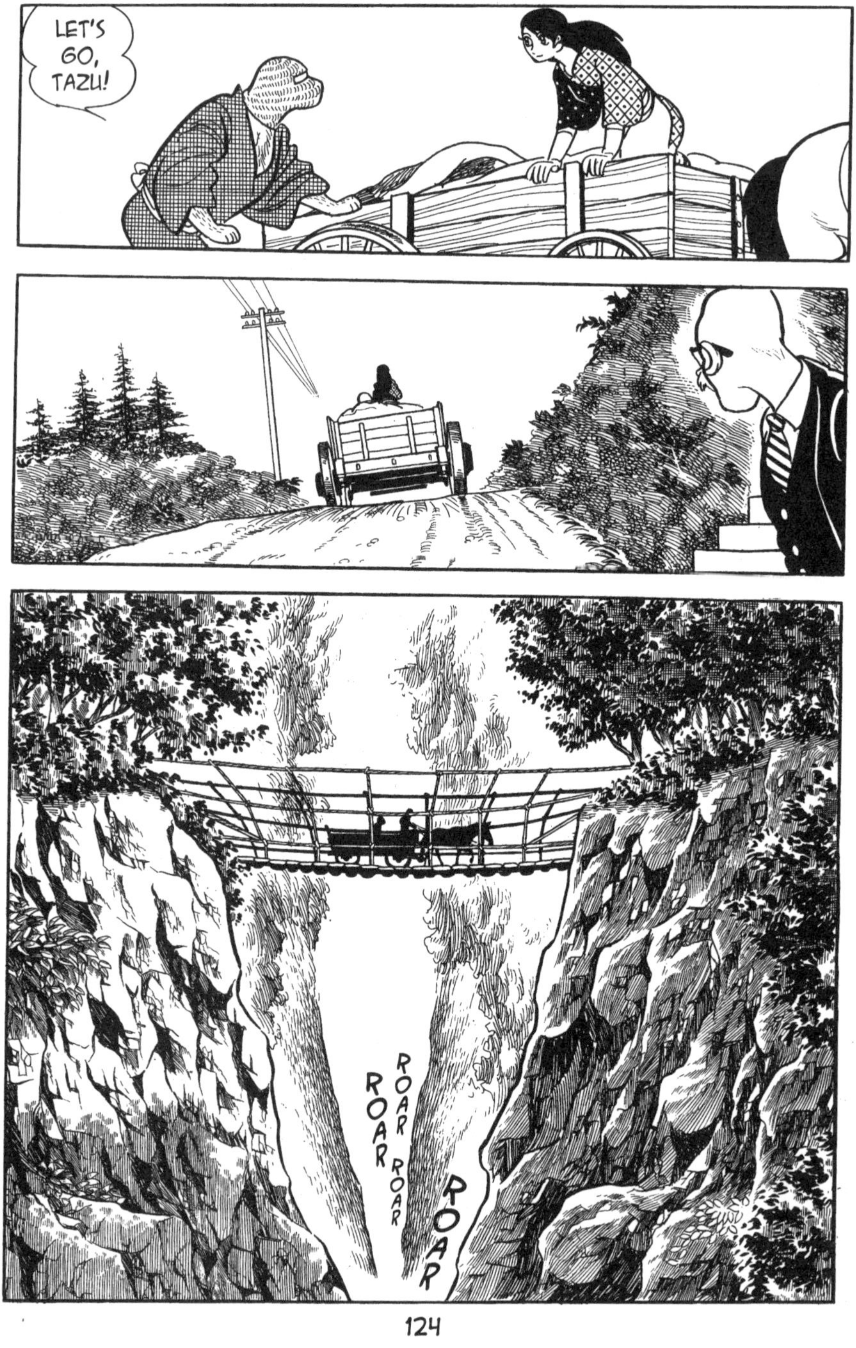
LET'S GO, TAZU!
ROAR ROAR ROAR ROAR ROAR

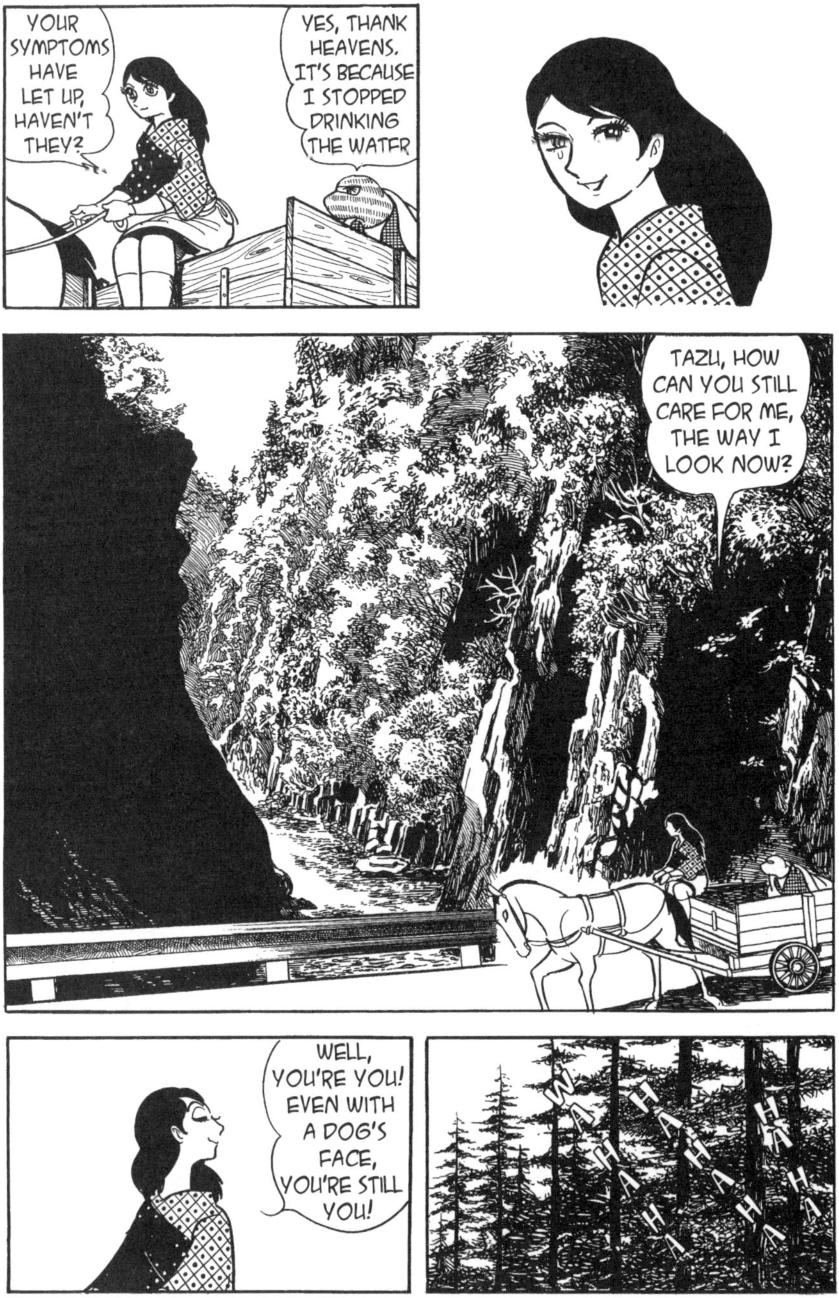
YOUR SYMPTOMS HAVE LET UP, HAVEN'T THEY?
YES, THANK HEAVENS. IT'S BECAUSE I STOPPED DRINKING THE WATER
TAZU, HOW CAN YOU STILL CARE FOR ME, THE WAY I LOOK NOW?
WELL, YOU'RE YOU! EVEN WITH A DOG'S FACE, YOU'RE STILL YOU!
WAHA HAHA HAHA HAHA

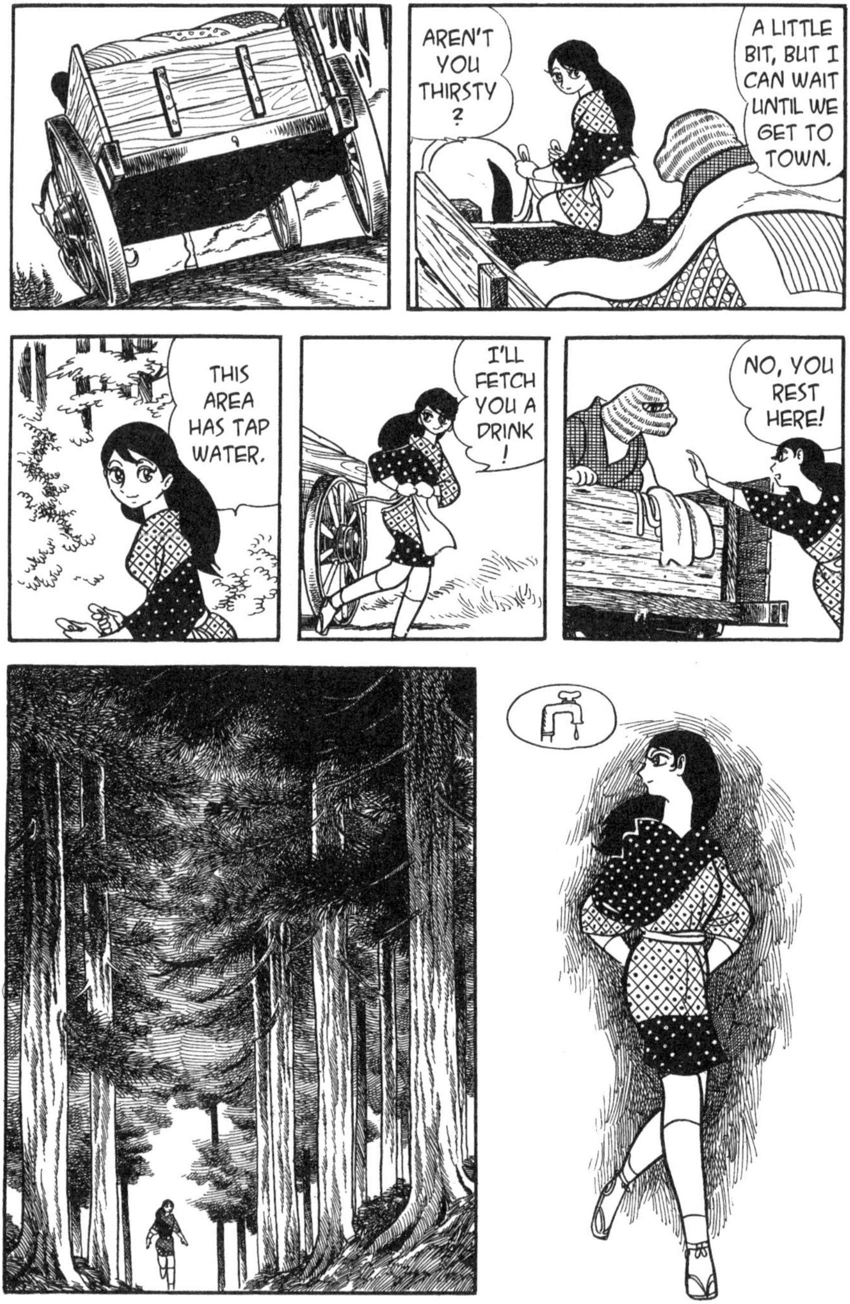
AREN'T YOU THIRSTY?
A LITTLE BIT, BUT I CAN WAIT UNTIL WE GET TO TOWN.
THIS AREA HAS TAP WATER.
I'LL FETCH YOU A DRINK!
NO, YOU REST HERE!

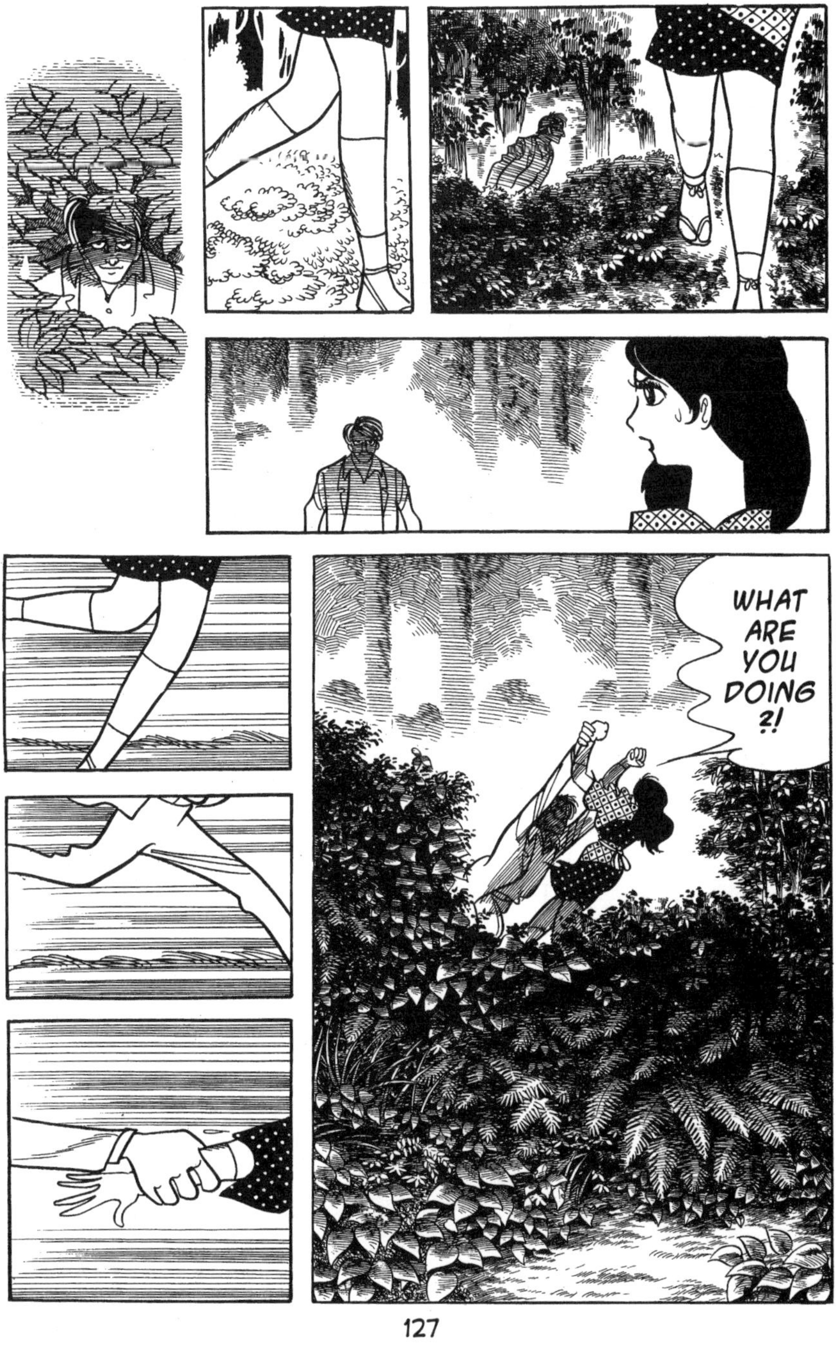
WHAT ARE YOU DOING ?!

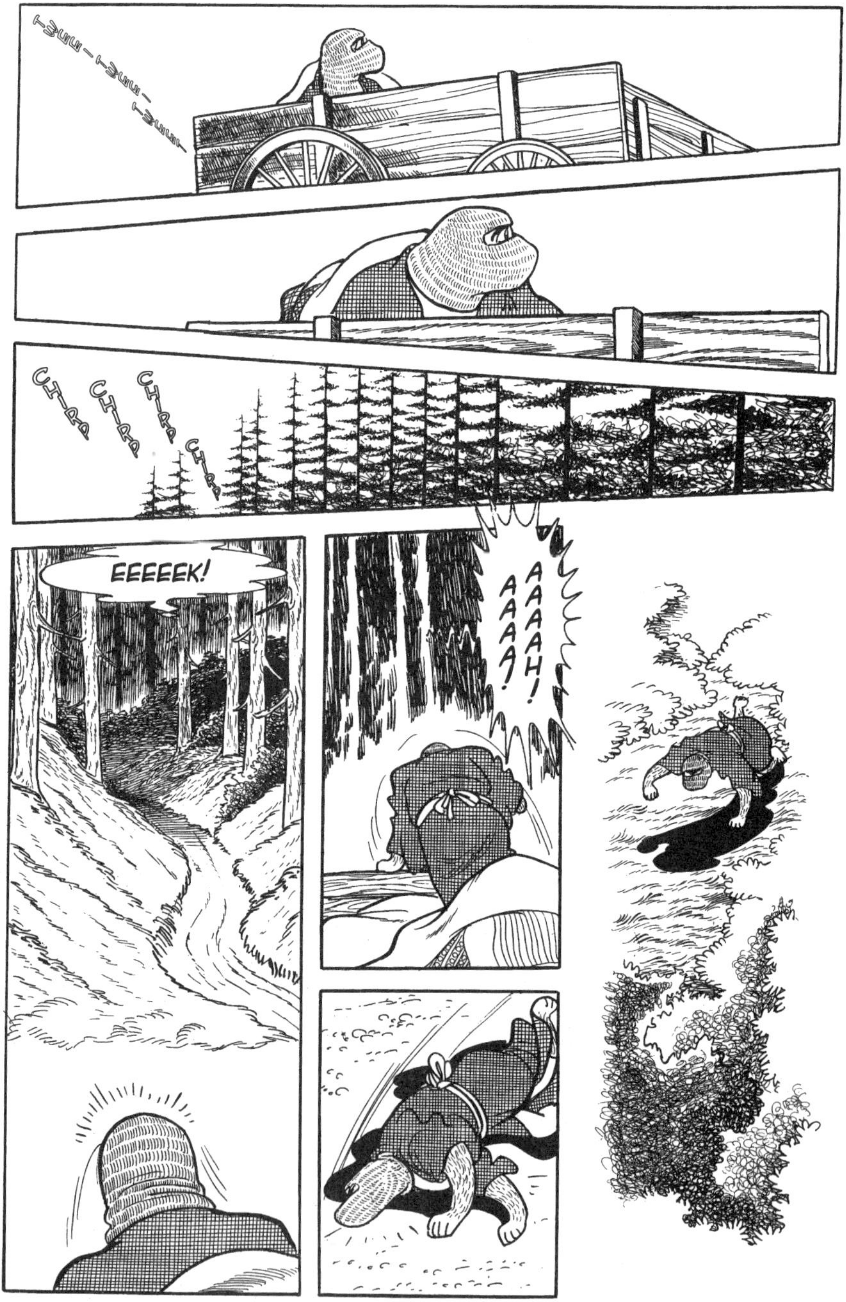
CHIRP
CHIRP
CHIRP
CHIRP
EEEEEK!
AAAAA!
AAAAAH!

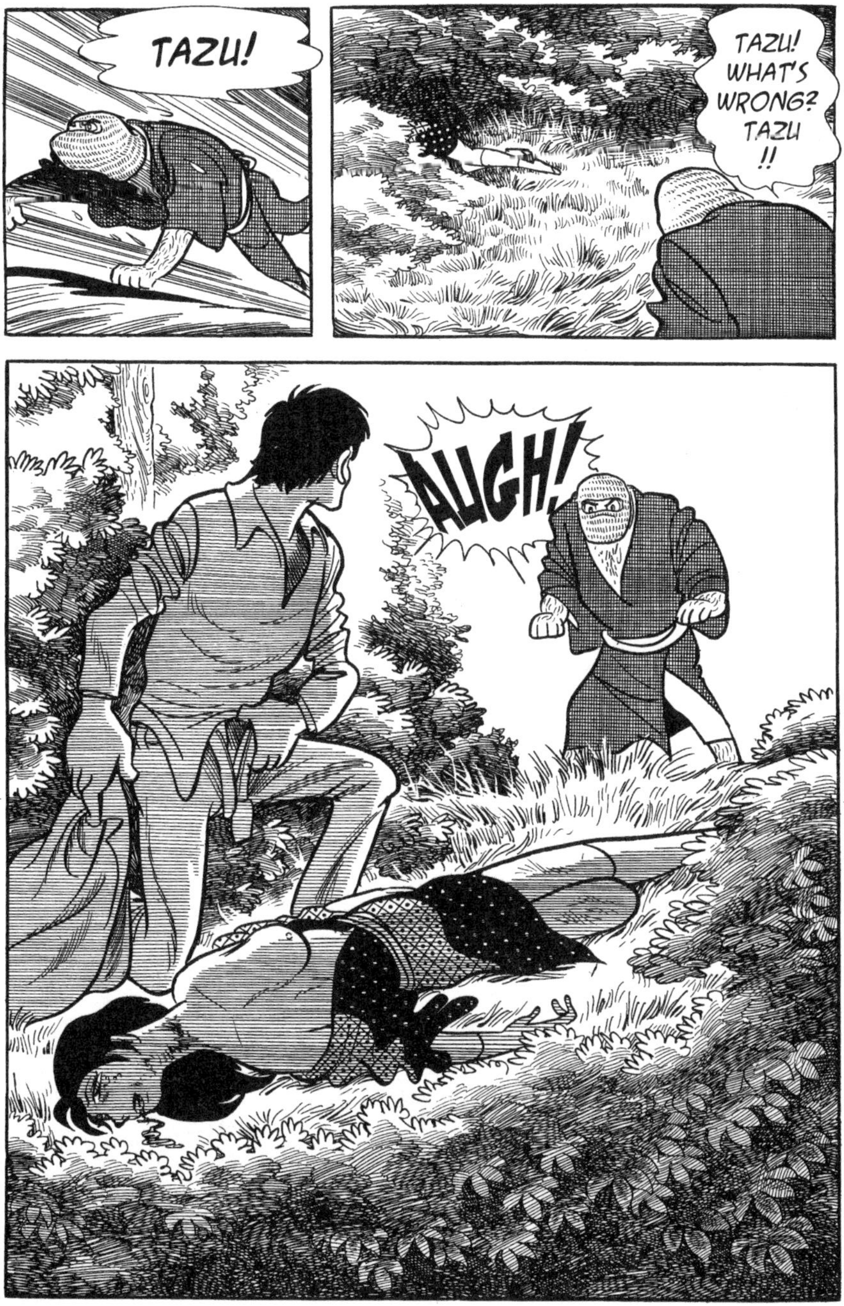
TAZU!
TAZU! WHAT'S WRONG? TAZU !!
AUGH!

TAZU !!
YOU FILTHY...!!
STOP!

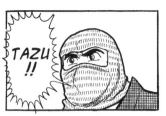

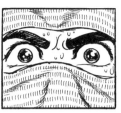

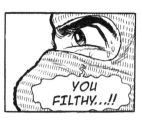

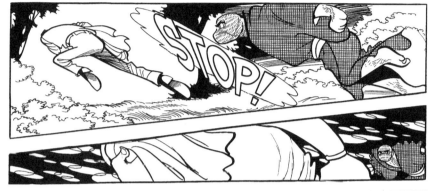

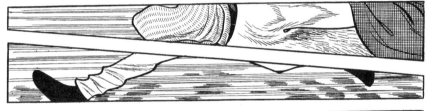

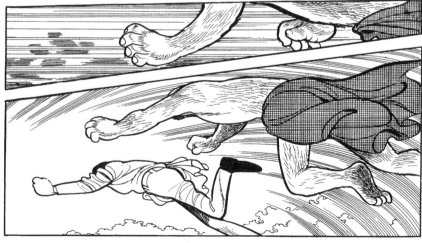

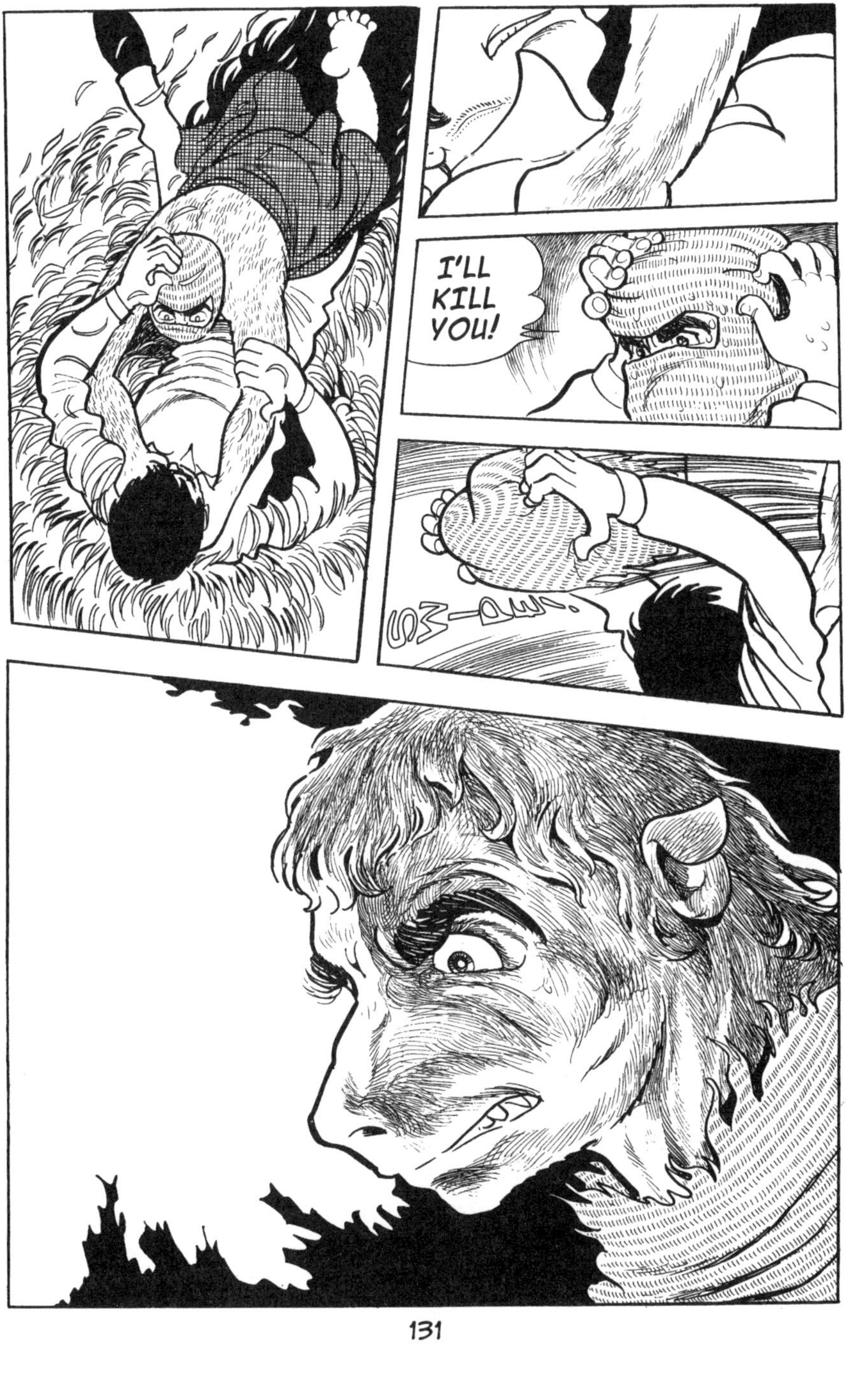
I'LL KILL YOU!

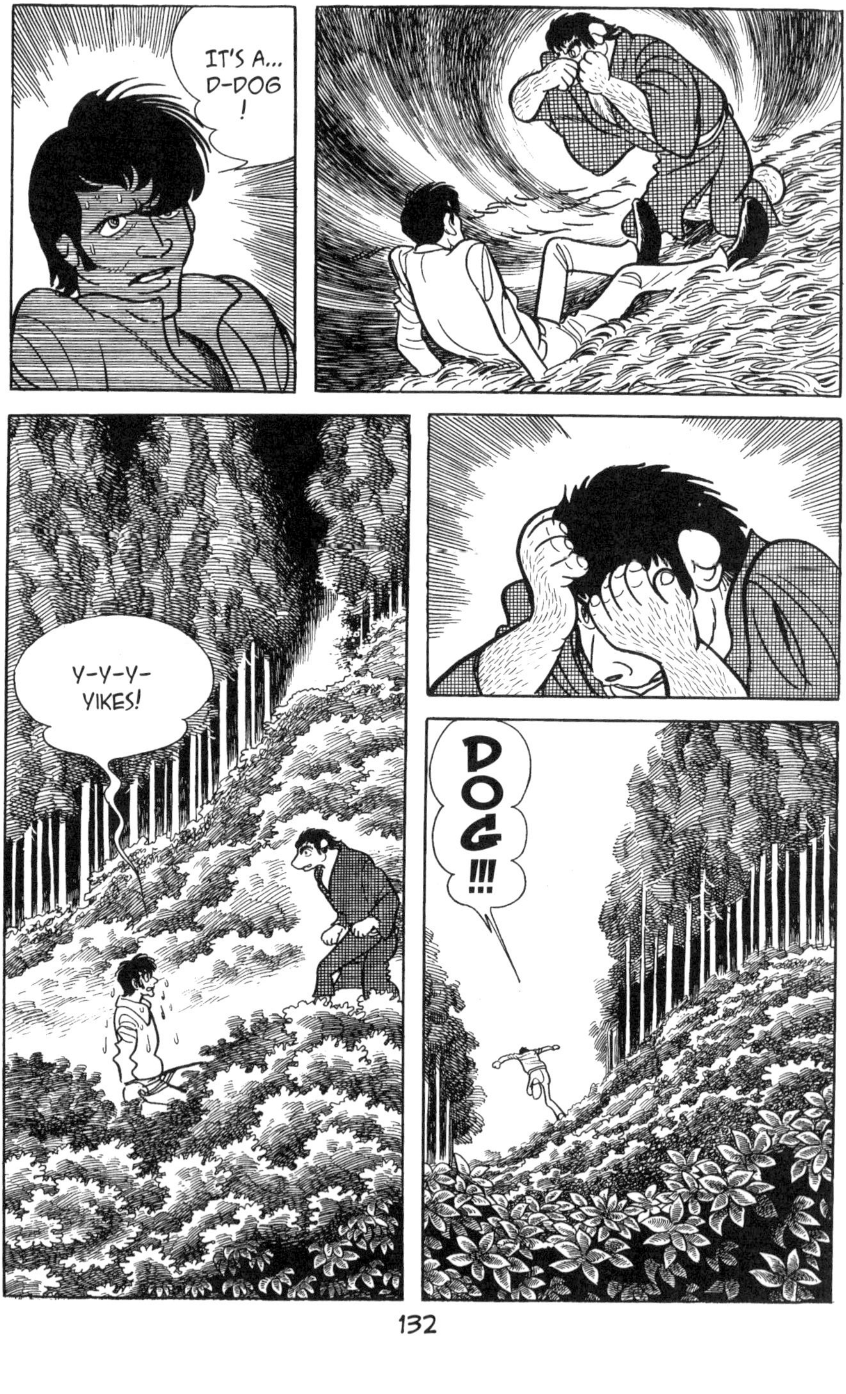
IT'S A... D-DOG !
Y-Y-Y-YIKES!
DOG!!!

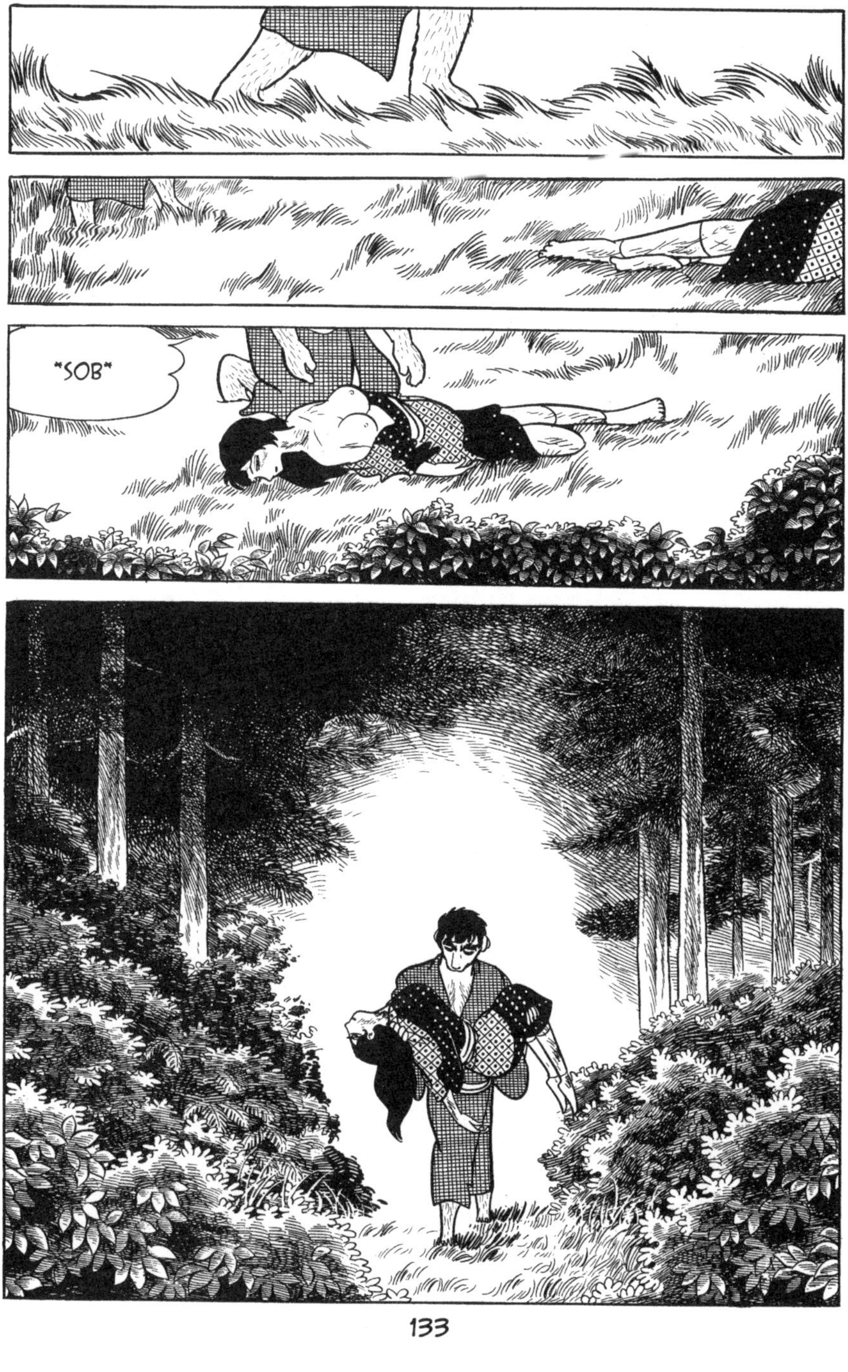
SOB

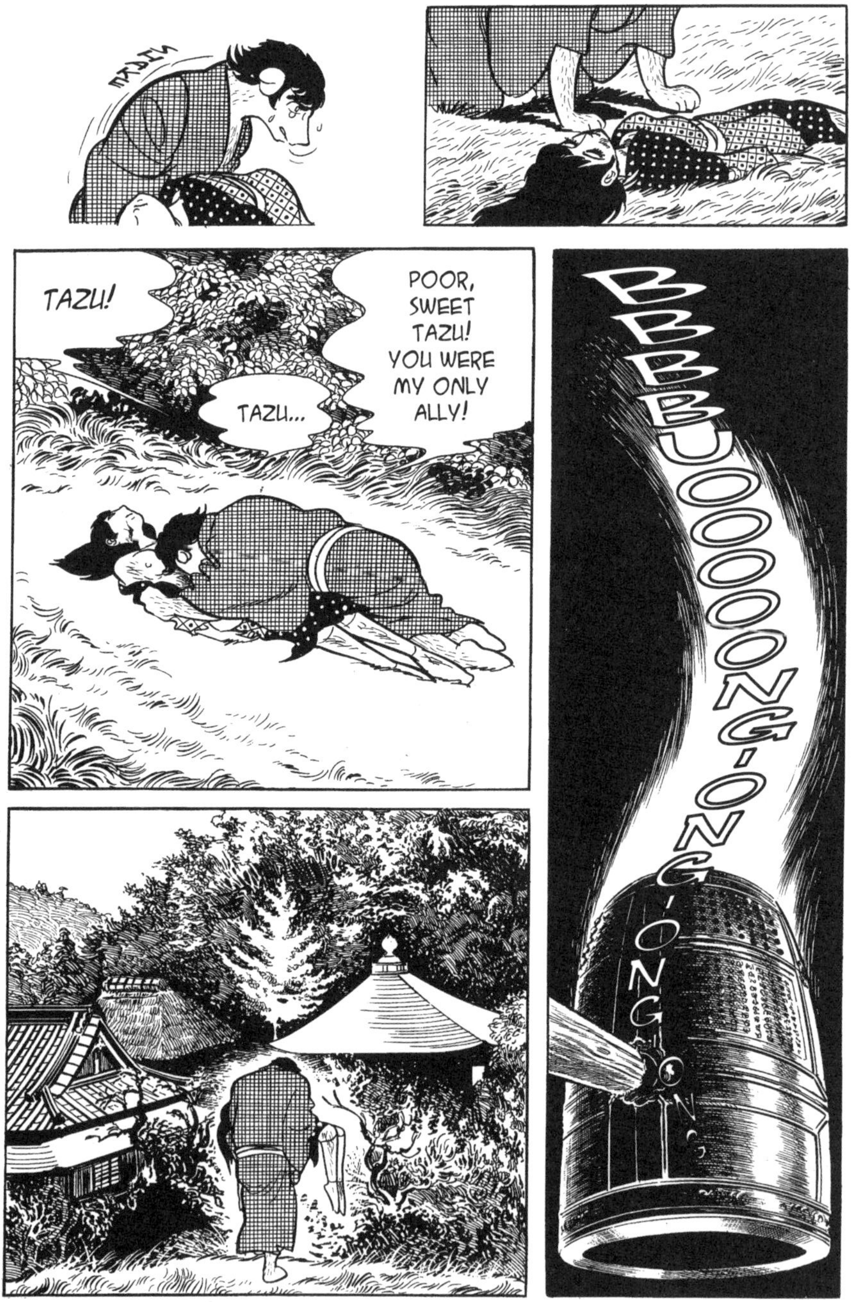
TAZU!
POOR, SWEET TAZU! YOU WERE MY ONLY ALLY!
TAZU...
BBBBUOOOOOONG-ONG-ONG-ONG

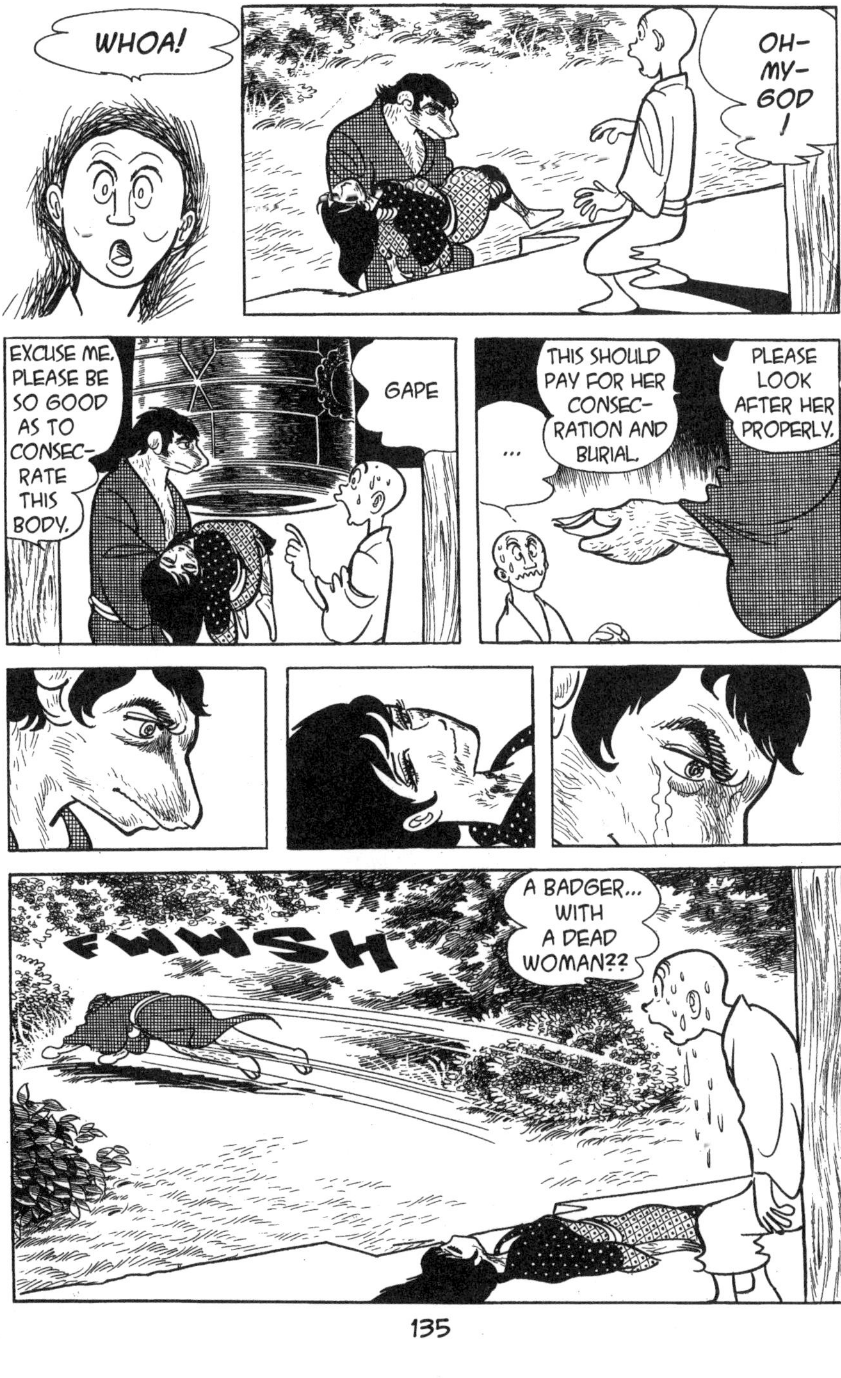
WHOA!
OH-MY-GOD!
EXCUSE ME. PLEASE BE SO GOOD AS TO CONSECRATE THIS BODY.
GAPE
PLEASE LOOK AFTER HER PROPERLY.
THIS SHOULD PAY FOR HER CONSECRATION AND BURIAL.
...
FWWSH
A BADGER... WITH A DEAD WOMAN??

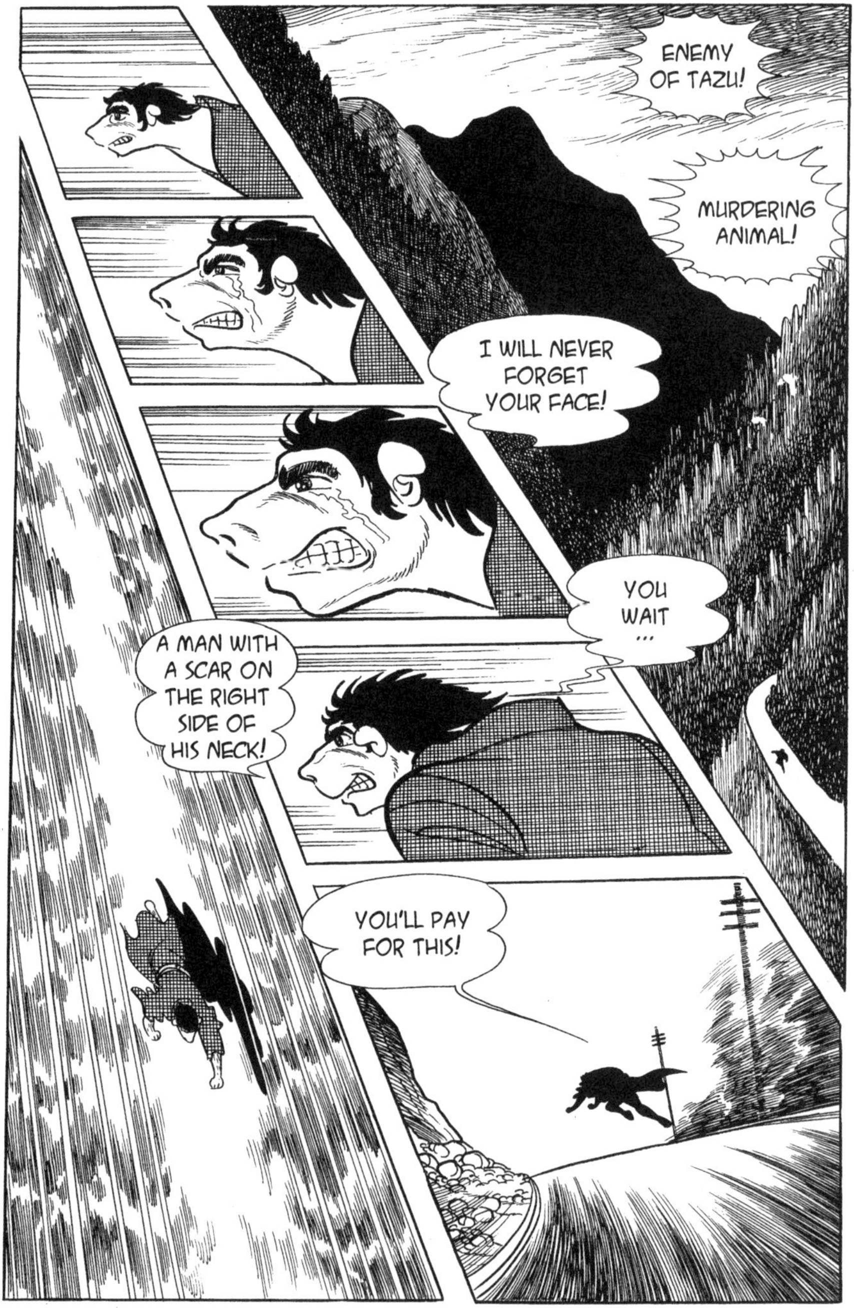
ENEMY OF TAZU!
MURDERING ANIMAL!
I WILL NEVER FORGET YOUR FACE!
YOU WAIT ...
A MAN WITH A SCAR ON THE RIGHT SIDE OF HIS NECK!
YOU'LL PAY FOR THIS!

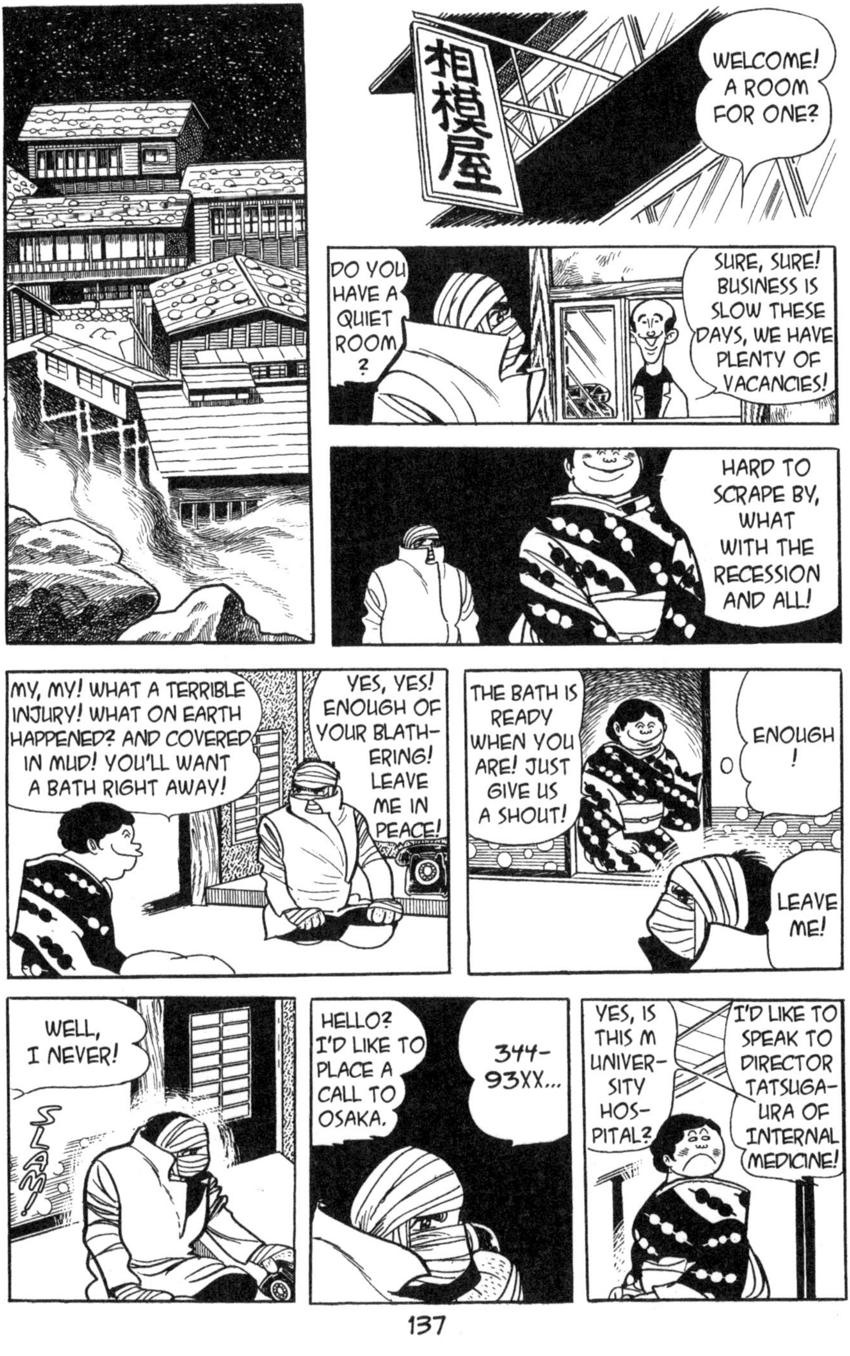
相模屋
WELCOME! A ROOM FOR ONE?
DO YOU HAVE A QUIET ROOM?
SURE, SURE! BUSINESS IS SLOW THESE DAYS, WE HAVE PLENTY OF VACANCIES!
HARD TO SCRAPE BY, WHAT WITH THE RECESSION AND ALL!
MY, MY! WHAT A TERRIBLE INJURY! WHAT ON EARTH HAPPENED? AND COVERED IN MUD! YOU'LL WANT A BATH RIGHT AWAY!
YES, YES! ENOUGH OF YOUR BLATH-ERING! LEAVE ME IN PEACE!
THE BATH IS READY WHEN YOU ARE! JUST GIVE US A SHOUT!
ENOUGH!
LEAVE ME!
WELL, I NEVER!
SLAM!
HELLO? I'D LIKE TO PLACE A CALL TO OSAKA.
344-93XX...
YES, IS THIS M UNIVER-SITY HOS-PITAL?
I'D LIKE TO SPEAK TO DIRECTOR TATSUGA-URA OF INTERNAL MEDICINE!

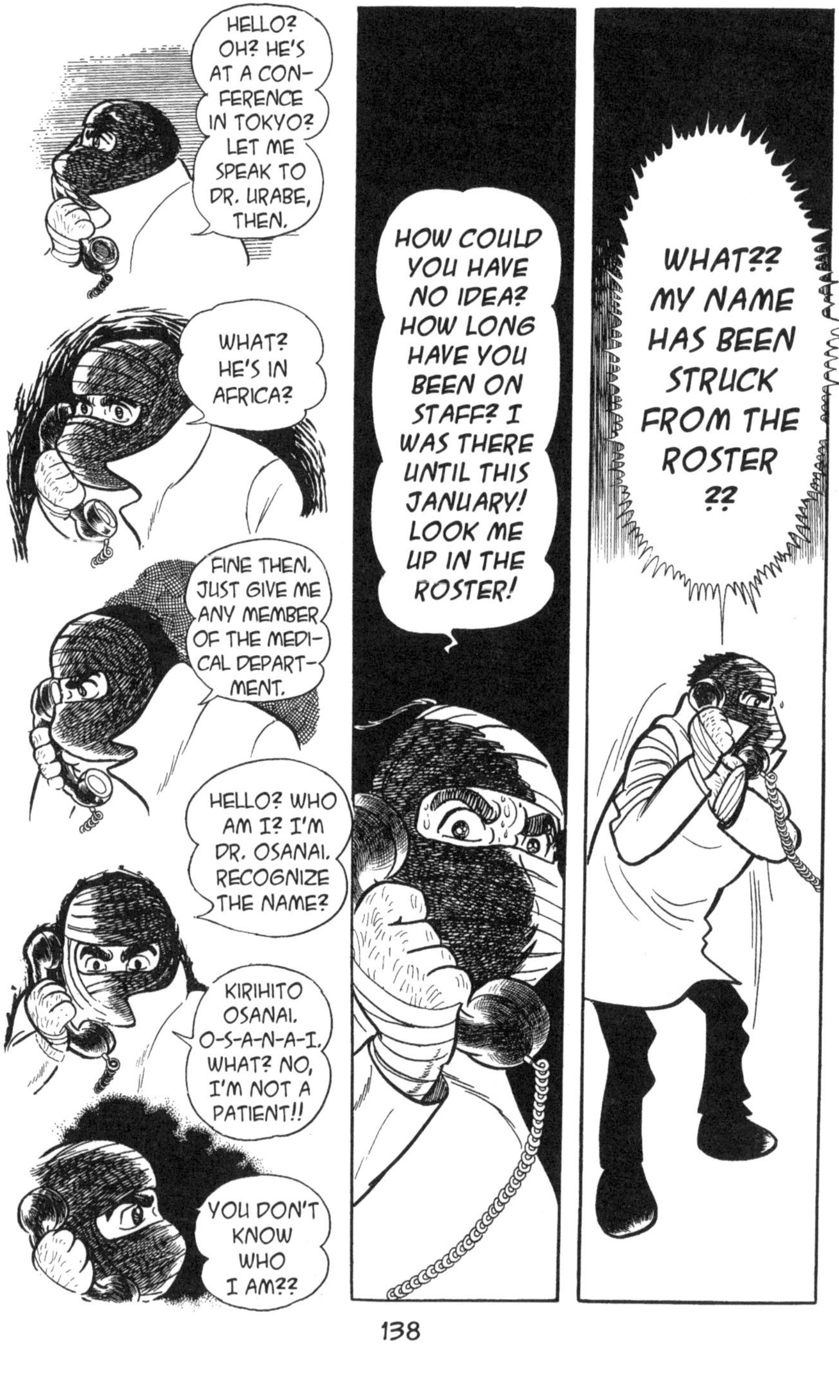
HELLO? OH? HE'S AT A CON-FERENCE IN TOKYO? LET ME SPEAK TO DR. URABE, THEN.
WHAT? HE'S IN AFRICA?
FINE THEN. JUST GIVE ME ANY MEMBER OF THE MEDI-CAL DEPART-MENT.
HELLO? WHO AM I? I'M DR. OSANAI. RECOGNIZE THE NAME?
KIRIHITO OSANAI. O-S-A-N-A-I. WHAT? NO, I'M NOT A PATIENT!!
YOU DON'T KNOW WHO I AM??
HOW COULD YOU HAVE NO IDEA? HOW LONG HAVE YOU BEEN ON STAFF? I WAS THERE UNTIL THIS JANUARY! LOOK ME UP IN THE ROSTER!
WHAT?? MY NAME HAS BEEN STRUCK FROM THE ROSTER ??

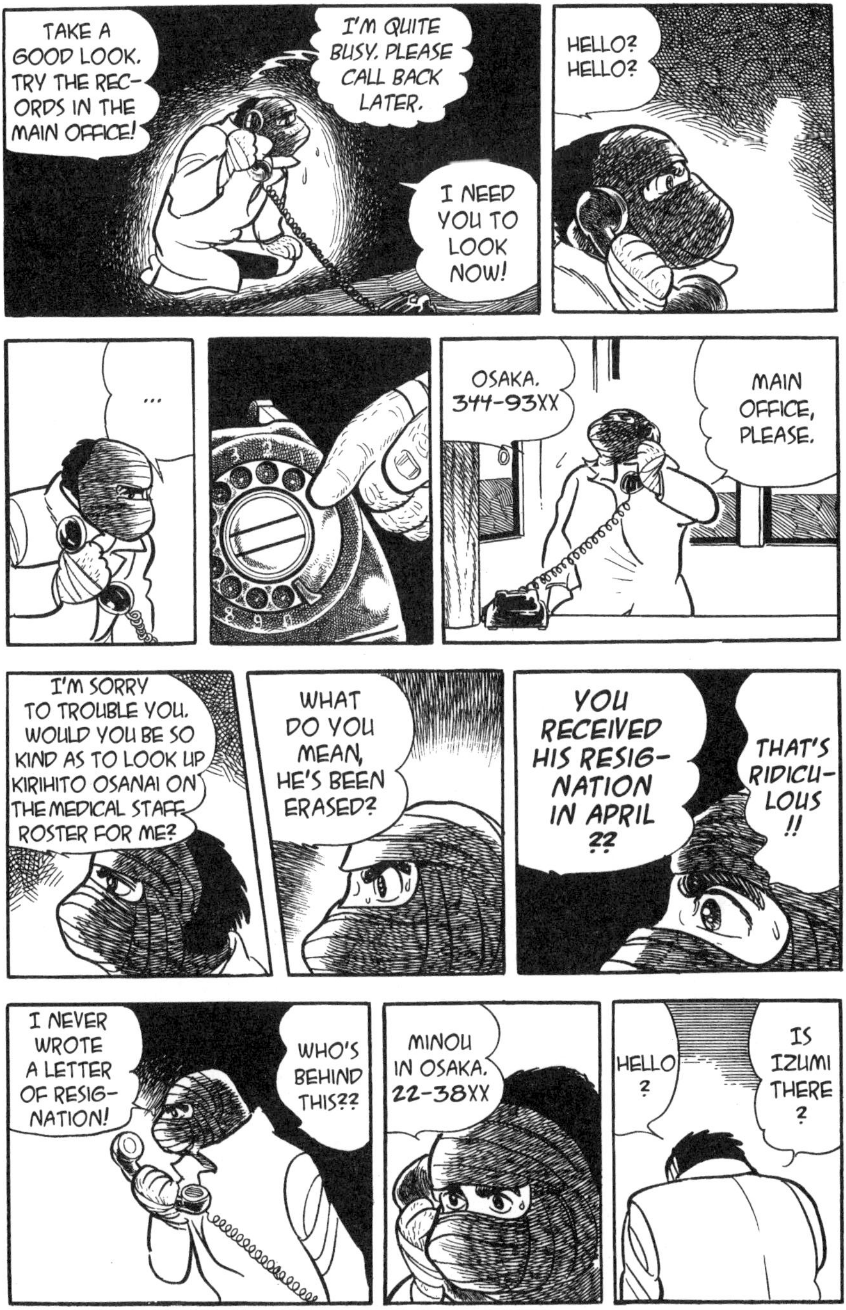
TAKE A GOOD LOOK. TRY THE RECORDS IN THE MAIN OFFICE!
I'M QUITE BUSY. PLEASE CALL BACK LATER.
I NEED YOU TO LOOK NOW!
HELLO? HELLO?
...
OSAKA. 344-93XX
MAIN OFFICE, PLEASE.
I'M SORRY TO TROUBLE YOU. WOULD YOU BE SO KIND AS TO LOOK UP KIRIHITO OSANAI ON THE MEDICAL STAFF ROSTER FOR ME?
WHAT DO YOU MEAN, HE'S BEEN ERASED?
YOU RECEIVED HIS RESIGNATION IN APRIL ??
THAT'S RIDICULOUS !!
I NEVER WROTE A LETTER OF RESIGNATION!
WHO'S BEHIND THIS??
MINOU IN OSAKA. 22-38XX
HELLO ?
IS IZUMI THERE ?

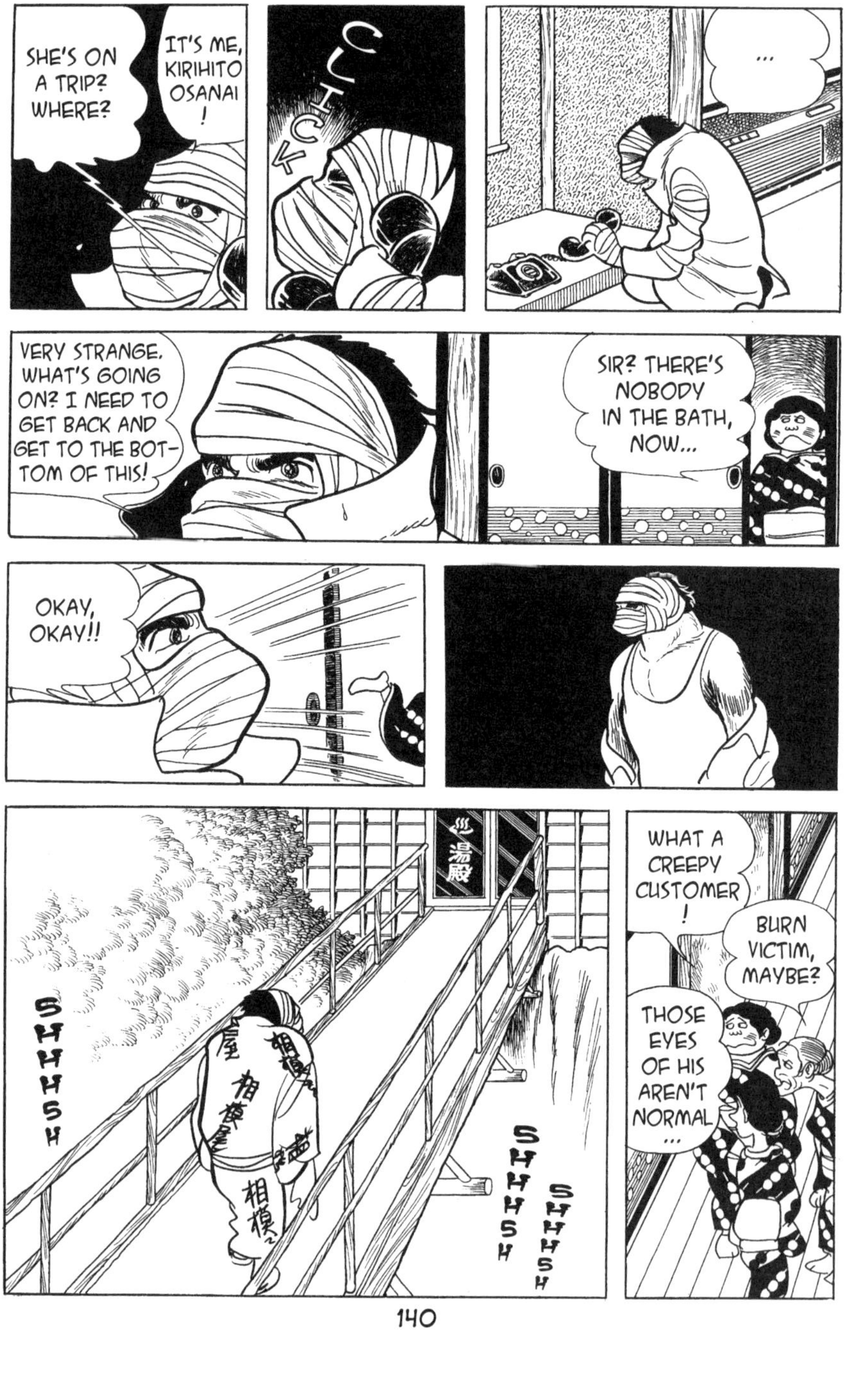
SHE'S ON A TRIP? WHERE?
IT'S ME, KIRIHITO OSANAI!
CLICK
...
VERY STRANGE. WHAT'S GOING ON? I NEED TO GET BACK AND GET TO THE BOTTOM OF THIS!
SIR? THERE'S NOBODY IN THE BATH, NOW...
OKAY, OKAY!!
湯殿
SHHHSH
SHHHSH
SHHHSH
WHAT A CREEPY CUSTOMER!
BURN VICTIM, MAYBE?
THOSE EYES OF HIS AREN'T NORMAL...

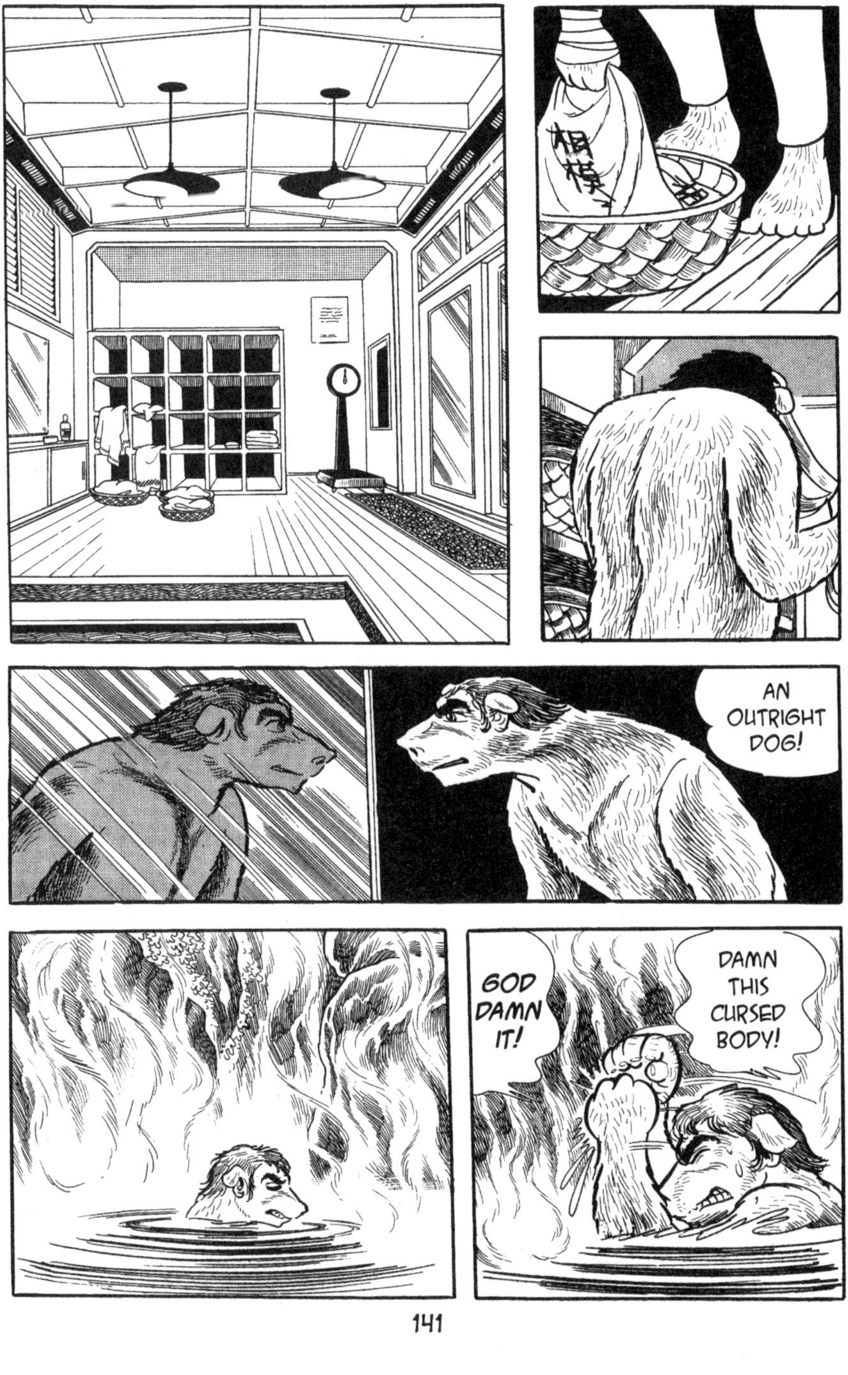
AN OUTRIGHT DOG!
GOD DAMN IT!
DAMN THIS CURSED BODY!

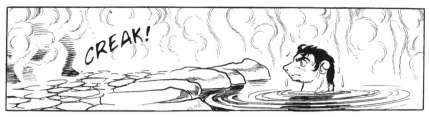

UGH! WILL YOU LOOK AT THAT! THERE'S A DOG IN THE BATH!

PHEW!

YIPES!!!

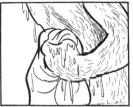

CHOMP!

EEEEEK! WHAT ARE YOU DOING?!?!

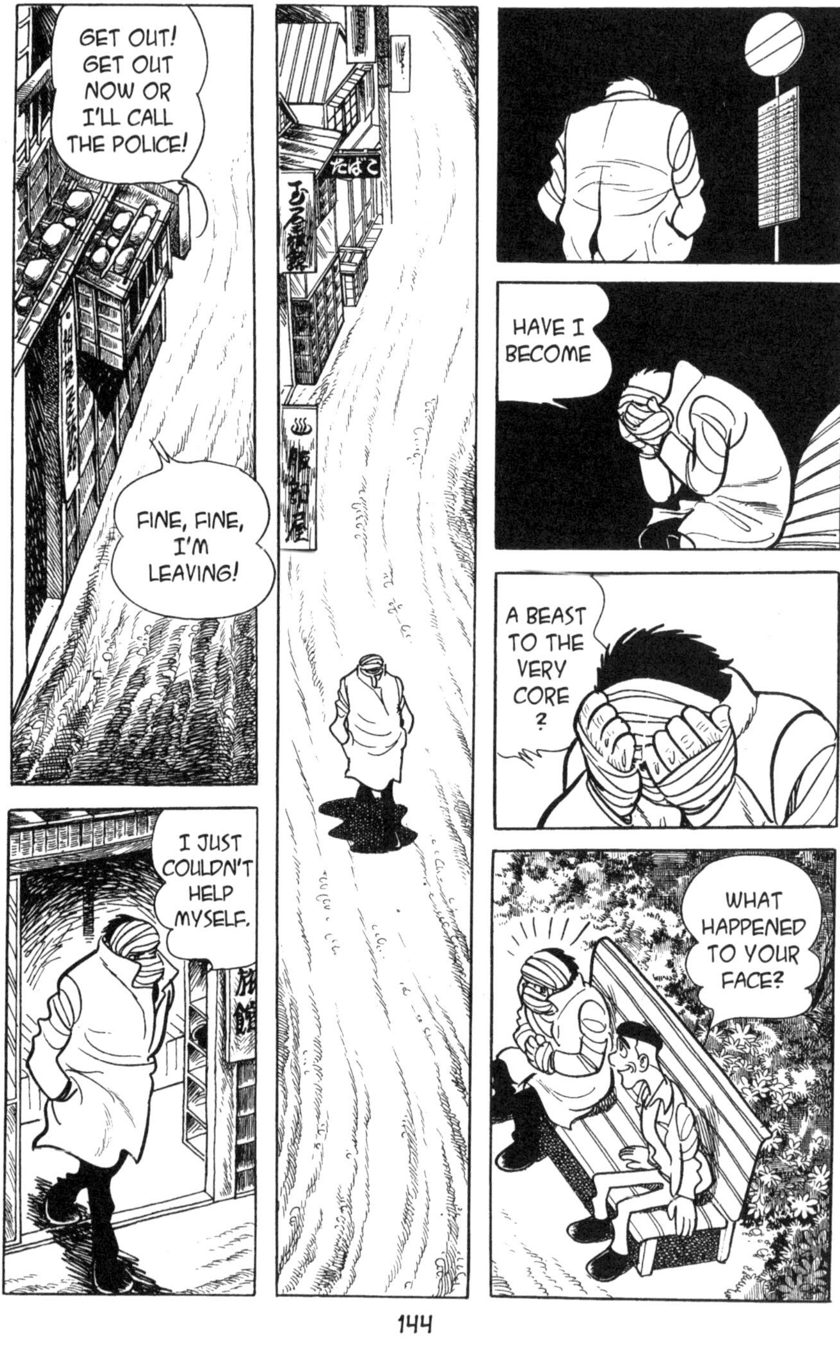
GET OUT! GET OUT NOW OR I'LL CALL THE POLICE!
FINE, FINE, I'M LEAVING!
I JUST COULDN'T HELP MYSELF.
たばこ
HAVE I BECOME
A BEAST TO THE VERY CORE ?
WHAT HAPPENED TO YOUR FACE?

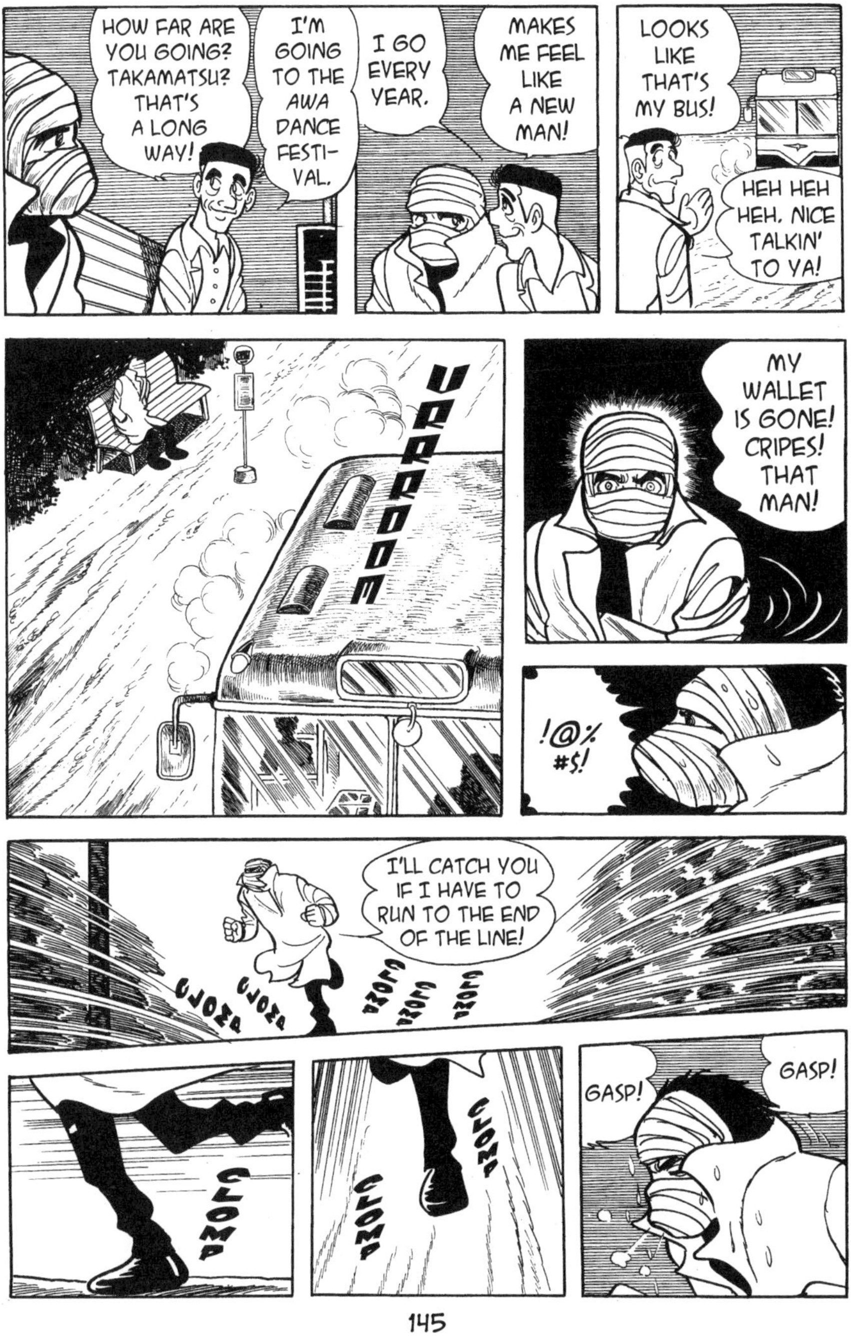
HOW FAR ARE YOU GOING? TAKAMATSU? THAT'S A LONG WAY!
I'M GOING TO THE AWA DANCE FESTI-VAL.
I GO EVERY YEAR.
MAKES ME FEEL LIKE A NEW MAN!
LOOKS LIKE THAT'S MY BUS!
HEH HEH HEH. NICE TALKIN' TO YA!
VRRROOOM
MY WALLET IS GONE! CRIPES! THAT MAN!
!@%#$!
I'LL CATCH YOU IF I HAVE TO RUN TO THE END OF THE LINE!
CLOMP CLOMP CLOMP CLOMP CLOMP
CLOMP
CLOMP CLOMP
GASP!
GASP!

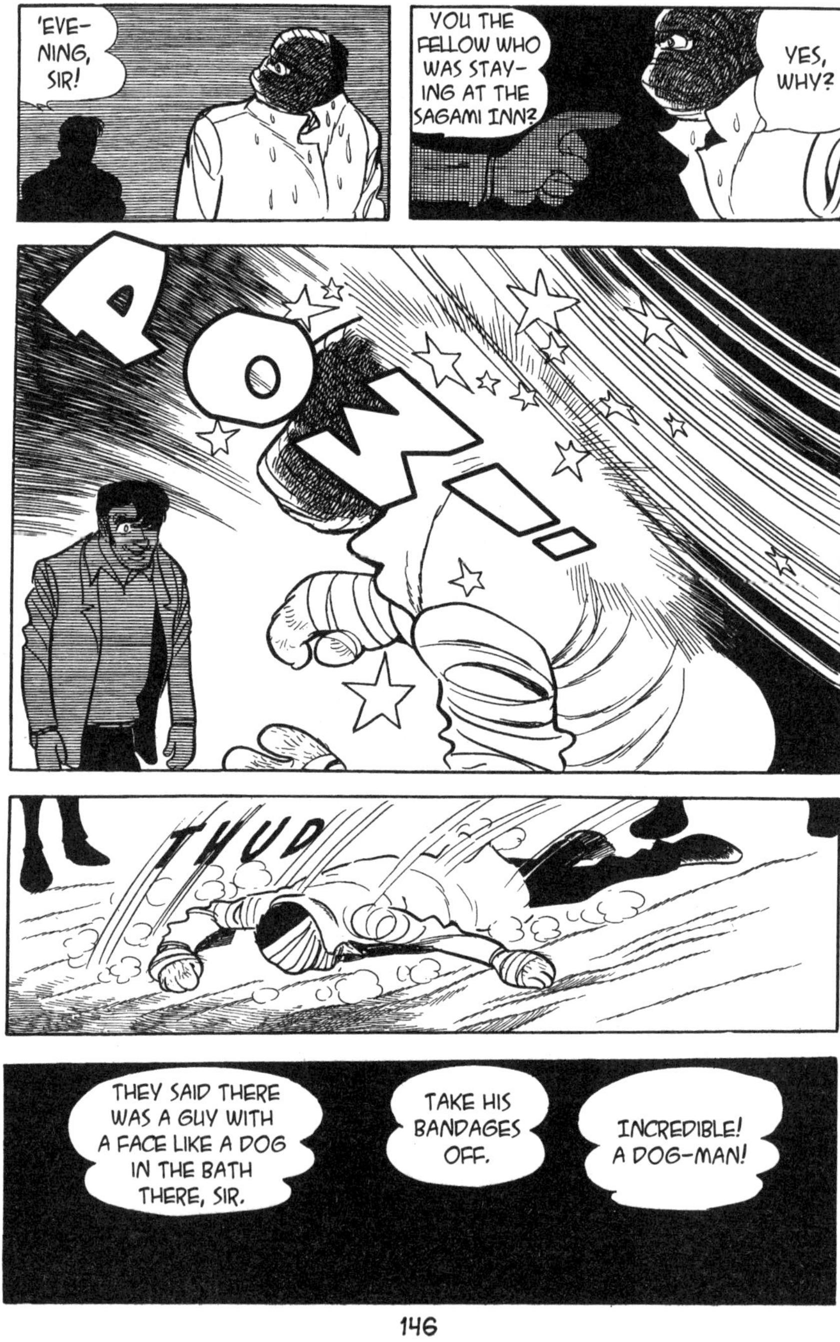
'EVE-NING, SIR!
YOU THE FELLOW WHO WAS STAY-ING AT THE SAGAMI INN?
YES, WHY?
POW!!
THUD
THEY SAID THERE WAS A GUY WITH A FACE LIKE A DOG IN THE BATH THERE, SIR.
TAKE HIS BANDAGES OFF.
INCREDIBLE! A DOG-MAN!

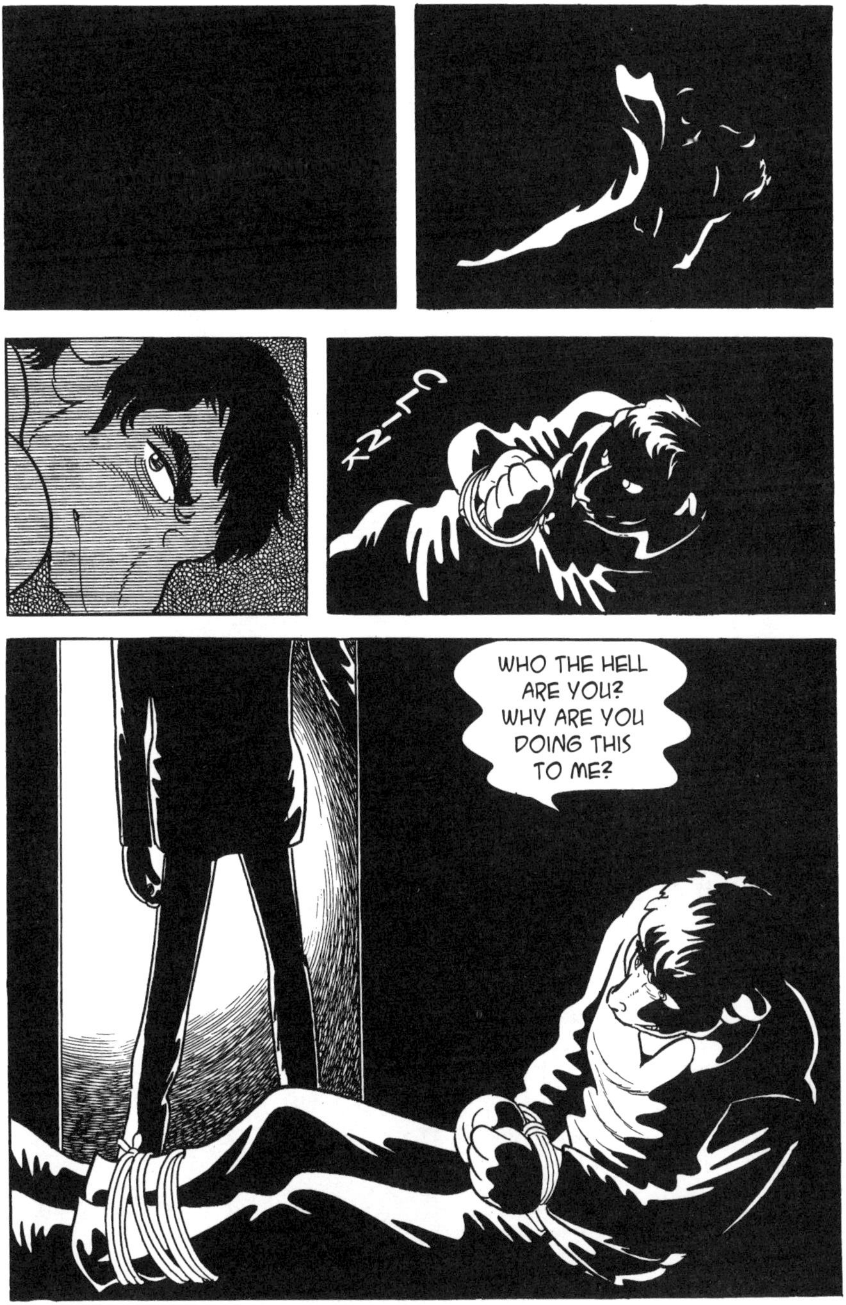
CL-I-NK
WHO THE HELL ARE YOU? WHY ARE YOU DOING THIS TO ME?

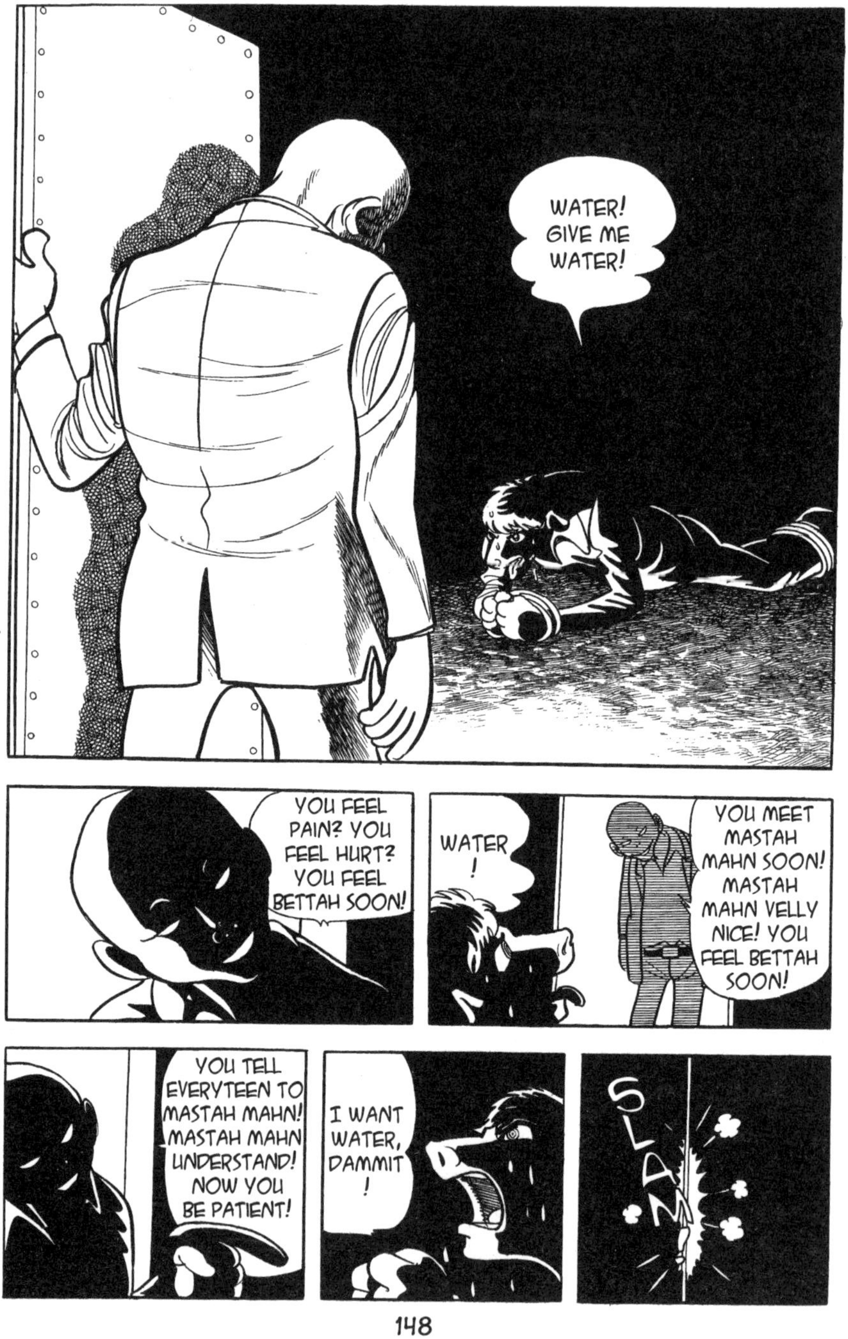
WATER! GIVE ME WATER!
YOU FEEL PAIN? YOU FEEL HURT? YOU FEEL BETTAH SOON!
WATER!
YOU MEET MASTAH MAHN SOON! MASTAH MAHN VELLY NICE! YOU FEEL BETTAH SOON!
YOU TELL EVERYTEEN TO MASTAH MAHN! MASTAH MAHN UNDERSTAND! NOW YOU BE PATIENT!
I WANT WATER, DAMMIT!
SLAM

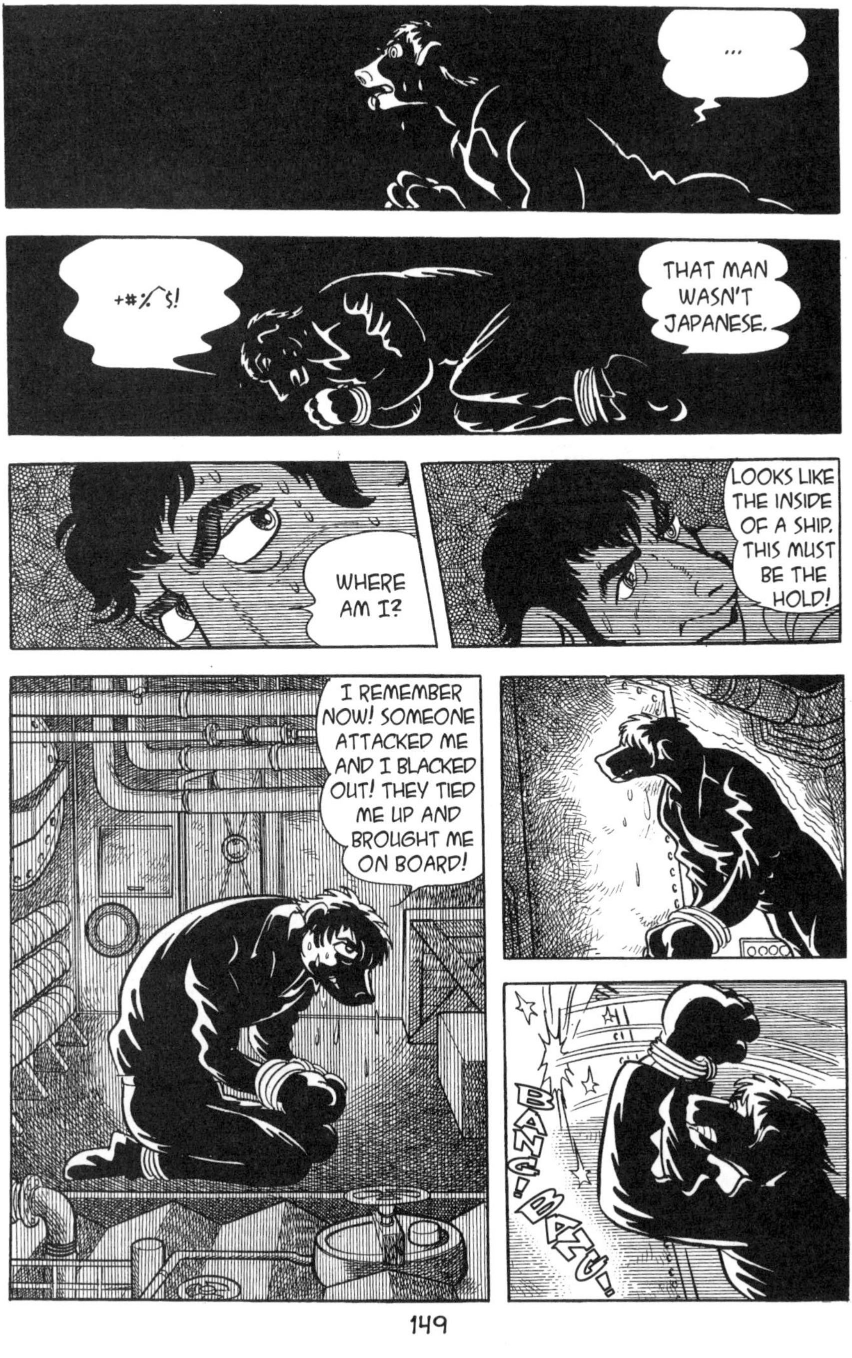
...
+#%^$!
THAT MAN WASN'T JAPANESE.
WHERE AM I?
LOOKS LIKE THE INSIDE OF A SHIP. THIS MUST BE THE HOLD!
I REMEMBER NOW! SOMEONE ATTACKED ME AND I BLACKED OUT! THEY TIED ME UP AND BROUGHT ME ON BOARD!
BANG! BAZU!

HEY!
WATER... WATER...
PANT
PANT
PANT
PANT
PANT
PANT

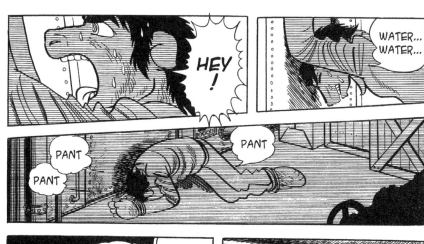

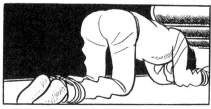

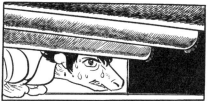

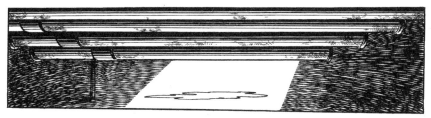

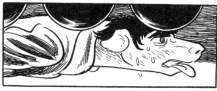

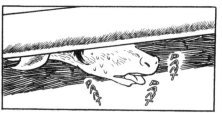

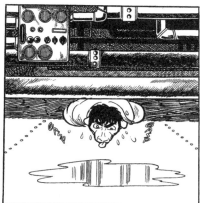

AARGH! SALT WATER!

LAP LAP
LAP LAP

...

GASP

GASP

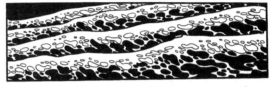

WE'RE AT SEA ...

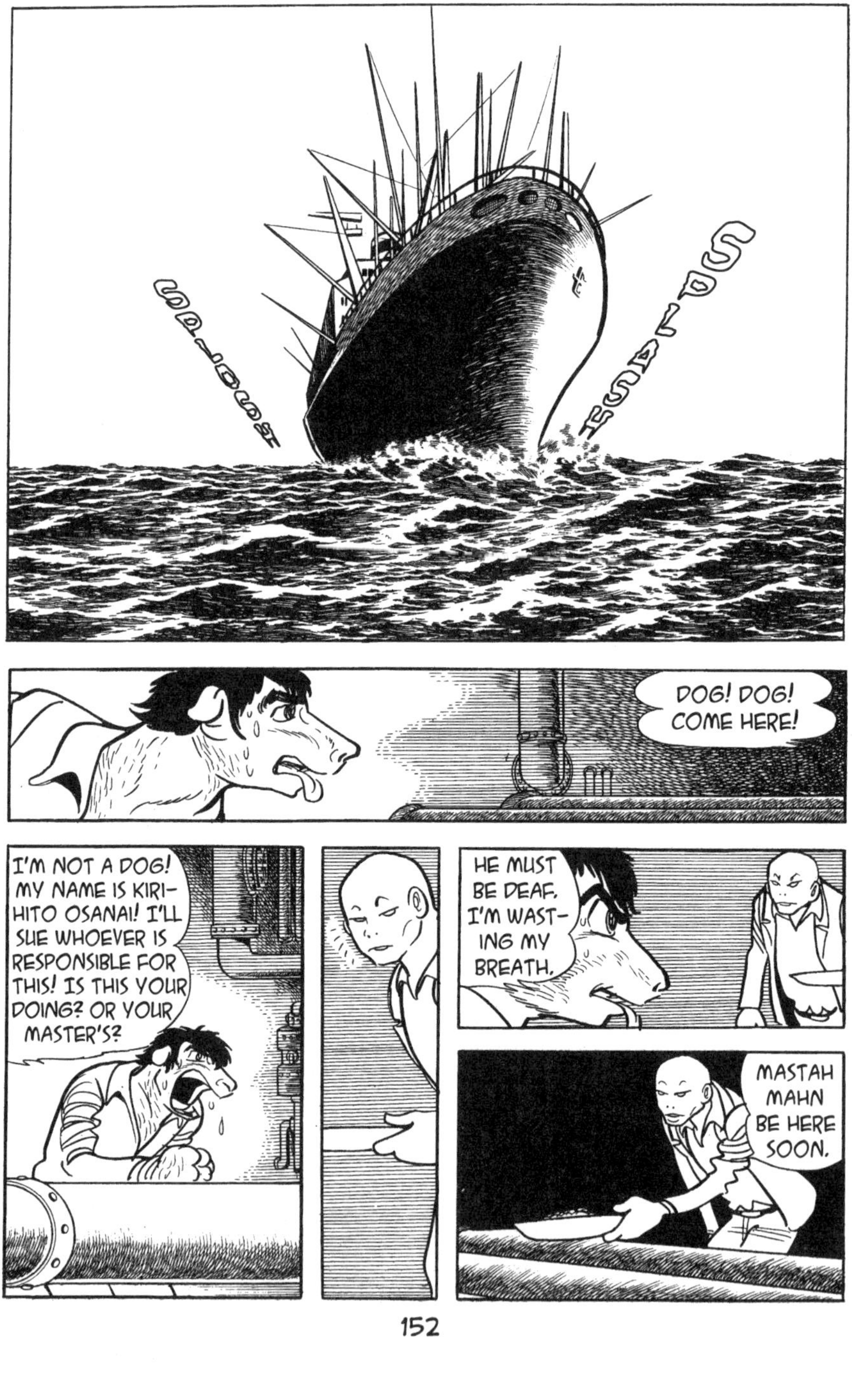
SPLOOSH
SPLASH
DOG! DOG! COME HERE!
I'M NOT A DOG! MY NAME IS KIRI-HITO OSANAI! I'LL SUE WHOEVER IS RESPONSIBLE FOR THIS! IS THIS YOUR DOING? OR YOUR MASTER'S?
HE MUST BE DEAF. I'M WAST-ING MY BREATH.
MASTAH MAHN BE HERE SOON.

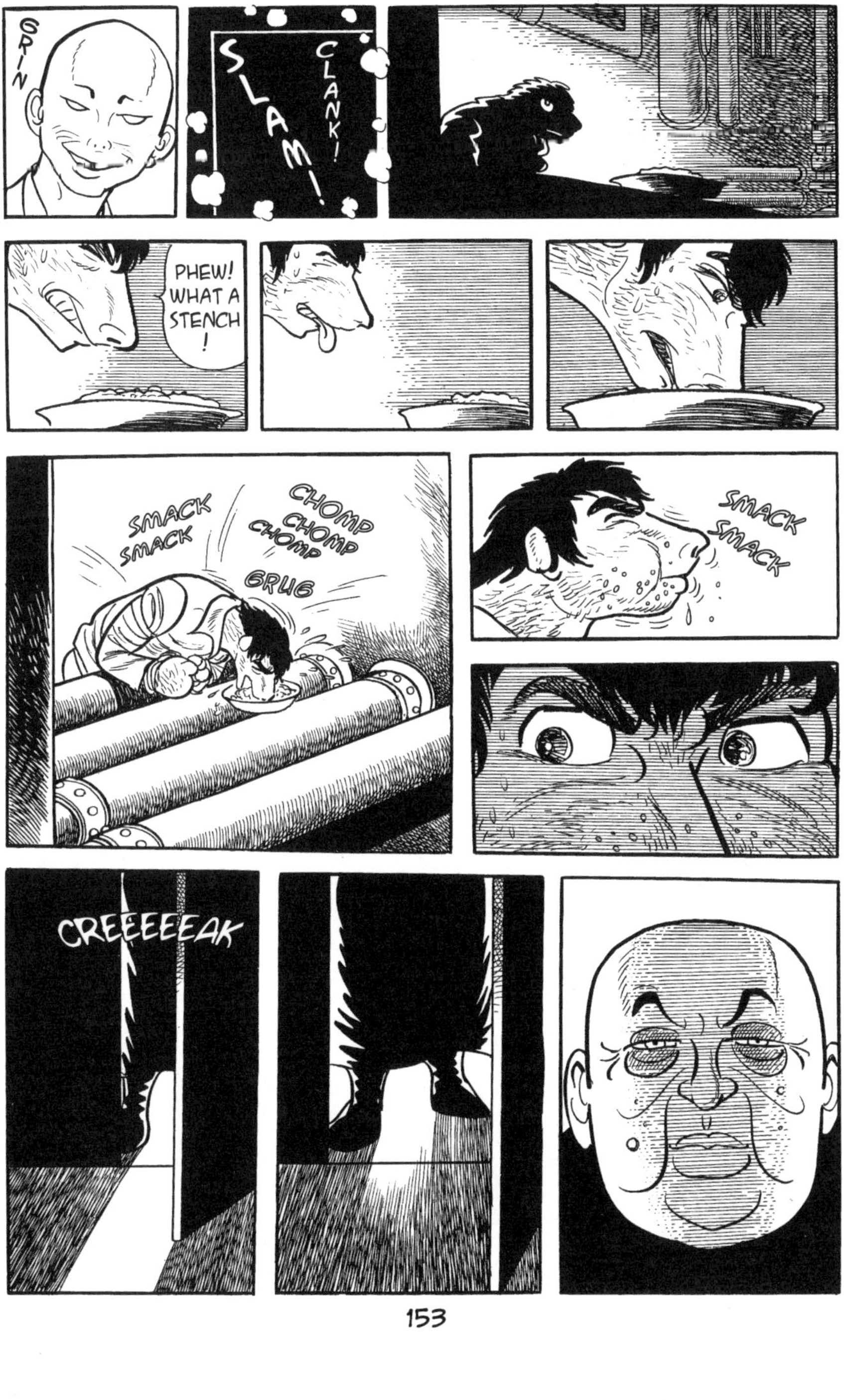
GRIN
SLAM!
CLANK!
PHEW! WHAT A STENCH!
SMACK SMACK
CHOMP CHOMP CHOMP
GRUG
SMACK SMACK
CREEEEEEAK

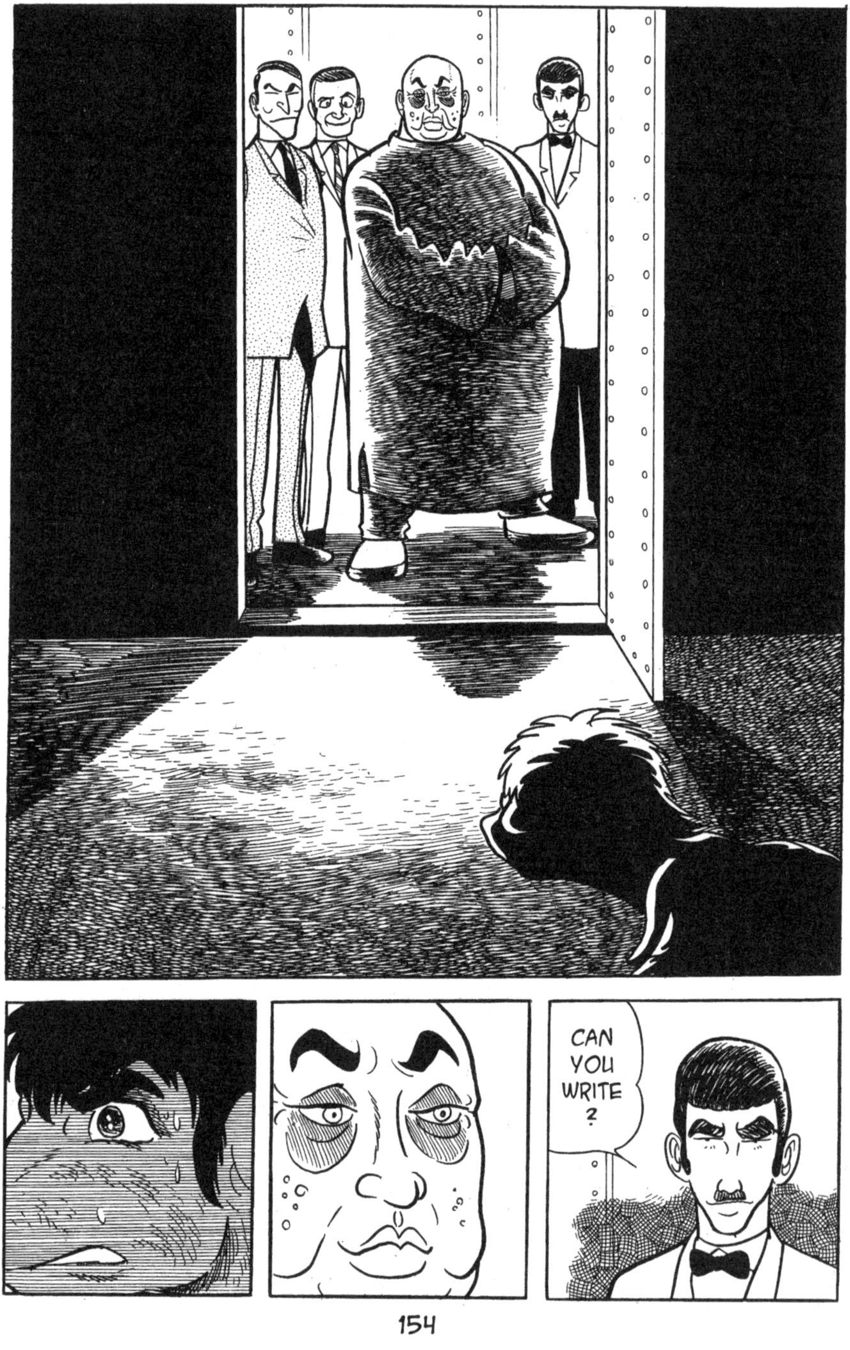
CAN YOU WRITE ?

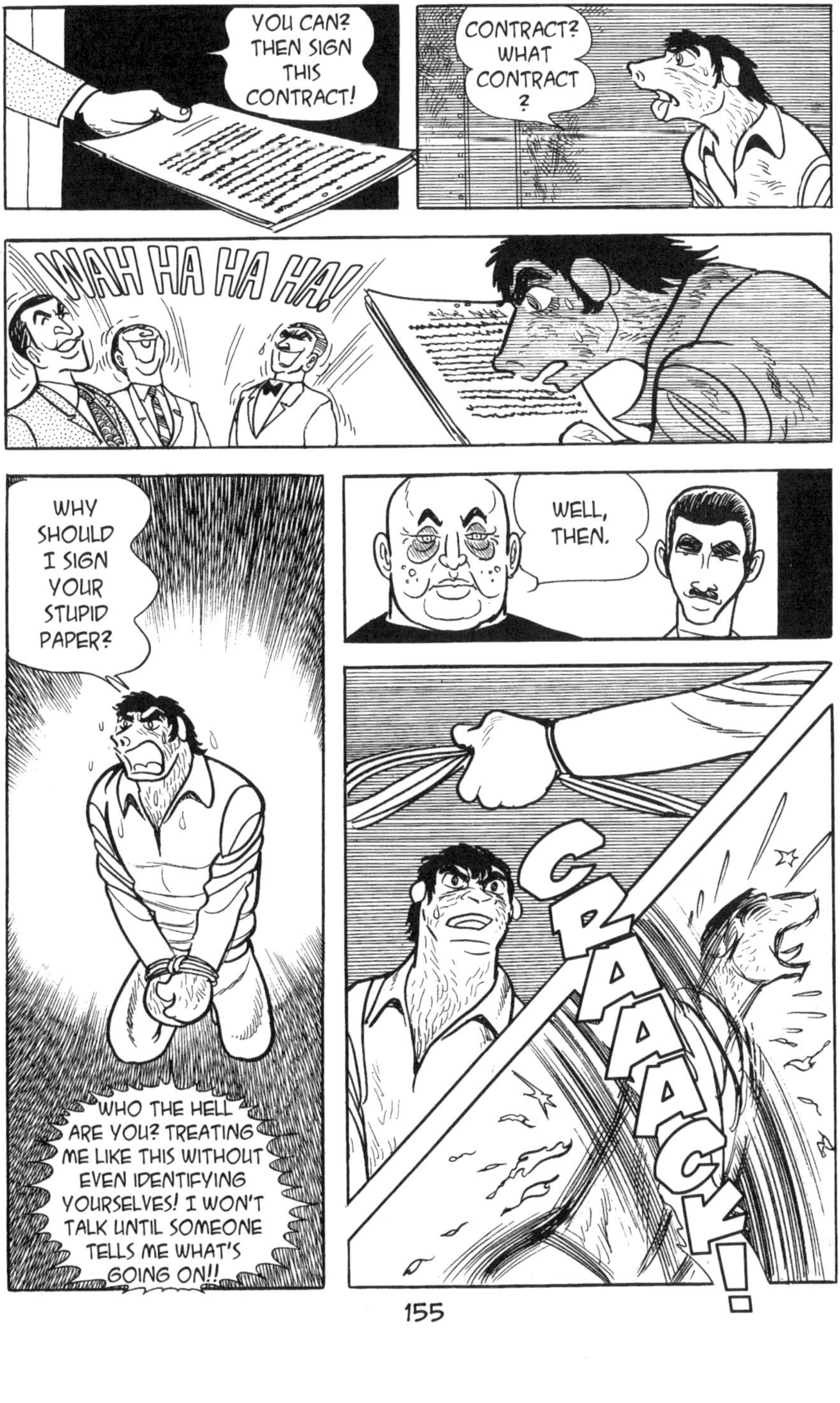
YOU CAN? THEN SIGN THIS CONTRACT!
CONTRACT? WHAT CONTRACT ?
WAH HA HA HA!
WHY SHOULD I SIGN YOUR STUPID PAPER?
WHO THE HELL ARE YOU? TREATING ME LIKE THIS WITHOUT EVEN IDENTIFYING YOURSELVES! I WON'T TALK UNTIL SOMEONE TELLS ME WHAT'S GOING ON!!
WELL, THEN.
CRAAAACK!

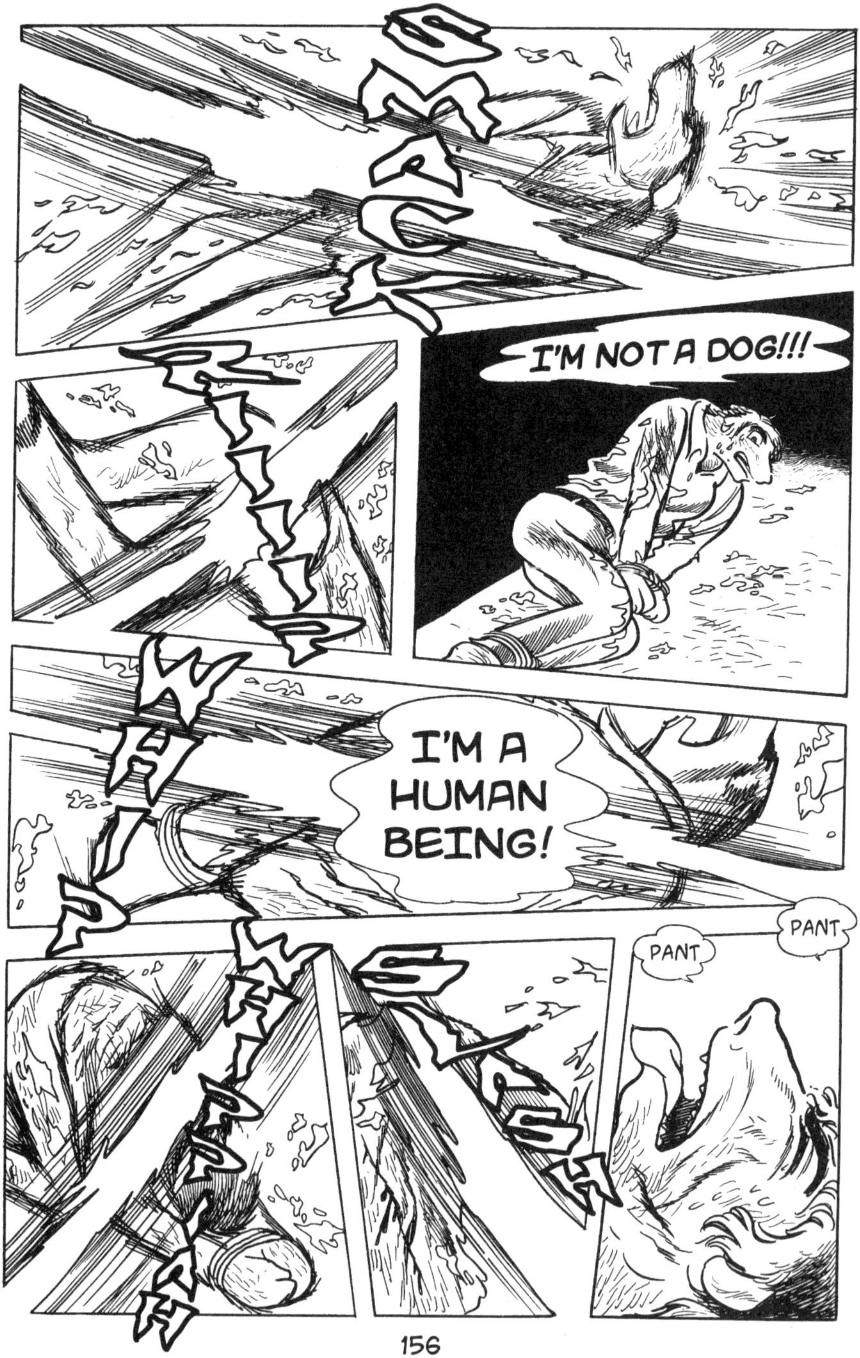
SMACK
RIIIIP
I'M NOT A DOG!!!
WHAP
I'M A HUMAN BEING!
SWISH
PANT
PANT

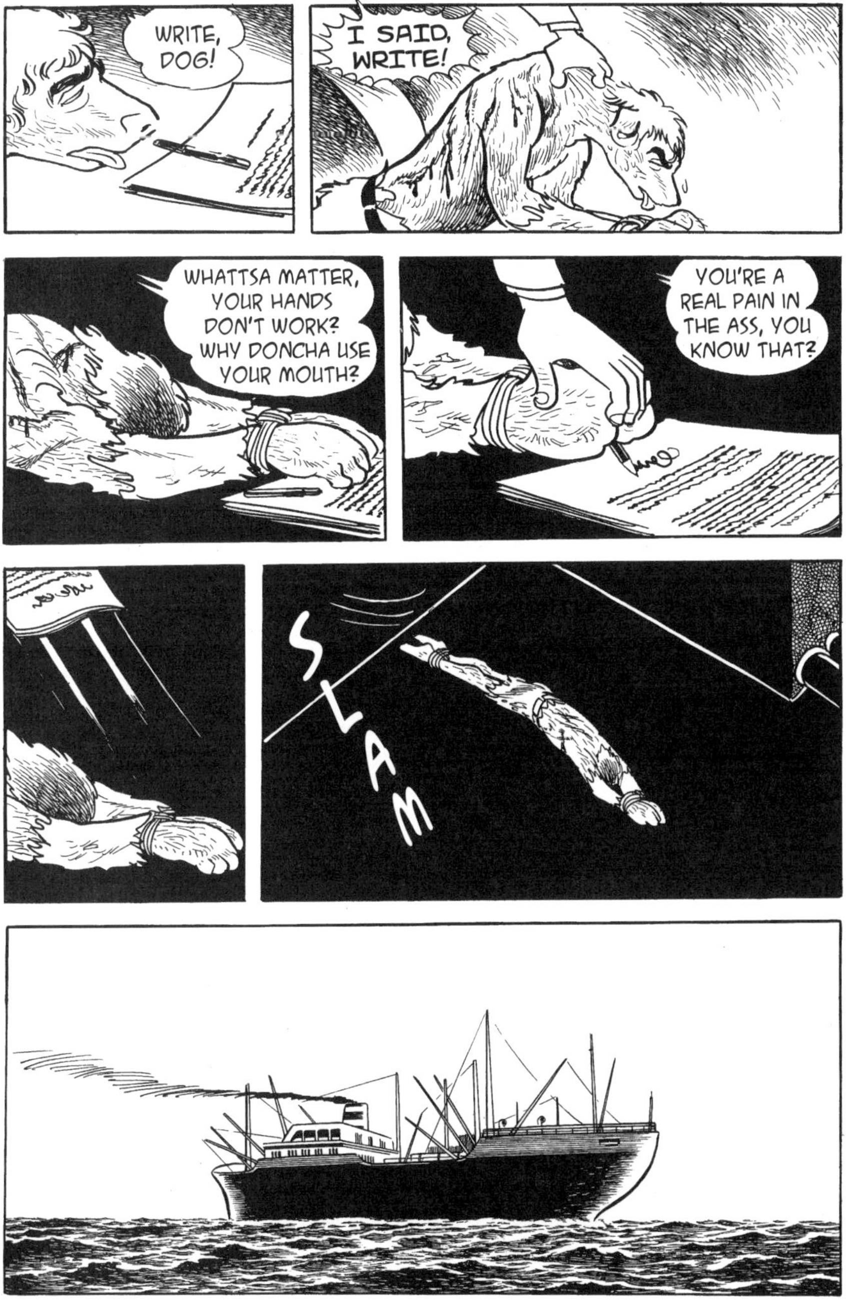
WRITE, DOG!
I SAID, WRITE!
WHATTSA MATTER, YOUR HANDS DON'T WORK? WHY DONCHA USE YOUR MOUTH?
YOU'RE A REAL PAIN IN THE ASS, YOU KNOW THAT?
SLAM

CHAPTER 5

GOLGOTHA HILL

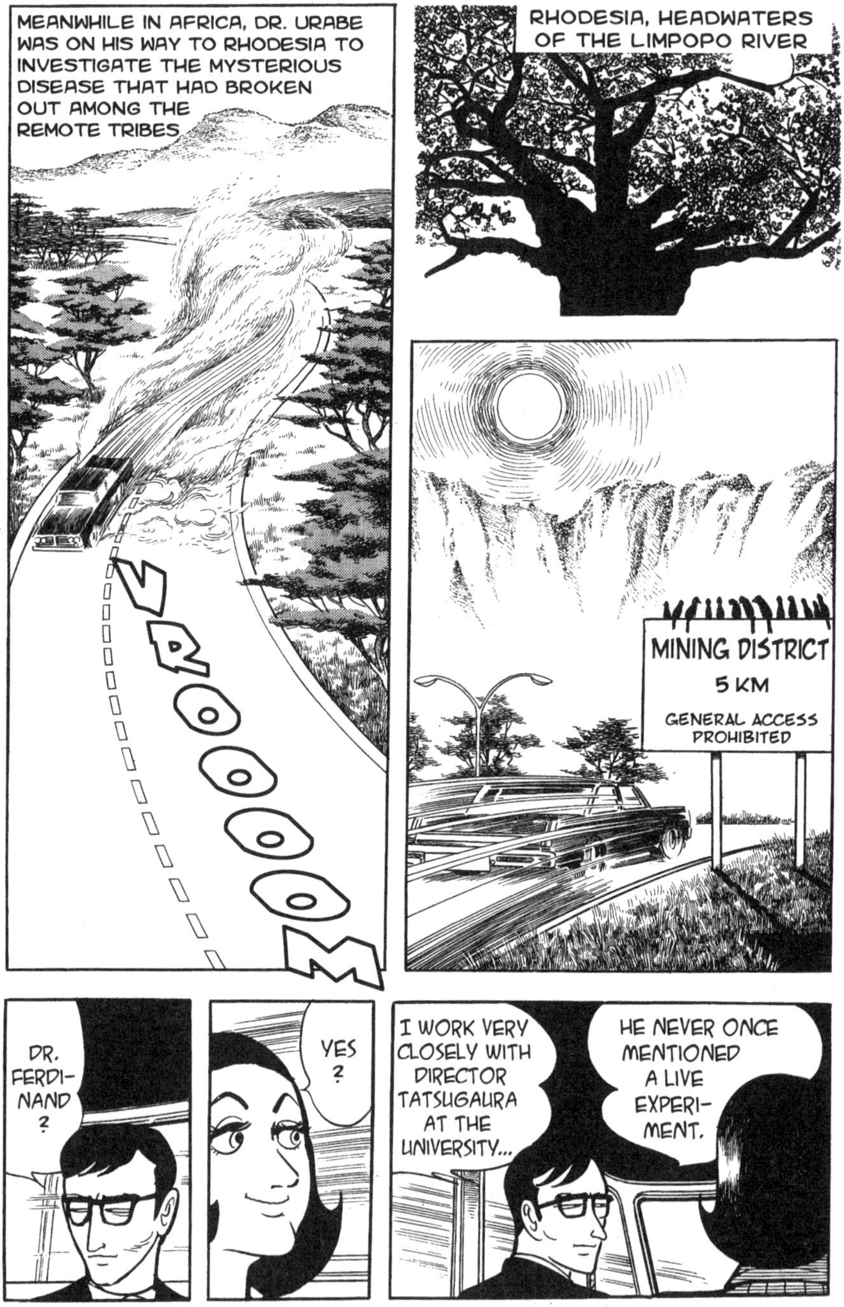
MEANWHILE IN AFRICA, DR. URABE WAS ON HIS WAY TO RHODESIA TO INVESTIGATE THE MYSTERIOUS DISEASE THAT HAD BROKEN OUT AMONG THE REMOTE TRIBES
RHODESIA, HEADWATERS OF THE LIMPOPO RIVER
VROOOOOM
MINING DISTRICT 5 KM GENERAL ACCESS PROHIBITED
DR. FERDI-NAND?
YES?
I WORK VERY CLOSELY WITH DIRECTOR TATSUGAURA AT THE UNIVERSITY...
HE NEVER ONCE MENTIONED A LIVE EXPERI-MENT.

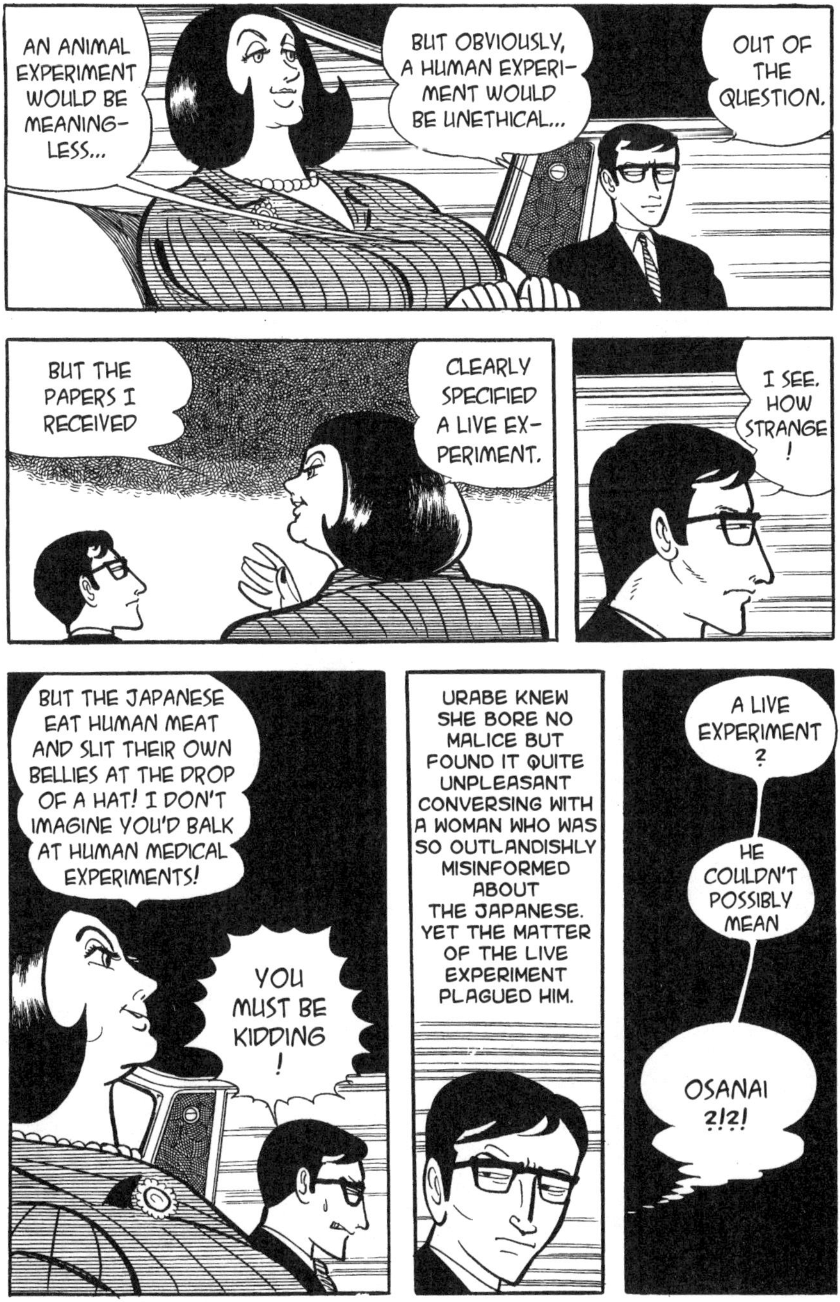
AN ANIMAL EXPERIMENT WOULD BE MEANING-LESS...
BUT OBVIOUSLY, A HUMAN EXPERI-MENT WOULD BE UNETHICAL...
OUT OF THE QUESTION.
BUT THE PAPERS I RECEIVED
CLEARLY SPECIFIED A LIVE EX-PERIMENT.
I SEE. HOW STRANGE!
BUT THE JAPANESE EAT HUMAN MEAT AND SLIT THEIR OWN BELLIES AT THE DROP OF A HAT! I DON'T IMAGINE YOU'D BALK AT HUMAN MEDICAL EXPERIMENTS!
YOU MUST BE KIDDING!
URABE KNEW SHE BORE NO MALICE BUT FOUND IT QUITE UNPLEASANT CONVERSING WITH A WOMAN WHO WAS SO OUTLANDISHLY MISINFORMED ABOUT THE JAPANESE. YET THE MATTER OF THE LIVE EXPERIMENT PLAGUED HIM.
A LIVE EXPERIMENT?
HE COULDN'T POSSIBLY MEAN
OSANAI ?!?!

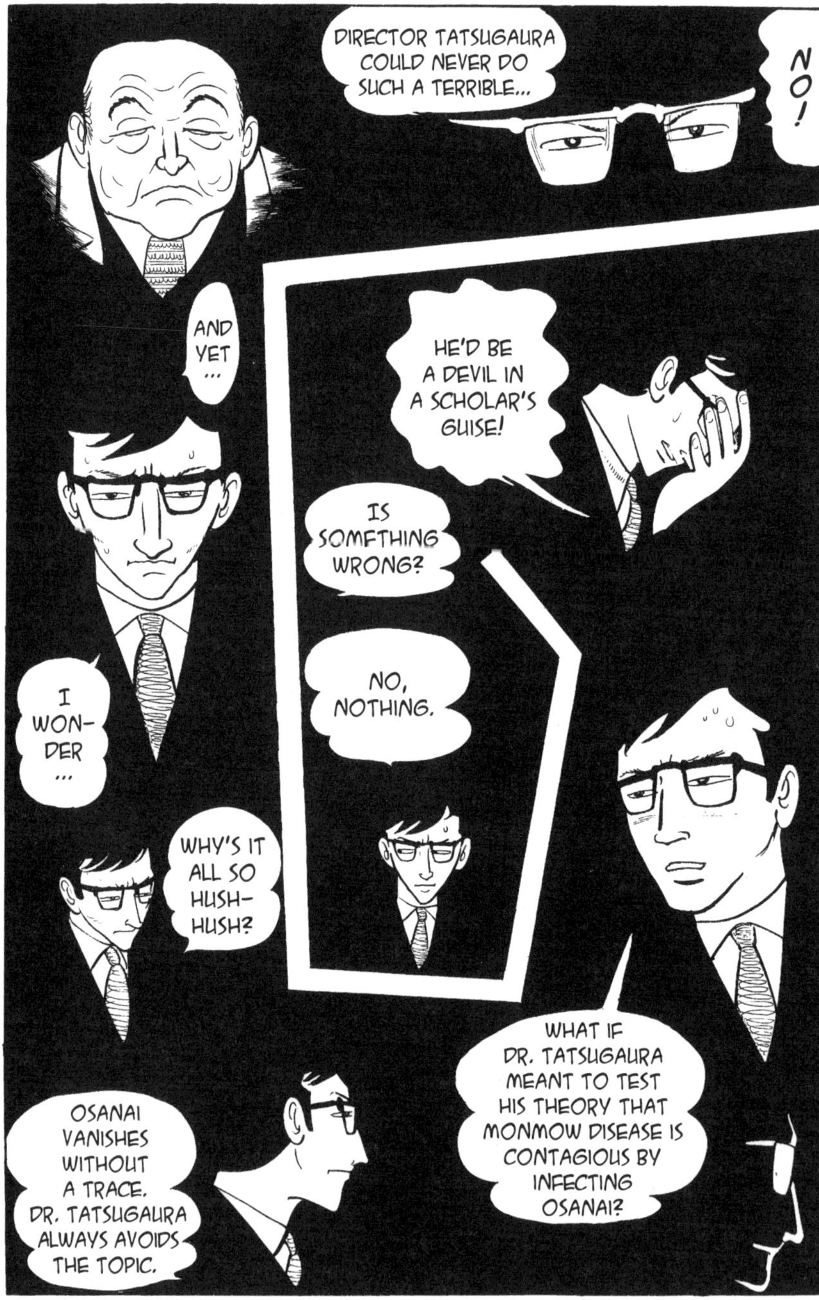
DIRECTOR TATSUGAURA COULD NEVER DO SUCH A TERRIBLE...
NO!
AND YET ...
HE'D BE A DEVIL IN A SCHOLAR'S GUISE!
IS SOMFTHING WRONG?
I WONDER ...
NO, NOTHING.
WHY'S IT ALL SO HUSH-HUSH?
WHAT IF DR. TATSUGAURA MEANT TO TEST HIS THEORY THAT MONMOW DISEASE IS CONTAGIOUS BY INFECTING OSANAI?
OSANAI VANISHES WITHOUT A TRACE. DR. TATSUGAURA ALWAYS AVOIDS THE TOPIC.

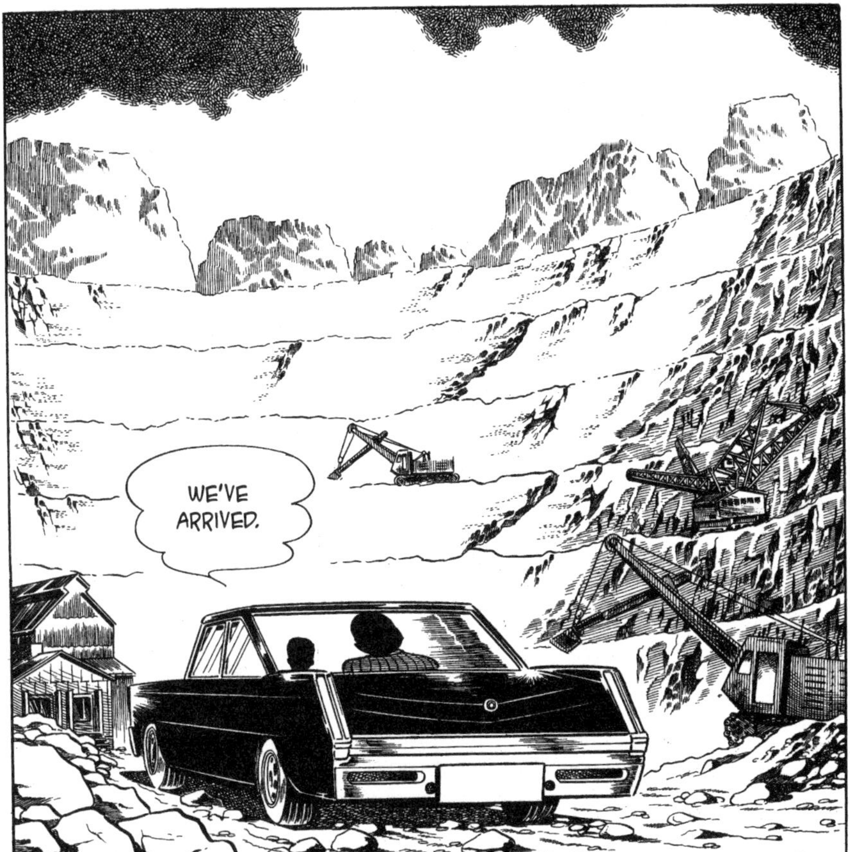
WE'VE ARRIVED.

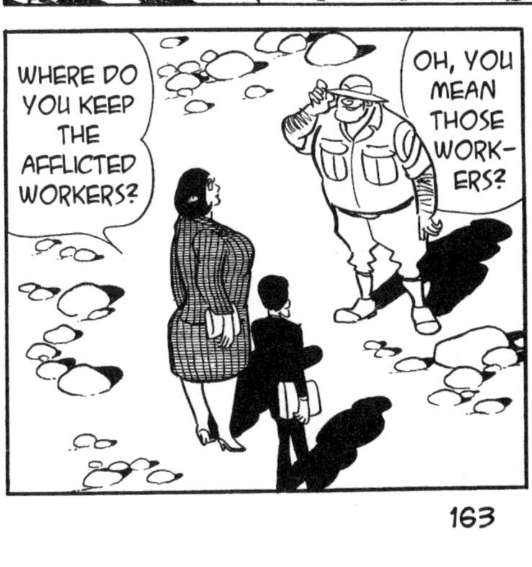
WHERE DO YOU KEEP THE AFFLICTED WORKERS?
OH, YOU MEAN THOSE WORK-ERS?

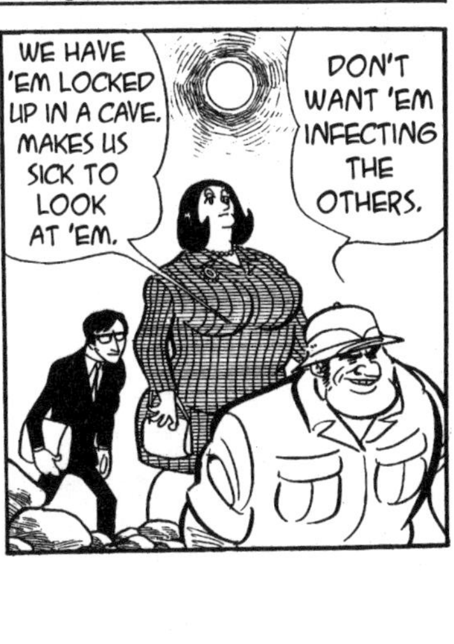
WE HAVE 'EM LOCKED UP IN A CAVE. MAKES US SICK TO LOOK AT 'EM.
DON'T WANT 'EM INFECTING THE OTHERS.

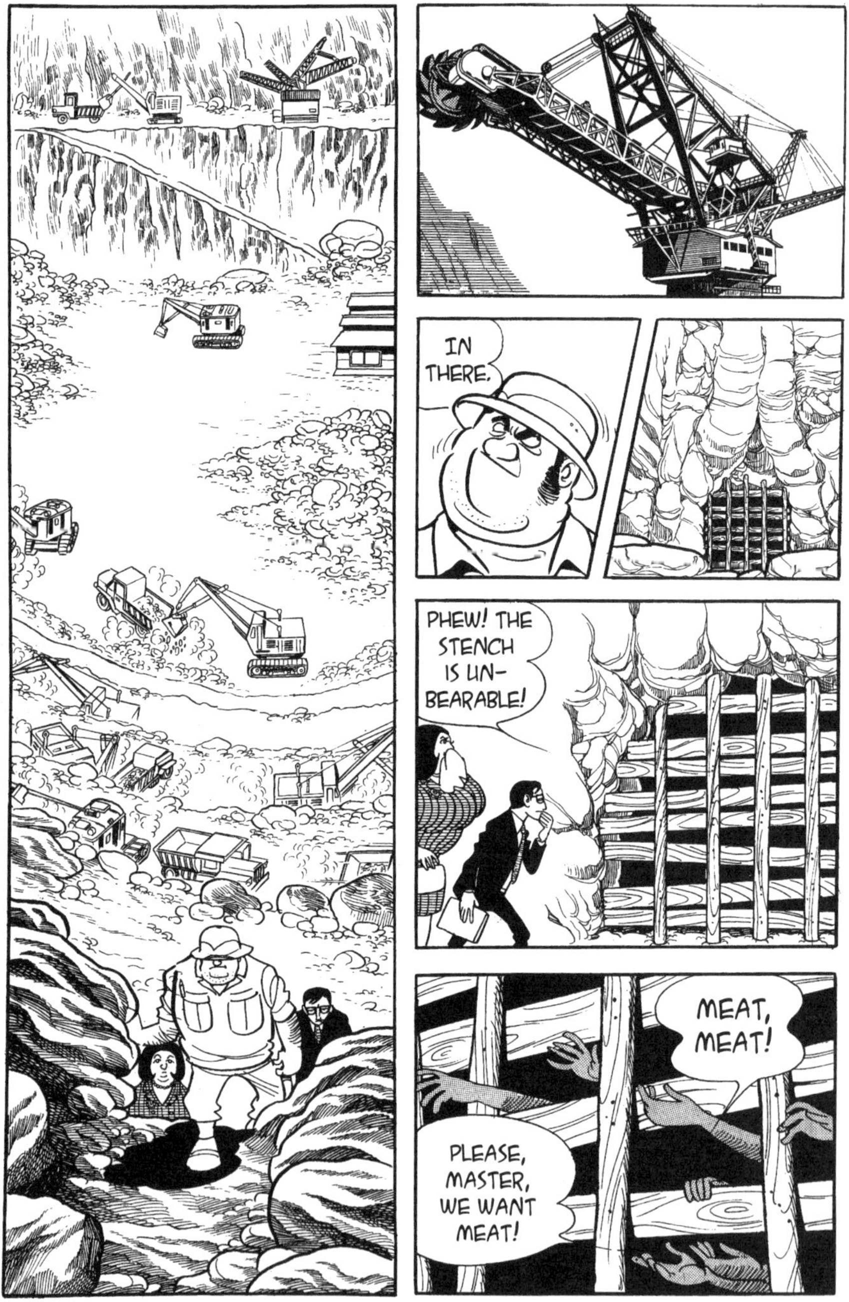
IN THERE.
PHEW! THE STENCH IS UN-BEARABLE!
MEAT, MEAT!
PLEASE, MASTER, WE WANT MEAT!

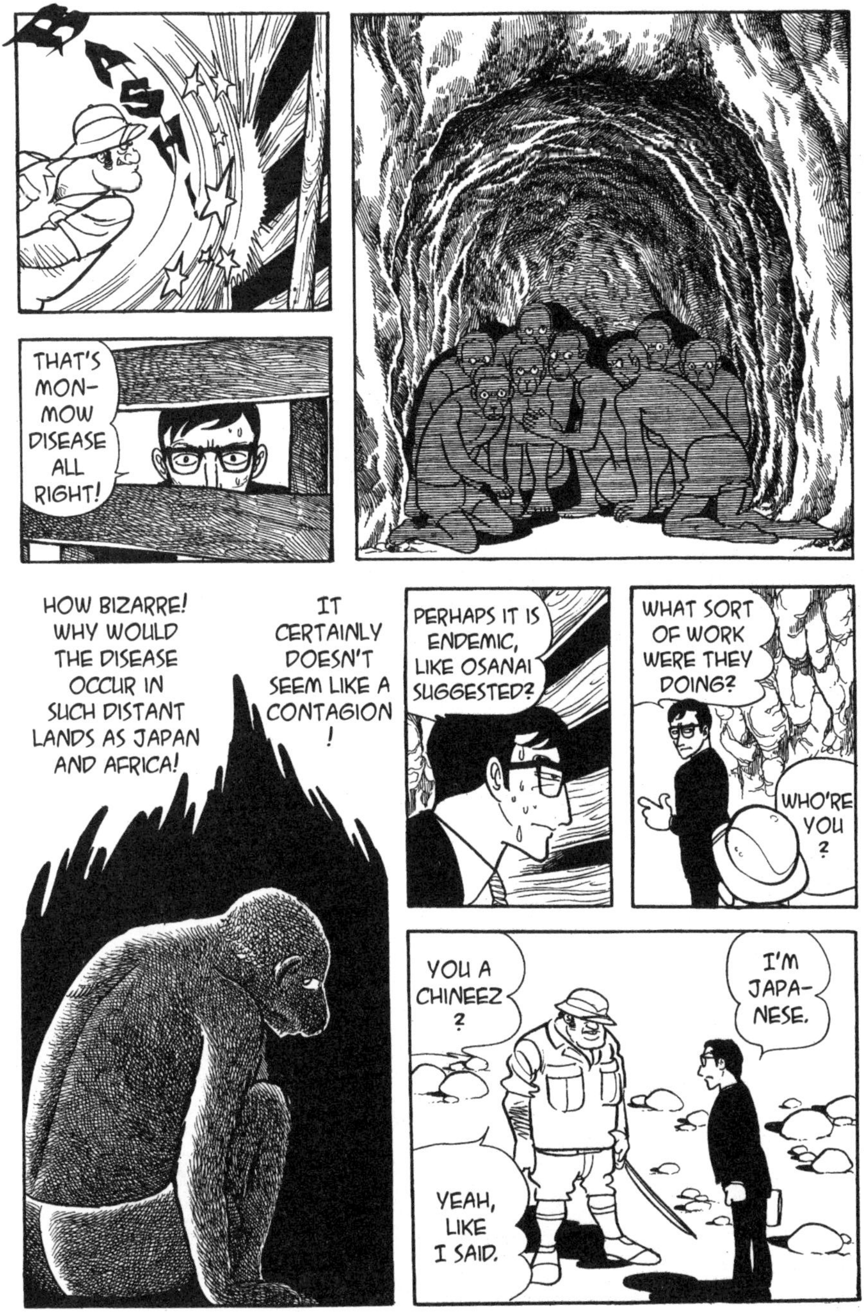
BASH
THAT'S MON-MOW DISEASE ALL RIGHT!
HOW BIZARRE! WHY WOULD THE DISEASE OCCUR IN SUCH DISTANT LANDS AS JAPAN AND AFRICA!
IT CERTAINLY DOESN'T SEEM LIKE A CONTAGION!
PERHAPS IT IS ENDEMIC, LIKE OSANAI SUGGESTED?
WHAT SORT OF WORK WERE THEY DOING?
WHO'RE YOU?
I'M JAPA-NESE.
YOU A CHINEEZ?
YEAH, LIKE I SAID.

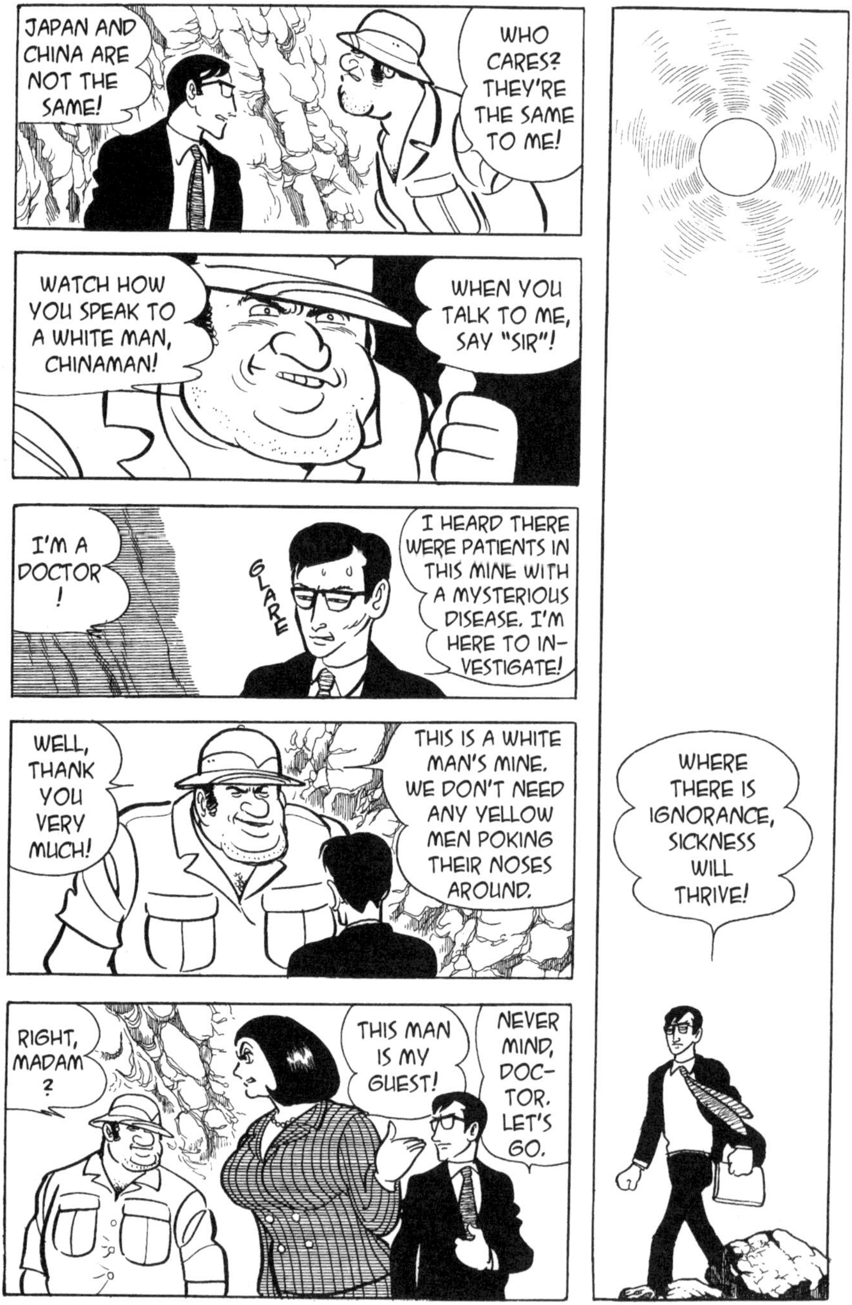
JAPAN AND CHINA ARE NOT THE SAME!
WHO CARES? THEY'RE THE SAME TO ME!
WATCH HOW YOU SPEAK TO A WHITE MAN, CHINAMAN!
WHEN YOU TALK TO ME, SAY "SIR"!
I'M A DOCTOR!
GLARE
I HEARD THERE WERE PATIENTS IN THIS MINE WITH A MYSTERIOUS DISEASE. I'M HERE TO IN-VESTIGATE!
WELL, THANK YOU VERY MUCH!
THIS IS A WHITE MAN'S MINE. WE DON'T NEED ANY YELLOW MEN POKING THEIR NOSES AROUND.
RIGHT, MADAM?
THIS MAN IS MY GUEST!
NEVER MIND, DOC-TOR. LET'S GO.
WHERE THERE IS IGNORANCE, SICKNESS WILL THRIVE!

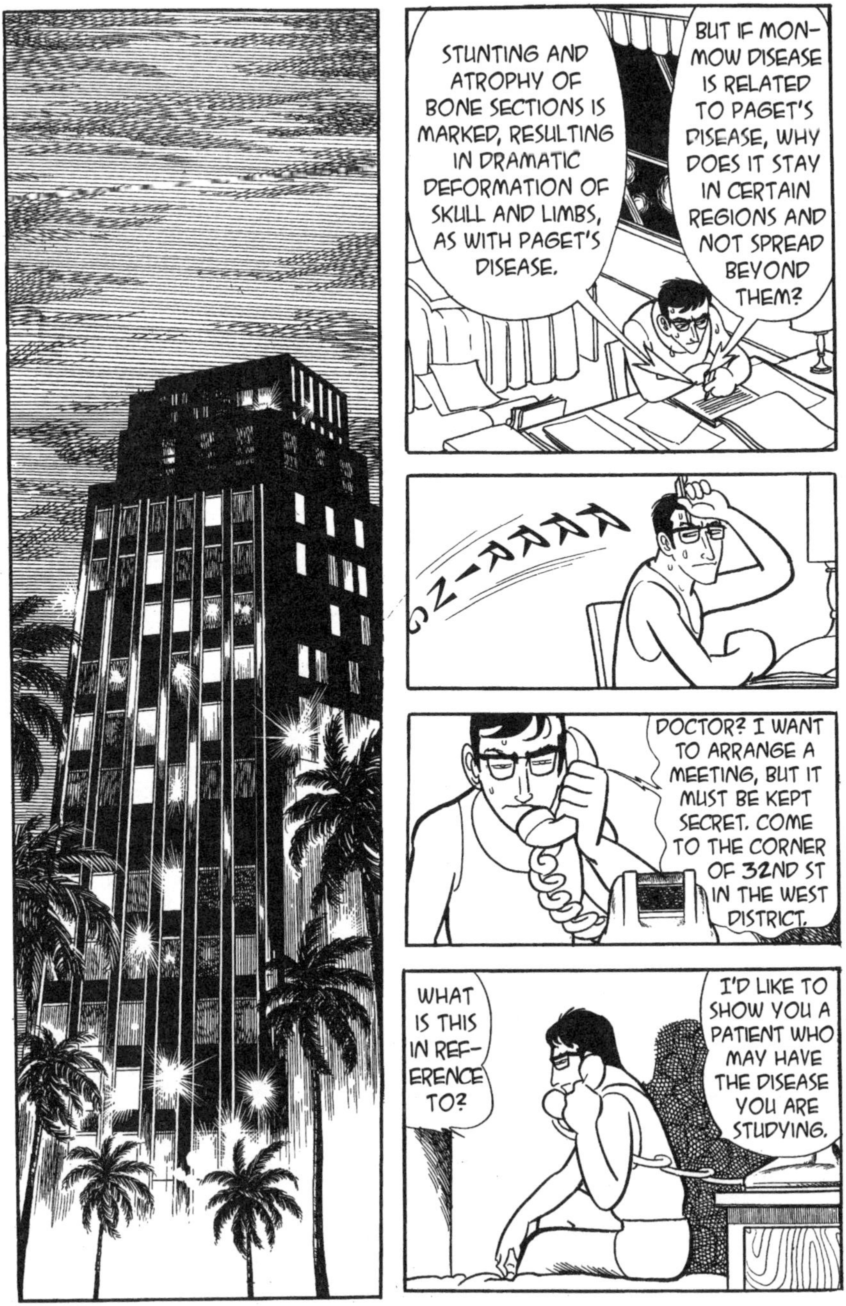
STUNTING AND ATROPHY OF BONE SECTIONS IS MARKED, RESULTING IN DRAMATIC DEFORMATION OF SKULL AND LIMBS, AS WITH PAGET'S DISEASE.
BUT IF MON-MOW DISEASE IS RELATED TO PAGET'S DISEASE, WHY DOES IT STAY IN CERTAIN REGIONS AND NOT SPREAD BEYOND THEM?
Z-RRRR
DOCTOR? I WANT TO ARRANGE A MEETING, BUT IT MUST BE KEPT SECRET. COME TO THE CORNER OF 32ND ST IN THE WEST DISTRICT.
WHAT IS THIS IN REF-ERENCE TO?
I'D LIKE TO SHOW YOU A PATIENT WHO MAY HAVE THE DISEASE YOU ARE STUDYING.

THANK YOU FOR COMING. MY NAME IS MCCRACKEN.

YOU SAID A PATIENT WITH MON-MOW DISEASE?

BEFORE I SHOW YOU

YOU MUST PROMISE NOT TO TELL ANYONE.

I CAN'T PROMISE ANYTHING WITHOUT SEEING THE PATIENT.

...

SHOW ME THE PATIENT FIRST.

...

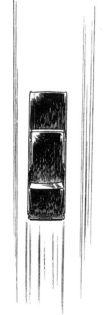

HERE? IN THE CONVENT?

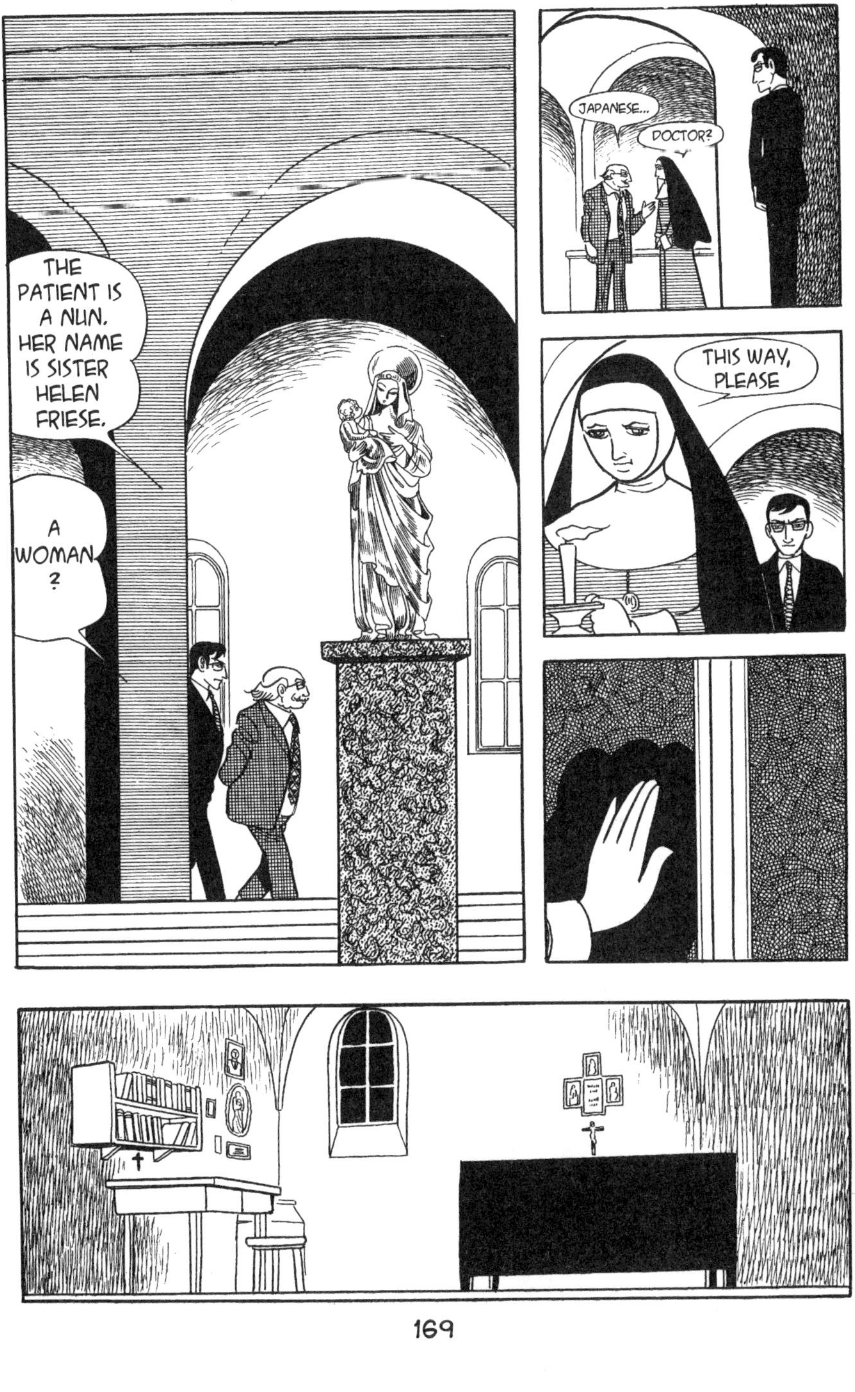
THE PATIENT IS A NUN. HER NAME IS SISTER HELEN FRIESE.
A WOMAN?
JAPANESE...
DOCTOR?
THIS WAY, PLEASE

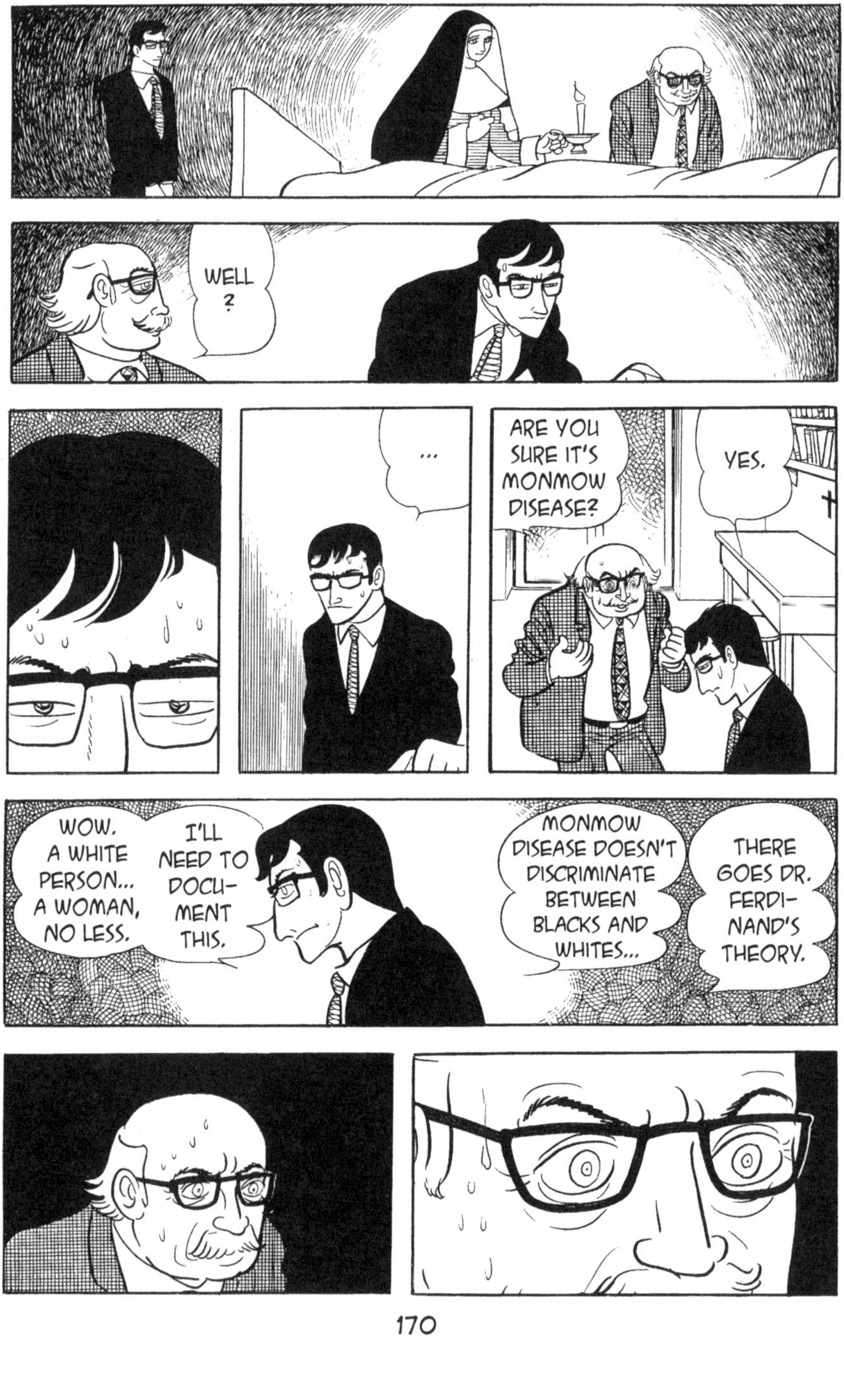
WELL ?
...
ARE YOU SURE IT'S MONMOW DISEASE?
YES.
WOW. A WHITE PERSON... A WOMAN, NO LESS.
I'LL NEED TO DOCU-MENT THIS.
MONMOW DISEASE DOESN'T DISCRIMINATE BETWEEN BLACKS AND WHITES...
THERE GOES DR. FERDI-NAND'S THEORY.

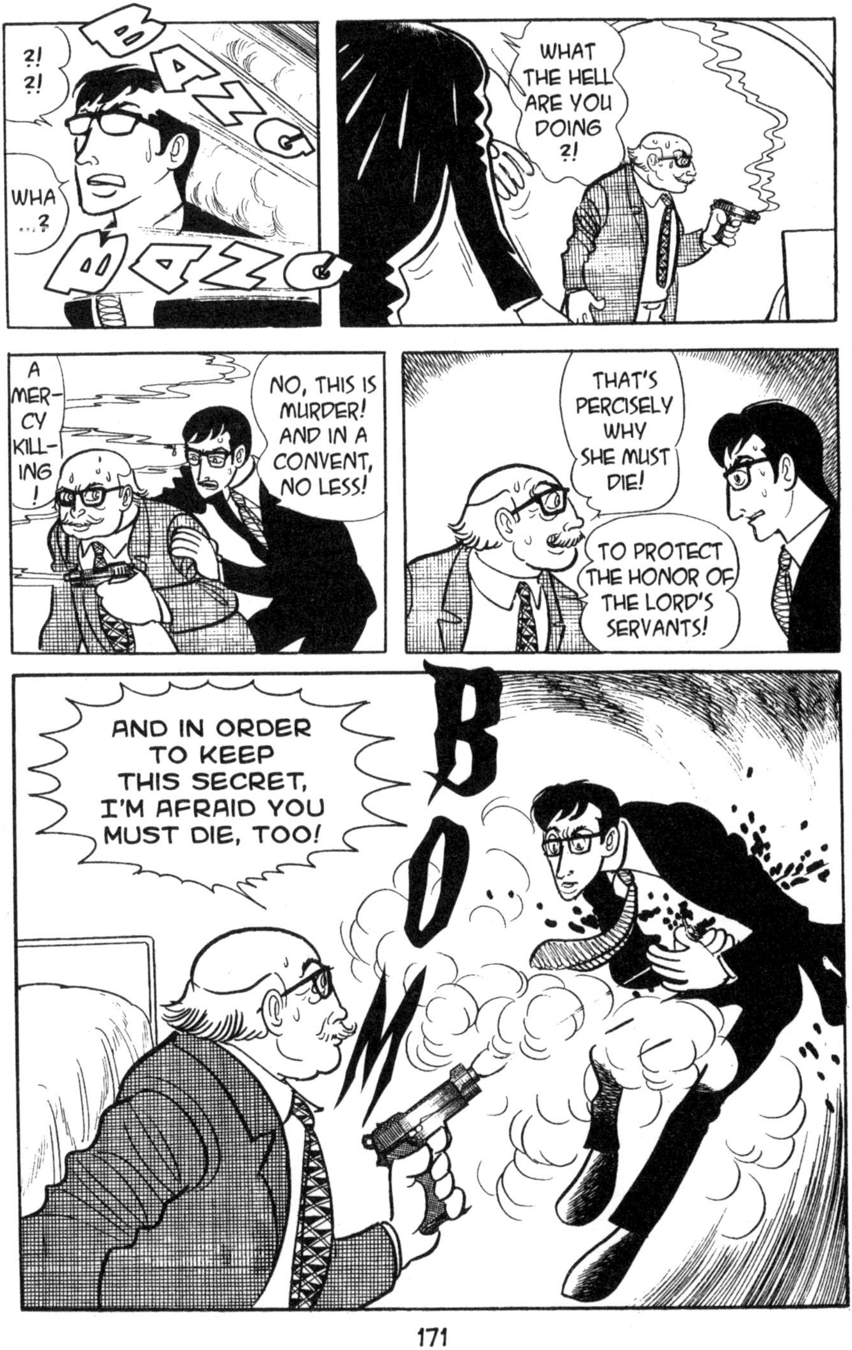
?!
?!
BAZG
WHA ...?
BAZG
WHAT THE HELL ARE YOU DOING ?!
A MERCY KILLING!
NO, THIS IS MURDER! AND IN A CONVENT, NO LESS!
THAT'S PERCISELY WHY SHE MUST DIE!
TO PROTECT THE HONOR OF THE LORD'S SERVANTS!
AND IN ORDER TO KEEP THIS SECRET, I'M AFRAID YOU MUST DIE, TOO!
BOOM

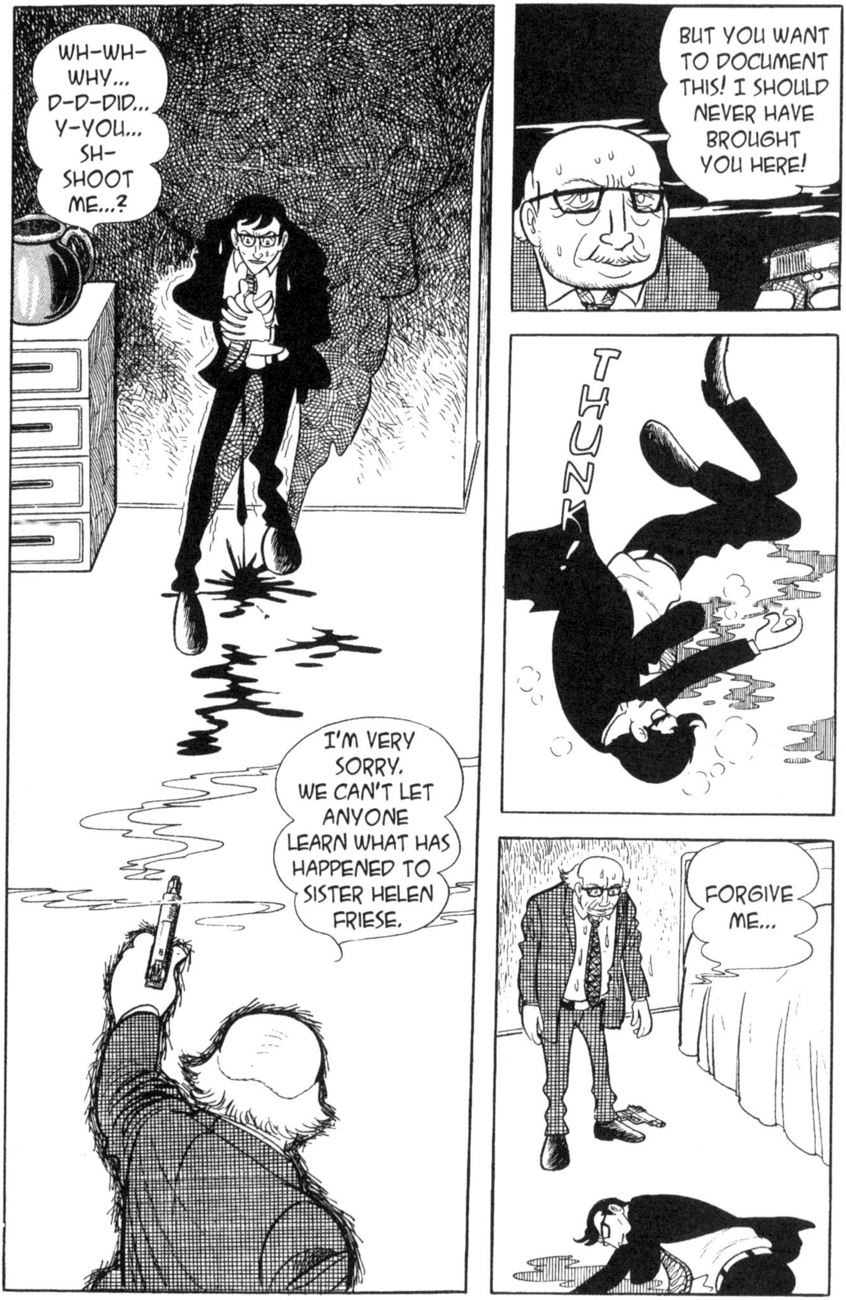
WH-WH-WHY... D-D-DID... Y-YOU... SH-SHOOT ME...?
I'M VERY SORRY. WE CAN'T LET ANYONE LEARN WHAT HAS HAPPENED TO SISTER HELEN FRIESE.
BUT YOU WANT TO DOCUMENT THIS! I SHOULD NEVER HAVE BROUGHT YOU HERE!
THUNK
FORGIVE ME...

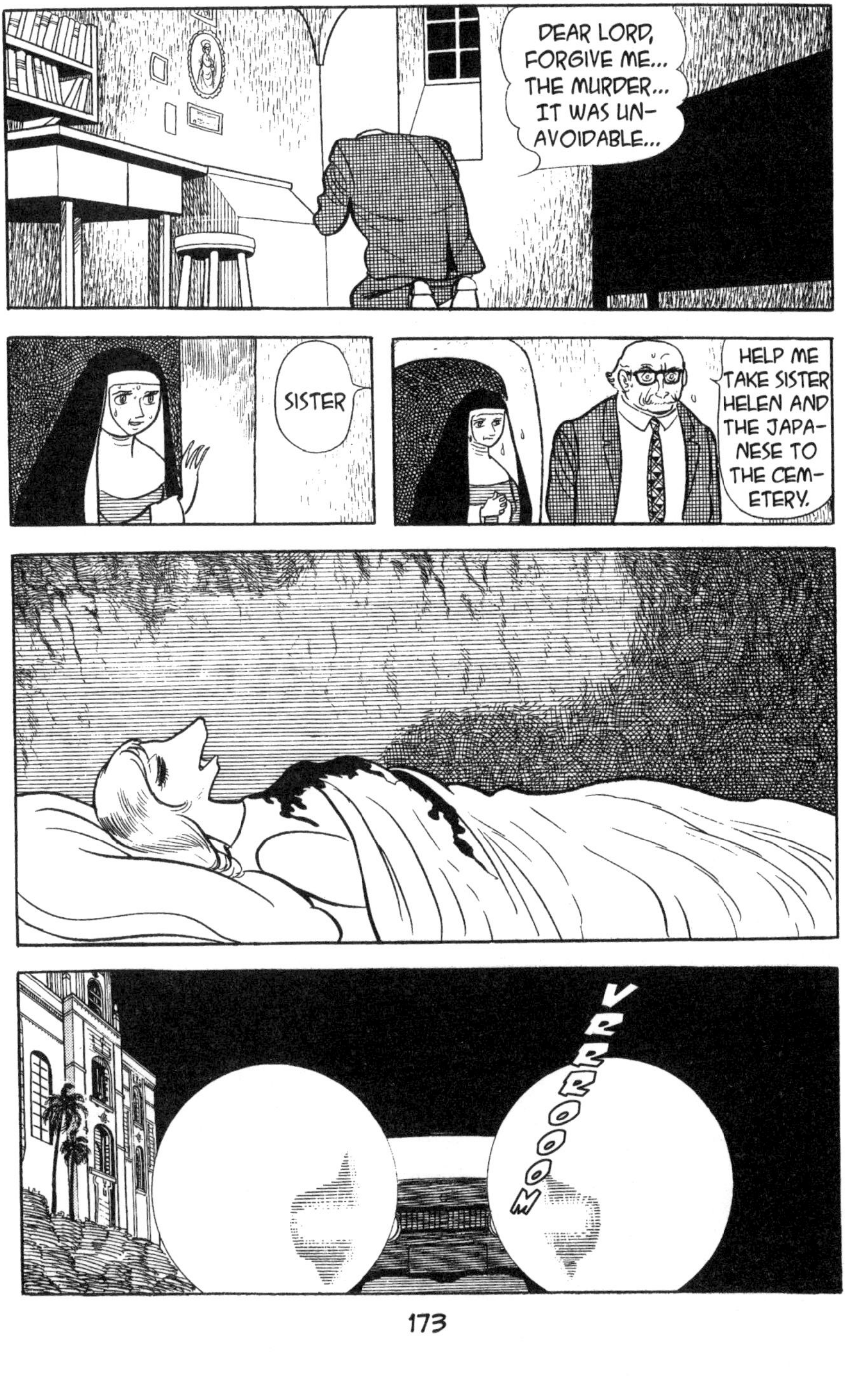
DEAR LORD, FORGIVE ME... THE MURDER... IT WAS UN-AVOIDABLE...
SISTER
HELP ME TAKE SISTER HELEN AND THE JAPANESE TO THE CEMETERY.
VRRROOOOM

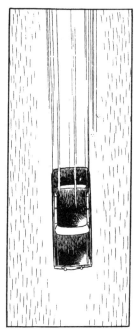

WE CAN PUT THEM IN THE VAULT FOR NOW. THAT SHOULD GIVE US TIME TO FIGURE OUT WHAT TO DO.

WON'T THE POLICE COME LOOKING FOR THE JAPANESE MAN?

NOBODY KNOWS THAT HE CAME TO SEE US.

I'M SO SCARED...

I AM, TOO, SISTER.

BUT THIS IS TO PRO- TECT THE CHURCH'S HONOR!

IF ANY- BODY SEES US, IT'S ALL OVER.

174

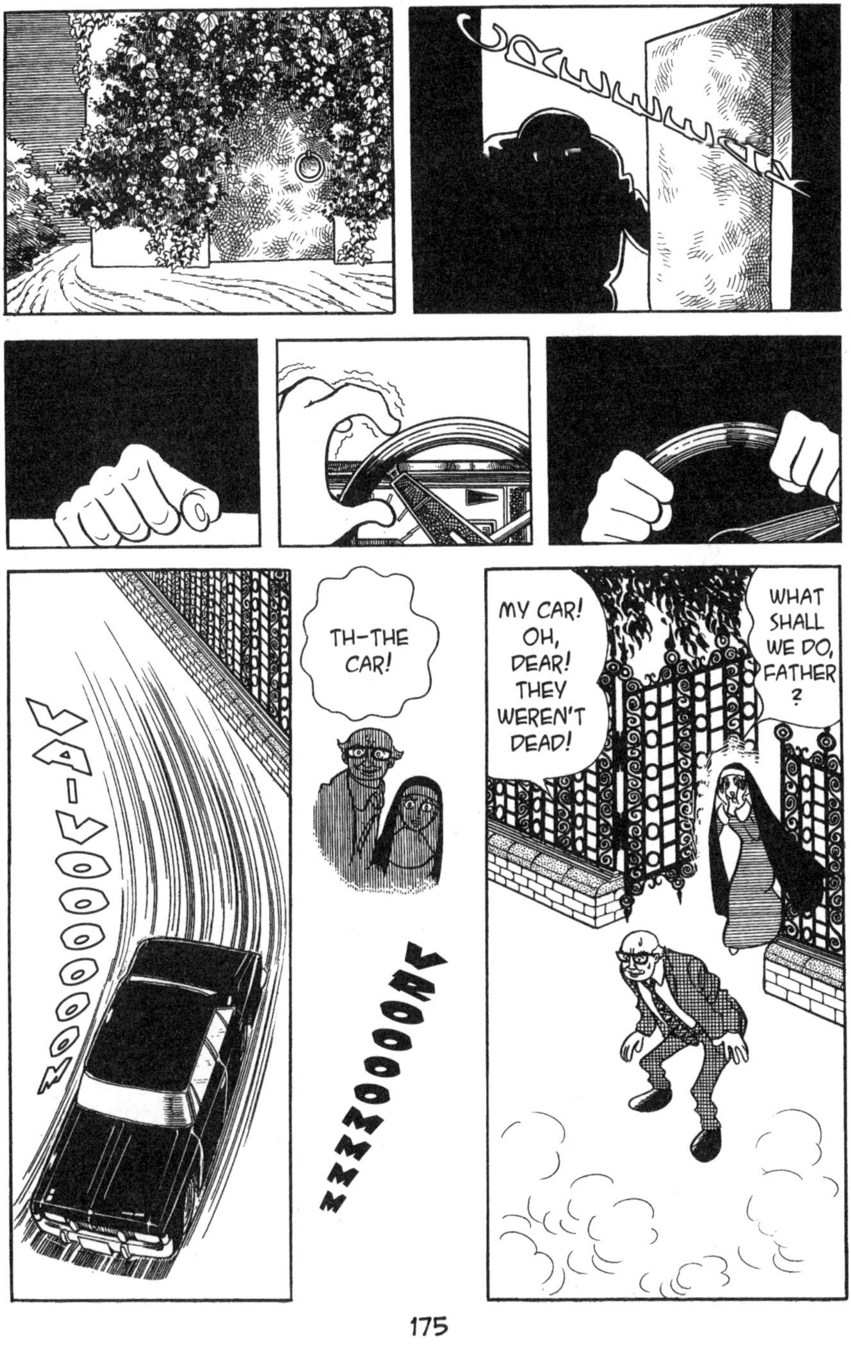
TH-THE CAR!
MY CAR! OH, DEAR! THEY WEREN'T DEAD!
WHAT SHALL WE DO, FATHER?

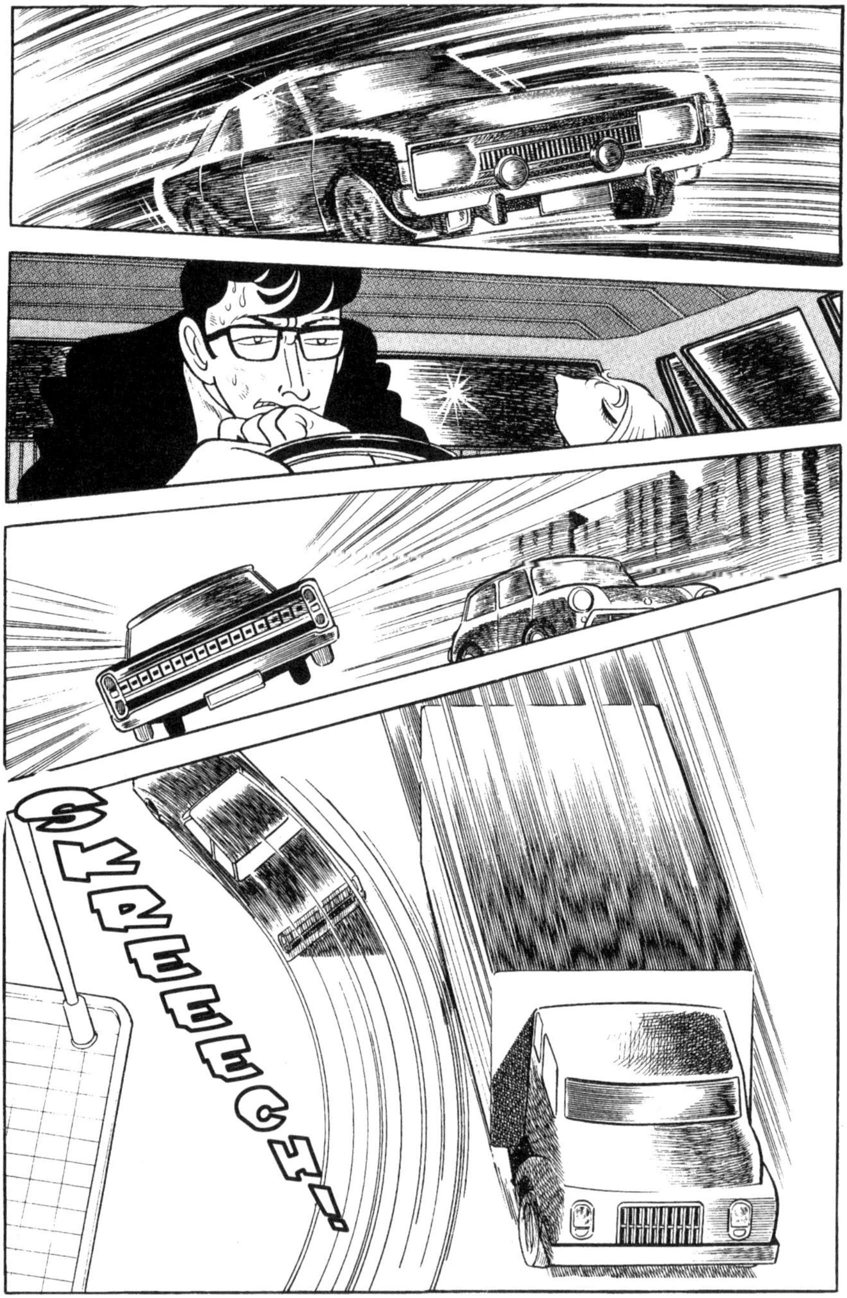
SKREEECH!

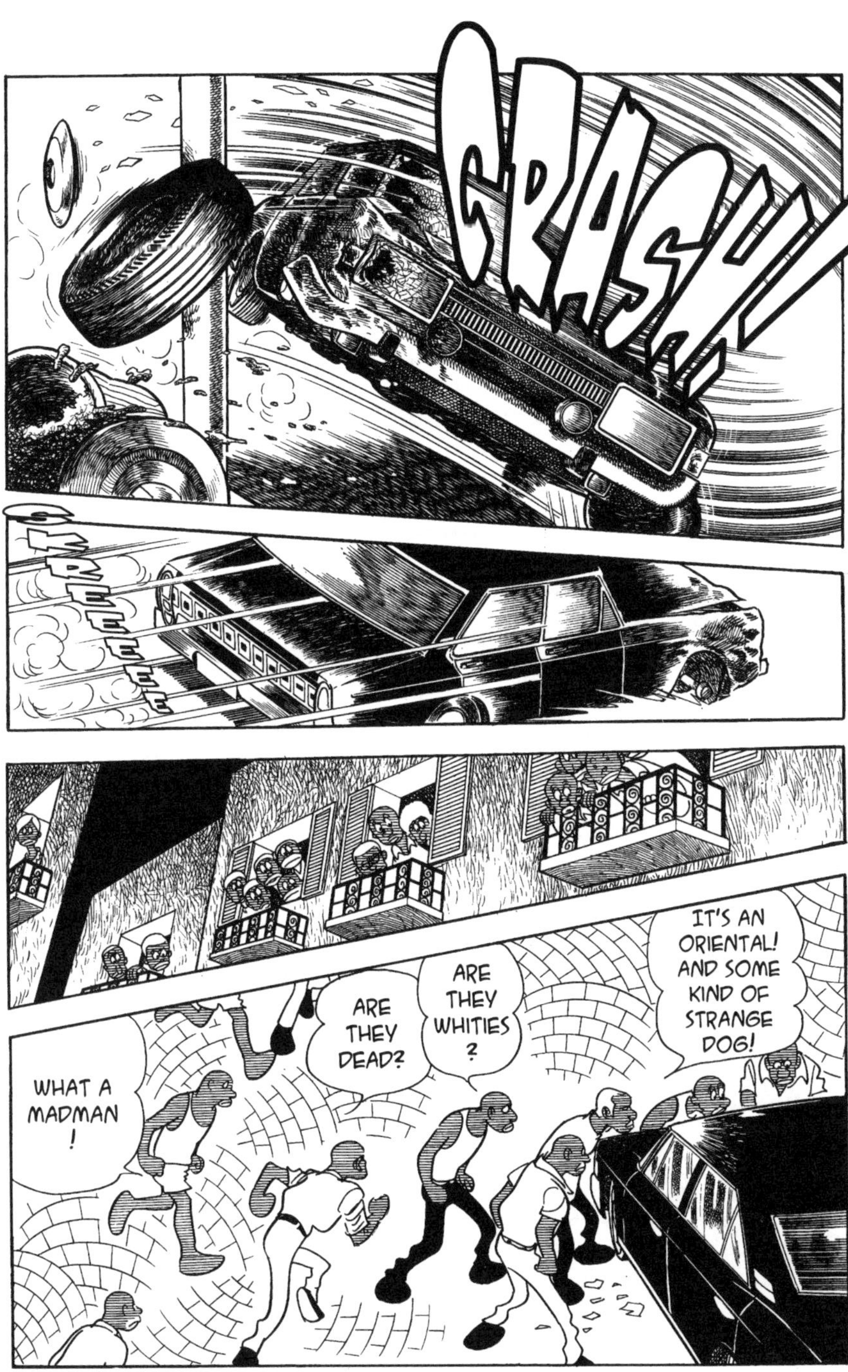
CRASH!!
WHAT A MADMAN!
ARE THEY DEAD?
ARE THEY WHITIES?
IT'S AN ORIENTAL! AND SOME KIND OF STRANGE DOG!

WOW!

BOTH THE FELLOW AND THE DOG HAVE BEEN SHOT! THERE'S BEEN A CRIME!

TAKE THEM TO DR. WORTHINTON.

WHAT IS IT, MAMA?

OFF TO BED WITH YOU!

THE BULLETS HAVE MISSED THE VITAL ORGANS, BUT THERE IS SEVERE BLOOD LOSS. THEY'LL NEED BLOOD TRANSFUSIONS.

WHO WANTS TO DONATE?

BUY MY BLOOD!

MINE, TOO!

I DON'T HAVE ANY MONEY!

THE ORIENTAL MUST HAVE SOME. HE CAN PAY!

OKAY, DONORS, LINE UP! WE'LL TEST YOUR BLOOD TYPES!

178

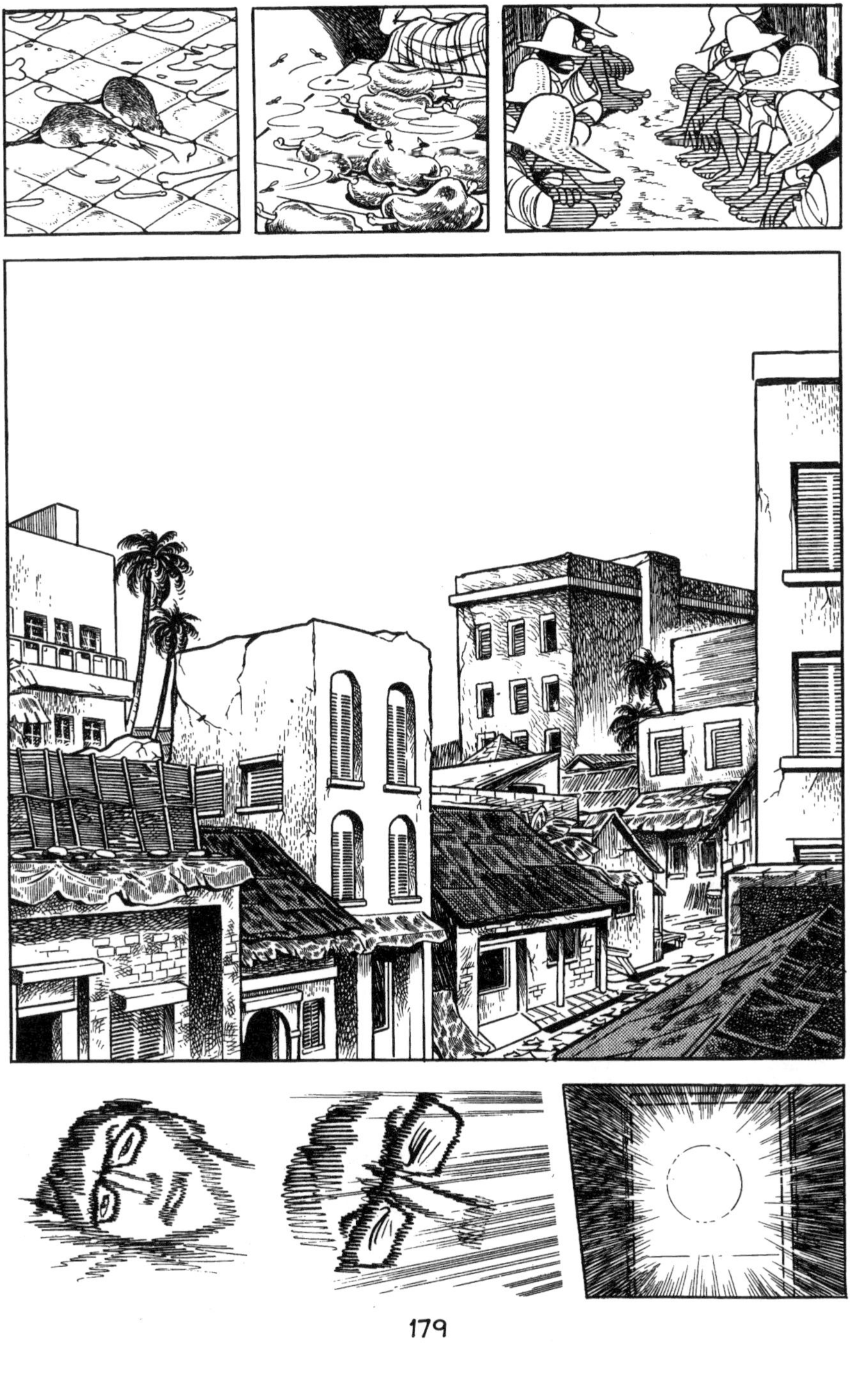

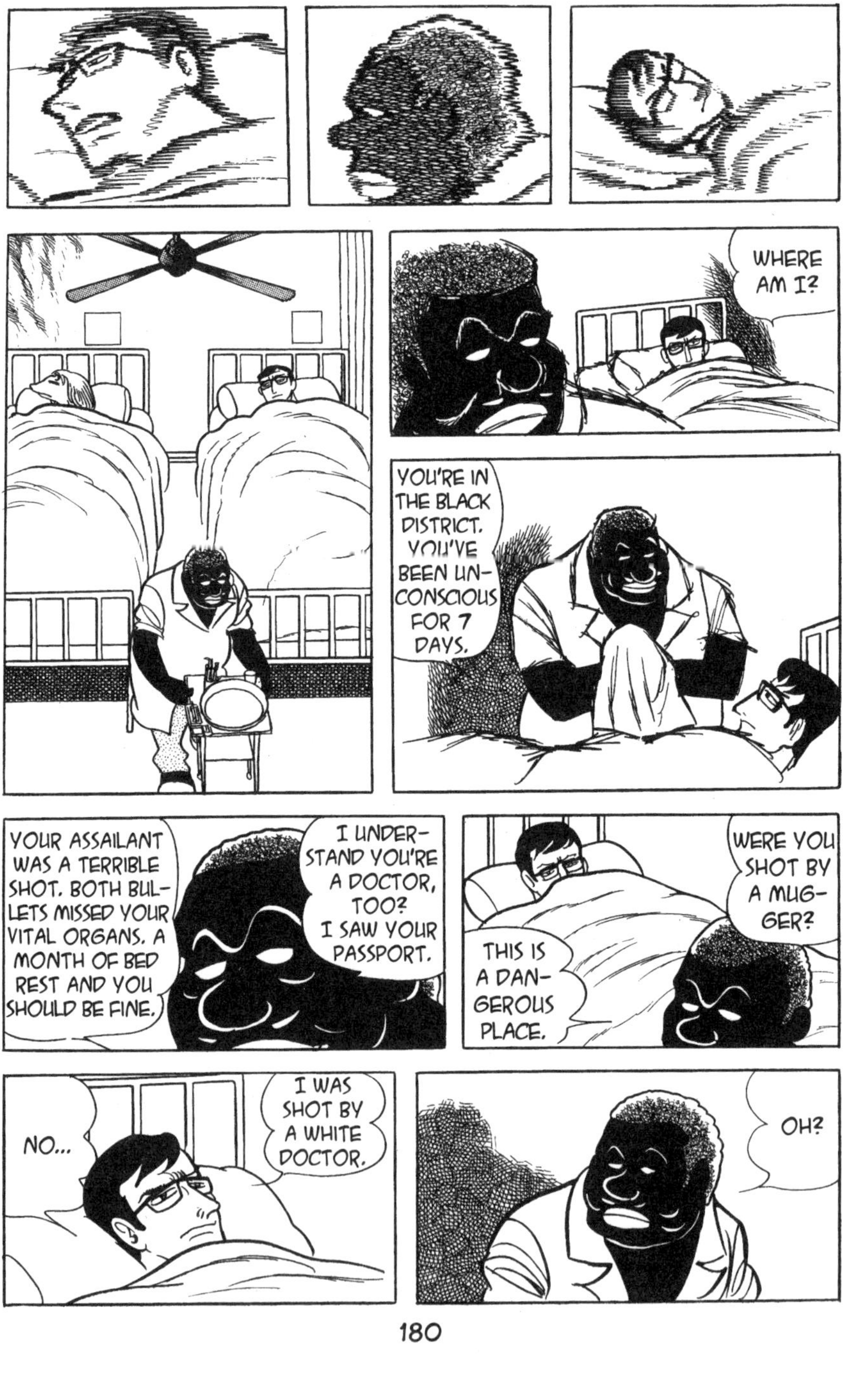

WHERE AM I?
YOU'RE IN THE BLACK DISTRICT. YOU'VE BEEN UNCONSCIOUS FOR 7 DAYS.
YOUR ASSAILANT WAS A TERRIBLE SHOT. BOTH BULLETS MISSED YOUR VITAL ORGANS. A MONTH OF BED REST AND YOU SHOULD BE FINE.
I UNDERSTAND YOU'RE A DOCTOR, TOO? I SAW YOUR PASSPORT.
WERE YOU SHOT BY A MUGGER?
THIS IS A DANGEROUS PLACE.
NO...
I WAS SHOT BY A WHITE DOCTOR.
OH?

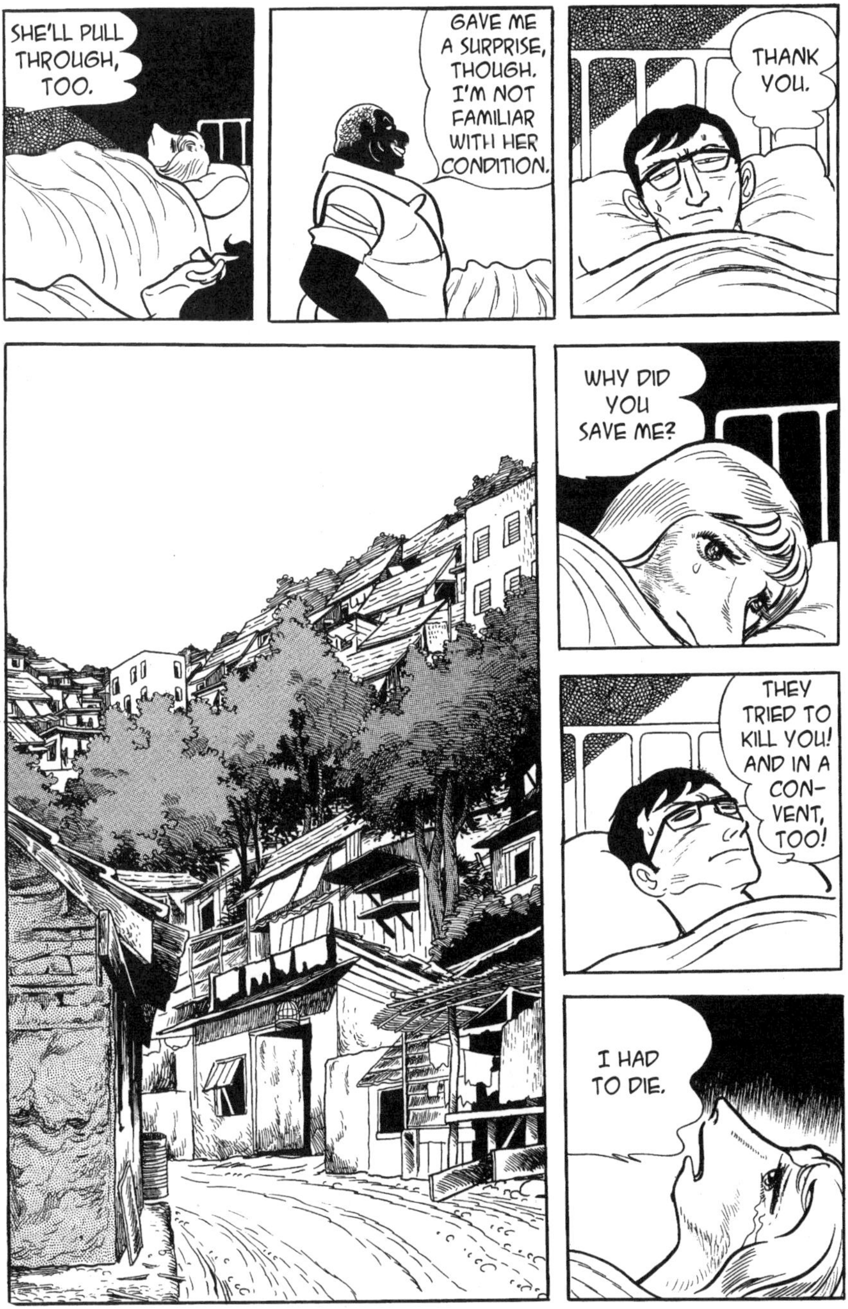
SHE'LL PULL THROUGH, TOO.
GAVE ME A SURPRISE, THOUGH. I'M NOT FAMILIAR WITH HER CONDITION.
THANK YOU.
WHY DID YOU SAVE ME?
THEY TRIED TO KILL YOU! AND IN A CON-VENT, TOO!
I HAD TO DIE.

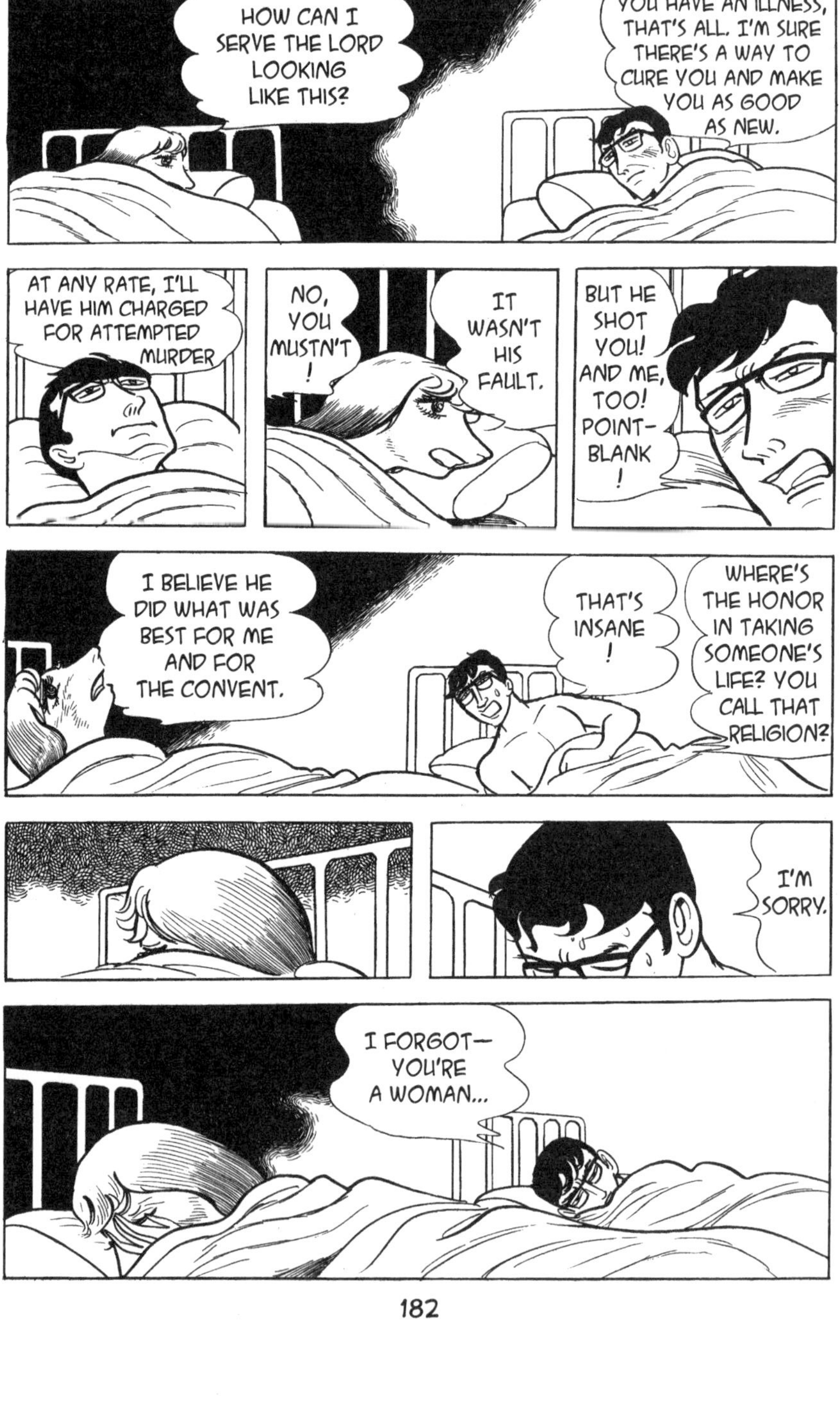
HOW CAN I SERVE THE LORD LOOKING LIKE THIS?
YOU HAVE AN ILLNESS, THAT'S ALL. I'M SURE THERE'S A WAY TO CURE YOU AND MAKE YOU AS GOOD AS NEW.
AT ANY RATE, I'LL HAVE HIM CHARGED FOR ATTEMPTED MURDER
NO, YOU MUSTN'T!
IT WASN'T HIS FAULT.
BUT HE SHOT YOU! AND ME, TOO! POINT-BLANK!
I BELIEVE HE DID WHAT WAS BEST FOR ME AND FOR THE CONVENT.
THAT'S INSANE!
WHERE'S THE HONOR IN TAKING SOMEONE'S LIFE? YOU CALL THAT RELIGION?
I'M SORRY.
I FORGOT— YOU'RE A WOMAN...

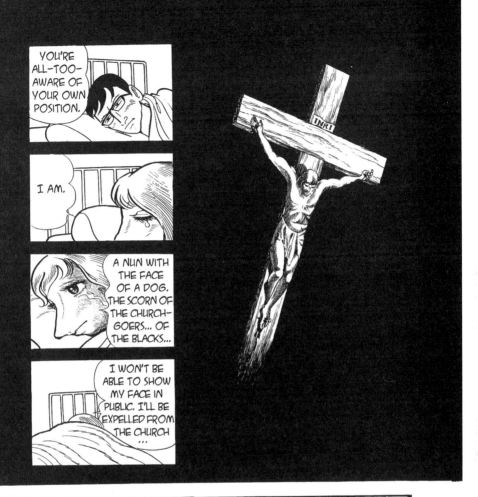

YOU'RE ALL-TOO-AWARE OF YOUR OWN POSITION.

I AM.

A NUN WITH THE FACE OF A DOG, THE SCORN OF THE CHURCH-GOERS... OF THE BLACKS...

I WON'T BE ABLE TO SHOW MY FACE IN PUBLIC. I'LL BE EXPELLED FROM THE CHURCH...

SISTER, I'M NOT A CHRISTIAN, BUT I KNOW THE STORY OF CHRIST'S LIFE! JESUS SAID HE WOULD SUFFER FOR ALL OF HUMANITY! THOSE WERE BRAVE WORDS.

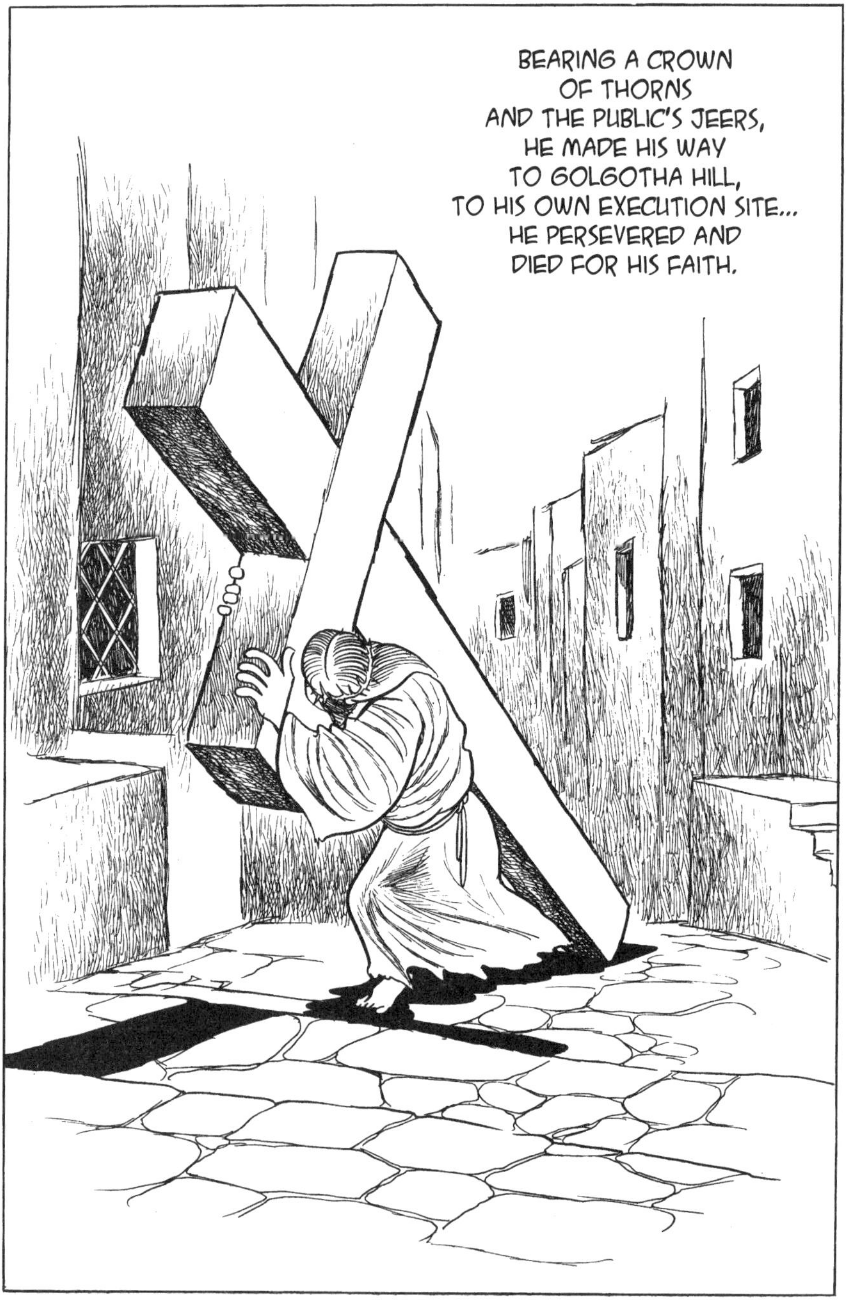
BEARING A CROWN
OF THORNS
AND THE PUBLIC'S JEERS,
HE MADE HIS WAY
TO GOLGOTHA HILL,
TO HIS OWN EXECUTION SITE...
HE PERSEVERED AND
DIED FOR HIS FAITH.

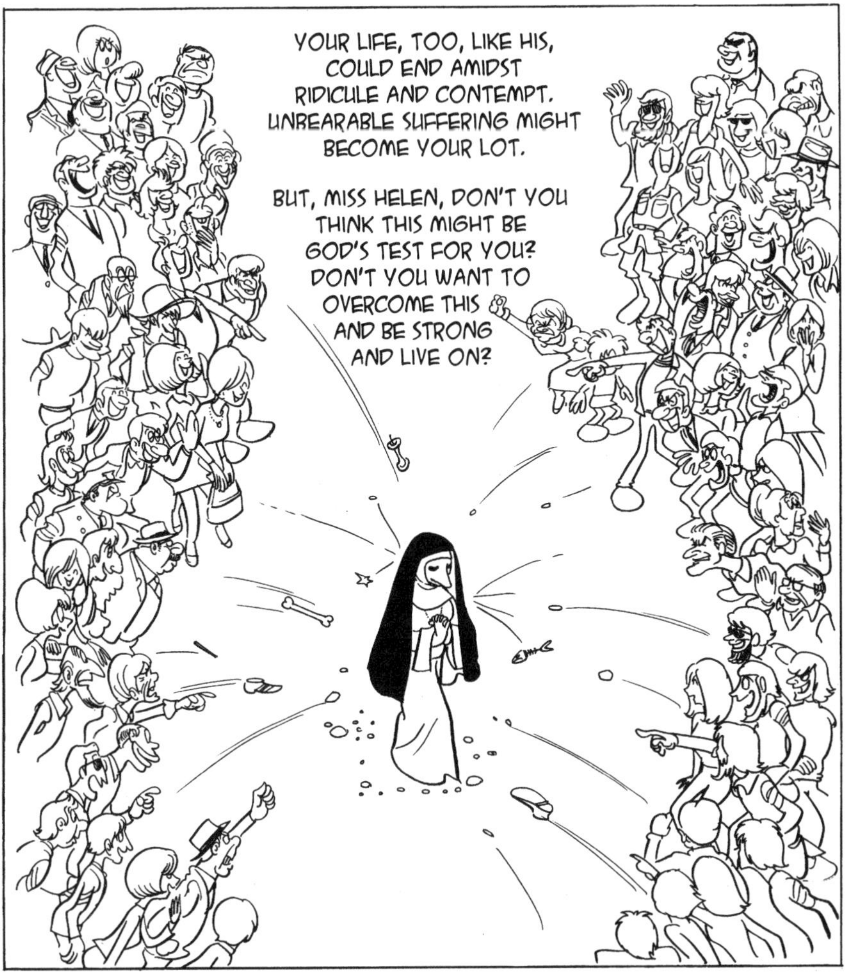
YOUR LIFE, TOO, LIKE HIS, COULD END AMIDST RIDICULE AND CONTEMPT. UNBEARABLE SUFFERING MIGHT BECOME YOUR LOT.
BUT, MISS HELEN, DON'T YOU THINK THIS MIGHT BE GOD'S TEST FOR YOU? DON'T YOU WANT TO OVERCOME THIS AND BE STRONG AND LIVE ON?

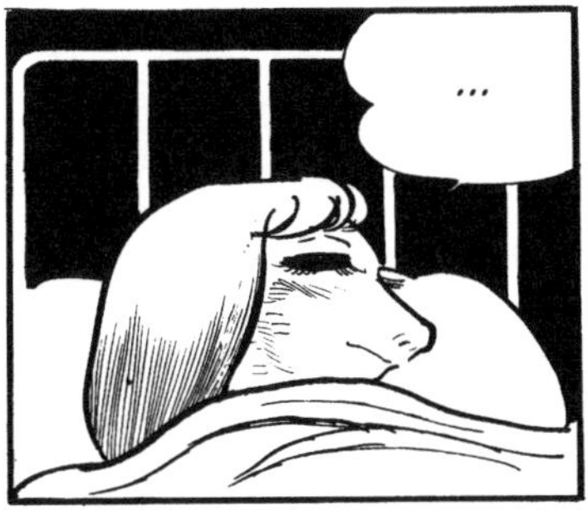
...

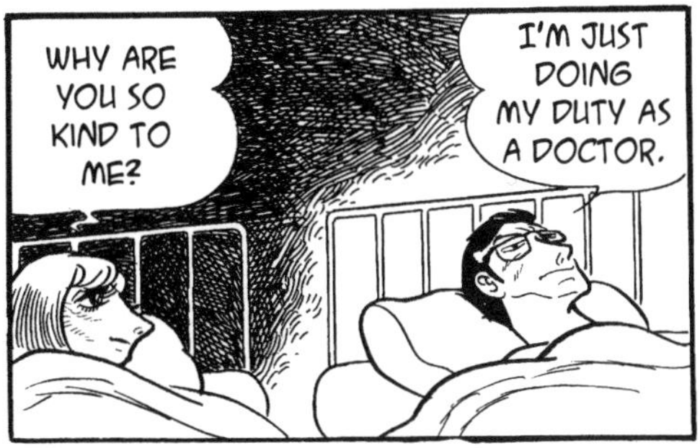
WHY ARE YOU SO KIND TO ME?
I'M JUST DOING MY DUTY AS A DOCTOR.

CHAPTER 6

PALACE OF FOLLIES

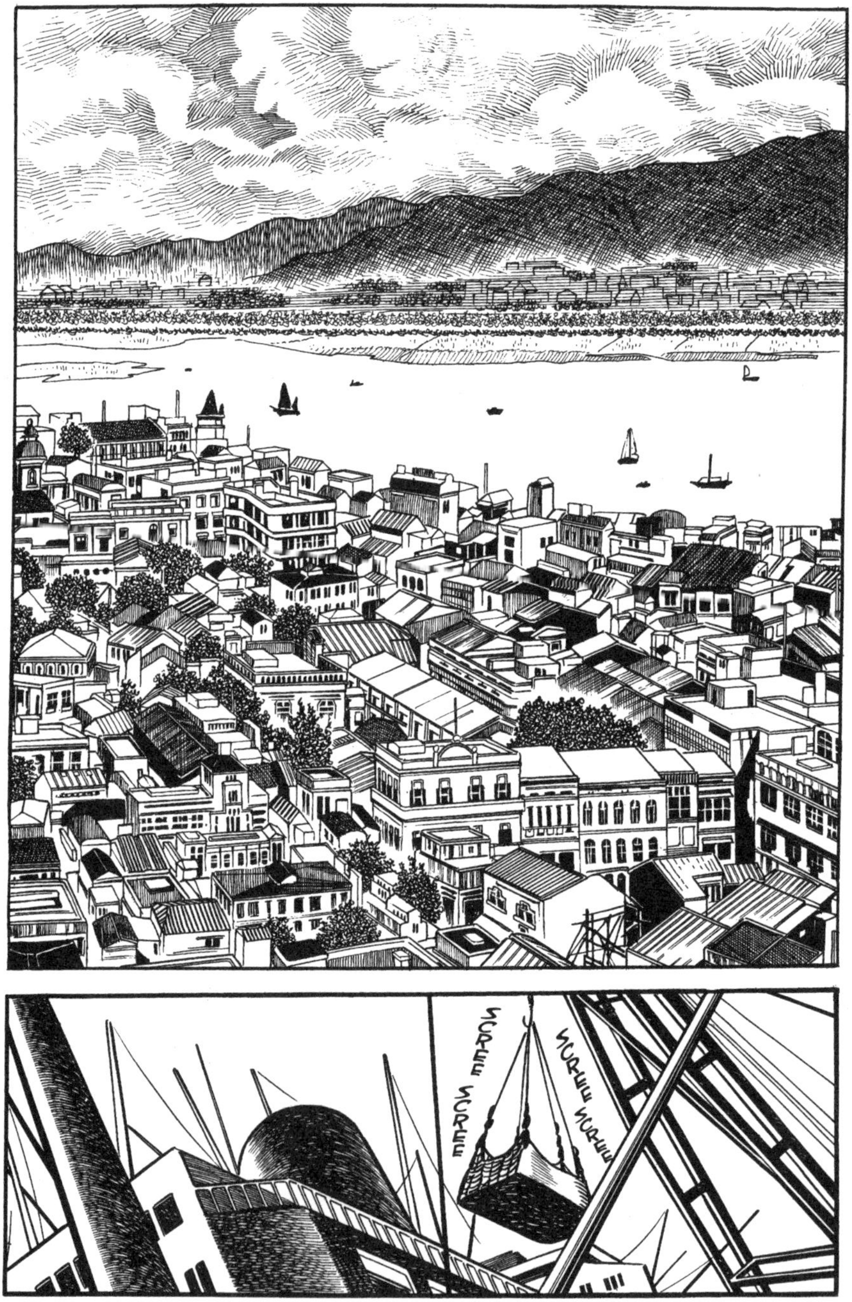
SCREE SCREE
SCREE SCREE

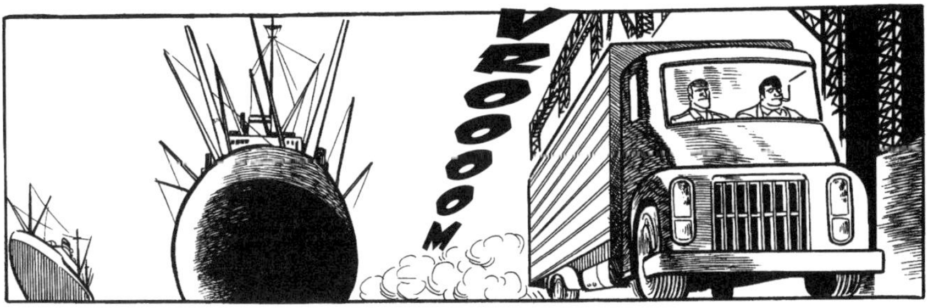
VROOOOM

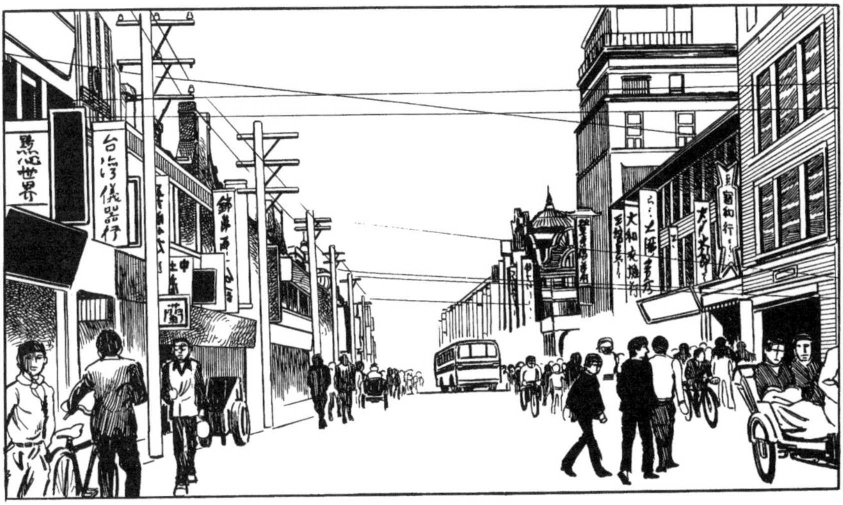

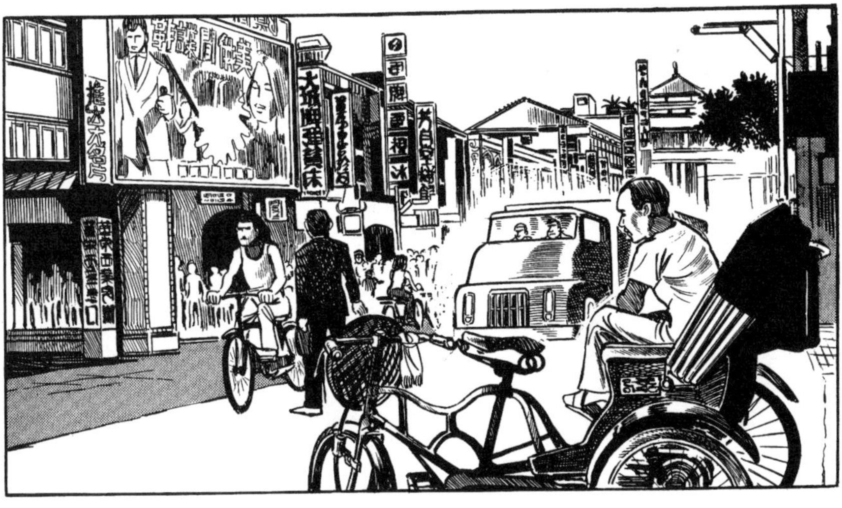

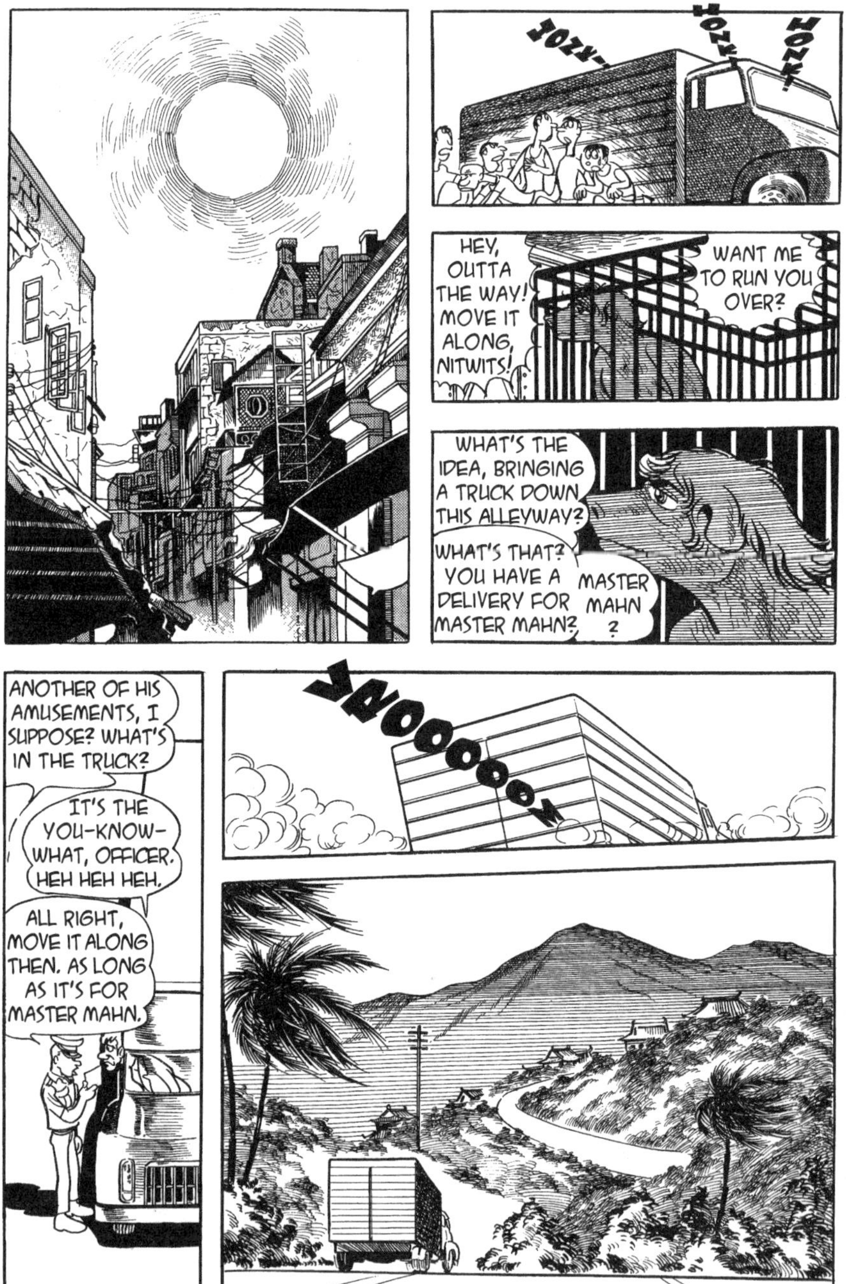
HONK!
HONK!
HEY, OUTTA THE WAY! MOVE IT ALONG, NITWITS!
WANT ME TO RUN YOU OVER?
WHAT'S THE IDEA, BRINGING A TRUCK DOWN THIS ALLEYWAY?
WHAT'S THAT? YOU HAVE A DELIVERY FOR MASTER MAHN?
MASTER MAHN ?
ANOTHER OF HIS AMUSEMENTS, I SUPPOSE? WHAT'S IN THE TRUCK?
IT'S THE YOU-KNOW-WHAT, OFFICER. HEH HEH HEH.
ALL RIGHT, MOVE IT ALONG THEN. AS LONG AS IT'S FOR MASTER MAHN.

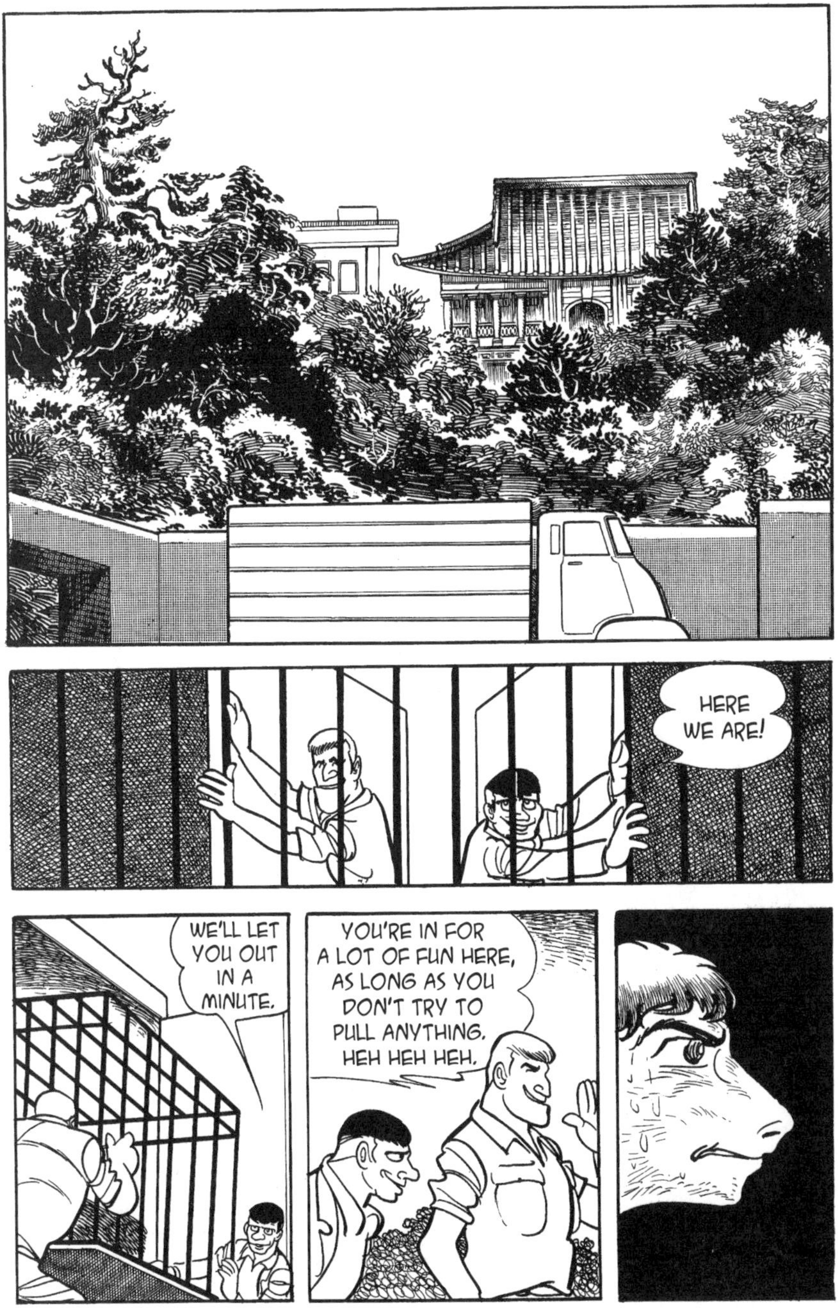
HERE WE ARE!
WE'LL LET YOU OUT IN A MINUTE.
YOU'RE IN FOR A LOT OF FUN HERE, AS LONG AS YOU DON'T TRY TO PULL ANYTHING. HEH HEH HEH.

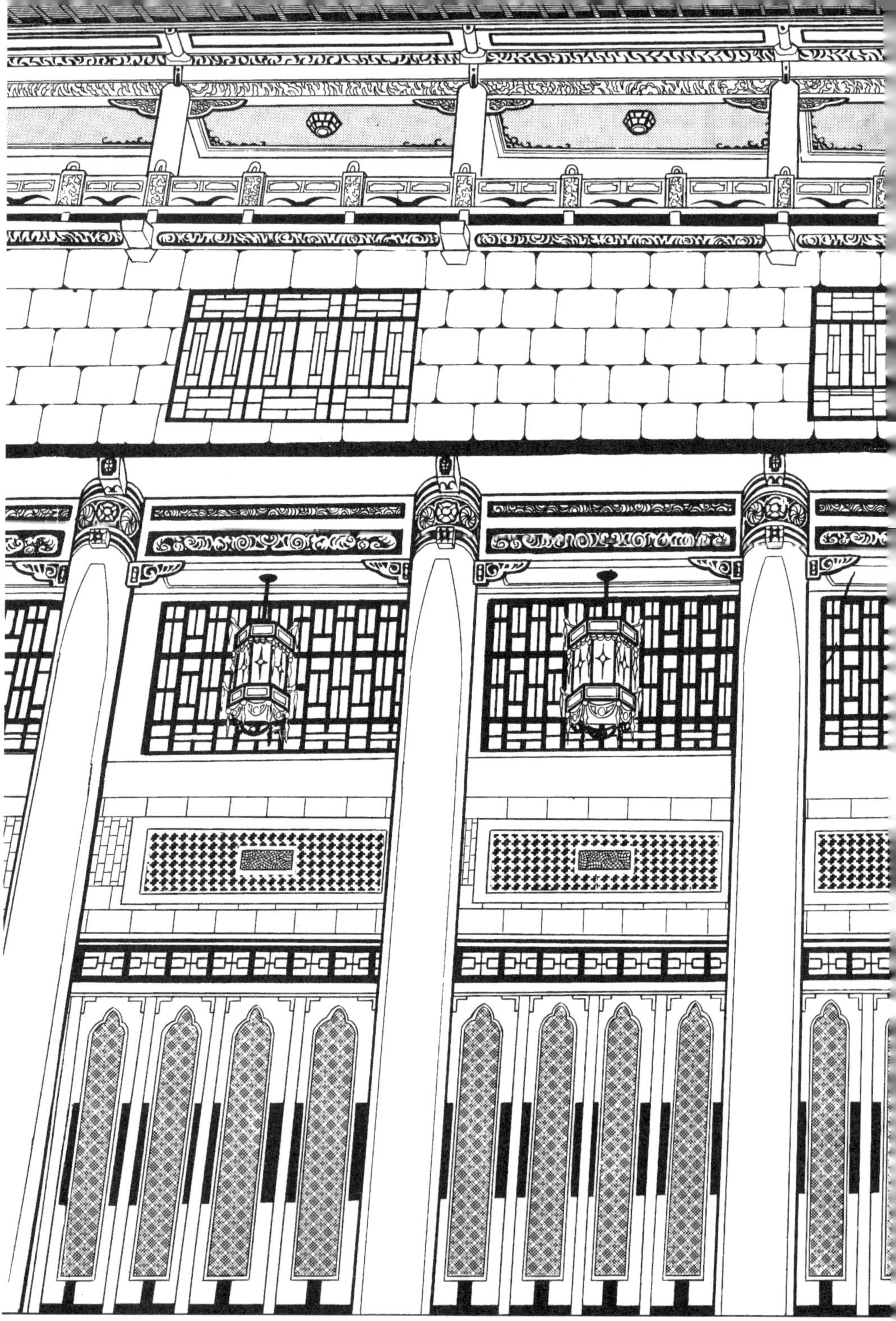

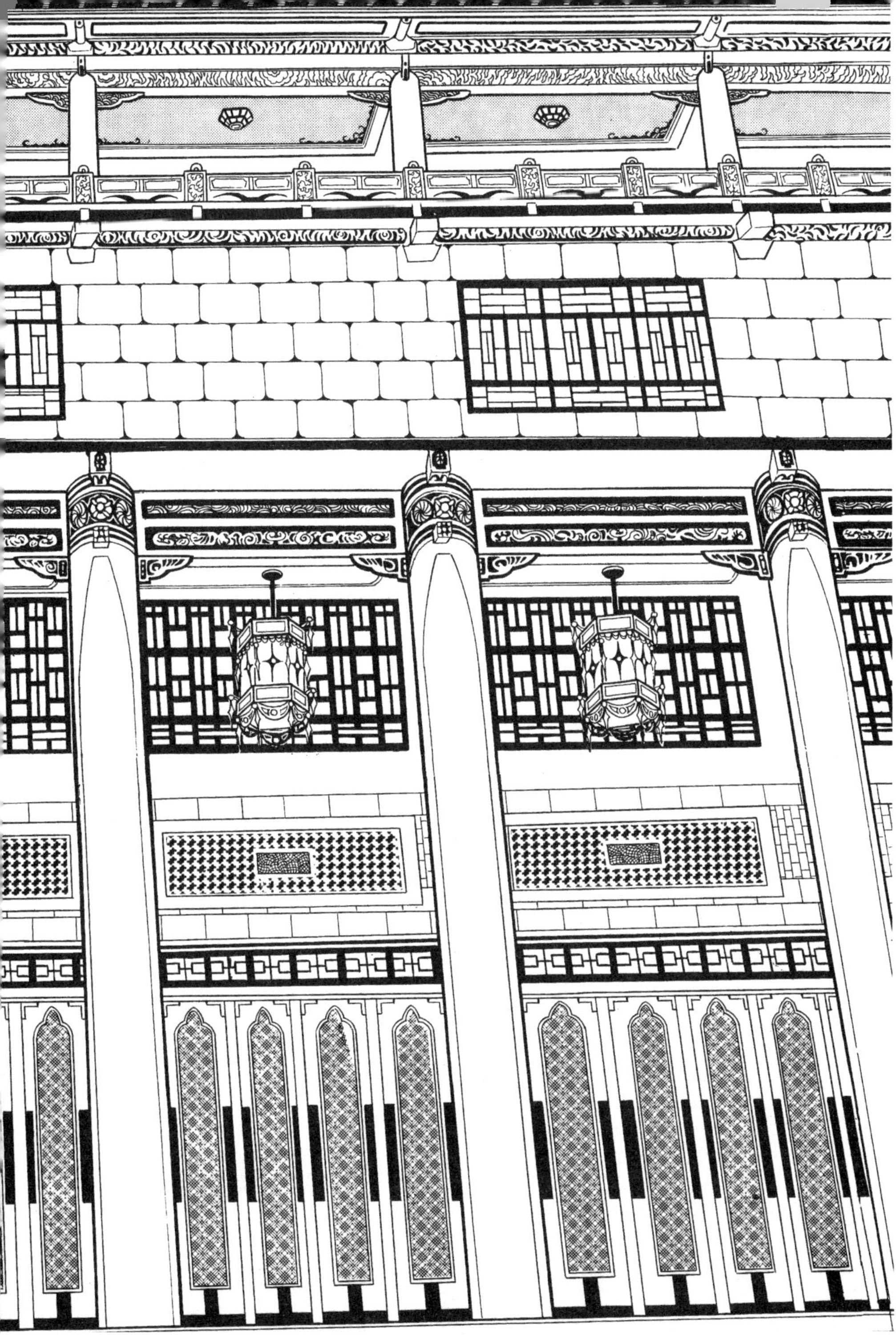

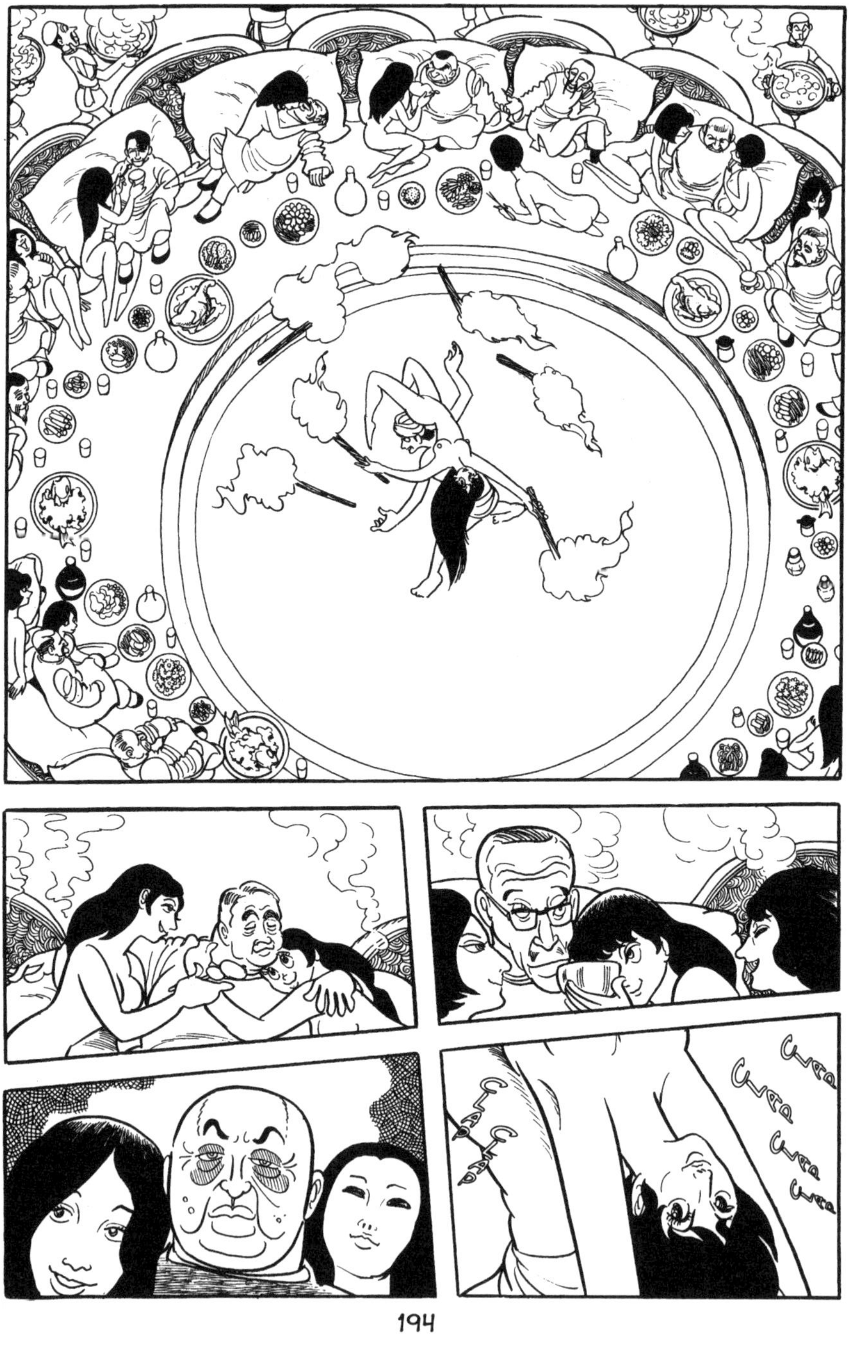
CLAP
CLAP

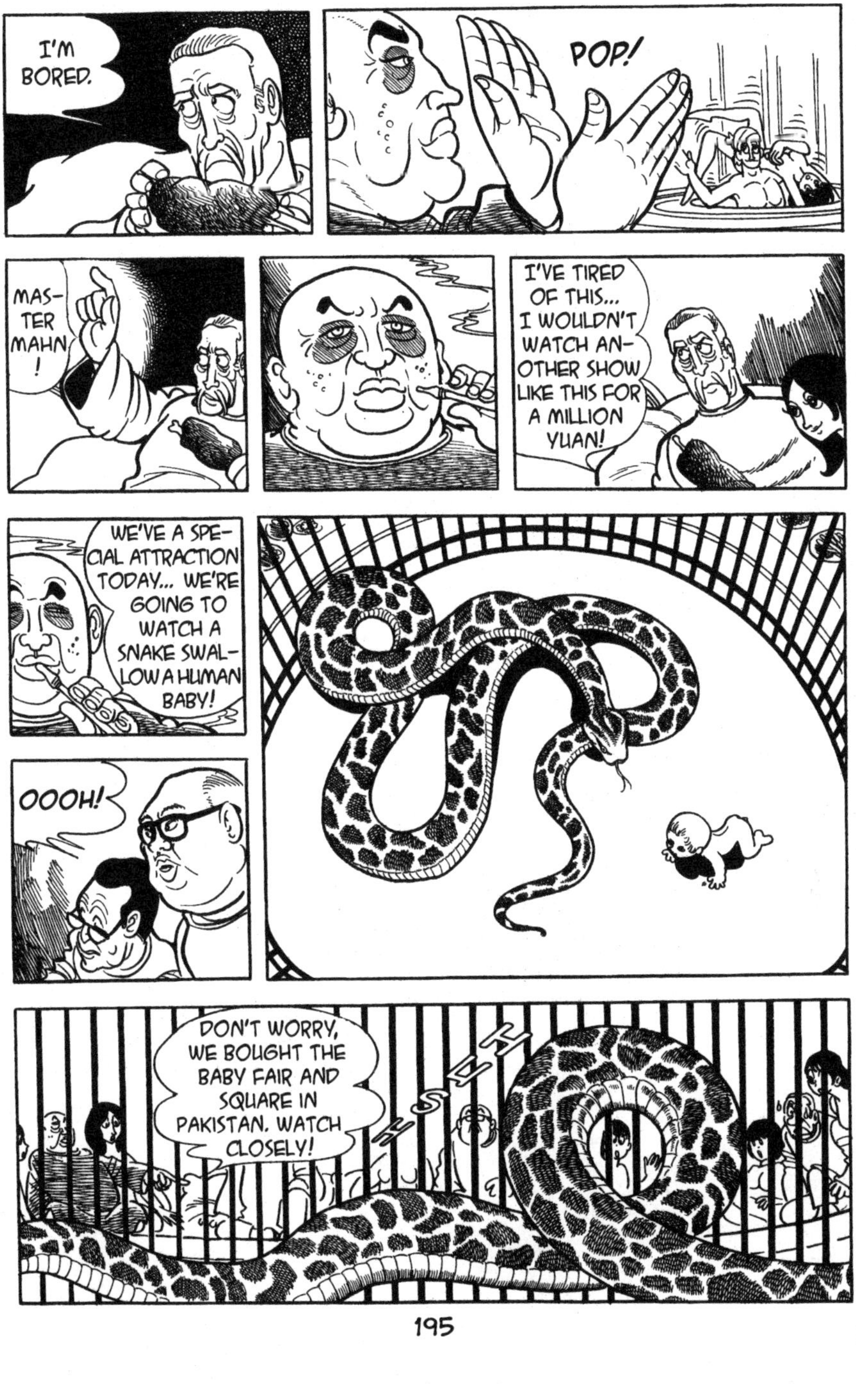
I'M BORED.
POP!
MAS-TER MAHN!
I'VE TIRED OF THIS... I WOULDN'T WATCH AN-OTHER SHOW LIKE THIS FOR A MILLION YUAN!
WE'VE A SPE-CIAL ATTRACTION TODAY... WE'RE GOING TO WATCH A SNAKE SWAL-LOW A HUMAN BABY!
OOOH!
DON'T WORRY, WE BOUGHT THE BABY FAIR AND SQUARE IN PAKISTAN. WATCH CLOSELY!
HSSH

SOB!

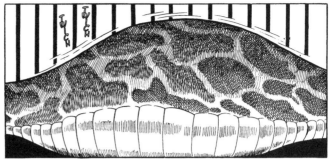

BORING! ALL YOU NEED IS MONEY TO BUY A SNAKE AND A BABY. I WANT TO SEE SOMETHING THAT EVEN MONEY CAN'T BUY!

HAH HAH HAH. FINE, NEXT WEEK I'LL SHOW YOU SOMETHING FROM JAPAN THAT'LL KNOCK YOU OFF YOUR FEET!

ARE YOU REALLY HUMAN? CAN YOU SPEAK? I SPEAK JAPANESE. IT'S BEST NOT TO MAKE TROUBLE HERE.

HAVE I BEEN SOLD INTO SLAVERY?

MASTER MAHN HAS A VAST FORTUNE OF HUNDREDS OF THOUSANDS OF YUAN. HE HAS EVERYTHING HE DESIRES.

AND WHAT DOES HE DO HERE IN THIS PALACE?

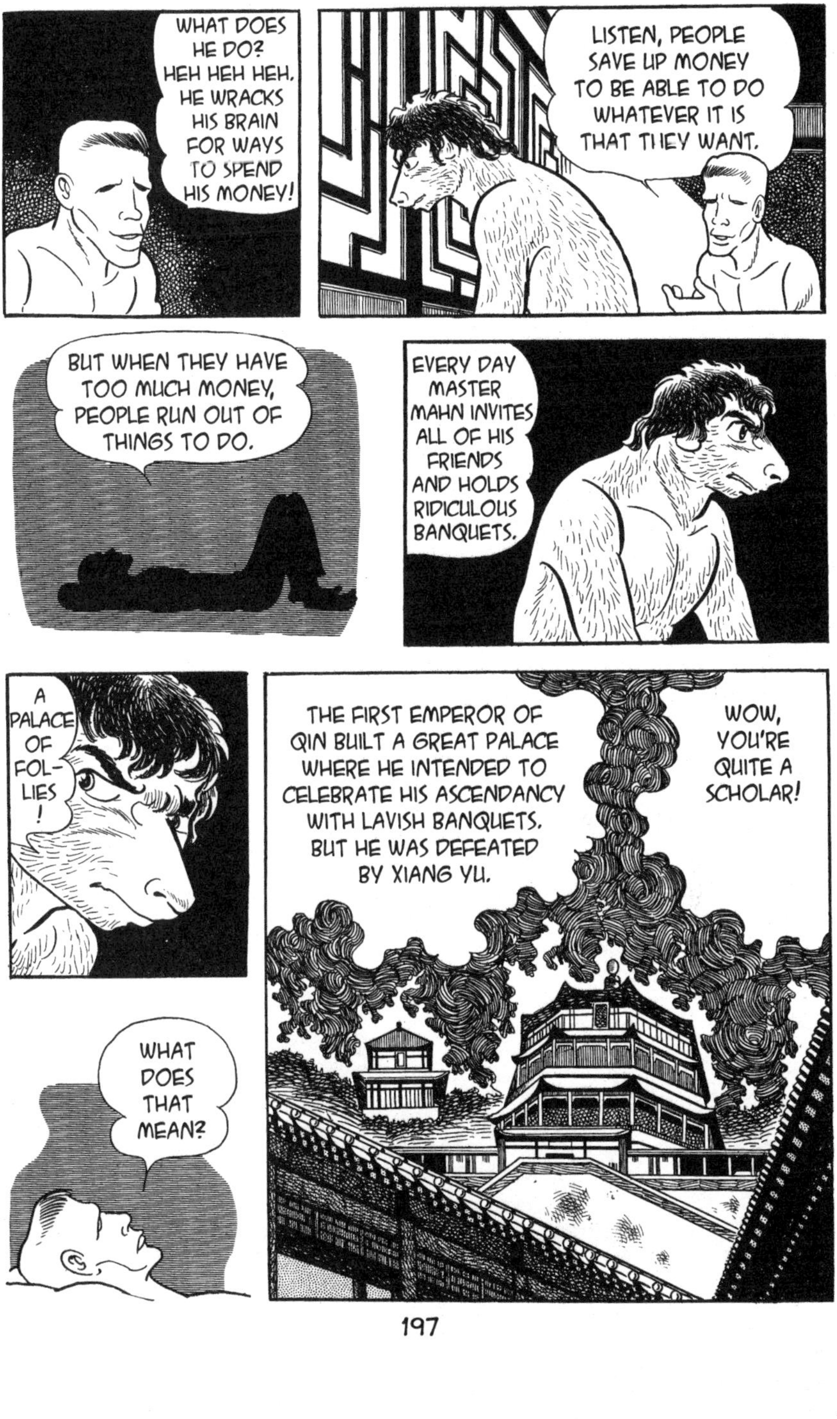

WHAT DOES HE DO? HEH HEH HEH. HE WRACKS HIS BRAIN FOR WAYS TO SPEND HIS MONEY!
LISTEN, PEOPLE SAVE UP MONEY TO BE ABLE TO DO WHATEVER IT IS THAT THEY WANT.
BUT WHEN THEY HAVE TOO MUCH MONEY, PEOPLE RUN OUT OF THINGS TO DO.
EVERY DAY MASTER MAHN INVITES ALL OF HIS FRIENDS AND HOLDS RIDICULOUS BANQUETS.
A PALACE OF FOL-LIES!
WHAT DOES THAT MEAN?
THE FIRST EMPEROR OF QIN BUILT A GREAT PALACE WHERE HE INTENDED TO CELEBRATE HIS ASCENDANCY WITH LAVISH BANQUETS. BUT HE WAS DEFEATED BY XIANG YU.
WOW, YOU'RE QUITE A SCHOLAR!

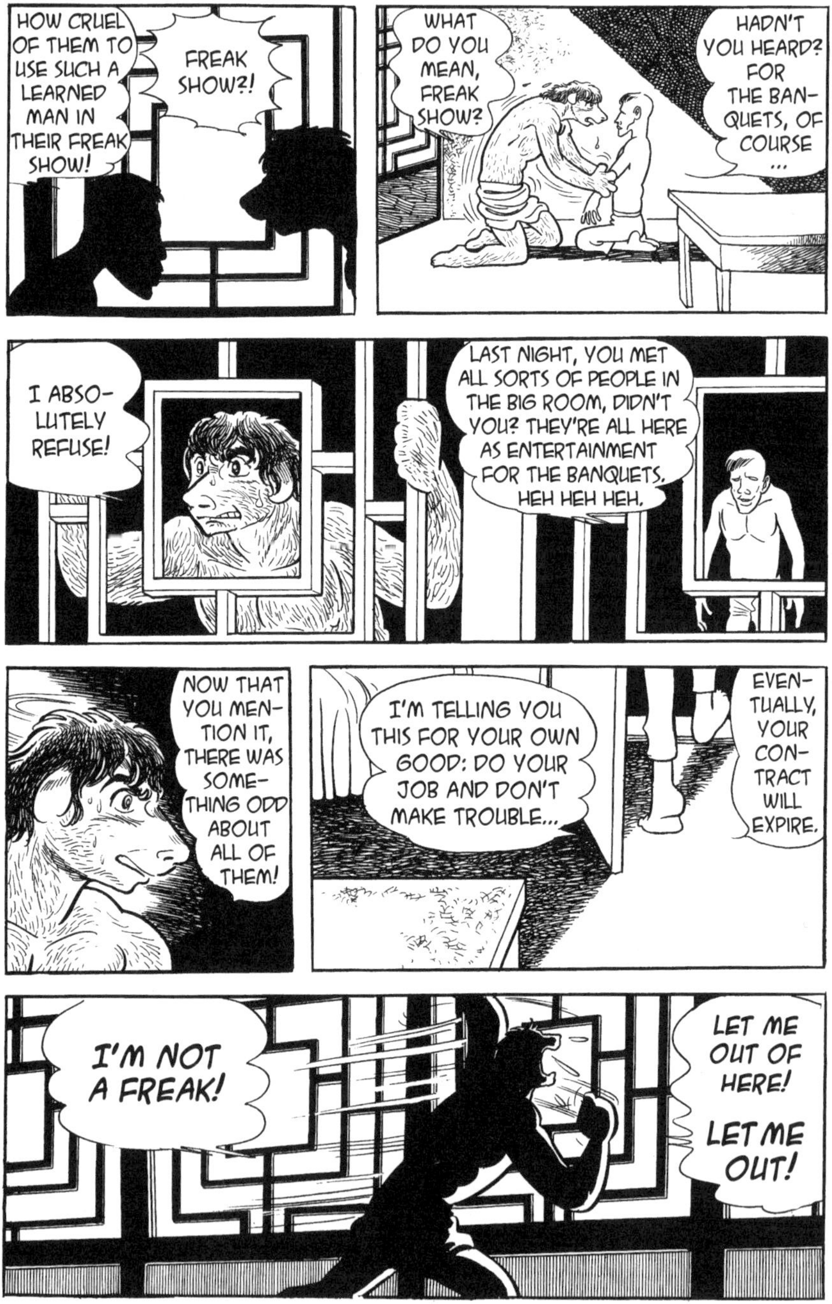

HOW CRUEL OF THEM TO USE SUCH A LEARNED MAN IN THEIR FREAK SHOW!
FREAK SHOW?!
WHAT DO YOU MEAN, FREAK SHOW?
HADN'T YOU HEARD? FOR THE BANQUETS, OF COURSE ...
I ABSOLUTELY REFUSE!
LAST NIGHT, YOU MET ALL SORTS OF PEOPLE IN THE BIG ROOM, DIDN'T YOU? THEY'RE ALL HERE AS ENTERTAINMENT FOR THE BANQUETS. HEH HEH HEH.
NOW THAT YOU MENTION IT, THERE WAS SOMETHING ODD ABOUT ALL OF THEM!
I'M TELLING YOU THIS FOR YOUR OWN GOOD: DO YOUR JOB AND DON'T MAKE TROUBLE...
EVENTUALLY, YOUR CONTRACT WILL EXPIRE.
I'M NOT A FREAK!
LET ME OUT OF HERE!
LET ME OUT!

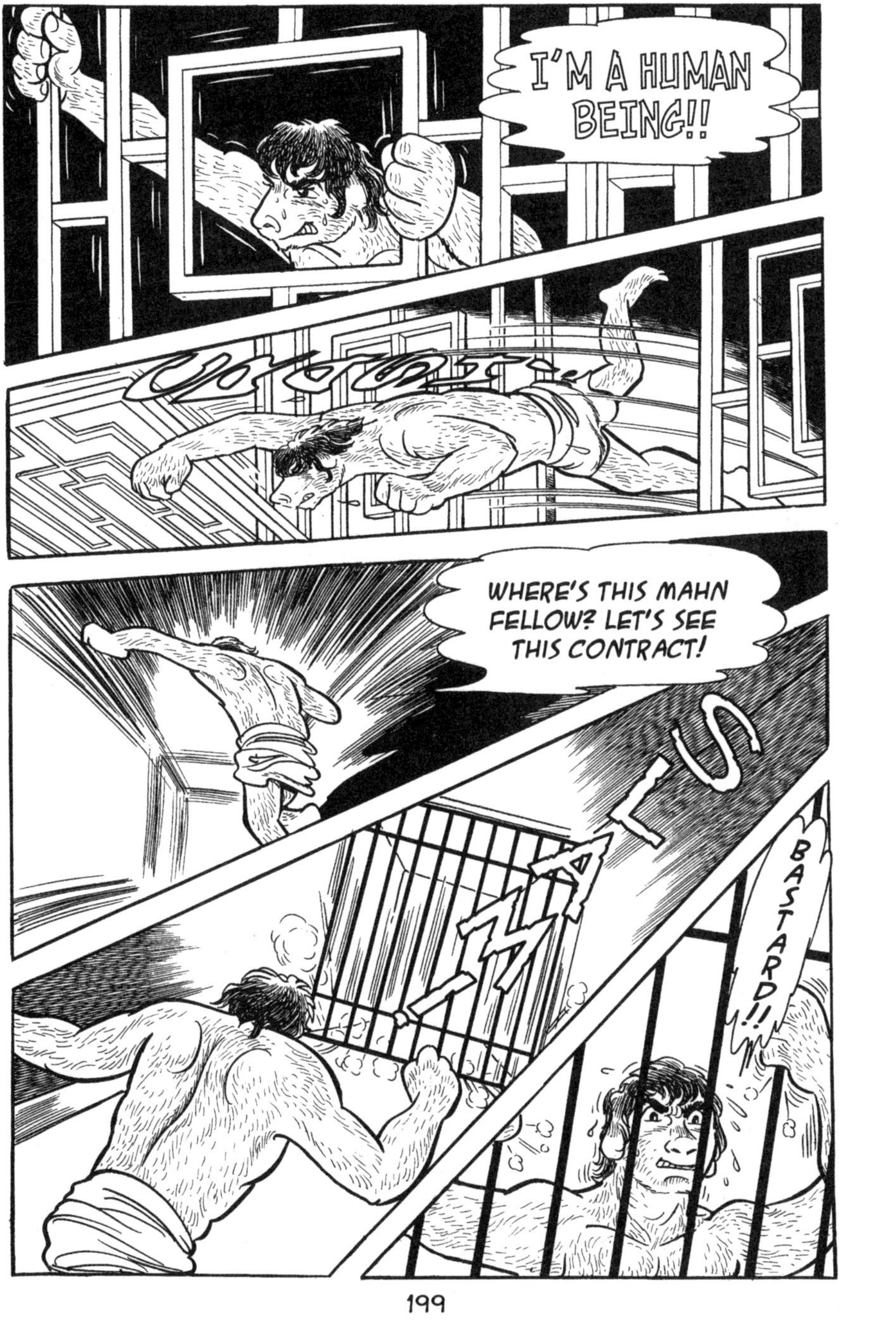
I'M A HUMAN BEING!!
WHERE'S THIS MAHN FELLOW? LET'S SEE THIS CONTRACT!
SMASH
BASTARD!!

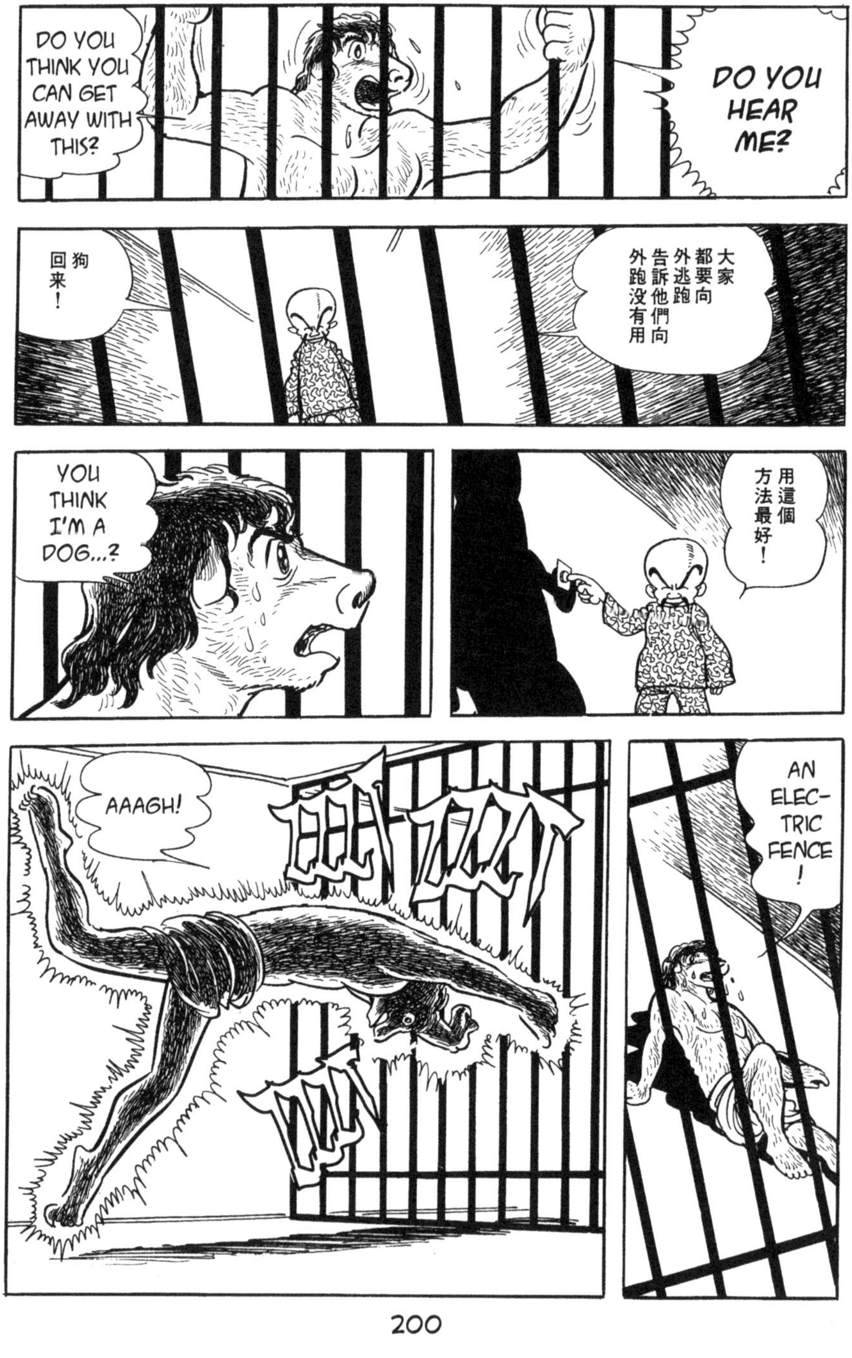
DO YOU THINK YOU CAN GET AWAY WITH THIS?
DO YOU HEAR ME?
大家都要向外逃跑告訴他們向外跑沒有用
狗回来！
YOU THINK I'M A DOG...?
用這個方法最好！
AAAGH!
AN ELEC-TRIC FENCE!

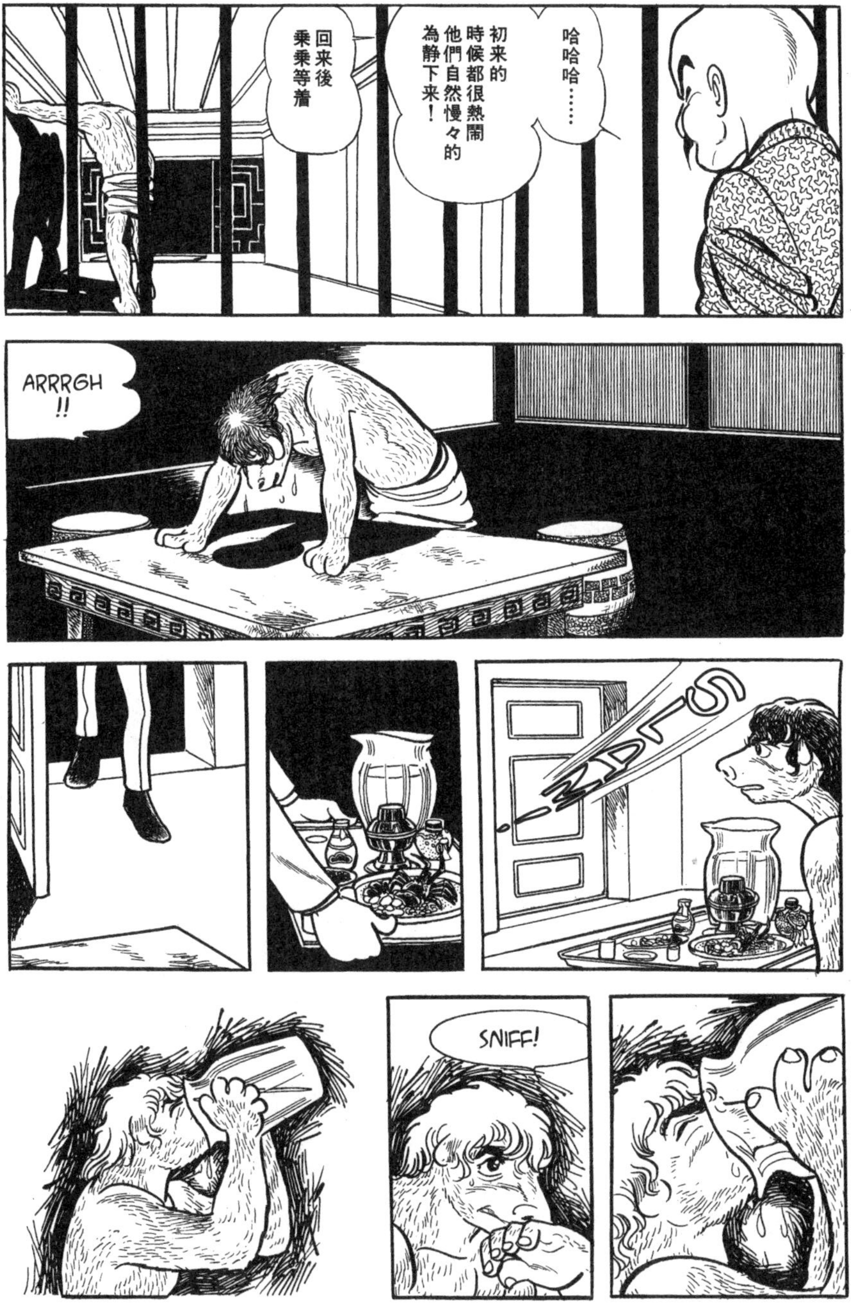
哈哈哈……
初来的時候都很熱鬧他們自然慢々的為静下来！
回来後乘乘等着
ARRRGH !!
SNIFF!

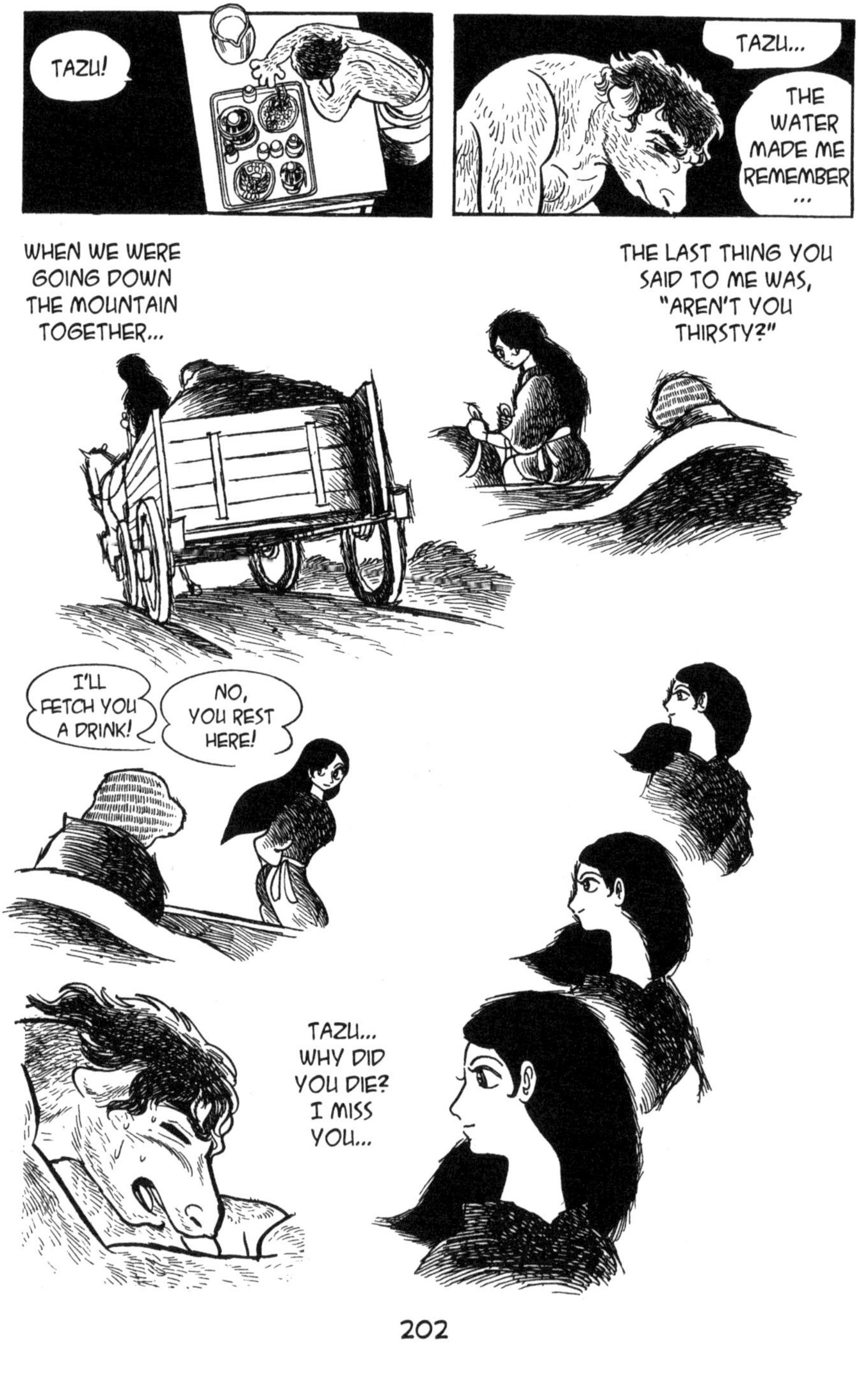
TAZU!
TAZU...
THE WATER MADE ME REMEMBER ...
WHEN WE WERE GOING DOWN THE MOUNTAIN TOGETHER...
THE LAST THING YOU SAID TO ME WAS, "AREN'T YOU THIRSTY?"
I'LL FETCH YOU A DRINK!
NO, YOU REST HERE!
TAZU... WHY DID YOU DIE? I MISS YOU...

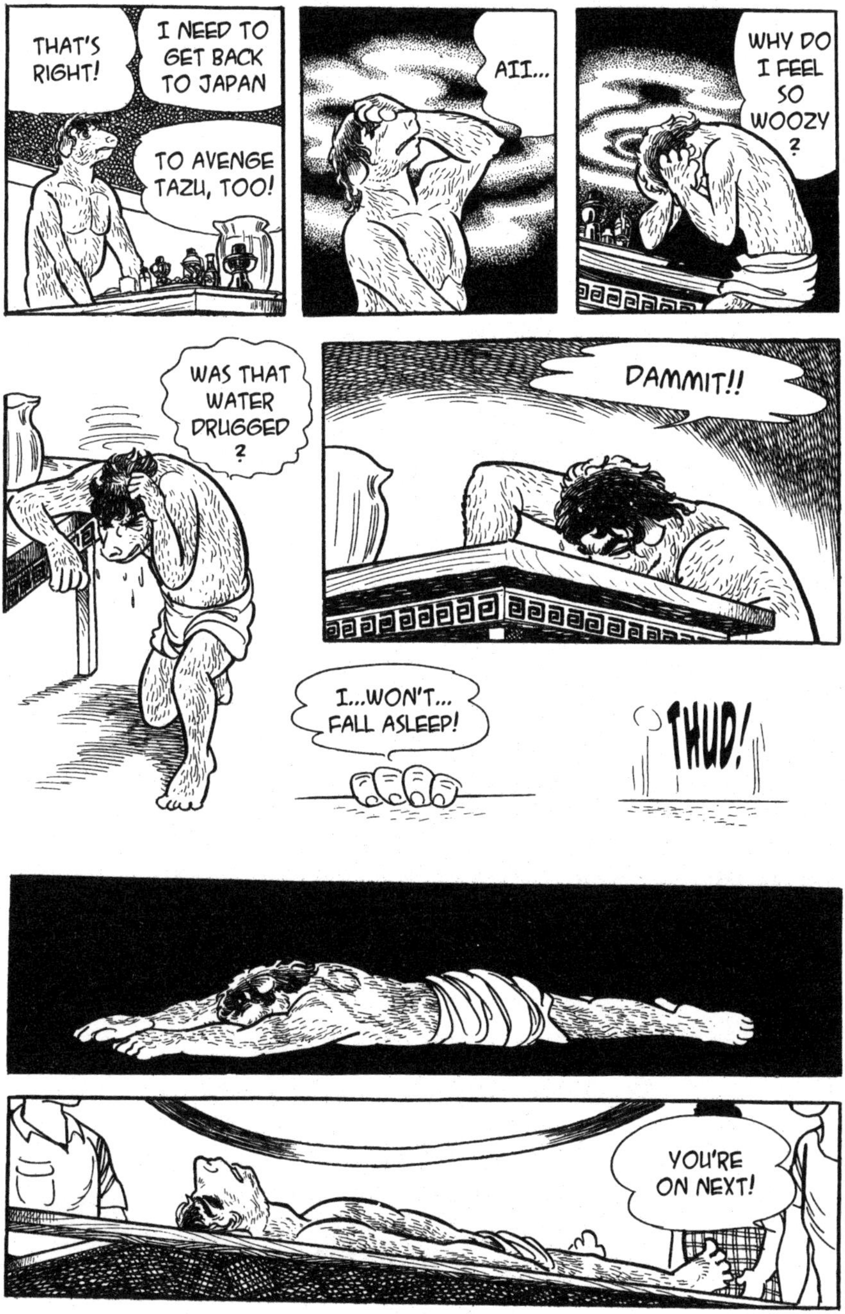
THAT'S RIGHT!
I NEED TO GET BACK TO JAPAN
TO AVENGE TAZU, TOO!
AII...
WHY DO I FEEL SO WOOZY ?
WAS THAT WATER DRUGGED ?
DAMMIT!!
I...WON'T... FALL ASLEEP!
THUD!
YOU'RE ON NEXT!

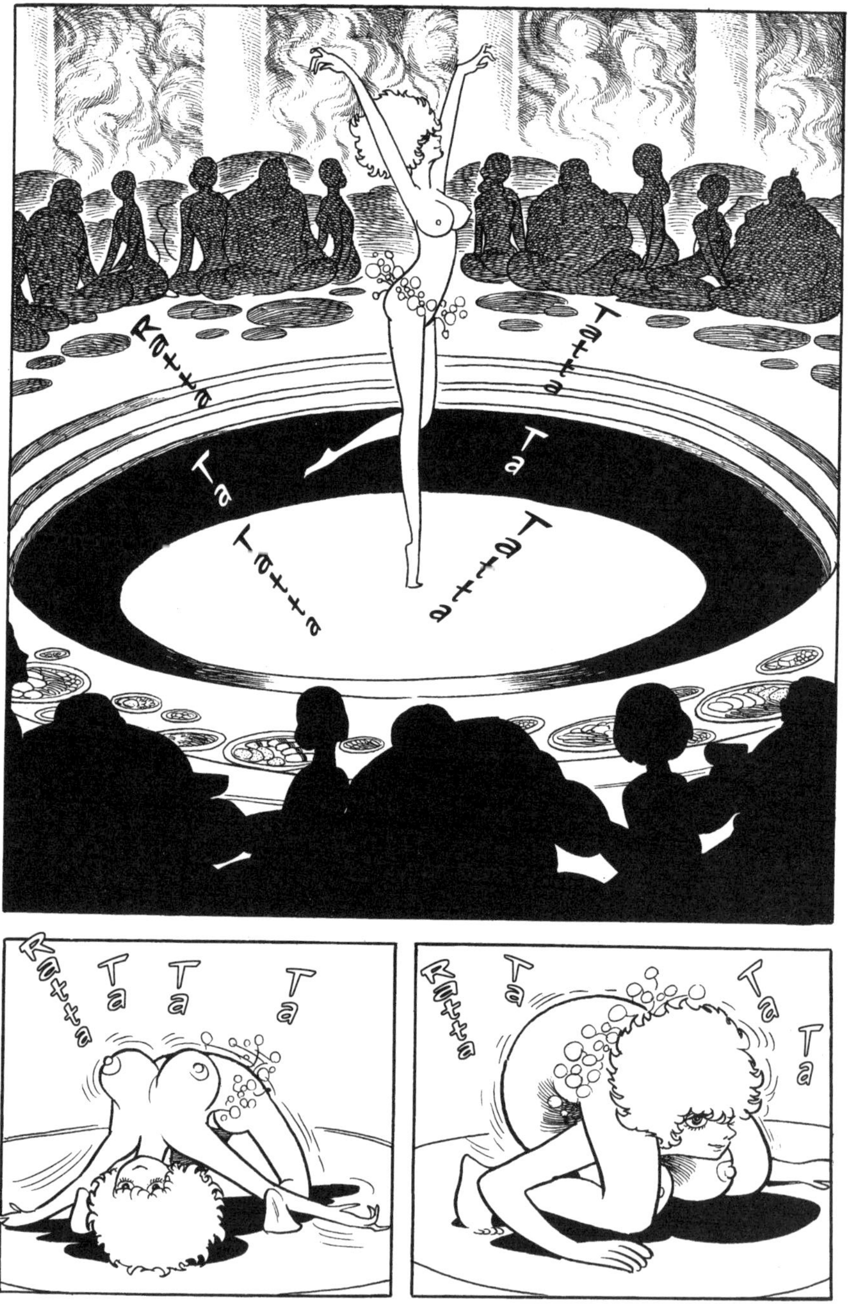
Ratta
Tatta
Ta
Ta
Tatta
Tatta
Ratta
Ta
Ta
Ta
Ratta
Ta
Ta
Ta

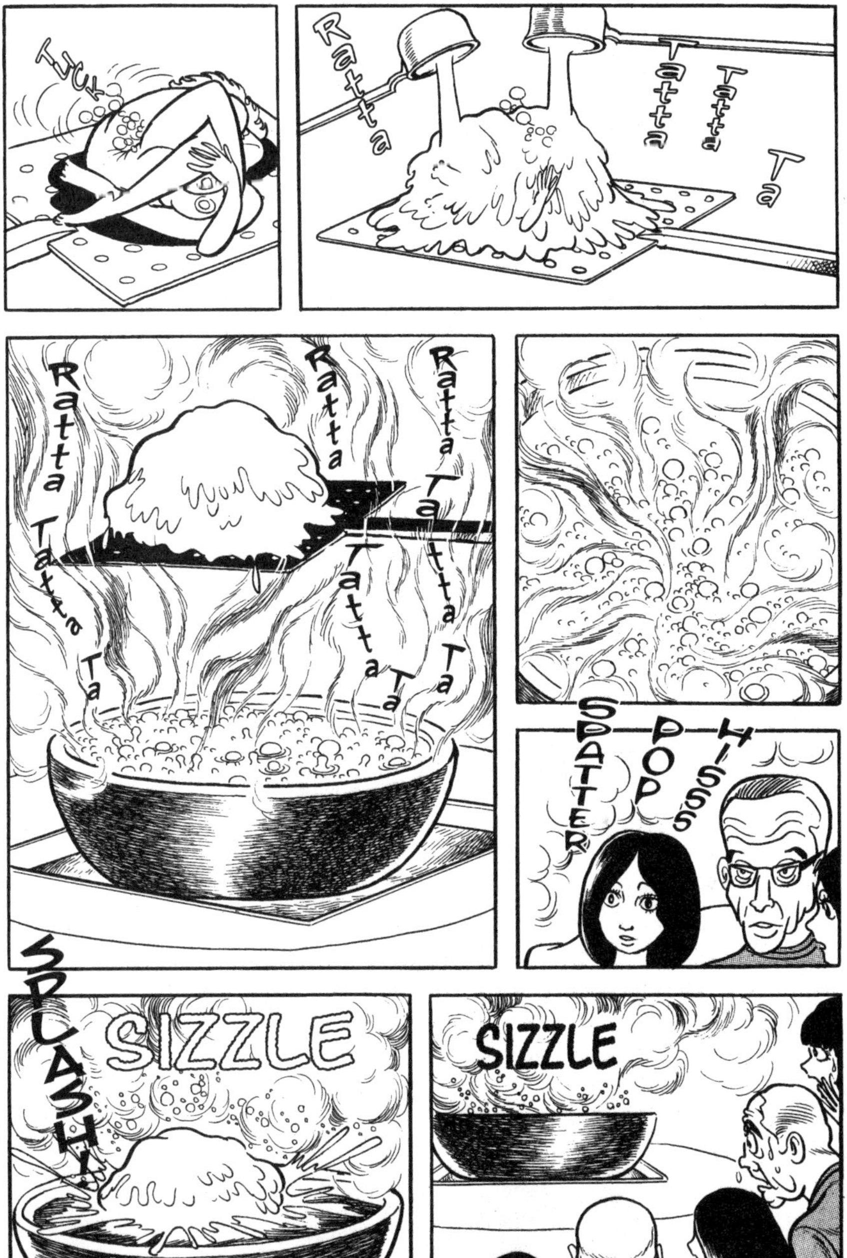
TUCK
Ratta
Tatta
Tatta
Ta
Ratta Tatta Ta
Ratta Tatta Ta
Ratta Tatta Ta
SPATTER
POP
HISSS
SPLASH!
SIZZLE
SIZZLE

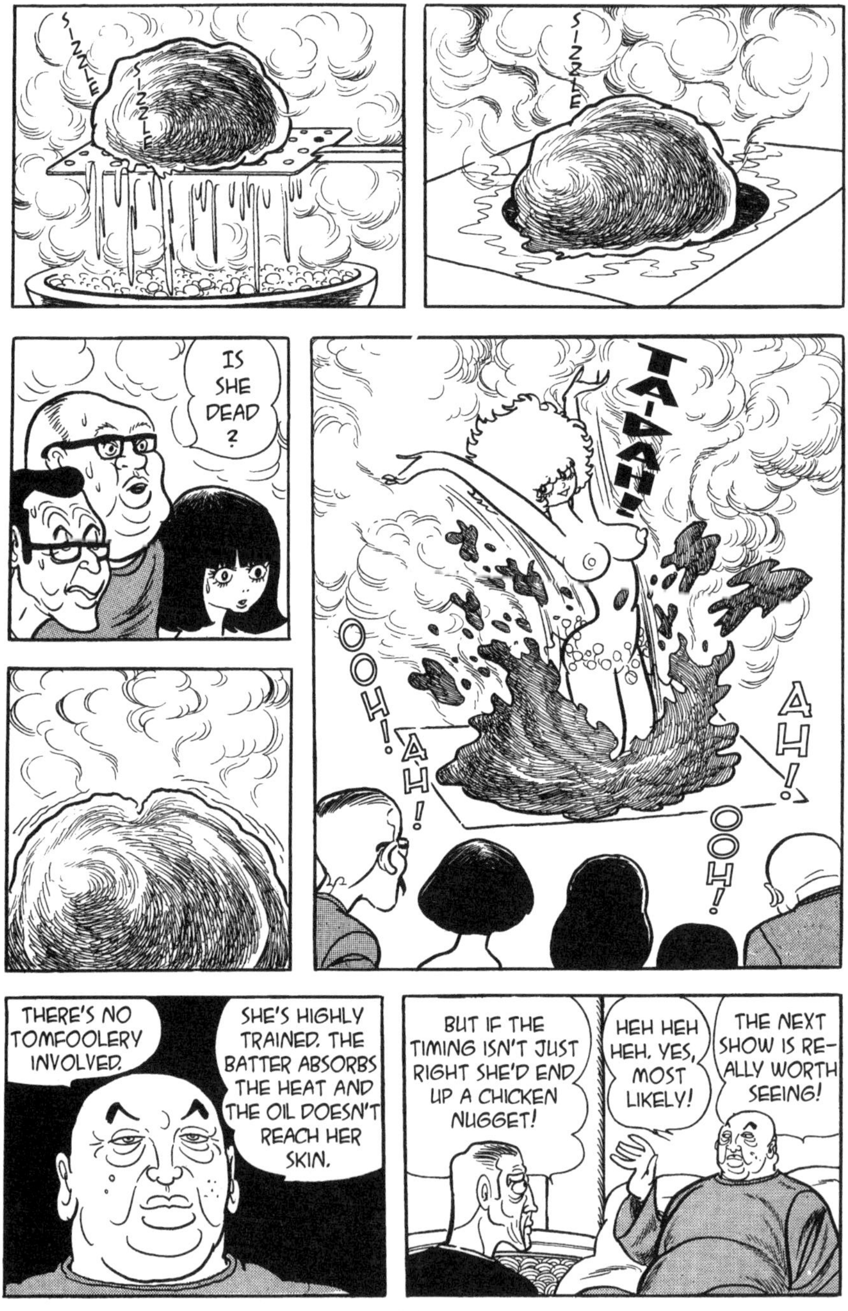
SIZZLE
SIZZLE
SIZZLE
IS SHE DEAD?
TA-DAH!
OOOH! AH!
AH! OOOH!
THERE'S NO TOMFOOLERY INVOLVED.
SHE'S HIGHLY TRAINED. THE BATTER ABSORBS THE HEAT AND THE OIL DOESN'T REACH HER SKIN.
BUT IF THE TIMING ISN'T JUST RIGHT SHE'D END UP A CHICKEN NUGGET!
HEH HEH HEH. YES, MOST LIKELY!
THE NEXT SHOW IS REALLY WORTH SEEING!

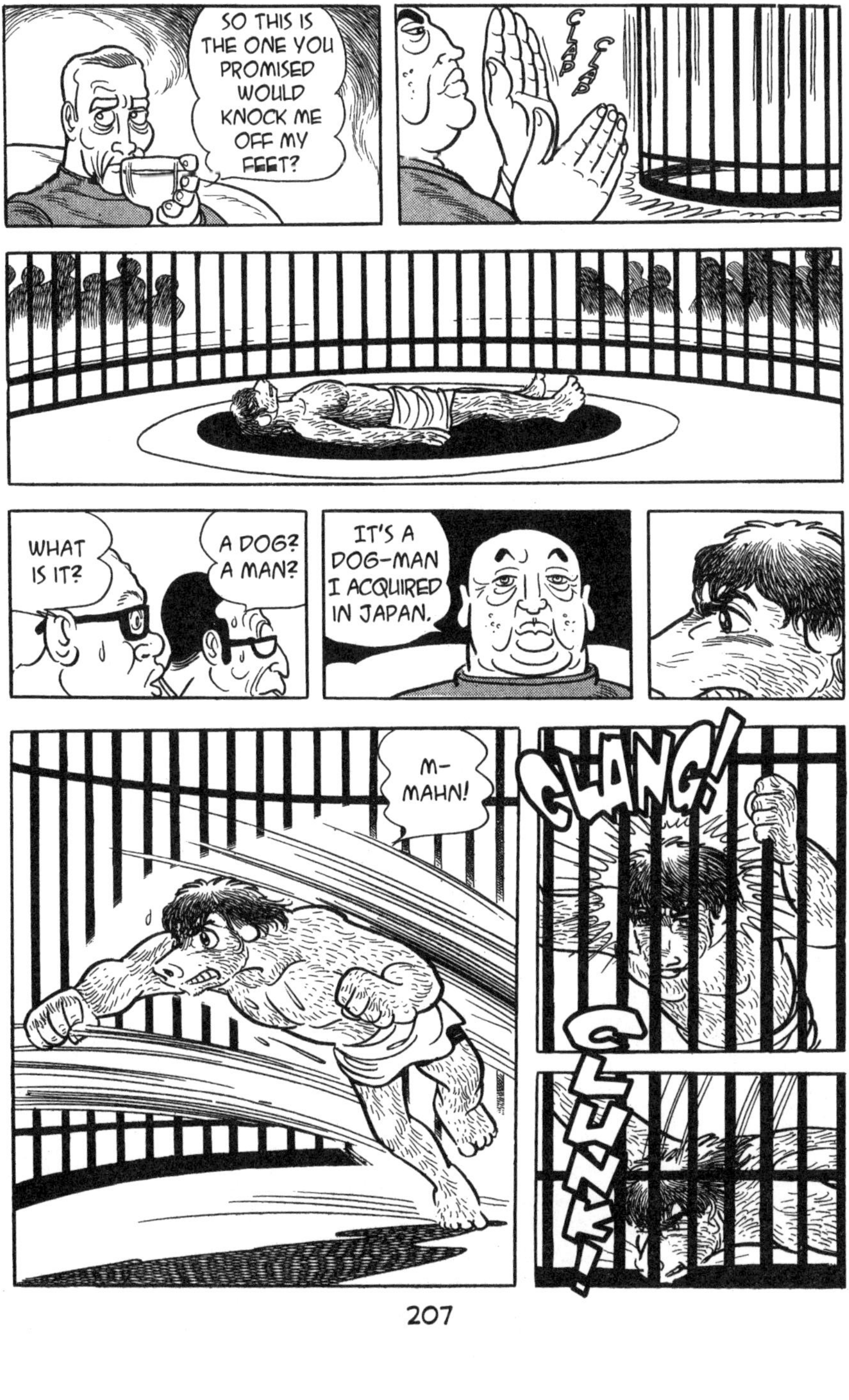

SO THIS IS THE ONE YOU PROMISED WOULD KNOCK ME OFF MY FEET?
CLAP CLAP
WHAT IS IT?
A DOG? A MAN?
IT'S A DOG-MAN I ACQUIRED IN JAPAN.
M-MAHN!
CLANG!
CLUNK!

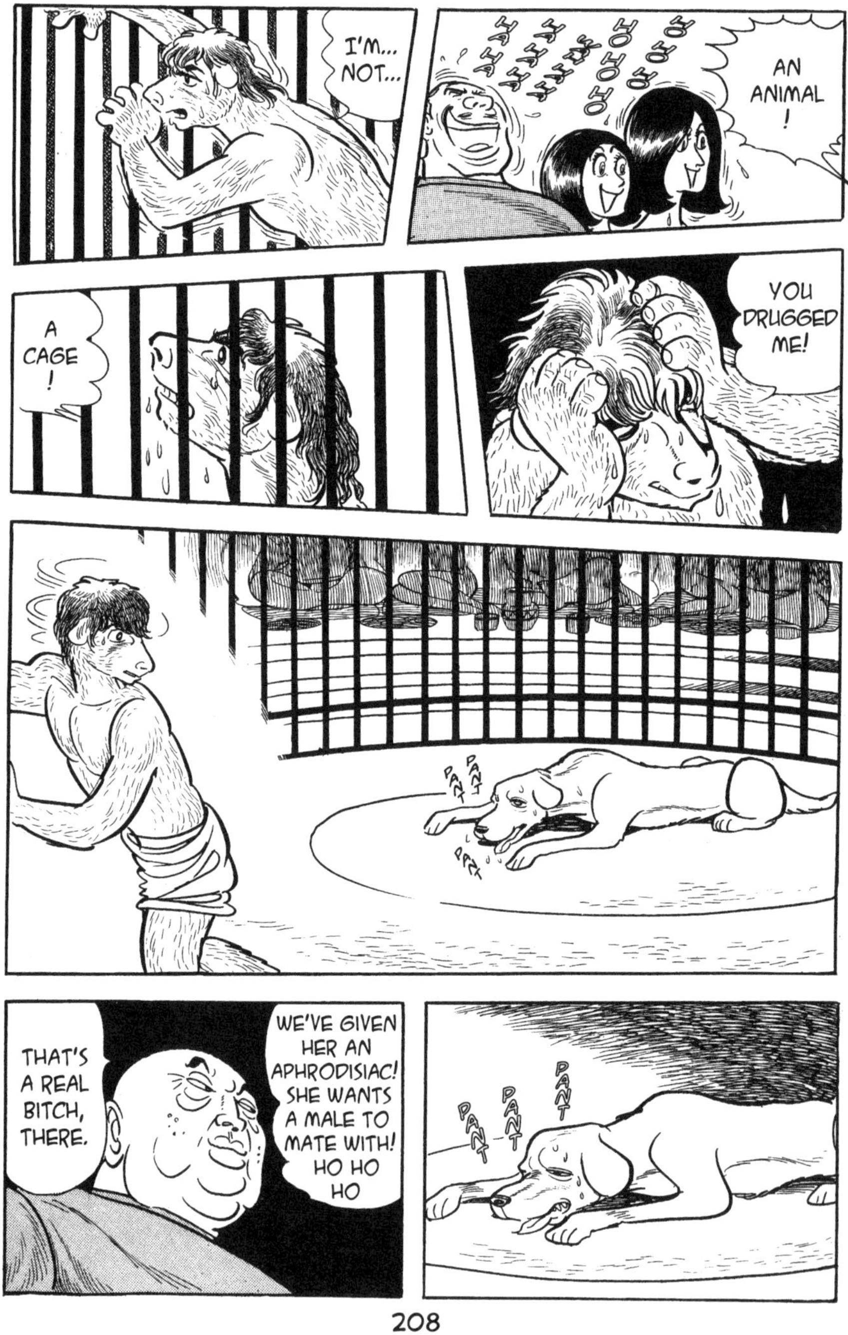
I'M... NOT...
HOHOHO
HOHOHO
HAHAHA
HAHA
AN ANIMAL!
A CAGE!
YOU DRUGGED ME!
PANT PANT
PANT
THAT'S A REAL BITCH, THERE.
WE'VE GIVEN HER AN APHRODISIAC! SHE WANTS A MALE TO MATE WITH! HO HO HO
PANT
PANT
PANT

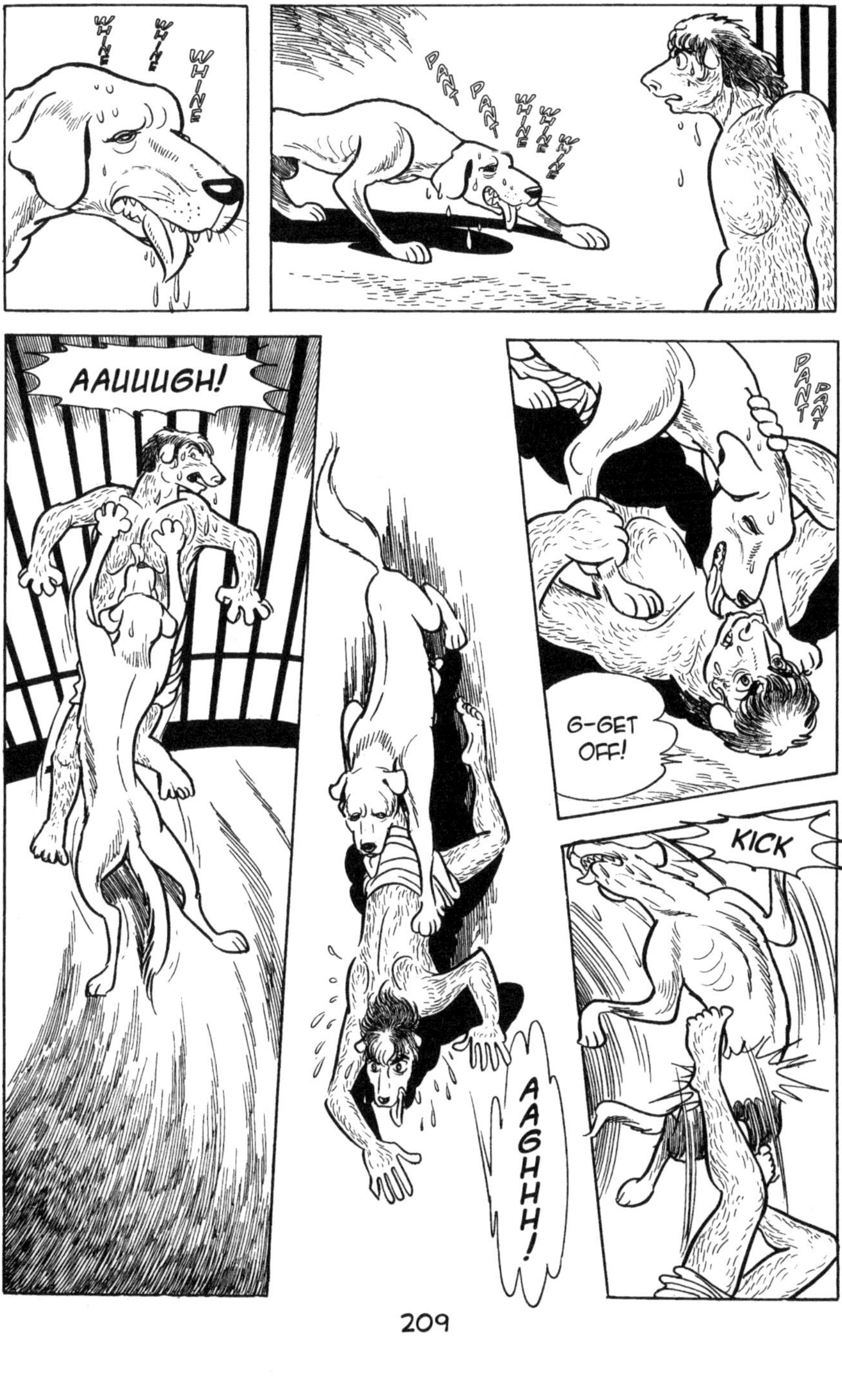
WHINE
WHINE
WHINE
PANT
PANT
WHINE
WHINE
WHINE
AAUUUGH!
PANT
PANT
G-GET OFF!
AAGHHH!
KICK

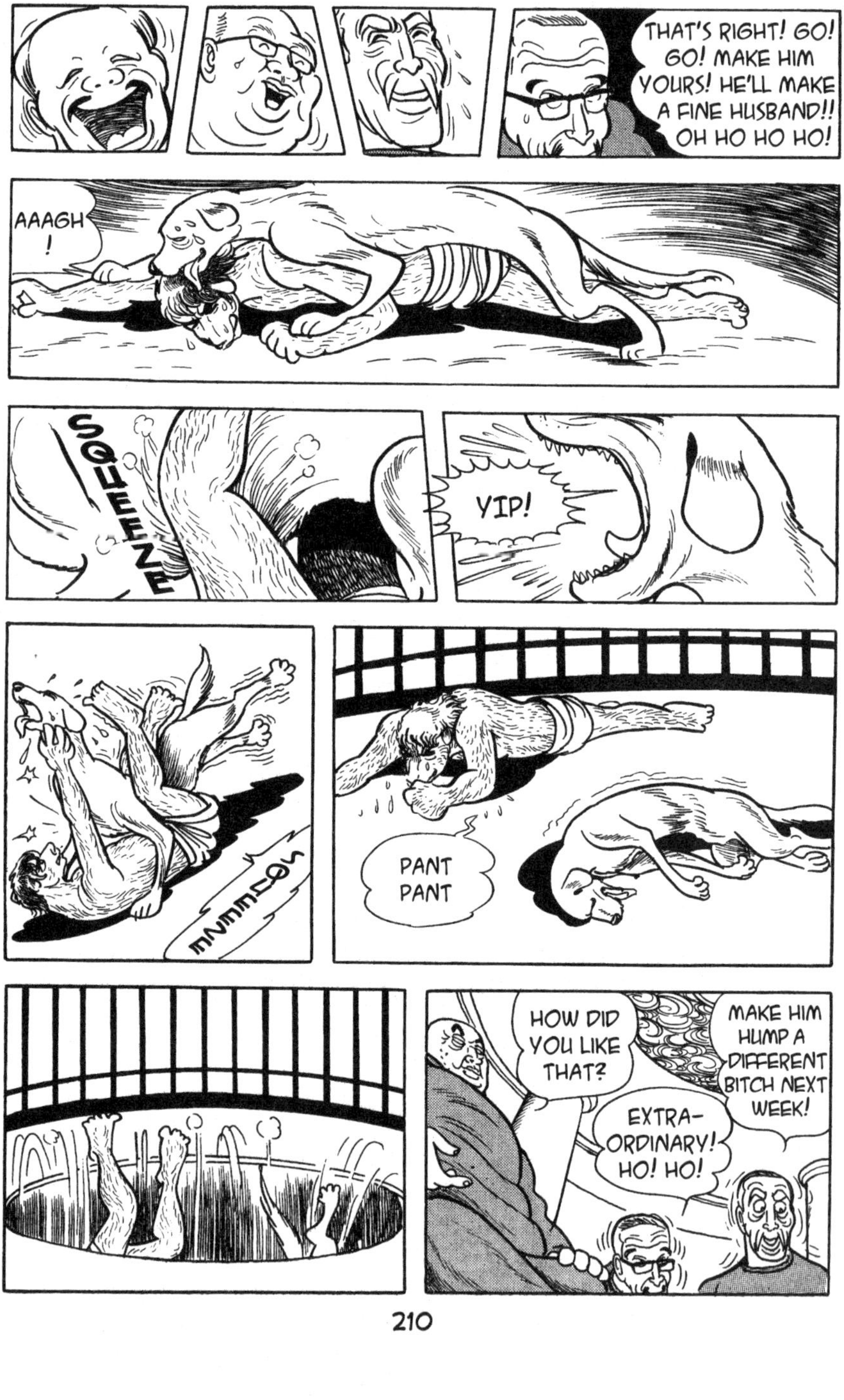
THAT'S RIGHT! GO! GO! MAKE HIM YOURS! HE'LL MAKE A FINE HUSBAND!! OH HO HO HO!
AAAGH !
SQUEEZE
YIP!
SQUEEEZE
PANT PANT
HOW DID YOU LIKE THAT?
MAKE HIM HUMP A DIFFERENT BITCH NEXT WEEK!
EXTRA-ORDINARY! HO! HO!

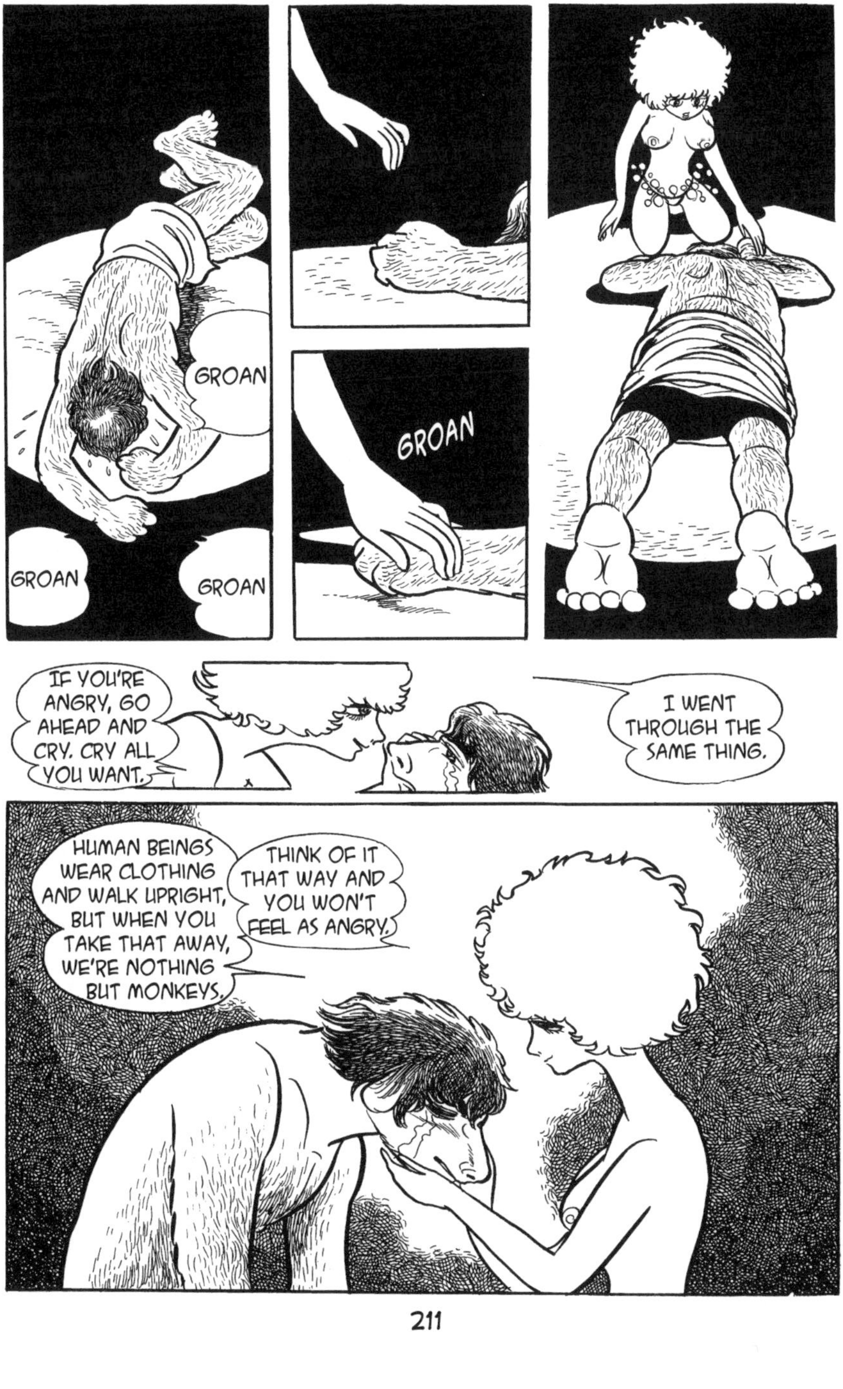
GROAN
GROAN
GROAN
GROAN
IF YOU'RE ANGRY, GO AHEAD AND CRY. CRY ALL YOU WANT.
I WENT THROUGH THE SAME THING.
HUMAN BEINGS WEAR CLOTHING AND WALK UPRIGHT, BUT WHEN YOU TAKE THAT AWAY, WE'RE NOTHING BUT MONKEYS.
THINK OF IT THAT WAY AND YOU WON'T FEEL AS ANGRY.

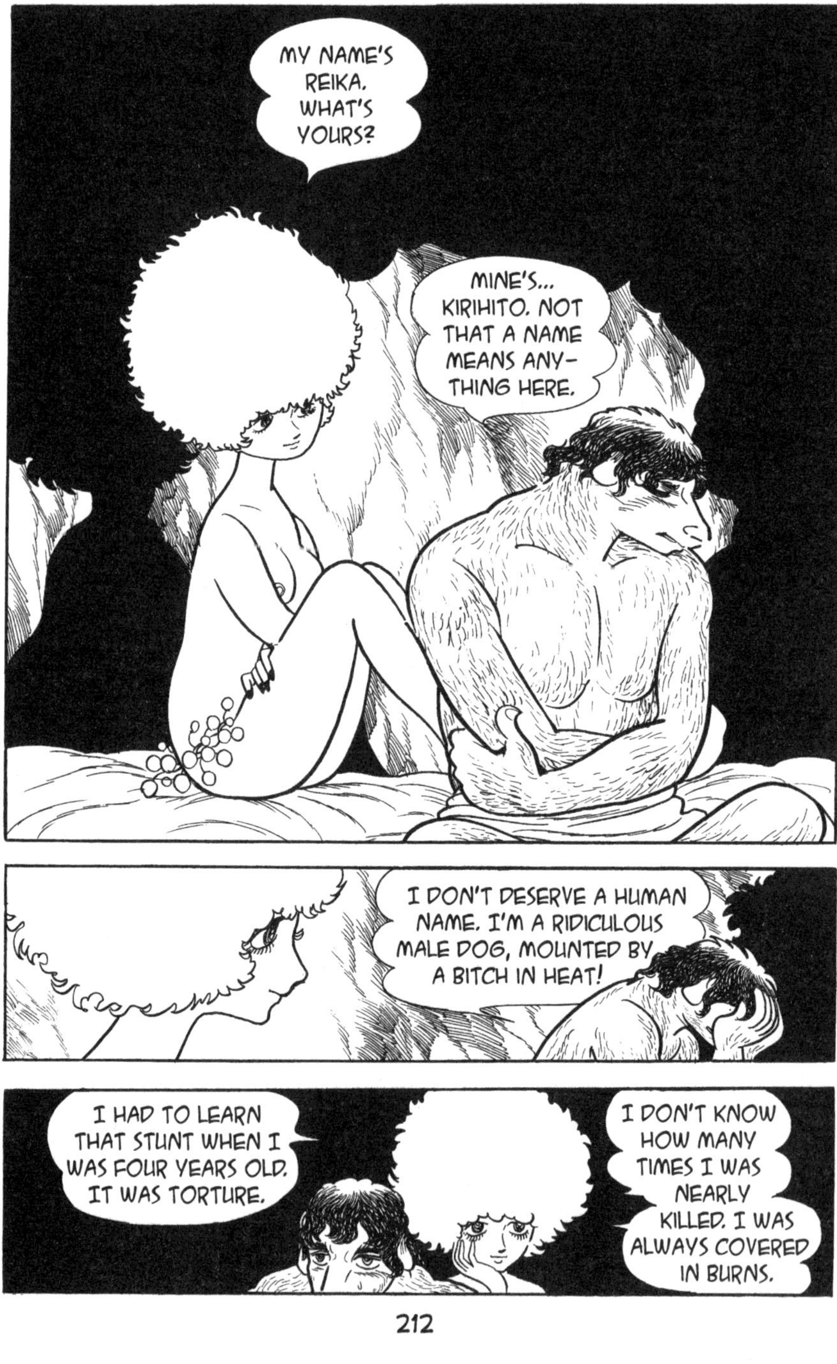
MY NAME'S REIKA. WHAT'S YOURS?
MINE'S... KIRIHITO. NOT THAT A NAME MEANS ANY-THING HERE.
I DON'T DESERVE A HUMAN NAME. I'M A RIDICULOUS MALE DOG, MOUNTED BY A BITCH IN HEAT!
I HAD TO LEARN THAT STUNT WHEN I WAS FOUR YEARS OLD. IT WAS TORTURE.
I DON'T KNOW HOW MANY TIMES I WAS NEARLY KILLED. I WAS ALWAYS COVERED IN BURNS.

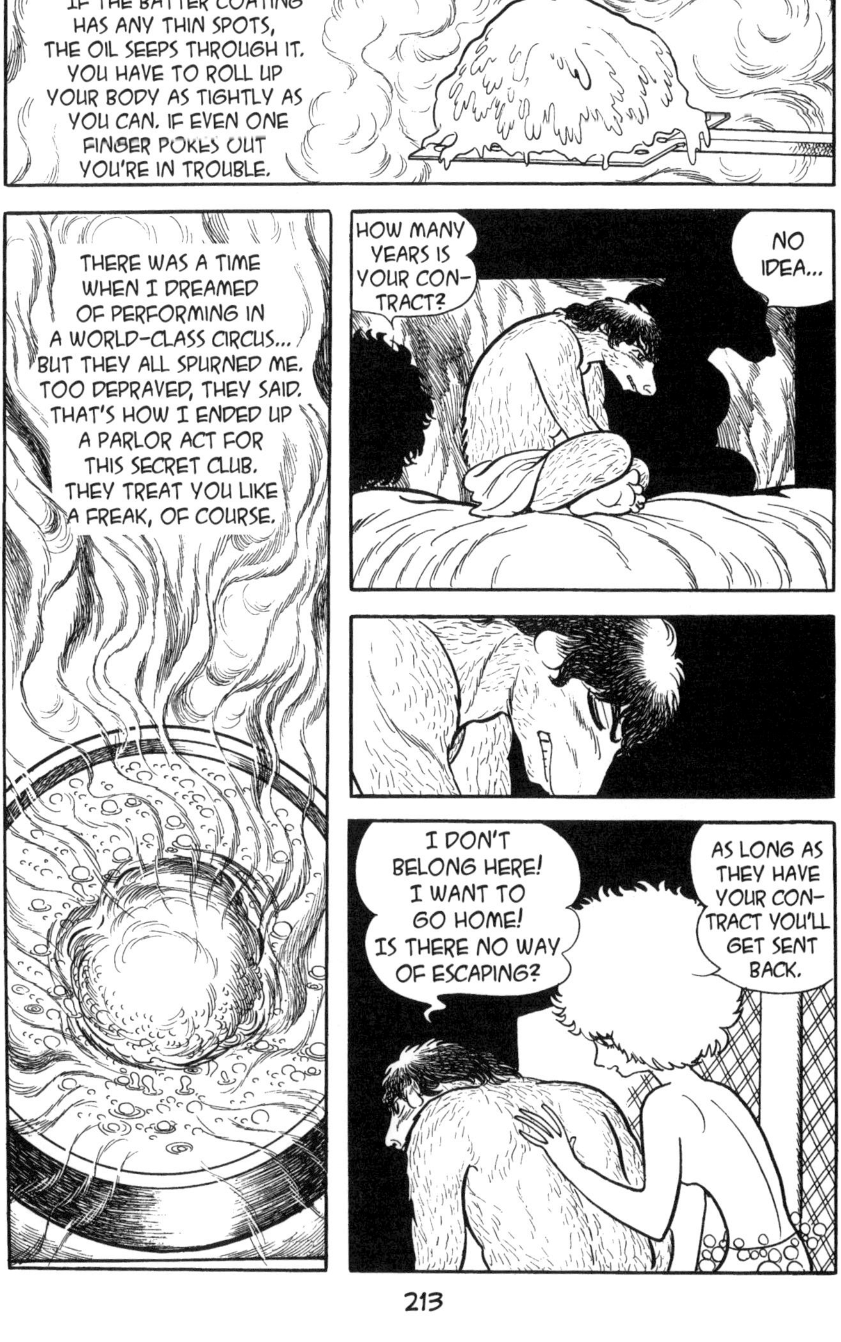
IF THE BATTER COATING HAS ANY THIN SPOTS, THE OIL SEEPS THROUGH IT. YOU HAVE TO ROLL UP YOUR BODY AS TIGHTLY AS YOU CAN. IF EVEN ONE FINGER POKES OUT YOU'RE IN TROUBLE.
THERE WAS A TIME WHEN I DREAMED OF PERFORMING IN A WORLD-CLASS CIRCUS... BUT THEY ALL SPURNED ME. TOO DEPRAVED, THEY SAID. THAT'S HOW I ENDED UP A PARLOR ACT FOR THIS SECRET CLUB. THEY TREAT YOU LIKE A FREAK, OF COURSE.
HOW MANY YEARS IS YOUR CON-TRACT?
NO IDEA...
I DON'T BELONG HERE! I WANT TO GO HOME! IS THERE NO WAY OF ESCAPING?
AS LONG AS THEY HAVE YOUR CON-TRACT YOU'LL GET SENT BACK.

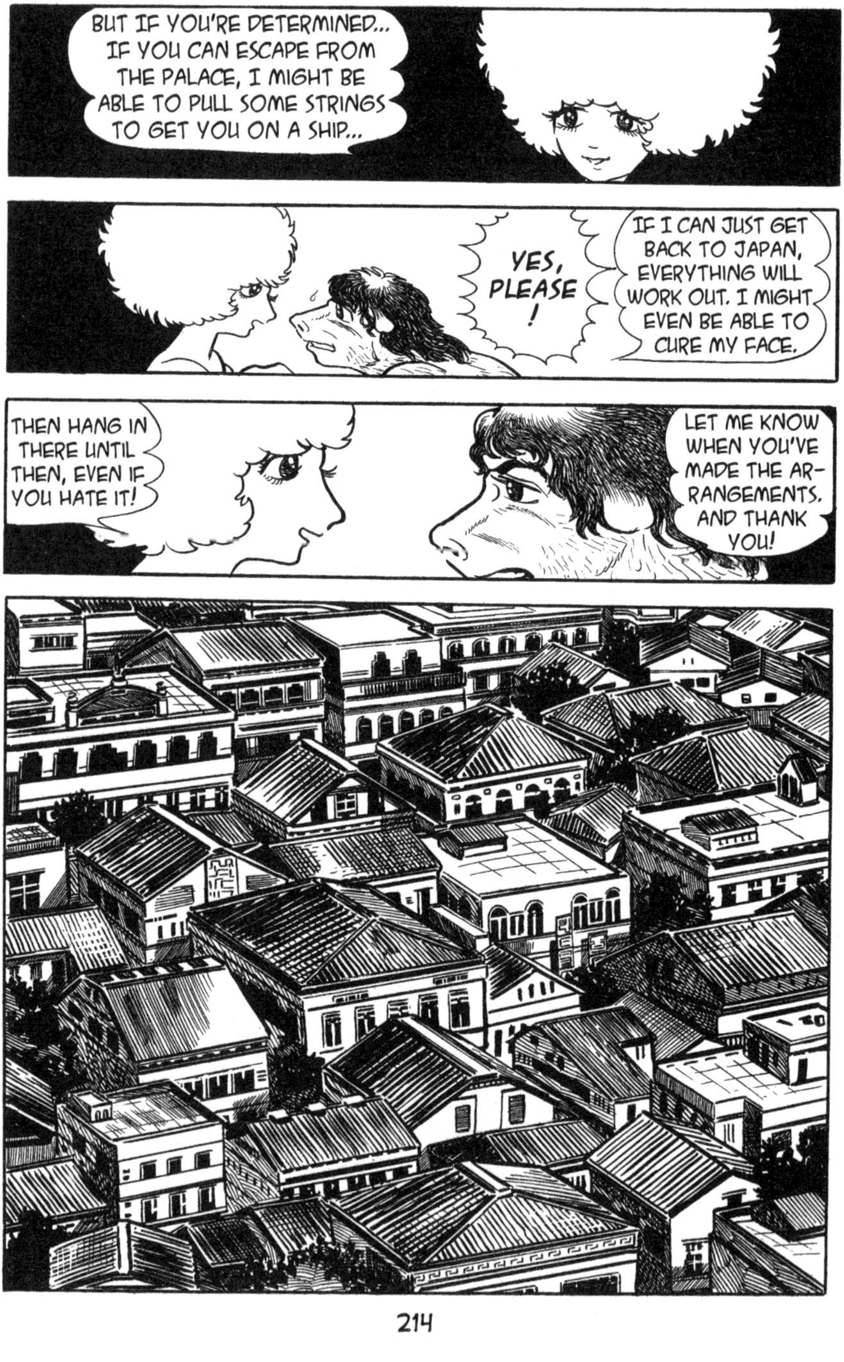
BUT IF YOU'RE DETERMINED... IF YOU CAN ESCAPE FROM THE PALACE, I MIGHT BE ABLE TO PULL SOME STRINGS TO GET YOU ON A SHIP...
IF I CAN JUST GET BACK TO JAPAN, EVERYTHING WILL WORK OUT. I MIGHT EVEN BE ABLE TO CURE MY FACE.
YES, PLEASE!
LET ME KNOW WHEN YOU'VE MADE THE AR-RANGEMENTS. AND THANK YOU!
THEN HANG IN THERE UNTIL THEN, EVEN IF YOU HATE IT!

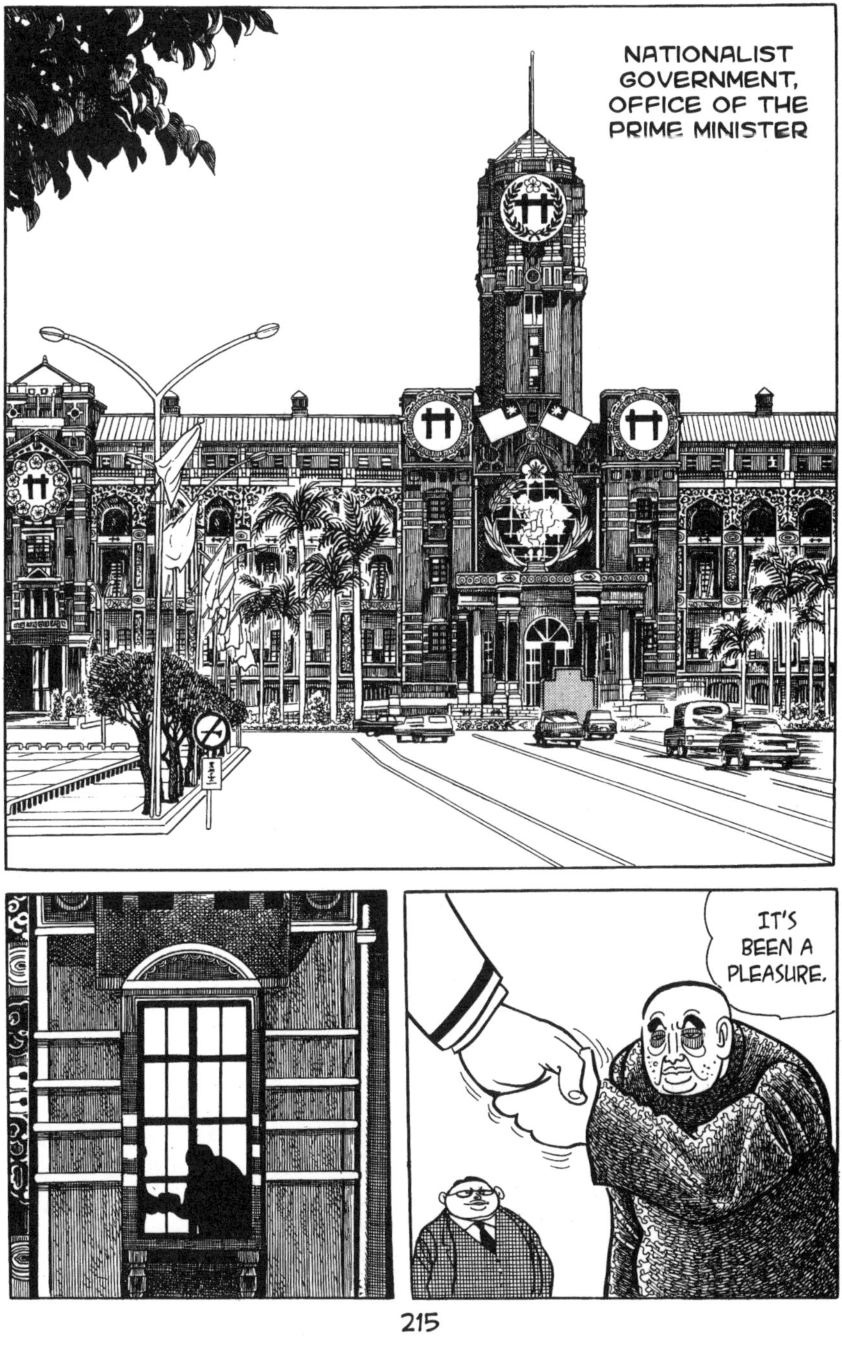
NATIONALIST GOVERNMENT, OFFICE OF THE PRIME MINISTER
IT'S BEEN A PLEASURE.

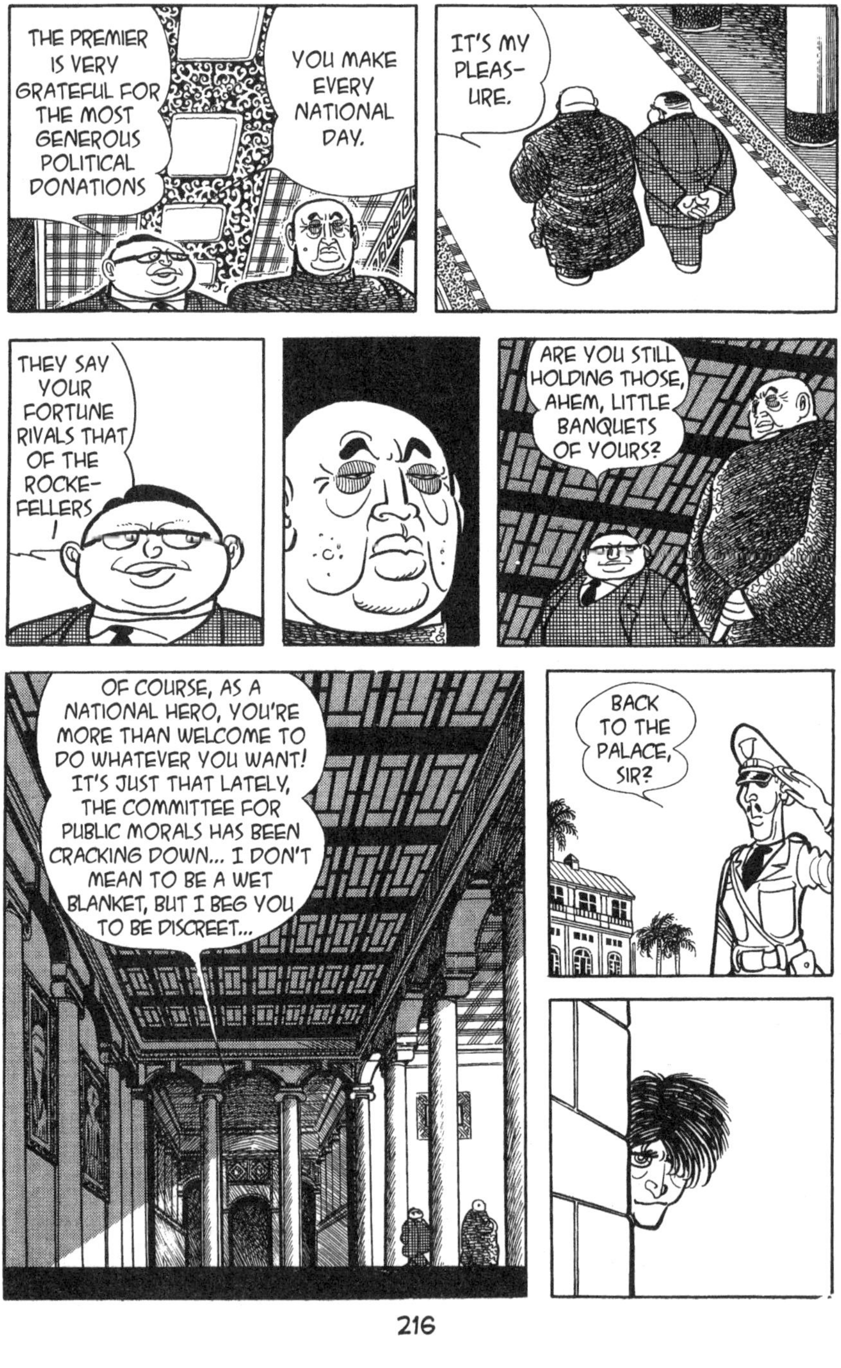
THE PREMIER IS VERY GRATEFUL FOR THE MOST GENEROUS POLITICAL DONATIONS
YOU MAKE EVERY NATIONAL DAY.
IT'S MY PLEASURE.
THEY SAY YOUR FORTUNE RIVALS THAT OF THE ROCKEFELLERS!
ARE YOU STILL HOLDING THOSE, AHEM, LITTLE BANQUETS OF YOURS?
OF COURSE, AS A NATIONAL HERO, YOU'RE MORE THAN WELCOME TO DO WHATEVER YOU WANT! IT'S JUST THAT LATELY, THE COMMITTEE FOR PUBLIC MORALS HAS BEEN CRACKING DOWN... I DON'T MEAN TO BE A WET BLANKET, BUT I BEG YOU TO BE DISCREET...
BACK TO THE PALACE, SIR?

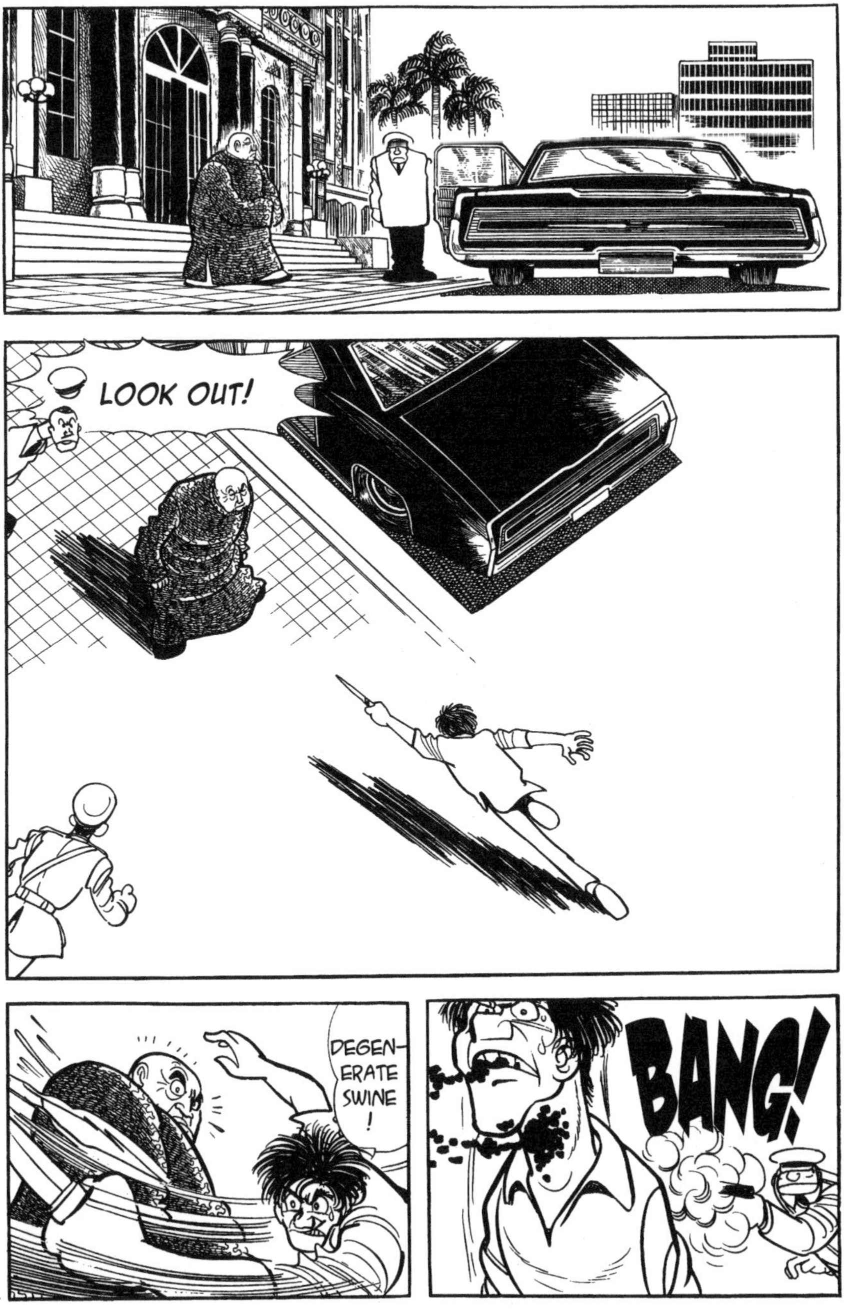
LOOK OUT!
DEGEN-ERATE SWINE!
BANG!

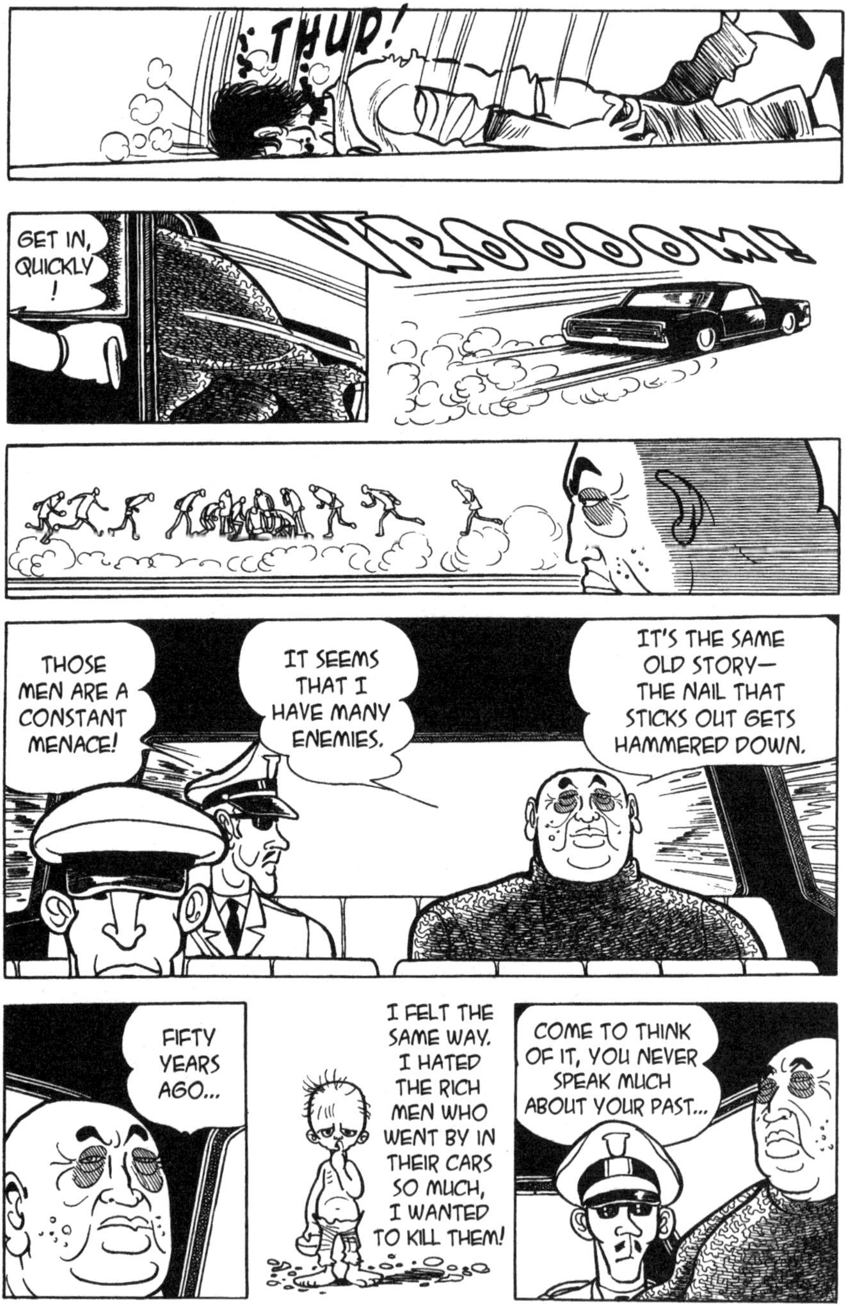
THUD!
GET IN, QUICKLY!
VROOOOOM!
THOSE MEN ARE A CONSTANT MENACE!
IT SEEMS THAT I HAVE MANY ENEMIES.
IT'S THE SAME OLD STORY— THE NAIL THAT STICKS OUT GETS HAMMERED DOWN.
FIFTY YEARS AGO...
I FELT THE SAME WAY. I HATED THE RICH MEN WHO WENT BY IN THEIR CARS SO MUCH, I WANTED TO KILL THEM!
COME TO THINK OF IT, YOU NEVER SPEAK MUCH ABOUT YOUR PAST...

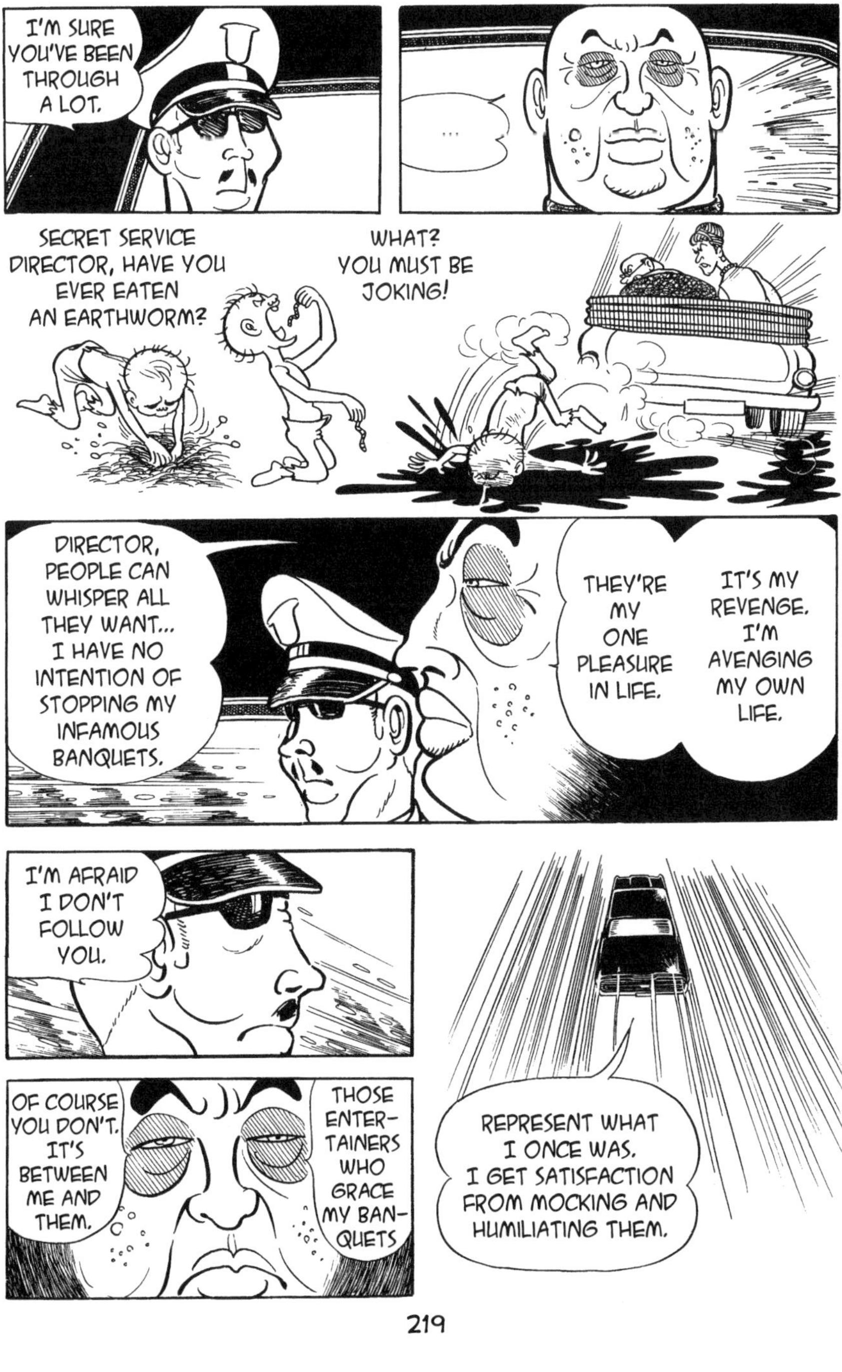
I'M SURE YOU'VE BEEN THROUGH A LOT.
...
SECRET SERVICE DIRECTOR, HAVE YOU EVER EATEN AN EARTHWORM?
WHAT? YOU MUST BE JOKING!
DIRECTOR, PEOPLE CAN WHISPER ALL THEY WANT... I HAVE NO INTENTION OF STOPPING MY INFAMOUS BANQUETS.
THEY'RE MY ONE PLEASURE IN LIFE.
IT'S MY REVENGE. I'M AVENGING MY OWN LIFE.
I'M AFRAID I DON'T FOLLOW YOU.
OF COURSE YOU DON'T. IT'S BETWEEN ME AND THEM.
THOSE ENTER-TAINERS WHO GRACE MY BAN-QUETS
REPRESENT WHAT I ONCE WAS. I GET SATISFACTION FROM MOCKING AND HUMILIATING THEM.

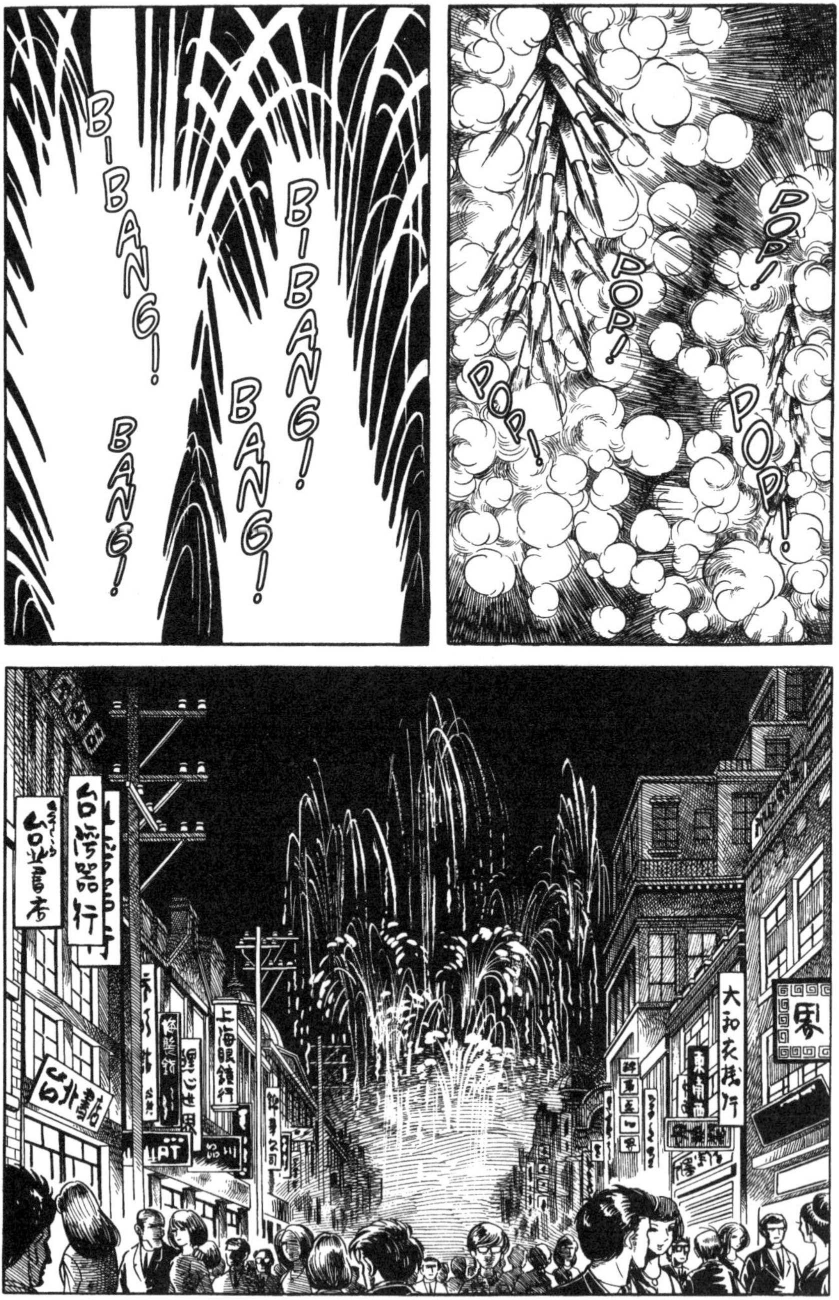
BIBANG!
BANG!
BIBANG!
BANG!
POP!
POP!
POP!
POP!

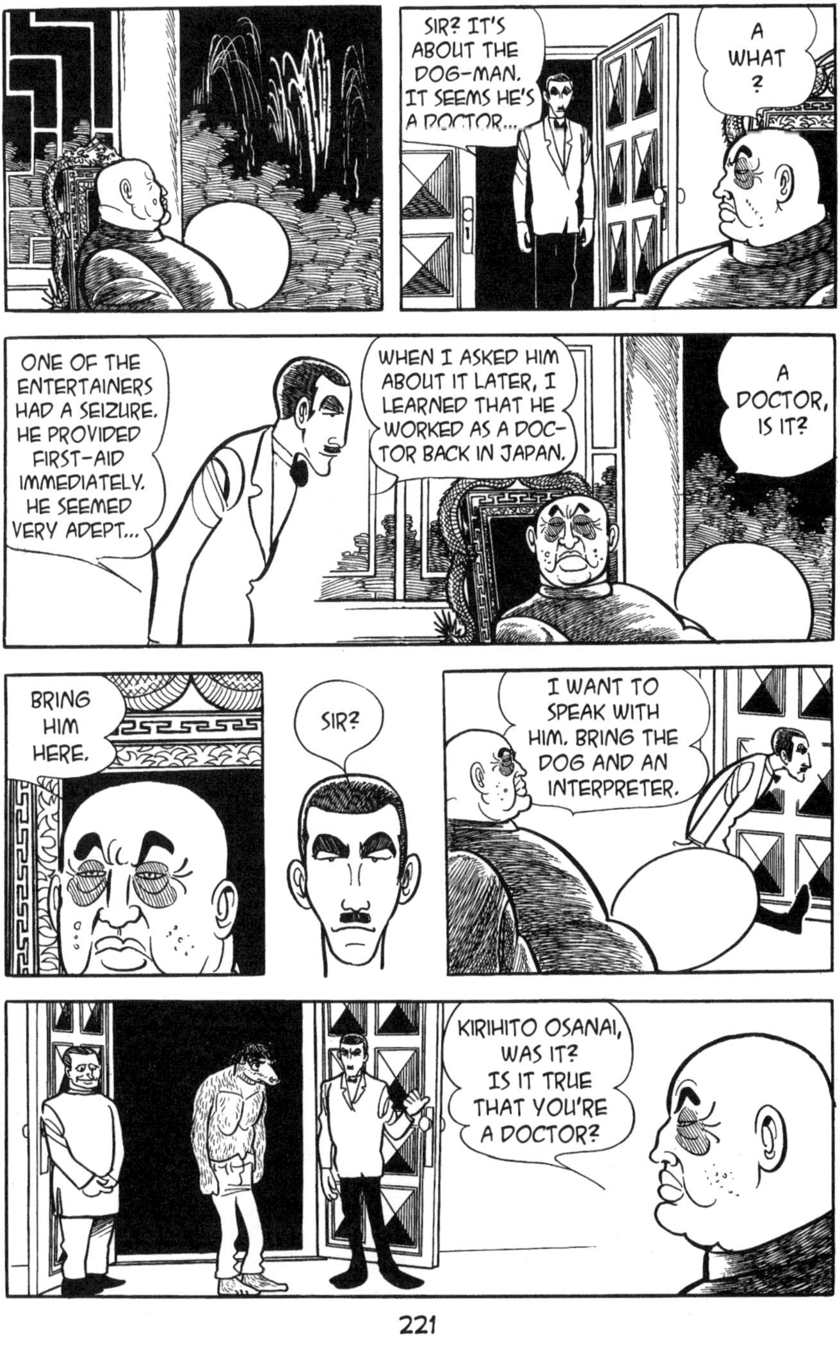
SIR? IT'S ABOUT THE DOG-MAN. IT SEEMS HE'S A DOCTOR...
A WHAT?
ONE OF THE ENTERTAINERS HAD A SEIZURE. HE PROVIDED FIRST-AID IMMEDIATELY. HE SEEMED VERY ADEPT...
WHEN I ASKED HIM ABOUT IT LATER, I LEARNED THAT HE WORKED AS A DOCTOR BACK IN JAPAN.
A DOCTOR, IS IT?
BRING HIM HERE.
SIR?
I WANT TO SPEAK WITH HIM. BRING THE DOG AND AN INTERPRETER.
KIRIHITO OSANAI, WAS IT? IS IT TRUE THAT YOU'RE A DOCTOR?

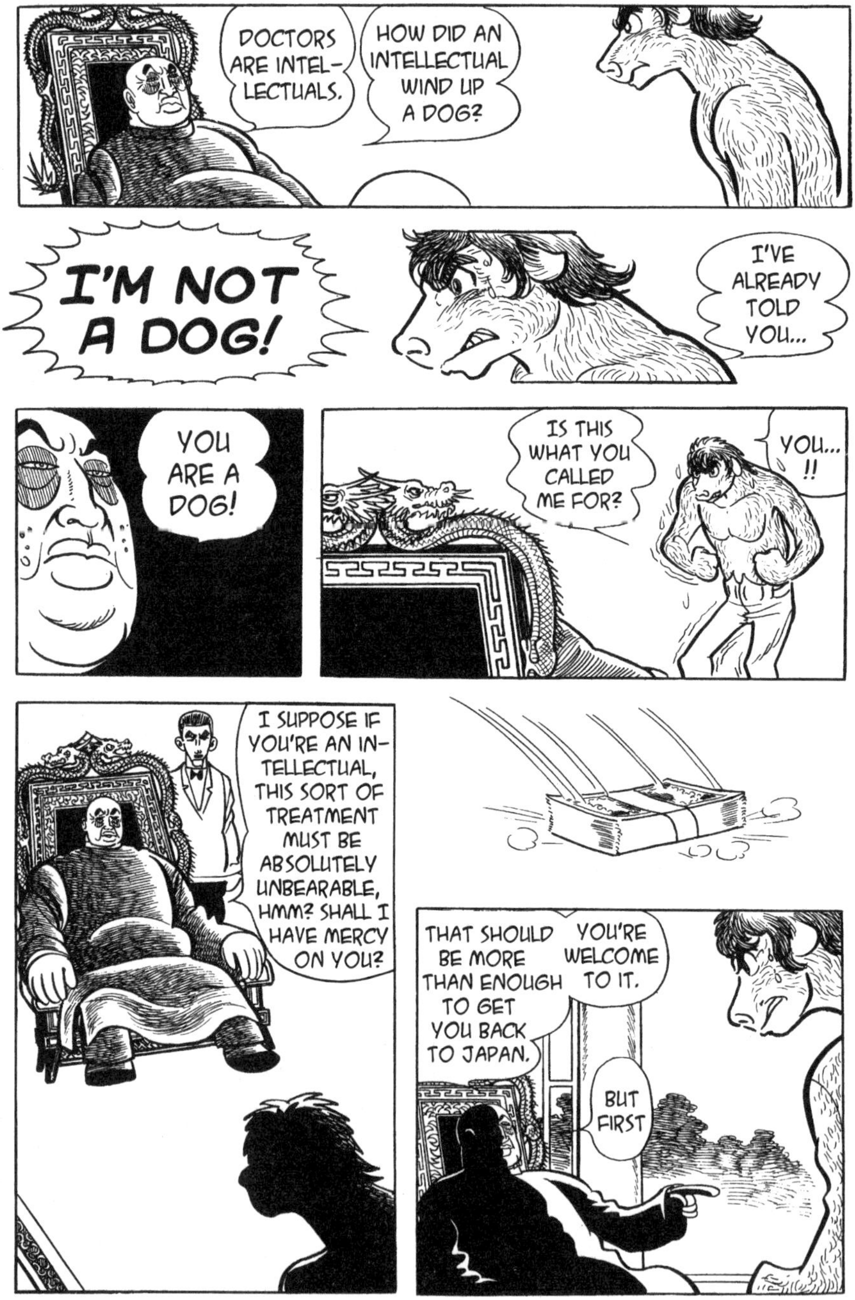
DOCTORS ARE INTEL-LECTUALS.
HOW DID AN INTELLECTUAL WIND UP A DOG?
I'M NOT A DOG!
I'VE ALREADY TOLD YOU...
YOU ARE A DOG!
IS THIS WHAT YOU CALLED ME FOR?
YOU... !!
I SUPPOSE IF YOU'RE AN IN-TELLECTUAL, THIS SORT OF TREATMENT MUST BE ABSOLUTELY UNBEARABLE, HMM? SHALL I HAVE MERCY ON YOU?
THAT SHOULD BE MORE THAN ENOUGH TO GET YOU BACK TO JAPAN.
YOU'RE WELCOME TO IT.
BUT FIRST

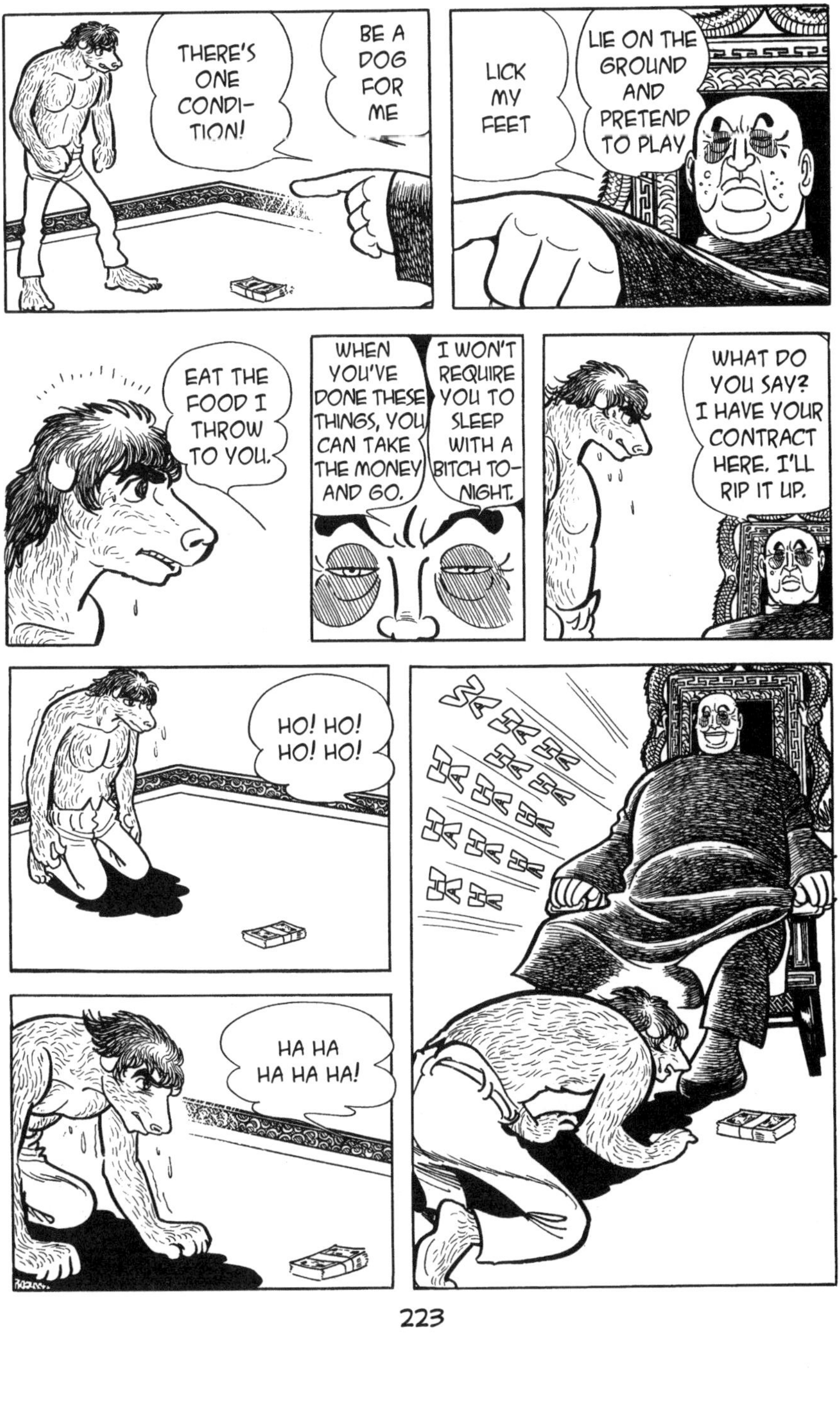
THERE'S ONE CONDITION!
BE A DOG FOR ME
LICK MY FEET
LIE ON THE GROUND AND PRETEND TO PLAY
EAT THE FOOD I THROW TO YOU.
WHEN YOU'VE DONE THESE THINGS, YOU CAN TAKE THE MONEY AND GO.
I WON'T REQUIRE YOU TO SLEEP WITH A BITCH TO-NIGHT.
WHAT DO YOU SAY? I HAVE YOUR CONTRACT HERE. I'LL RIP IT UP.
HO! HO! HO! HO!
WA HA HA HA HA HA HA HA HA HA HA HA HA HA HA HA HA HA
HA HA HA HA HA!

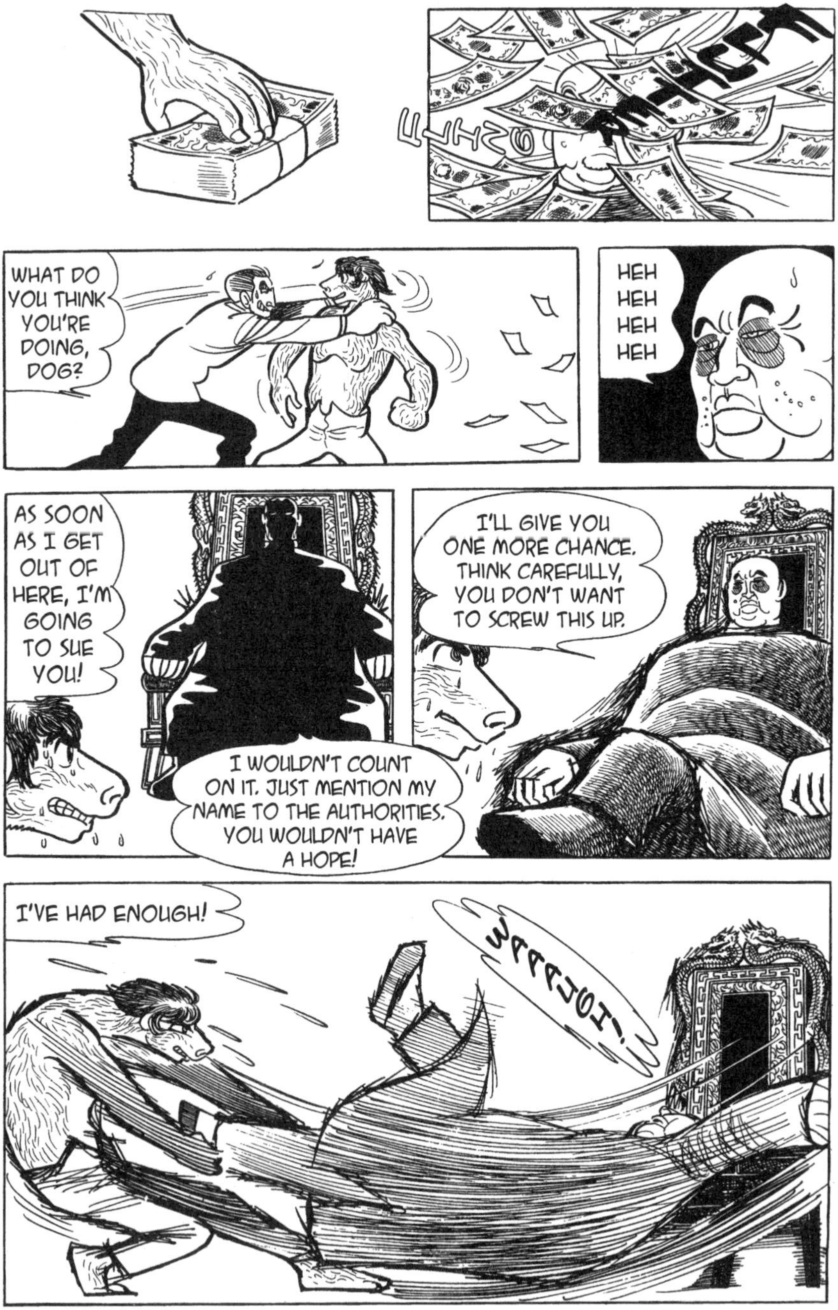
WHAT DO YOU THINK YOU'RE DOING, DOG?
HEH HEH HEH HEH
AS SOON AS I GET OUT OF HERE, I'M GOING TO SUE YOU!
I WOULDN'T COUNT ON IT. JUST MENTION MY NAME TO THE AUTHORITIES. YOU WOULDN'T HAVE A HOPE!
I'LL GIVE YOU ONE MORE CHANCE. THINK CAREFULLY, YOU DON'T WANT TO SCREW THIS UP.
I'VE HAD ENOUGH!

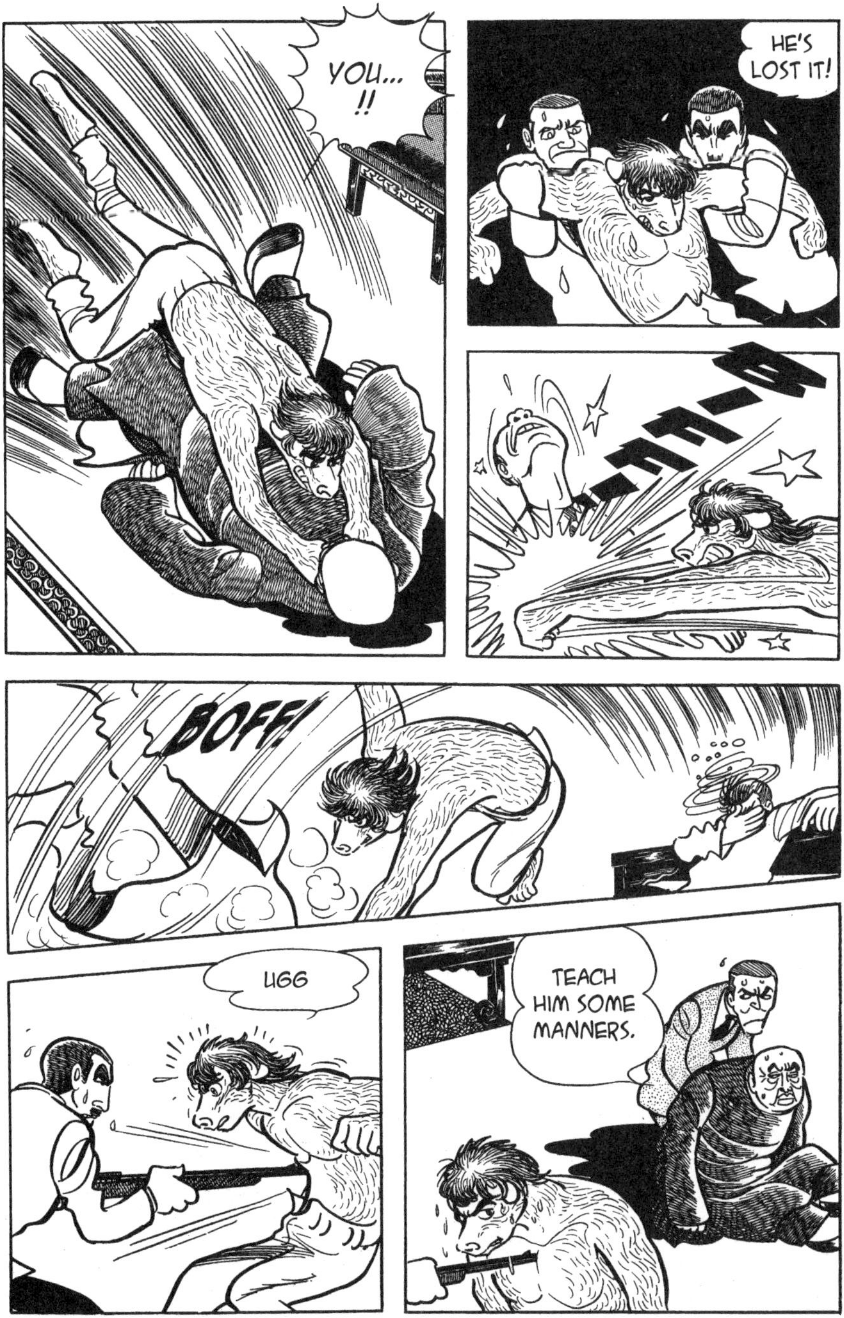
YOU... !!
HE'S LOST IT!
BOFF!
UGG
TEACH HIM SOME MANNERS.

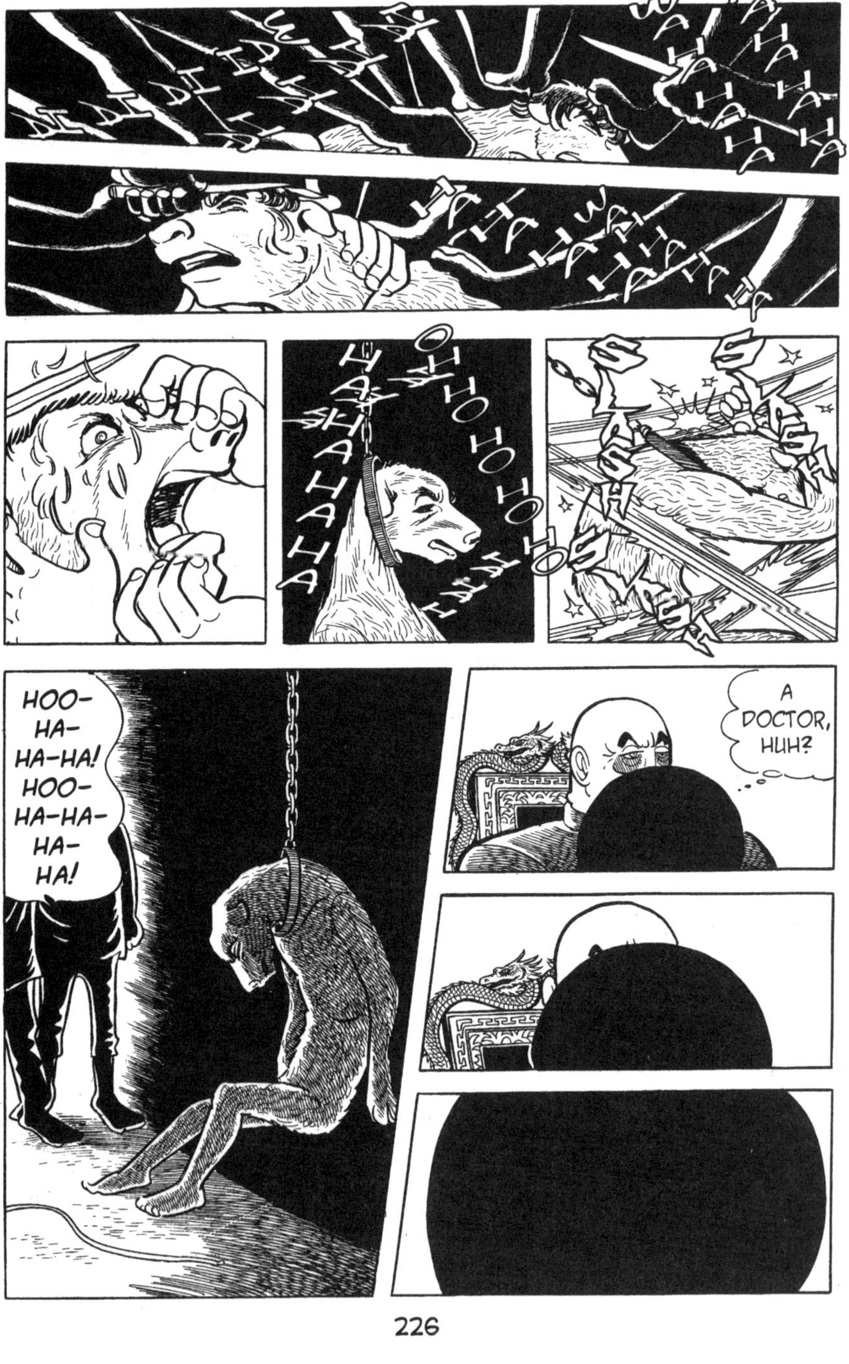
HOO-HA-HA-HA! HOO-HA-HA-HA-HA!
A DOCTOR, HUH?

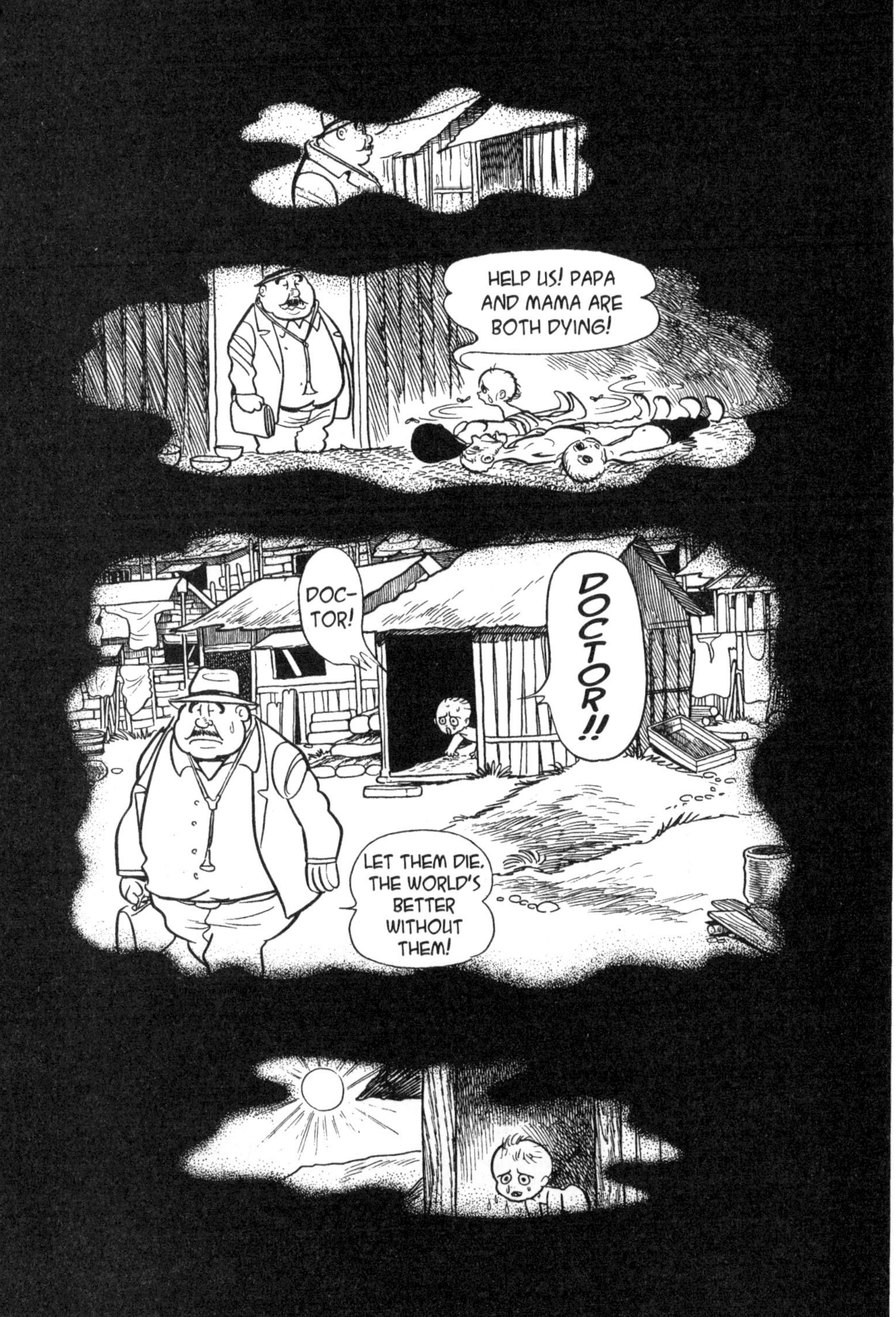
HELP US! PAPA AND MAMA ARE BOTH DYING!
DOCTOR!!
DOC-TOR!
LET THEM DIE. THE WORLD'S BETTER WITHOUT THEM!

IT WAS HOT THAT DAY. I STILL RE-MEMBER IT CLEARLY...

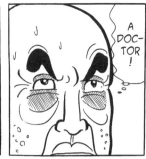

A DOC-TOR!

REIKA...

I BROUGHT A FILE.

I GOT IT FROM THE MAN YOU TREATED.

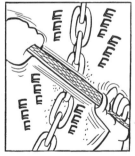

YOU POOR THING.

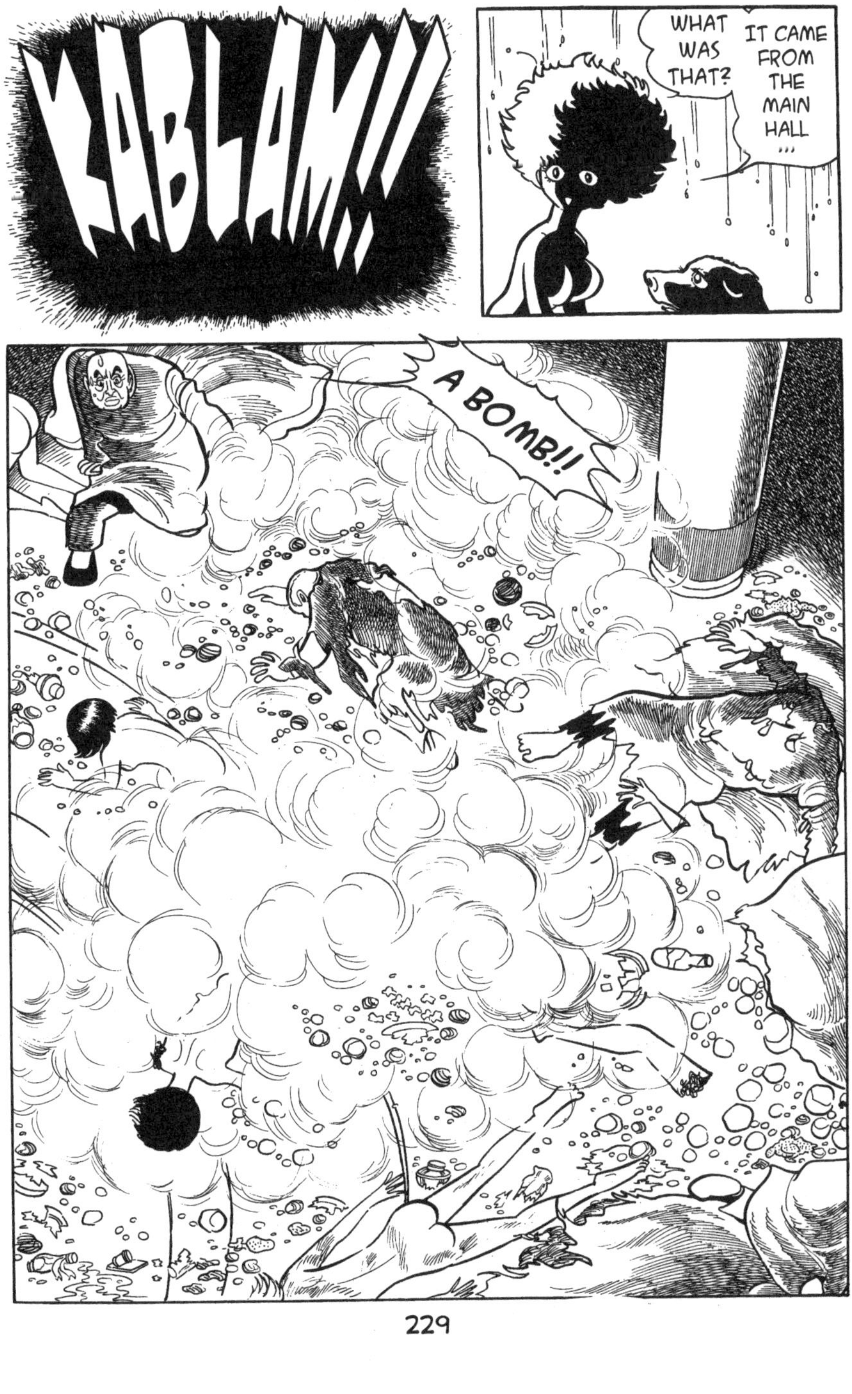
KABLAM!!
WHAT WAS THAT?
IT CAME FROM THE MAIN HALL ...
A BOMB!!

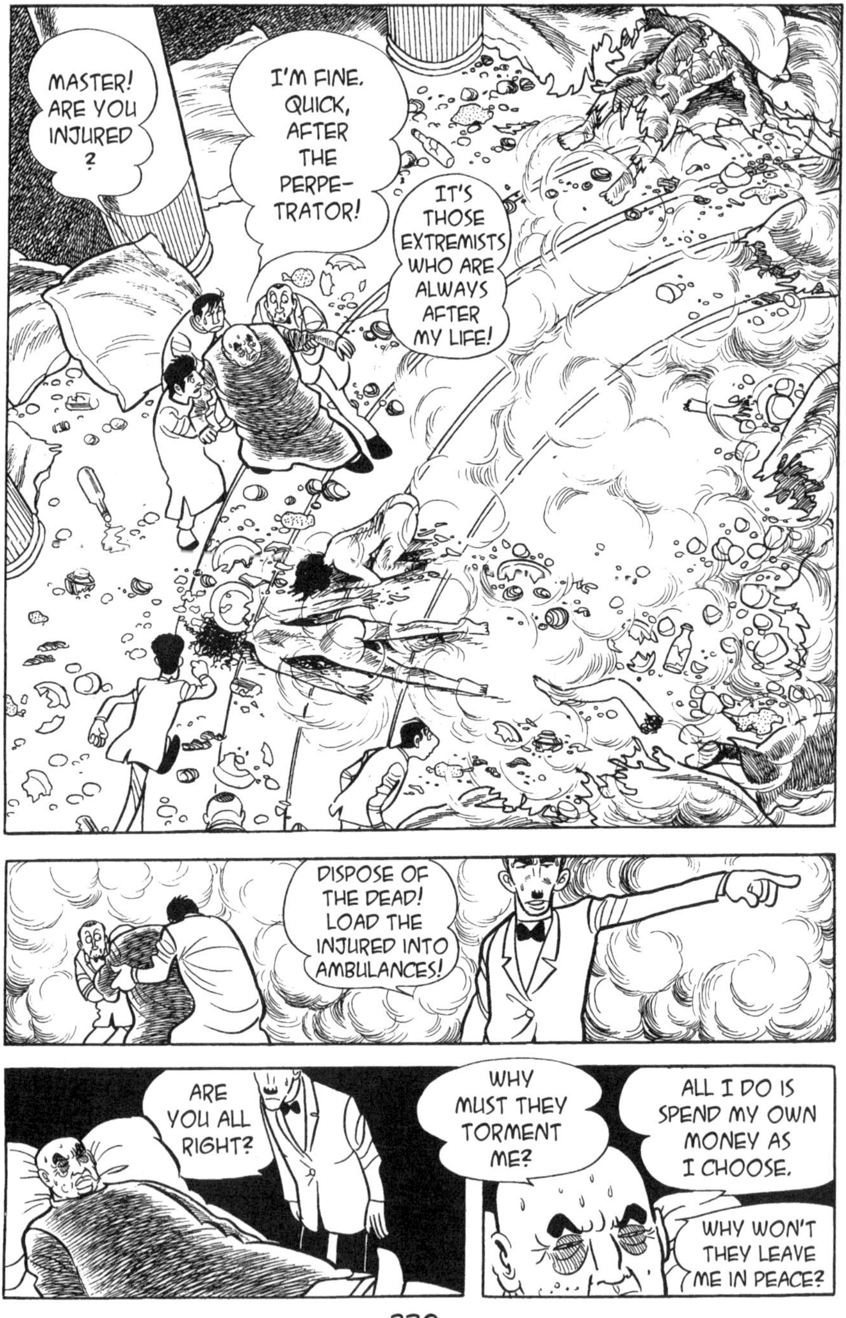
MASTER! ARE YOU INJURED?
I'M FINE. QUICK, AFTER THE PERPETRATOR!
IT'S THOSE EXTREMISTS WHO ARE ALWAYS AFTER MY LIFE!
DISPOSE OF THE DEAD! LOAD THE INJURED INTO AMBULANCES!
ARE YOU ALL RIGHT?
WHY MUST THEY TORMENT ME?
ALL I DO IS SPEND MY OWN MONEY AS I CHOOSE.
WHY WON'T THEY LEAVE ME IN PEACE?

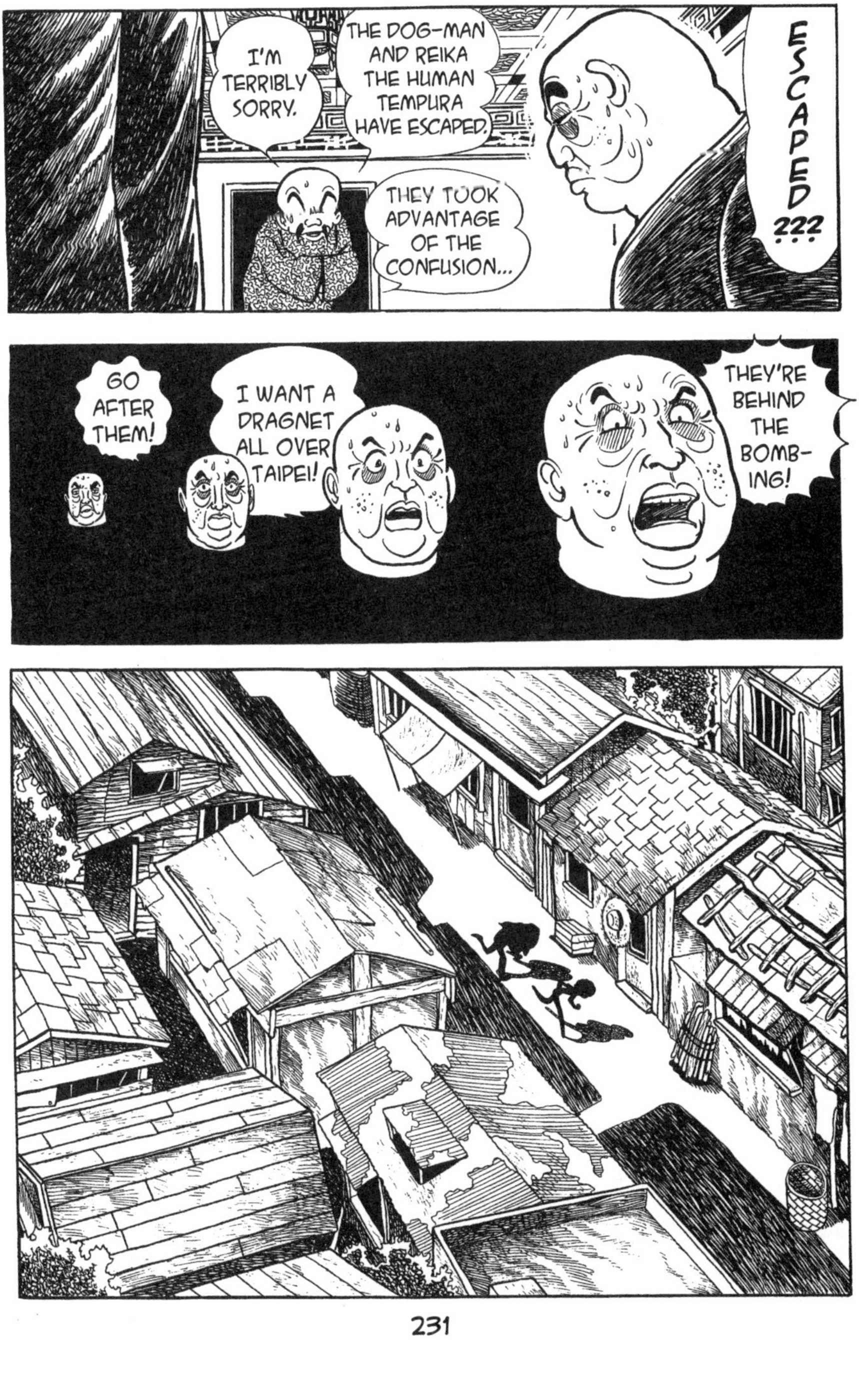
I'M TERRIBLY SORRY.
THE DOG-MAN AND REIKA THE HUMAN TEMPURA HAVE ESCAPED.
THEY TOOK ADVANTAGE OF THE CONFUSION...
ESCAPED???
GO AFTER THEM!
I WANT A DRAGNET ALL OVER TAIPEI!
THEY'RE BEHIND THE BOMB-ING!

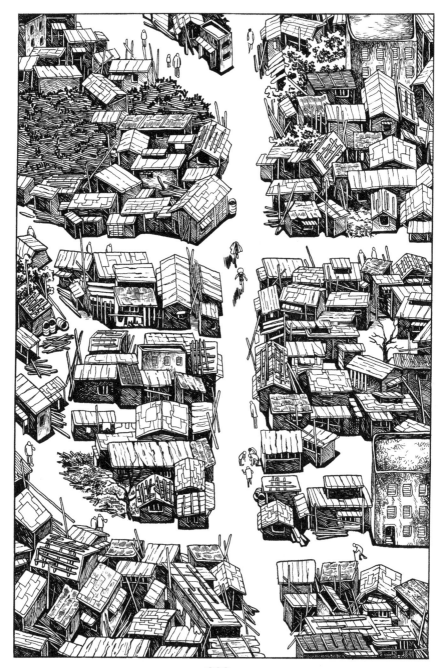

232

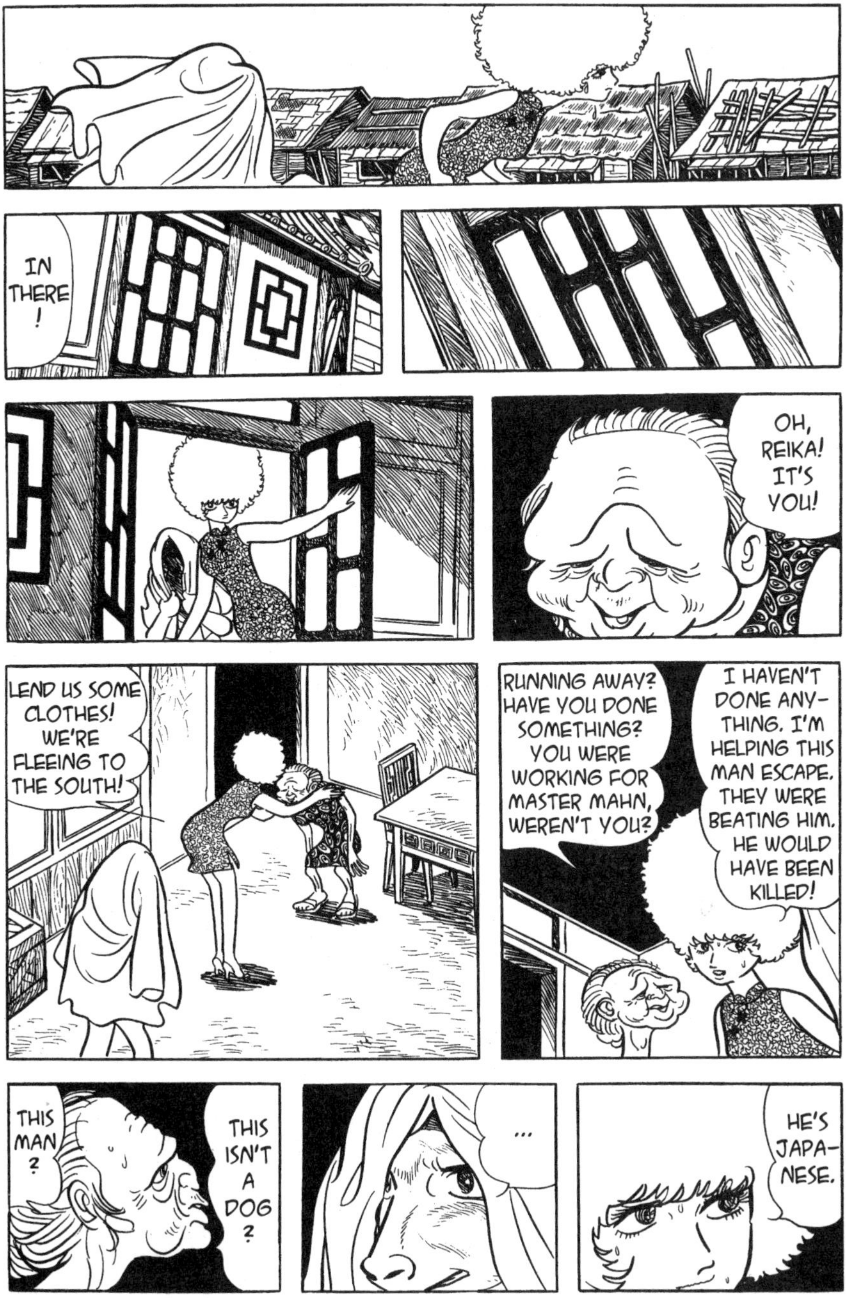

IN THERE!
OH, REIKA! IT'S YOU!
LEND US SOME CLOTHES! WE'RE FLEEING TO THE SOUTH!
RUNNING AWAY? HAVE YOU DONE SOMETHING? YOU WERE WORKING FOR MASTER MAHN, WEREN'T YOU?
I HAVEN'T DONE ANY-THING. I'M HELPING THIS MAN ESCAPE. THEY WERE BEATING HIM. HE WOULD HAVE BEEN KILLED!
THIS MAN?
THIS ISN'T A DOG?
...
HE'S JAPA-NESE.

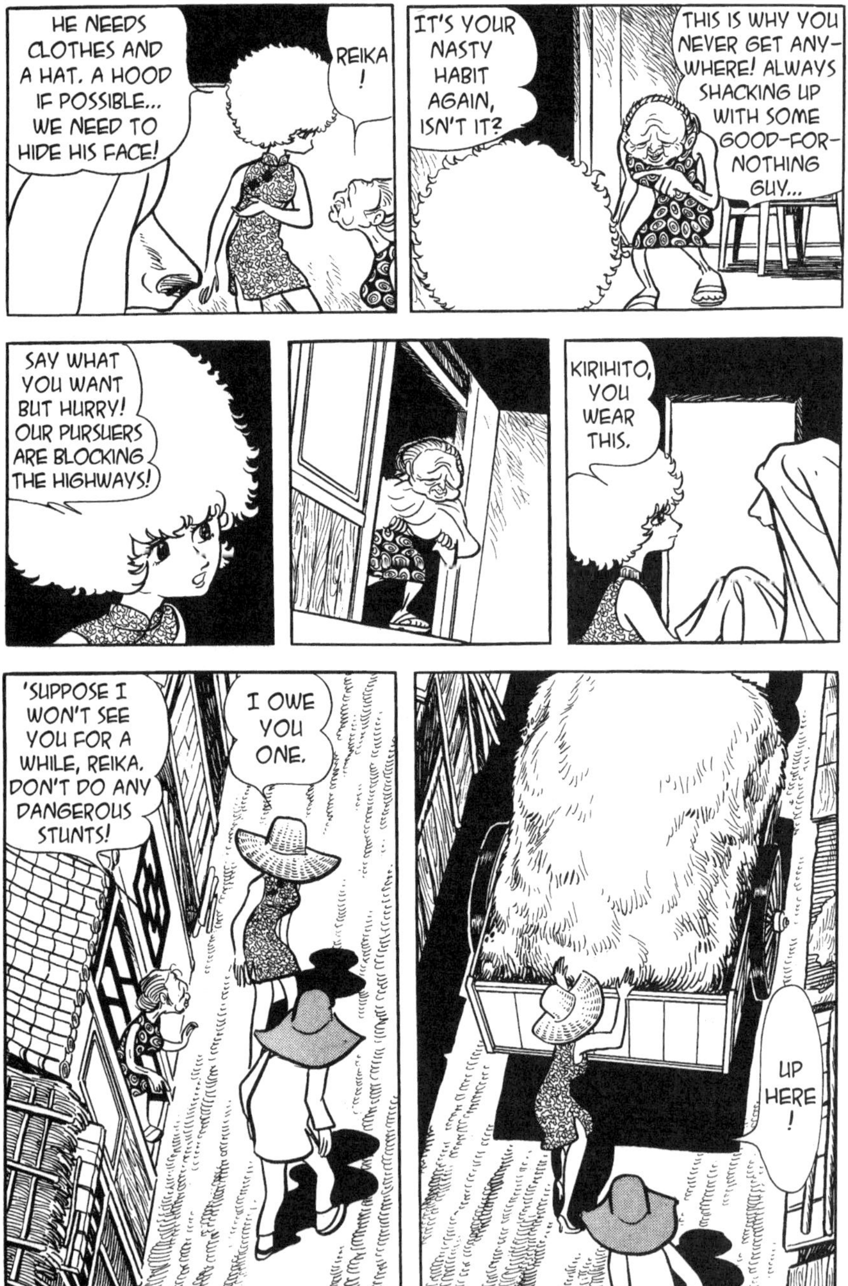
HE NEEDS CLOTHES AND A HAT. A HOOD IF POSSIBLE... WE NEED TO HIDE HIS FACE!
REIKA!
IT'S YOUR NASTY HABIT AGAIN, ISN'T IT?
THIS IS WHY YOU NEVER GET ANY-WHERE! ALWAYS SHACKING UP WITH SOME GOOD-FOR-NOTHING GUY...
SAY WHAT YOU WANT BUT HURRY! OUR PURSUERS ARE BLOCKING THE HIGHWAYS!
KIRIHITO, YOU WEAR THIS.
'SUPPOSE I WON'T SEE YOU FOR A WHILE, REIKA. DON'T DO ANY DANGEROUS STUNTS!
I OWE YOU ONE.
UP HERE!

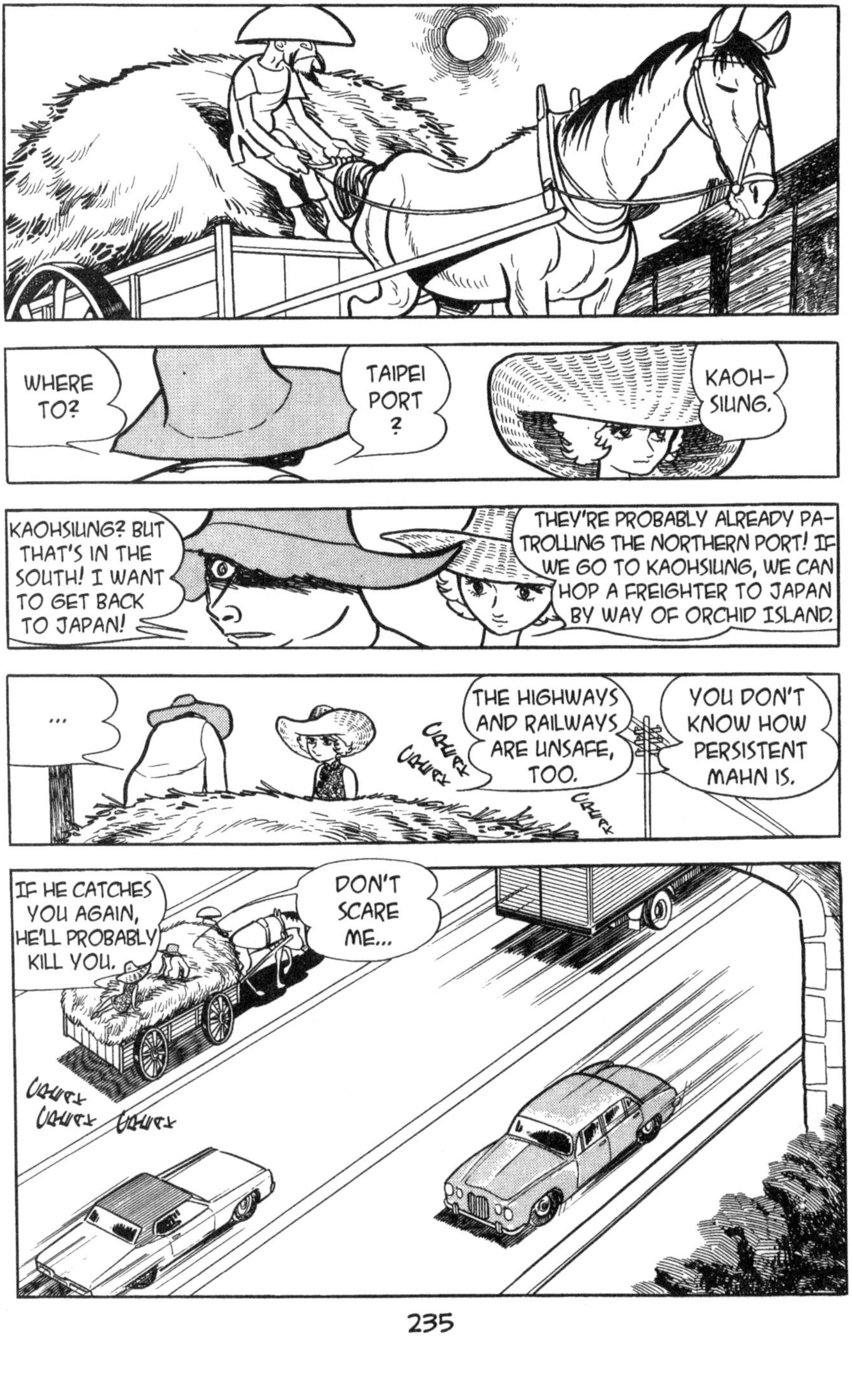
WHERE TO?
TAIPEI PORT ?
KAOH-SIUNG.
KAOHSIUNG? BUT THAT'S IN THE SOUTH! I WANT TO GET BACK TO JAPAN!
THEY'RE PROBABLY ALREADY PATROLLING THE NORTHERN PORT! IF WE GO TO KAOHSIUNG, WE CAN HOP A FREIGHTER TO JAPAN BY WAY OF ORCHID ISLAND.
...
THE HIGHWAYS AND RAILWAYS ARE UNSAFE, TOO.
YOU DON'T KNOW HOW PERSISTENT MAHN IS.
IF HE CATCHES YOU AGAIN, HE'LL PROBABLY KILL YOU.
DON'T SCARE ME...

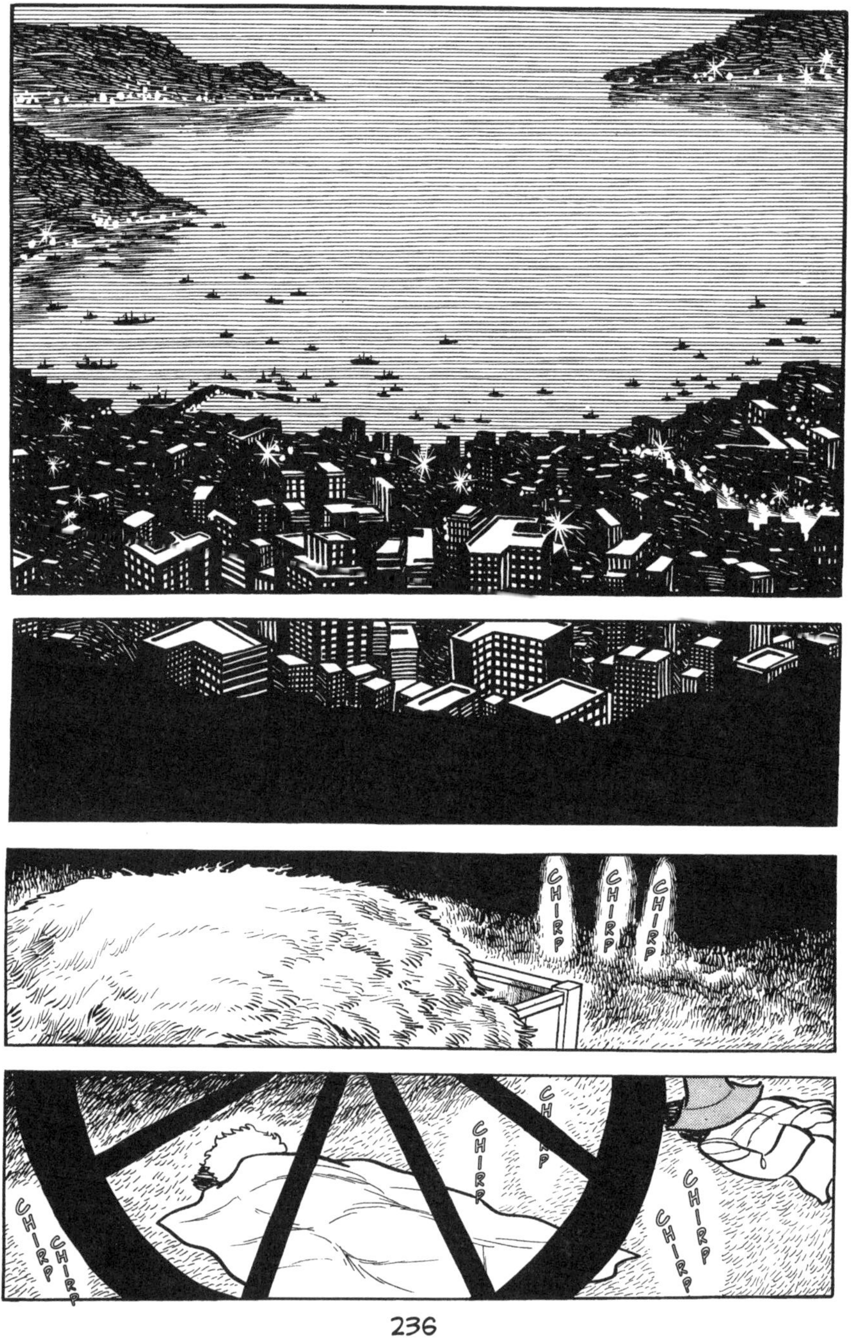
CHIRP
CHIRP
CHIRP
CHIRP
CHIRP
CHIRP
CHIRP
CHIRP
CHIRP

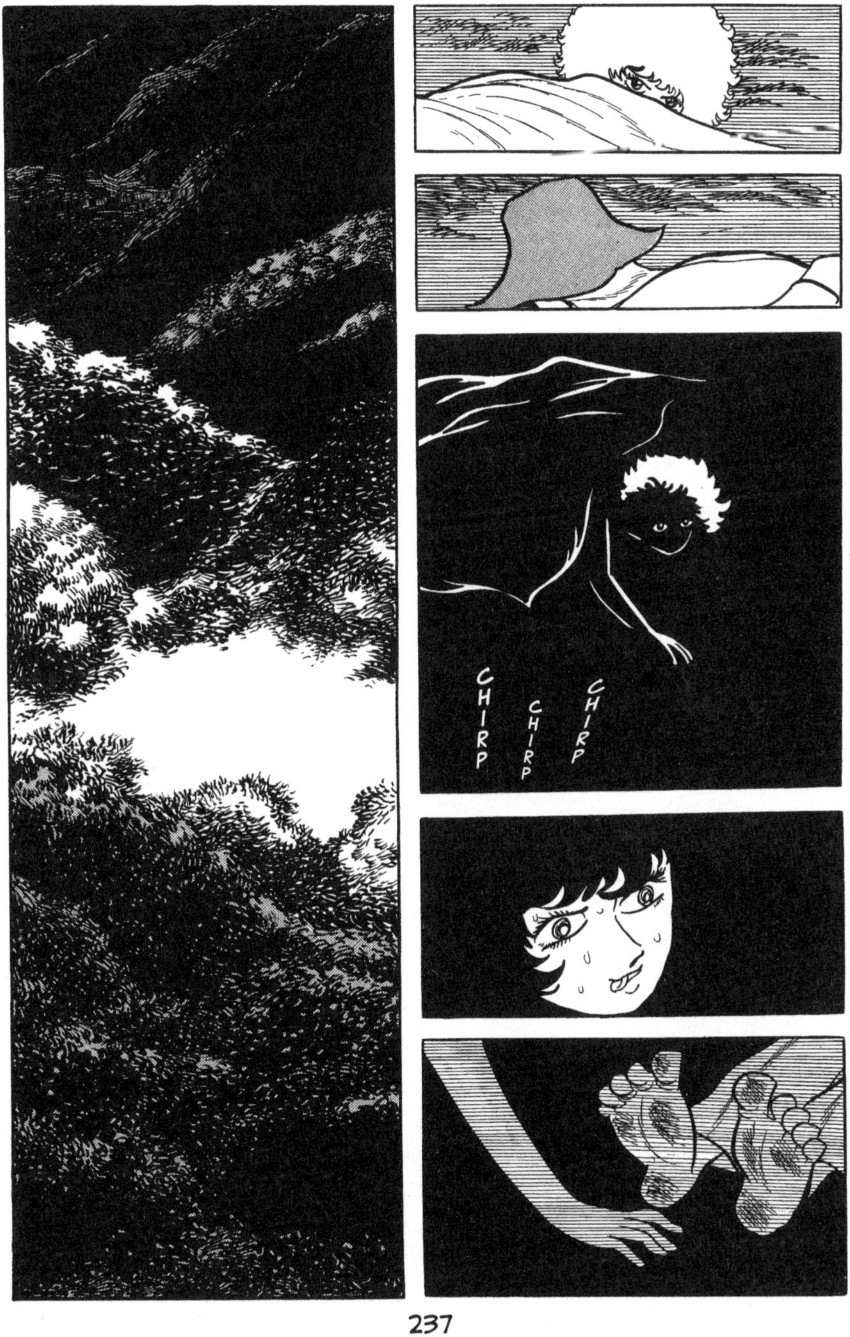
CHIRP
CHIRP
CHIRP

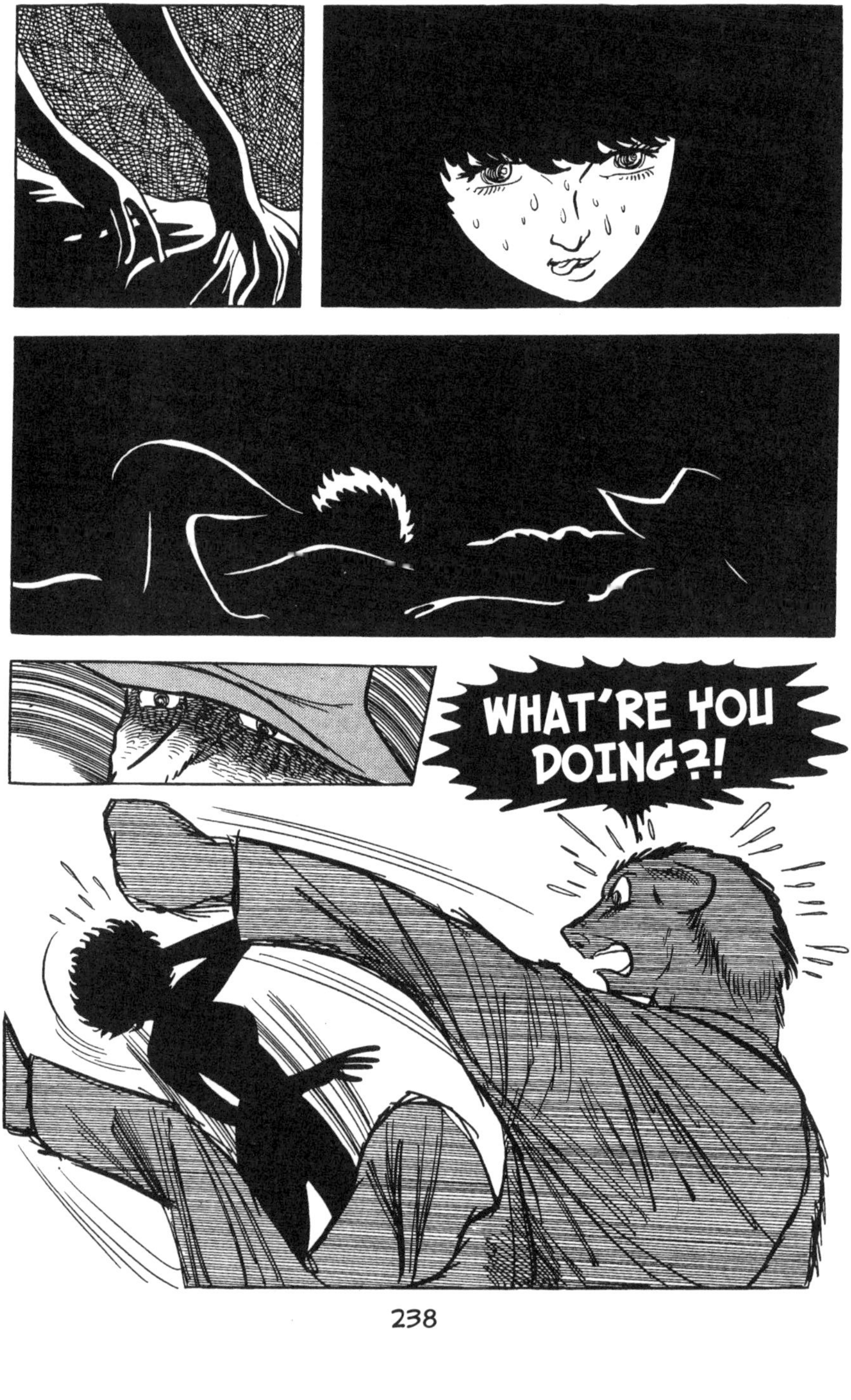
WHAT'RE YOU DOING?!

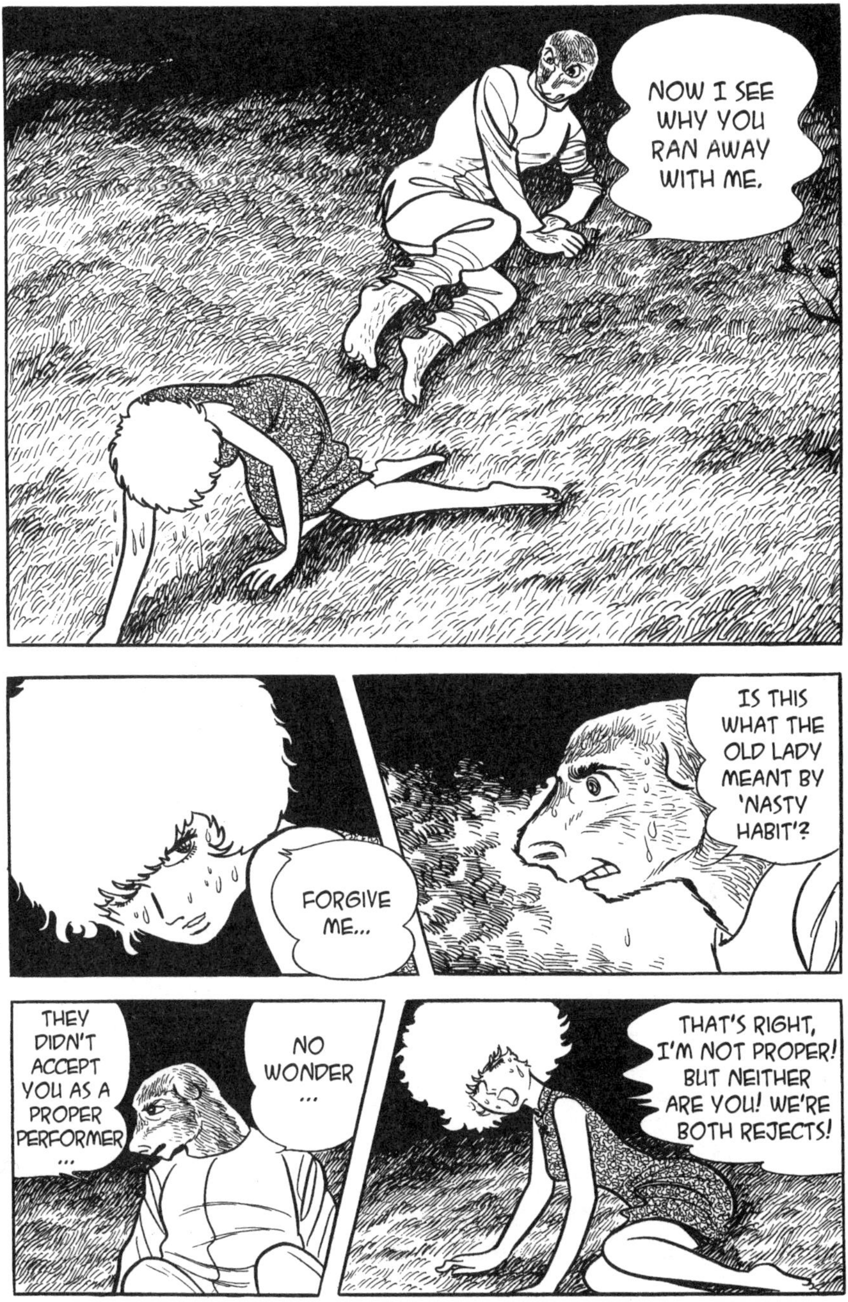
NOW I SEE WHY YOU RAN AWAY WITH ME.
IS THIS WHAT THE OLD LADY MEANT BY 'NASTY HABIT'?
FORGIVE ME...
NO WONDER ...
THEY DIDN'T ACCEPT YOU AS A PROPER PERFORMER ...
THAT'S RIGHT, I'M NOT PROPER! BUT NEITHER ARE YOU! WE'RE BOTH REJECTS!

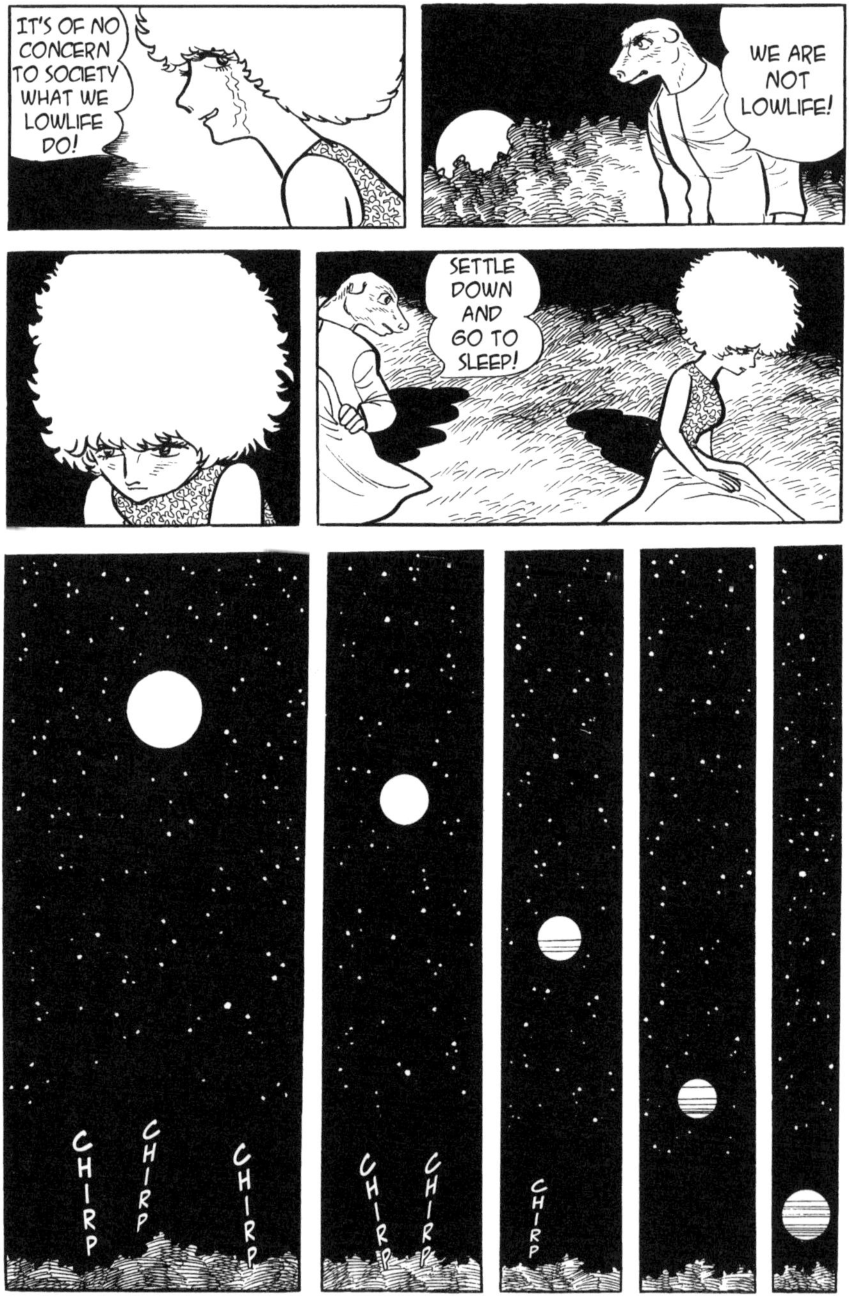
IT'S OF NO CONCERN TO SOCIETY WHAT WE LOWLIFE DO!
WE ARE NOT LOWLIFE!
SETTLE DOWN AND GO TO SLEEP!
CHIRP
CHIRP
CHIRP
CHIRP
CHIRP
CHIRP

CHAPTER 7

DARK GULLEY

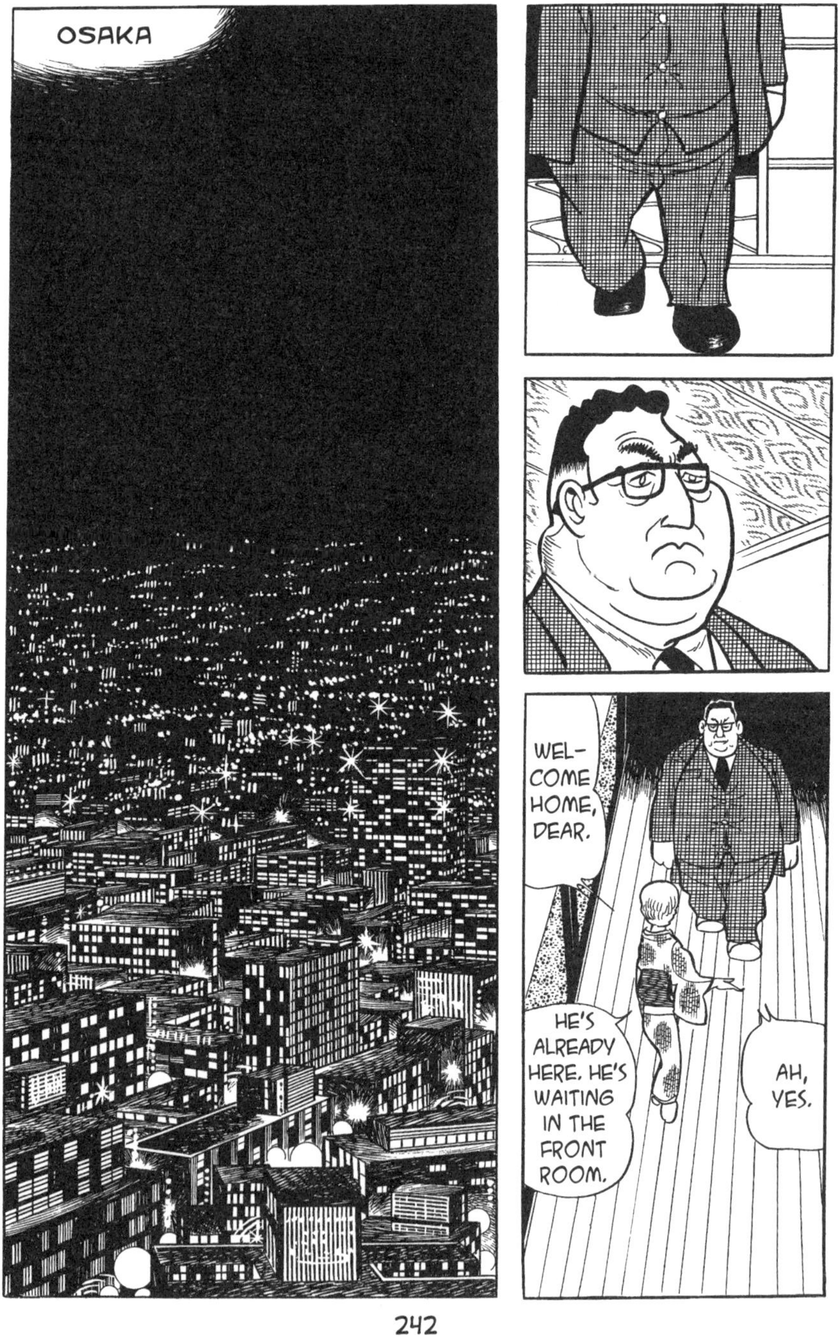
OSAKA
WEL-COME HOME, DEAR.
HE'S ALREADY HERE. HE'S WAITING IN THE FRONT ROOM.
AH, YES.

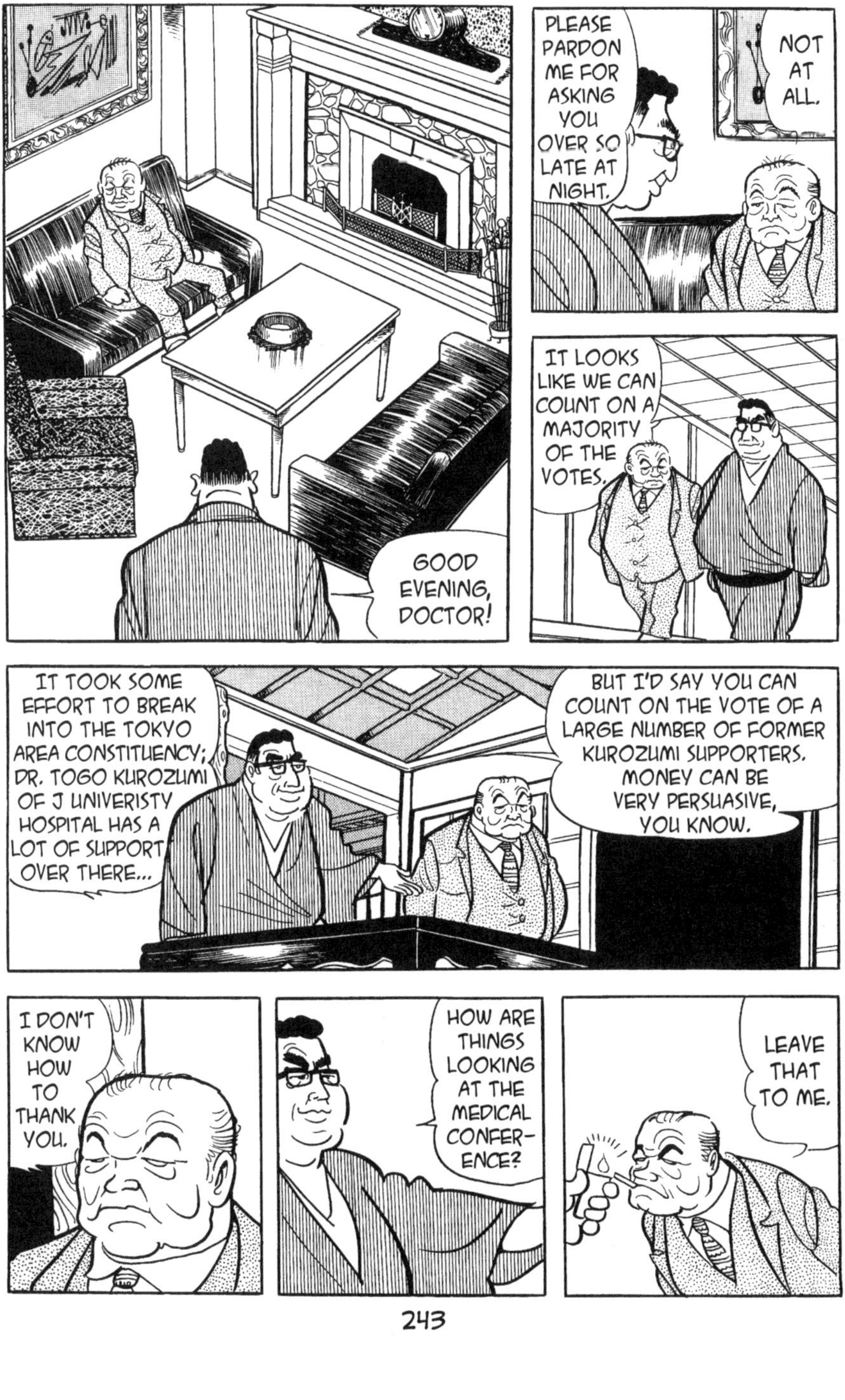
GOOD EVENING, DOCTOR!
PLEASE PARDON ME FOR ASKING YOU OVER SO LATE AT NIGHT.
NOT AT ALL.
IT LOOKS LIKE WE CAN COUNT ON A MAJORITY OF THE VOTES.
IT TOOK SOME EFFORT TO BREAK INTO THE TOKYO AREA CONSTITUENCY; DR. TOGO KUROZUMI OF J UNIVERISTY HOSPITAL HAS A LOT OF SUPPORT OVER THERE...
BUT I'D SAY YOU CAN COUNT ON THE VOTE OF A LARGE NUMBER OF FORMER KUROZUMI SUPPORTERS. MONEY CAN BE VERY PERSUASIVE, YOU KNOW.
I DON'T KNOW HOW TO THANK YOU.
HOW ARE THINGS LOOKING AT THE MEDICAL CONFERENCE?
LEAVE THAT TO ME.

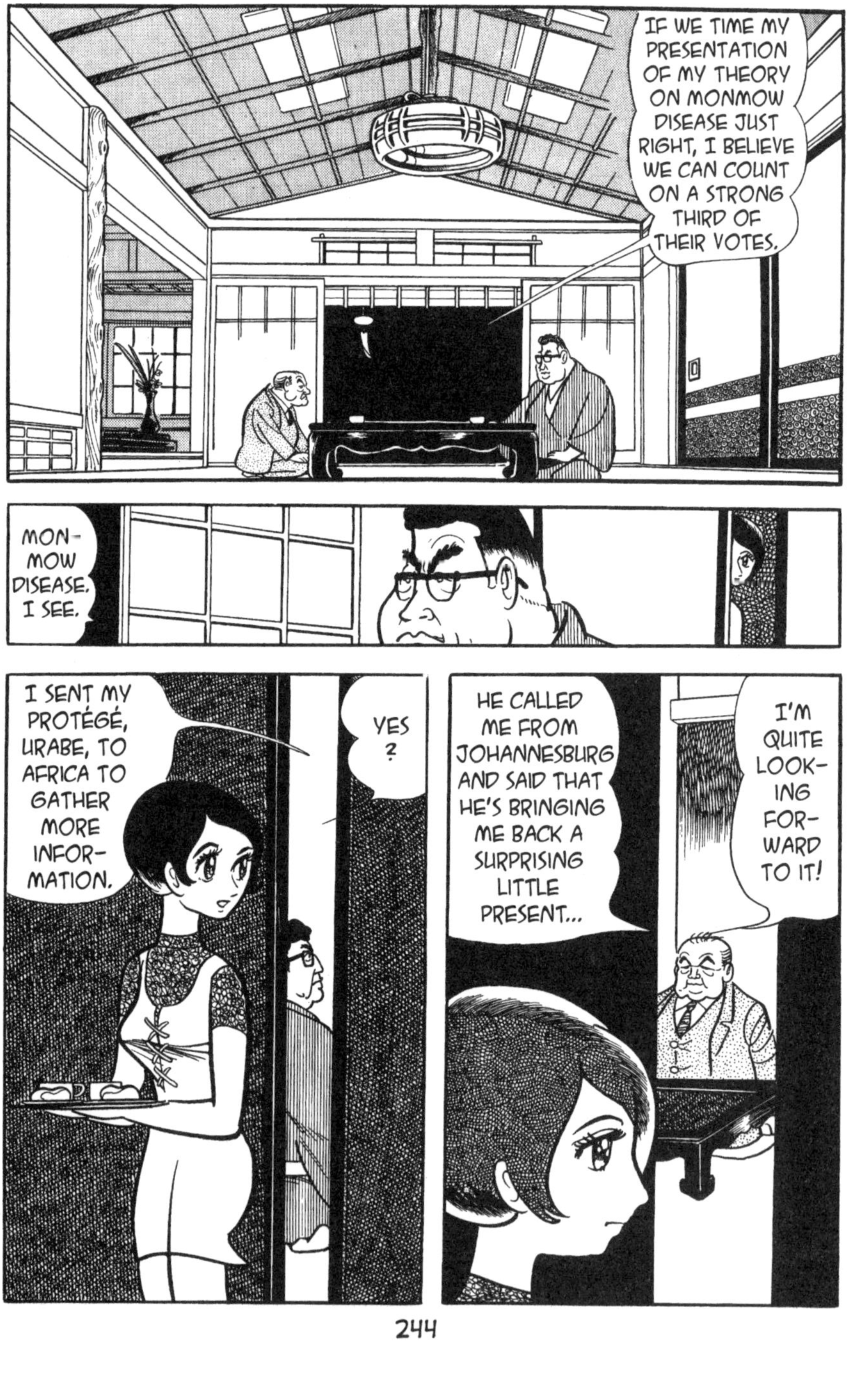
IF WE TIME MY PRESENTATION OF MY THEORY ON MONMOW DISEASE JUST RIGHT, I BELIEVE WE CAN COUNT ON A STRONG THIRD OF THEIR VOTES.
MON-MOW DISEASE. I SEE.
I SENT MY PROTÉGÉ, URABE, TO AFRICA TO GATHER MORE INFOR-MATION.
YES ?
HE CALLED ME FROM JOHANNESBURG AND SAID THAT HE'S BRINGING ME BACK A SURPRISING LITTLE PRESENT...
I'M QUITE LOOK-ING FOR-WARD TO IT!

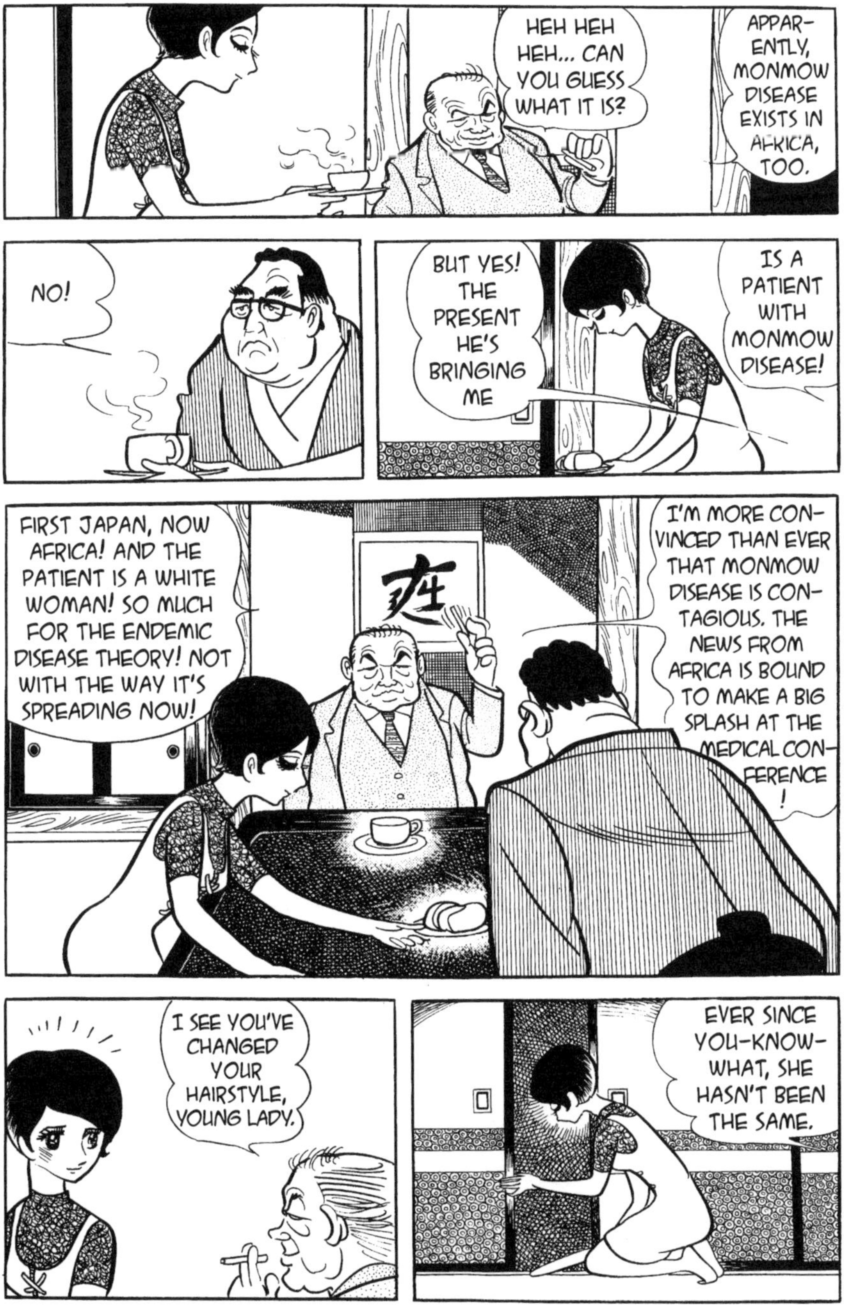
HEH HEH HEH... CAN YOU GUESS WHAT IT IS?
APPARENTLY, MONMOW DISEASE EXISTS IN AFRICA, TOO.
NO!
BUT YES! THE PRESENT HE'S BRINGING ME
IS A PATIENT WITH MONMOW DISEASE!
FIRST JAPAN, NOW AFRICA! AND THE PATIENT IS A WHITE WOMAN! SO MUCH FOR THE ENDEMIC DISEASE THEORY! NOT WITH THE WAY IT'S SPREADING NOW!
I'M MORE CONVINCED THAN EVER THAT MONMOW DISEASE IS CONTAGIOUS. THE NEWS FROM AFRICA IS BOUND TO MAKE A BIG SPLASH AT THE MEDICAL CONFERENCE!
I SEE YOU'VE CHANGED YOUR HAIRSTYLE, YOUNG LADY.
EVER SINCE YOU-KNOW-WHAT, SHE HASN'T BEEN THE SAME.

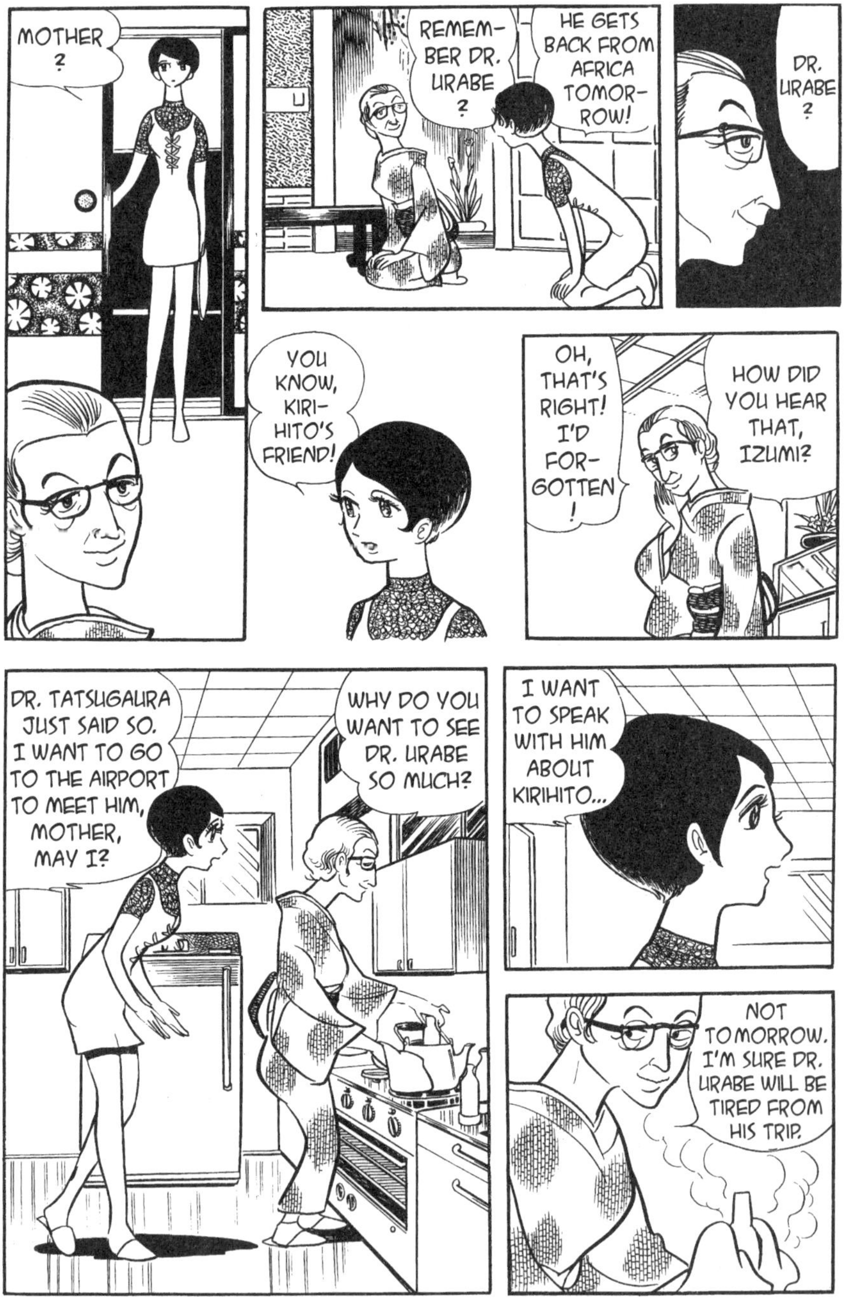
MOTHER?
REMEMBER DR. URABE?
HE GETS BACK FROM AFRICA TOMORROW!
DR. URABE?
YOU KNOW, KIRIHITO'S FRIEND!
OH, THAT'S RIGHT! I'D FORGOTTEN!
HOW DID YOU HEAR THAT, IZUMI?
DR. TATSUGAURA JUST SAID SO. I WANT TO GO TO THE AIRPORT TO MEET HIM, MOTHER, MAY I?
WHY DO YOU WANT TO SEE DR. URABE SO MUCH?
I WANT TO SPEAK WITH HIM ABOUT KIRIHITO...
NOT TOMORROW. I'M SURE DR. URABE WILL BE TIRED FROM HIS TRIP.

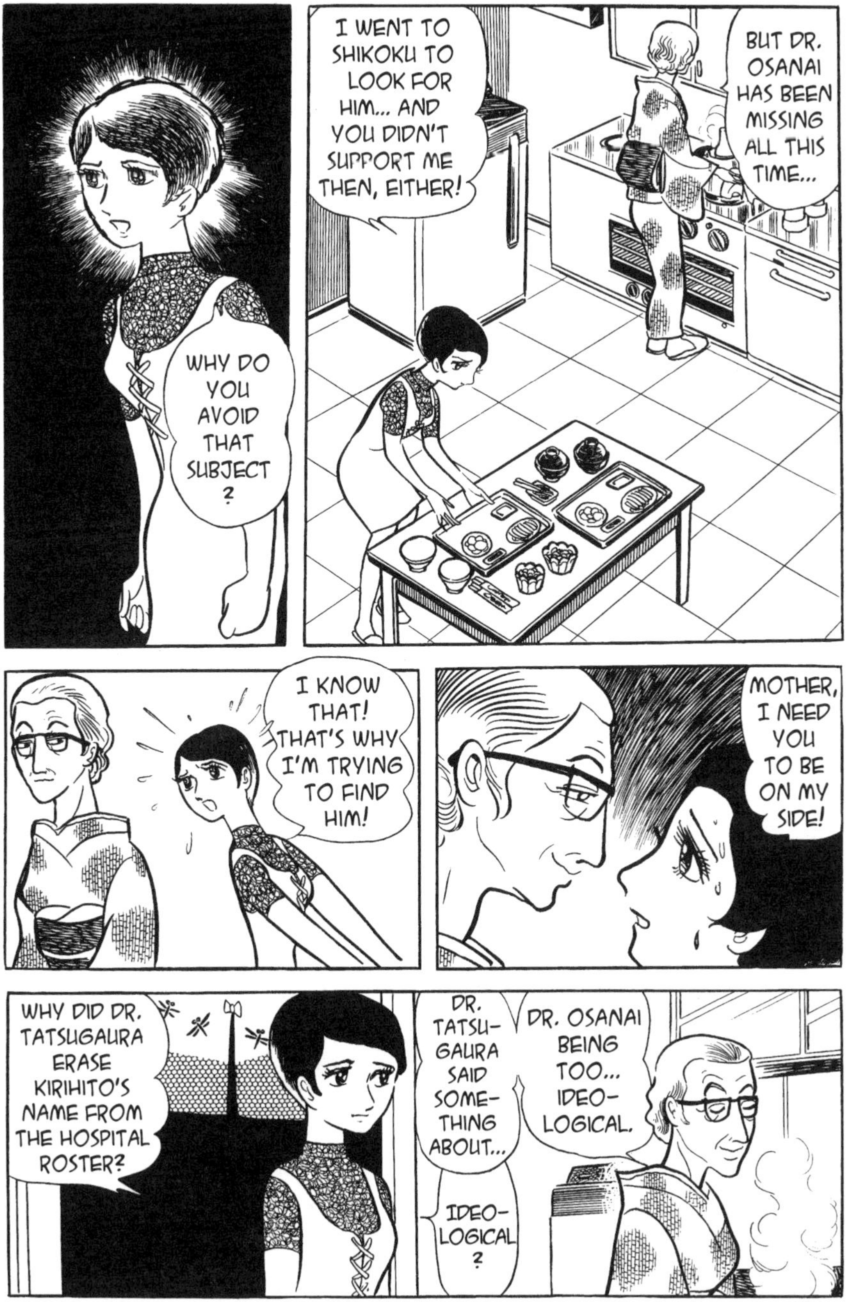
WHY DO YOU AVOID THAT SUBJECT?
I WENT TO SHIKOKU TO LOOK FOR HIM... AND YOU DIDN'T SUPPORT ME THEN, EITHER!
BUT DR. OSANAI HAS BEEN MISSING ALL THIS TIME...
I KNOW THAT! THAT'S WHY I'M TRYING TO FIND HIM!
MOTHER, I NEED YOU TO BE ON MY SIDE!
WHY DID DR. TATSUGAURA ERASE KIRIHITO'S NAME FROM THE HOSPITAL ROSTER?
DR. TATSU-GAURA SAID SOME-THING ABOUT...
DR. OSANAI BEING TOO... IDEO-LOGICAL.
IDEO-LOGICAL?

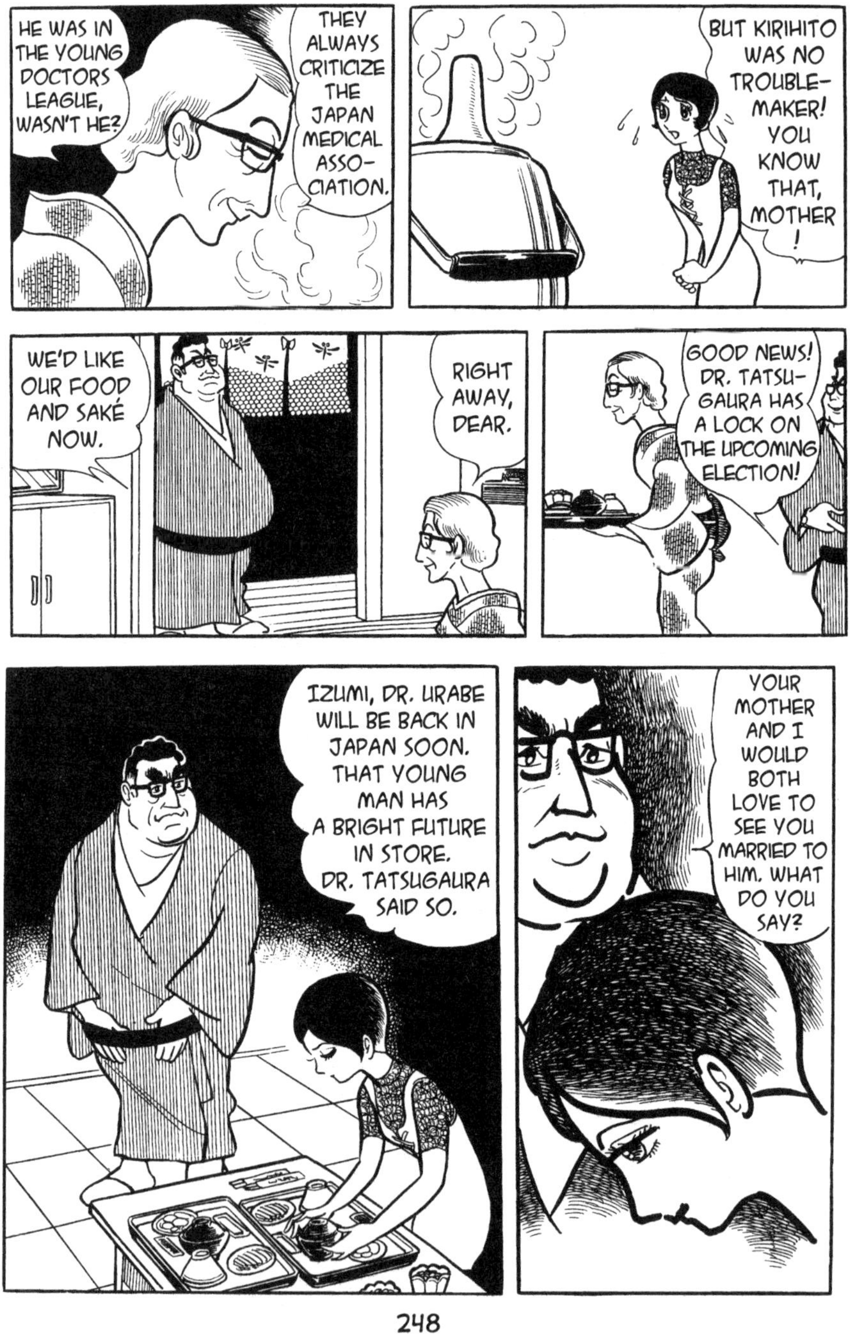
HE WAS IN THE YOUNG DOCTORS LEAGUE, WASN'T HE?
THEY ALWAYS CRITICIZE THE JAPAN MEDICAL ASSO-CIATION.
BUT KIRIHITO WAS NO TROUBLE-MAKER! YOU KNOW THAT, MOTHER!
WE'D LIKE OUR FOOD AND SAKÉ NOW.
RIGHT AWAY, DEAR.
GOOD NEWS! DR. TATSU-GAURA HAS A LOCK ON THE UPCOMING ELECTION!
IZUMI, DR. URABE WILL BE BACK IN JAPAN SOON. THAT YOUNG MAN HAS A BRIGHT FUTURE IN STORE. DR. TATSUGAURA SAID SO.
YOUR MOTHER AND I WOULD BOTH LOVE TO SEE YOU MARRIED TO HIM. WHAT DO YOU SAY?

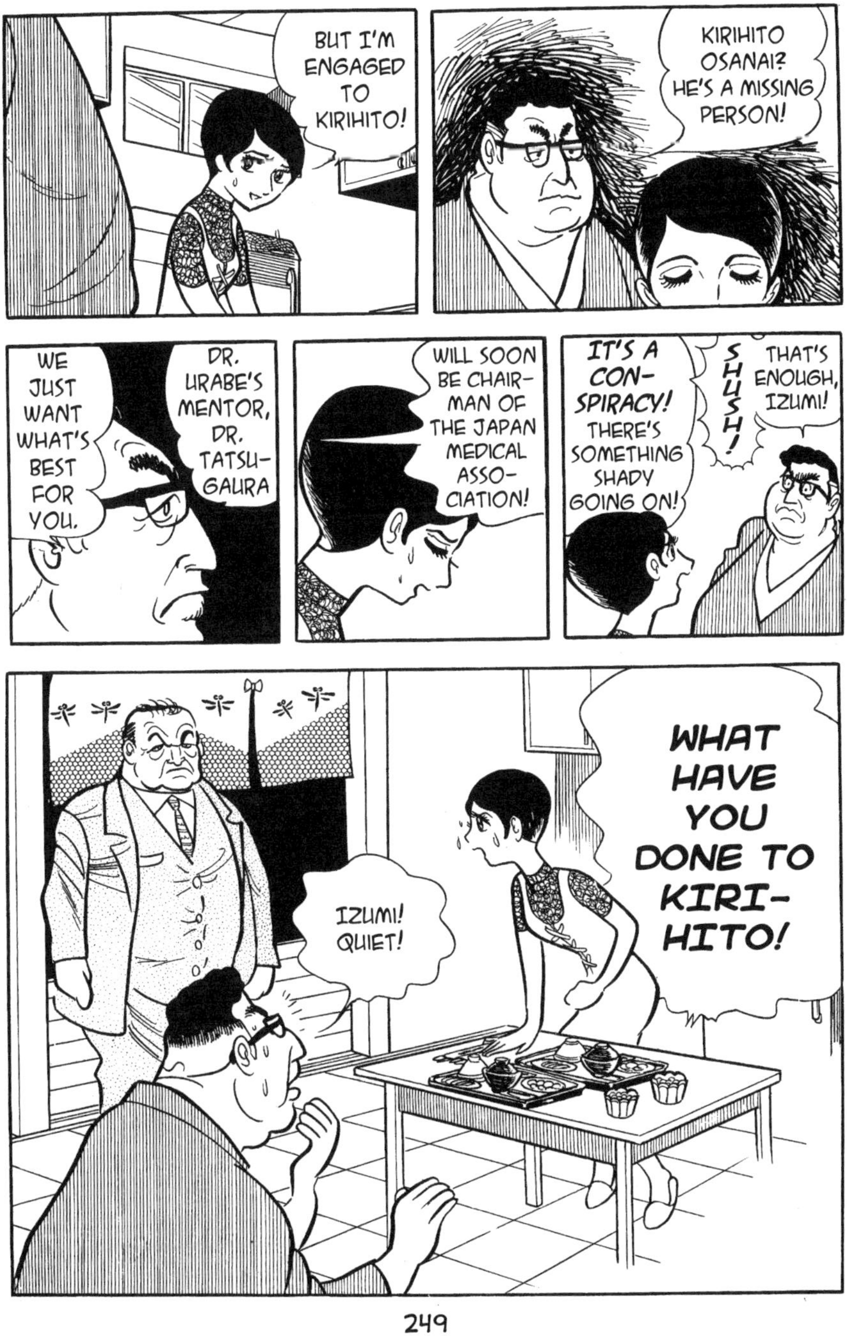
BUT I'M ENGAGED TO KIRIHITO!
KIRIHITO OSANAI? HE'S A MISSING PERSON!
WE JUST WANT WHAT'S BEST FOR YOU.
DR. URABE'S MENTOR, DR. TATSU-GAURA
WILL SOON BE CHAIR-MAN OF THE JAPAN MEDICAL ASSO-CIATION!
IT'S A CON-SPIRACY! THERE'S SOMETHING SHADY GOING ON!
SHUSH!
THAT'S ENOUGH, IZUMI!
WHAT HAVE YOU DONE TO KIRI-HITO!
IZUMI! QUIET!

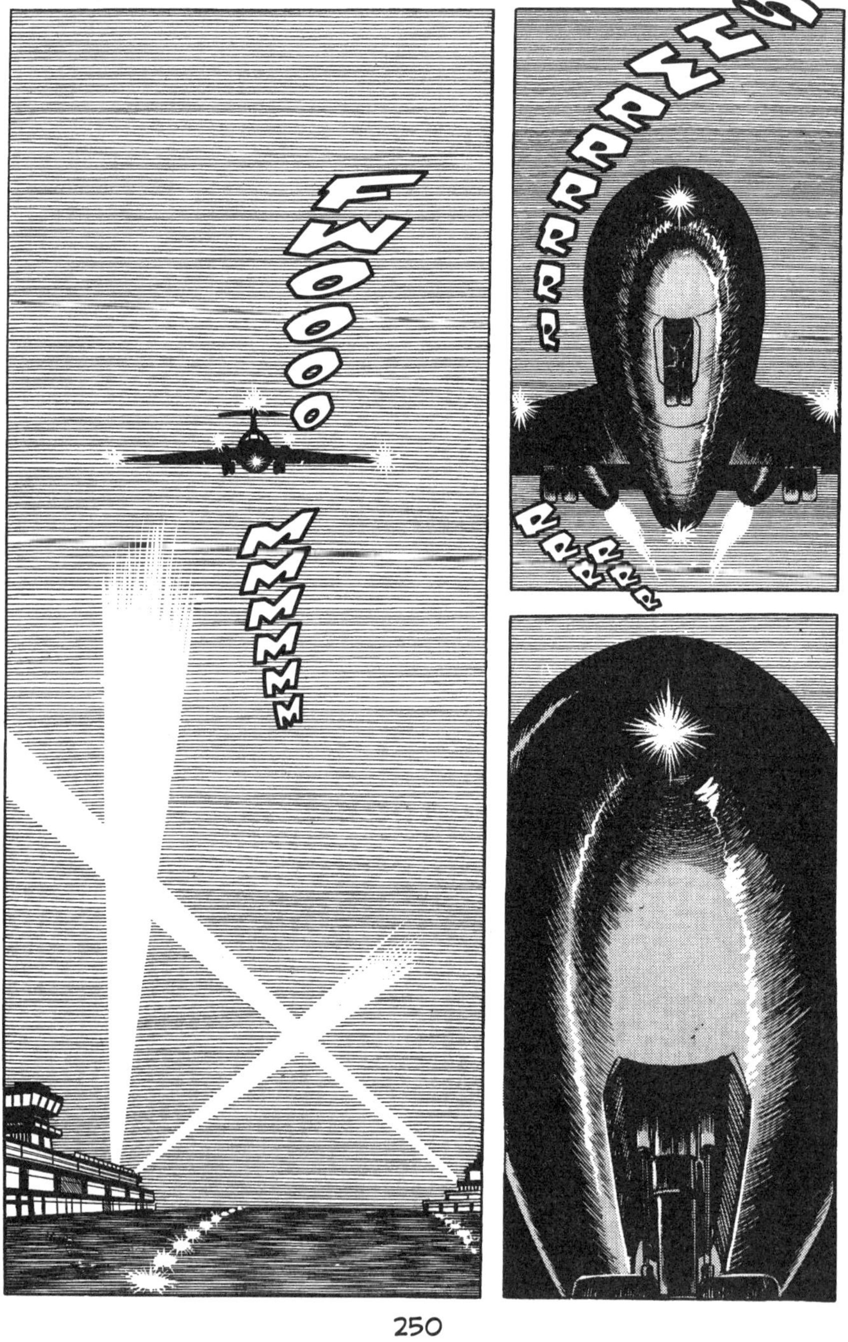
FWOOOOOMMMMMMM

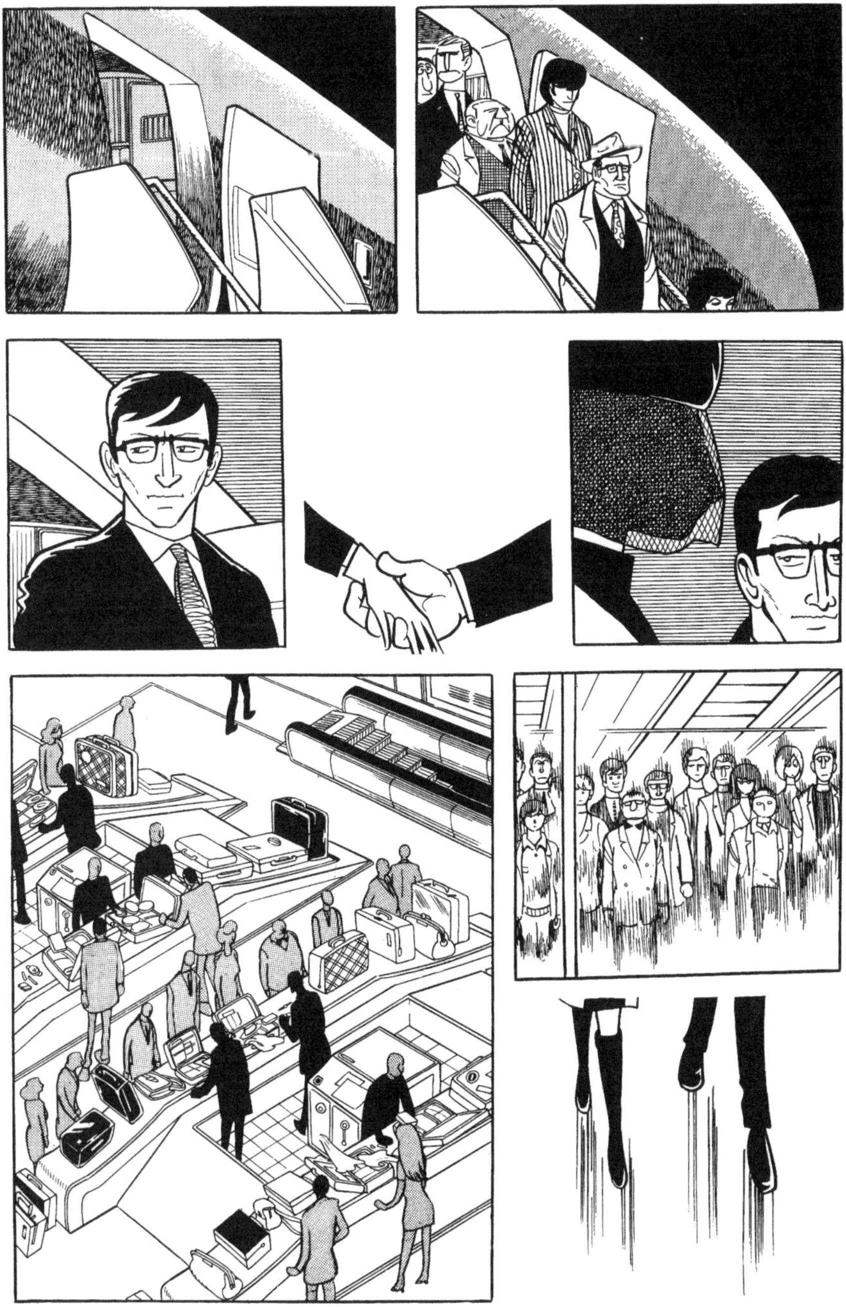

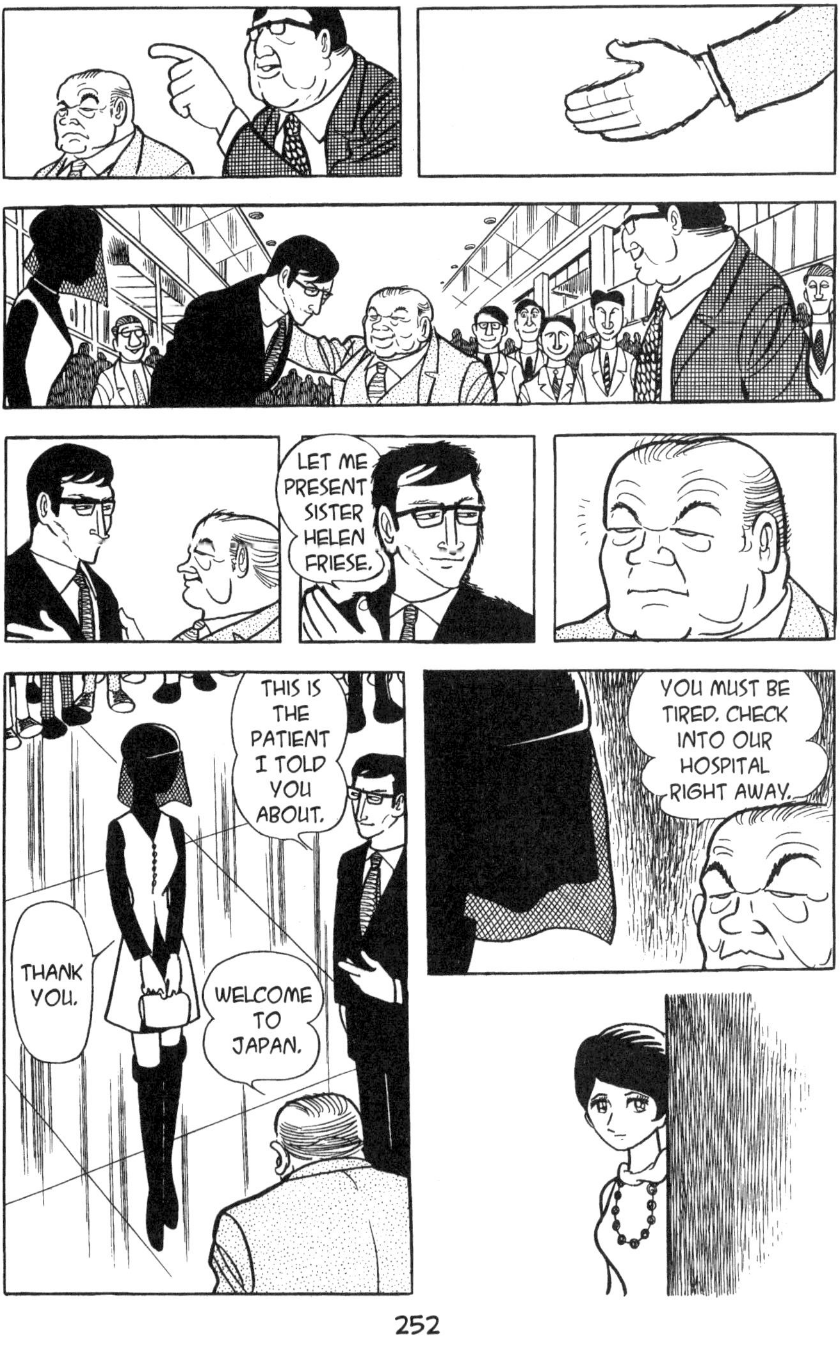
LET ME PRESENT SISTER HELEN FRIESE.
THIS IS THE PATIENT I TOLD YOU ABOUT.
THANK YOU.
WELCOME TO JAPAN.
YOU MUST BE TIRED. CHECK INTO OUR HOSPITAL RIGHT AWAY.

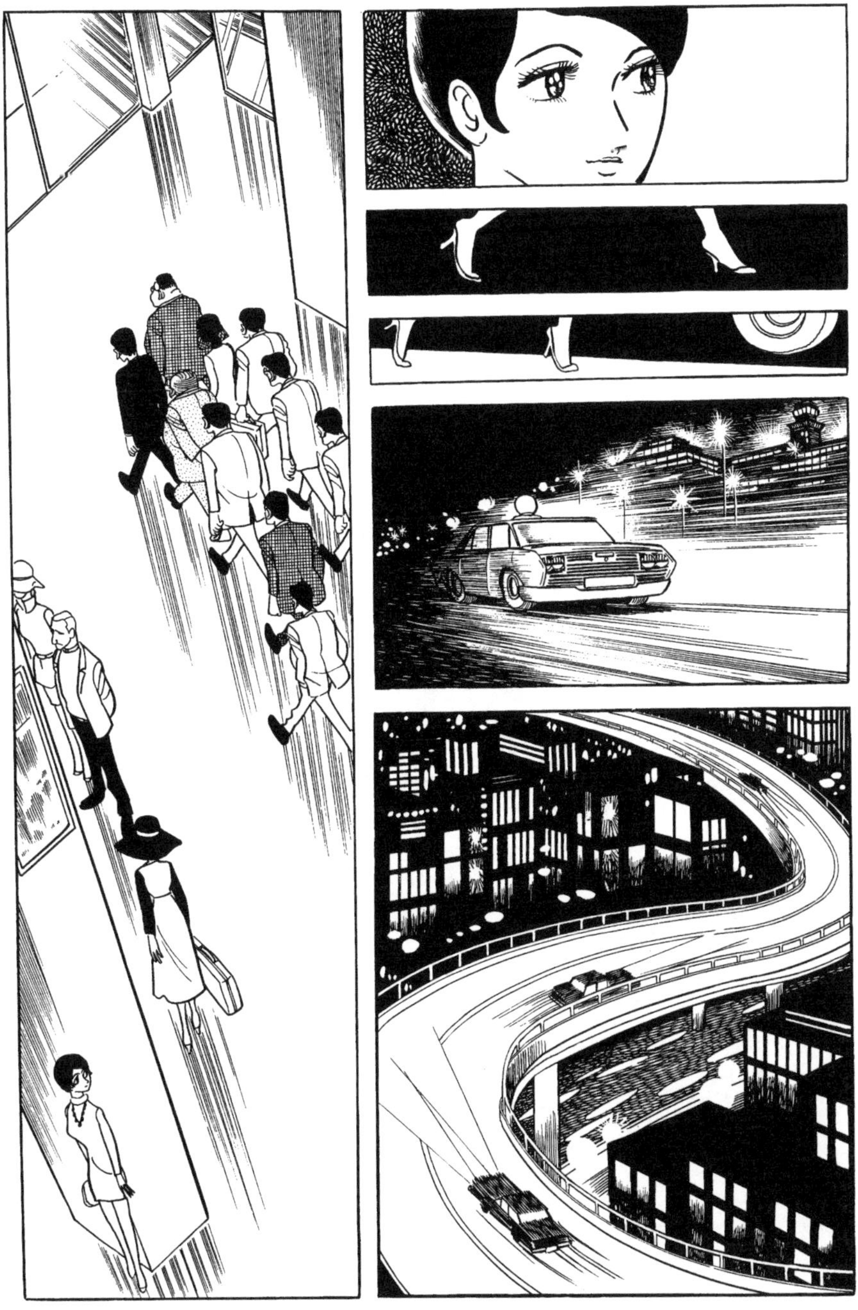

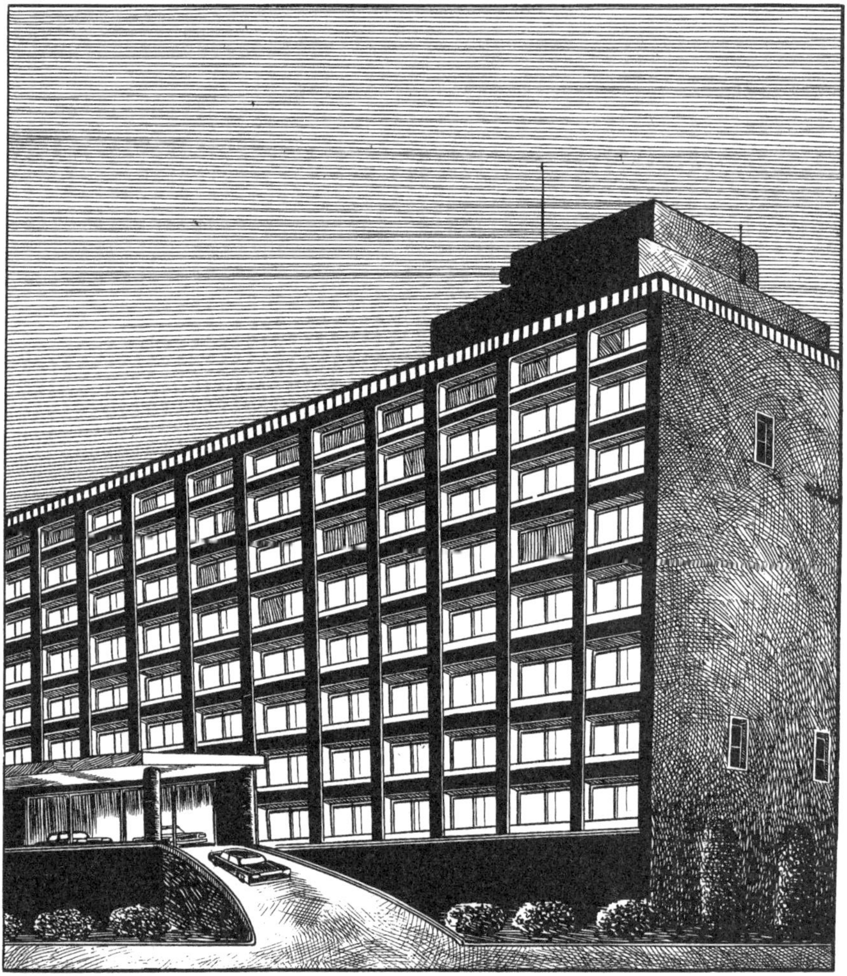

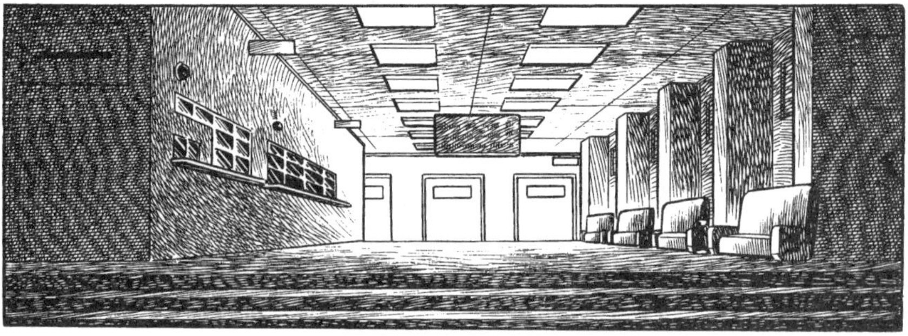

YOU MUST BE TIRED. GO HOME AND REST, WE CAN TALK TOMORROW.

THANK YOU.

I'VE HAD YOUR PATIENT PUT IN ROOM 67.

HERE'S MY REPORT AND THE DOCUMENTS FROM THE CONFER- ENCE...

IF WE'RE ABLE TO ISOLATE THE PATHOGEN THROUGH HER, PERHAPS WE SHOULD NAME IT VIRUS URABENSIS...

PATHO-GEN?

THAT'S RIGHT. IT'S OBVIOUSLY CAUSED BY AN INFECTIOUS PATHOGEN...

HAVE YOU IDENTIFIED IT ALREADY, DOCTOR?

NO, BUT IT'S ONLY A MATTER OF TIME, NOW...

ACTUALLY, MONMOW IS LOOKING MORE LIKE AN ENDEMIC DISEASE TO ME...

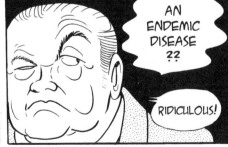

AN ENDEMIC DISEASE ??

RIDICULOUS!

255

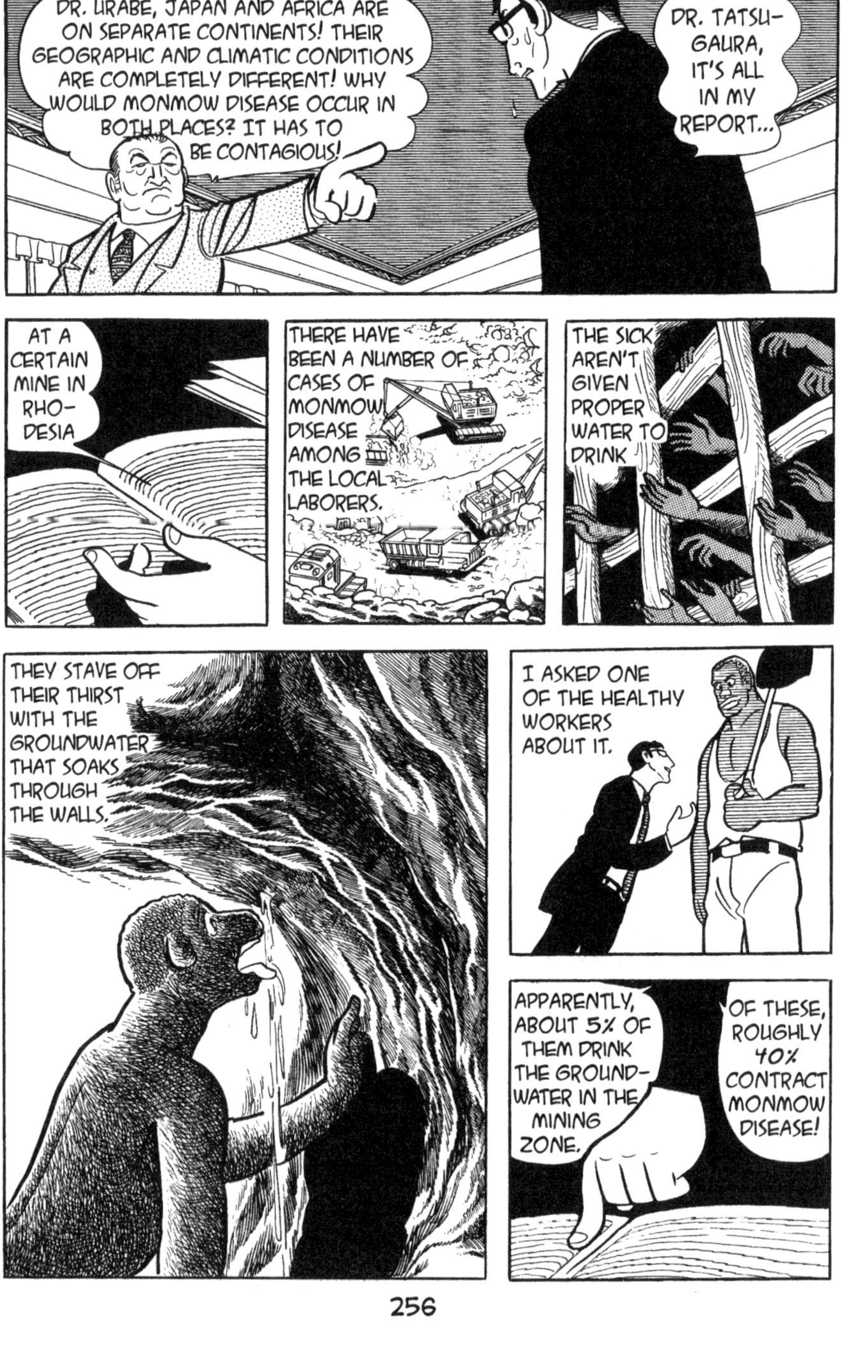

DR. URABE, JAPAN AND AFRICA ARE ON SEPARATE CONTINENTS! THEIR GEOGRAPHIC AND CLIMATIC CONDITIONS ARE COMPLETELY DIFFERENT! WHY WOULD MONMOW DISEASE OCCUR IN BOTH PLACES? IT HAS TO BE CONTAGIOUS!
DR. TATSUGAURA, IT'S ALL IN MY REPORT...
AT A CERTAIN MINE IN RHODESIA
THERE HAVE BEEN A NUMBER OF CASES OF MONMOW DISEASE AMONG THE LOCAL LABORERS.
THE SICK AREN'T GIVEN PROPER WATER TO DRINK
THEY STAVE OFF THEIR THIRST WITH THE GROUNDWATER THAT SOAKS THROUGH THE WALLS.
I ASKED ONE OF THE HEALTHY WORKERS ABOUT IT.
APPARENTLY, ABOUT 5% OF THEM DRINK THE GROUNDWATER IN THE MINING ZONE.
OF THESE, ROUGHLY 40% CONTRACT MONMOW DISEASE!

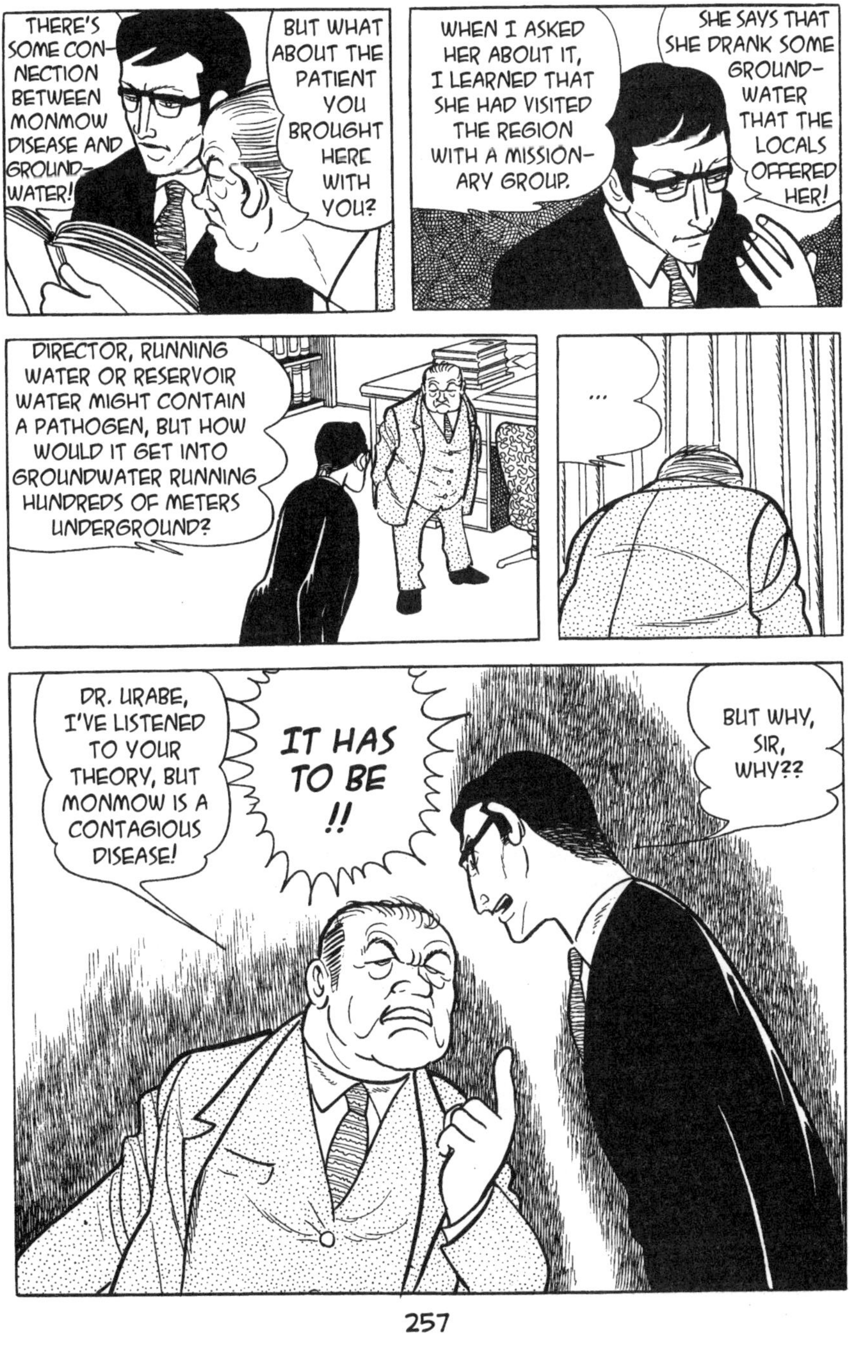
THERE'S SOME CONNECTION BETWEEN MONMOW DISEASE AND GROUNDWATER!
BUT WHAT ABOUT THE PATIENT YOU BROUGHT HERE WITH YOU?
WHEN I ASKED HER ABOUT IT, I LEARNED THAT SHE HAD VISITED THE REGION WITH A MISSIONARY GROUP.
SHE SAYS THAT SHE DRANK SOME GROUNDWATER THAT THE LOCALS OFFERED HER!
DIRECTOR, RUNNING WATER OR RESERVOIR WATER MIGHT CONTAIN A PATHOGEN, BUT HOW WOULD IT GET INTO GROUNDWATER RUNNING HUNDREDS OF METERS UNDERGROUND?
...
DR. URABE, I'VE LISTENED TO YOUR THEORY, BUT MONMOW IS A CONTAGIOUS DISEASE!
IT HAS TO BE !!
BUT WHY, SIR, WHY??

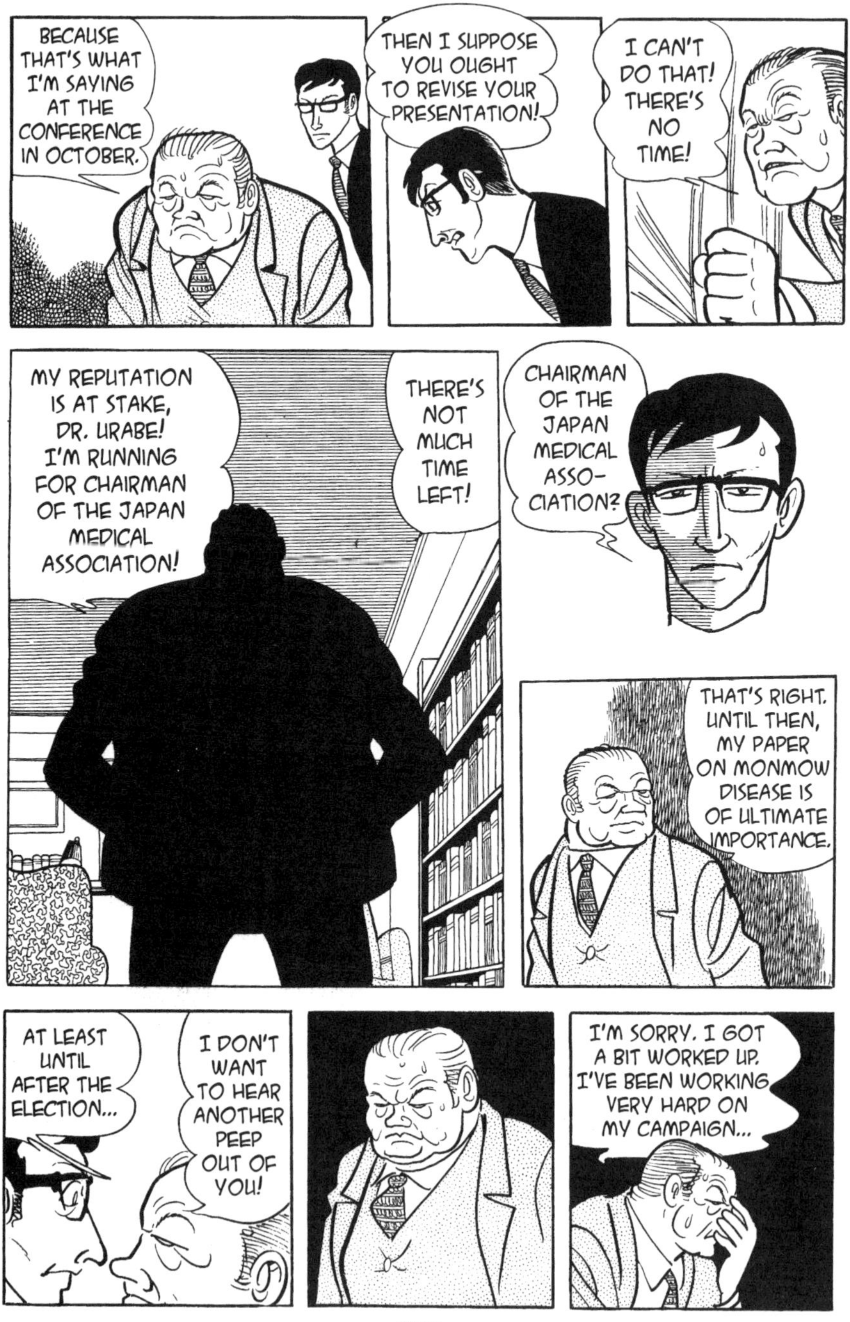
BECAUSE THAT'S WHAT I'M SAYING AT THE CONFERENCE IN OCTOBER.
THEN I SUPPOSE YOU OUGHT TO REVISE YOUR PRESENTATION!
I CAN'T DO THAT! THERE'S NO TIME!
MY REPUTATION IS AT STAKE, DR. URABE! I'M RUNNING FOR CHAIRMAN OF THE JAPAN MEDICAL ASSOCIATION!
THERE'S NOT MUCH TIME LEFT!
CHAIRMAN OF THE JAPAN MEDICAL ASSO-CIATION?
THAT'S RIGHT. UNTIL THEN, MY PAPER ON MONMOW DISEASE IS OF ULTIMATE IMPORTANCE.
AT LEAST UNTIL AFTER THE ELECTION...
I DON'T WANT TO HEAR ANOTHER PEEP OUT OF YOU!
I'M SORRY. I GOT A BIT WORKED UP. I'VE BEEN WORKING VERY HARD ON MY CAMPAIGN...

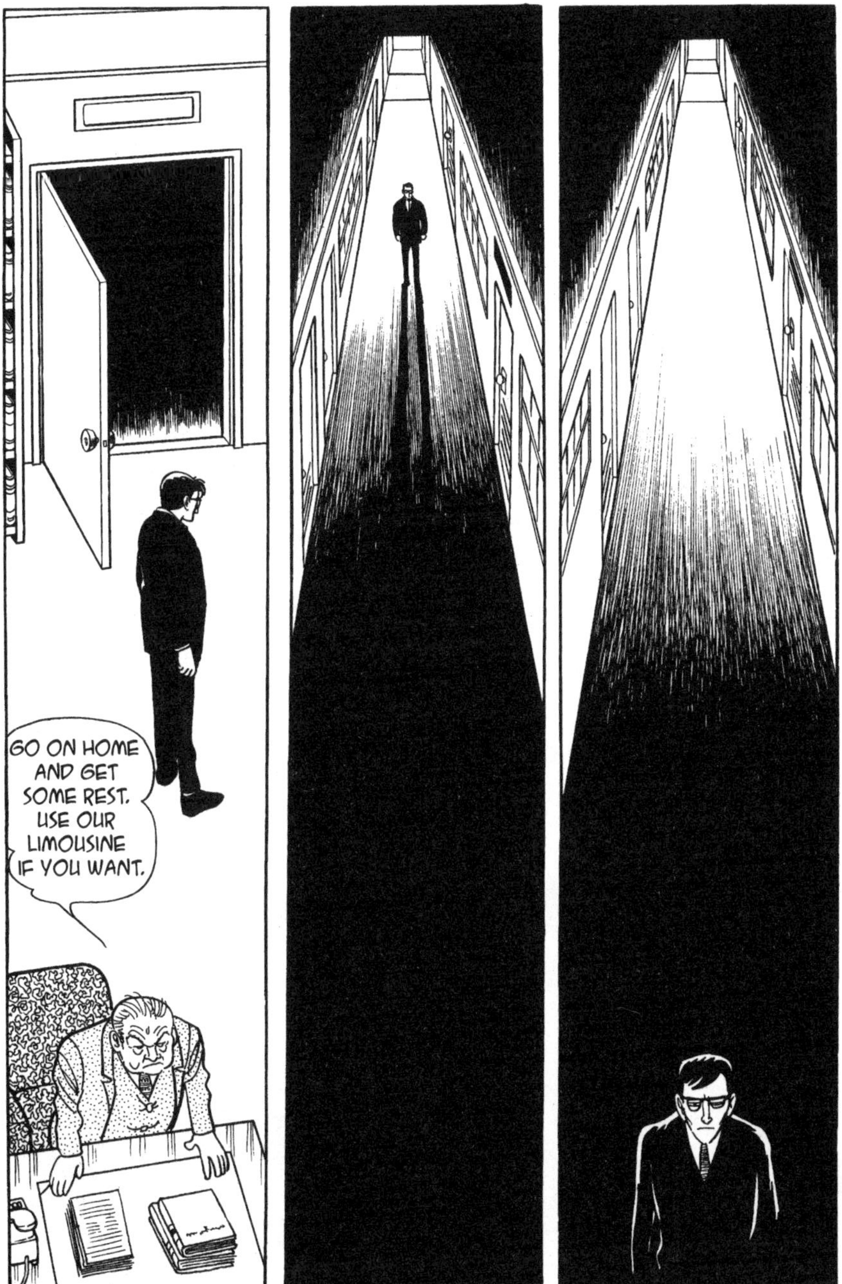
GO ON HOME AND GET SOME REST. USE OUR LIMOUSINE IF YOU WANT.

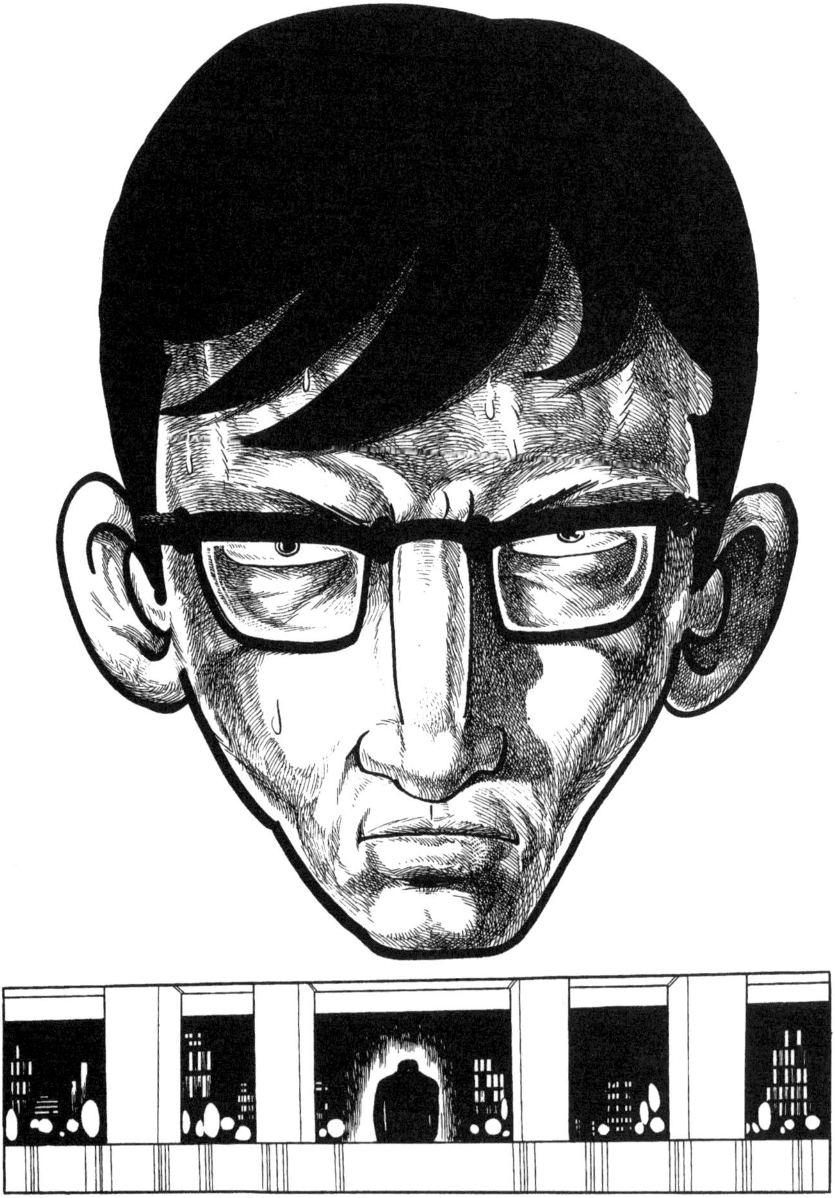

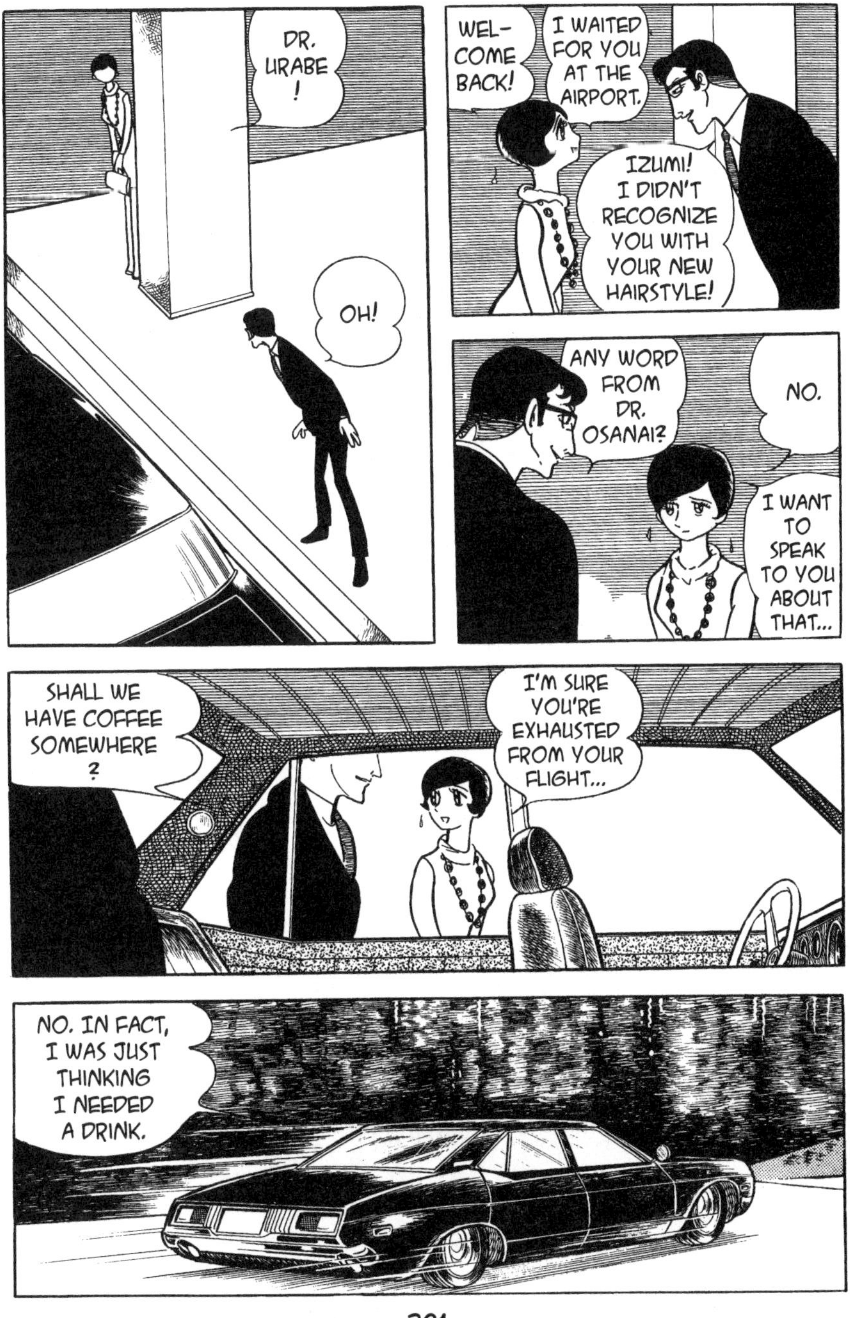
DR. URABE!
OH!
WEL-COME BACK!
I WAITED FOR YOU AT THE AIRPORT.
IZUMI! I DIDN'T RECOGNIZE YOU WITH YOUR NEW HAIRSTYLE!
ANY WORD FROM DR. OSANAI?
NO.
I WANT TO SPEAK TO YOU ABOUT THAT...
SHALL WE HAVE COFFEE SOMEWHERE?
I'M SURE YOU'RE EXHAUSTED FROM YOUR FLIGHT...
NO. IN FACT, I WAS JUST THINKING I NEEDED A DRINK.

I SEE... ARE YOU SURE YOU AREN'T JUMPING TO CONCLUSIONS?

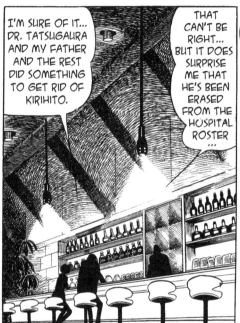

I'M SURE OF IT... DR. TATSUGAURA AND MY FATHER AND THE REST DID SOMETHING TO GET RID OF KIRIHITO.

THAT CAN'T BE RIGHT... BUT IT DOES SURPRISE ME THAT HE'S BEEN ERASED FROM THE HOSPITAL ROSTER ...

THEY SAY IT'S BECAUSE HE'S MISSING ...

DR. URABE, KIRIHITO WAS IN THE YOUNG DOCTORS LEAGUE, WASN'T HE?

WELL, YES, BUT HE WASN'T REALLY ACTIVELY INVOLVED...

YOU KNOW OSANAI, HE WASN'T ONE TO ROCK THE BOAT.

IT SOUNDS LIKE THAT'S WHY THEY WANTED TO GET RID OF HIM.

THAT DOESN'T SEEM POSSIBLE, EITHER...

262

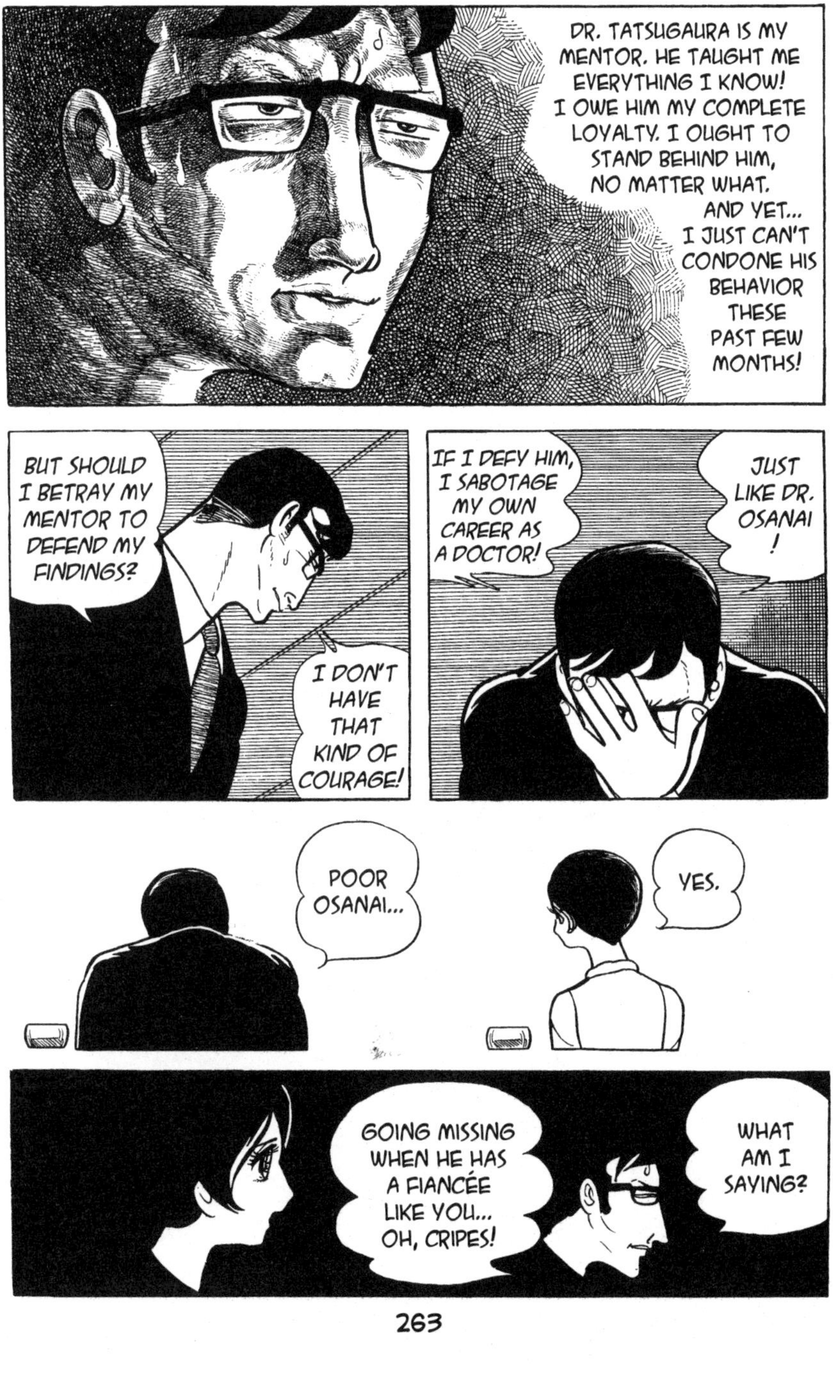

DR. TATSUGAURA IS MY MENTOR. HE TAUGHT ME EVERYTHING I KNOW! I OWE HIM MY COMPLETE LOYALTY. I OUGHT TO STAND BEHIND HIM, NO MATTER WHAT.
AND YET... I JUST CAN'T CONDONE HIS BEHAVIOR THESE PAST FEW MONTHS!
BUT SHOULD I BETRAY MY MENTOR TO DEFEND MY FINDINGS?
I DON'T HAVE THAT KIND OF COURAGE!
IF I DEFY HIM, I SABOTAGE MY OWN CAREER AS A DOCTOR!
JUST LIKE DR. OSANAI!
POOR OSANAI...
YES.
GOING MISSING WHEN HE HAS A FIANCÉE LIKE YOU... OH, CRIPES!
WHAT AM I SAYING?

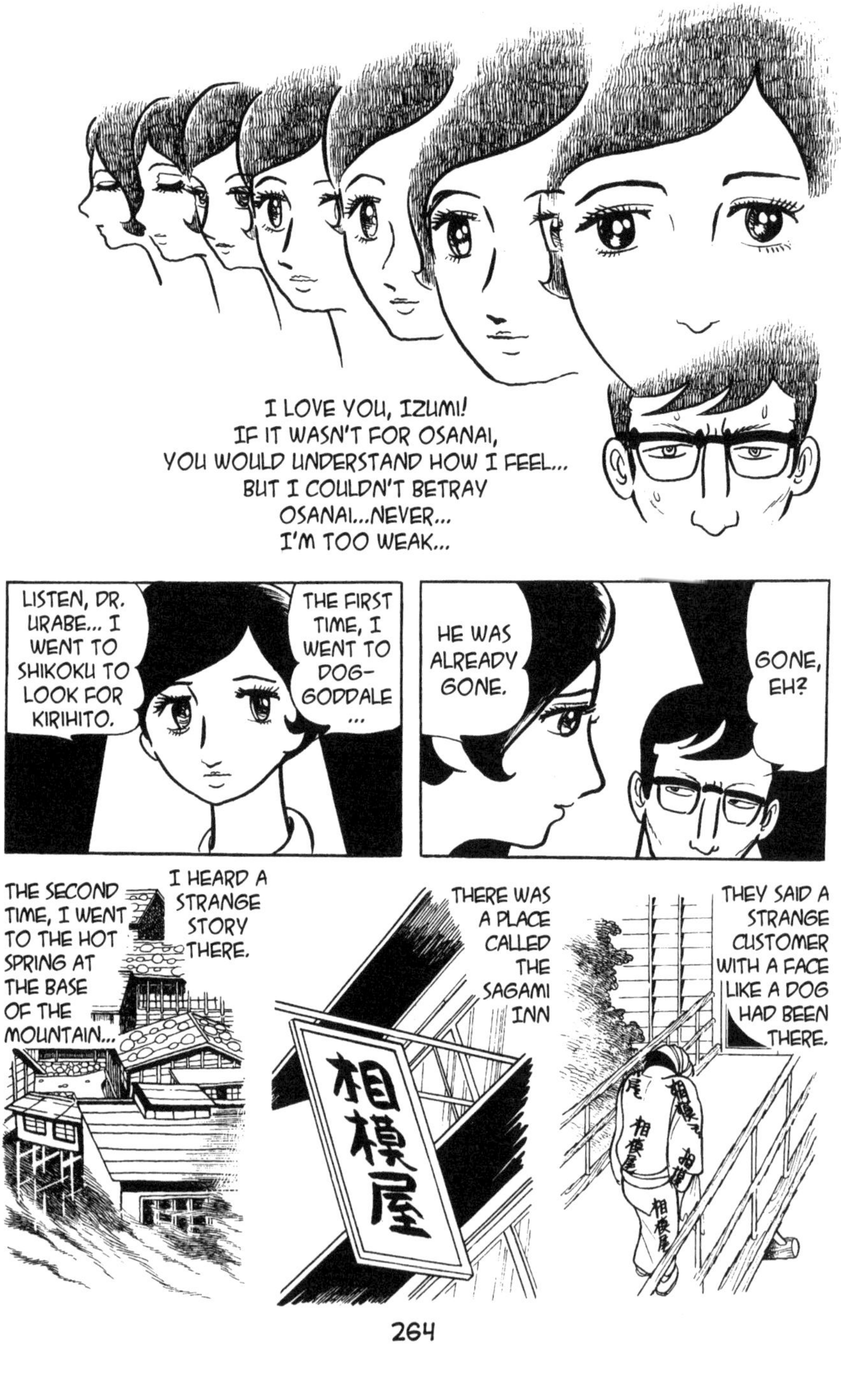
I LOVE YOU, IZUMI!
IF IT WASN'T FOR OSANAI,
YOU WOULD UNDERSTAND HOW I FEEL...
BUT I COULDN'T BETRAY
OSANAI...NEVER...
I'M TOO WEAK...
LISTEN, DR. URABE... I WENT TO SHIKOKU TO LOOK FOR KIRIHITO.
THE FIRST TIME, I WENT TO DOG-GODDALE ...
HE WAS ALREADY GONE.
GONE, EH?
THE SECOND TIME, I WENT TO THE HOT SPRING AT THE BASE OF THE MOUNTAIN...
I HEARD A STRANGE STORY THERE.
THERE WAS A PLACE CALLED THE SAGAMI INN
相模屋
THEY SAID A STRANGE CUSTOMER WITH A FACE LIKE A DOG HAD BEEN THERE.

THEY DISCOVERED HIM WOLFING DOWN RAW MEAT IN THE INN'S KITCHEN!

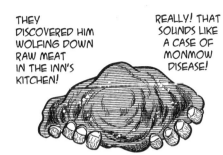

REALLY! THAT SOUNDS LIKE A CASE OF MONMOW DISEASE!

LISTEN TO THIS... A MAID AT THE INN HEARD THE MAN PLACING A PHONE CALL TO M UNIVERSITY HOSPITAL!

THE M.U.H. ??

THERE'S MORE...

AT A TEMPLE DOWN-STREAM FROM DOGGOD RIVER

THEY SAY A MAN WHO LOOKED LIKE A BADGER DROPPED OFF THE BODY OF A DEAD WOMAN AND DIS-APPEARED

HE ASKED THEM TO CONSE-CRATE THE BODY...

ARE YOU SUGGEST-ING...?

YOU THINK OSANAI DEVELOPED MONMOW DISEASE?

I DON'T KNOW.

BUT I JUST CAN'T STOP WONDERING ABOUT HIM...

IZUMI, YOU AND I WILL FIND OSANAI, NO MATTER WHAT!

I'M ASHAMED TO SAY IT, BUT I FEEL LOST TOO, WITHOUT HIM.

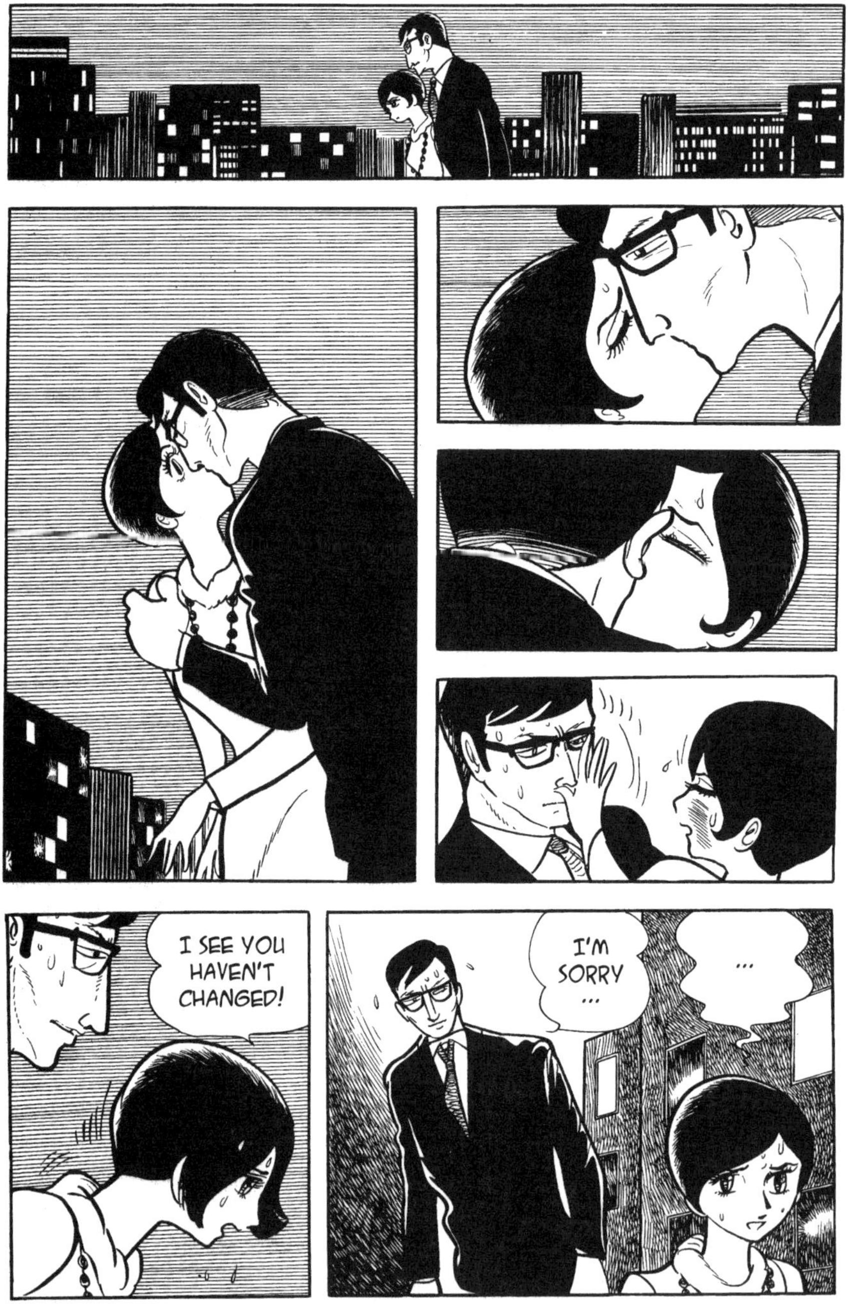
I SEE YOU HAVEN'T CHANGED!
I'M SORRY ...
...

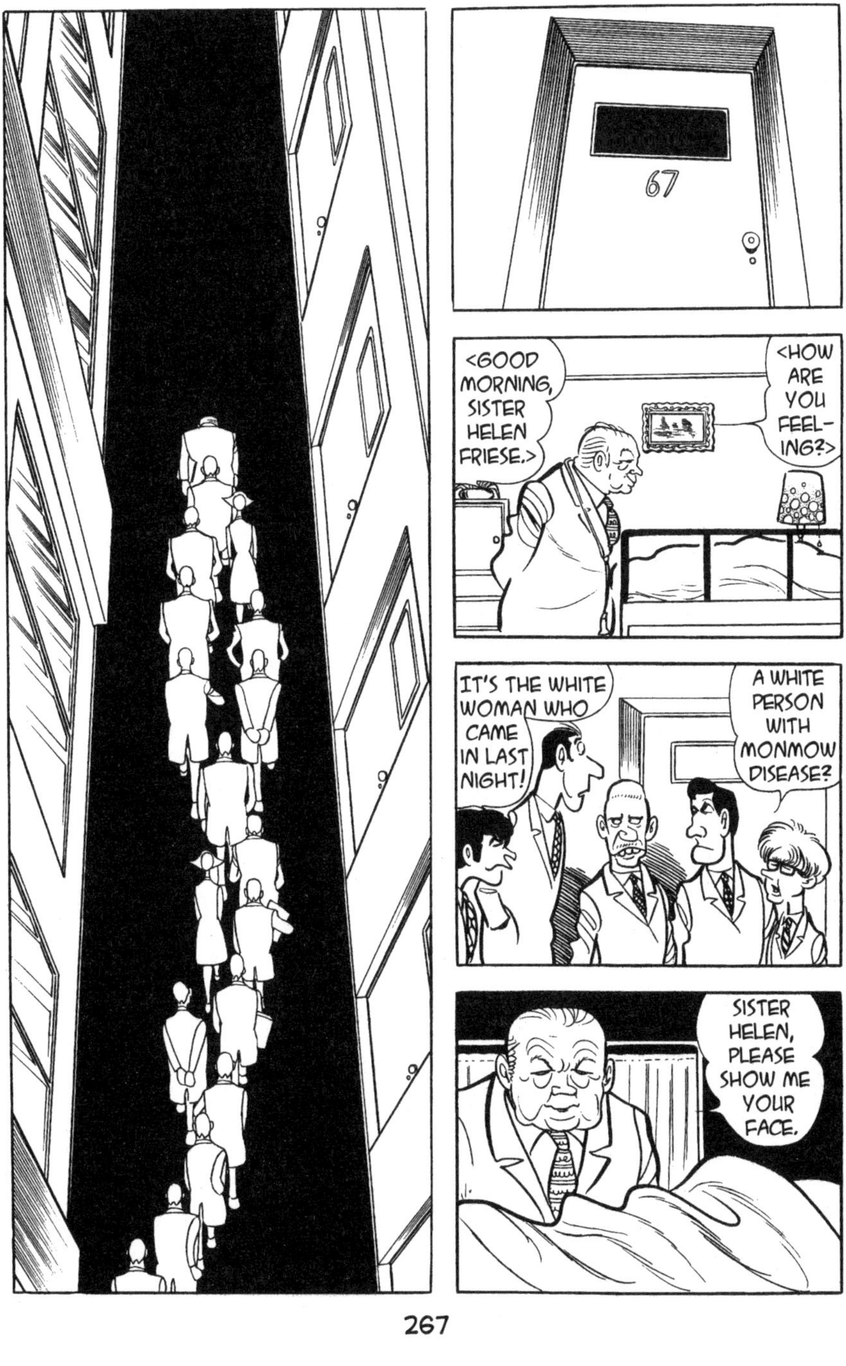
67
<GOOD MORNING, SISTER HELEN FRIESE.>
<HOW ARE YOU FEELING?>
IT'S THE WHITE WOMAN WHO CAME IN LAST NIGHT!
A WHITE PERSON WITH MONMOW DISEASE?
SISTER HELEN, PLEASE SHOW ME YOUR FACE.

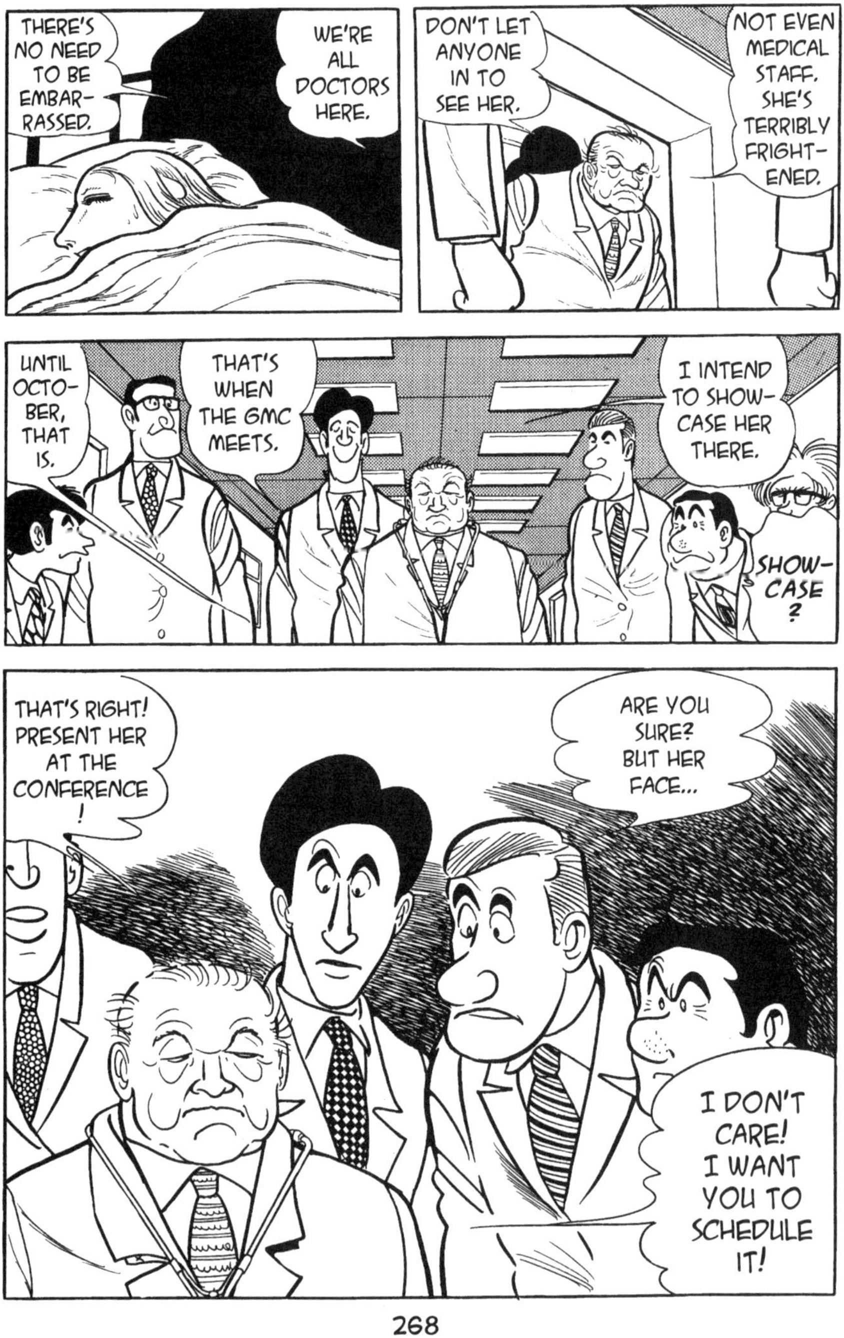
THERE'S NO NEED TO BE EMBARRASSED.
WE'RE ALL DOCTORS HERE.
DON'T LET ANYONE IN TO SEE HER.
NOT EVEN MEDICAL STAFF. SHE'S TERRIBLY FRIGHTENED.
UNTIL OCTOBER, THAT IS.
THAT'S WHEN THE GMC MEETS.
I INTEND TO SHOWCASE HER THERE.
SHOWCASE?
THAT'S RIGHT! PRESENT HER AT THE CONFERENCE!
ARE YOU SURE? BUT HER FACE...
I DON'T CARE! I WANT YOU TO SCHEDULE IT!

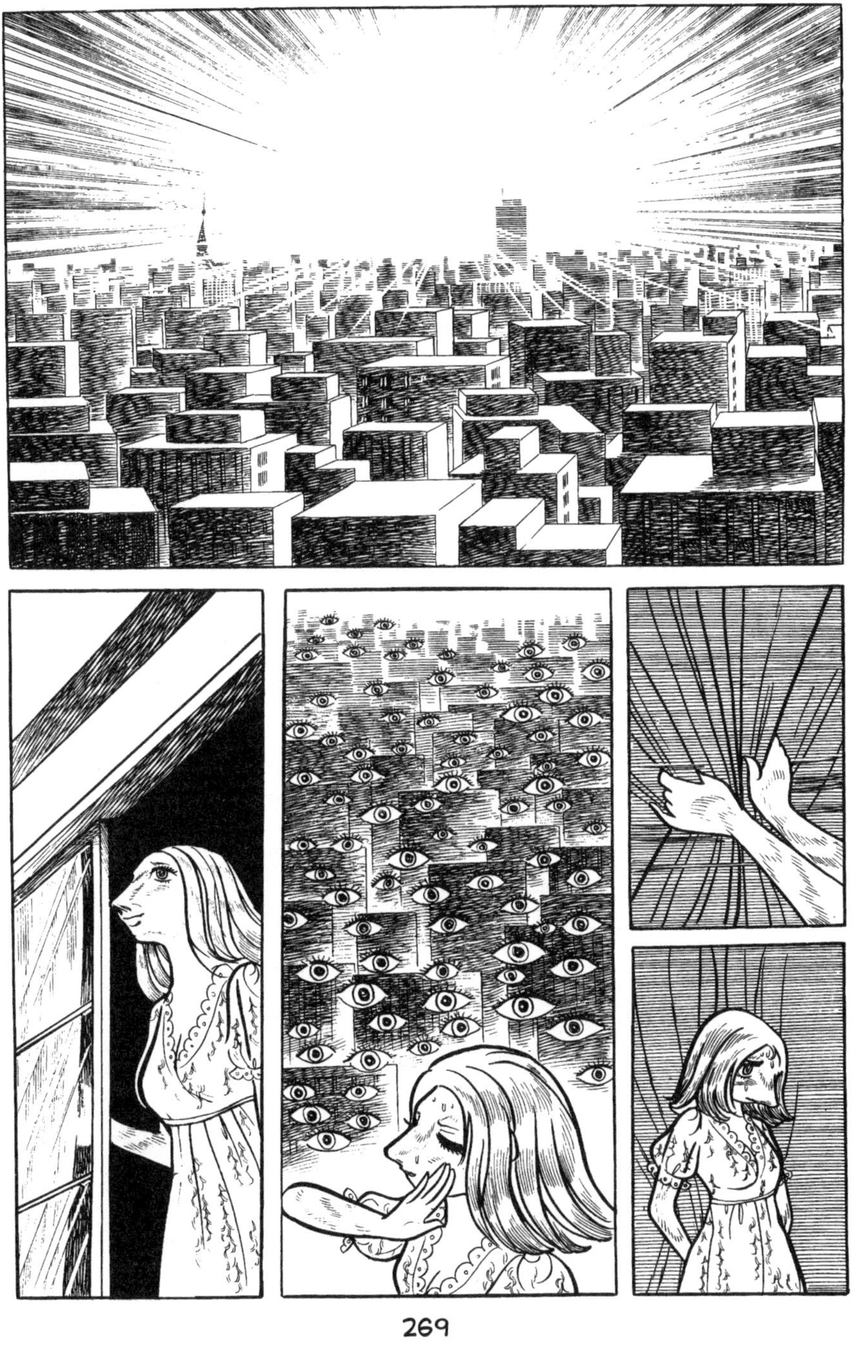

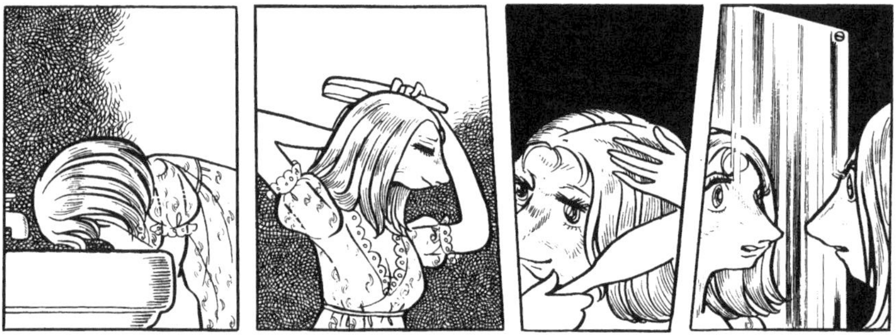

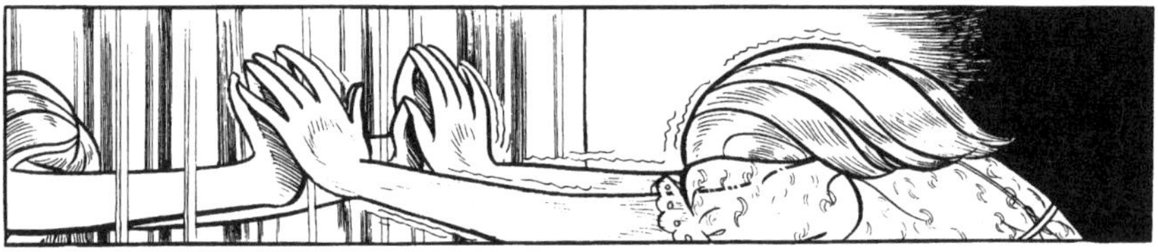

THEREFORE I SAY UNTO YOU, IS NOT THE LIFE MORE THAN MEAT,
AND THE BODY THAN RAIMENT? BEHOLD THE FOWLS OF THE AIR:
FOR THEY SOW NOT, NEITHER DO THEY REAP, NOR GATHER INTO BARNS;
YET YOUR HEAVENLY FATHER FEEDETH THEM. ARE YE NOT MUCH
BETTER THAN THEY? CONSIDER THE LILIES OF THE FIELD, HOW THEY GROW;
THEY TOIL NOT, NEITHER DO THEY SPIN: AND YET I SAY UNTO YOU,
THAT EVEN SOLOMON IN ALL HIS GLORY WAS NOT ARRAYED LIKE
ONE OF THESE. WHEREFORE, IF GOD SO CLOTHE THE GRASS OF THE FIELD,
WHICH TO DAY IS, AND TO MORROW
IS CAST INTO THE OVEN,
SHALL HE NOT
MUCH MORE
CLOTHE YOU?

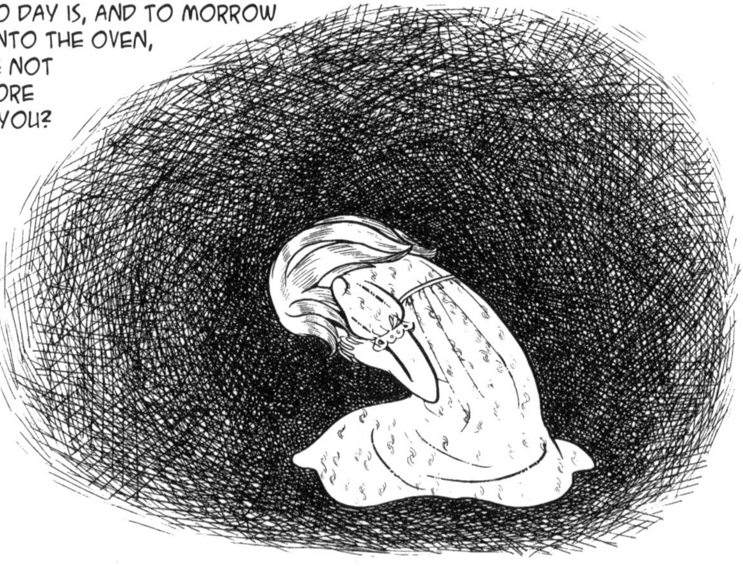

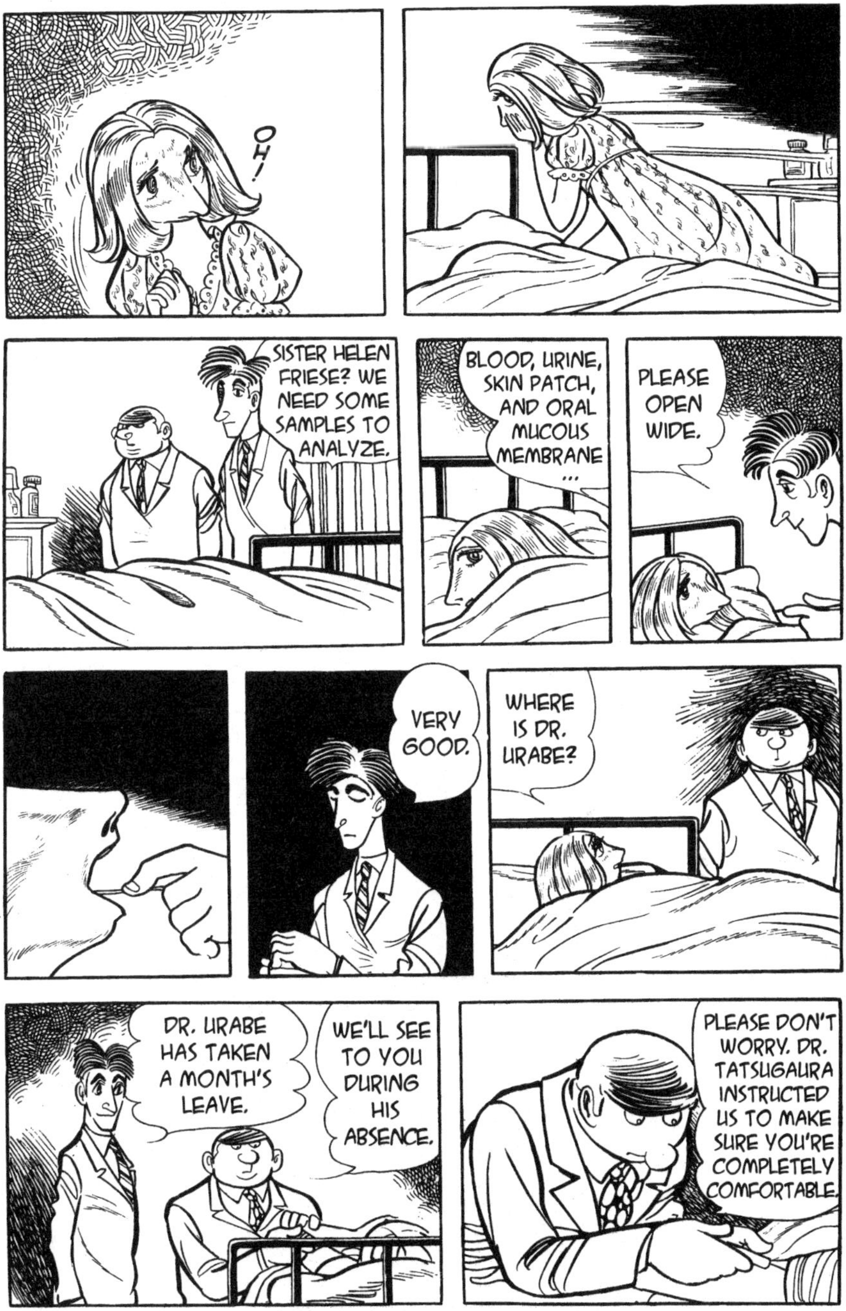
OH!
SISTER HELEN FRIESE? WE NEED SOME SAMPLES TO ANALYZE.
BLOOD, URINE, SKIN PATCH, AND ORAL MUCOUS MEMBRANE ...
PLEASE OPEN WIDE.
VERY GOOD.
WHERE IS DR. URABE?
DR. URABE HAS TAKEN A MONTH'S LEAVE.
WE'LL SEE TO YOU DURING HIS ABSENCE.
PLEASE DON'T WORRY. DR. TATSUGAURA INSTRUCTED US TO MAKE SURE YOU'RE COMPLETELY COMFORTABLE.

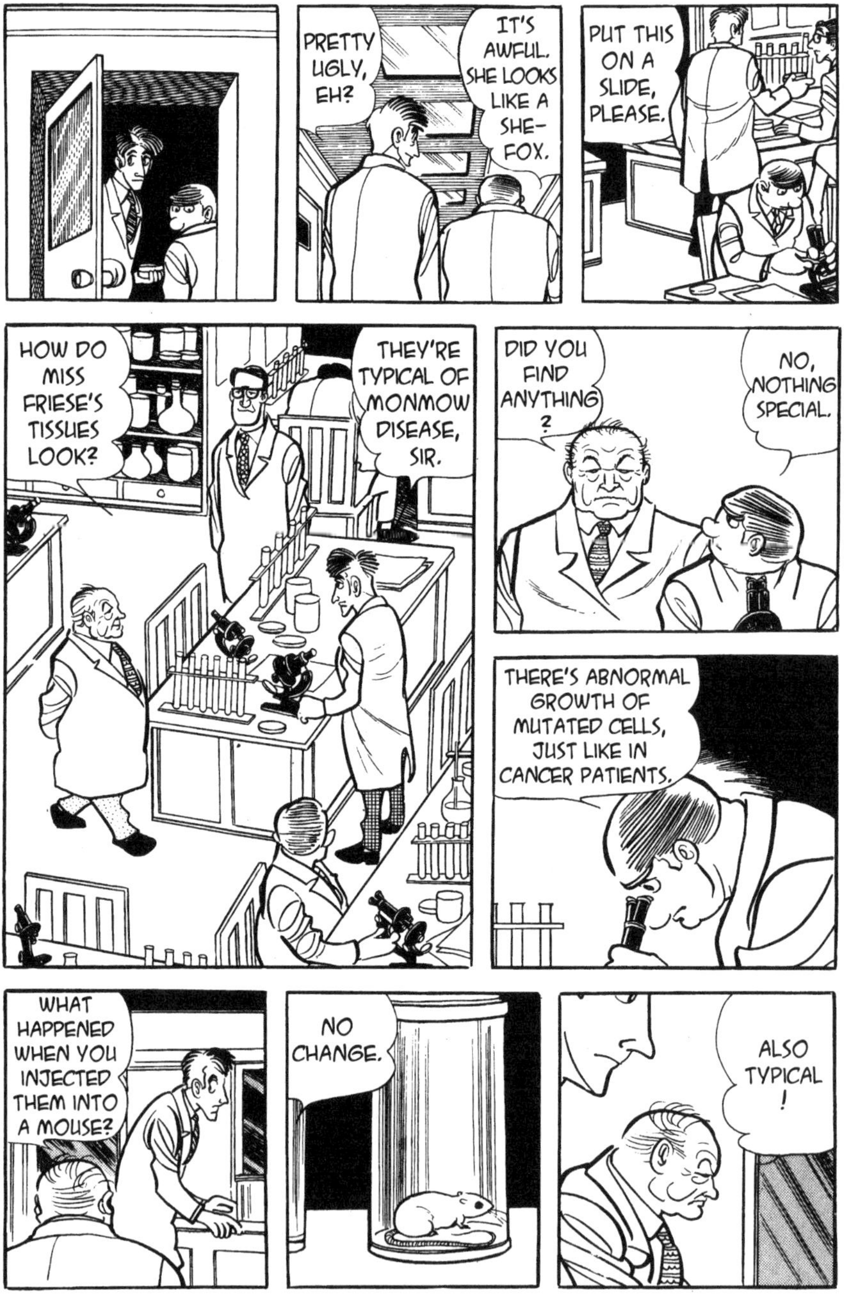
PRETTY UGLY, EH?
IT'S AWFUL. SHE LOOKS LIKE A SHE-FOX.
PUT THIS ON A SLIDE, PLEASE.
HOW DO MISS FRIESE'S TISSUES LOOK?
THEY'RE TYPICAL OF MONMOW DISEASE, SIR.
DID YOU FIND ANYTHING?
NO, NOTHING SPECIAL.
THERE'S ABNORMAL GROWTH OF MUTATED CELLS, JUST LIKE IN CANCER PATIENTS.
WHAT HAPPENED WHEN YOU INJECTED THEM INTO A MOUSE?
NO CHANGE.
ALSO TYPICAL!

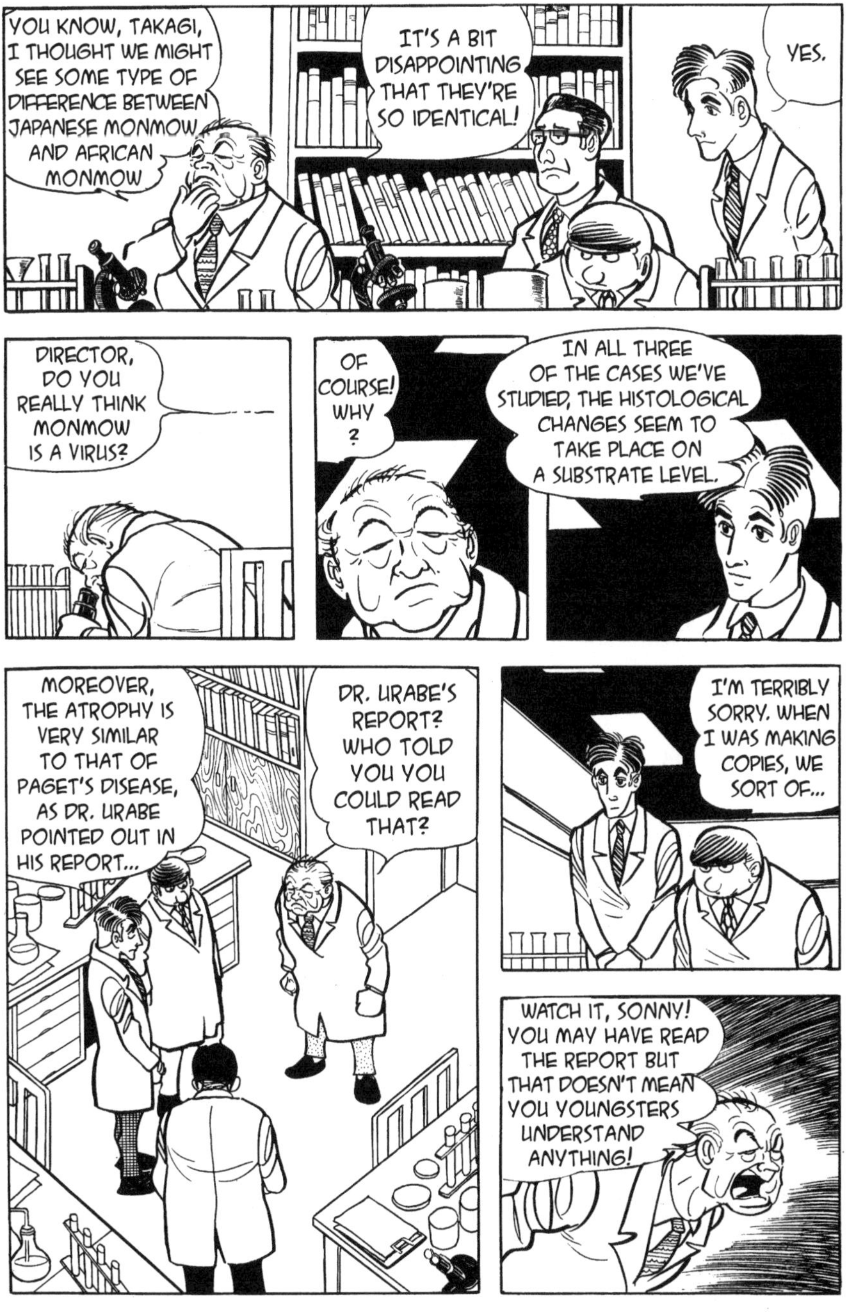
YOU KNOW, TAKAGI, I THOUGHT WE MIGHT SEE SOME TYPE OF DIFFERENCE BETWEEN JAPANESE MONMOW AND AFRICAN MONMOW
IT'S A BIT DISAPPOINTING THAT THEY'RE SO IDENTICAL!
YES.
DIRECTOR, DO YOU REALLY THINK MONMOW IS A VIRUS?
OF COURSE! WHY ?
IN ALL THREE OF THE CASES WE'VE STUDIED, THE HISTOLOGICAL CHANGES SEEM TO TAKE PLACE ON A SUBSTRATE LEVEL.
MOREOVER, THE ATROPHY IS VERY SIMILAR TO THAT OF PAGET'S DISEASE, AS DR. URABE POINTED OUT IN HIS REPORT...
DR. URABE'S REPORT? WHO TOLD YOU YOU COULD READ THAT?
I'M TERRIBLY SORRY. WHEN I WAS MAKING COPIES, WE SORT OF...
WATCH IT, SONNY! YOU MAY HAVE READ THE REPORT BUT THAT DOESN'T MEAN YOU YOUNGSTERS UNDERSTAND ANYTHING!

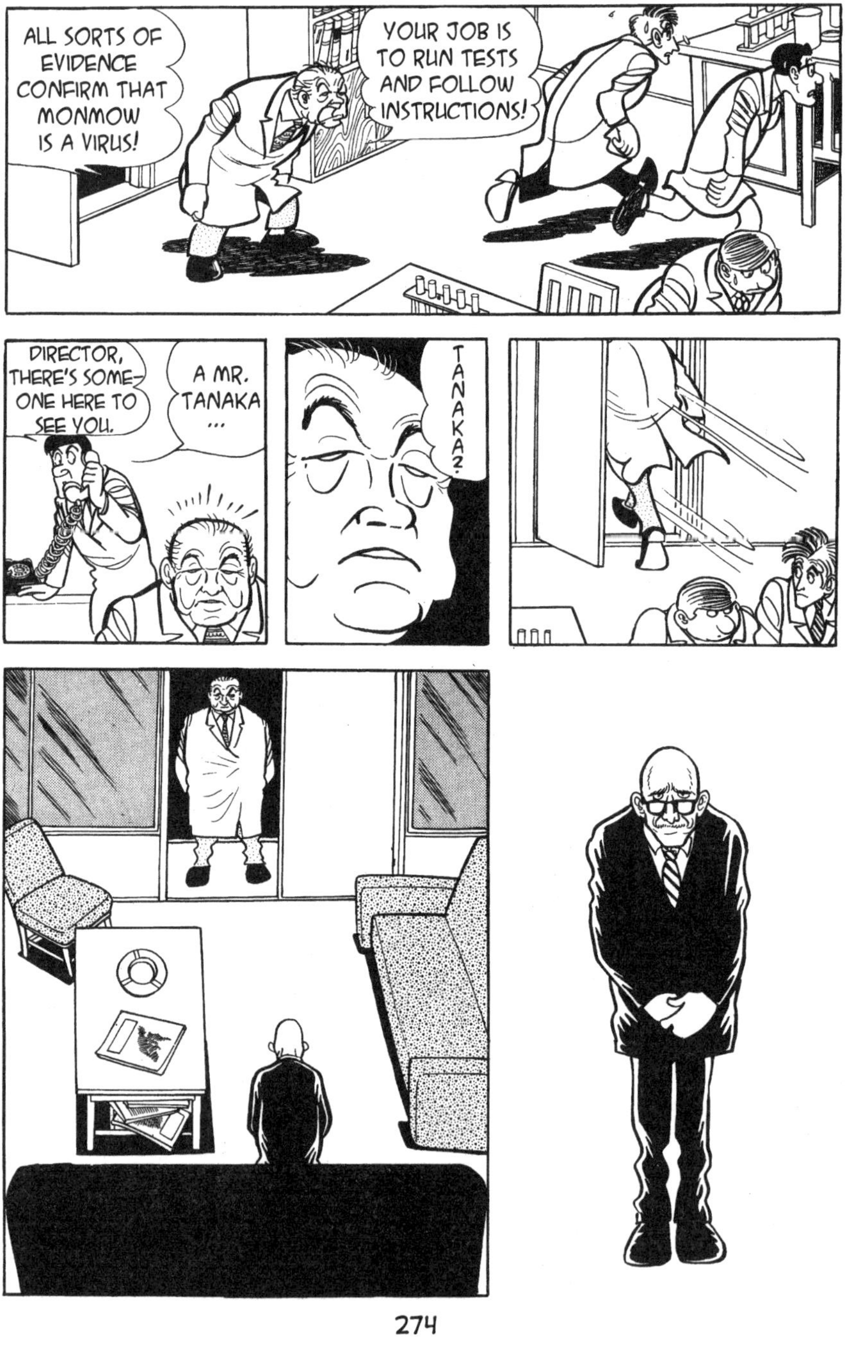
ALL SORTS OF EVIDENCE CONFIRM THAT MONMOW IS A VIRUS!
YOUR JOB IS TO RUN TESTS AND FOLLOW INSTRUCTIONS!
DIRECTOR, THERE'S SOME-ONE HERE TO SEE YOU.
A MR. TANAKA ...
TANAKA?

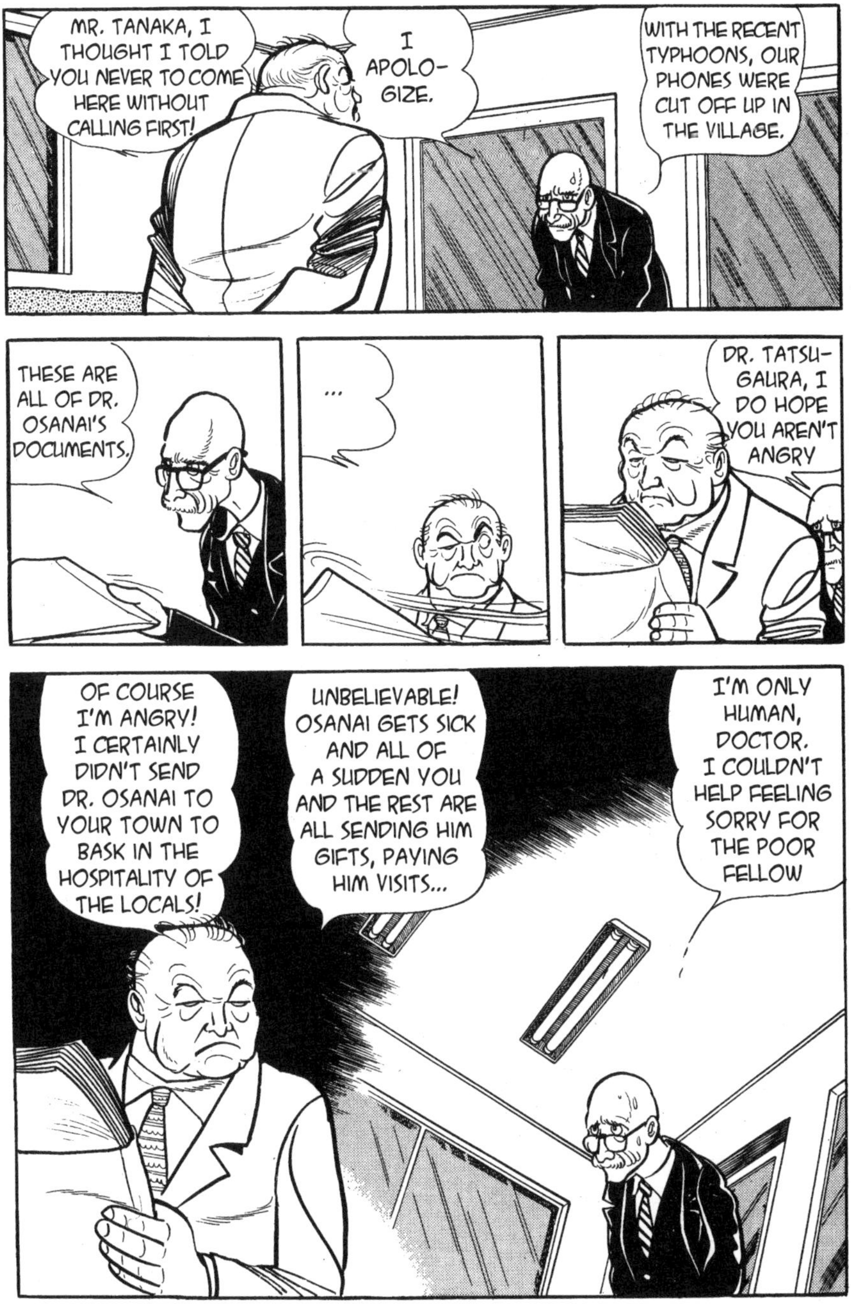
MR. TANAKA, I THOUGHT I TOLD YOU NEVER TO COME HERE WITHOUT CALLING FIRST!
I APOLOGIZE.
WITH THE RECENT TYPHOONS, OUR PHONES WERE CUT OFF UP IN THE VILLAGE.
THESE ARE ALL OF DR. OSANAI'S DOCUMENTS.
...
DR. TATSUGAURA, I DO HOPE YOU AREN'T ANGRY
OF COURSE I'M ANGRY! I CERTAINLY DIDN'T SEND DR. OSANAI TO YOUR TOWN TO BASK IN THE HOSPITALITY OF THE LOCALS!
UNBELIEVABLE! OSANAI GETS SICK AND ALL OF A SUDDEN YOU AND THE REST ARE ALL SENDING HIM GIFTS, PAYING HIM VISITS...
I'M ONLY HUMAN, DOCTOR. I COULDN'T HELP FEELING SORRY FOR THE POOR FELLOW

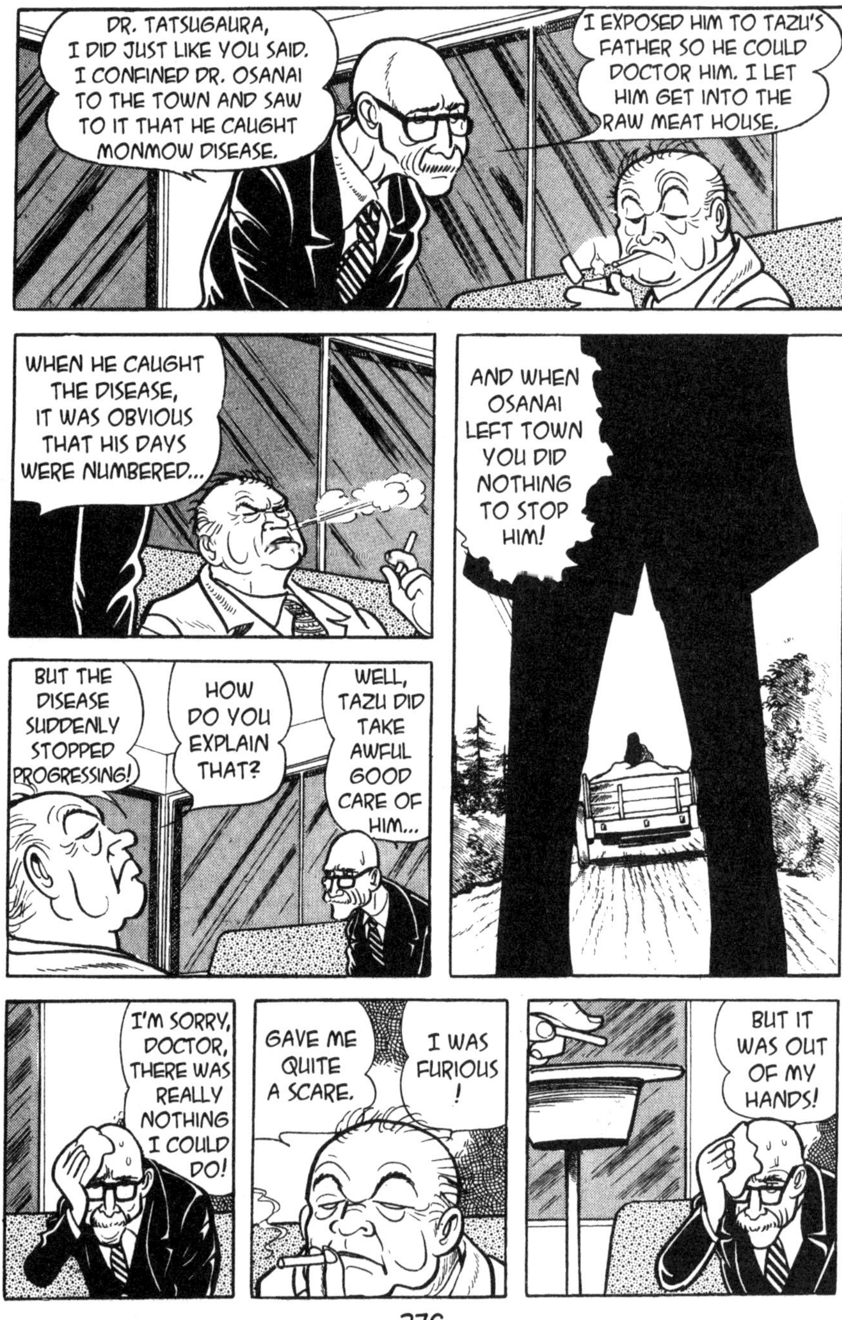
DR. TATSUGAURA, I DID JUST LIKE YOU SAID. I CONFINED DR. OSANAI TO THE TOWN AND SAW TO IT THAT HE CAUGHT MONMOW DISEASE.
I EXPOSED HIM TO TAZU'S FATHER SO HE COULD DOCTOR HIM. I LET HIM GET INTO THE RAW MEAT HOUSE.
WHEN HE CAUGHT THE DISEASE, IT WAS OBVIOUS THAT HIS DAYS WERE NUMBERED...
AND WHEN OSANAI LEFT TOWN YOU DID NOTHING TO STOP HIM!
BUT THE DISEASE SUDDENLY STOPPED PROGRESSING!
HOW DO YOU EXPLAIN THAT?
WELL, TAZU DID TAKE AWFUL GOOD CARE OF HIM...
I'M SORRY, DOCTOR, THERE WAS REALLY NOTHING I COULD DO!
GAVE ME QUITE A SCARE.
I WAS FURIOUS!
BUT IT WAS OUT OF MY HANDS!

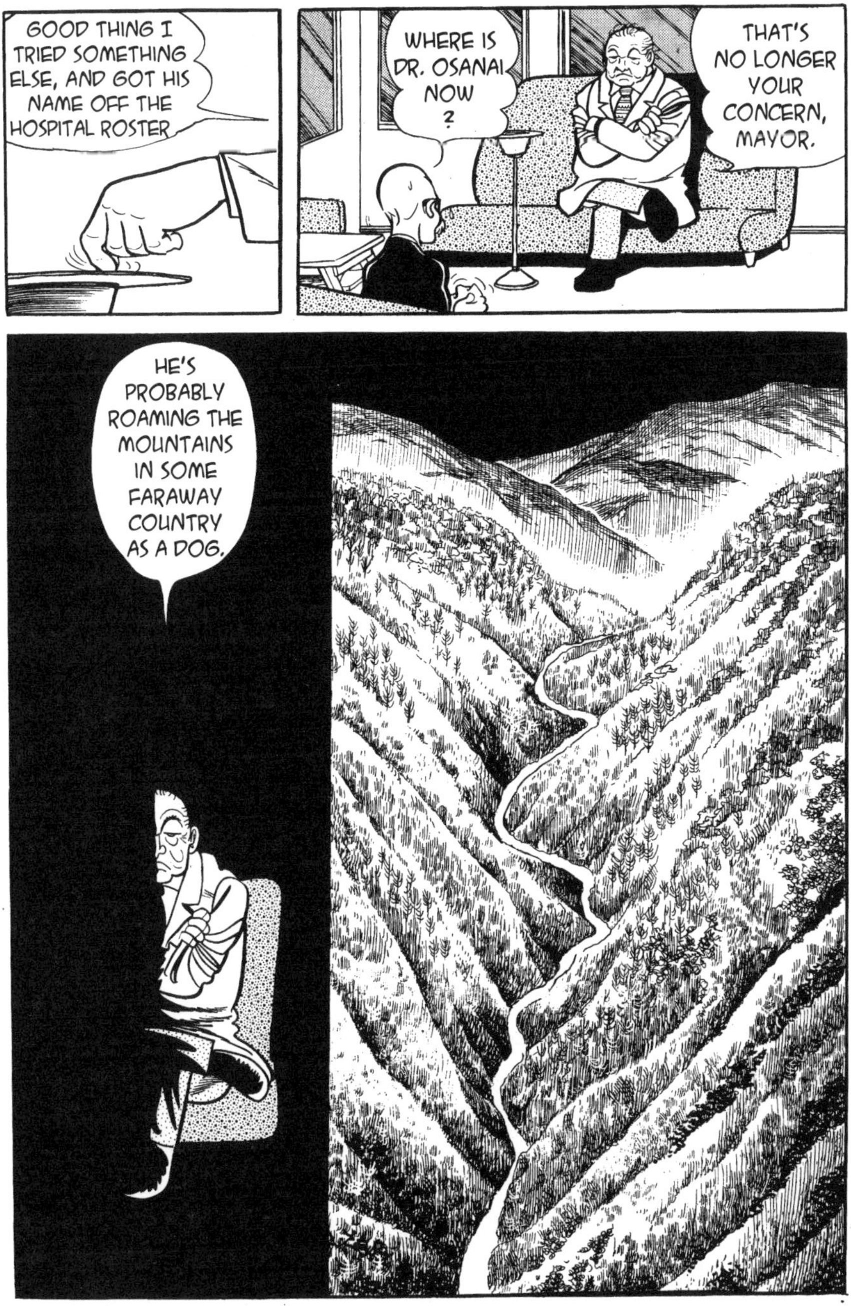
GOOD THING I TRIED SOMETHING ELSE, AND GOT HIS NAME OFF THE HOSPITAL ROSTER
WHERE IS DR. OSANAI NOW ?
THAT'S NO LONGER YOUR CONCERN, MAYOR.
HE'S PROBABLY ROAMING THE MOUNTAINS IN SOME FARAWAY COUNTRY AS A DOG.

CHAPTER 8

DISSOLUTION

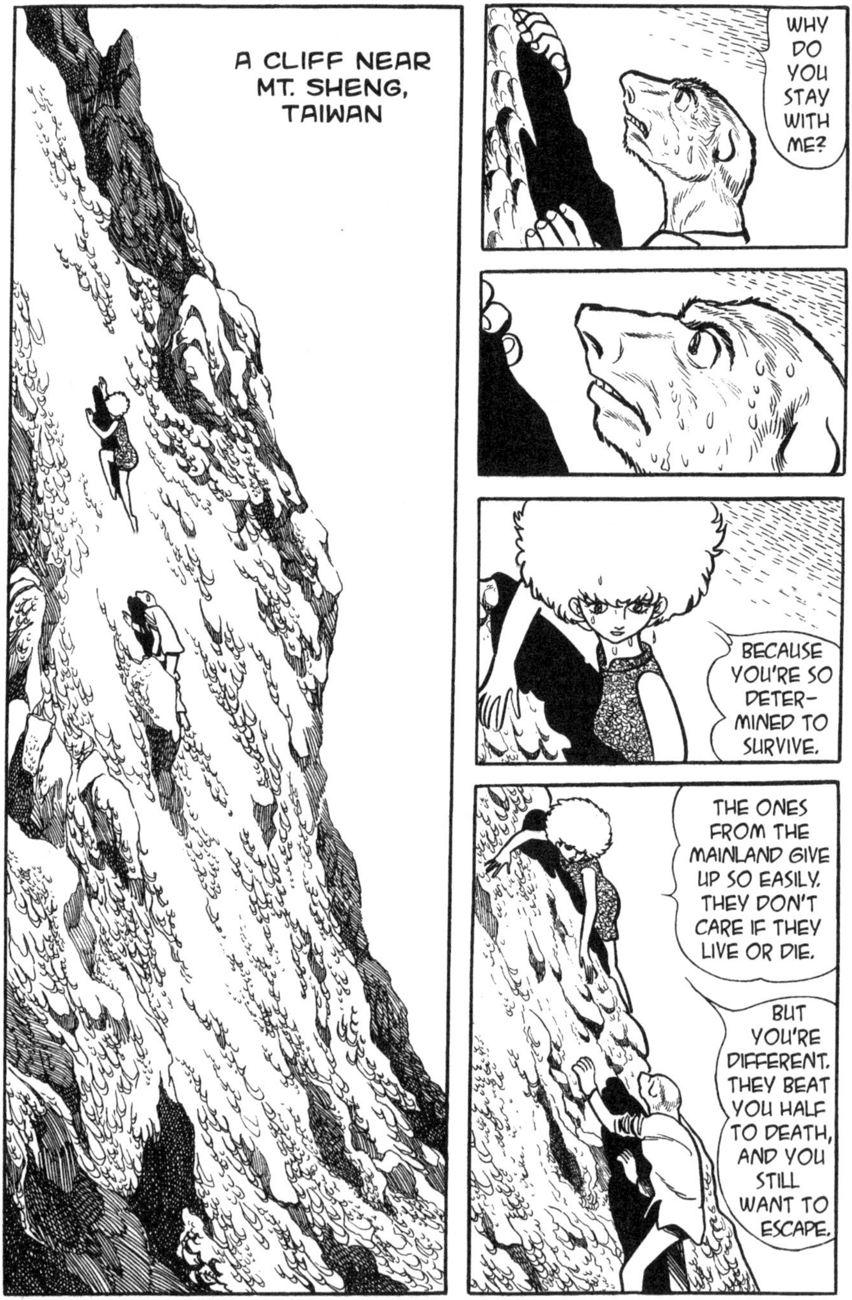
A CLIFF NEAR MT. SHENG, TAIWAN
WHY DO YOU STAY WITH ME?
BECAUSE YOU'RE SO DETER-MINED TO SURVIVE.
THE ONES FROM THE MAINLAND GIVE UP SO EASILY. THEY DON'T CARE IF THEY LIVE OR DIE.
BUT YOU'RE DIFFERENT. THEY BEAT YOU HALF TO DEATH, AND YOU STILL WANT TO ESCAPE.

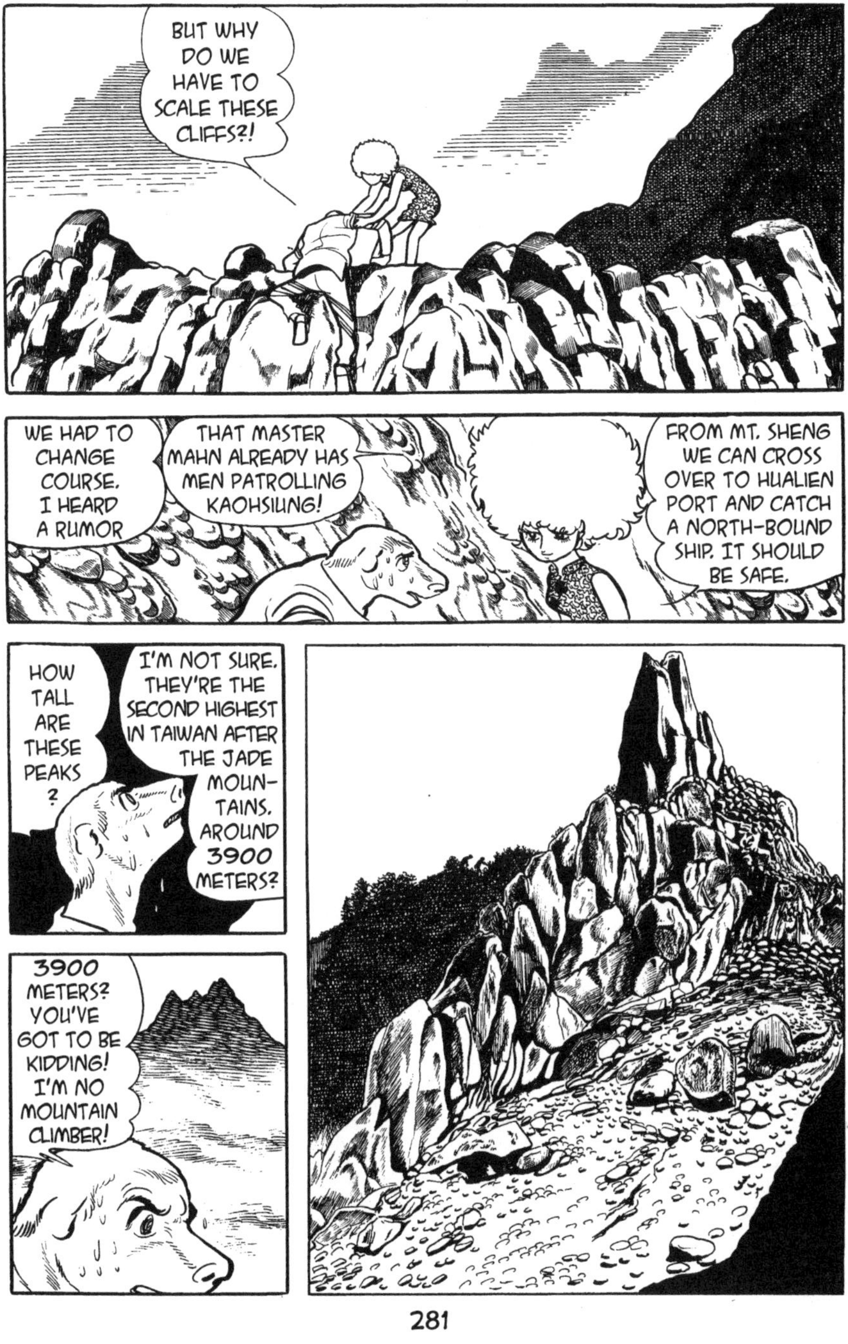
BUT WHY DO WE HAVE TO SCALE THESE CLIFFS?!
WE HAD TO CHANGE COURSE. I HEARD A RUMOR
THAT MASTER MAHN ALREADY HAS MEN PATROLLING KAOHSIUNG!
FROM MT. SHENG WE CAN CROSS OVER TO HUALIEN PORT AND CATCH A NORTH-BOUND SHIP. IT SHOULD BE SAFE.
HOW TALL ARE THESE PEAKS?
I'M NOT SURE. THEY'RE THE SECOND HIGHEST IN TAIWAN AFTER THE JADE MOUNTAINS. AROUND 3900 METERS?
3900 METERS? YOU'VE GOT TO BE KIDDING! I'M NO MOUNTAIN CLIMBER!

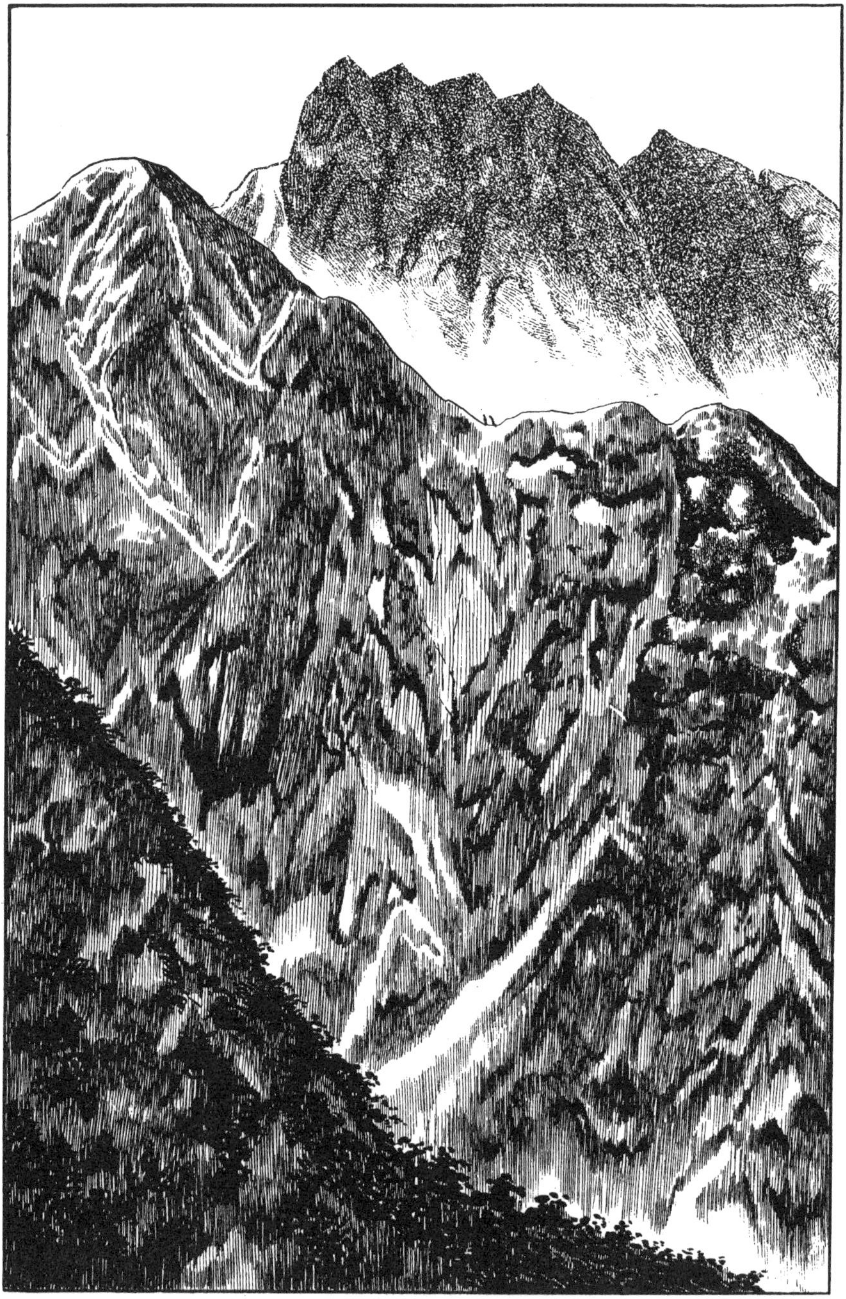

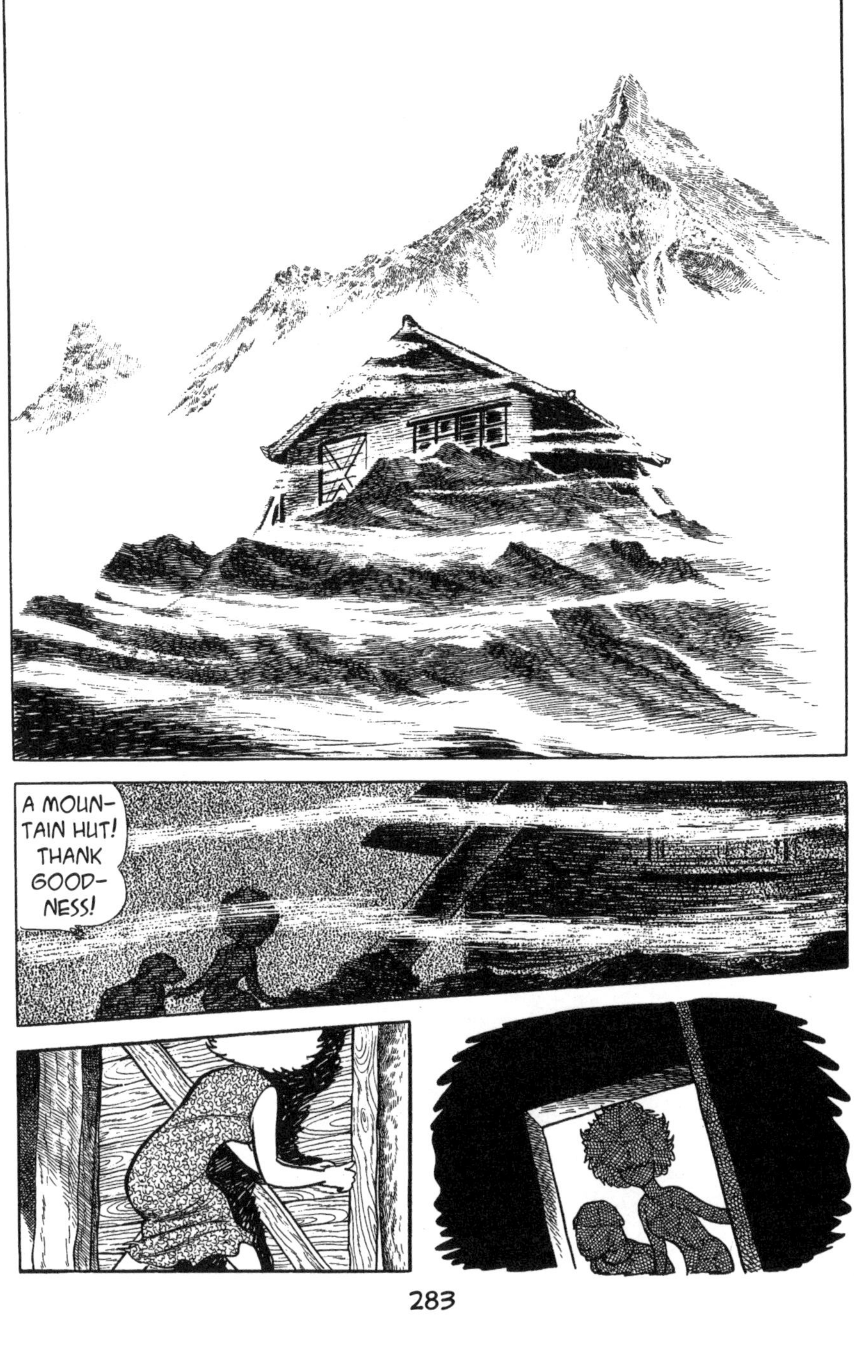
A MOUNTAIN HUT! THANK GOODNESS!

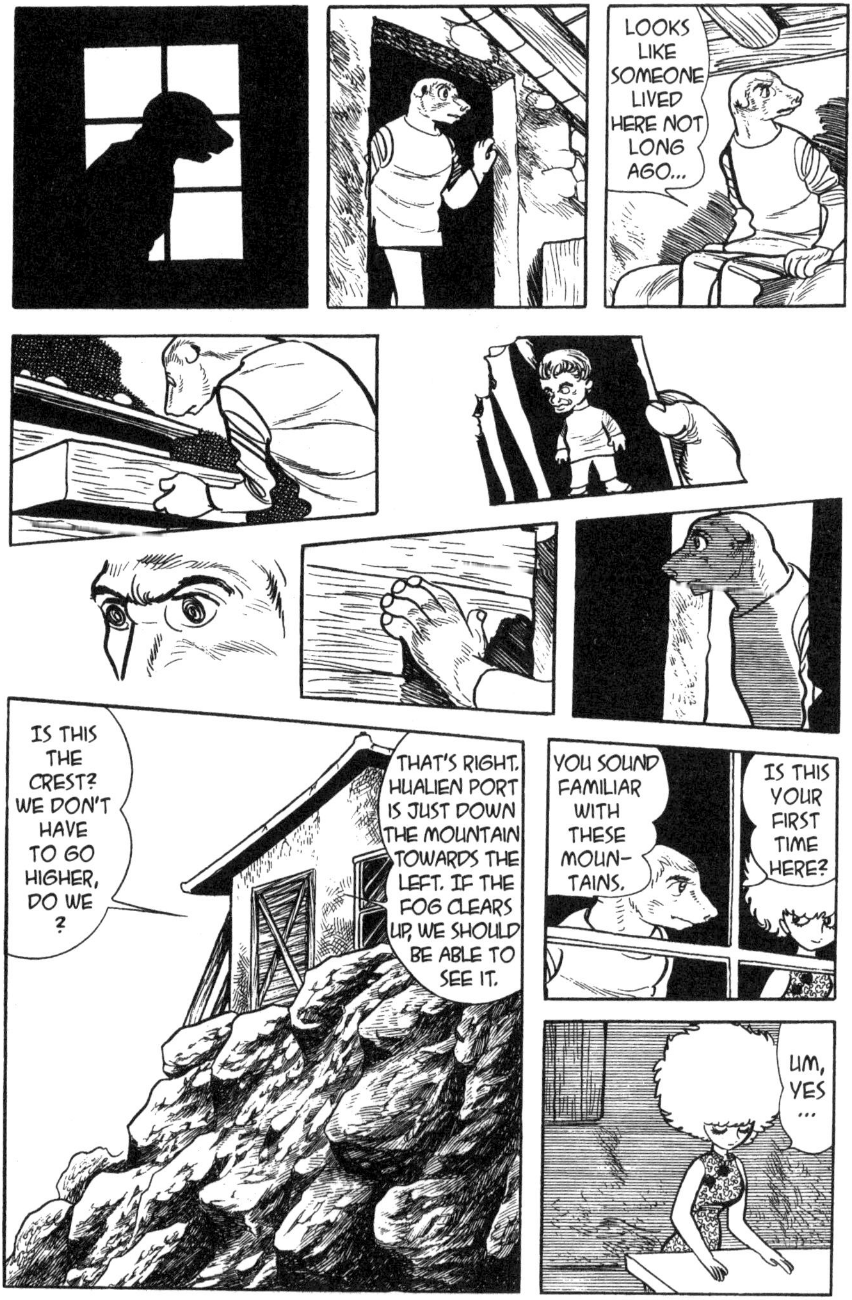
LOOKS LIKE SOMEONE LIVED HERE NOT LONG AGO...
IS THIS THE CREST? WE DON'T HAVE TO GO HIGHER, DO WE?
THAT'S RIGHT. HUALIEN PORT IS JUST DOWN THE MOUNTAIN TOWARDS THE LEFT. IF THE FOG CLEARS UP, WE SHOULD BE ABLE TO SEE IT.
YOU SOUND FAMILIAR WITH THESE MOUN-TAINS.
IS THIS YOUR FIRST TIME HERE?
UM, YES ...

TELL ME MORE ABOUT MONMOW DISEASE. WHAT CAUSES IT?

THE TECHNICAL TERM IS AN INCRETION IMBALANCE. BASICALLY, THE HORMONES THAT MAINTAIN THE BODY'S BALANCE GO OUT OF WHACK. EVER HEARD OF RICKETS?

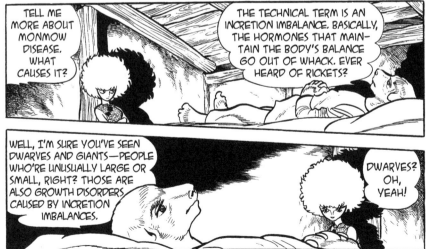

WELL, I'M SURE YOU'VE SEEN DWARVES AND GIANTS—PEOPLE WHO'RE UNUSUALLY LARGE OR SMALL, RIGHT? THOSE ARE ALSO GROWTH DISORDERS CAUSED BY INCRETION IMBALANCES.

DWARVES? OH, YEAH!

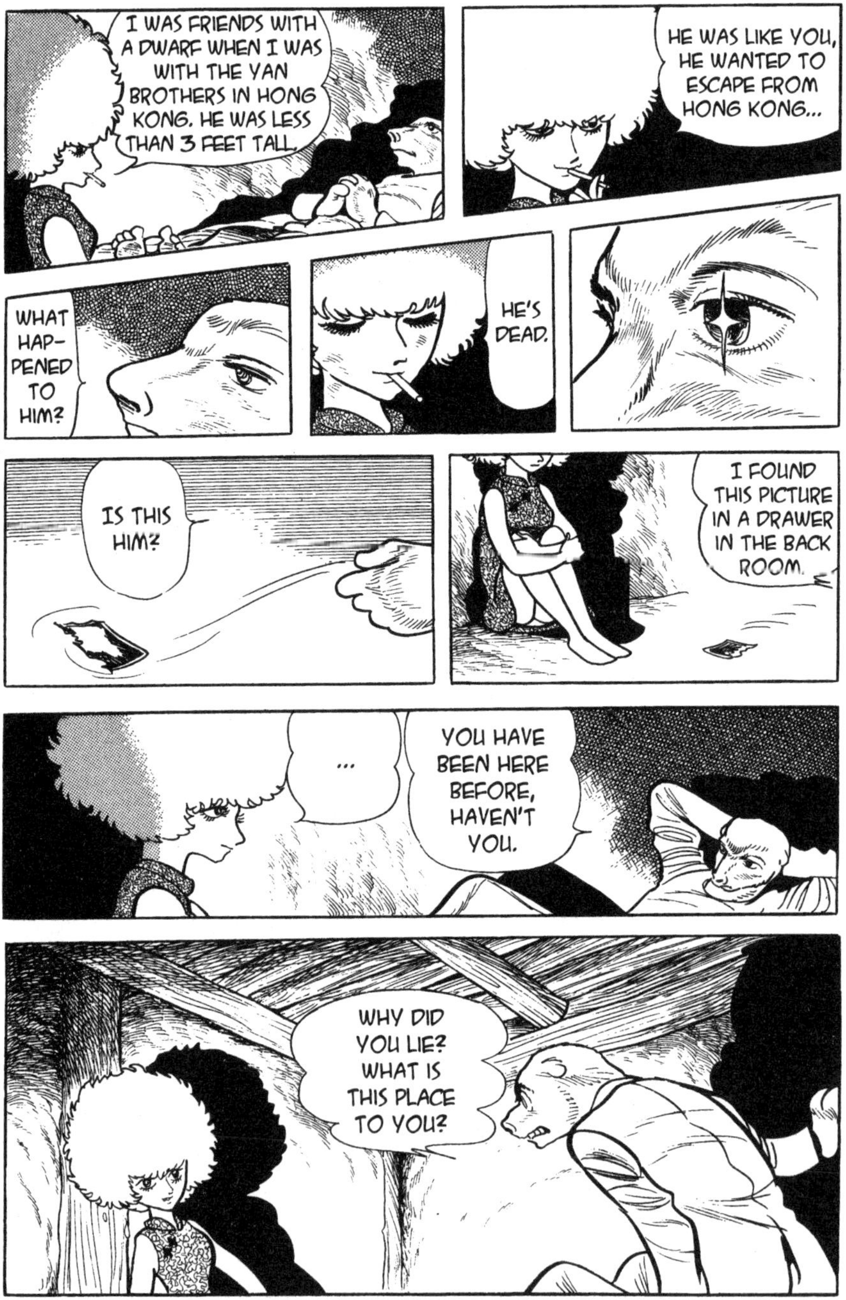
I WAS FRIENDS WITH A DWARF WHEN I WAS WITH THE YAN BROTHERS IN HONG KONG. HE WAS LESS THAN 3 FEET TALL.
HE WAS LIKE YOU, HE WANTED TO ESCAPE FROM HONG KONG...
WHAT HAP-PENED TO HIM?
HE'S DEAD.
IS THIS HIM?
I FOUND THIS PICTURE IN A DRAWER IN THE BACK ROOM.
...
YOU HAVE BEEN HERE BEFORE, HAVEN'T YOU.
WHY DID YOU LIE? WHAT IS THIS PLACE TO YOU?

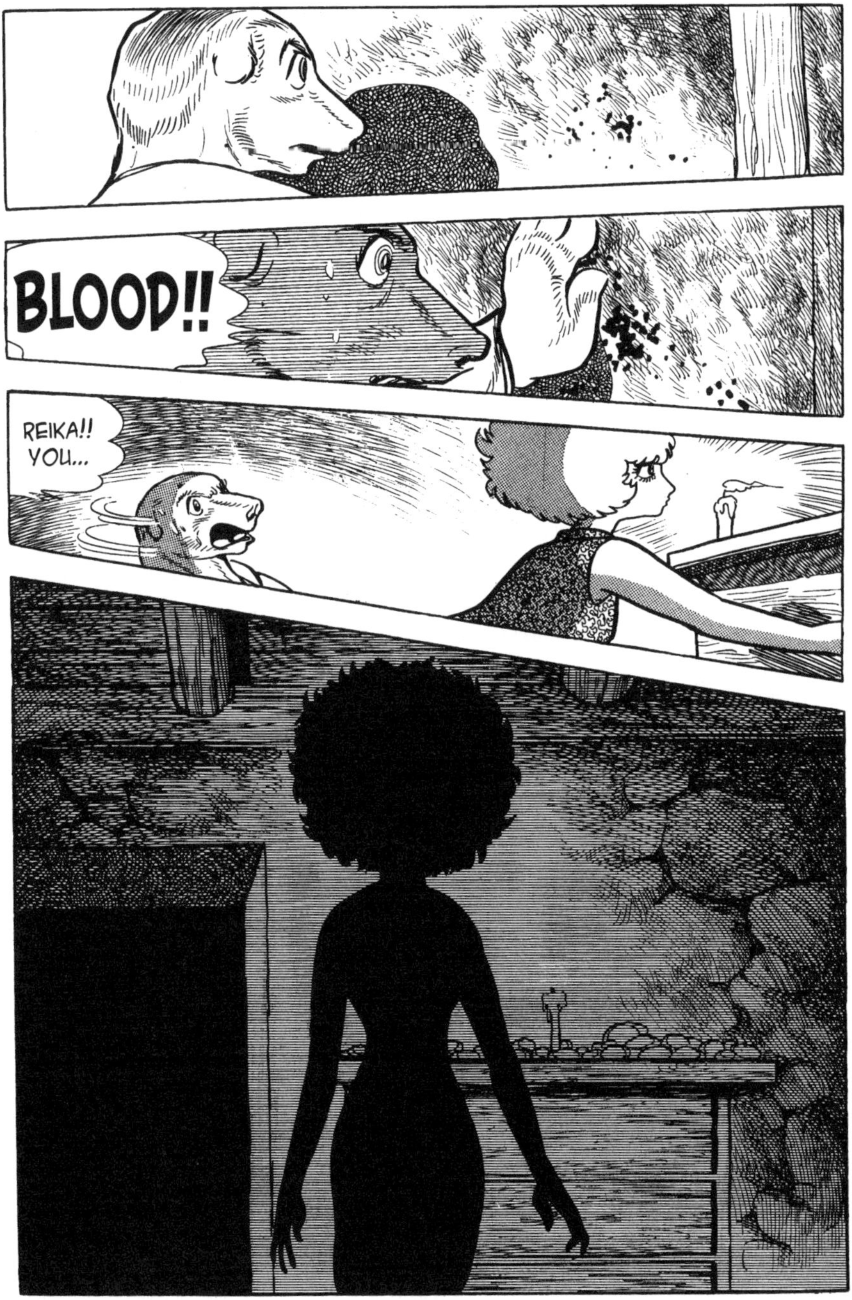
BLOOD!!
REIKA!! YOU...

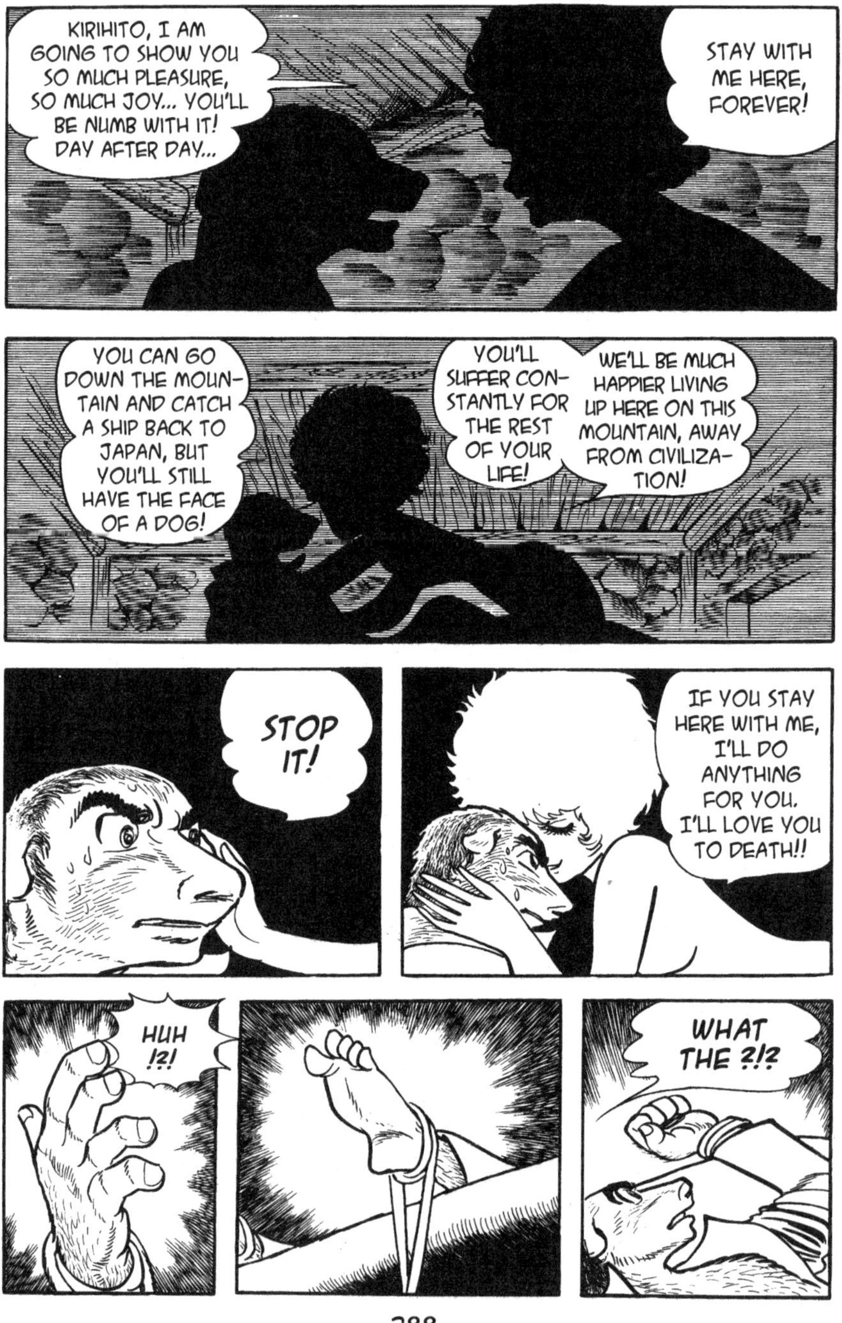
KIRIHITO, I AM GOING TO SHOW YOU SO MUCH PLEASURE, SO MUCH JOY... YOU'LL BE NUMB WITH IT! DAY AFTER DAY...
STAY WITH ME HERE, FOREVER!
YOU CAN GO DOWN THE MOUNTAIN AND CATCH A SHIP BACK TO JAPAN, BUT YOU'LL STILL HAVE THE FACE OF A DOG!
YOU'LL SUFFER CONSTANTLY FOR THE REST OF YOUR LIFE!
WE'LL BE MUCH HAPPIER LIVING UP HERE ON THIS MOUNTAIN, AWAY FROM CIVILIZATION!
STOP IT!
IF YOU STAY HERE WITH ME, I'LL DO ANYTHING FOR YOU. I'LL LOVE YOU TO DEATH!!
HUH !?!
WHAT THE ?!?

OH HO HO HO HO HO HO HO HO HO

SO, THIS IS WHY YOU BROUGHT ME HERE!

VERY CLEVER. PRETENDING TO CARESS ME AND SLIPPING NOOSES OVER MY WRISTS AND ANKLES...

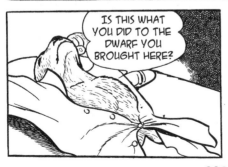

IS THIS WHAT YOU DID TO THE DWARF YOU BROUGHT HERE?

HEH HEH HEH

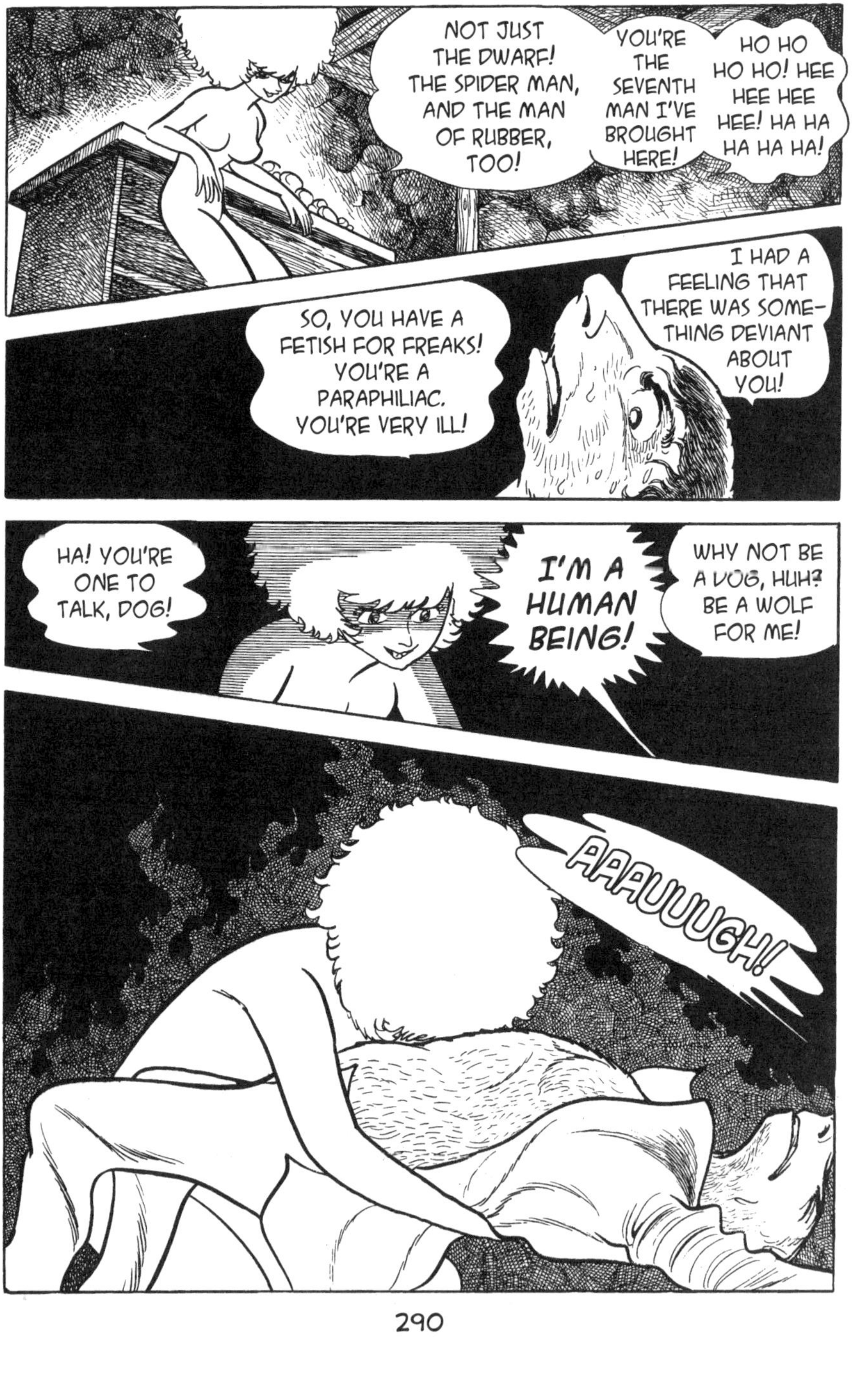
NOT JUST THE DWARF! THE SPIDER MAN, AND THE MAN OF RUBBER, TOO!
YOU'RE THE SEVENTH MAN I'VE BROUGHT HERE!
HO HO HO HO! HEE HEE HEE HEE! HA HA HA HA HA!
I HAD A FEELING THAT THERE WAS SOME-THING DEVIANT ABOUT YOU!
SO, YOU HAVE A FETISH FOR FREAKS! YOU'RE A PARAPHILIAC. YOU'RE VERY ILL!
HA! YOU'RE ONE TO TALK, DOG!
I'M A HUMAN BEING!
WHY NOT BE A DOG, HUH? BE A WOLF FOR ME!
AAAUUUGH!

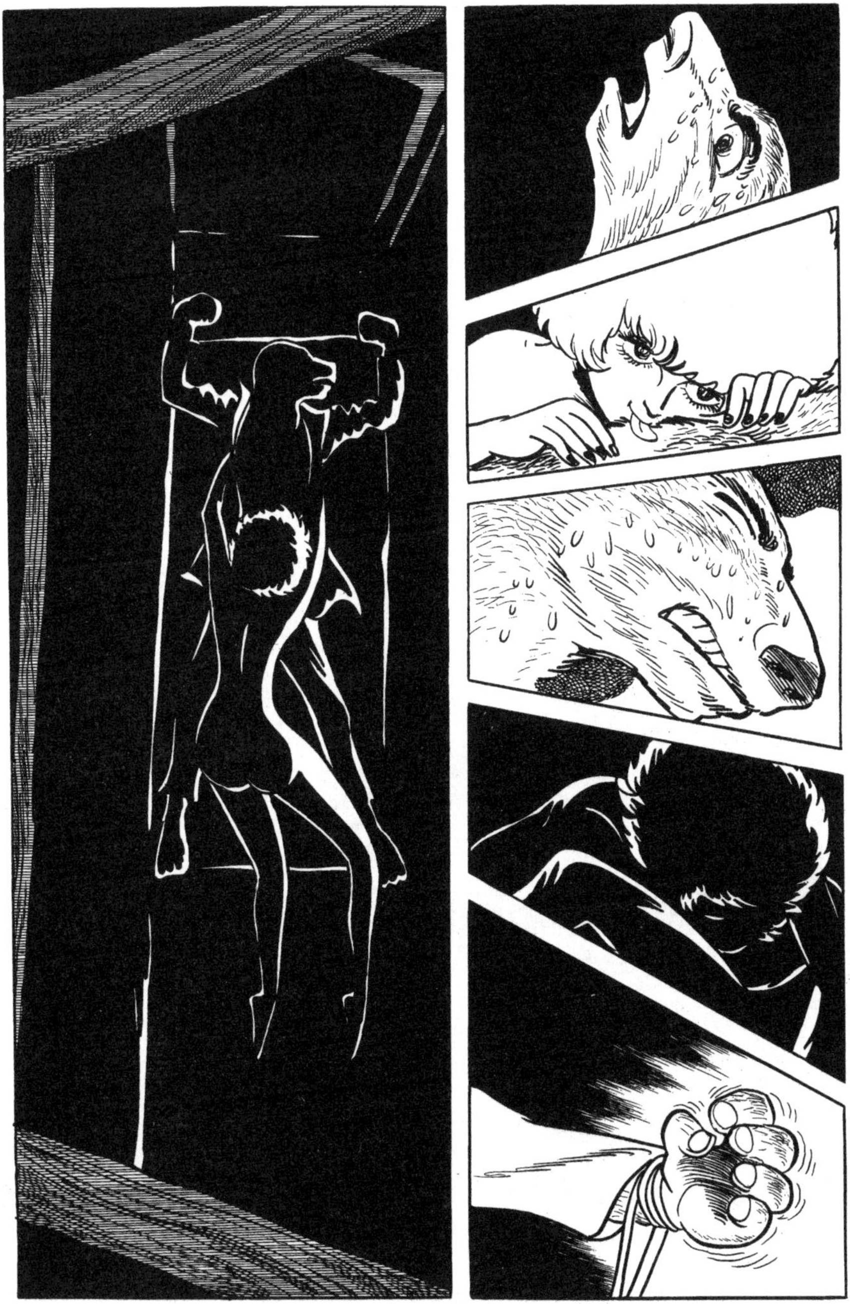

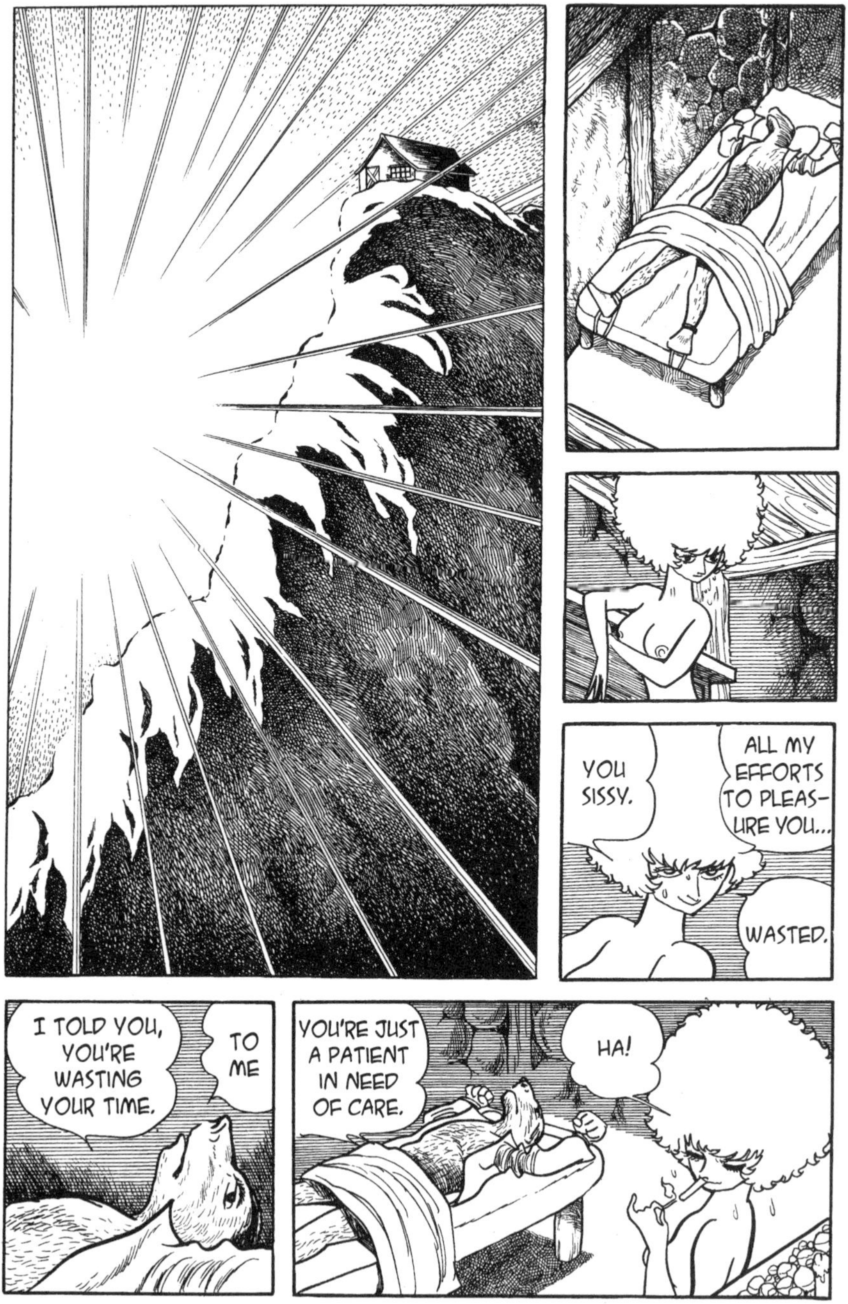

YOU SISSY.
ALL MY EFFORTS TO PLEAS-URE YOU...
WASTED.
I TOLD YOU, YOU'RE WASTING YOUR TIME.
TO ME
YOU'RE JUST A PATIENT IN NEED OF CARE.
HA!

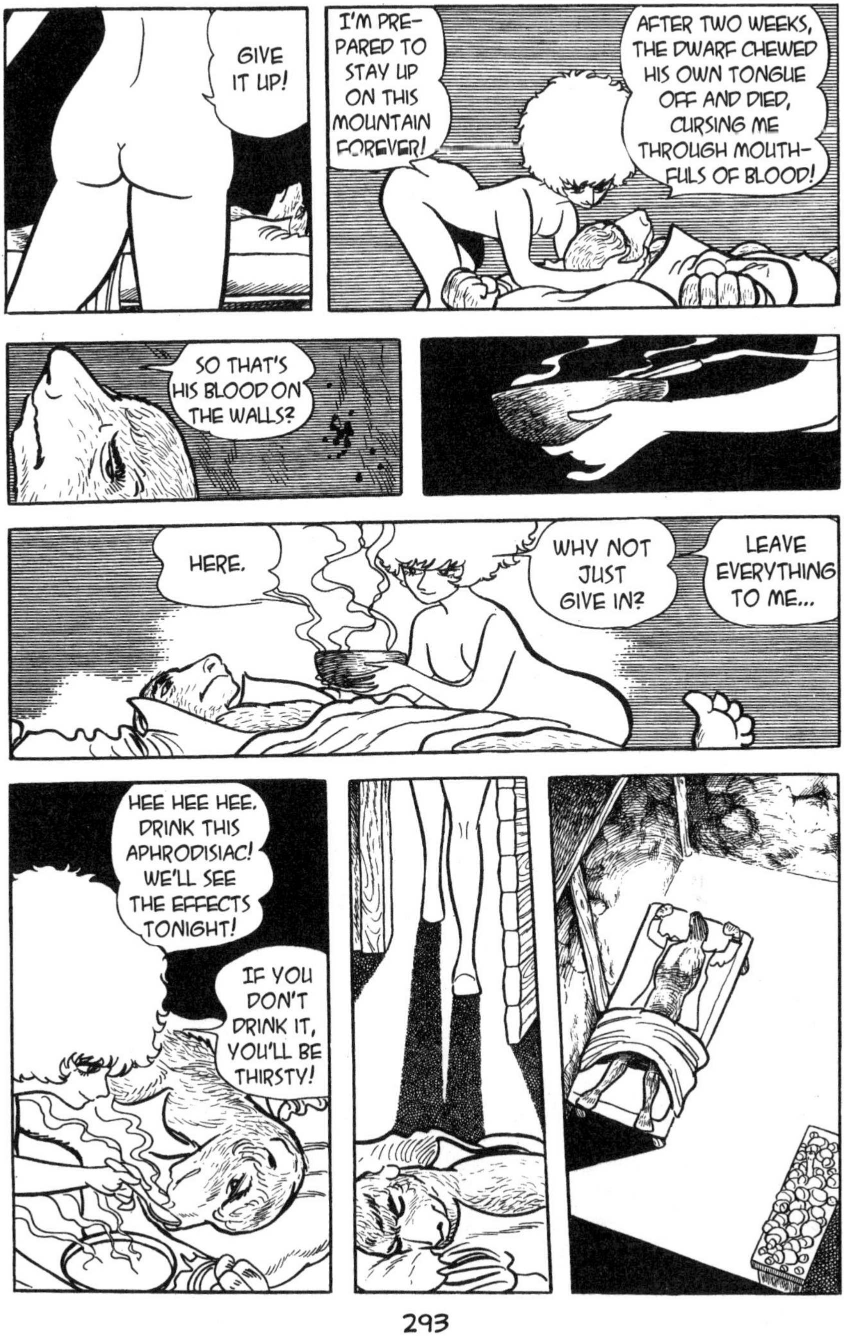
GIVE IT UP!
I'M PREPARED TO STAY UP ON THIS MOUNTAIN FOREVER!
AFTER TWO WEEKS, THE DWARF CHEWED HIS OWN TONGUE OFF AND DIED, CURSING ME THROUGH MOUTHFULS OF BLOOD!
SO THAT'S HIS BLOOD ON THE WALLS?
HERE.
WHY NOT JUST GIVE IN?
LEAVE EVERYTHING TO ME...
HEE HEE HEE. DRINK THIS APHRODISIAC! WE'LL SEE THE EFFECTS TONIGHT!
IF YOU DON'T DRINK IT, YOU'LL BE THIRSTY!

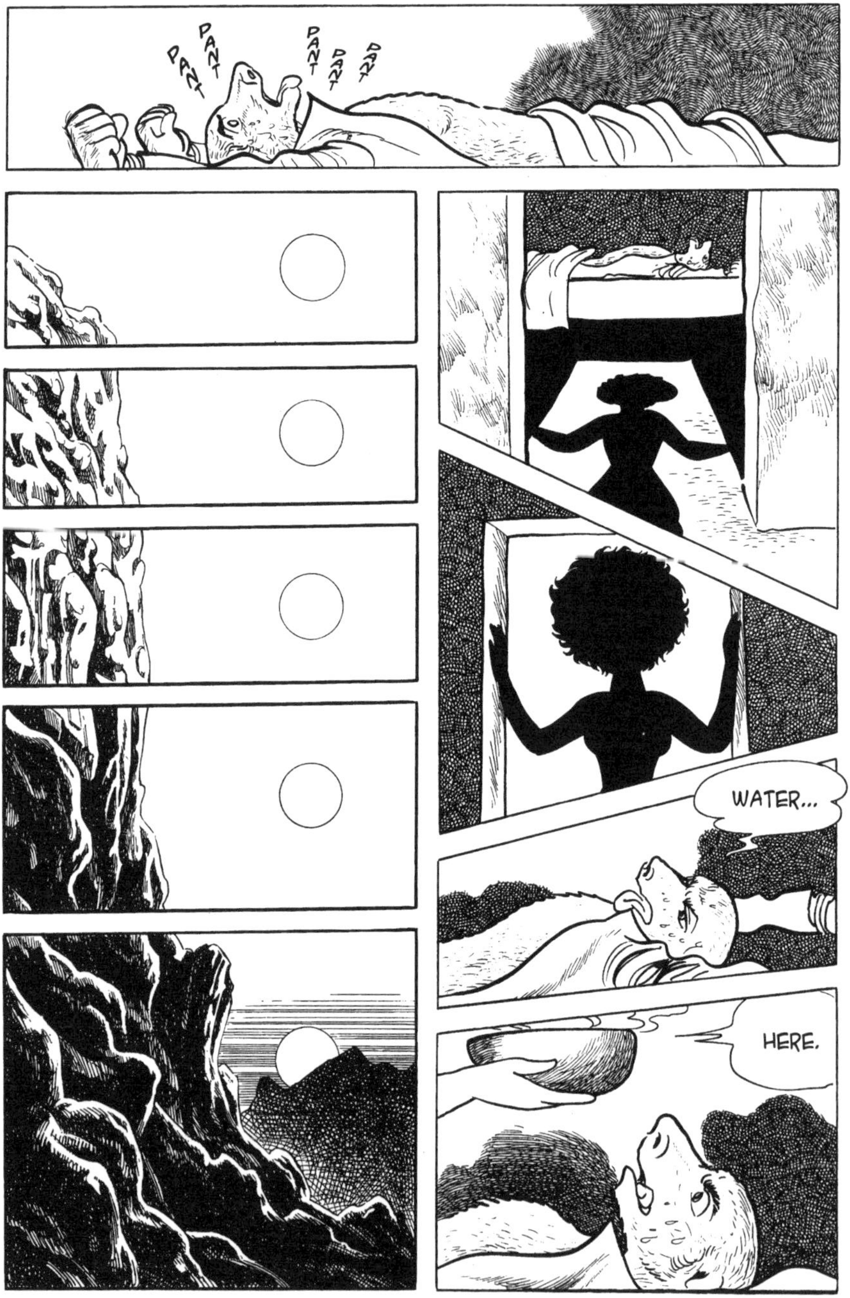
PANT PANT
PANT PANT PANT
WATER...
HERE.

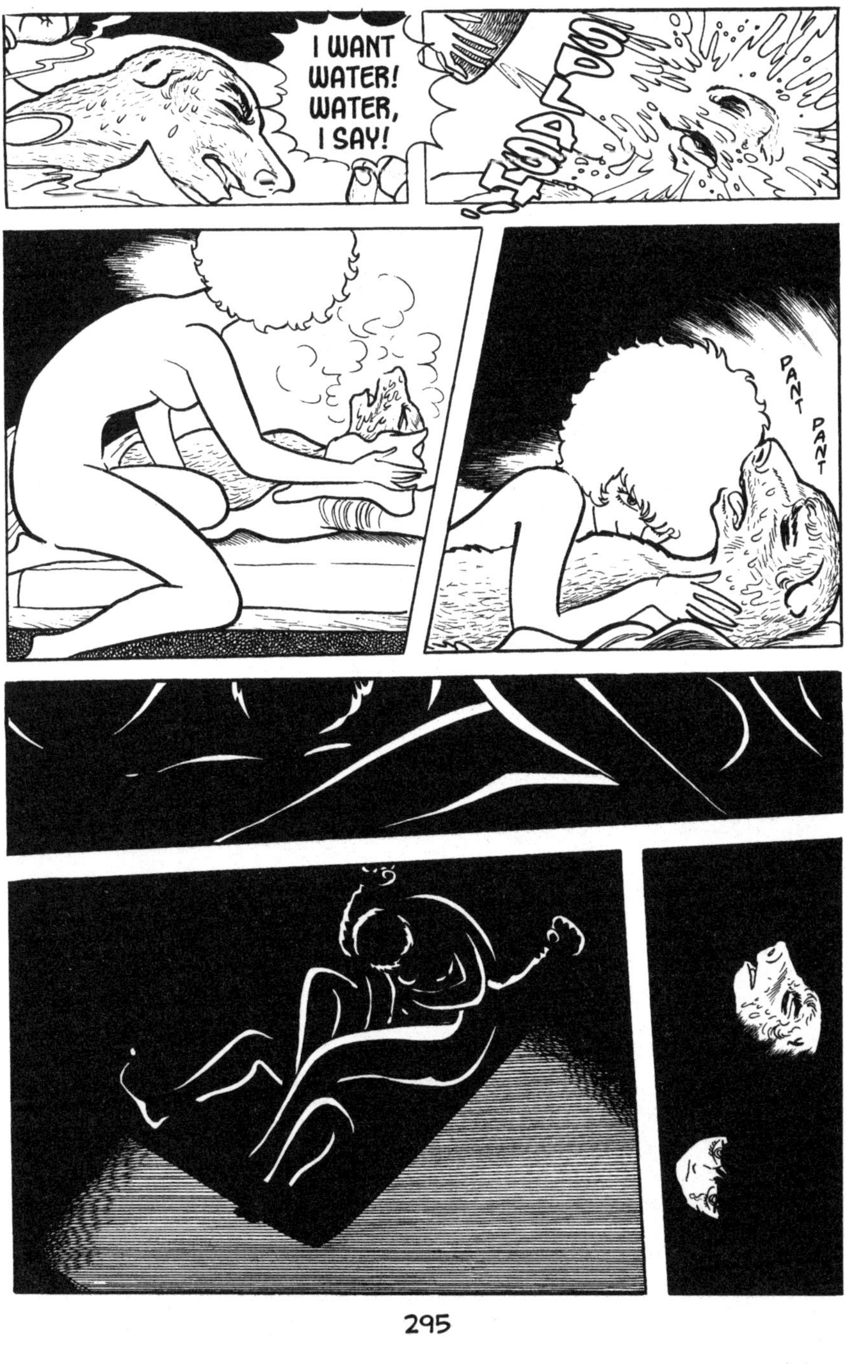
I WANT WATER! WATER, I SAY!
SPLASH
PANT PANT

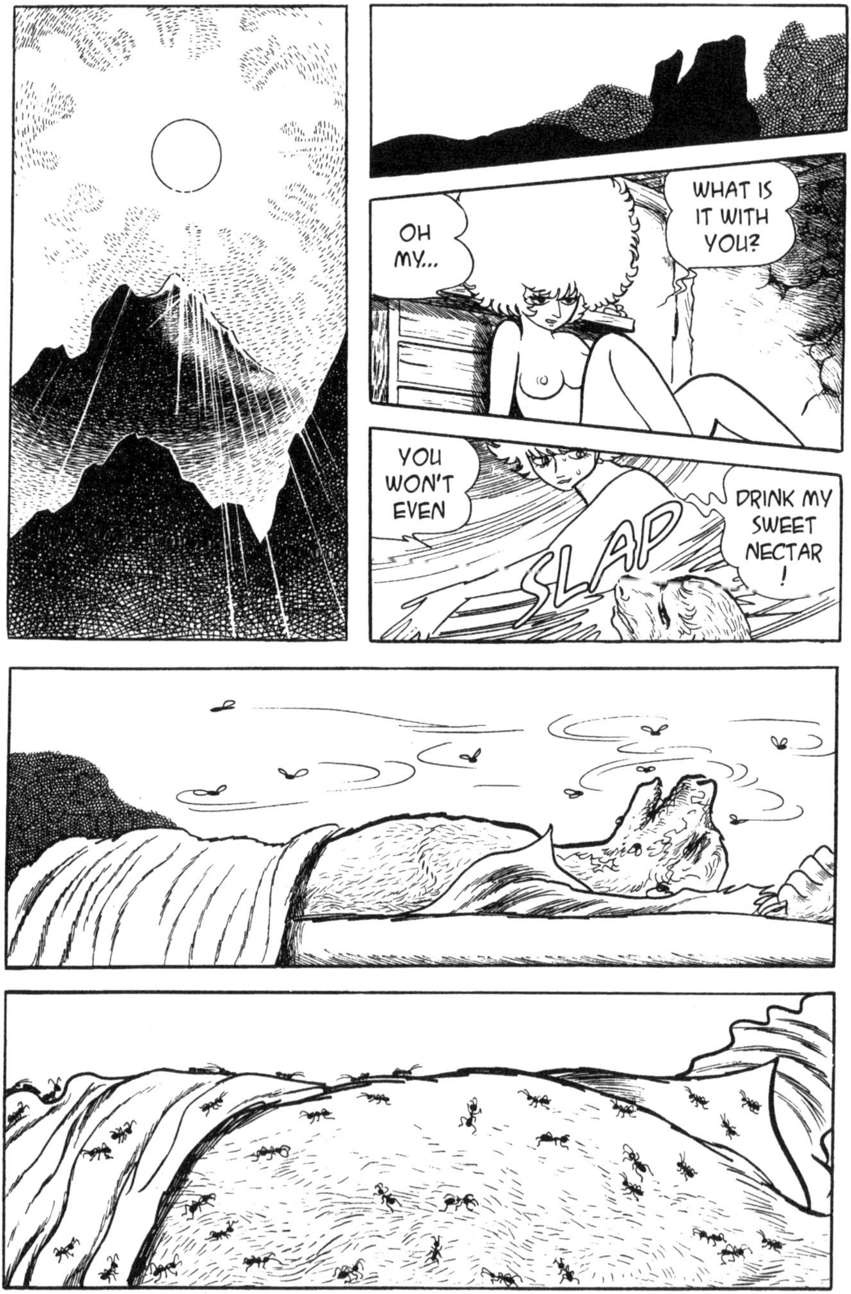
OH MY...
WHAT IS IT WITH YOU?
YOU WON'T EVEN
DRINK MY SWEET NECTAR !
SLAP

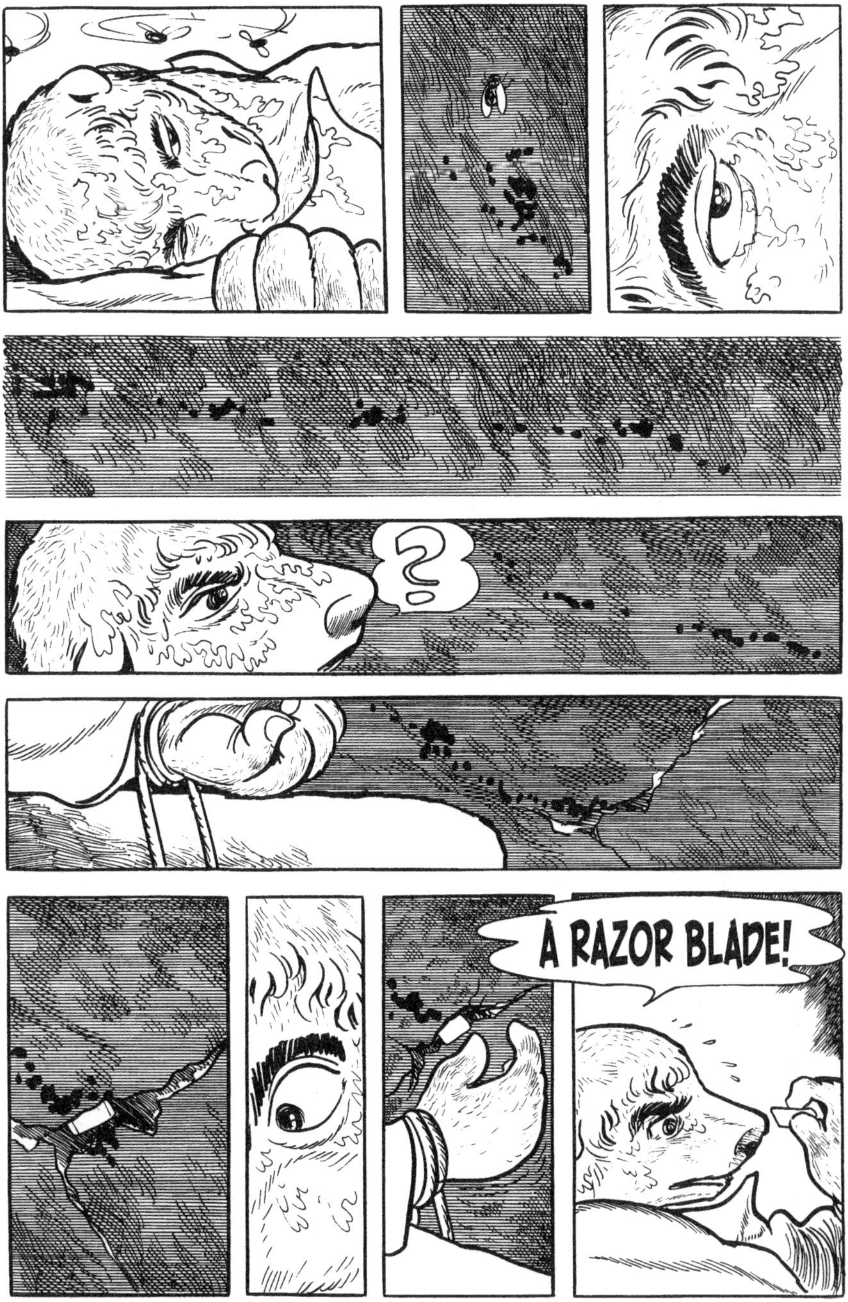
?
A RAZOR BLADE!

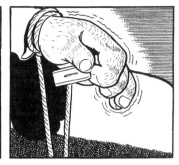

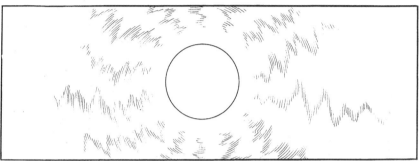

IT'S BEEN FORTY DAYS!

THIS IS IT.

IF YOU REFUSE MY ADVANCES ONCE MORE, I'LL KILL YOU AND PUSH YOU OVER THE CLIFF.

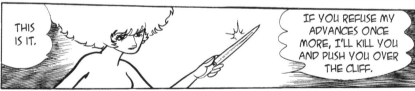

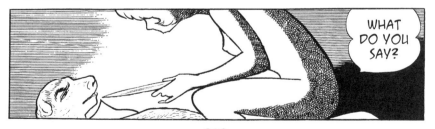

WHAT DO YOU SAY?

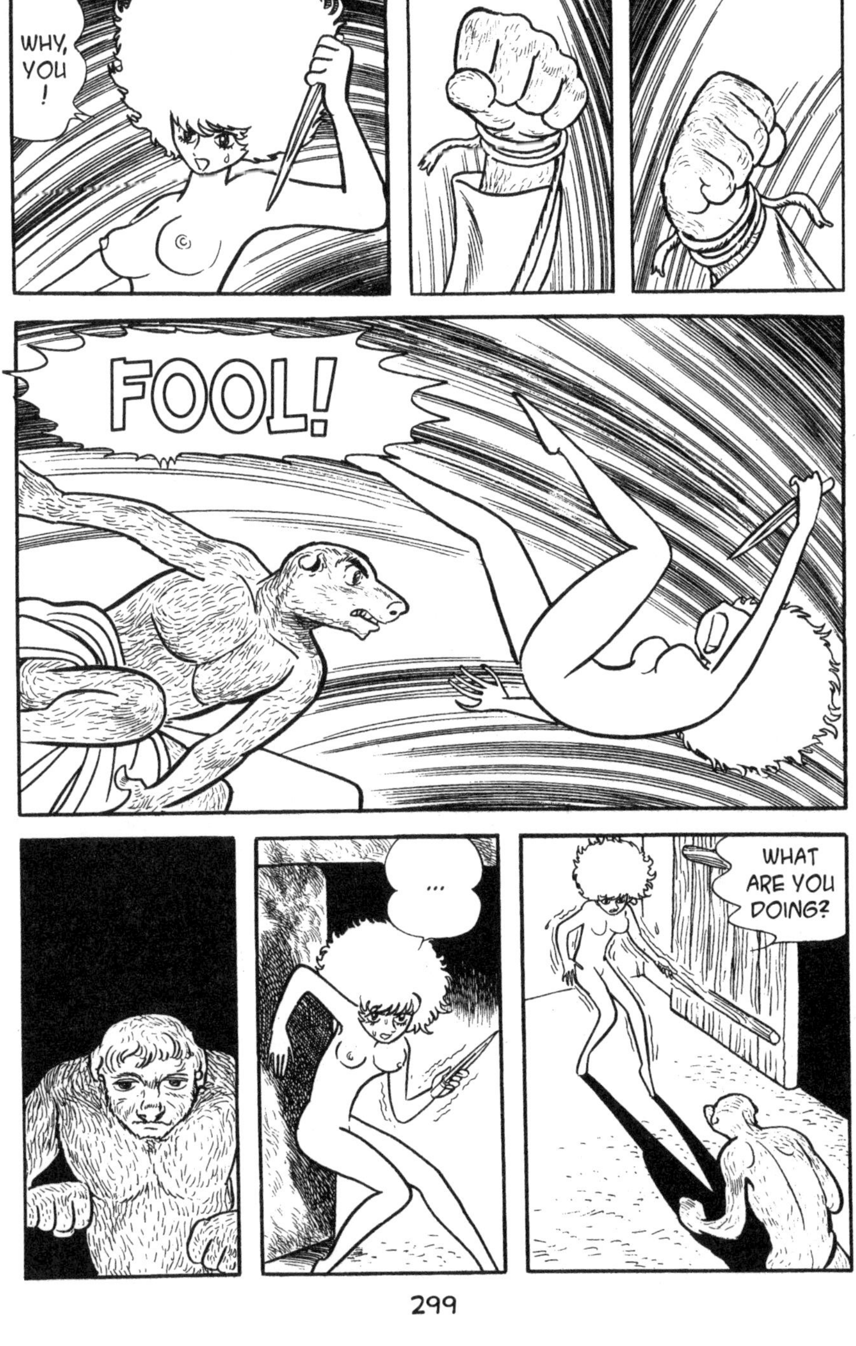
WHY, YOU !
FOOL!
...
WHAT ARE YOU DOING?

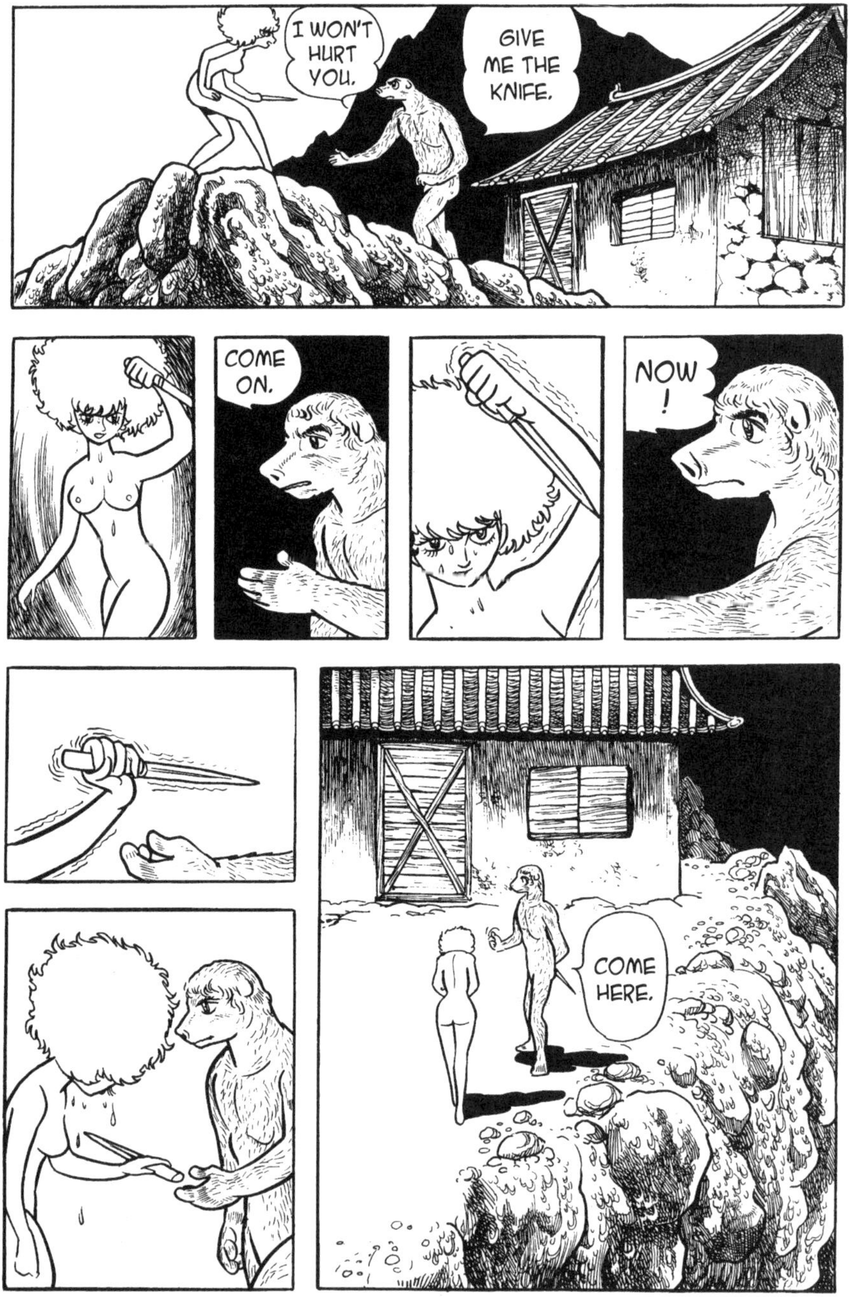
I WON'T HURT YOU.
GIVE ME THE KNIFE.
COME ON.
NOW !
COME HERE.

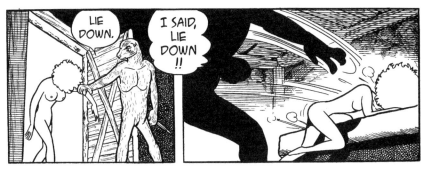

LIE DOWN.

I SAID, LIE DOWN!!

YOU'RE NOT WELL, REIKA. YOU'RE DEEPLY WOUNDED, PSYCHO- LOGICALLY.

I WILL DO EVERYTHING I CAN FOR YOU.

BUT YOU WON'T GET BETTER UNLESS YOU DO AS I SAY.

CLOSE YOUR EYES AND CALM DOWN.

THIS GIRL'S STUNT PUTS HER UNDER EXTREME STRESS. PERHAPS HER ABNORMAL LIBIDO AROSE FROM THAT PSYCHOLOGICAL TRAUMA.

PERHAPS I CAN USE THE HYPNOTIC TREATMENT DEVELOPED BY DR. INOUE OF JOSO HOS- PITAL.

CLOSE YOUR EYES, REIKA. YOUR EYELIDS ARE GROWING HEAVY. SO VERY HEAVY...

YOU'RE GOING BACK IN TIME TO YOUR CHILDHOOD. YOU'RE QUITTING YOUR CIRCUS TRAINING.

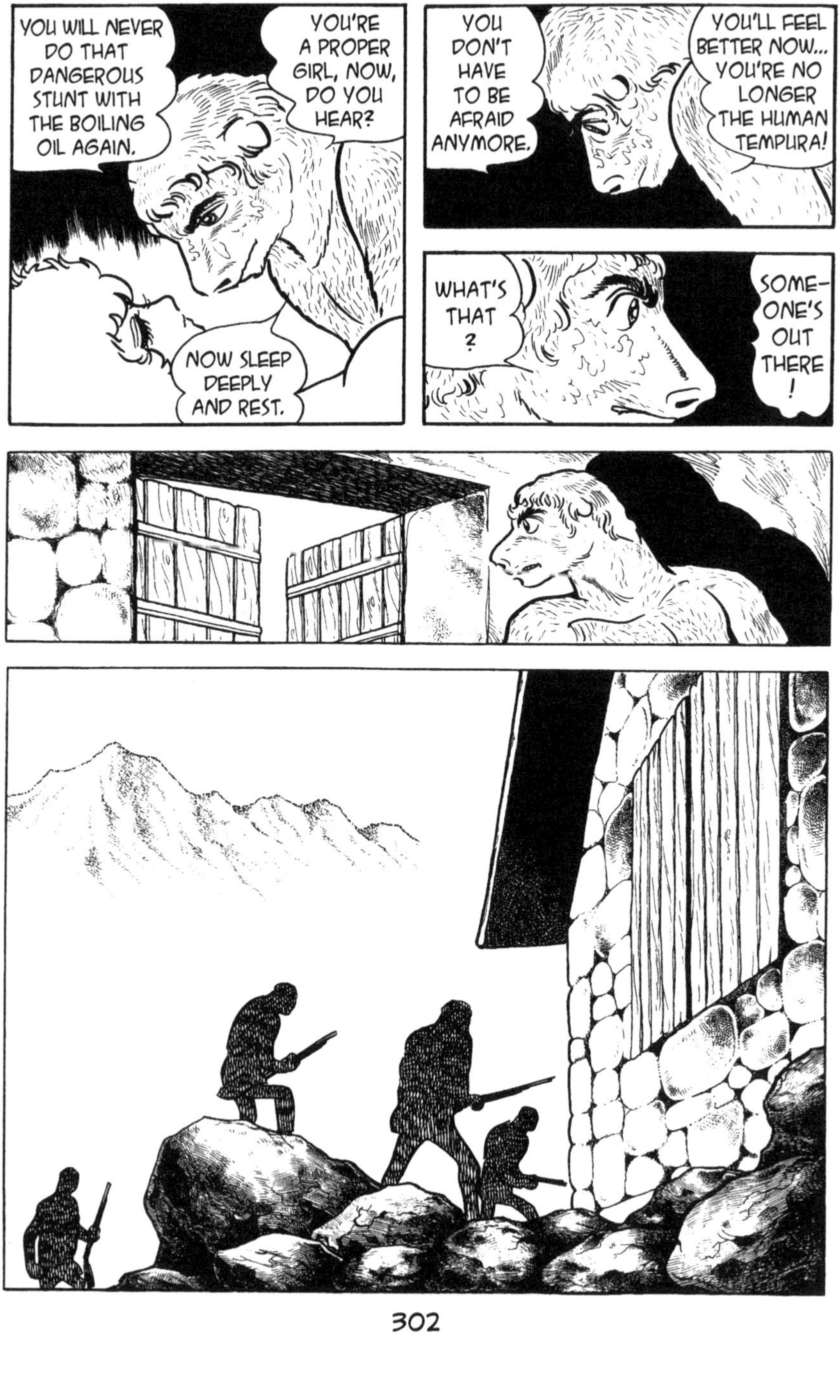

YOU WILL NEVER DO THAT DANGEROUS STUNT WITH THE BOILING OIL AGAIN.
YOU'RE A PROPER GIRL, NOW, DO YOU HEAR?
NOW SLEEP DEEPLY AND REST.
YOU DON'T HAVE TO BE AFRAID ANYMORE.
YOU'LL FEEL BETTER NOW... YOU'RE NO LONGER THE HUMAN TEMPURA!
WHAT'S THAT ?
SOME-ONE'S OUT THERE !

WHAT DO YOU WANT?
STOP!
大概是我耳朵的關係
這是人的声音

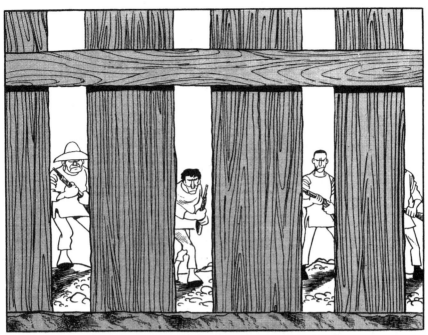

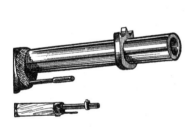

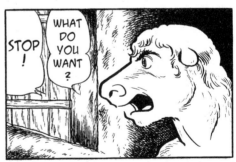

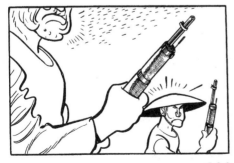

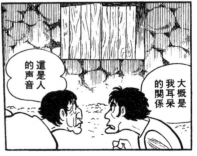

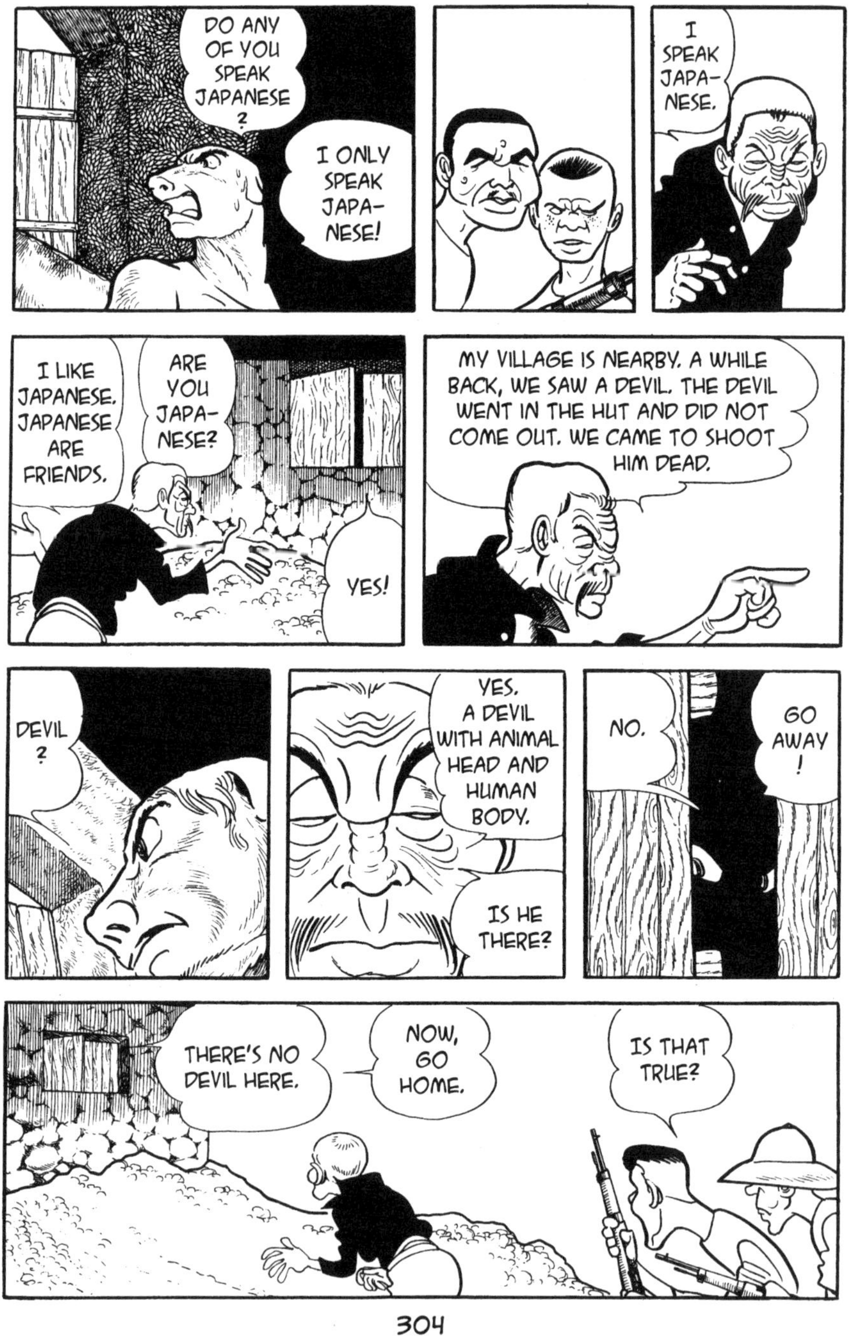
DO ANY OF YOU SPEAK JAPANESE?
I ONLY SPEAK JAPANESE!
I SPEAK JAPANESE.
ARE YOU JAPANESE?
YES!
I LIKE JAPANESE. JAPANESE ARE FRIENDS.
MY VILLAGE IS NEARBY. A WHILE BACK, WE SAW A DEVIL. THE DEVIL WENT IN THE HUT AND DID NOT COME OUT. WE CAME TO SHOOT HIM DEAD.
DEVIL?
YES. A DEVIL WITH ANIMAL HEAD AND HUMAN BODY.
IS HE THERE?
NO.
GO AWAY!
THERE'S NO DEVIL HERE.
NOW, GO HOME.
IS THAT TRUE?

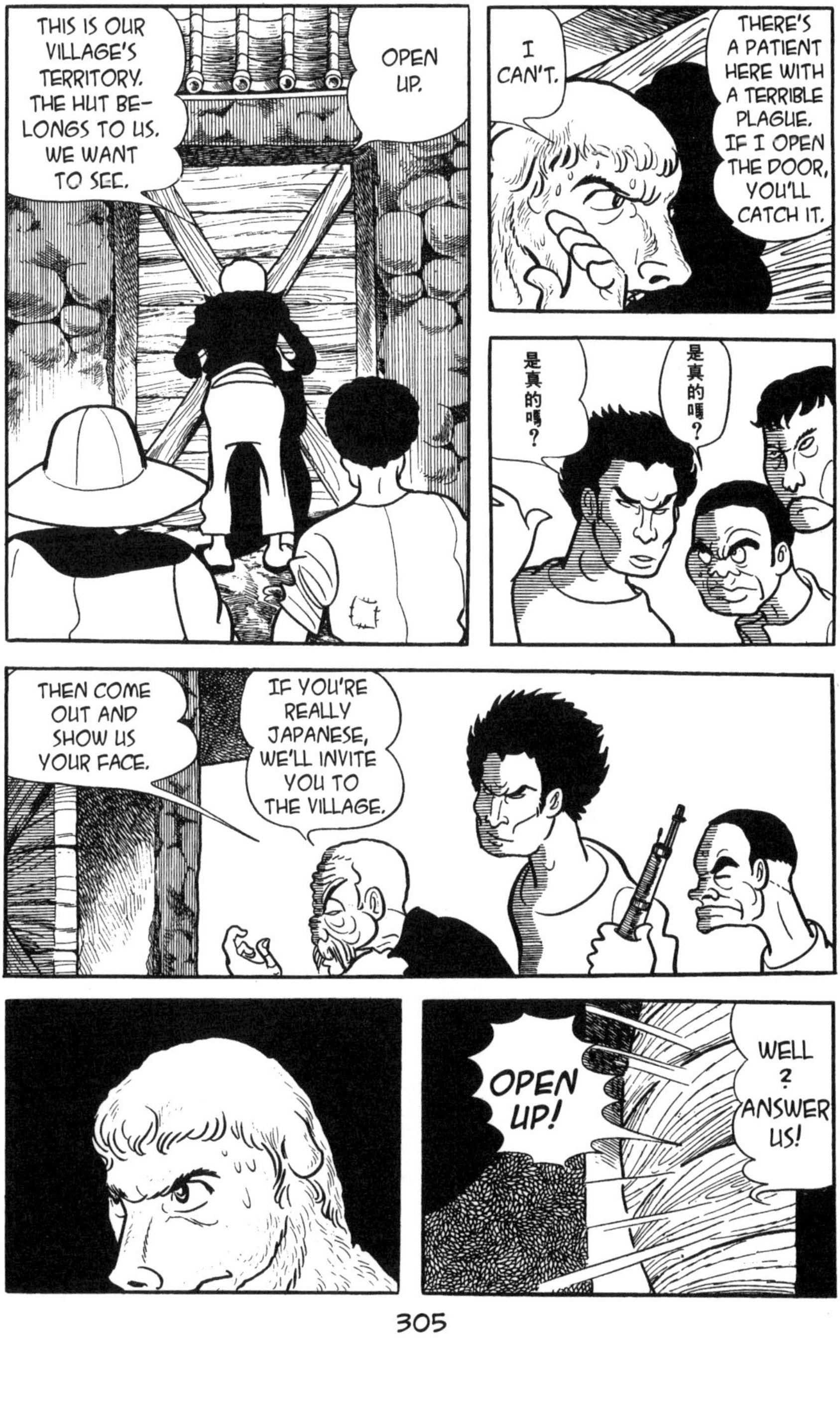
THIS IS OUR VILLAGE'S TERRITORY. THE HUT BELONGS TO US. WE WANT TO SEE.
OPEN UP.
I CAN'T.
THERE'S A PATIENT HERE WITH A TERRIBLE PLAGUE. IF I OPEN THE DOOR, YOU'LL CATCH IT.
是真的嗎？
是真的嗎？
THEN COME OUT AND SHOW US YOUR FACE.
IF YOU'RE REALLY JAPANESE, WE'LL INVITE YOU TO THE VILLAGE.
OPEN UP!
WELL? ANSWER US!

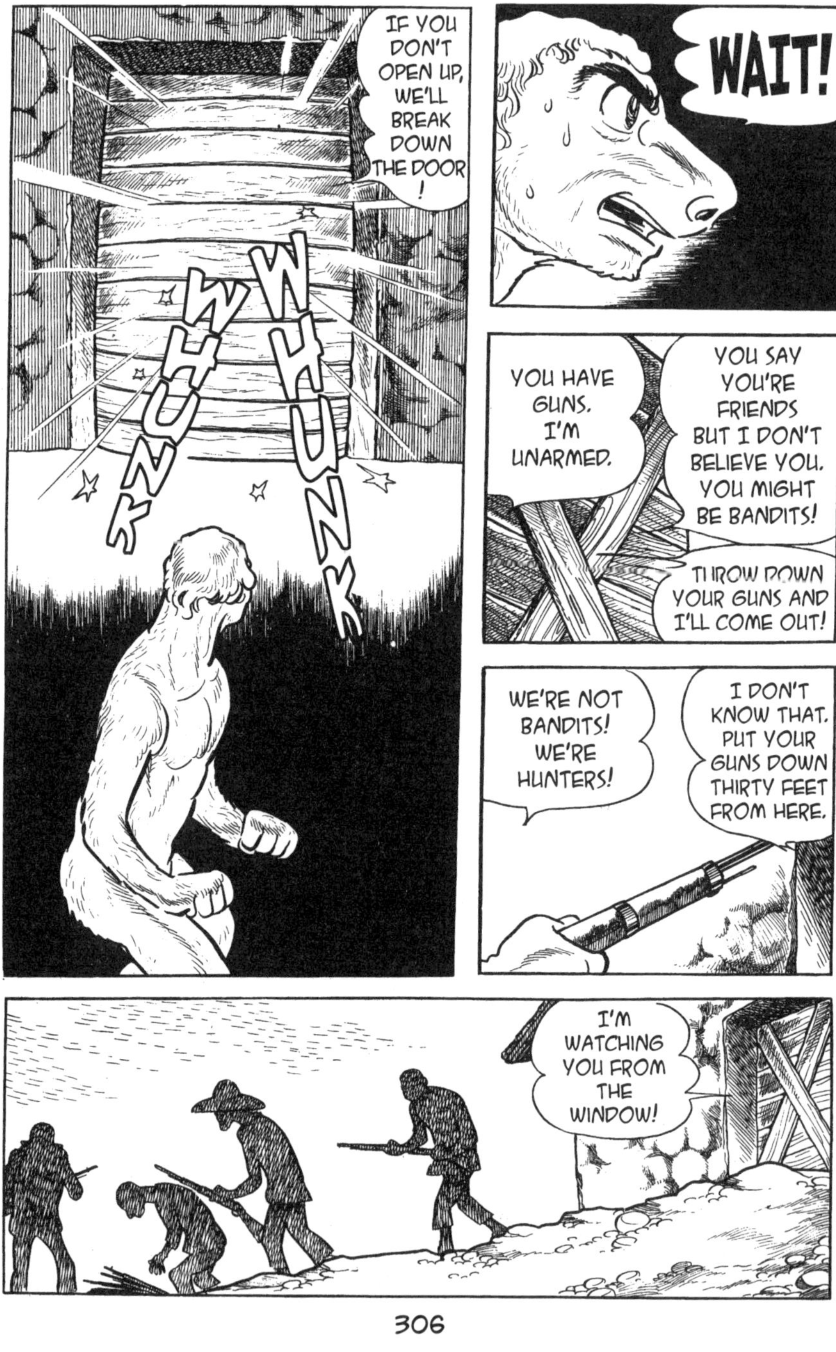
IF YOU DON'T OPEN UP, WE'LL BREAK DOWN THE DOOR!
WHUNK
WHUNK
WAIT!
YOU HAVE GUNS. I'M UNARMED.
YOU SAY YOU'RE FRIENDS BUT I DON'T BELIEVE YOU. YOU MIGHT BE BANDITS!
THROW DOWN YOUR GUNS AND I'LL COME OUT!
WE'RE NOT BANDITS! WE'RE HUNTERS!
I DON'T KNOW THAT. PUT YOUR GUNS DOWN THIRTY FEET FROM HERE.
I'M WATCHING YOU FROM THE WINDOW!

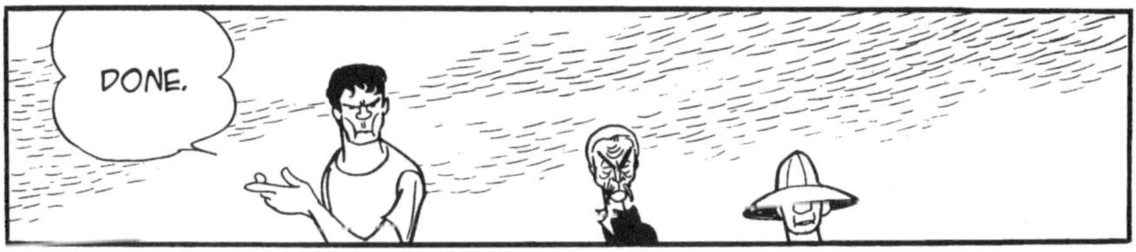
DONE.
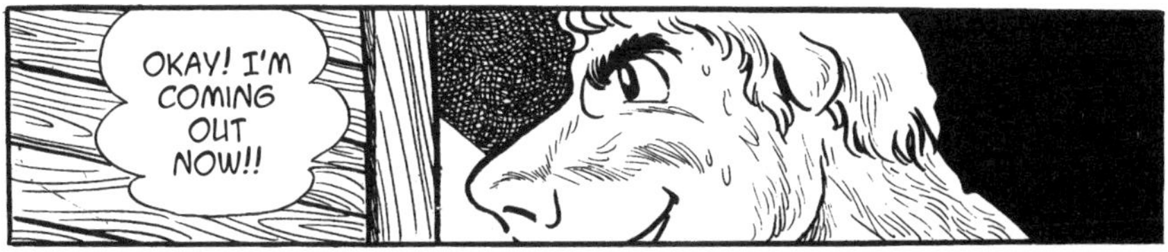
OKAY! I'M COMING OUT NOW!!
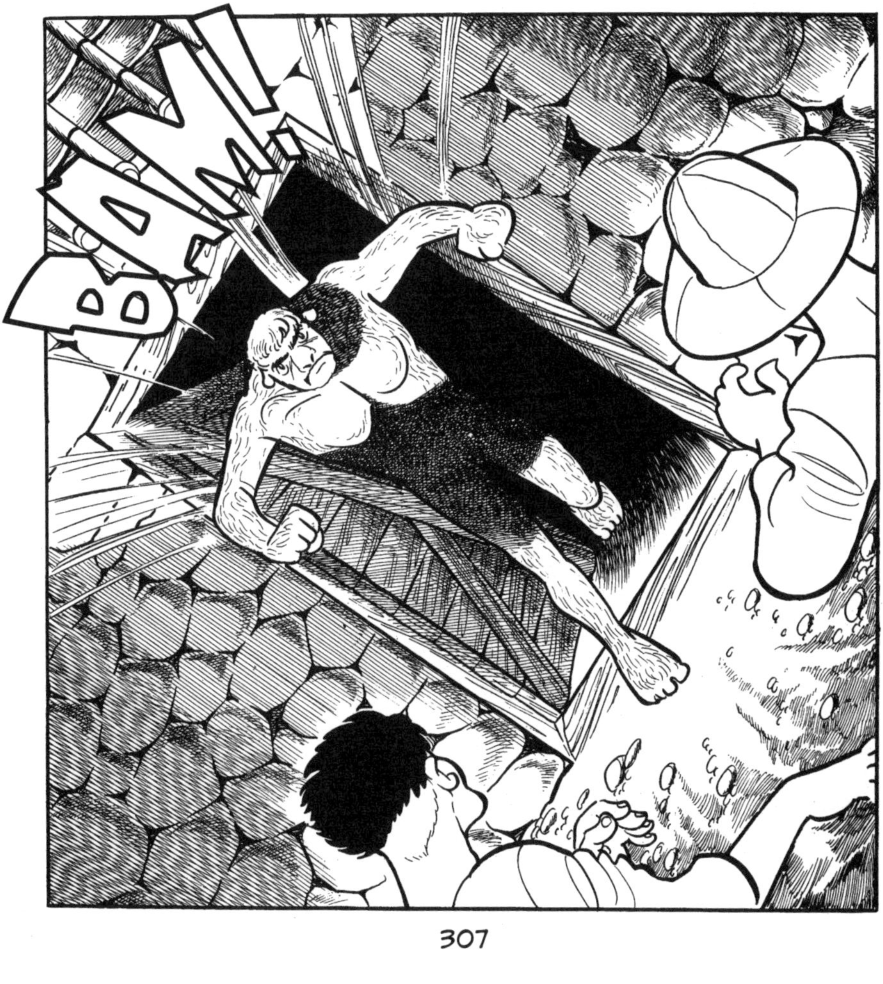
BAM!!

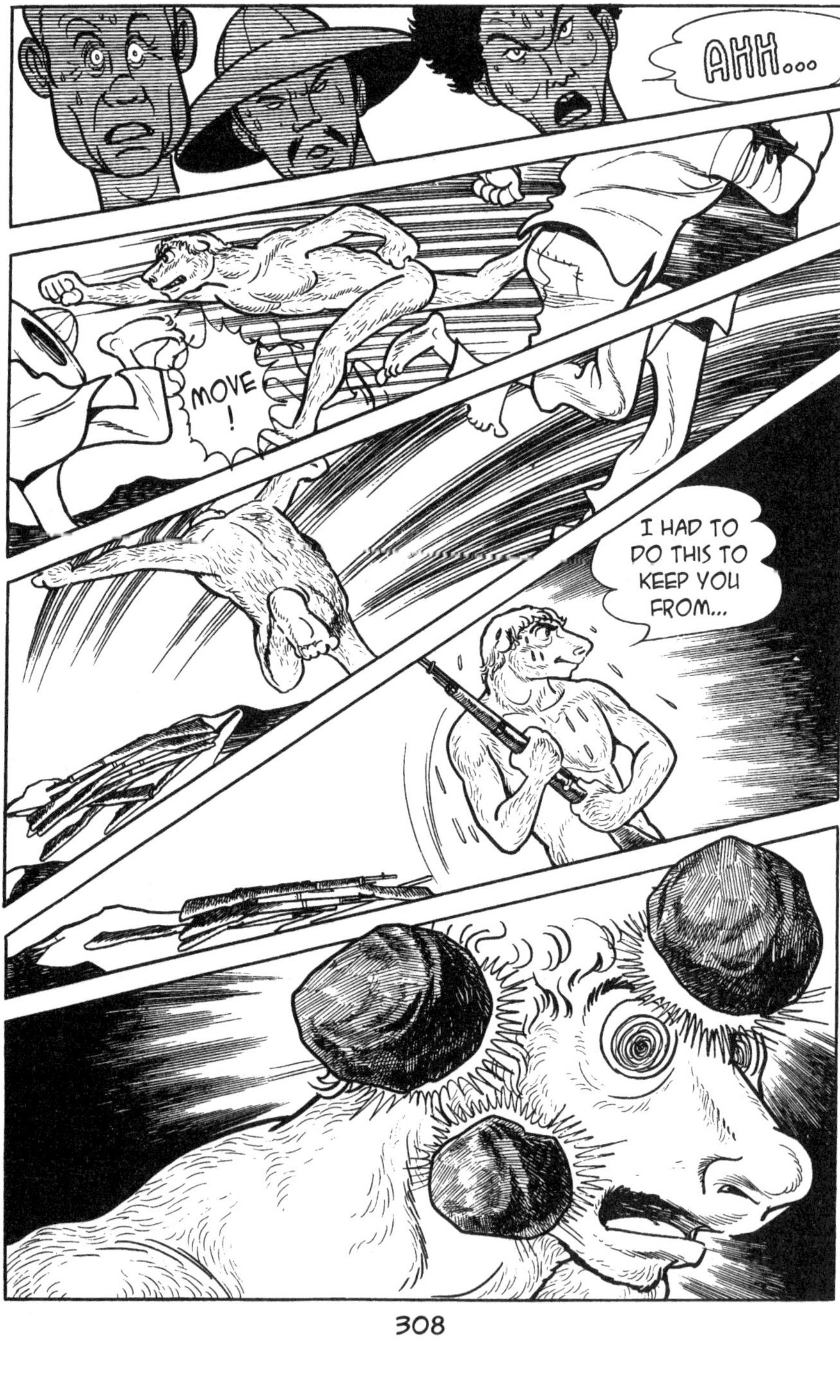
AHH...
MOVE !
I HAD TO DO THIS TO KEEP YOU FROM...

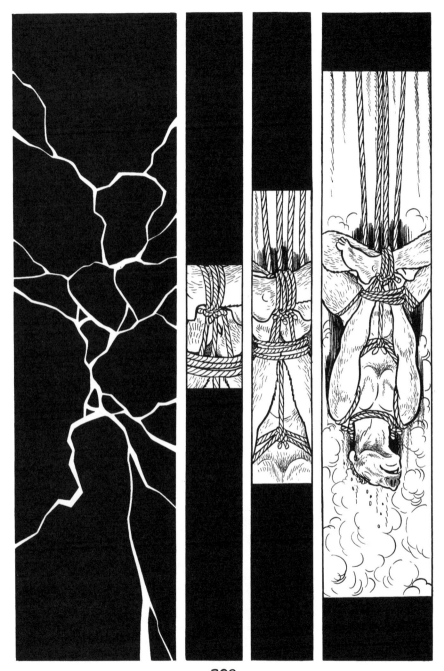

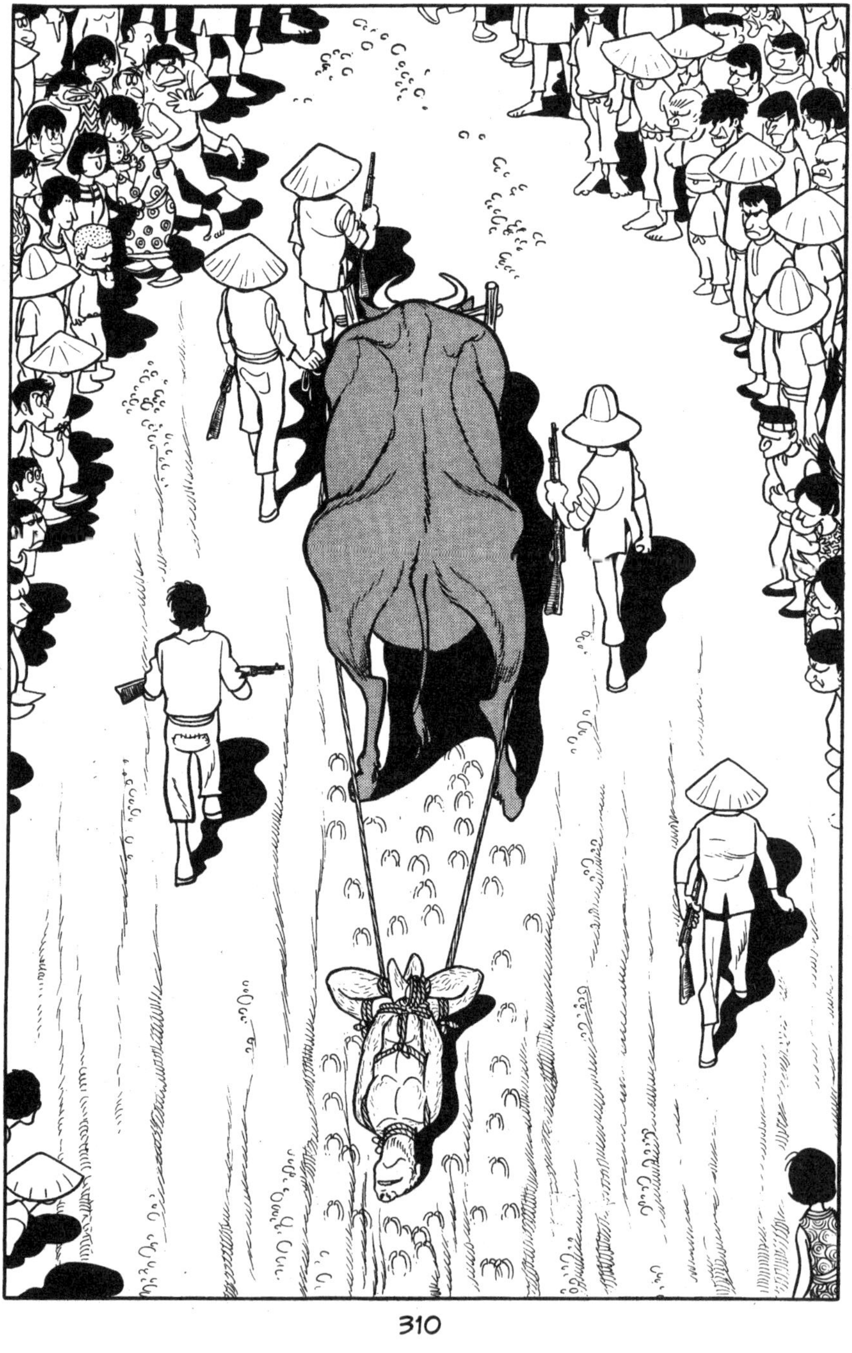

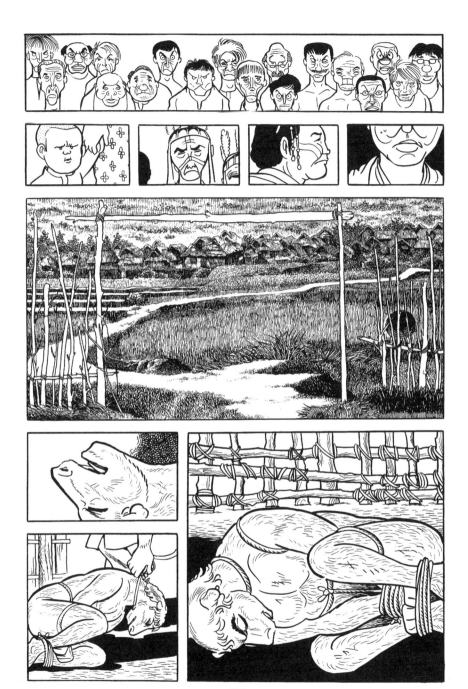

311

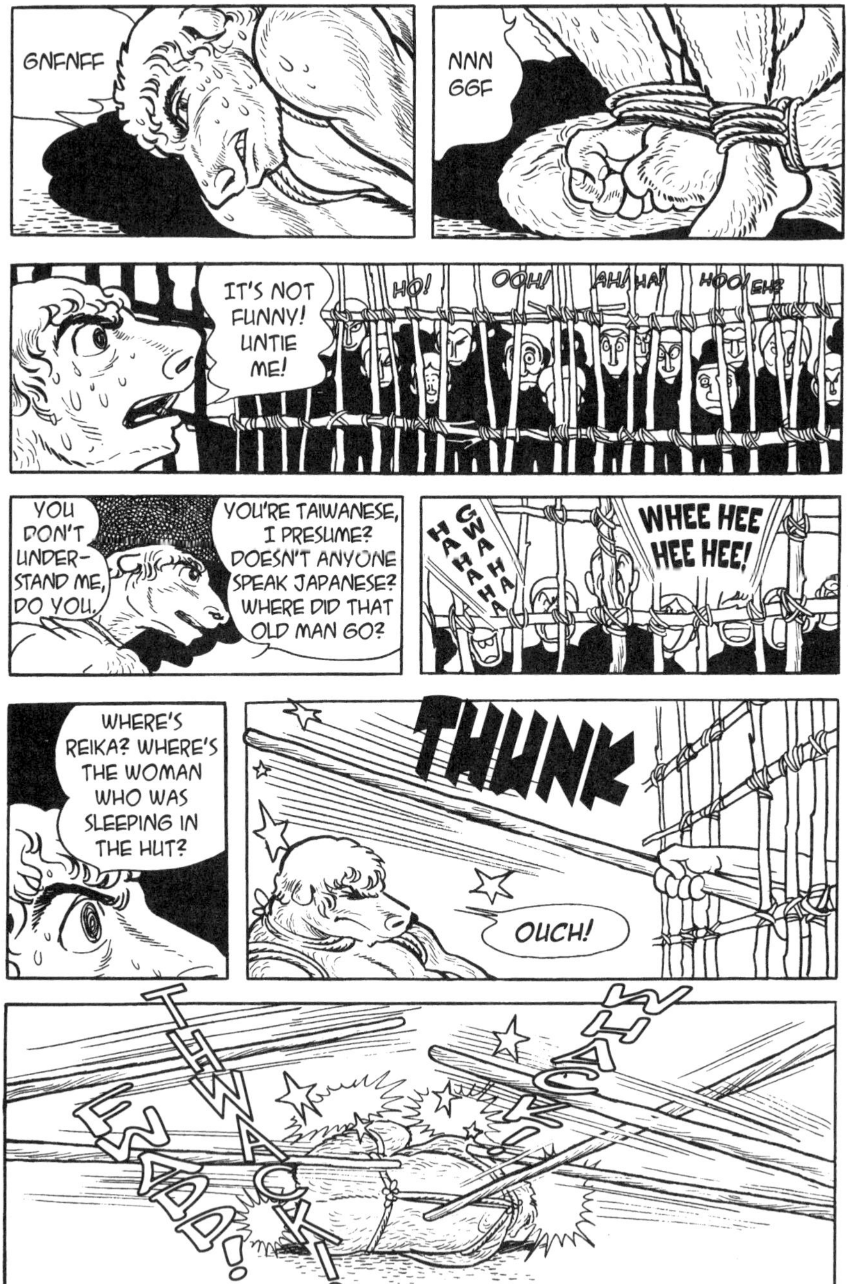
GNFNFF
NNN GGF
IT'S NOT FUNNY! UNTIE ME!
HO! OOH! AH! HA! HOO! EH?
YOU DON'T UNDER-STAND ME, DO YOU.
YOU'RE TAIWANESE, I PRESUME? DOESN'T ANYONE SPEAK JAPANESE? WHERE DID THAT OLD MAN GO?
HAHAHAHA
GWAHAHA
WHEE HEE HEE HEE!
WHERE'S REIKA? WHERE'S THE WOMAN WHO WAS SLEEPING IN THE HUT?
THUNK
OUCH!
THWACK!
WHACK!
WADD!

THWACK!
FWADD!
THUNK
EAT.

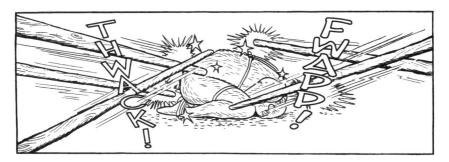

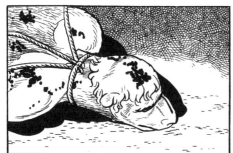

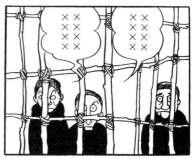

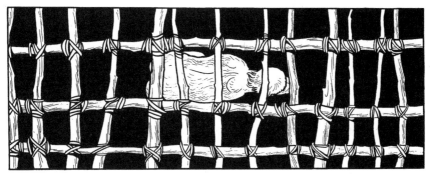

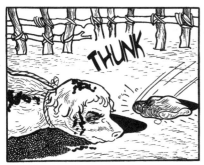

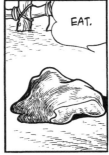

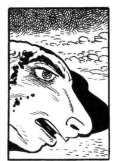

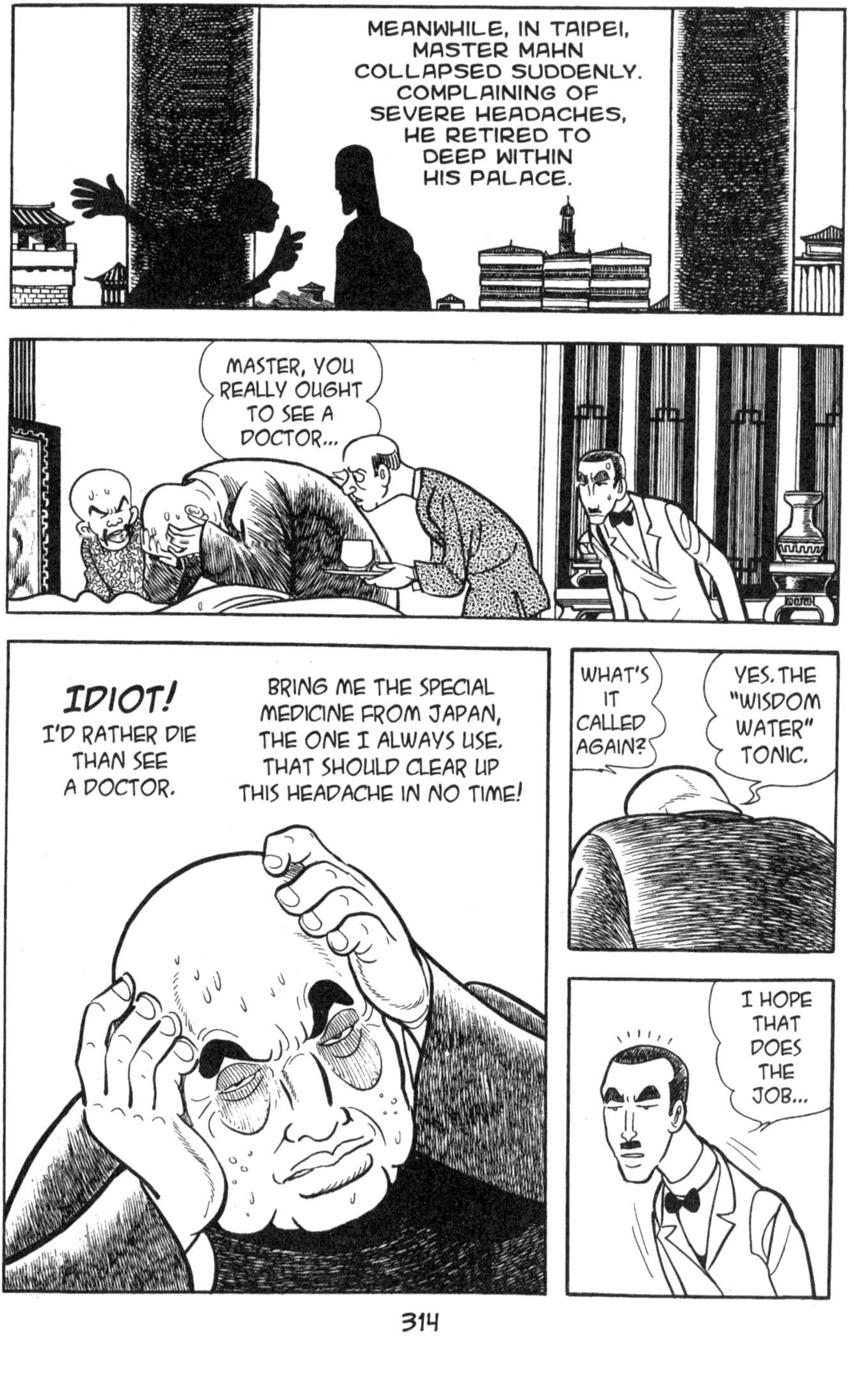

MEANWHILE, IN TAIPEI, MASTER MAHN COLLAPSED SUDDENLY. COMPLAINING OF SEVERE HEADACHES, HE RETIRED TO DEEP WITHIN HIS PALACE.
MASTER, YOU REALLY OUGHT TO SEE A DOCTOR...
IDIOT! I'D RATHER DIE THAN SEE A DOCTOR.
BRING ME THE SPECIAL MEDICINE FROM JAPAN, THE ONE I ALWAYS USE. THAT SHOULD CLEAR UP THIS HEADACHE IN NO TIME!
WHAT'S IT CALLED AGAIN?
YES. THE "WISDOM WATER" TONIC.
I HOPE THAT DOES THE JOB...

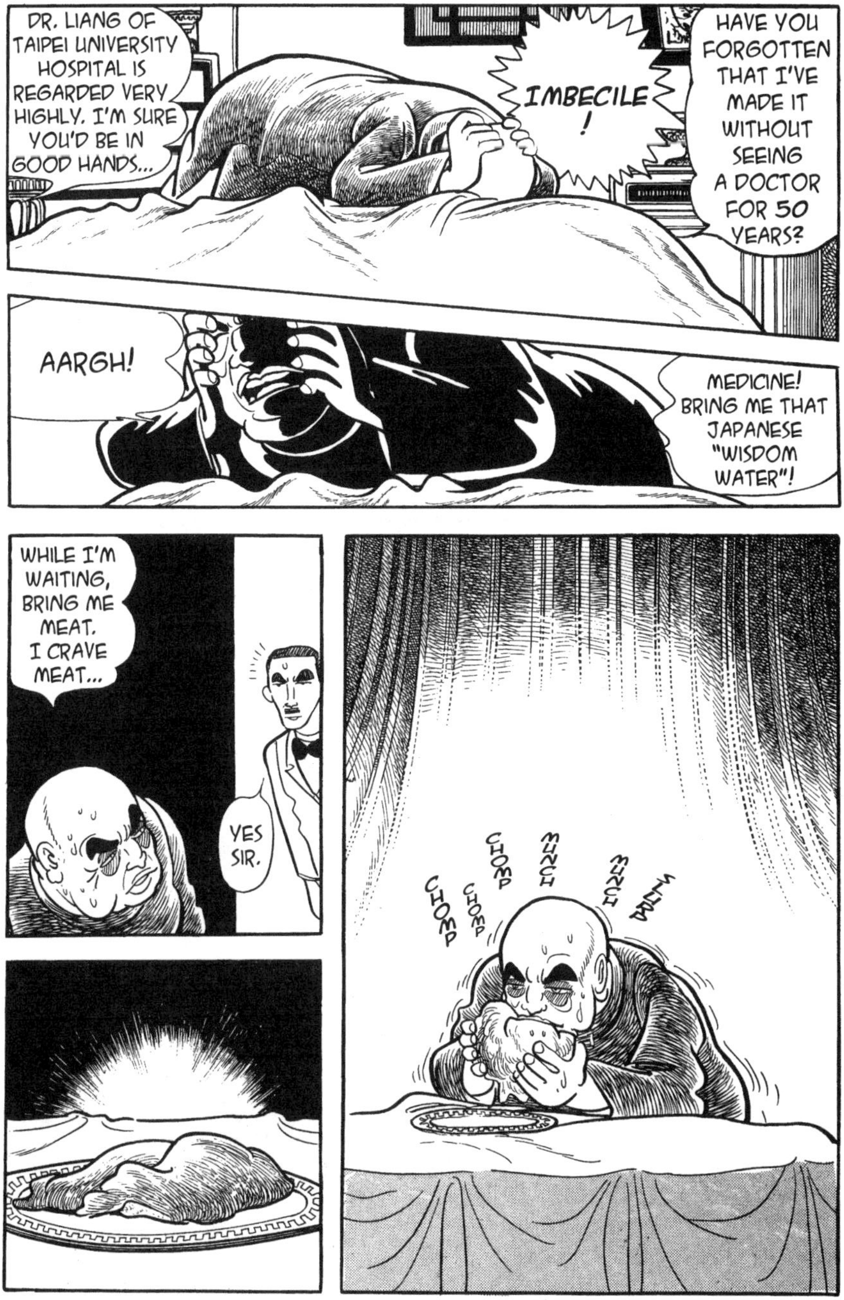
DR. LIANG OF TAIPEI UNIVERSITY HOSPITAL IS REGARDED VERY HIGHLY. I'M SURE YOU'D BE IN GOOD HANDS...
IMBECILE!
HAVE YOU FORGOTTEN THAT I'VE MADE IT WITHOUT SEEING A DOCTOR FOR 50 YEARS?
AARGH!
MEDICINE! BRING ME THAT JAPANESE "WISDOM WATER"!
WHILE I'M WAITING, BRING ME MEAT. I CRAVE MEAT...
YES SIR.
CHOMP
CHOMP
CHOMP
MUNCH
MUNCH
SLURP

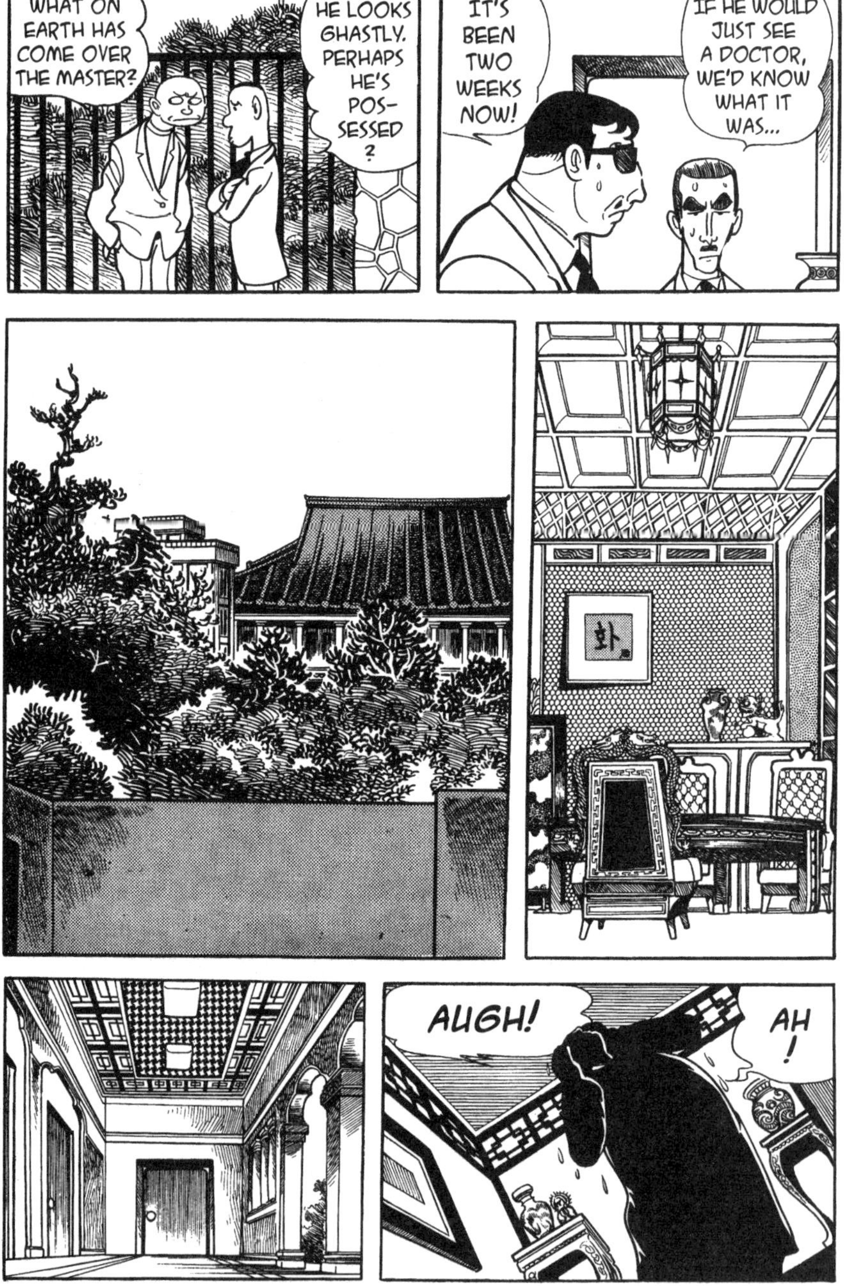

WHAT ON EARTH HAS COME OVER THE MASTER?
HE LOOKS GHASTLY. PERHAPS HE'S POS-SESSED?
IT'S BEEN TWO WEEKS NOW!
IF HE WOULD JUST SEE A DOCTOR, WE'D KNOW WHAT IT WAS...
화
AUGH!
AH!

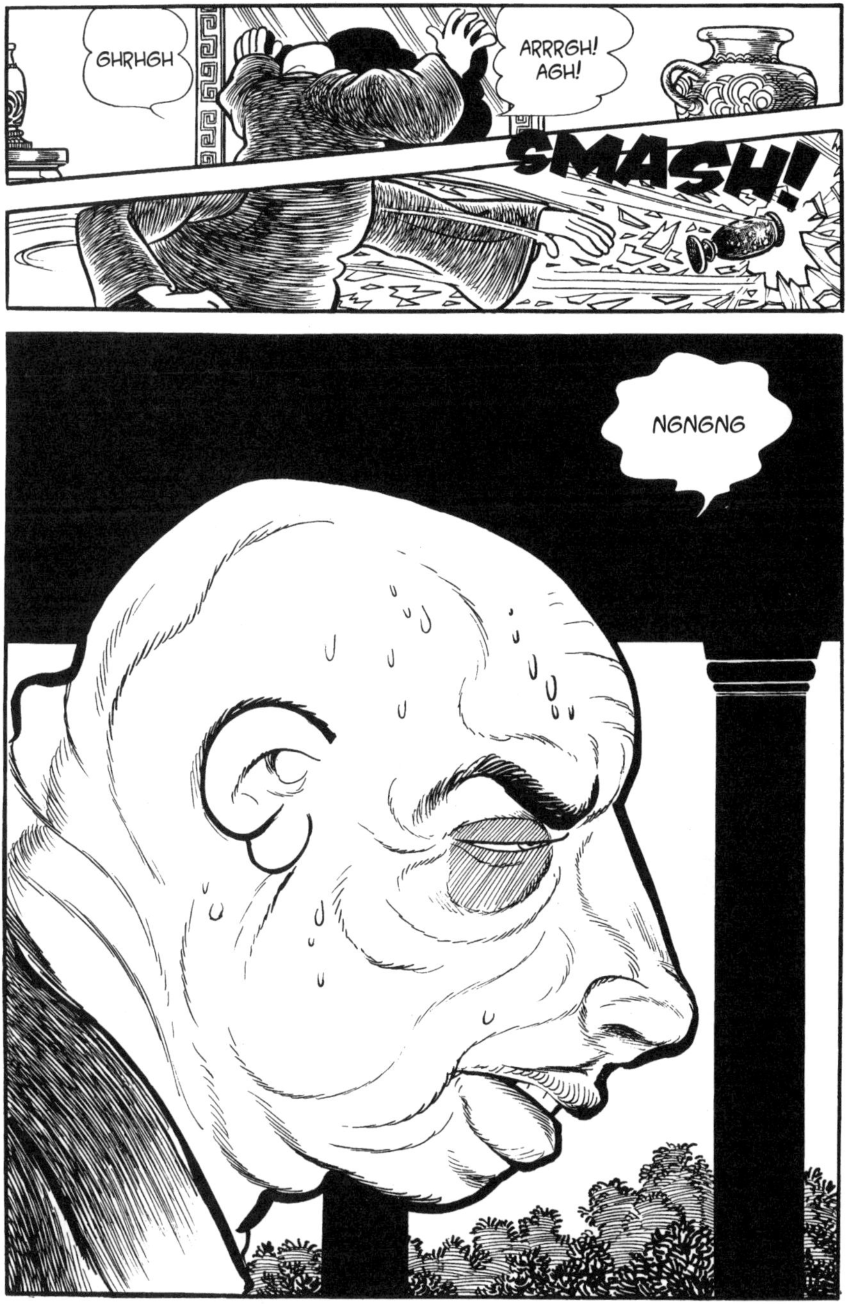
GHRHGH
ARRRGH! AGH!
SMASH!
NGNGNG

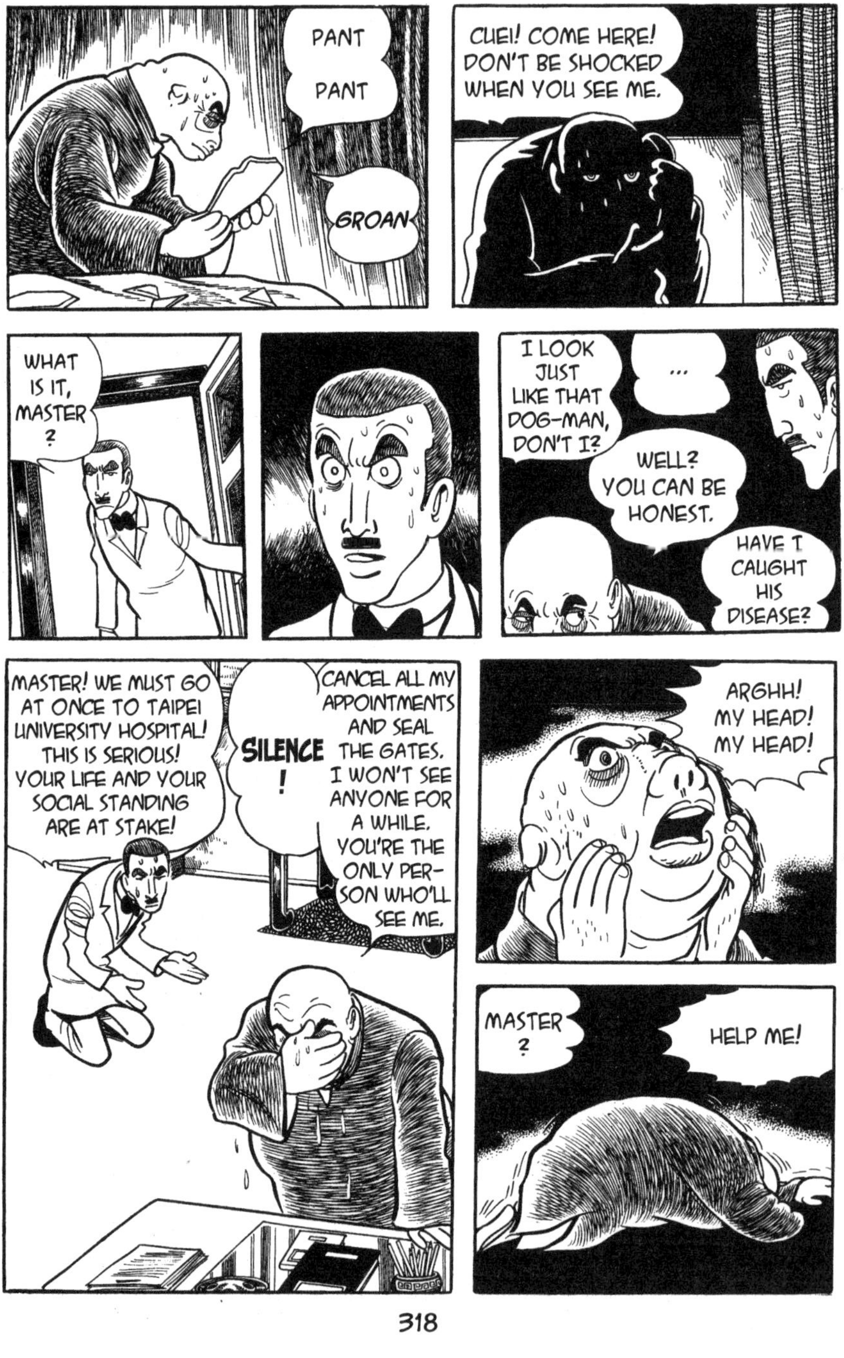

PANT PANT
GROAN
CUEI! COME HERE! DON'T BE SHOCKED WHEN YOU SEE ME.
WHAT IS IT, MASTER?
I LOOK JUST LIKE THAT DOG-MAN, DON'T I?
...
WELL? YOU CAN BE HONEST.
HAVE I CAUGHT HIS DISEASE?
MASTER! WE MUST GO AT ONCE TO TAIPEI UNIVERSITY HOSPITAL! THIS IS SERIOUS! YOUR LIFE AND YOUR SOCIAL STANDING ARE AT STAKE!
SILENCE!
CANCEL ALL MY APPOINTMENTS AND SEAL THE GATES. I WON'T SEE ANYONE FOR A WHILE. YOU'RE THE ONLY PERSON WHO'LL SEE ME.
ARGHH! MY HEAD! MY HEAD!
MASTER?
HELP ME!

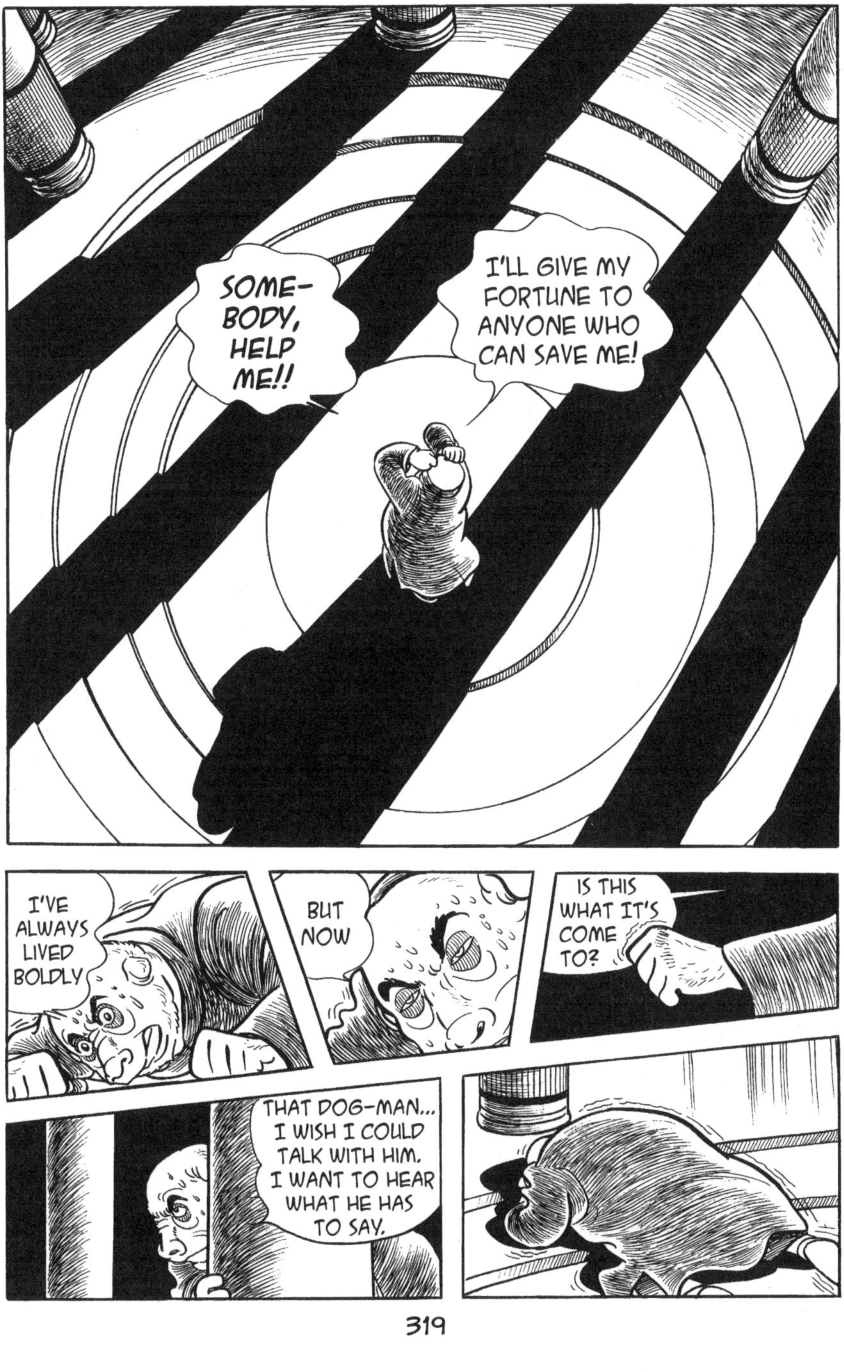
SOME-BODY, HELP ME!!
I'LL GIVE MY FORTUNE TO ANYONE WHO CAN SAVE ME!
I'VE ALWAYS LIVED BOLDLY
BUT NOW
IS THIS WHAT IT'S COME TO?
THAT DOG-MAN... I WISH I COULD TALK WITH HIM. I WANT TO HEAR WHAT HE HAS TO SAY.

CHAPTER 9

CRAZED BITCH

DR. TATSUGAURA, YOU'RE SAYING THAT YOU WANT TO DISPLAY ME AT THE GMC IN OCTOBER?

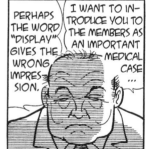

PERHAPS THE WORD "DISPLAY" GIVES THE WRONG IMPRESSION.

I WANT TO INTRODUCE YOU TO THE MEMBERS AS AN IMPORTANT MEDICAL CASE...

ARE YOU SURE?

ABSOLUTELY.

322

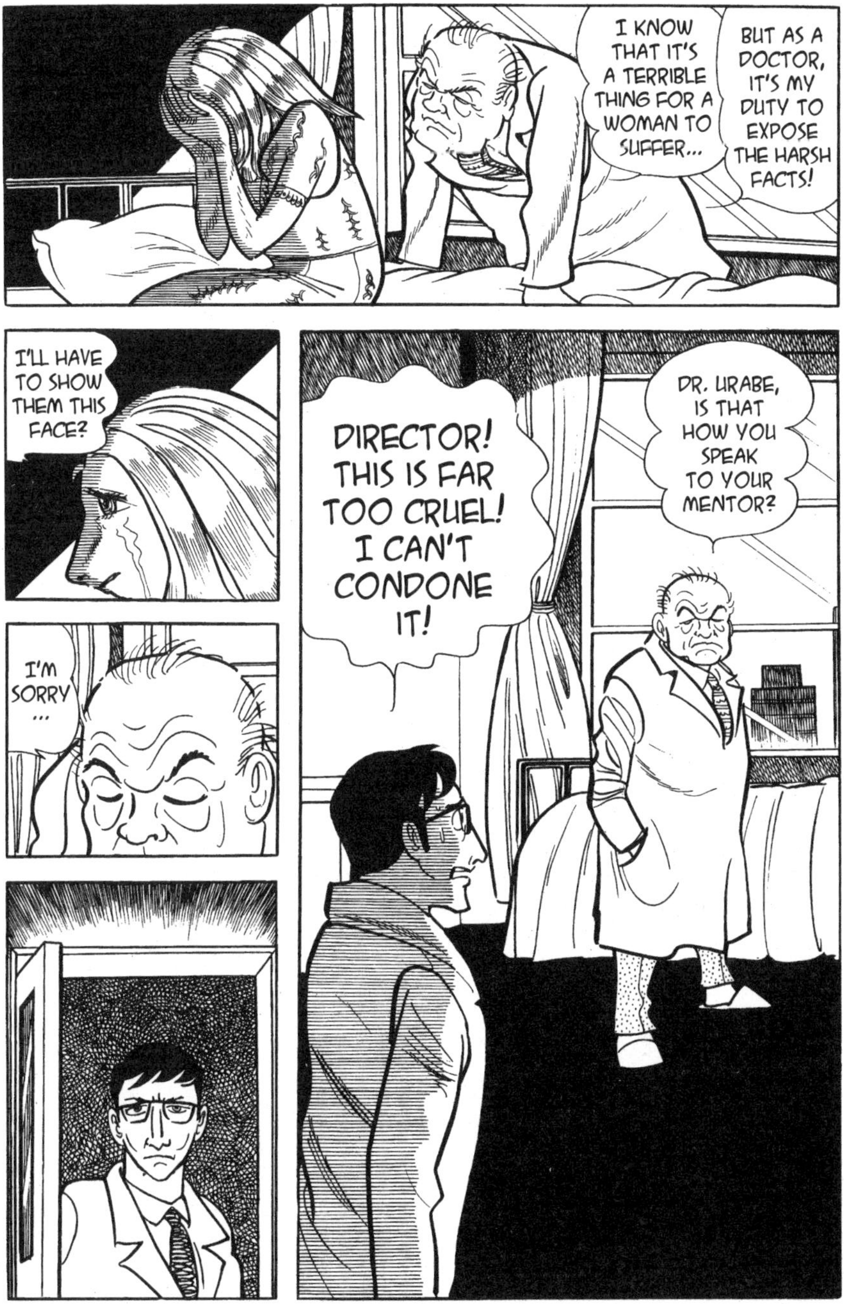
I KNOW THAT IT'S A TERRIBLE THING FOR A WOMAN TO SUFFER...
BUT AS A DOCTOR, IT'S MY DUTY TO EXPOSE THE HARSH FACTS!
I'LL HAVE TO SHOW THEM THIS FACE?
I'M SORRY ...
DIRECTOR! THIS IS FAR TOO CRUEL! I CAN'T CONDONE IT!
DR. URABE, IS THAT HOW YOU SPEAK TO YOUR MENTOR?

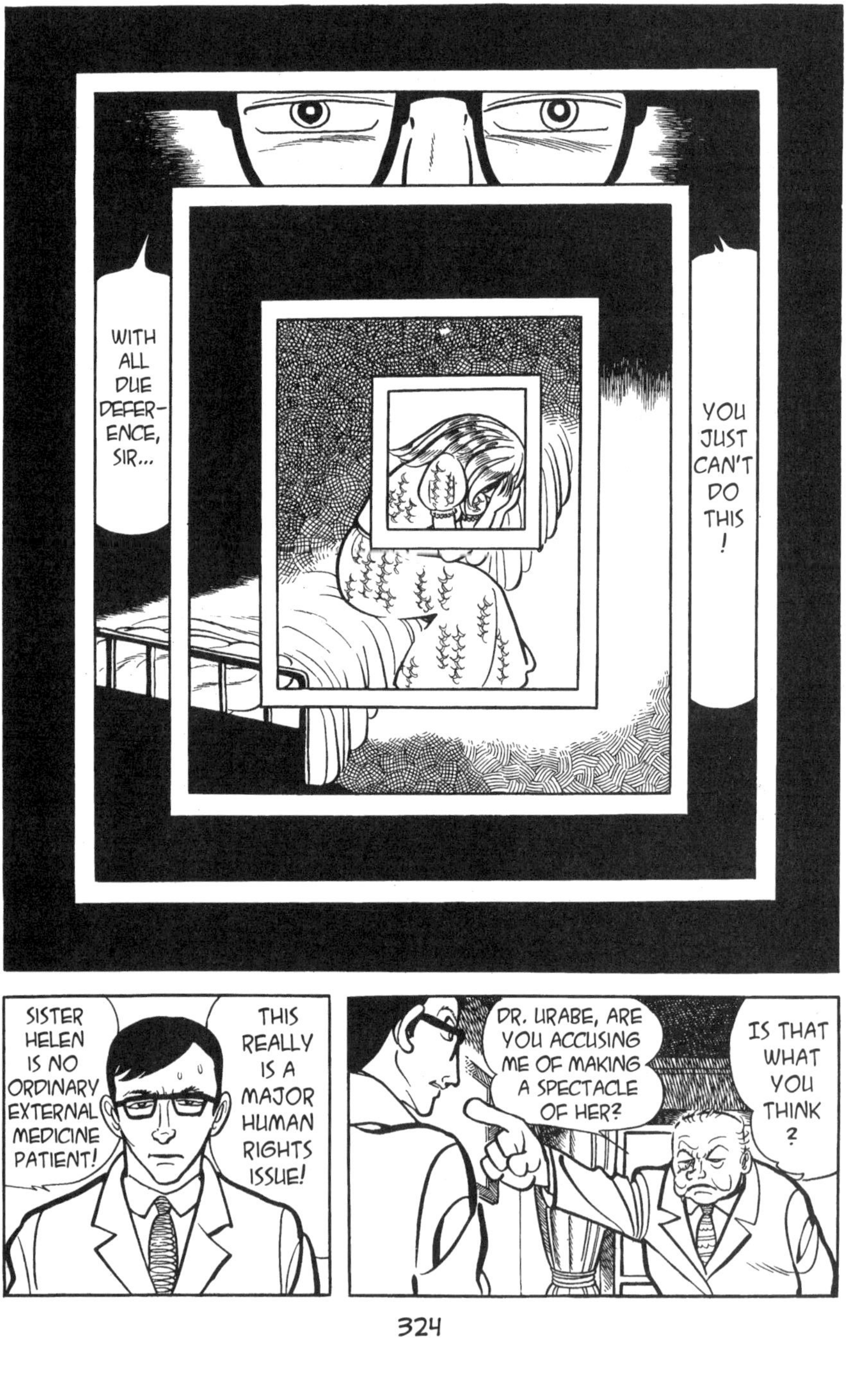
WITH ALL DUE DEFERENCE, SIR...
YOU JUST CAN'T DO THIS!
SISTER HELEN IS NO ORDINARY EXTERNAL MEDICINE PATIENT!
THIS REALLY IS A MAJOR HUMAN RIGHTS ISSUE!
DR. URABE, ARE YOU ACCUSING ME OF MAKING A SPECTACLE OF HER?
IS THAT WHAT YOU THINK?

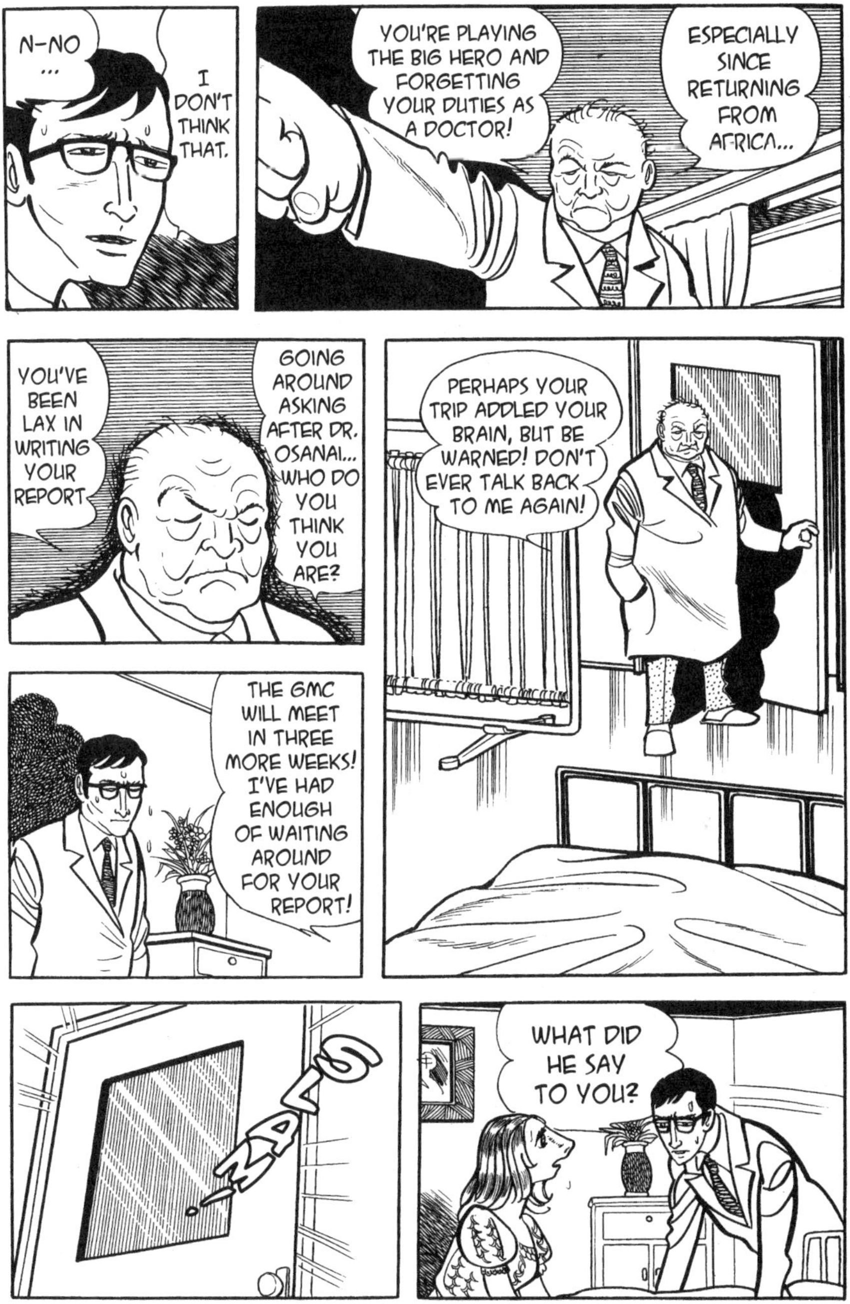
N-NO ...
I DON'T THINK THAT.
YOU'RE PLAYING THE BIG HERO AND FORGETTING YOUR DUTIES AS A DOCTOR!
ESPECIALLY SINCE RETURNING FROM AFRICA...
YOU'VE BEEN LAX IN WRITING YOUR REPORT.
GOING AROUND ASKING AFTER DR. OSANAI... WHO DO YOU THINK YOU ARE?
PERHAPS YOUR TRIP ADDLED YOUR BRAIN, BUT BE WARNED! DON'T EVER TALK BACK TO ME AGAIN!
THE GMC WILL MEET IN THREE MORE WEEKS! I'VE HAD ENOUGH OF WAITING AROUND FOR YOUR REPORT!
SLAM!
WHAT DID HE SAY TO YOU?

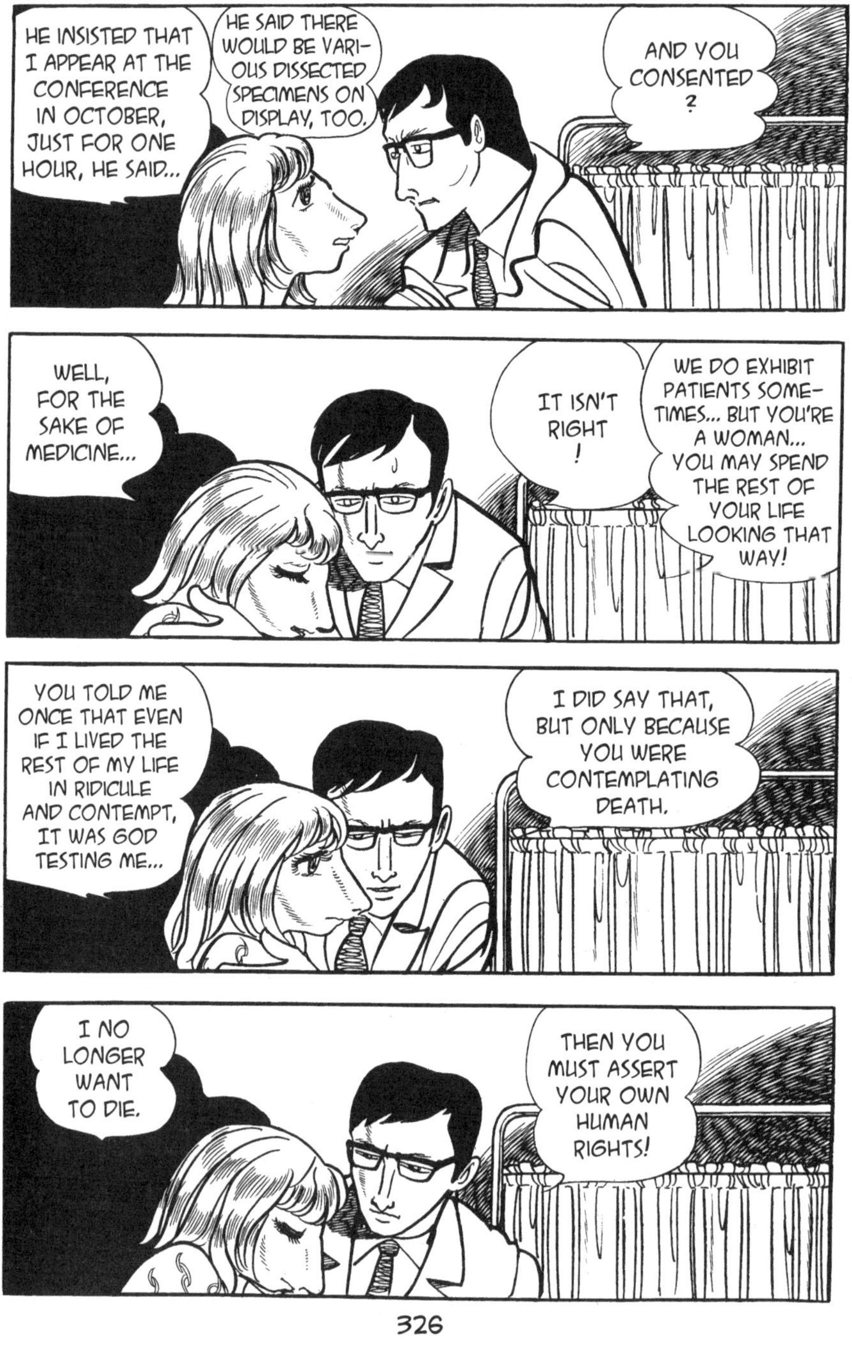
HE INSISTED THAT I APPEAR AT THE CONFERENCE IN OCTOBER, JUST FOR ONE HOUR, HE SAID...
HE SAID THERE WOULD BE VARI-OUS DISSECTED SPECIMENS ON DISPLAY, TOO.
AND YOU CONSENTED?
WELL, FOR THE SAKE OF MEDICINE...
IT ISN'T RIGHT!
WE DO EXHIBIT PATIENTS SOME-TIMES... BUT YOU'RE A WOMAN... YOU MAY SPEND THE REST OF YOUR LIFE LOOKING THAT WAY!
YOU TOLD ME ONCE THAT EVEN IF I LIVED THE REST OF MY LIFE IN RIDICULE AND CONTEMPT, IT WAS GOD TESTING ME...
I DID SAY THAT, BUT ONLY BECAUSE YOU WERE CONTEMPLATING DEATH.
I NO LONGER WANT TO DIE.
THEN YOU MUST ASSERT YOUR OWN HUMAN RIGHTS!

YOU HAVE THE RIGHT TO SAY NO!

I BROUGHT YOU TO JAPAN TO CURE YOU, NOT TO HAVE YOU DISPLAYED AS A MEDICAL SPECIMEN!

LISTEN, IF YOU REFUSE FIRMLY, YOU WON'T HAVE TO DO IT! THERE'S NO REASON TO FEEL OBLIGATED!

DON'T WORRY, I'LL HANDLE DR. TATSUGAURA...

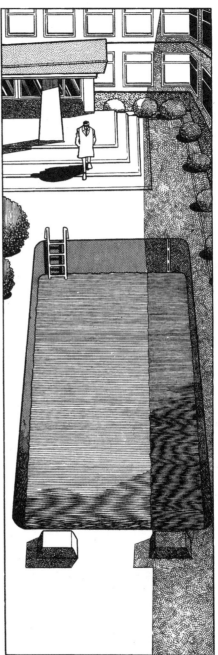

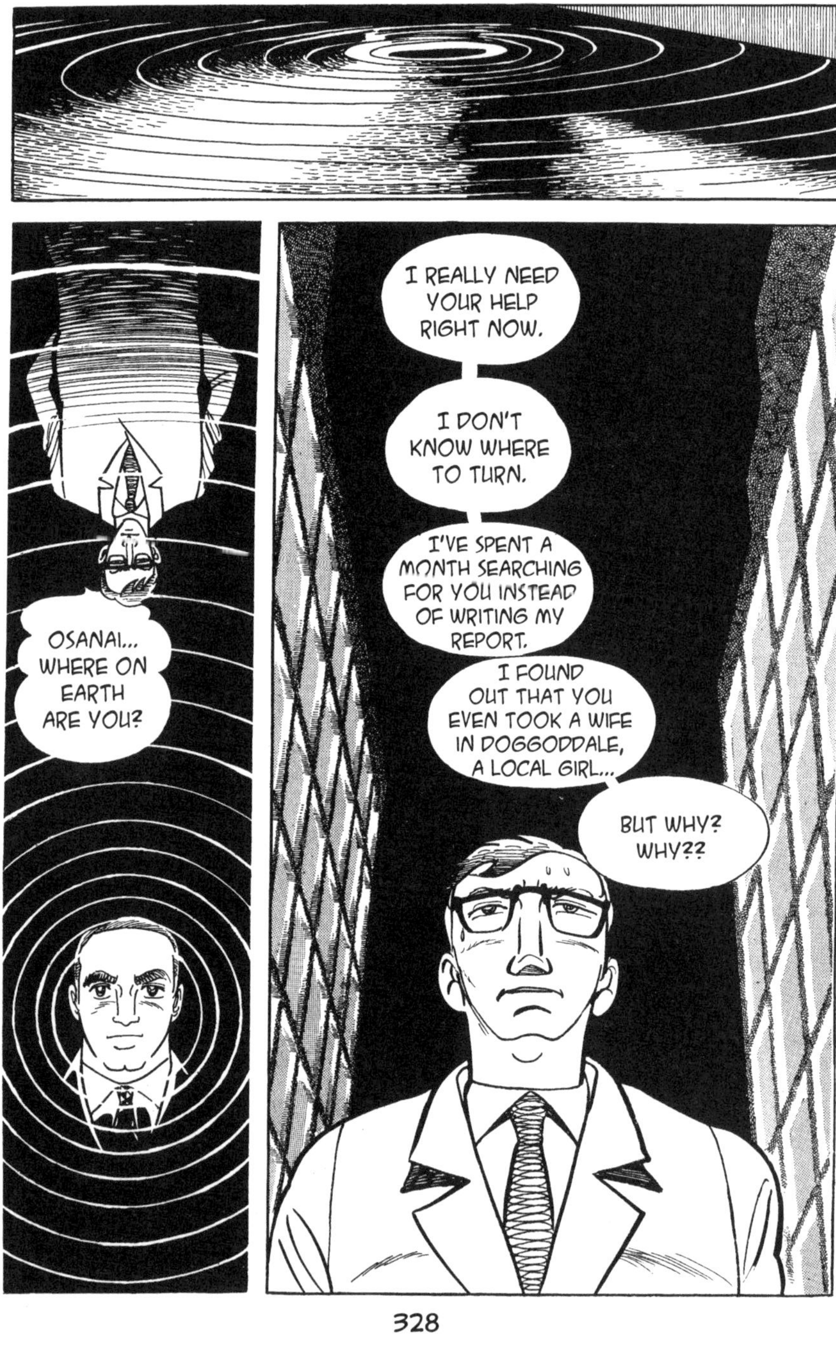
OSANAI... WHERE ON EARTH ARE YOU?
I REALLY NEED YOUR HELP RIGHT NOW.
I DON'T KNOW WHERE TO TURN.
I'VE SPENT A MONTH SEARCHING FOR YOU INSTEAD OF WRITING MY REPORT.
I FOUND OUT THAT YOU EVEN TOOK A WIFE IN DOGGODDALE, A LOCAL GIRL...
BUT WHY? WHY??

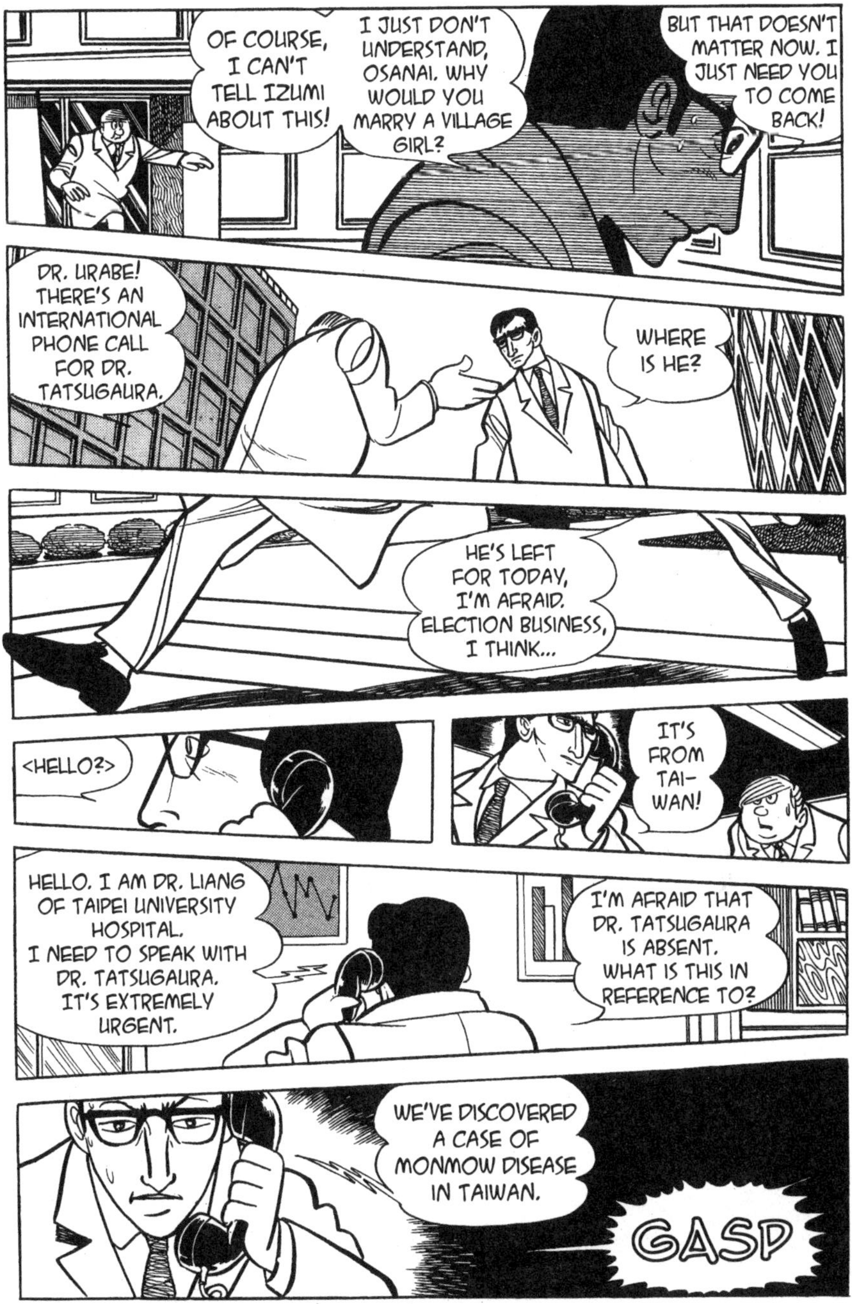

OF COURSE, I CAN'T TELL IZUMI ABOUT THIS!
I JUST DON'T UNDERSTAND, OSANAI. WHY WOULD YOU MARRY A VILLAGE GIRL?
BUT THAT DOESN'T MATTER NOW. I JUST NEED YOU TO COME BACK!
DR. URABE! THERE'S AN INTERNATIONAL PHONE CALL FOR DR. TATSUGAURA.
WHERE IS HE?
HE'S LEFT FOR TODAY, I'M AFRAID. ELECTION BUSINESS, I THINK...
<HELLO?>
IT'S FROM TAI-WAN!
HELLO. I AM DR. LIANG OF TAIPEI UNIVERSITY HOSPITAL. I NEED TO SPEAK WITH DR. TATSUGAURA. IT'S EXTREMELY URGENT.
I'M AFRAID THAT DR. TATSUGAURA IS ABSENT. WHAT IS THIS IN REFERENCE TO?
WE'VE DISCOVERED A CASE OF MONMOW DISEASE IN TAIWAN.
GASP

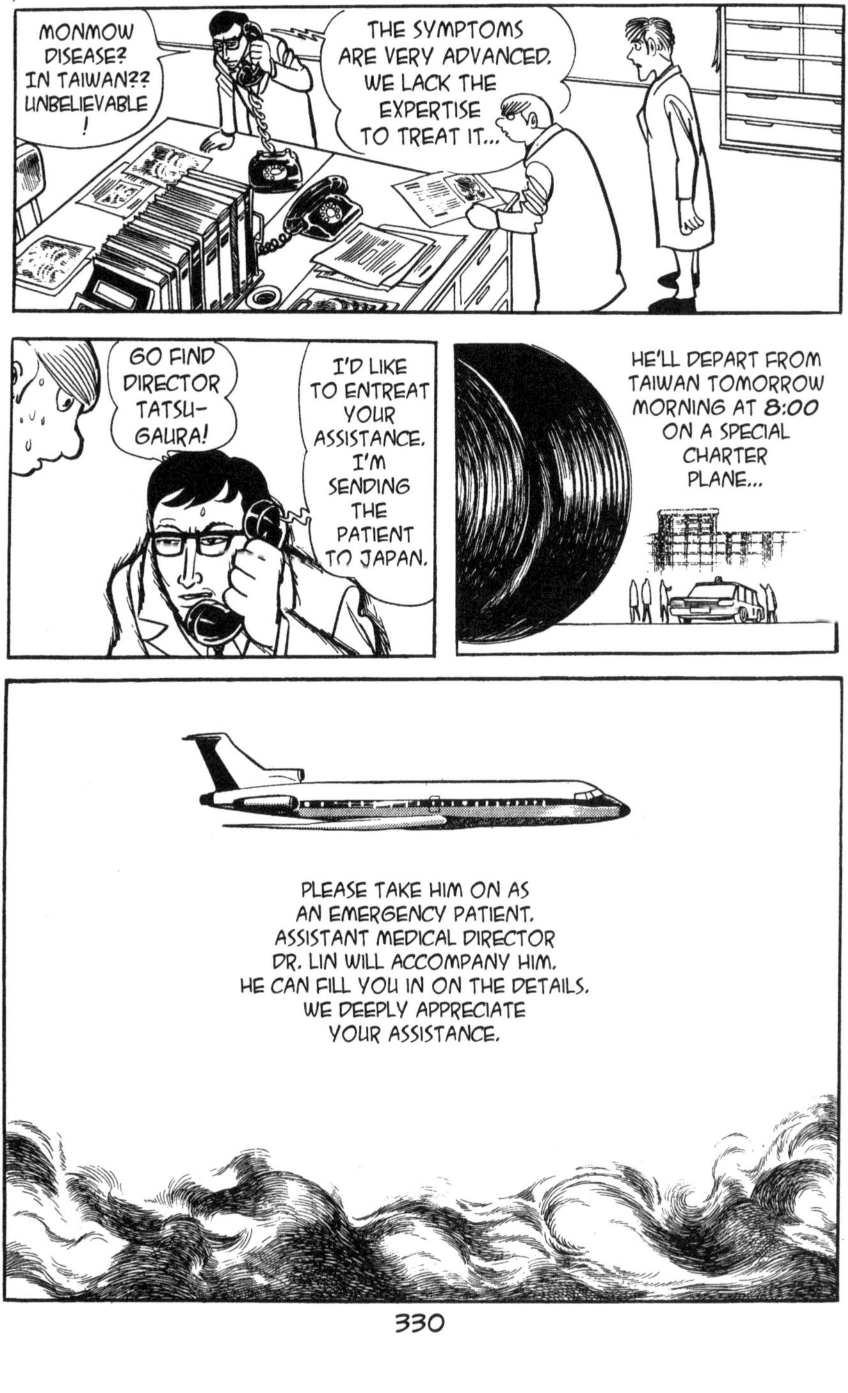
MONMOW DISEASE? IN TAIWAN?? UNBELIEVABLE!
THE SYMPTOMS ARE VERY ADVANCED. WE LACK THE EXPERTISE TO TREAT IT...
GO FIND DIRECTOR TATSU-GAURA!
I'D LIKE TO ENTREAT YOUR ASSISTANCE. I'M SENDING THE PATIENT TO JAPAN.
HE'LL DEPART FROM TAIWAN TOMORROW MORNING AT 8:00 ON A SPECIAL CHARTER PLANE...
PLEASE TAKE HIM ON AS AN EMERGENCY PATIENT. ASSISTANT MEDICAL DIRECTOR DR. LIN WILL ACCOMPANY HIM. HE CAN FILL YOU IN ON THE DETAILS. WE DEEPLY APPRECIATE YOUR ASSISTANCE.

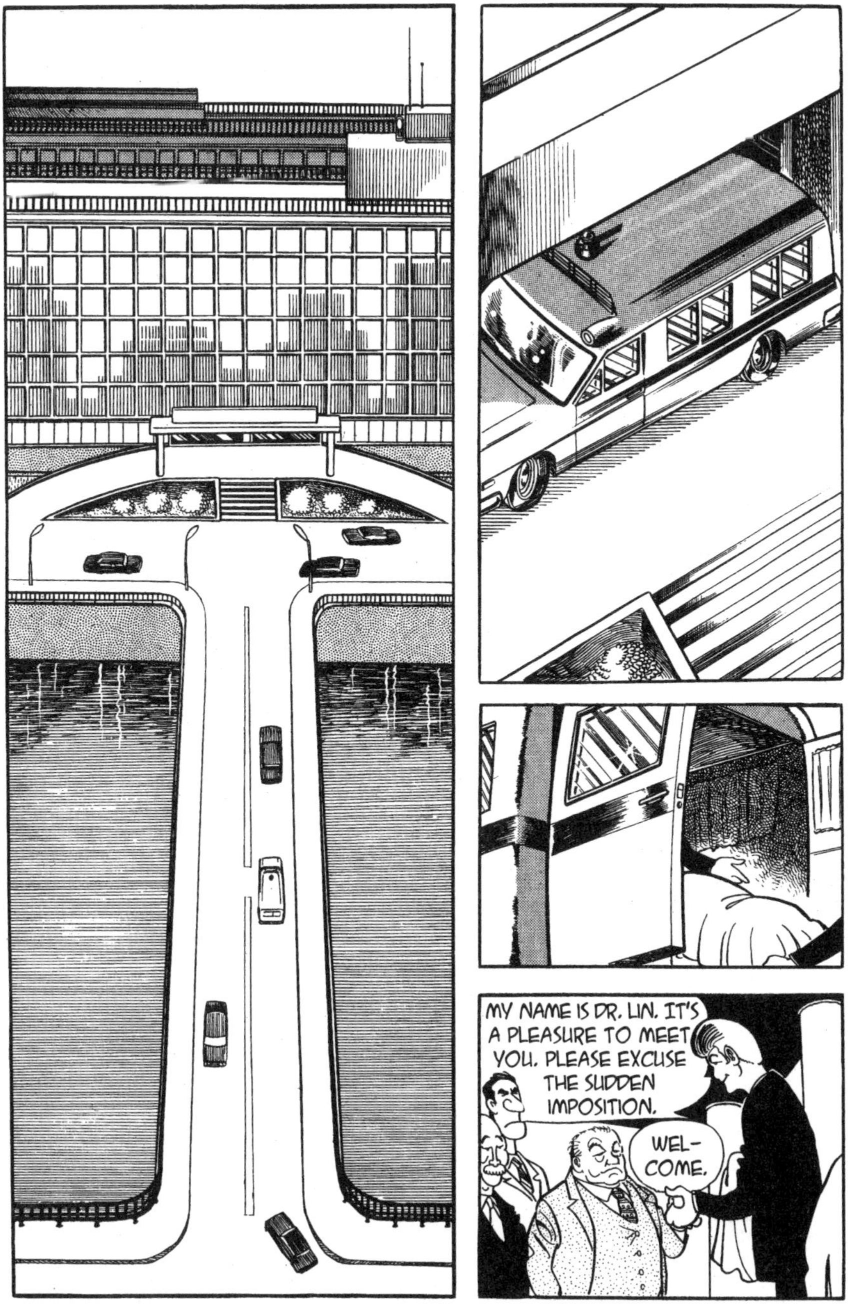
MY NAME IS DR. LIN. IT'S A PLEASURE TO MEET YOU. PLEASE EXCUSE THE SUDDEN IMPOSITION.
WEL-COME.

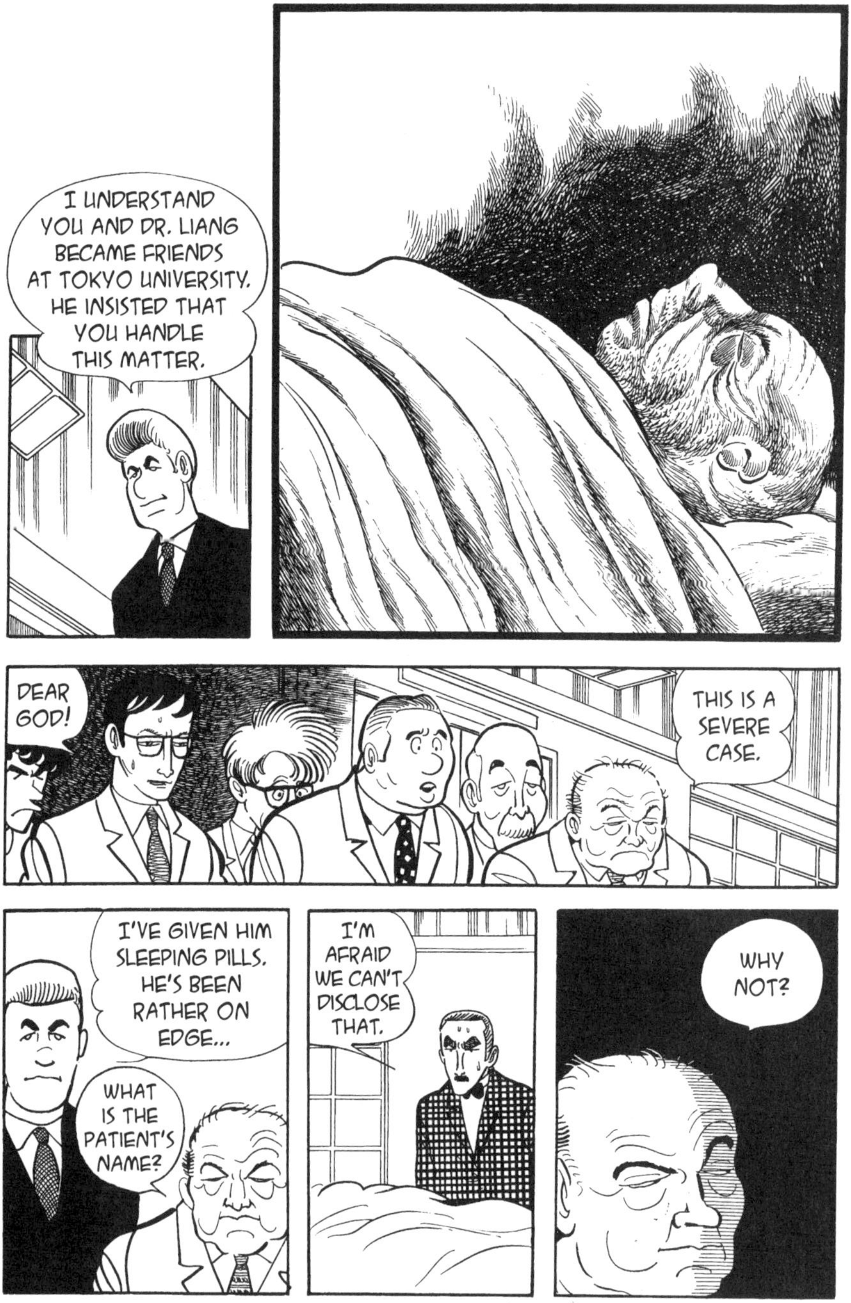
I UNDERSTAND YOU AND DR. LIANG BECAME FRIENDS AT TOKYO UNIVERSITY. HE INSISTED THAT YOU HANDLE THIS MATTER.
DEAR GOD!
THIS IS A SEVERE CASE.
I'VE GIVEN HIM SLEEPING PILLS. HE'S BEEN RATHER ON EDGE...
WHAT IS THE PATIENT'S NAME?
I'M AFRAID WE CAN'T DISCLOSE THAT.
WHY NOT?

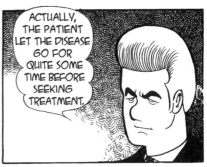

ACTUALLY, THE PATIENT LET THE DISEASE GO FOR QUITE SOME TIME BEFORE SEEKING TREATMENT.

THIS MAN IS AN EMINENT FIGURE IN OUR COUNTRY... IF HIS NAME IS LEAKED, IT WOULD CAUSE A MAJOR BLOW TO OUR ECONOMY... TO OUR POLITICAL SYSTEM, EVEN!

BUT WHY DID YOU WAIT SO LONG TO CONTACT US?

BUT WHY?

ER... HE HAS A PROFOUND AVERSION TO DOCTORS...

WHAT APPALLING IGNORANCE!

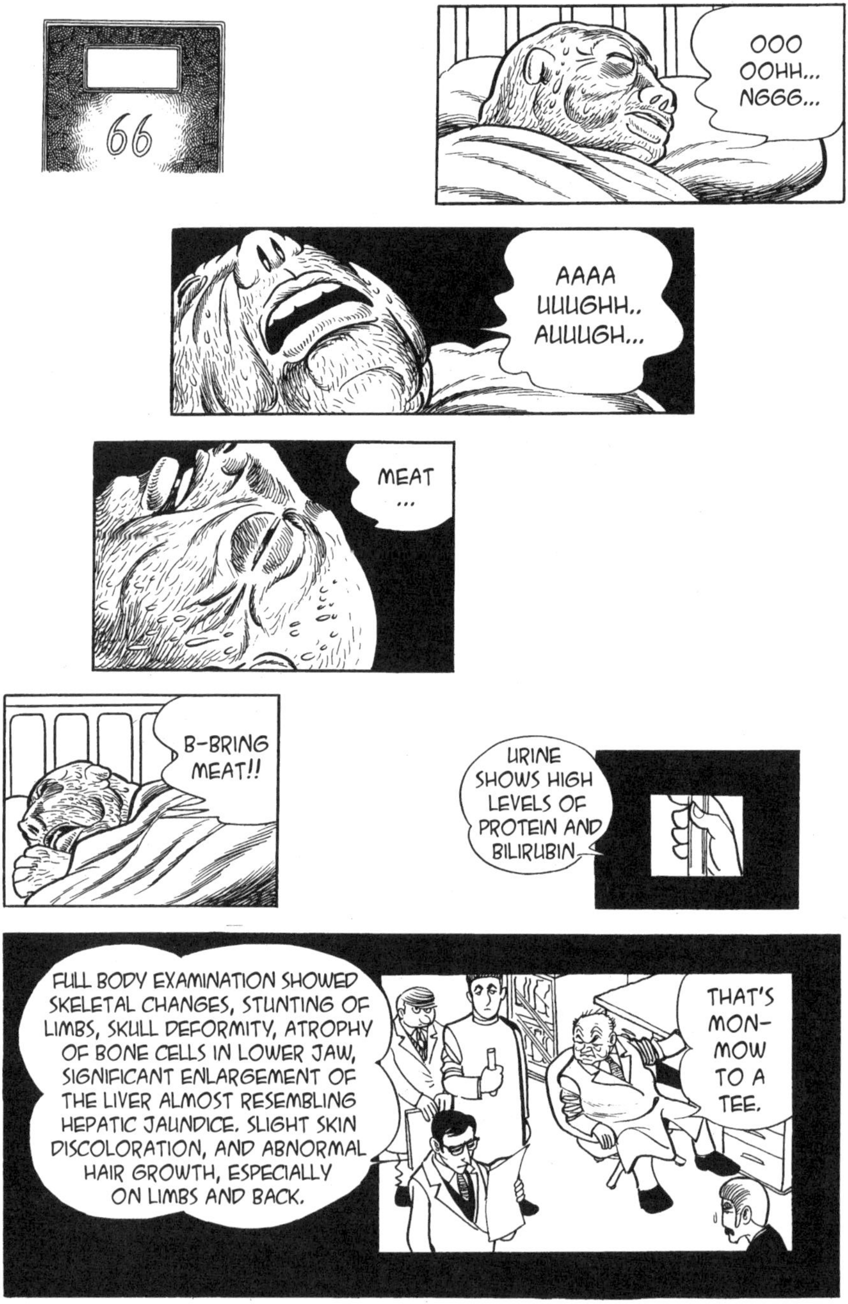
66
OOO OOHH... NGGG...
AAAA UUUGHH.. AUUUGH...
MEAT ...
B-BRING MEAT!!
URINE SHOWS HIGH LEVELS OF PROTEIN AND BILIRUBIN.
FULL BODY EXAMINATION SHOWED SKELETAL CHANGES, STUNTING OF LIMBS, SKULL DEFORMITY, ATROPHY OF BONE CELLS IN LOWER JAW, SIGNIFICANT ENLARGEMENT OF THE LIVER ALMOST RESEMBLING HEPATIC JAUNDICE. SLIGHT SKIN DISCOLORATION, AND ABNORMAL HAIR GROWTH, ESPECIALLY ON LIMBS AND BACK.
THAT'S MON-MOW TO A TEE.

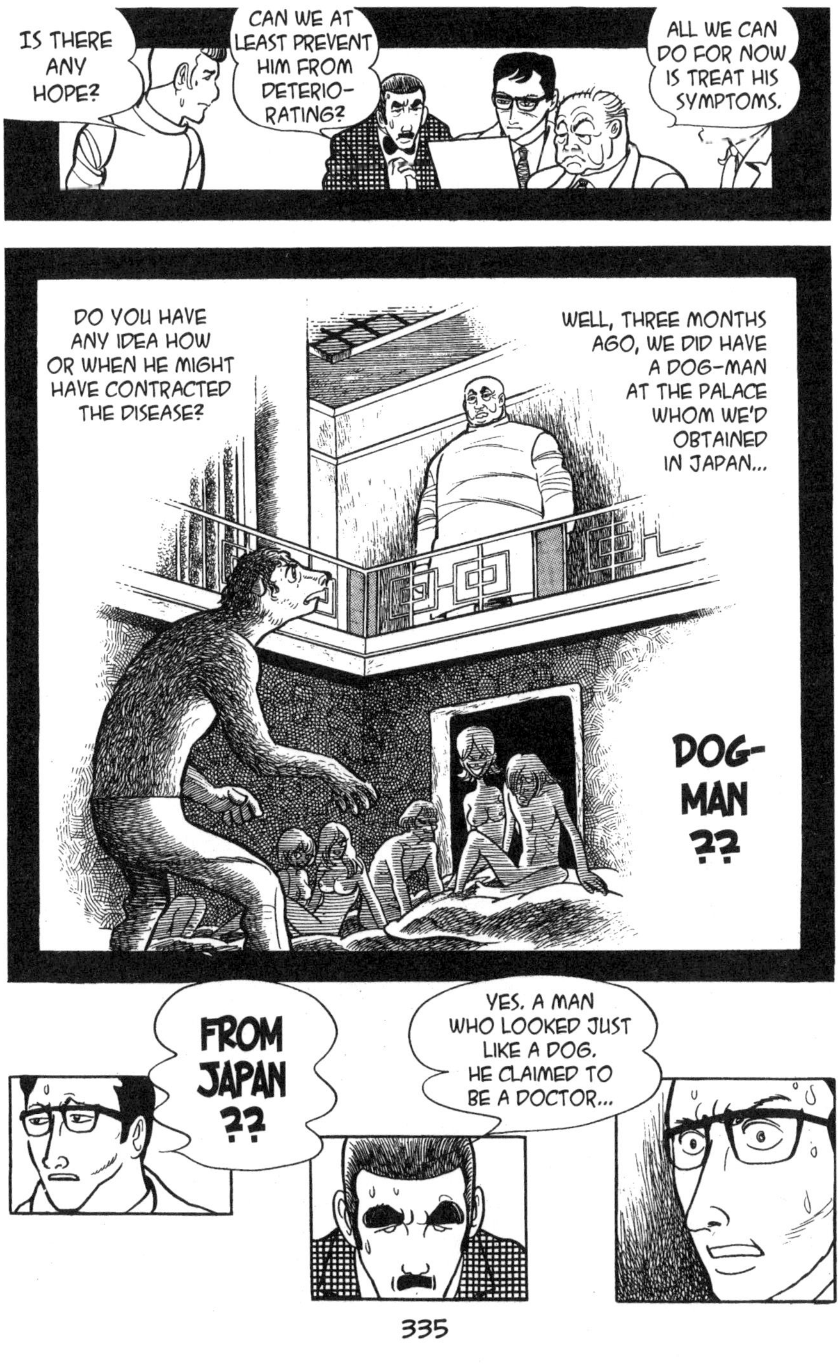
IS THERE ANY HOPE?
CAN WE AT LEAST PREVENT HIM FROM DETERIO-RATING?
ALL WE CAN DO FOR NOW IS TREAT HIS SYMPTOMS.
DO YOU HAVE ANY IDEA HOW OR WHEN HE MIGHT HAVE CONTRACTED THE DISEASE?
WELL, THREE MONTHS AGO, WE DID HAVE A DOG-MAN AT THE PALACE WHOM WE'D OBTAINED IN JAPAN...
DOG-MAN ??
FROM JAPAN ??
YES. A MAN WHO LOOKED JUST LIKE A DOG. HE CLAIMED TO BE A DOCTOR...

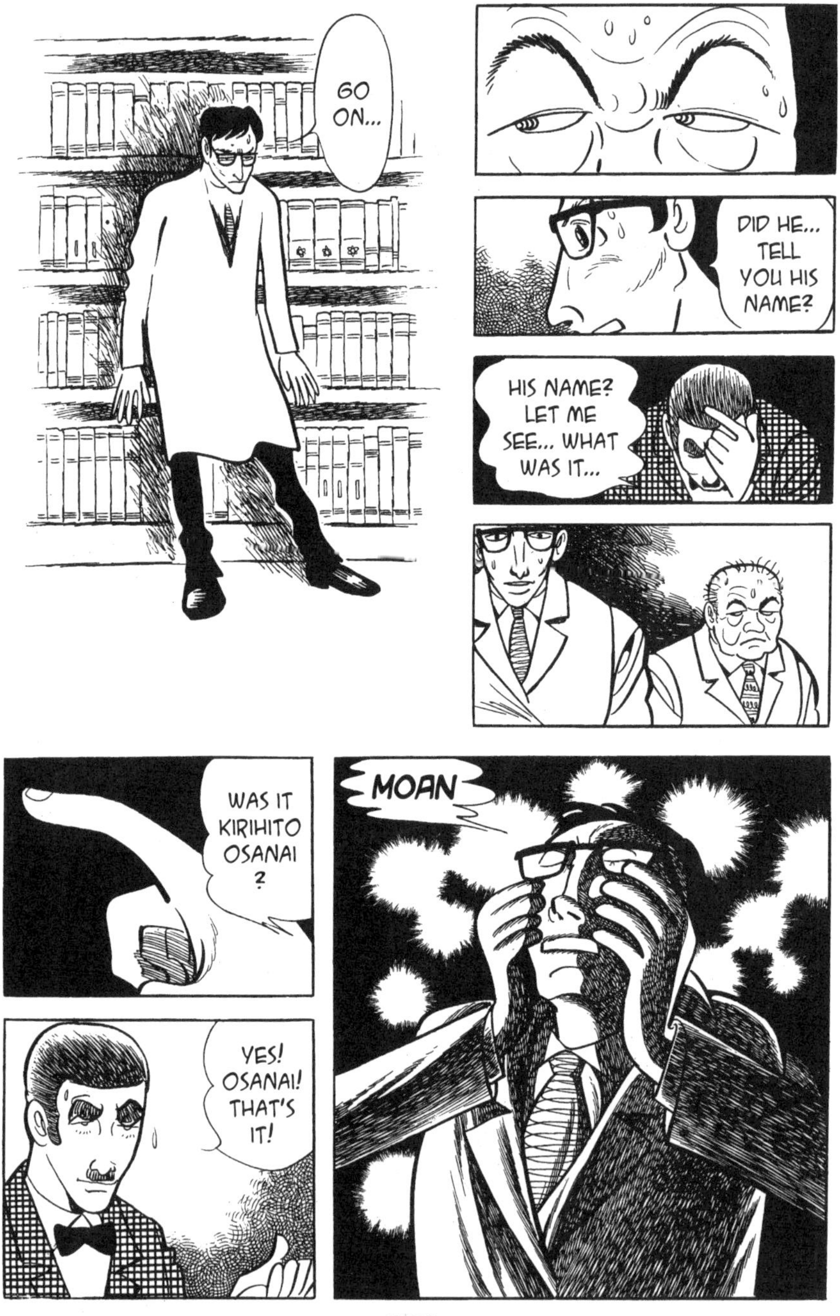
GO ON...
DID HE... TELL YOU HIS NAME?
HIS NAME? LET ME SEE... WHAT WAS IT...
WAS IT KIRIHITO OSANAI?
YES! OSANAI! THAT'S IT!
MOAN

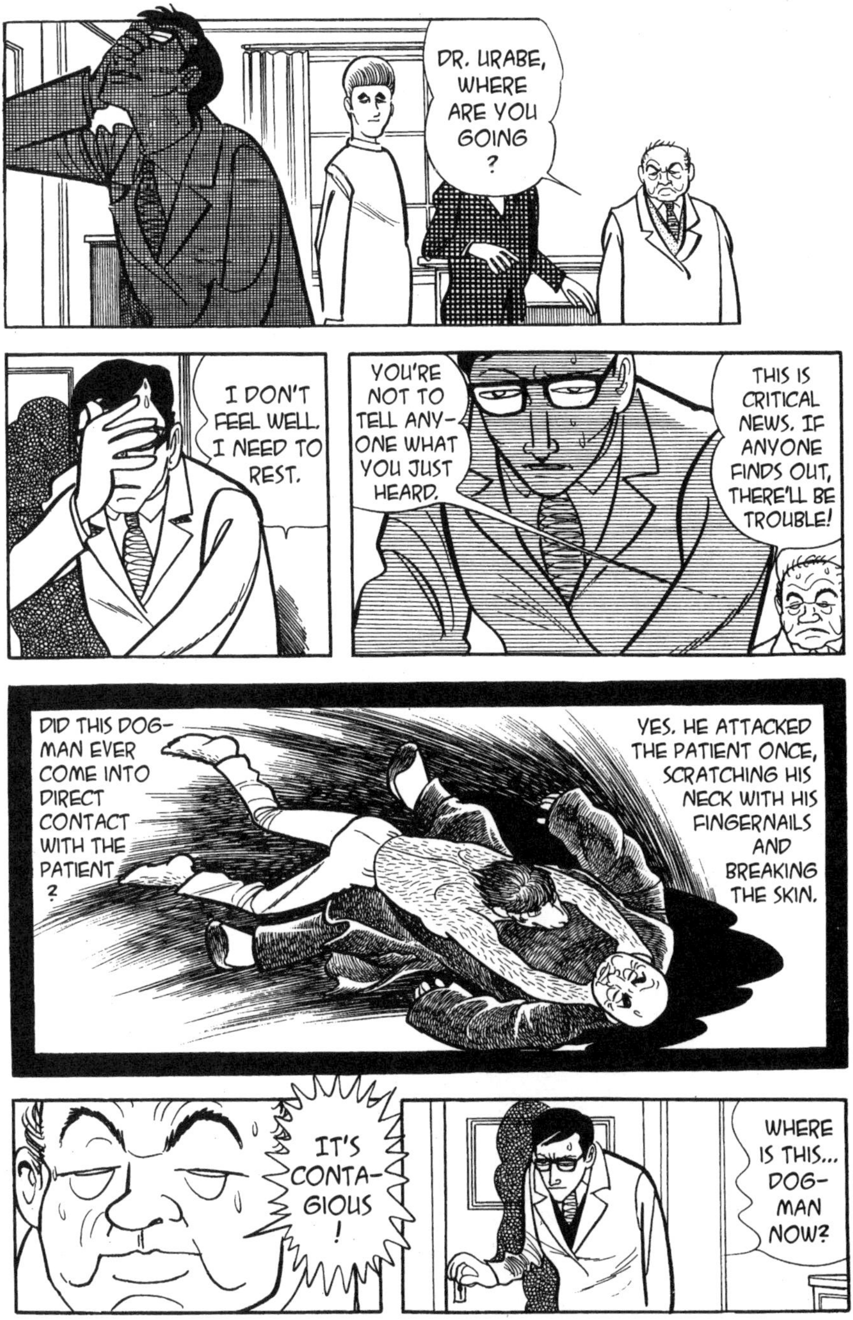
DR. URABE, WHERE ARE YOU GOING ?
I DON'T FEEL WELL. I NEED TO REST.
YOU'RE NOT TO TELL ANY-ONE WHAT YOU JUST HEARD.
THIS IS CRITICAL NEWS. IF ANYONE FINDS OUT, THERE'LL BE TROUBLE!
DID THIS DOG-MAN EVER COME INTO DIRECT CONTACT WITH THE PATIENT ?
YES. HE ATTACKED THE PATIENT ONCE, SCRATCHING HIS NECK WITH HIS FINGERNAILS AND BREAKING THE SKIN.
IT'S CONTA-GIOUS !
WHERE IS THIS... DOG-MAN NOW?

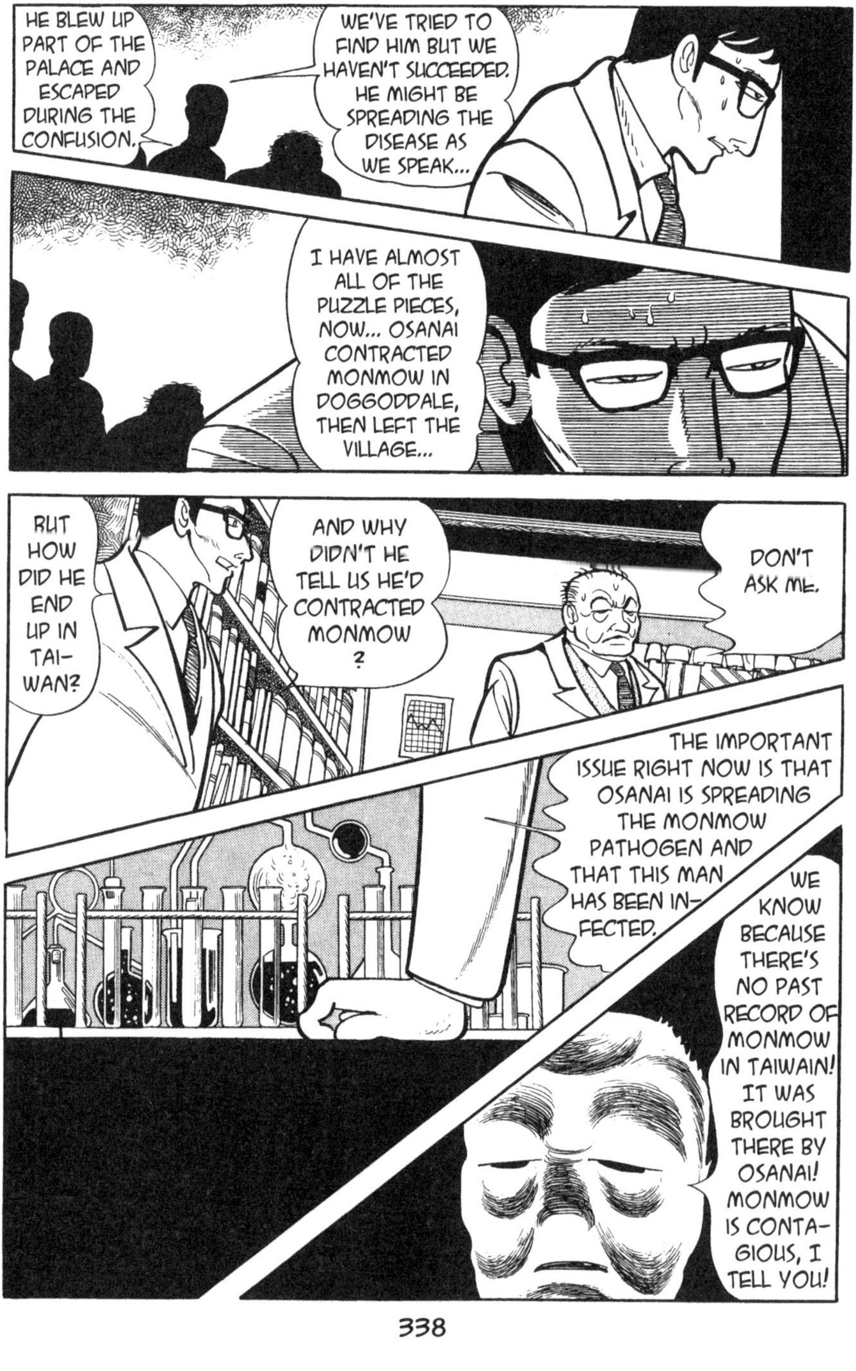

HE BLEW UP PART OF THE PALACE AND ESCAPED DURING THE CONFUSION.
WE'VE TRIED TO FIND HIM BUT WE HAVEN'T SUCCEEDED. HE MIGHT BE SPREADING THE DISEASE AS WE SPEAK...
I HAVE ALMOST ALL OF THE PUZZLE PIECES, NOW... OSANAI CONTRACTED MONMOW IN DOGGODDALE, THEN LEFT THE VILLAGE...
BUT HOW DID HE END UP IN TAI-WAN?
AND WHY DIDN'T HE TELL US HE'D CONTRACTED MONMOW ?
DON'T ASK ME.
THE IMPORTANT ISSUE RIGHT NOW IS THAT OSANAI IS SPREADING THE MONMOW PATHOGEN AND THAT THIS MAN HAS BEEN IN-FECTED.
WE KNOW BECAUSE THERE'S NO PAST RECORD OF MONMOW IN TAIWAIN! IT WAS BROUGHT THERE BY OSANAI! MONMOW IS CONTA-GIOUS, I TELL YOU!

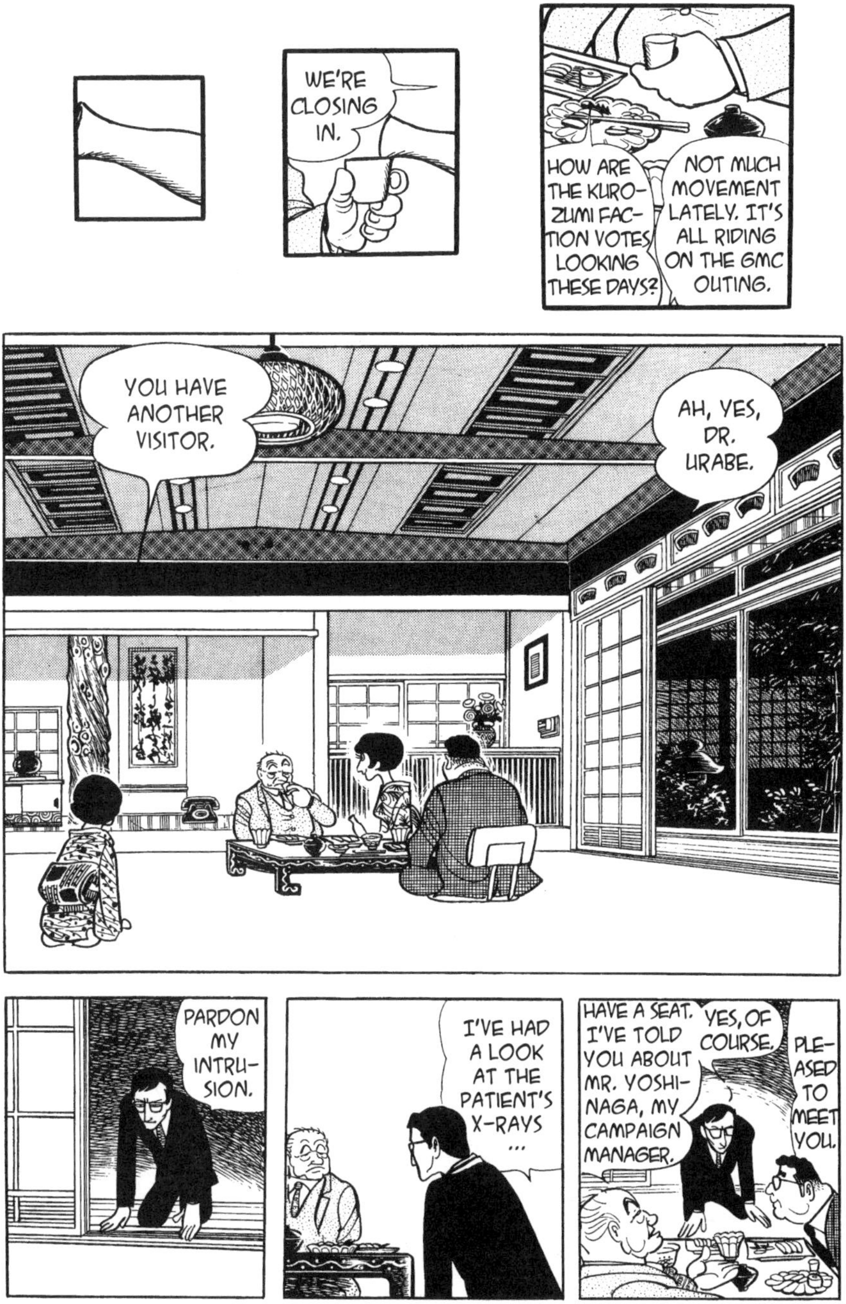
WE'RE CLOSING IN.
HOW ARE THE KURO-ZUMI FAC-TION VOTES LOOKING THESE DAYS?
NOT MUCH MOVEMENT LATELY. IT'S ALL RIDING ON THE GMC OUTING.
YOU HAVE ANOTHER VISITOR.
AH, YES, DR. URABE.
PARDON MY INTRU-SION.
I'VE HAD A LOOK AT THE PATIENT'S X-RAYS ...
HAVE A SEAT. I'VE TOLD YOU ABOUT MR. YOSHI-NAGA, MY CAMPAIGN MANAGER.
YES, OF COURSE.
PLE-ASED TO MEET YOU.

DR. URABE, I'M VERY CONCERNED TO HEAR THAT THE REPORT DR. TATSUGAURA IS PRESENTING AT THE CONFERENCE STILL ISN'T FINISHED...

I DON'T UNDERSTAND WHAT THE HOLD-UP IS. WE ONLY HAVE THREE MORE WEEKS. I DO HOPE THE REPORT WILL BE READY IN TIME.

...

I KNOW WHAT IT IS. YOU STILL HARBOR DOUBTS AS TO WHETHER OR NOT THE DISEASE IS CAUSED BY A VIRUS...

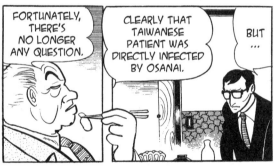

FORTUNATELY, THERE'S NO LONGER ANY QUESTION.

CLEARLY THAT TAIWANESE PATIENT WAS DIRECTLY INFECTED BY OSANAI.

BUT ...

YOU'RE CONCERNED BECAUSE WE STILL HAVEN'T ISOLATED THE PATHO-GEN?

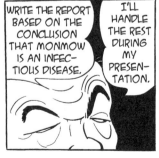

WRITE THE REPORT BASED ON THE CONCLUSION THAT MONMOW IS AN INFEC-TIOUS DISEASE.

I'LL HANDLE THE REST DURING MY PRESEN-TATION.

340

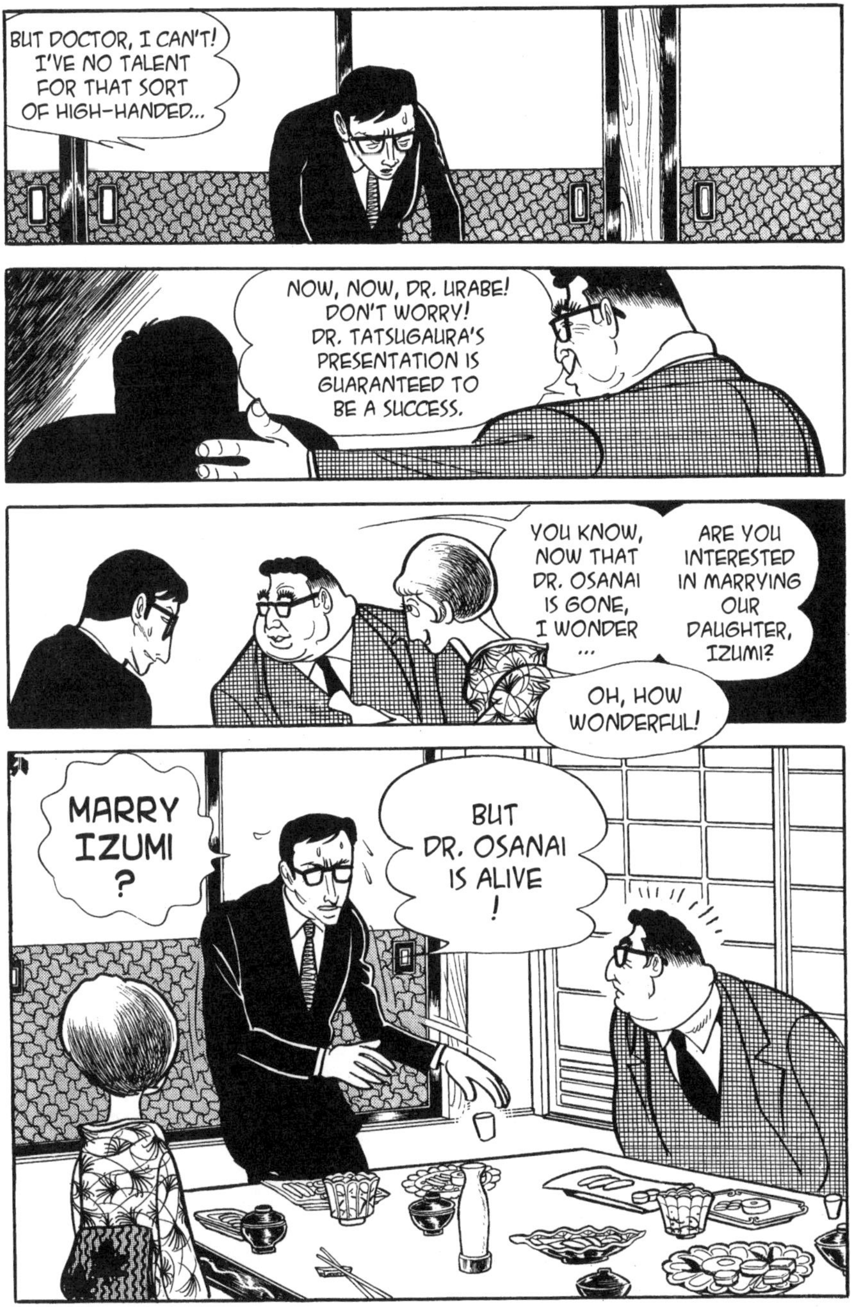

BUT DOCTOR, I CAN'T! I'VE NO TALENT FOR THAT SORT OF HIGH-HANDED...
NOW, NOW, DR. URABE! DON'T WORRY! DR. TATSUGAURA'S PRESENTATION IS GUARANTEED TO BE A SUCCESS.
YOU KNOW, NOW THAT DR. OSANAI IS GONE, I WONDER ...
ARE YOU INTERESTED IN MARRYING OUR DAUGHTER, IZUMI?
OH, HOW WONDERFUL!
MARRY IZUMI ?
BUT DR. OSANAI IS ALIVE !

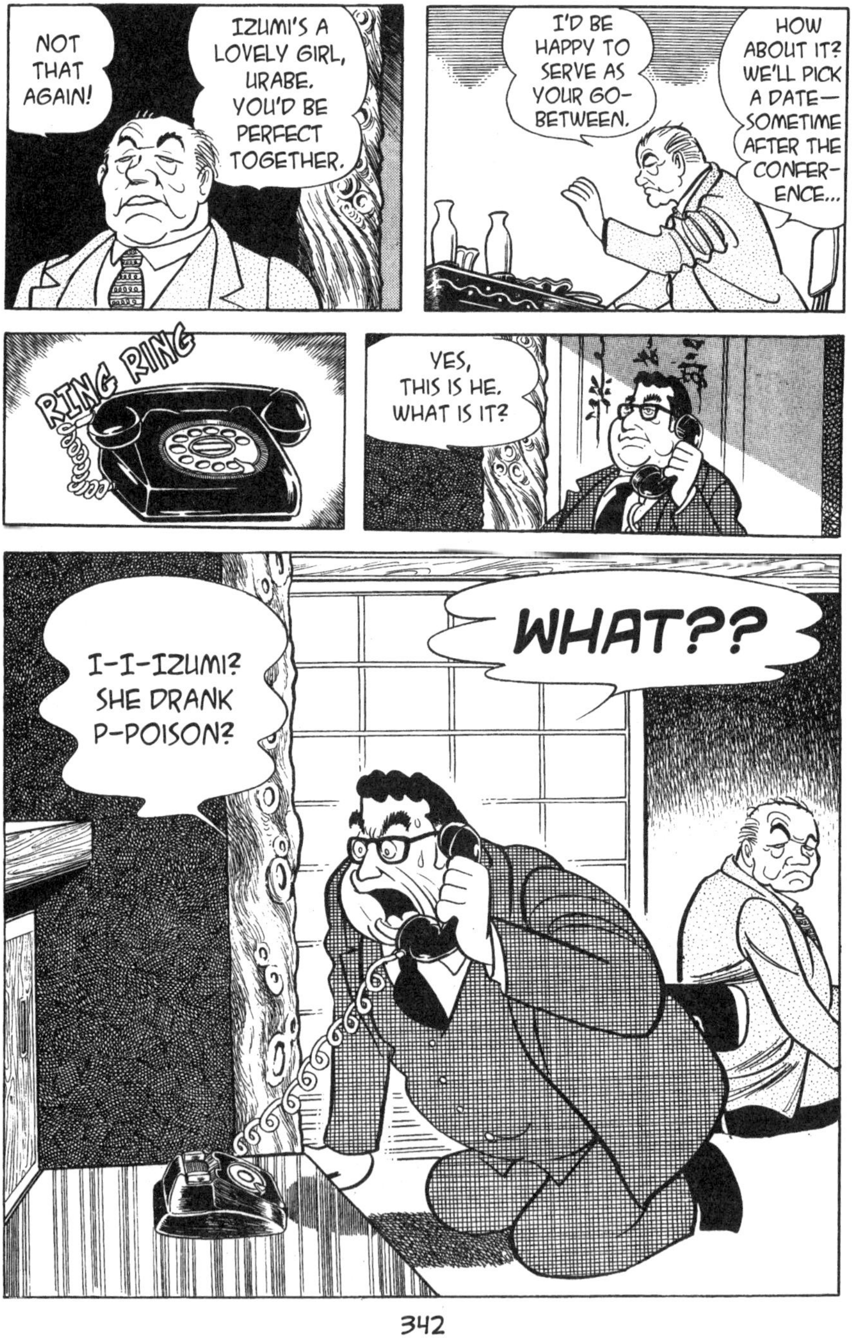
IZUMI'S A LOVELY GIRL, URABE. YOU'D BE PERFECT TOGETHER.
NOT THAT AGAIN!
I'D BE HAPPY TO SERVE AS YOUR GO-BETWEEN.
HOW ABOUT IT? WE'LL PICK A DATE— SOMETIME AFTER THE CONFERENCE...
RING RING
YES, THIS IS HE. WHAT IS IT?
I-I-IZUMI? SHE DRANK P-POISON?
WHAT??

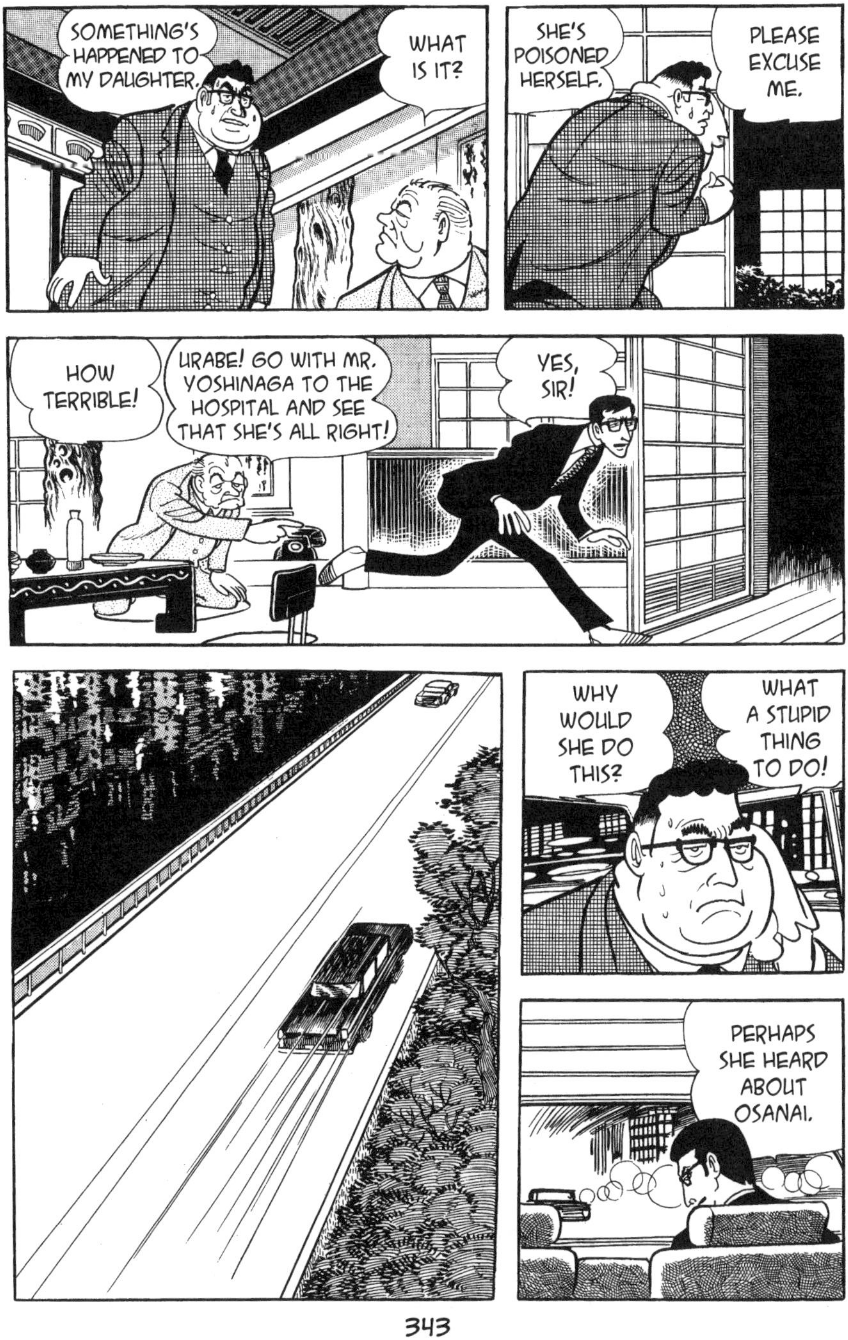

SOMETHING'S HAPPENED TO MY DAUGHTER.
WHAT IS IT?
SHE'S POISONED HERSELF.
PLEASE EXCUSE ME.
HOW TERRIBLE!
URABE! GO WITH MR. YOSHINAGA TO THE HOSPITAL AND SEE THAT SHE'S ALL RIGHT!
YES, SIR!
WHY WOULD SHE DO THIS?
WHAT A STUPID THING TO DO!
PERHAPS SHE HEARD ABOUT OSANAI.

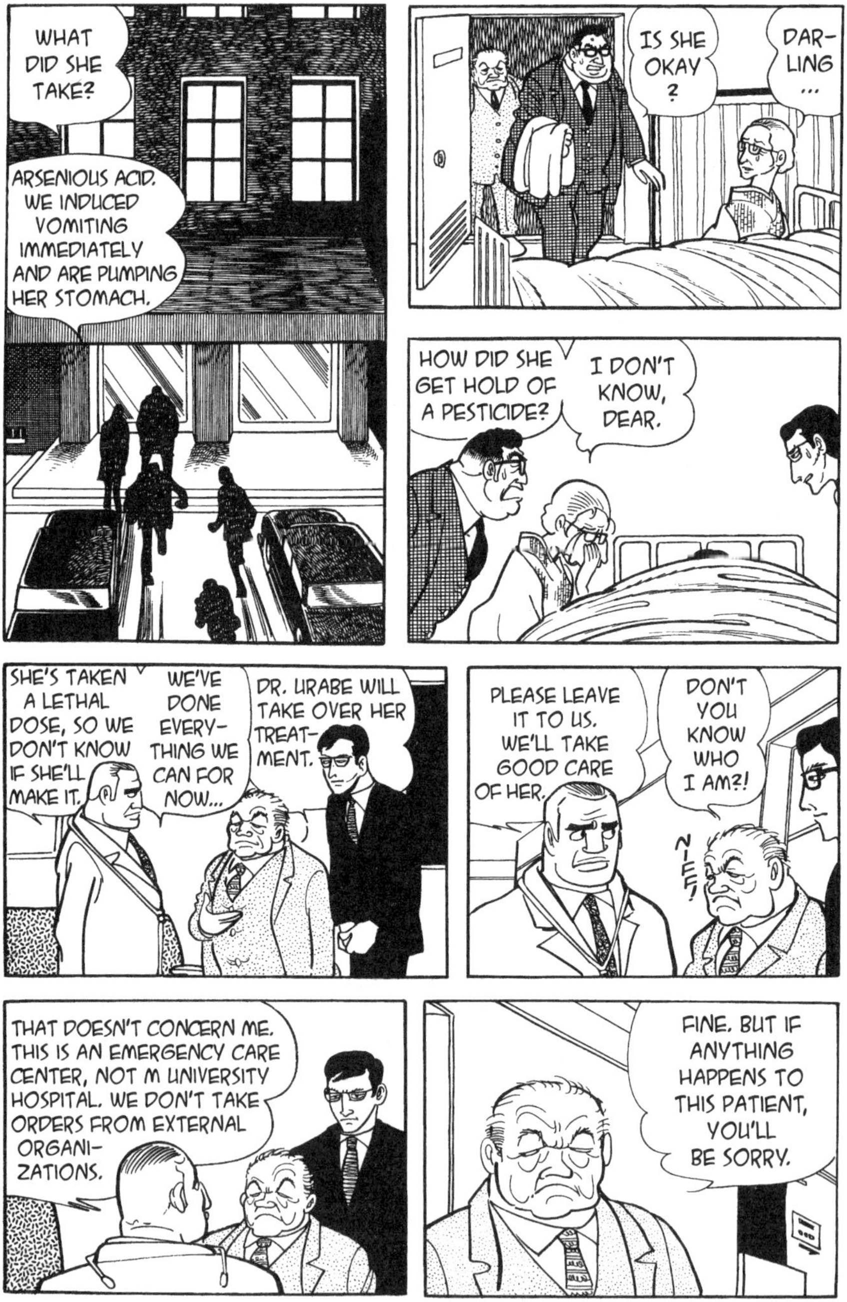
WHAT DID SHE TAKE?
ARSENIOUS ACID. WE INDUCED VOMITING IMMEDIATELY AND ARE PUMPING HER STOMACH.
IS SHE OKAY?
DARLING...
HOW DID SHE GET HOLD OF A PESTICIDE?
I DON'T KNOW, DEAR.
SHE'S TAKEN A LETHAL DOSE, SO WE DON'T KNOW IF SHE'LL MAKE IT.
WE'VE DONE EVERYTHING WE CAN FOR NOW...
DR. URABE WILL TAKE OVER HER TREATMENT.
PLEASE LEAVE IT TO US. WE'LL TAKE GOOD CARE OF HER.
DON'T YOU KNOW WHO I AM?!
NIFF!
THAT DOESN'T CONCERN ME. THIS IS AN EMERGENCY CARE CENTER, NOT M UNIVERSITY HOSPITAL. WE DON'T TAKE ORDERS FROM EXTERNAL ORGANIZATIONS.
FINE. BUT IF ANYTHING HAPPENS TO THIS PATIENT, YOU'LL BE SORRY.

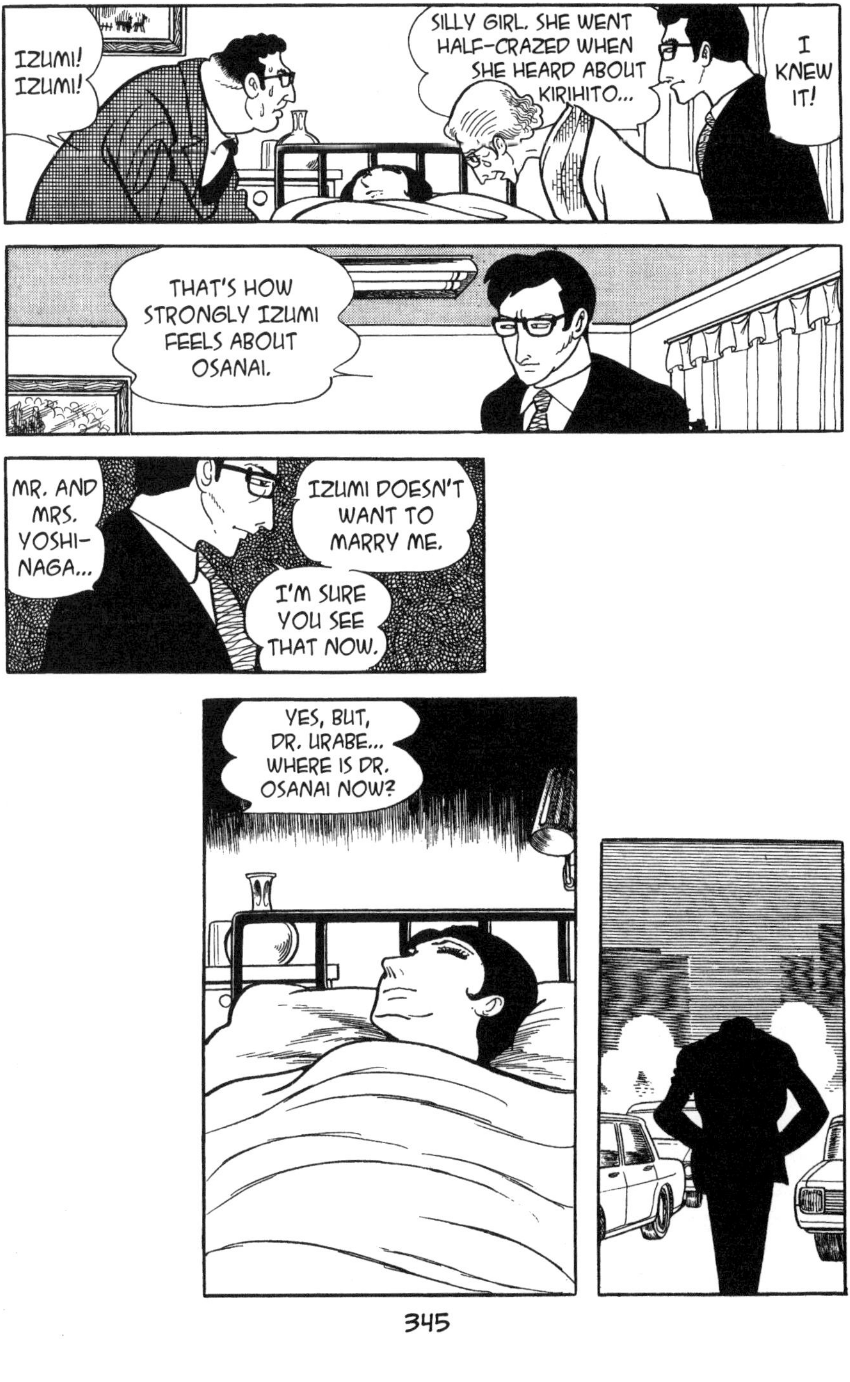
IZUMI! IZUMI!
SILLY GIRL. SHE WENT HALF-CRAZED WHEN SHE HEARD ABOUT KIRIHITO...
I KNEW IT!
THAT'S HOW STRONGLY IZUMI FEELS ABOUT OSANAI.
MR. AND MRS. YOSHI-NAGA...
IZUMI DOESN'T WANT TO MARRY ME.
I'M SURE YOU SEE THAT NOW.
YES, BUT, DR. URABE... WHERE IS DR. OSANAI NOW?

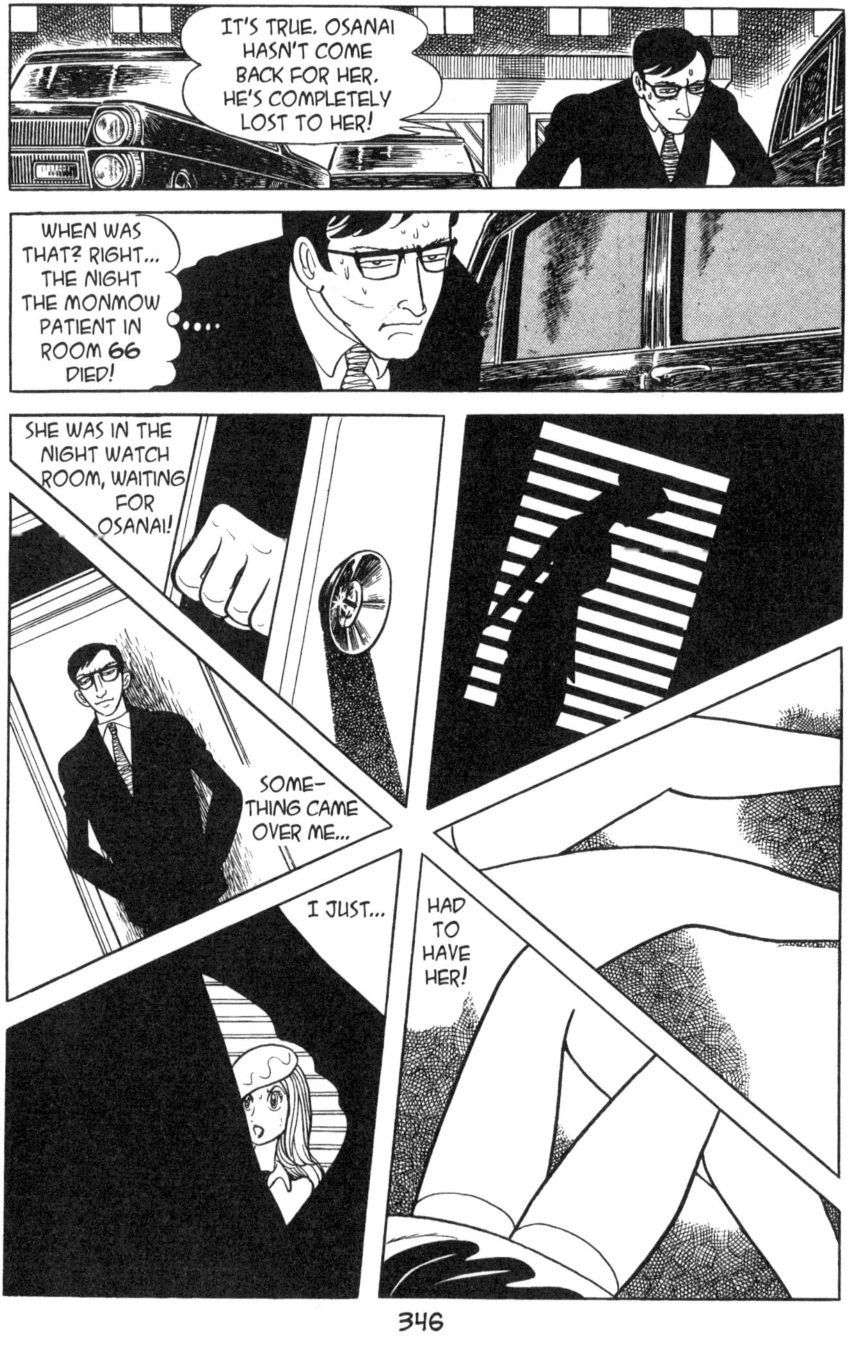
IT'S TRUE. OSANAI HASN'T COME BACK FOR HER. HE'S COMPLETELY LOST TO HER!
WHEN WAS THAT? RIGHT... THE NIGHT THE MONMOW PATIENT IN ROOM 66 DIED!
SHE WAS IN THE NIGHT WATCH ROOM, WAITING FOR OSANAI!
SOME-THING CAME OVER ME...
I JUST...
HAD TO HAVE HER!

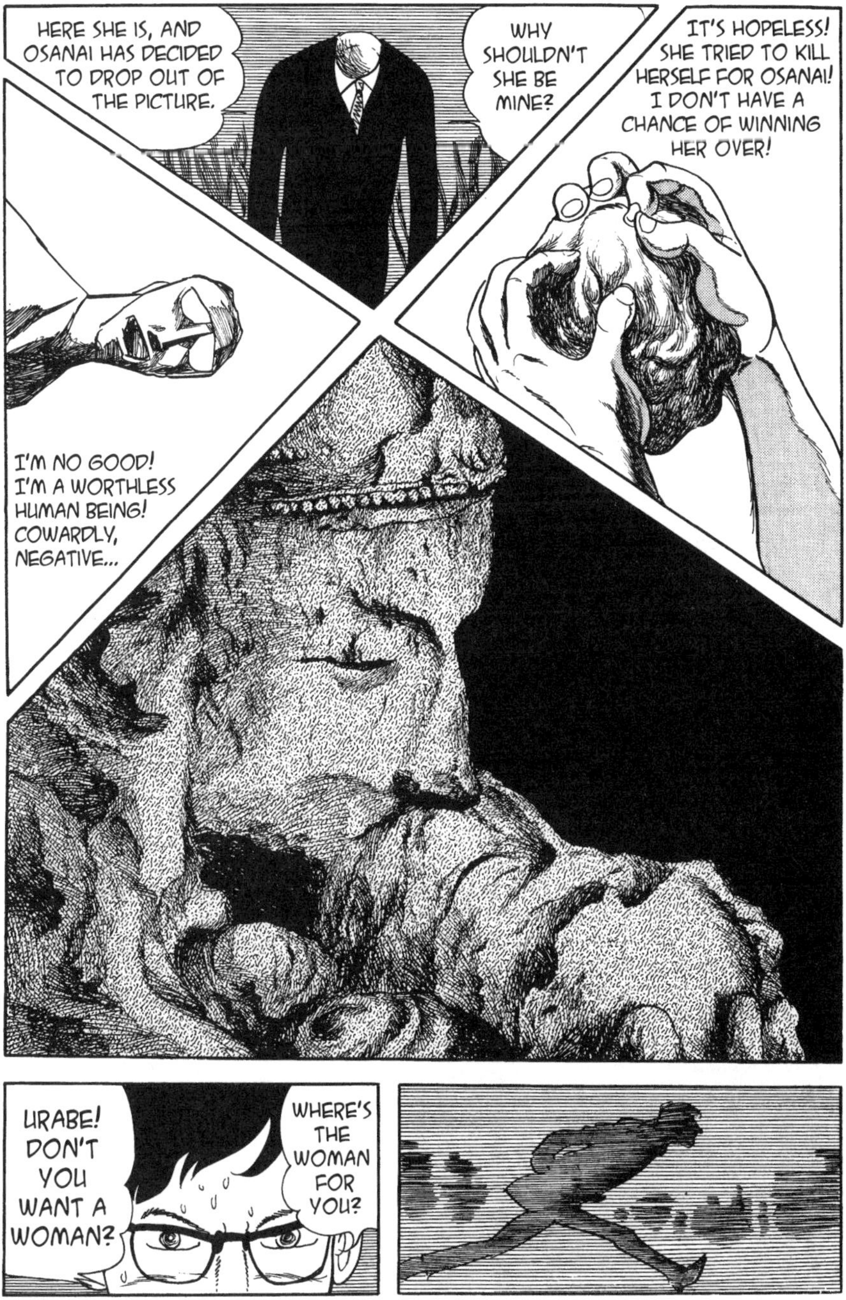
HERE SHE IS, AND OSANAI HAS DECIDED TO DROP OUT OF THE PICTURE.
WHY SHOULDN'T SHE BE MINE?
IT'S HOPELESS! SHE TRIED TO KILL HERSELF FOR OSANAI! I DON'T HAVE A CHANCE OF WINNING HER OVER!
I'M NO GOOD! I'M A WORTHLESS HUMAN BEING! COWARDLY, NEGATIVE...
URABE! DON'T YOU WANT A WOMAN?
WHERE'S THE WOMAN FOR YOU?

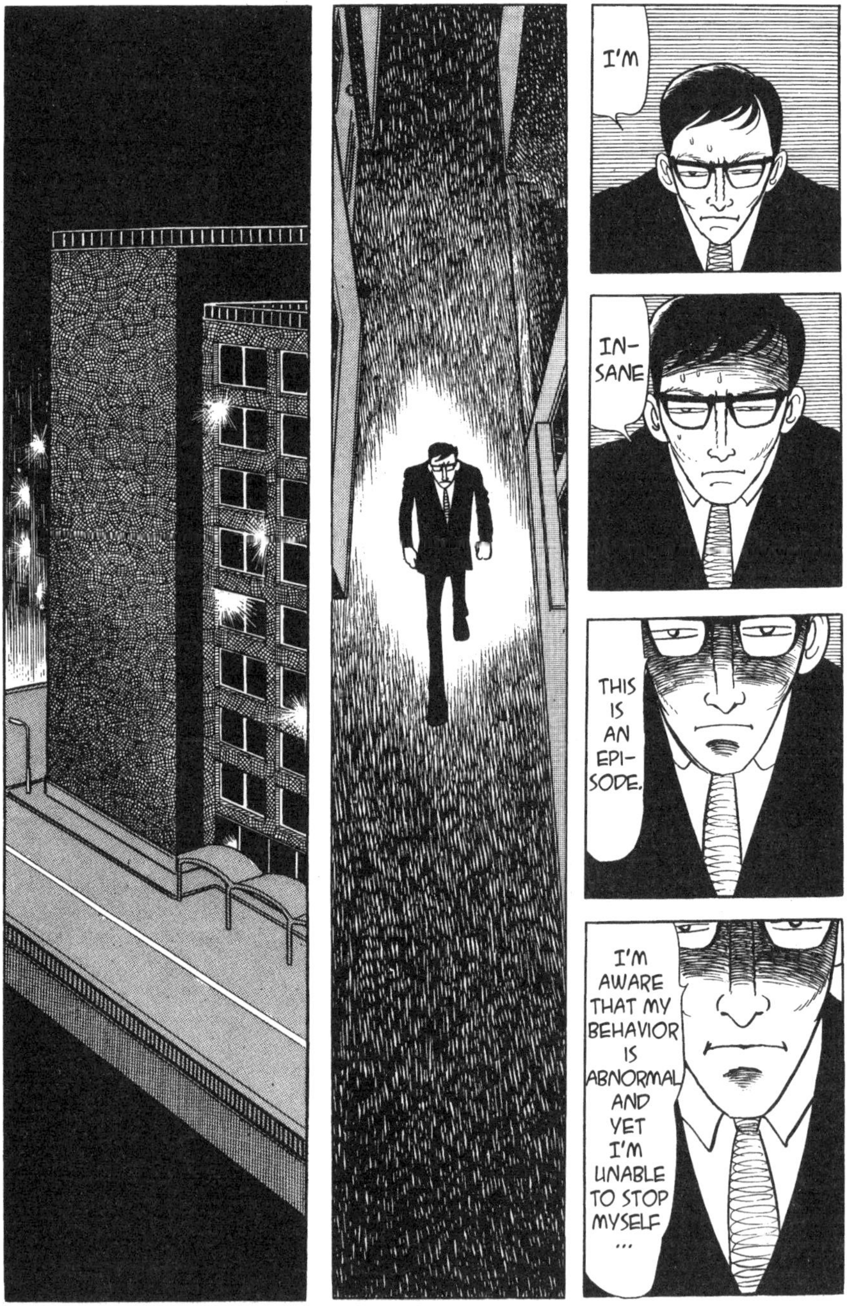
I'M
IN-SANE
THIS IS AN EPI-SODE.
I'M AWARE THAT MY BEHAVIOR IS ABNORMAL AND YET I'M UNABLE TO STOP MYSELF ...

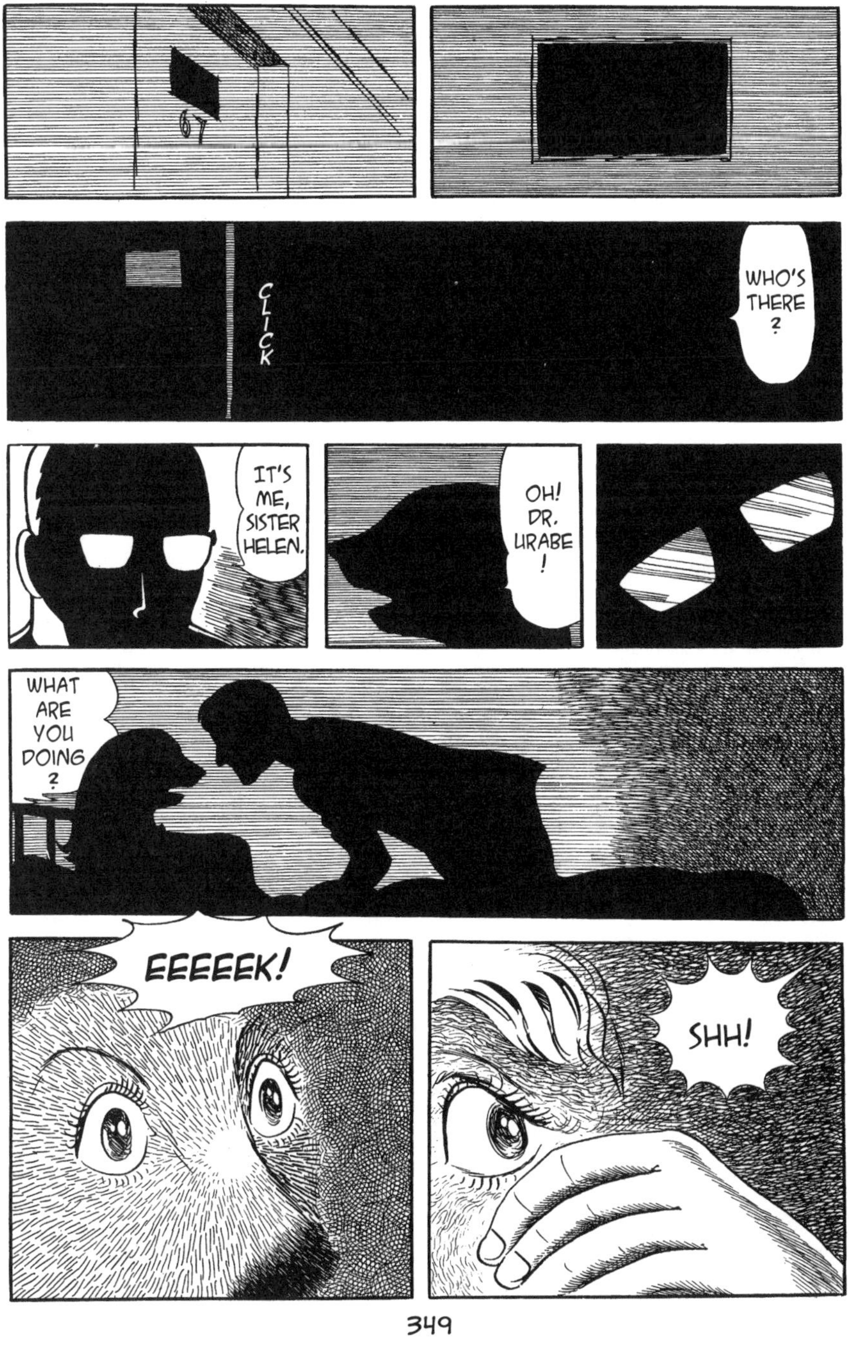
67
CLICK
WHO'S THERE?
IT'S ME, SISTER HELEN.
OH! DR. URABE!
WHAT ARE YOU DOING?
EEEEEK!
SHH!

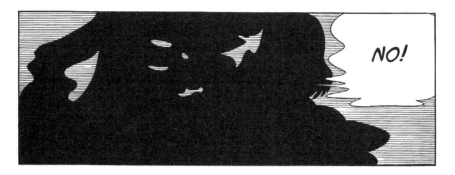

NO!

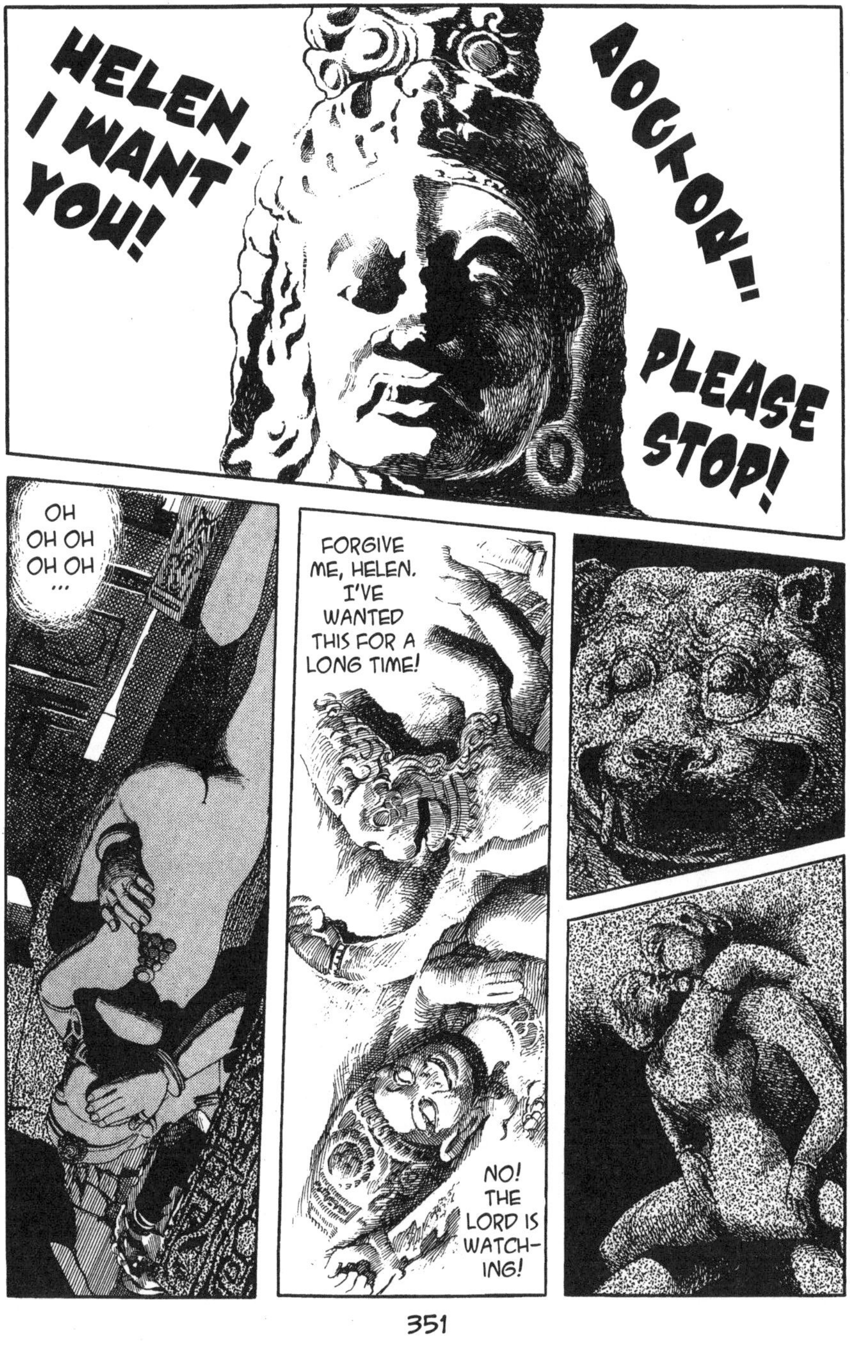
HELEN, I WANT YOU!
DOCTOR!
PLEASE STOP!
OH OH OH OH OH ...
FORGIVE ME, HELEN. I'VE WANTED THIS FOR A LONG TIME!
NO! THE LORD IS WATCHING!

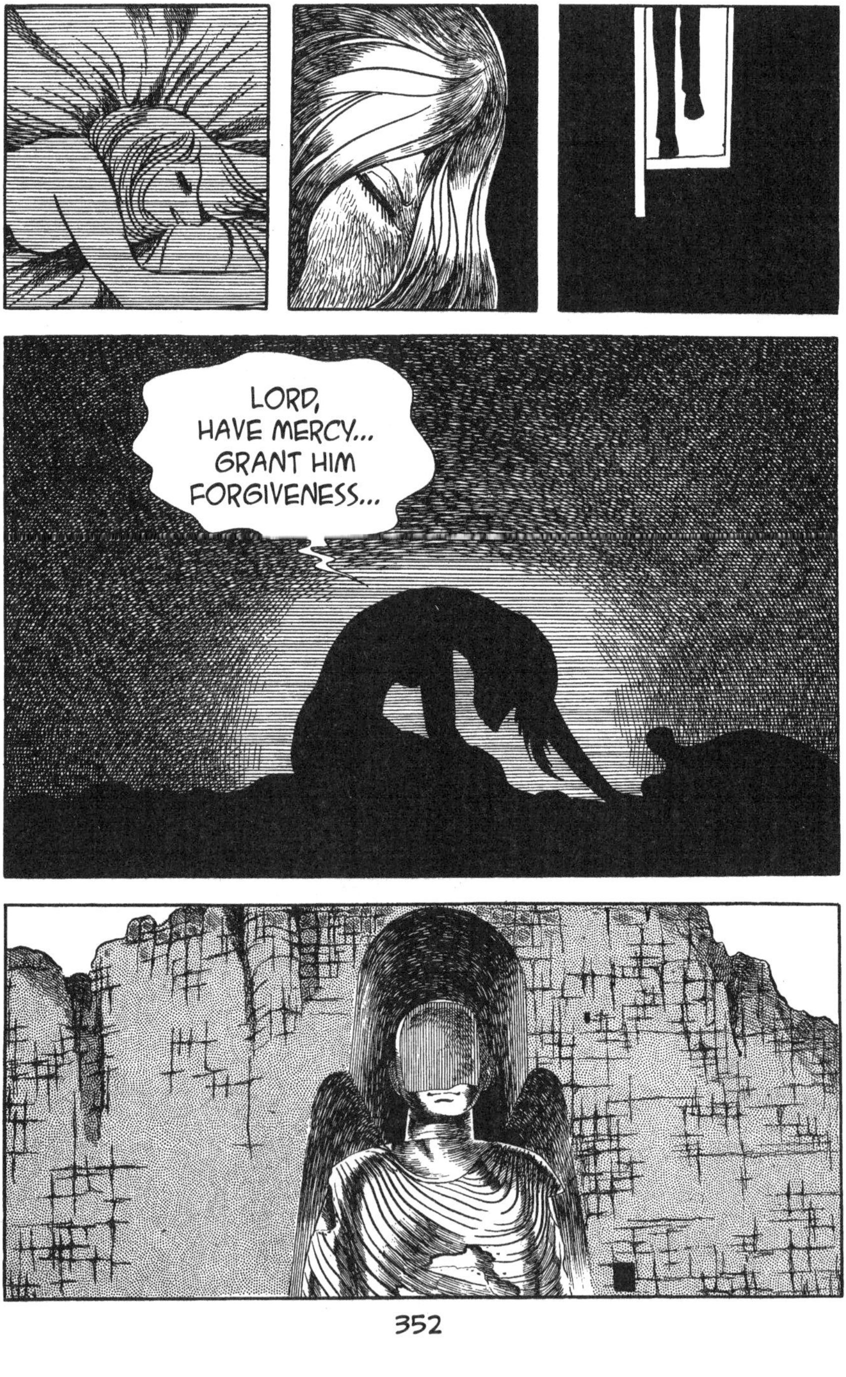
LORD, HAVE MERCY... GRANT HIM FORGIVENESS...

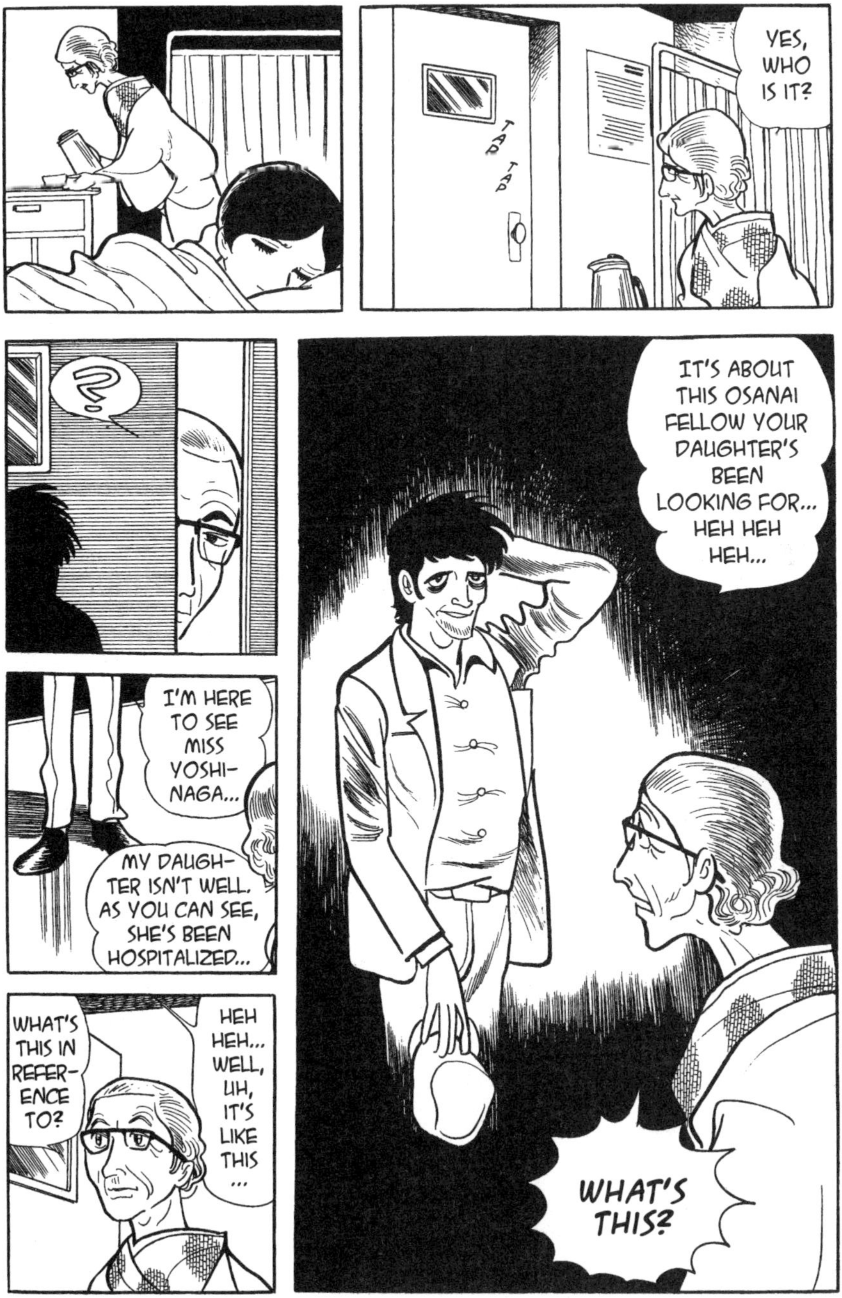
TAP TAP
YES, WHO IS IT?
?
I'M HERE TO SEE MISS YOSHI-NAGA...
MY DAUGH-TER ISN'T WELL. AS YOU CAN SEE, SHE'S BEEN HOSPITALIZED...
WHAT'S THIS IN REFER-ENCE TO?
HEH HEH... WELL, UH, IT'S LIKE THIS ...
IT'S ABOUT THIS OSANAI FELLOW YOUR DAUGHTER'S BEEN LOOKING FOR... HEH HEH HEH...
WHAT'S THIS?

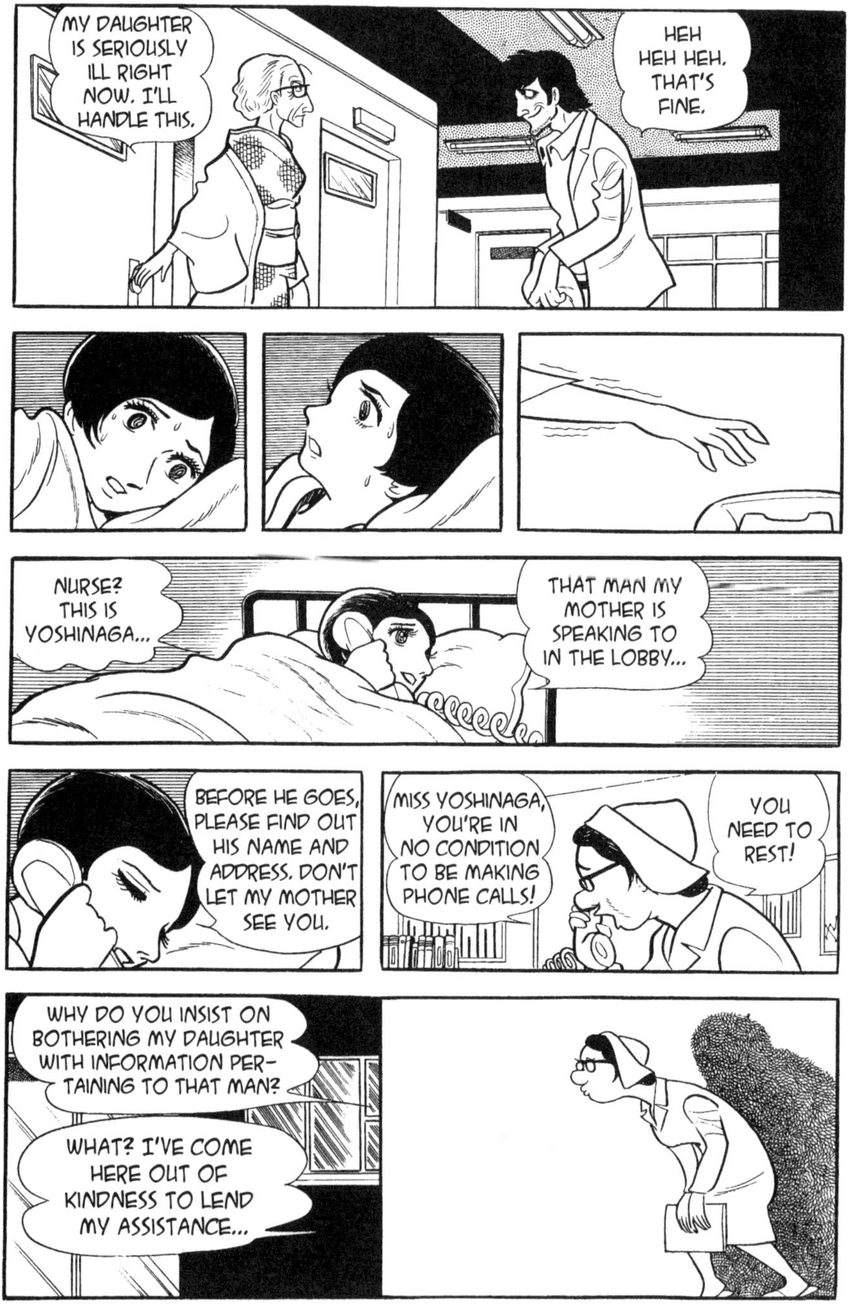

MY DAUGHTER IS SERIOUSLY ILL RIGHT NOW. I'LL HANDLE THIS.
HEH HEH HEH. THAT'S FINE.
NURSE? THIS IS YOSHINAGA...
THAT MAN MY MOTHER IS SPEAKING TO IN THE LOBBY...
BEFORE HE GOES, PLEASE FIND OUT HIS NAME AND ADDRESS. DON'T LET MY MOTHER SEE YOU.
MISS YOSHINAGA, YOU'RE IN NO CONDITION TO BE MAKING PHONE CALLS!
YOU NEED TO REST!
WHY DO YOU INSIST ON BOTHERING MY DAUGHTER WITH INFORMATION PERTAINING TO THAT MAN?
WHAT? I'VE COME HERE OUT OF KINDNESS TO LEND MY ASSISTANCE...

HOW VERY THOUGHTFUL. BUT I'M AFRAID THAT WON'T BE NECESSARY.

MY DAUGHTER NO LONGER HAS ANYTHING TO DO WITH THAT MAN.

COME ON, NOW, BE REASONABLE!

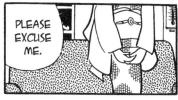

PLEASE EXCUSE ME.

...

WHAT NOW?

THIS IS SOMEWHAT AWKWARD...

I'VE TRAVELED HERE ALL THE WAY FROM SHIKOKU. I'D LIKE SOME COMPENSATION FOR MY TROUBLES.

SHALL I CALL THE POLICE?

OLD BAG!

355

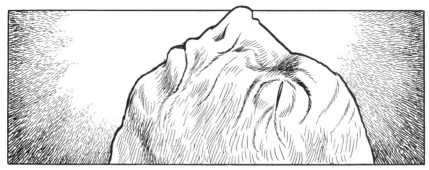

THE DISEASE HAS STOPPED PROGRESSING. PERHAPS THOSE PITUITARY HORMONES WORKED.

BUT THE BONE ATROPHY IS ALREADY VERY ADVANCED...

THERE'S ALSO A RISK THAT THE SKULL DEFORMATION IS PRESSURING THE BRAIN. THE PATIENT COULD DIE OF SHOCK.

IN ANY CASE, HE'S BEYOND HOPE.

IT'S MUCH TOO LATE.

TOO LATE??

DUE TO NEGLIGENT TREATMENT. THIS ISN'T OUR FAULT. IF ANYTHING, THE FAULT LIES WITH TAIPEI UNIVERSITY HOSPITAL.

THAT'S UNFAIR! IT WAS ALREADY TOO LATE WHEN THE PATIENT CAME UNDER OUR CARE!

SO YOU DECIDED TO PAWN HIM OFF ON US?

...

KEEP TREATING HIS SYMPTOMS.

THE BOSS IS IN A REALLY FOUL MOOD TODAY.

I WONDER IF SOMETHING HAPPENED LAST NIGHT.

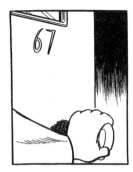

HOW IS SHE?

...

SHE HASN'T EATEN OR SPOKEN A WORD ALL DAY.

IS THAT SO?

SHE'S COMPLETELY DISTRAIT.

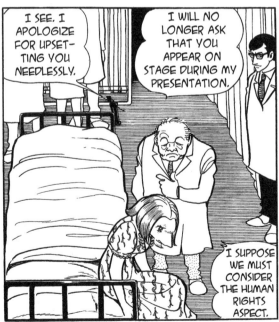

I SEE. I APOLOGIZE FOR UPSETTING YOU NEEDLESSLY.

I WILL NO LONGER ASK THAT YOU APPEAR ON STAGE DURING MY PRESENTATION.

I SUPPOSE WE MUST CONSIDER THE HUMAN RIGHTS ASPECT.

...

LET'S MOVE ON, DR. URABE.

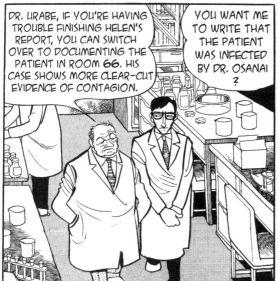

DR. URABE, IF YOU'RE HAVING TROUBLE FINISHING HELEN'S REPORT, YOU CAN SWITCH OVER TO DOCUMENTING THE PATIENT IN ROOM 66. HIS CASE SHOWS MORE CLEAR-CUT EVIDENCE OF CONTAGION.

YOU WANT ME TO WRITE THAT THE PATIENT WAS INFECTED BY DR. OSANAI?

THAT'S RIGHT.

AND DR. OSANAI'S NAME WILL APPEAR IN THE REPORT?

OF COURSE, WE HAVE TO DEMON-STRATE THE ROUTE OF INFECTION.

BUT DR. OSANAI'S CAREER WILL BE DESTROYED! THE MEDIA WILL BE ALL OVER IT...

WE CAN'T DO THAT TO HIM!

HIS CAREER IS OVER, ANYWAY.

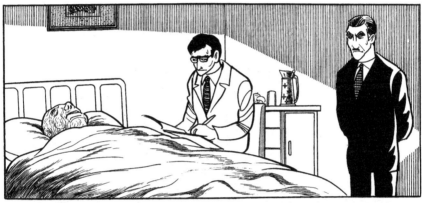

I SEE THAT DR. TATSUGAURA IS DETERMINED TO PUBLICIZE THE CASE.

WE CAN'T HAVE THAT.

THE ONLY WAY TO PREVENT IT

WOULD BE TO PROVE THAT THE DISEASE ISN'T INFECTIOUS.

THE THEORY THAT OSANAI INFECTED THE PATIENT WHEN HE SCRATCHED HIS NECK

IS STILL JUST A THEORY, AFTER ALL...

359

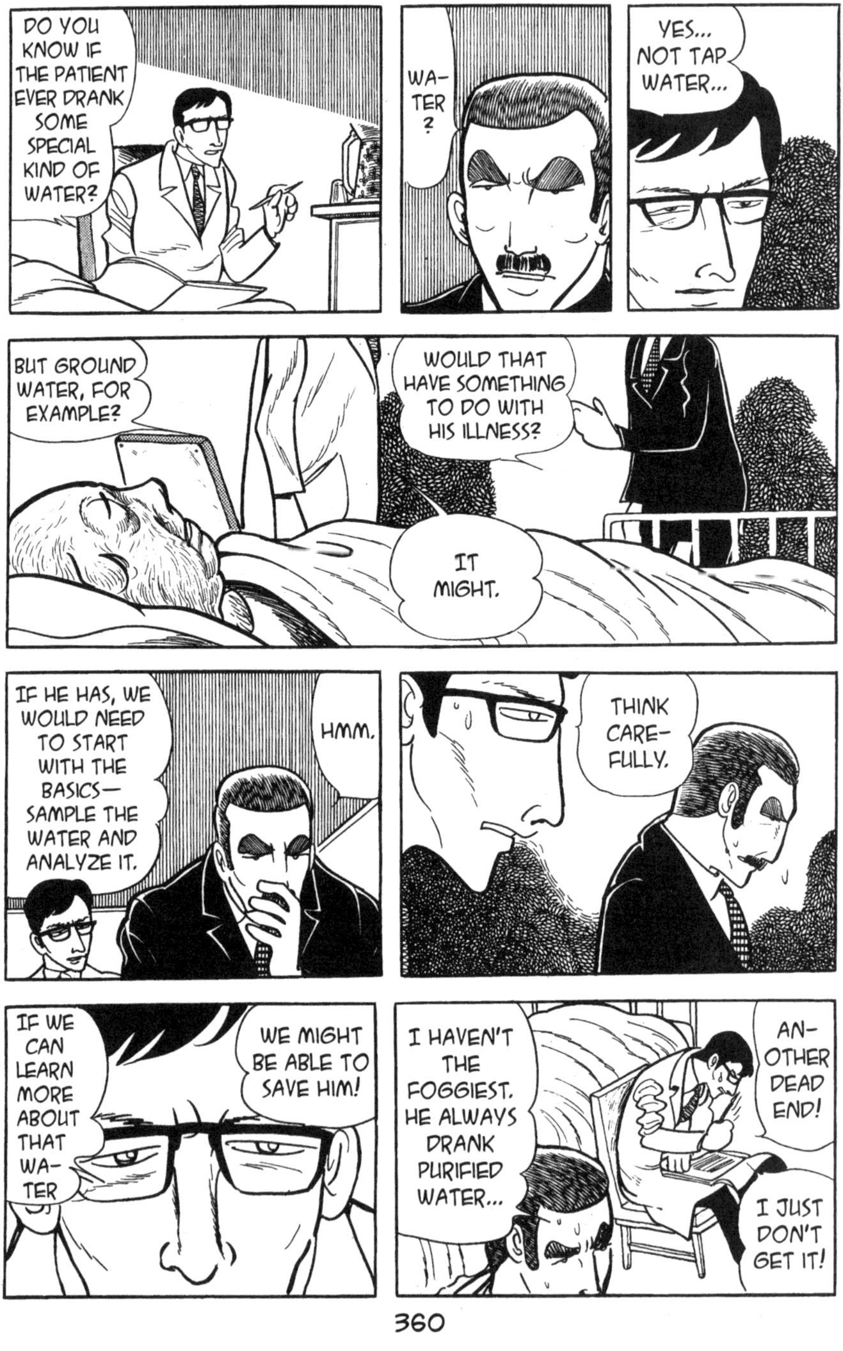
DO YOU KNOW IF THE PATIENT EVER DRANK SOME SPECIAL KIND OF WATER?
WA-TER?
YES... NOT TAP WATER...
BUT GROUND WATER, FOR EXAMPLE?
WOULD THAT HAVE SOMETHING TO DO WITH HIS ILLNESS?
IT MIGHT.
IF HE HAS, WE WOULD NEED TO START WITH THE BASICS—SAMPLE THE WATER AND ANALYZE IT.
HMM.
THINK CARE-FULLY.
IF WE CAN LEARN MORE ABOUT THAT WA-TER
WE MIGHT BE ABLE TO SAVE HIM!
I HAVEN'T THE FOGGIEST. HE ALWAYS DRANK PURIFIED WATER...
AN-OTHER DEAD END!
I JUST DON'T GET IT!

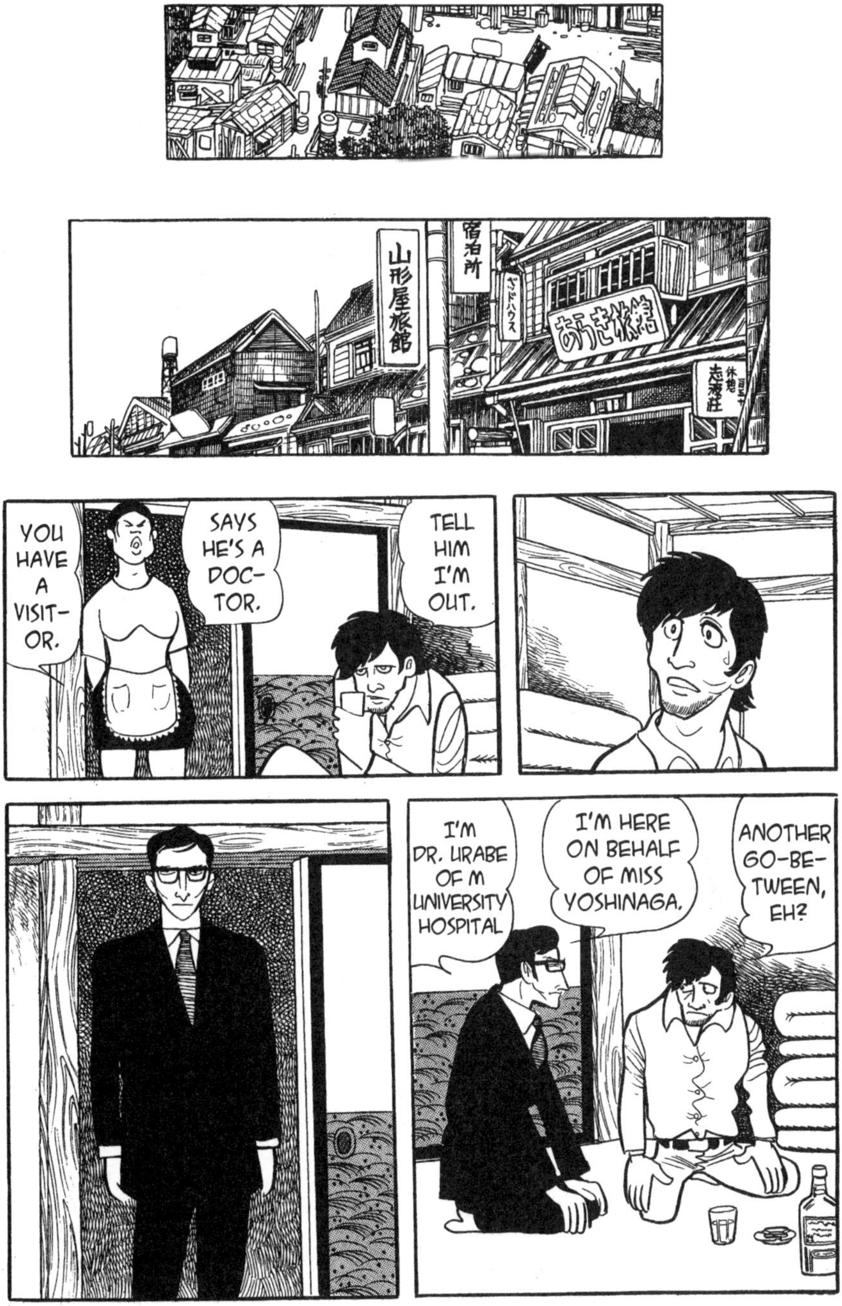
山形屋旅館
宿泊所
YOU HAVE A VISITOR.
SAYS HE'S A DOCTOR.
TELL HIM I'M OUT.
I'M DR. URABE OF M UNIVERSITY HOSPITAL
I'M HERE ON BEHALF OF MISS YOSHINAGA.
ANOTHER GO-BETWEEN, EH?

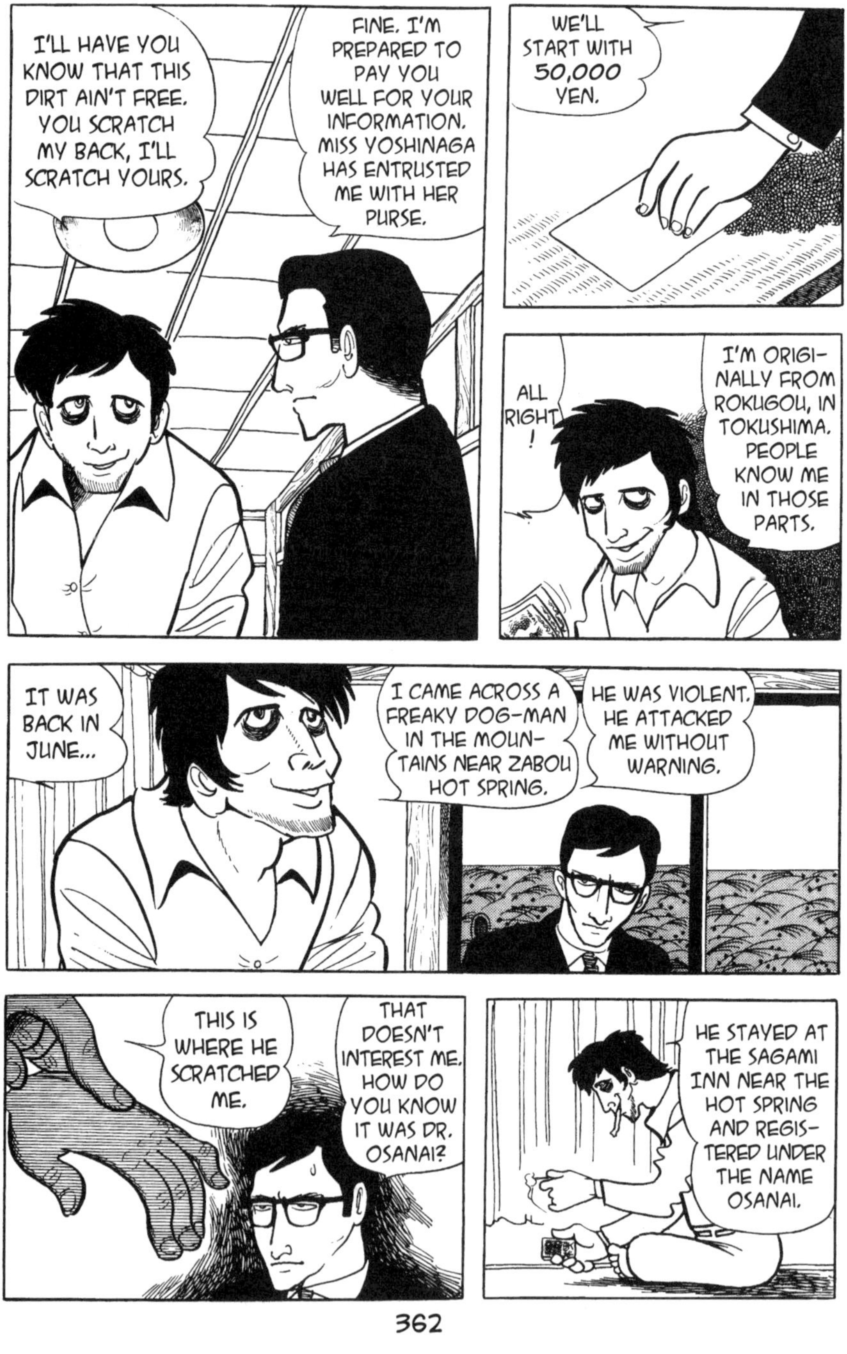
I'LL HAVE YOU KNOW THAT THIS DIRT AIN'T FREE. YOU SCRATCH MY BACK, I'LL SCRATCH YOURS.
FINE. I'M PREPARED TO PAY YOU WELL FOR YOUR INFORMATION. MISS YOSHINAGA HAS ENTRUSTED ME WITH HER PURSE.
WE'LL START WITH 50,000 YEN.
ALL RIGHT!
I'M ORIGINALLY FROM ROKUGOU, IN TOKUSHIMA. PEOPLE KNOW ME IN THOSE PARTS.
IT WAS BACK IN JUNE...
I CAME ACROSS A FREAKY DOG-MAN IN THE MOUNTAINS NEAR ZABOU HOT SPRING.
HE WAS VIOLENT. HE ATTACKED ME WITHOUT WARNING.
THIS IS WHERE HE SCRATCHED ME.
THAT DOESN'T INTEREST ME. HOW DO YOU KNOW IT WAS DR. OSANAI?
HE STAYED AT THE SAGAMI INN NEAR THE HOT SPRING AND REGISTERED UNDER THE NAME OSANAI.

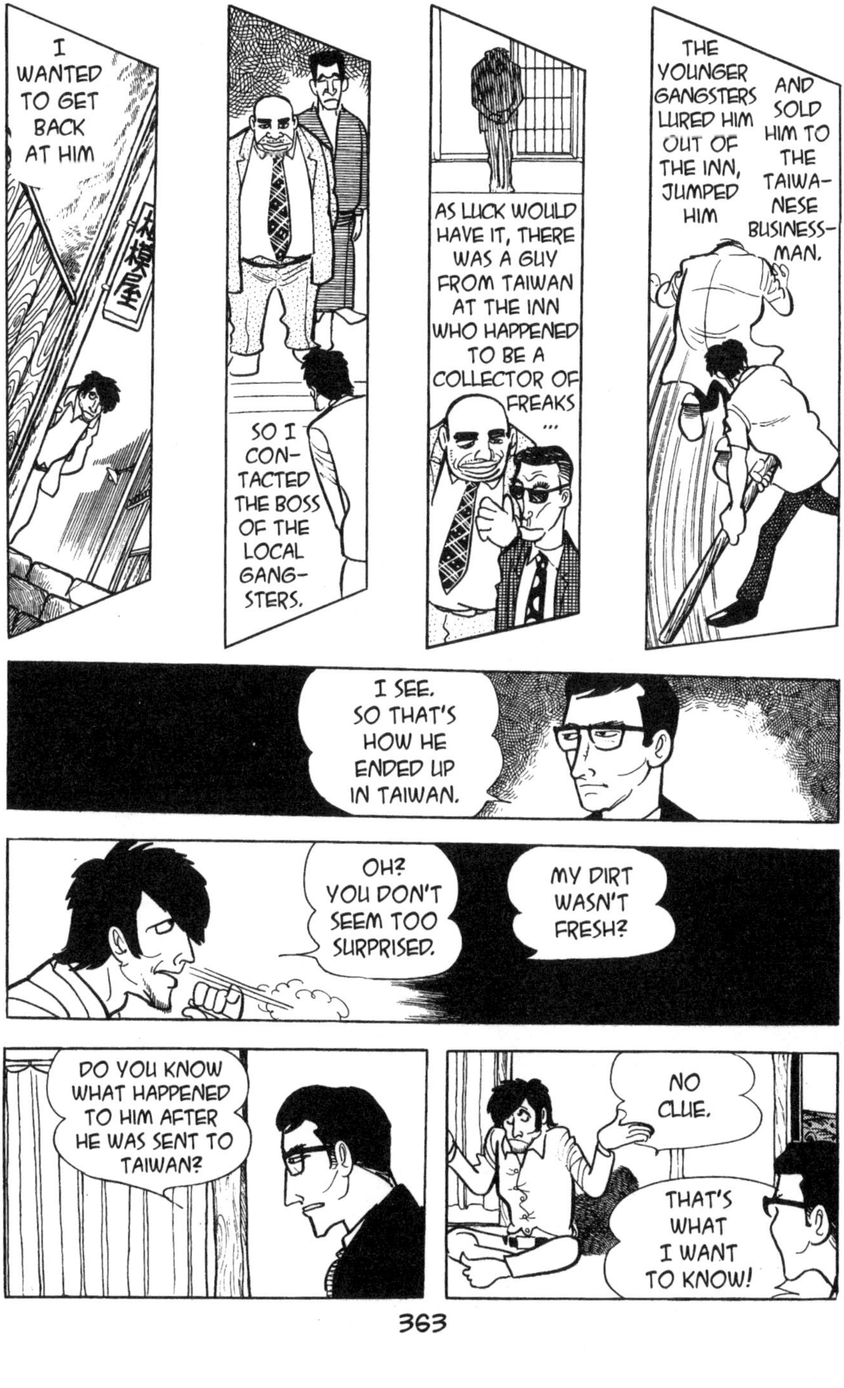
I WANTED TO GET BACK AT HIM
SO I CONTACTED THE BOSS OF THE LOCAL GANGSTERS.
AS LUCK WOULD HAVE IT, THERE WAS A GUY FROM TAIWAN AT THE INN WHO HAPPENED TO BE A COLLECTOR OF FREAKS ...
THE YOUNGER GANGSTERS LURED HIM OUT OF THE INN, JUMPED HIM
AND SOLD HIM TO THE TAIWANESE BUSINESSMAN.
I SEE. SO THAT'S HOW HE ENDED UP IN TAIWAN.
OH? YOU DON'T SEEM TOO SURPRISED.
MY DIRT WASN'T FRESH?
DO YOU KNOW WHAT HAPPENED TO HIM AFTER HE WAS SENT TO TAIWAN?
NO CLUE.
THAT'S WHAT I WANT TO KNOW!

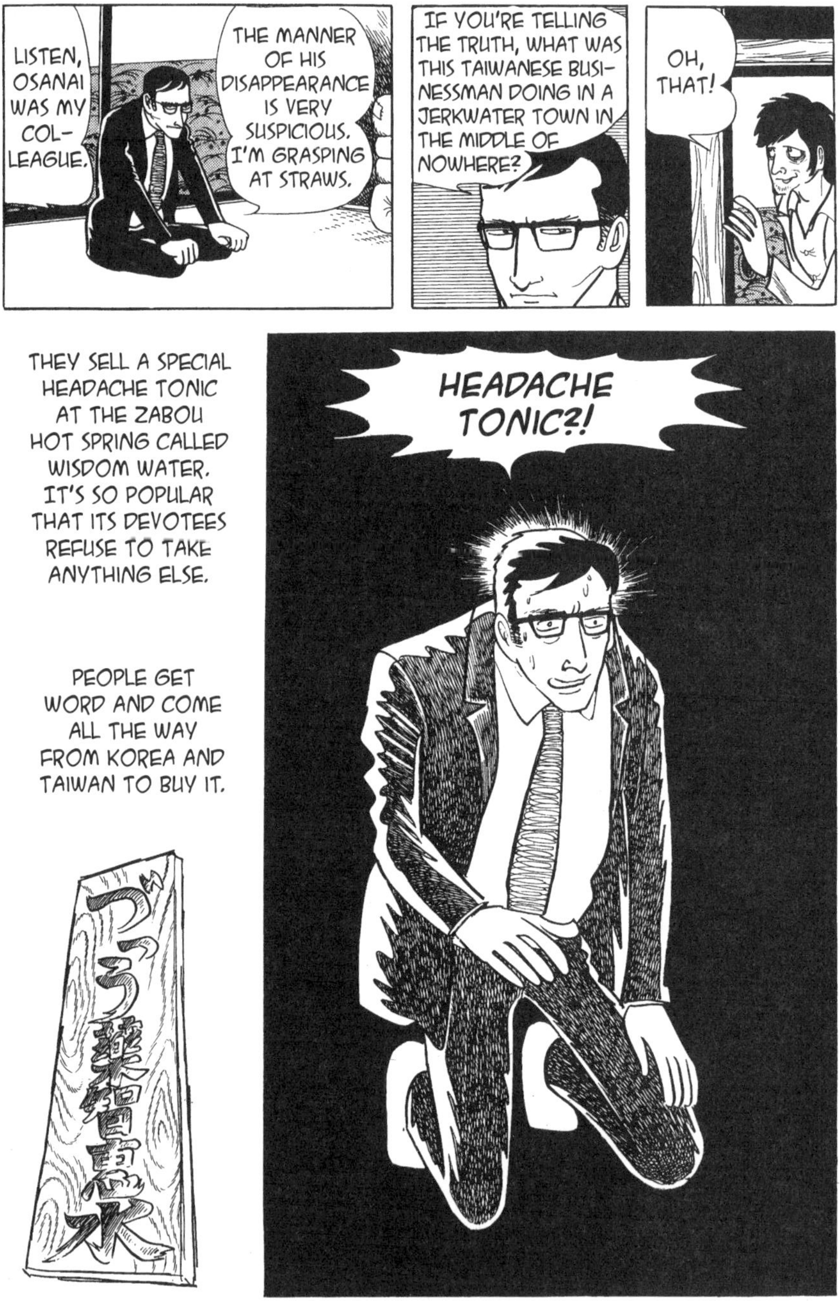
LISTEN, OSANAI WAS MY COL-LEAGUE.
THE MANNER OF HIS DISAPPEARANCE IS VERY SUSPICIOUS. I'M GRASPING AT STRAWS.
IF YOU'RE TELLING THE TRUTH, WHAT WAS THIS TAIWANESE BUSI-NESSMAN DOING IN A JERKWATER TOWN IN THE MIDDLE OF NOWHERE?
OH, THAT!
THEY SELL A SPECIAL HEADACHE TONIC AT THE ZABOU HOT SPRING CALLED WISDOM WATER. IT'S SO POPULAR THAT ITS DEVOTEES REFUSE TO TAKE ANYTHING ELSE.
PEOPLE GET WORD AND COME ALL THE WAY FROM KOREA AND TAIWAN TO BUY IT.
HEADACHE TONIC?!

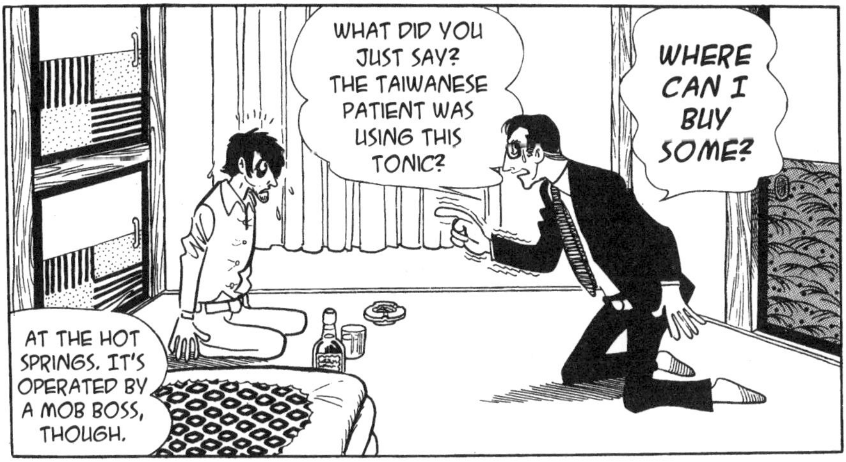
WHERE CAN I BUY SOME?
WHAT DID YOU JUST SAY? THE TAIWANESE PATIENT WAS USING THIS TONIC?
AT THE HOT SPRINGS. IT'S OPERATED BY A MOB BOSS, THOUGH.

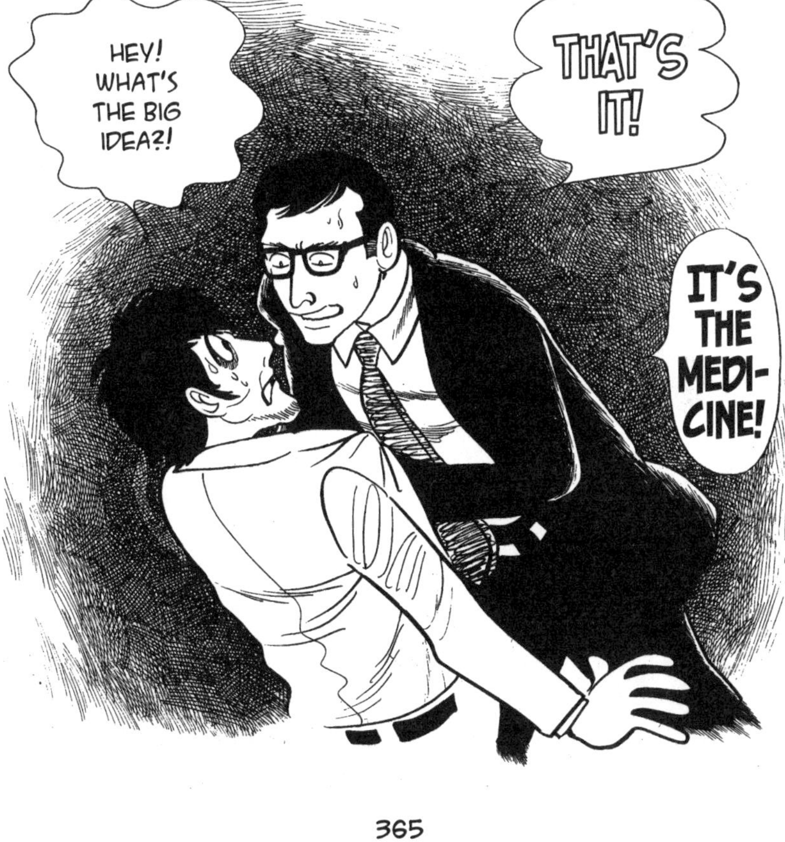
THAT'S IT!
IT'S THE MEDI-CINE!
HEY! WHAT'S THE BIG IDEA?!

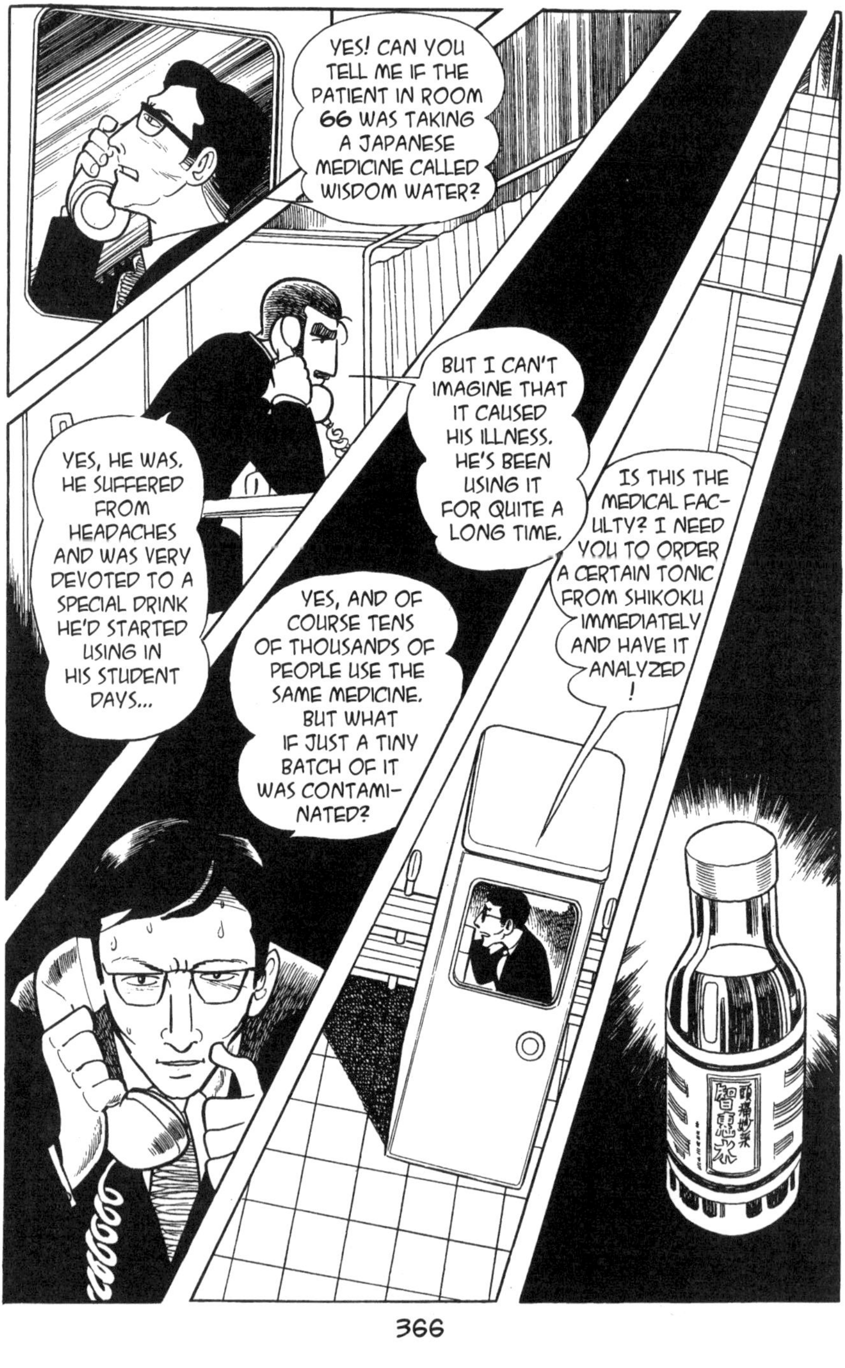
YES! CAN YOU TELL ME IF THE PATIENT IN ROOM 66 WAS TAKING A JAPANESE MEDICINE CALLED WISDOM WATER?
YES, HE WAS. HE SUFFERED FROM HEADACHES AND WAS VERY DEVOTED TO A SPECIAL DRINK HE'D STARTED USING IN HIS STUDENT DAYS...
BUT I CAN'T IMAGINE THAT IT CAUSED HIS ILLNESS. HE'S BEEN USING IT FOR QUITE A LONG TIME.
YES, AND OF COURSE TENS OF THOUSANDS OF PEOPLE USE THE SAME MEDICINE. BUT WHAT IF JUST A TINY BATCH OF IT WAS CONTAMINATED?
IS THIS THE MEDICAL FACULTY? I NEED YOU TO ORDER A CERTAIN TONIC FROM SHIKOKU IMMEDIATELY AND HAVE IT ANALYZED!

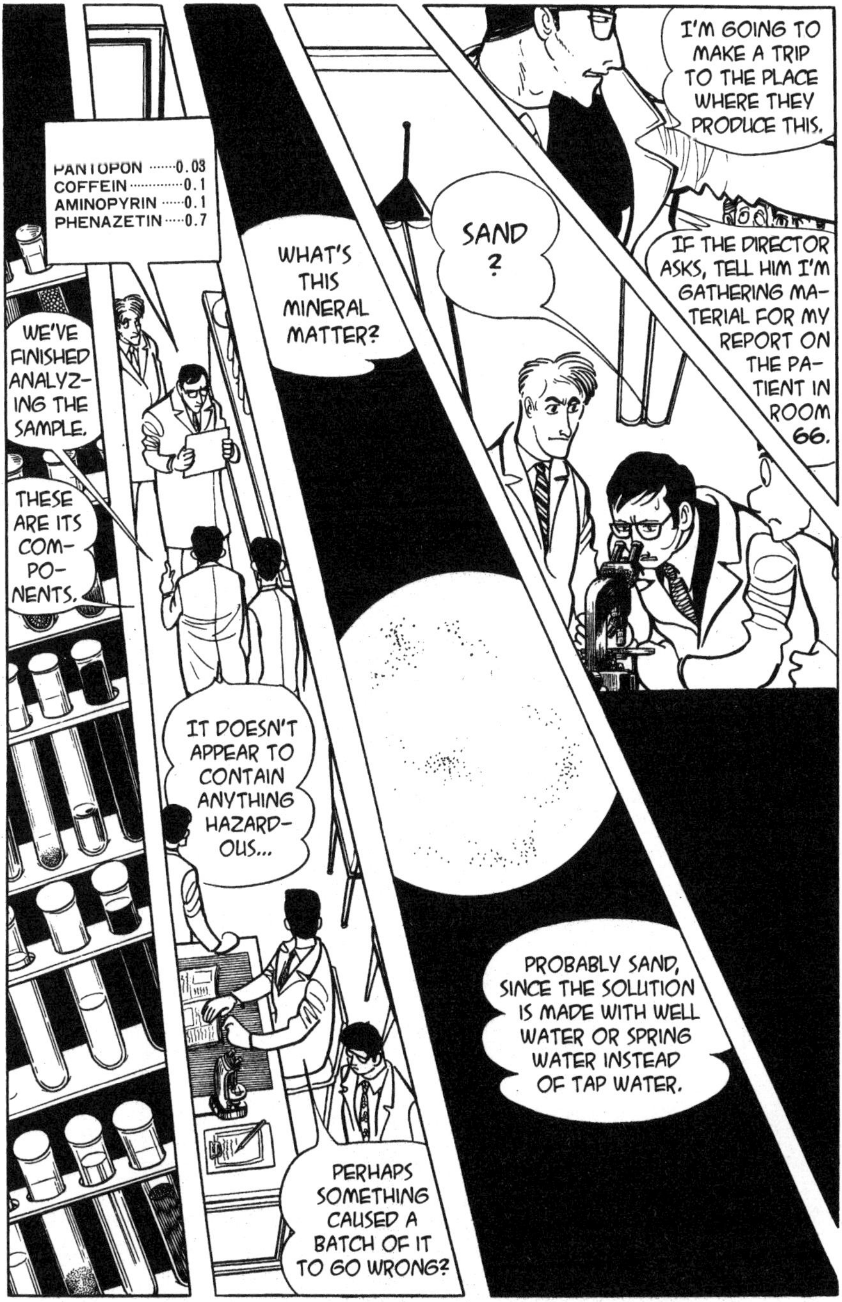

WE'VE FINISHED ANALYZING THE SAMPLE.
THESE ARE ITS COMPONENTS.
PANTOPON ······0.03
COFFEIN ··············0.1
AMINOPYRIN ······0.1
PHENAZETIN ·····0.7
IT DOESN'T APPEAR TO CONTAIN ANYTHING HAZARDOUS...
PERHAPS SOMETHING CAUSED A BATCH OF IT TO GO WRONG?
WHAT'S THIS MINERAL MATTER?
PROBABLY SAND, SINCE THE SOLUTION IS MADE WITH WELL WATER OR SPRING WATER INSTEAD OF TAP WATER.
SAND?
I'M GOING TO MAKE A TRIP TO THE PLACE WHERE THEY PRODUCE THIS.
IF THE DIRECTOR ASKS, TELL HIM I'M GATHERING MATERIAL FOR MY REPORT ON THE PATIENT IN ROOM 66.

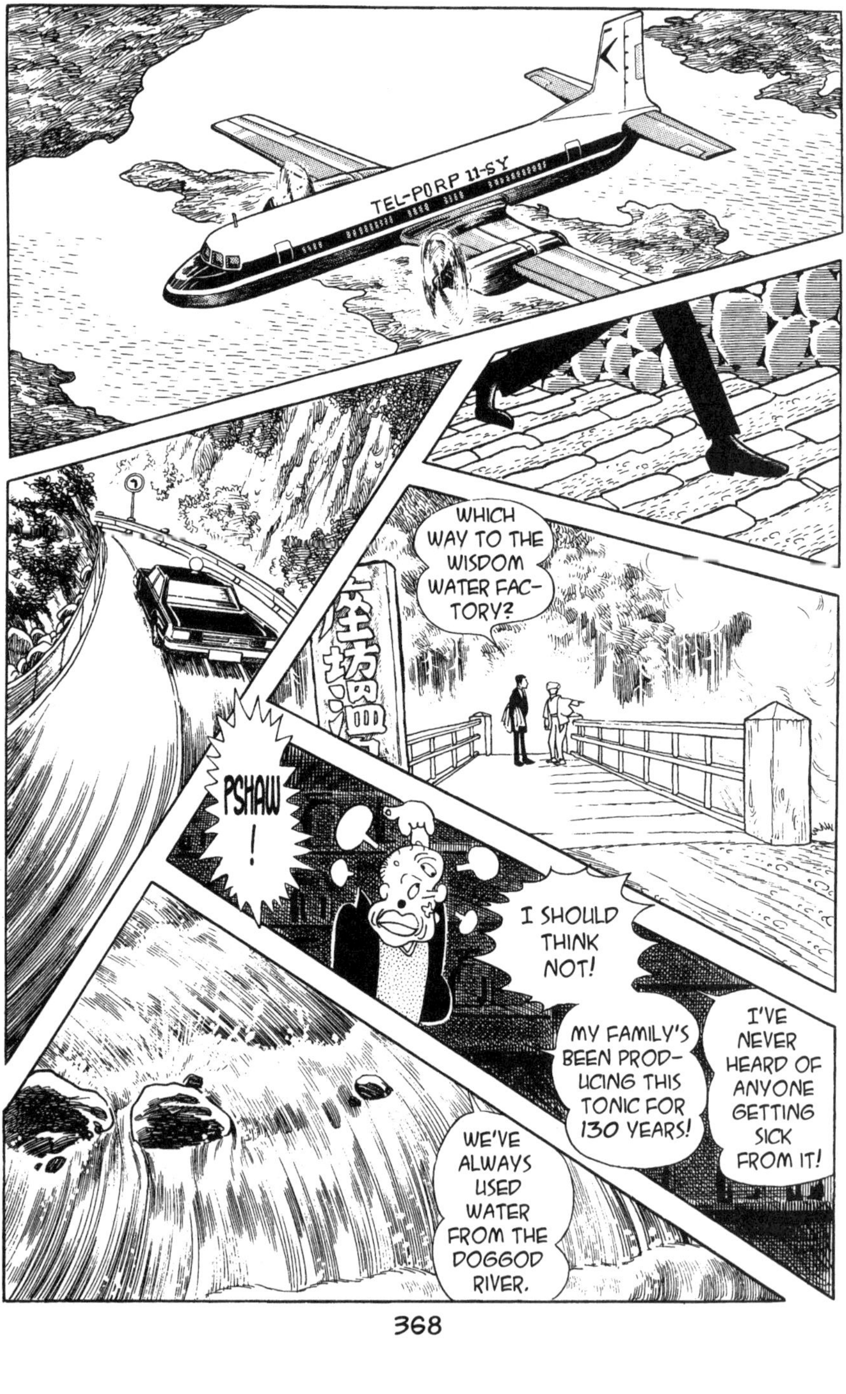
TEL-PORP 11-SY
WHICH WAY TO THE WISDOM WATER FAC-TORY?
PSHAW!
I SHOULD THINK NOT!
I'VE NEVER HEARD OF ANYONE GETTING SICK FROM IT!
MY FAMILY'S BEEN PROD-UCING THIS TONIC FOR 130 YEARS!
WE'VE ALWAYS USED WATER FROM THE DOGGOD RIVER.

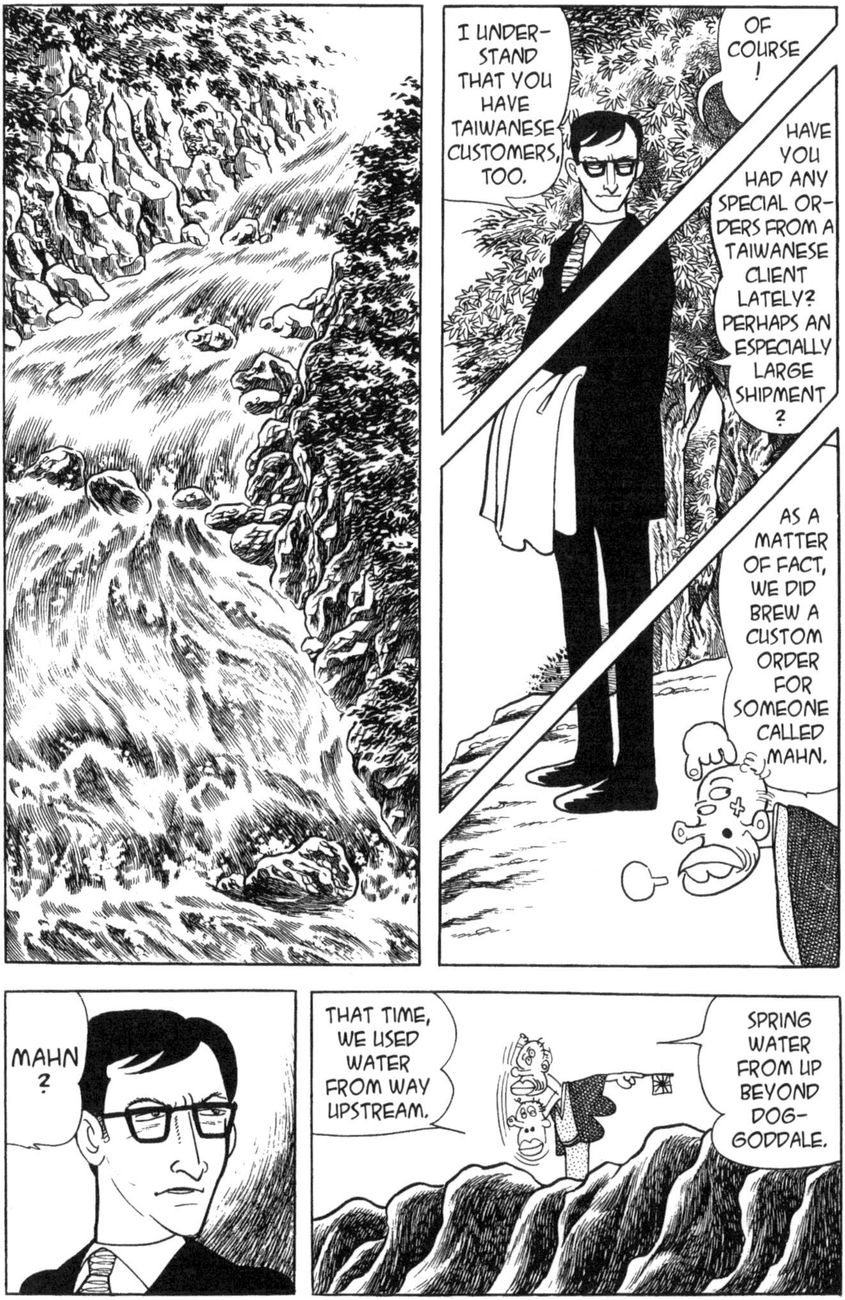

I UNDERSTAND THAT YOU HAVE TAIWANESE CUSTOMERS, TOO.
OF COURSE!
HAVE YOU HAD ANY SPECIAL ORDERS FROM A TAIWANESE CLIENT LATELY? PERHAPS AN ESPECIALLY LARGE SHIPMENT?
AS A MATTER OF FACT, WE DID BREW A CUSTOM ORDER FOR SOMEONE CALLED MAHN.
MAHN?
THAT TIME, WE USED WATER FROM WAY UPSTREAM.
SPRING WATER FROM UP BEYOND DOG-GODDALE.

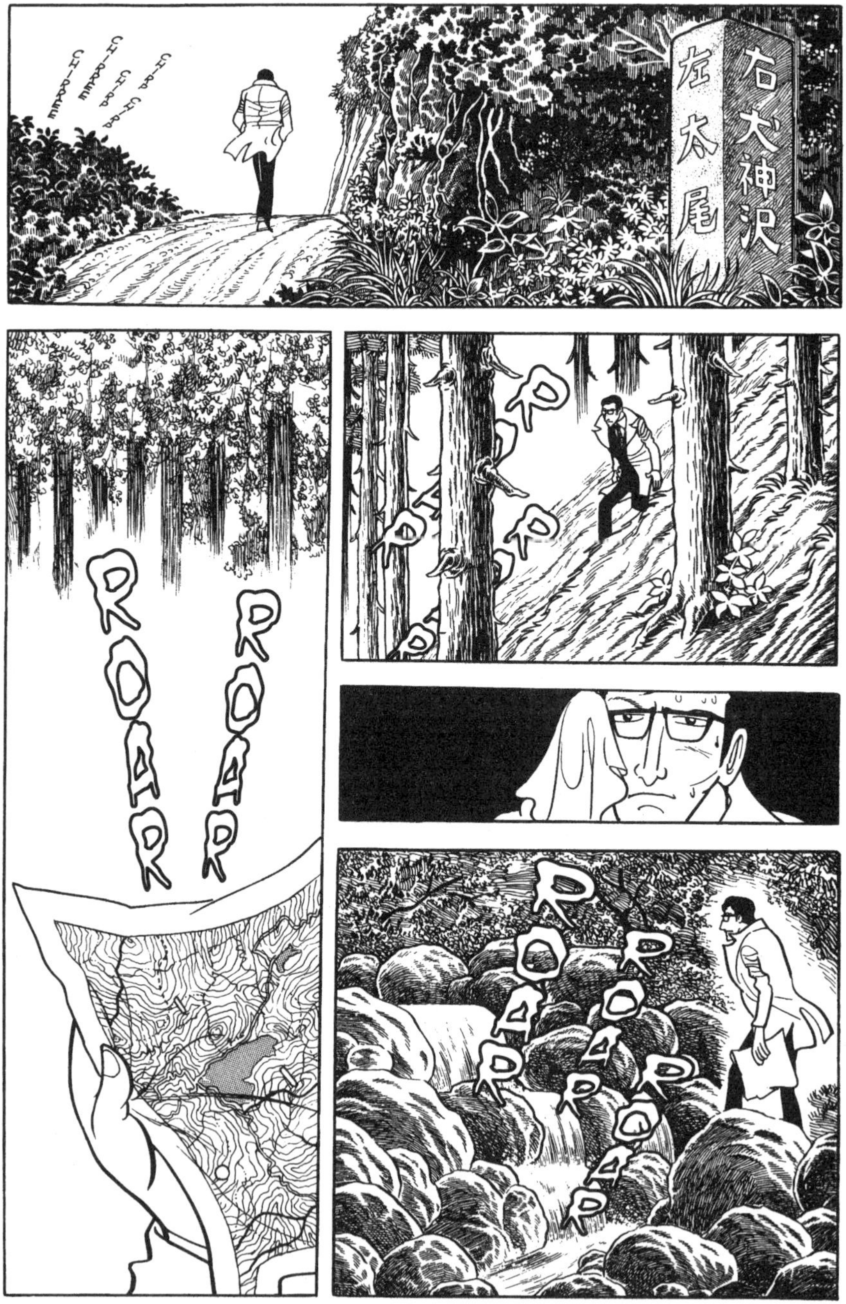
右犬神沢
左太尾
CHI-RP CHI-RP
CHI-RP CHI-RP
CHI-REEE
CHI-REEE
ROAR
ROAR
ROAR
ROAR
ROAR
ROAR
ROAR
ROAR

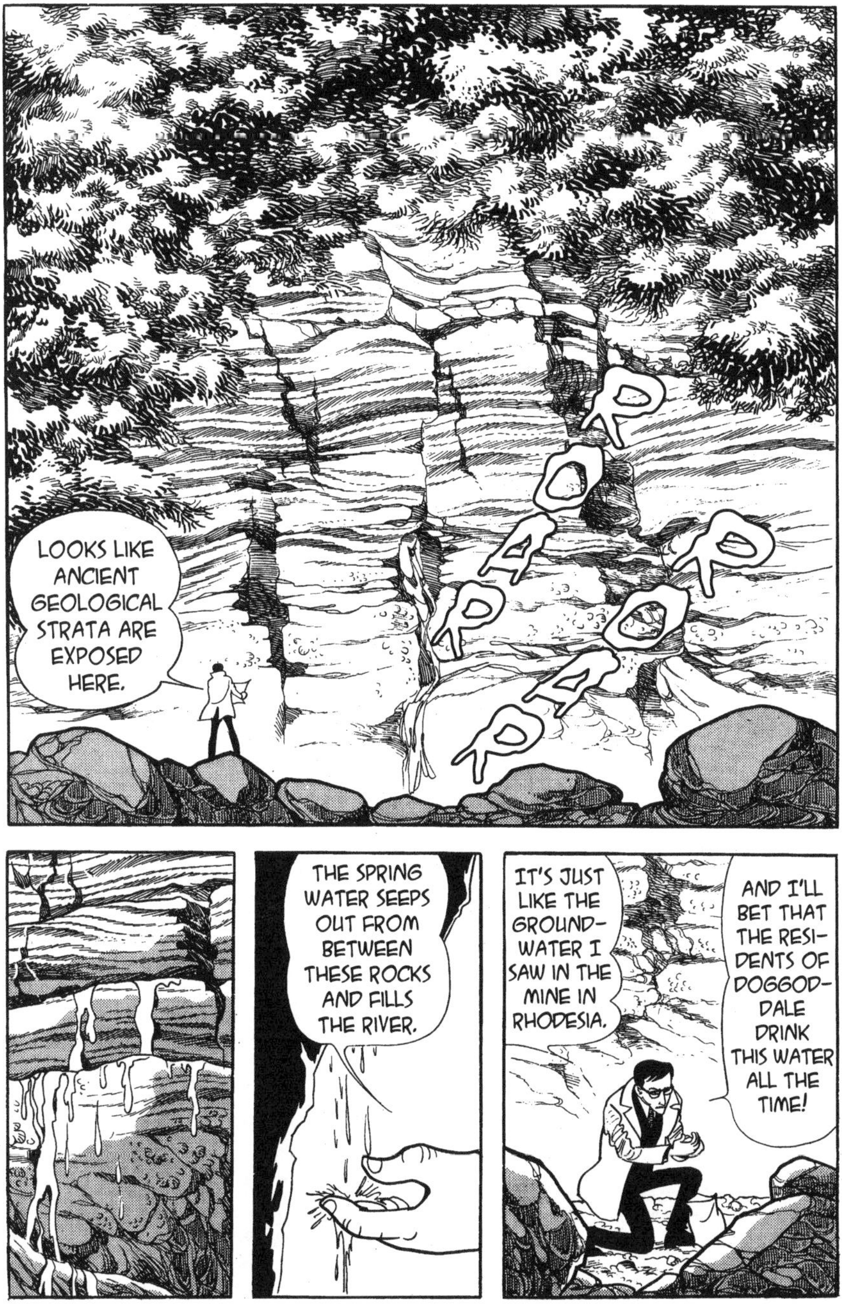
ROAR
ROAR
LOOKS LIKE ANCIENT GEOLOGICAL STRATA ARE EXPOSED HERE.
THE SPRING WATER SEEPS OUT FROM BETWEEN THESE ROCKS AND FILLS THE RIVER.
IT'S JUST LIKE THE GROUND-WATER I SAW IN THE MINE IN RHODESIA.
AND I'LL BET THAT THE RESI-DENTS OF DOGGOD-DALE DRINK THIS WATER ALL THE TIME!

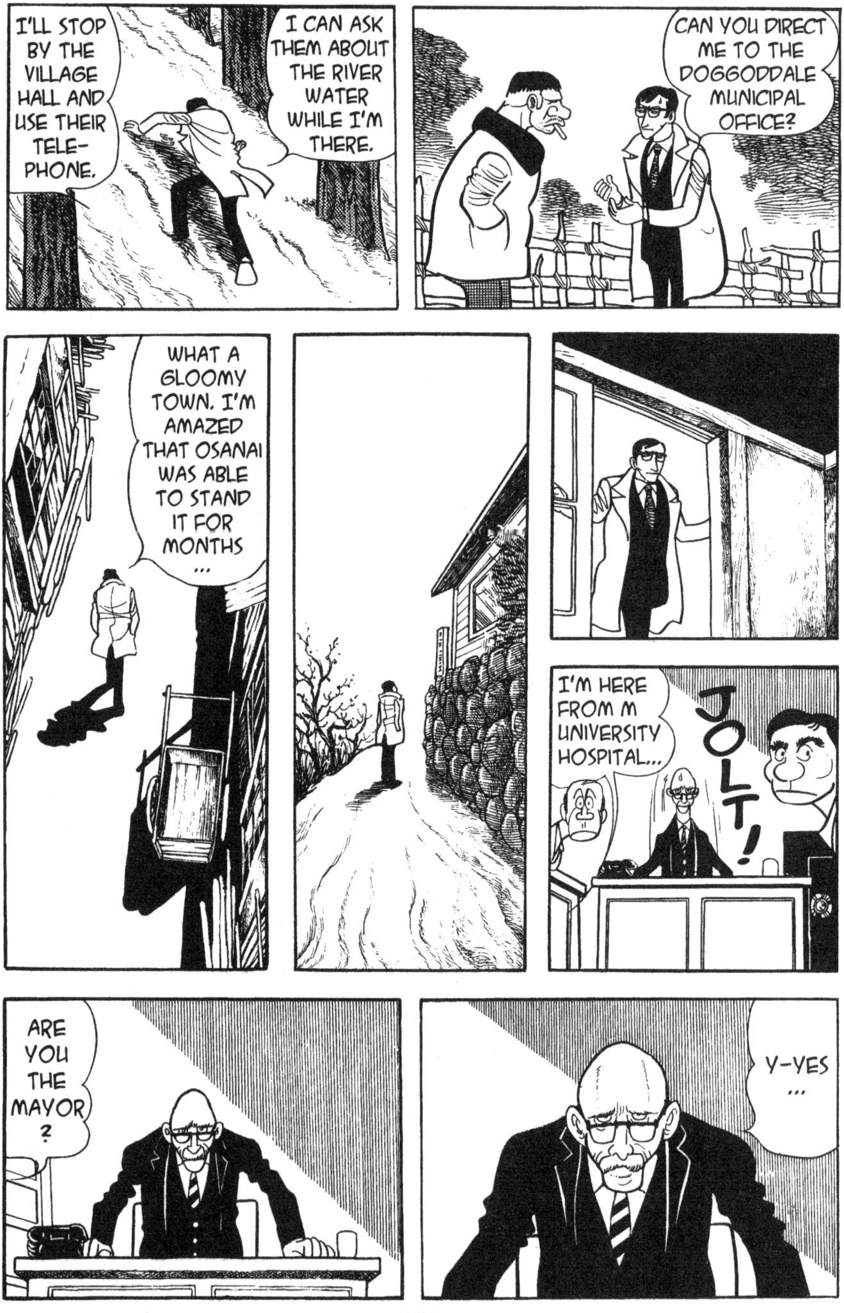
I'LL STOP BY THE VILLAGE HALL AND USE THEIR TELE-PHONE.
I CAN ASK THEM ABOUT THE RIVER WATER WHILE I'M THERE.
CAN YOU DIRECT ME TO THE DOGGODDALE MUNICIPAL OFFICE?
WHAT A GLOOMY TOWN. I'M AMAZED THAT OSANAI WAS ABLE TO STAND IT FOR MONTHS ...
I'M HERE FROM M UNIVERSITY HOSPITAL...
JOLT!
ARE YOU THE MAYOR ?
Y-YES ...

I'M DR. URABE OF THE FIRST DEPARTMENT OF INTERNAL MEDICINE.

THANK YOU FOR LOOKING AFTER MY COLLEAGUE, DR. OSANAI.

...

...

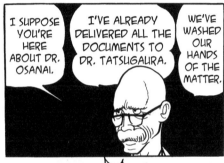

I SUPPOSE YOU'RE HERE ABOUT DR. OSANAI.

I'VE ALREADY DELIVERED ALL THE DOCUMENTS TO DR. TATSUGAURA.

WE'VE WASHED OUR HANDS OF THE MATTER.

TO DR. TATSU-GAURA?

THAT'S ODD. I'VE NEVER SEEN THEM.

WELL, YES, THE WHOLE THING WAS HIS PLAN, AFTER ALL!

WHAT WHOLE THING?

WHAT WAS ALL DR. TATSUGAURA'S PLAN?

DID YOU SAY SOMETHING YOU SHOULDN'T HAVE?

WHAT'S THIS ALL ABOUT?

...

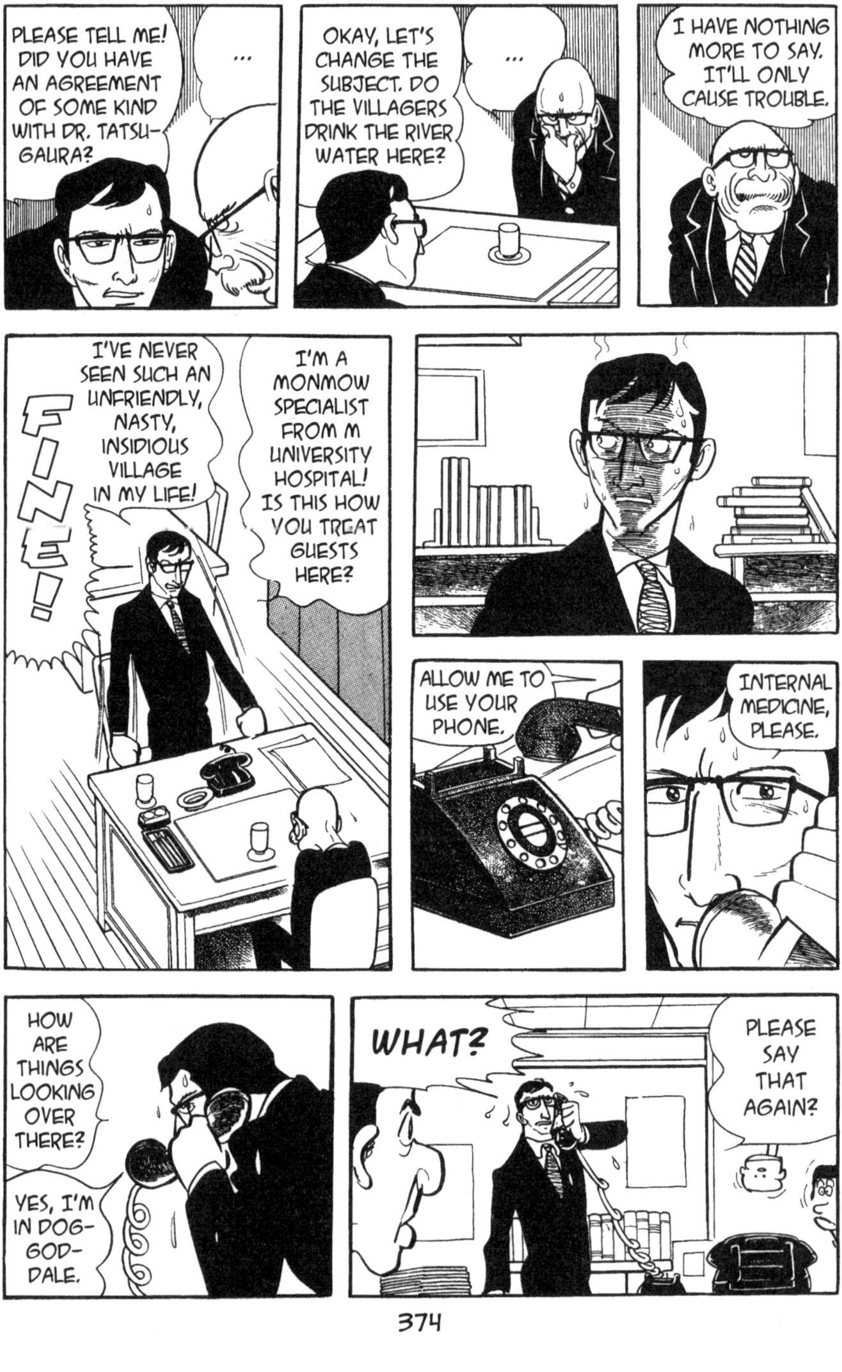
PLEASE TELL ME! DID YOU HAVE AN AGREEMENT OF SOME KIND WITH DR. TATSU-GAURA?
...
OKAY, LET'S CHANGE THE SUBJECT. DO THE VILLAGERS DRINK THE RIVER WATER HERE?
...
I HAVE NOTHING MORE TO SAY. IT'LL ONLY CAUSE TROUBLE.
FINE!
I'VE NEVER SEEN SUCH AN UNFRIENDLY, NASTY, INSIDIOUS VILLAGE IN MY LIFE!
I'M A MONMOW SPECIALIST FROM M UNIVERSITY HOSPITAL! IS THIS HOW YOU TREAT GUESTS HERE?
ALLOW ME TO USE YOUR PHONE.
INTERNAL MEDICINE, PLEASE.
HOW ARE THINGS LOOKING OVER THERE?
YES, I'M IN DOG-GOD-DALE.
WHAT?
PLEASE SAY THAT AGAIN?

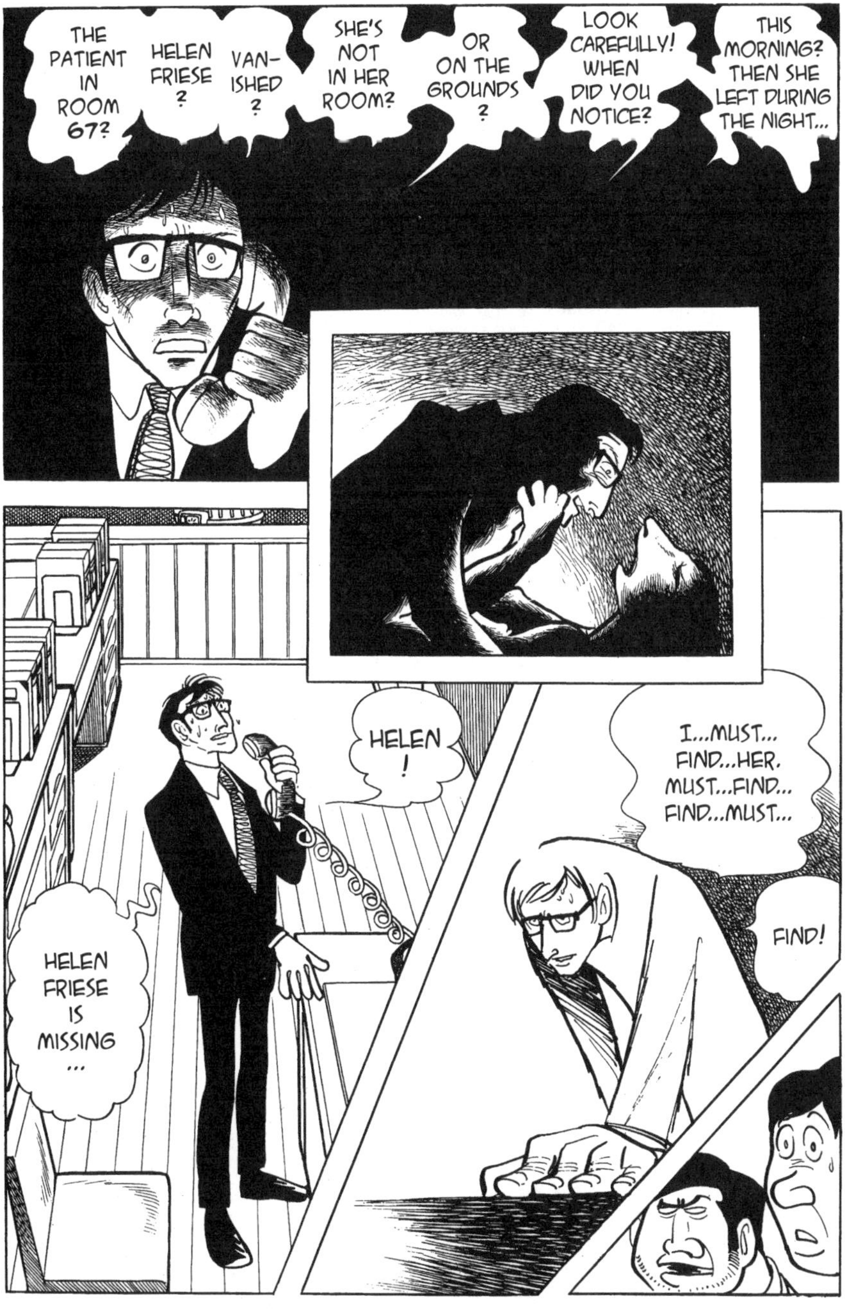
THE PATIENT IN ROOM 67?
HELEN FRIESE?
VAN-ISHED?
SHE'S NOT IN HER ROOM?
OR ON THE GROUNDS?
LOOK CAREFULLY! WHEN DID YOU NOTICE?
THIS MORNING? THEN SHE LEFT DURING THE NIGHT...
HELEN!
HELEN FRIESE IS MISSING...
I...MUST... FIND...HER. MUST...FIND... FIND...MUST...
FIND!

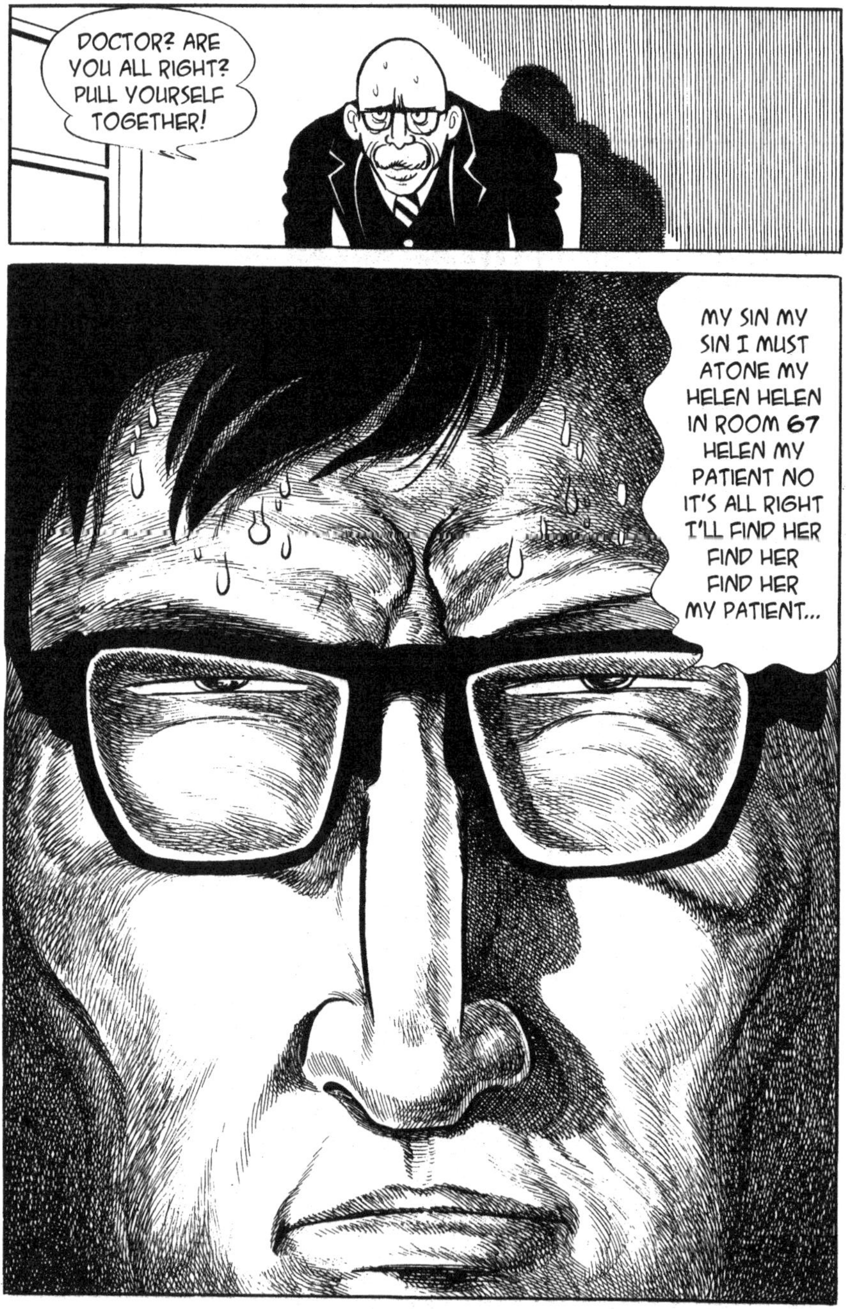
DOCTOR? ARE YOU ALL RIGHT? PULL YOURSELF TOGETHER!
MY SIN MY SIN I MUST ATONE MY HELEN HELEN IN ROOM 67 HELEN MY PATIENT NO IT'S ALL RIGHT I'LL FIND HER FIND HER FIND HER MY PATIENT...

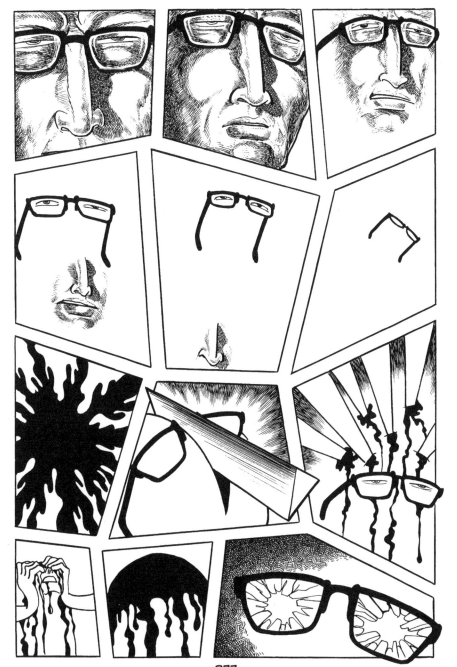

377

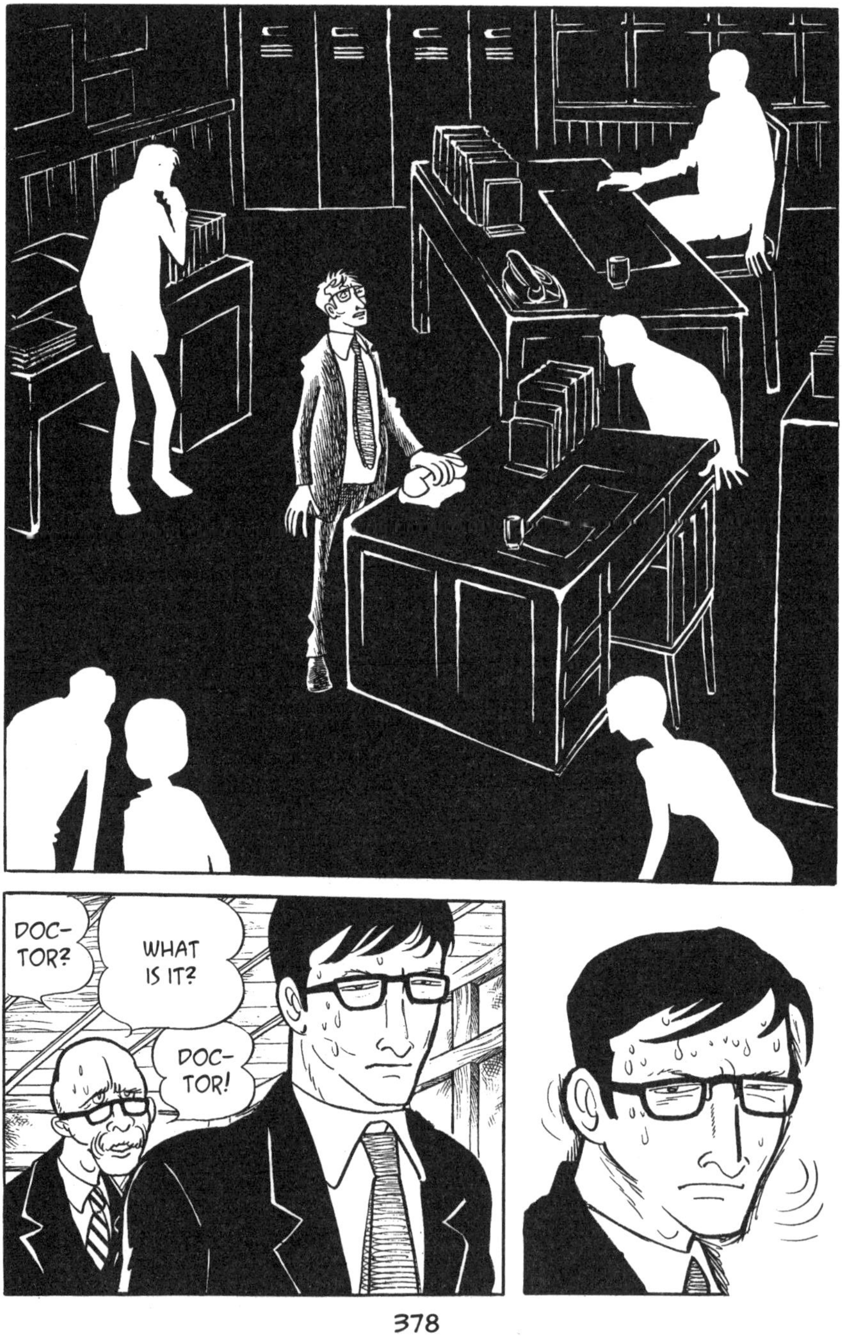

DOC-
TOR?
WHAT
IS IT?
DOC-
TOR!

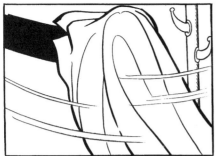

DOC-TOR!!

CLATTER

WHAT WAS THAT?

THAT LOOK IN HIS EYES!

THERE WAS SOMETHING WRONG WITH THAT MAN!

WHY WOULD M UNIVERISTY HOSPITAL KEEP A MAN LIKE THAT ON STAFF?

MAYOR, HE FORGOT SOMETHING.

RUN AND GIVE IT TO HIM.

NO! I'M SCARED!

WAIT!

LET'S LOOK INSIDE.

ROCKS?

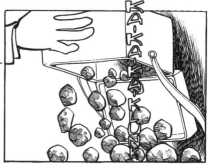

KA-KA-KA-KA-KA

ROCKS! ROCKS FROM THE RIVER BED!

WHAT DID HE WANT WITH THESE?

MUST BE A LOONY!

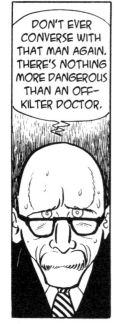

DON'T EVER CONVERSE WITH THAT MAN AGAIN. THERE'S NOTHING MORE DANGEROUS THAN AN OFF-KILTER DOCTOR.

CHAPTER 10

APPROACH TO GLORY

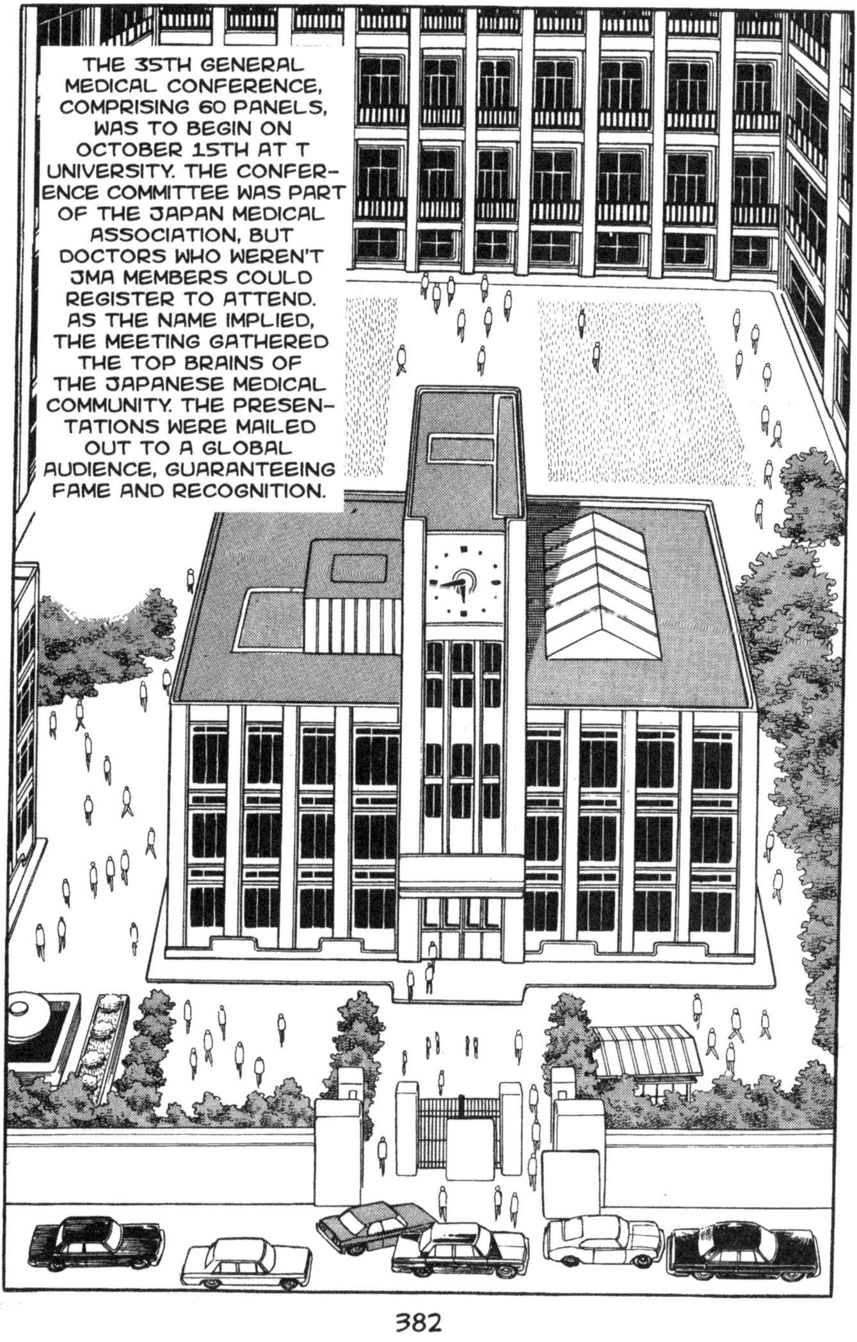
THE 35TH GENERAL MEDICAL CONFERENCE, COMPRISING 60 PANELS, WAS TO BEGIN ON OCTOBER 15TH AT T UNIVERSITY. THE CONFERENCE COMMITTEE WAS PART OF THE JAPAN MEDICAL ASSOCIATION, BUT DOCTORS WHO WEREN'T JMA MEMBERS COULD REGISTER TO ATTEND. AS THE NAME IMPLIED, THE MEETING GATHERED THE TOP BRAINS OF THE JAPANESE MEDICAL COMMUNITY. THE PRESENTATIONS WERE MAILED OUT TO A GLOBAL AUDIENCE, GUARANTEEING FAME AND RECOGNITION.

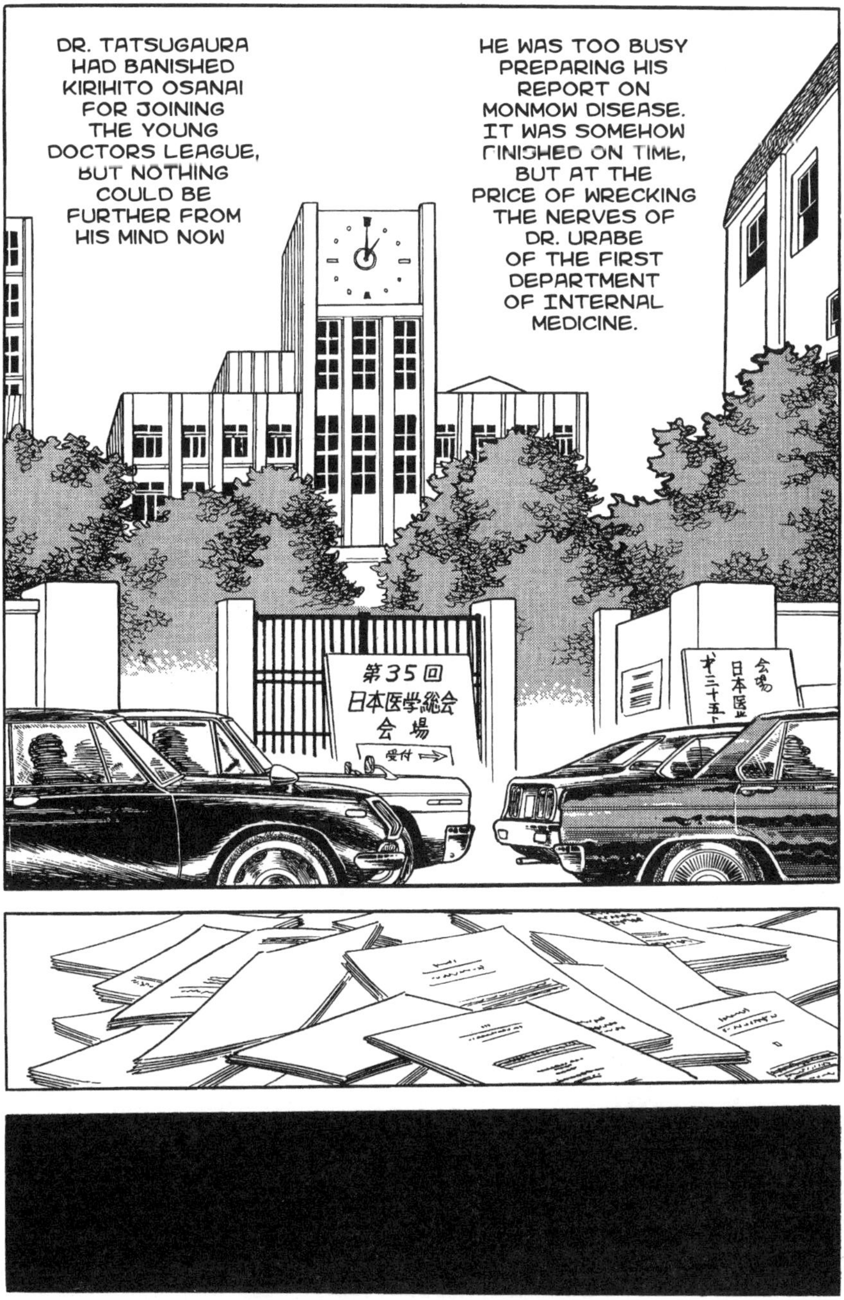
DR. TATSUGAURA HAD BANISHED KIRIHITO OSANAI FOR JOINING THE YOUNG DOCTORS LEAGUE, BUT NOTHING COULD BE FURTHER FROM HIS MIND NOW
HE WAS TOO BUSY PREPARING HIS REPORT ON MONMOW DISEASE. IT WAS SOMEHOW FINISHED ON TIME, BUT AT THE PRICE OF WRECKING THE NERVES OF DR. URABE OF THE FIRST DEPARTMENT OF INTERNAL MEDICINE.
第35回
日本医学総会
会場
受付

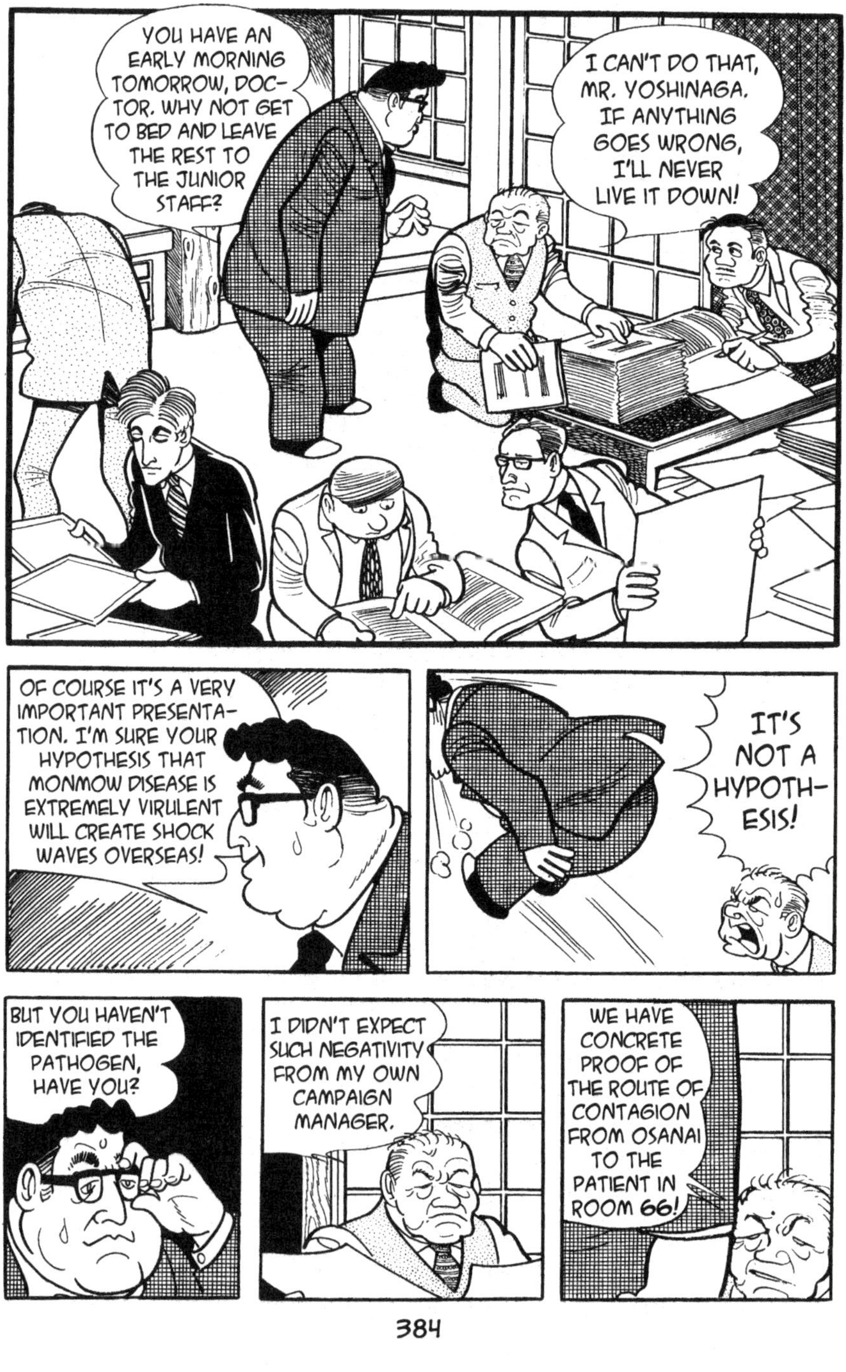
YOU HAVE AN EARLY MORNING TOMORROW, DOCTOR. WHY NOT GET TO BED AND LEAVE THE REST TO THE JUNIOR STAFF?
I CAN'T DO THAT, MR. YOSHINAGA. IF ANYTHING GOES WRONG, I'LL NEVER LIVE IT DOWN!
OF COURSE IT'S A VERY IMPORTANT PRESENTATION. I'M SURE YOUR HYPOTHESIS THAT MONMOW DISEASE IS EXTREMELY VIRULENT WILL CREATE SHOCK WAVES OVERSEAS!
IT'S NOT A HYPOTHESIS!
BUT YOU HAVEN'T IDENTIFIED THE PATHOGEN, HAVE YOU?
I DIDN'T EXPECT SUCH NEGATIVITY FROM MY OWN CAMPAIGN MANAGER.
WE HAVE CONCRETE PROOF OF THE ROUTE OF CONTAGION FROM OSANAI TO THE PATIENT IN ROOM 66!

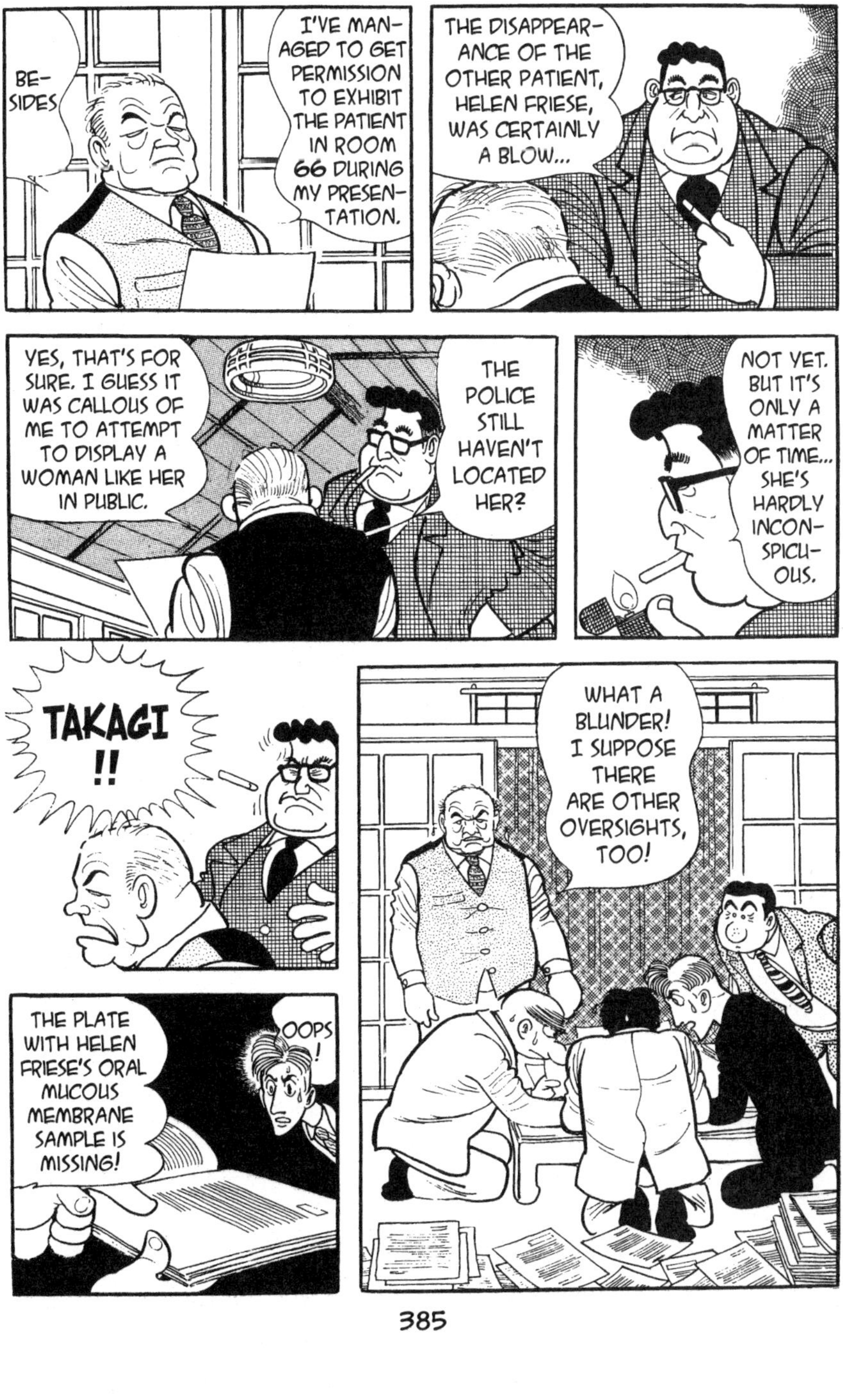
BE-SIDES
I'VE MAN-AGED TO GET PERMISSION TO EXHIBIT THE PATIENT IN ROOM 66 DURING MY PRESEN-TATION.
THE DISAPPEAR-ANCE OF THE OTHER PATIENT, HELEN FRIESE, WAS CERTAINLY A BLOW...
YES, THAT'S FOR SURE. I GUESS IT WAS CALLOUS OF ME TO ATTEMPT TO DISPLAY A WOMAN LIKE HER IN PUBLIC.
THE POLICE STILL HAVEN'T LOCATED HER?
NOT YET. BUT IT'S ONLY A MATTER OF TIME... SHE'S HARDLY INCON-SPICU-OUS.
TAKAGI !!
THE PLATE WITH HELEN FRIESE'S ORAL MUCOUS MEMBRANE SAMPLE IS MISSING!
OOPS !
WHAT A BLUNDER! I SUPPOSE THERE ARE OTHER OVERSIGHTS, TOO!

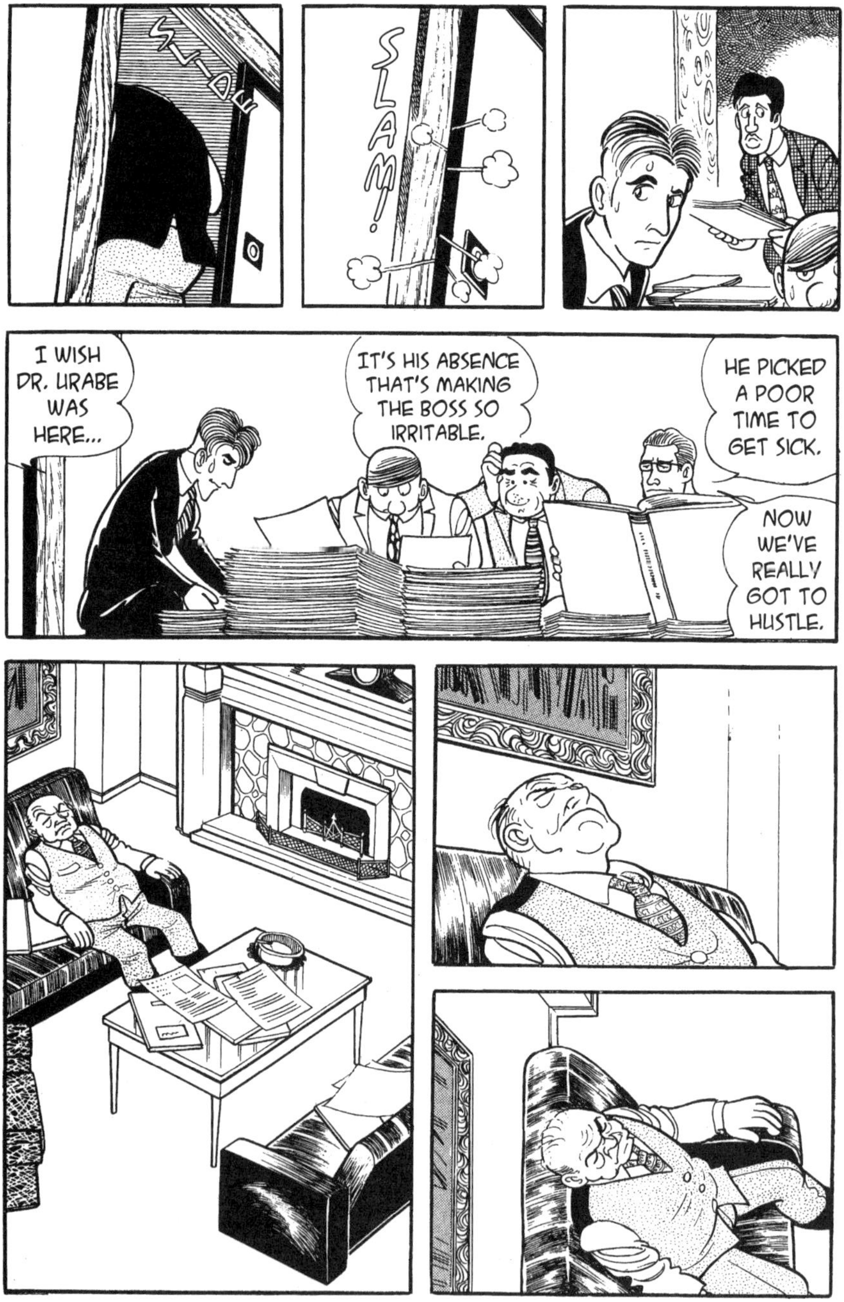
SLIDE
SLAM!
I WISH DR. URABE WAS HERE...
IT'S HIS ABSENCE THAT'S MAKING THE BOSS SO IRRITABLE.
HE PICKED A POOR TIME TO GET SICK.
NOW WE'VE REALLY GOT TO HUSTLE.

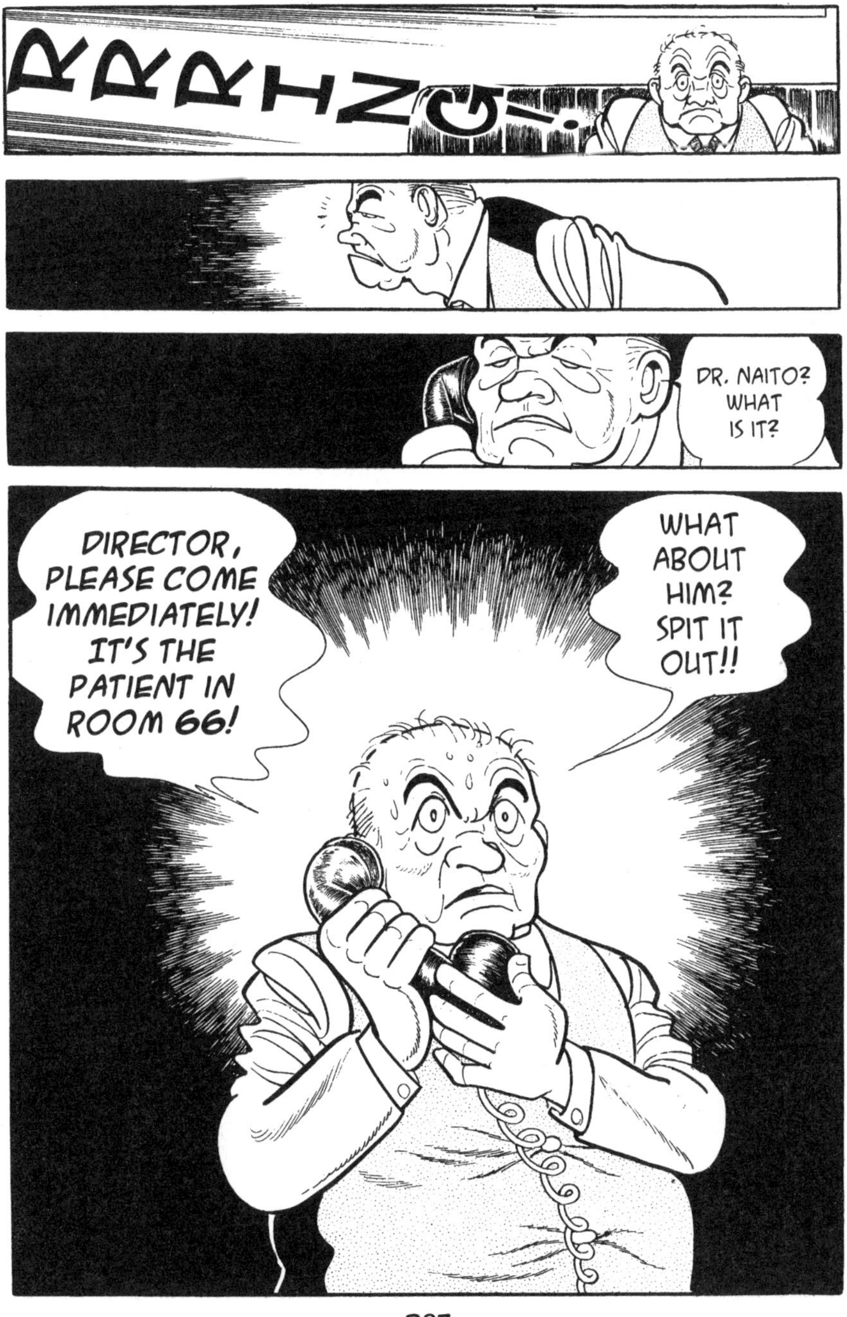
RRRHNG!!
DR. NAITO? WHAT IS IT?
DIRECTOR, PLEASE COME IMMEDIATELY! IT'S THE PATIENT IN ROOM 66!
WHAT ABOUT HIM? SPIT IT OUT!!

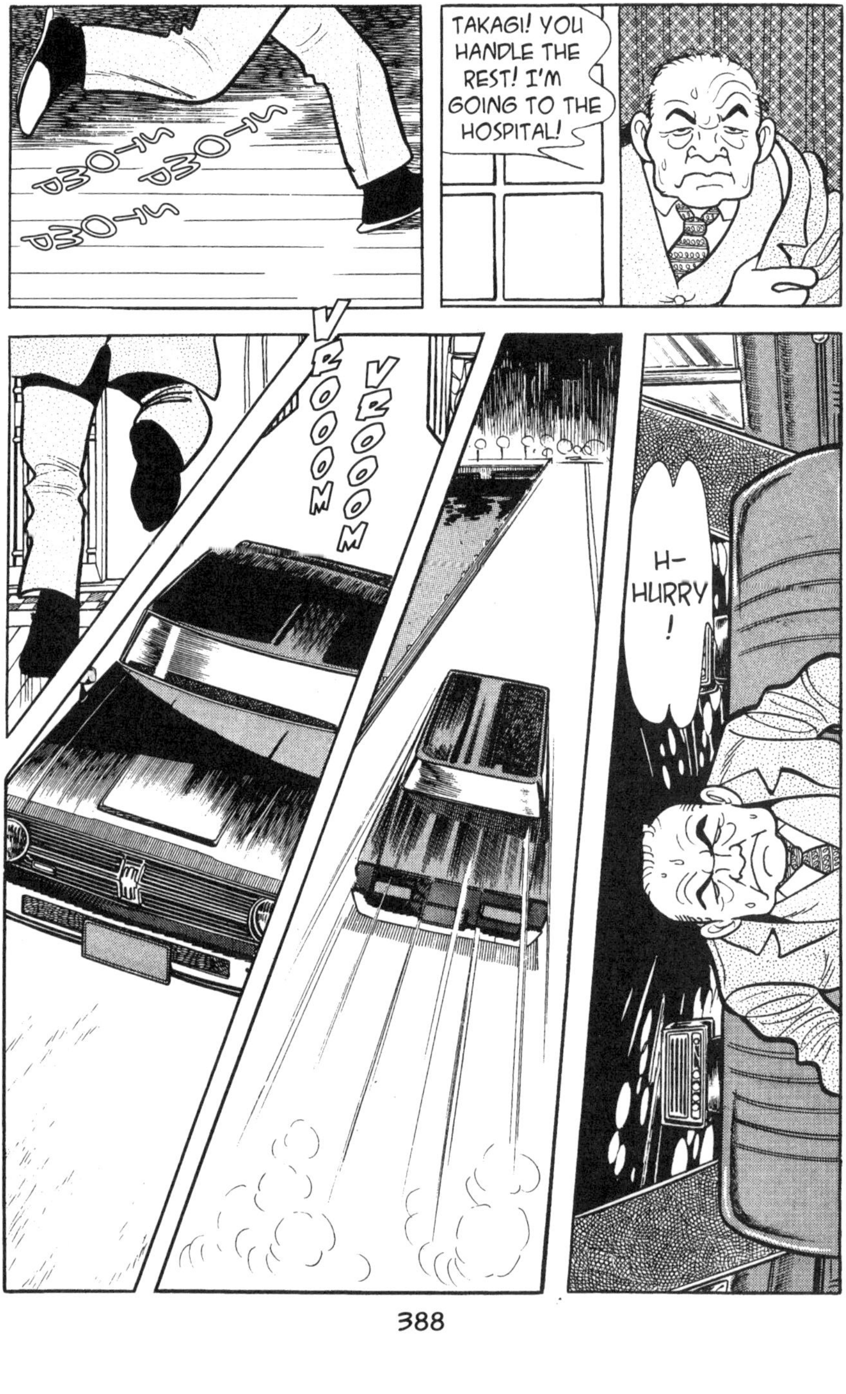
STOMP STOMP
STOMP
TAKAGI! YOU HANDLE THE REST! I'M GOING TO THE HOSPITAL!
VROOOOM
VROOOOM
H-HURRY!

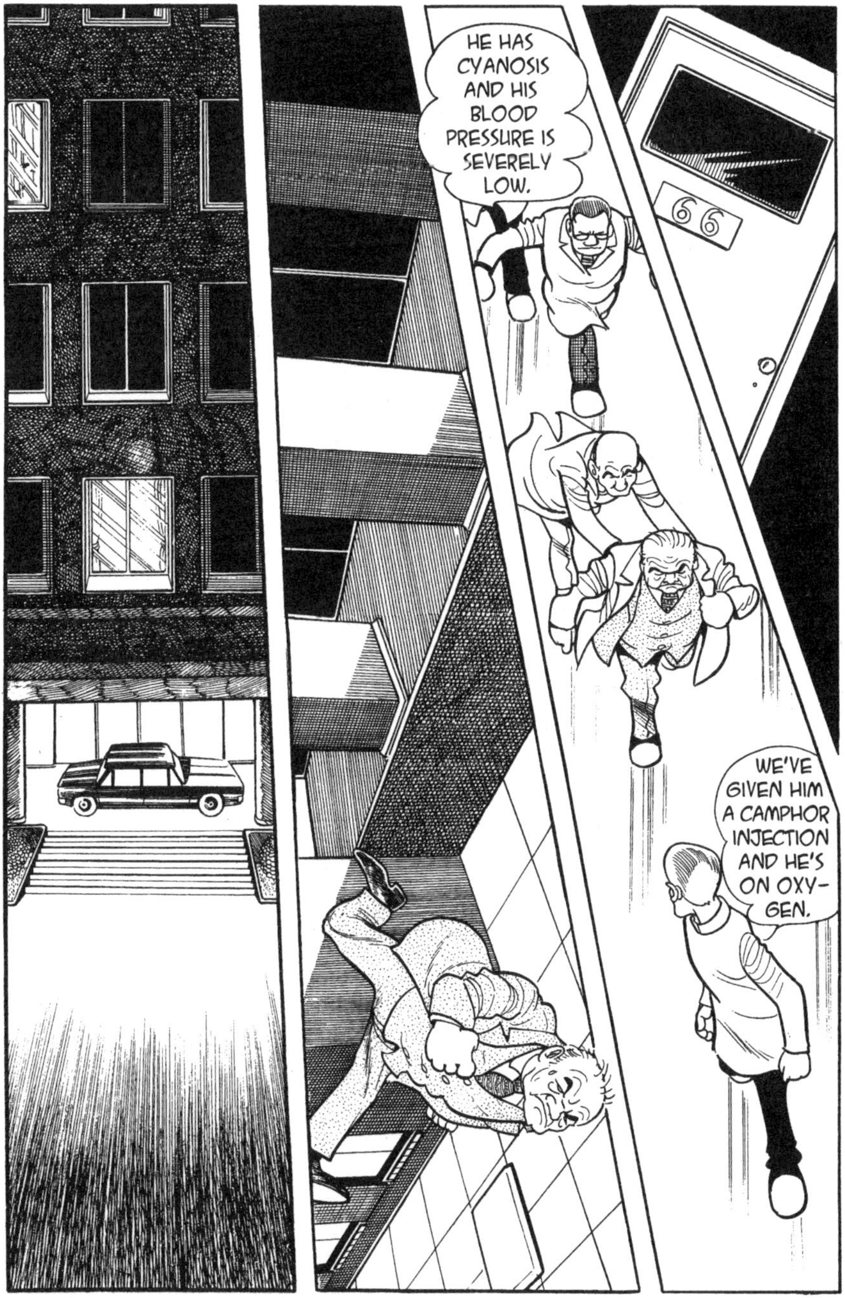
HE HAS CYANOSIS AND HIS BLOOD PRESSURE IS SEVERELY LOW.
66
WE'VE GIVEN HIM A CAMPHOR INJECTION AND HE'S ON OXY-GEN.

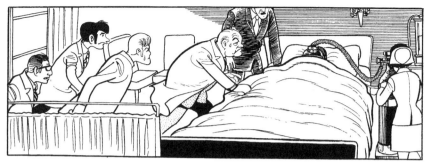

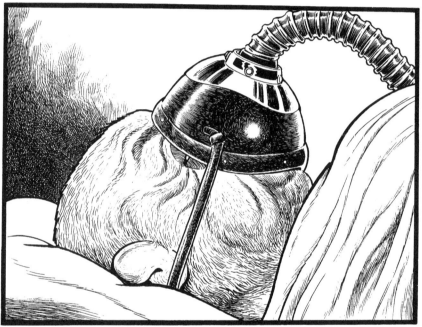

I WANT YOU TO DO EVERYTHING YOU CAN TO KEEP HIM ALIVE!

WHY WEREN'T YOU ABLE TO FORESEE THIS, EH? UN-ACCEPTABLE!

I'M TERRIBLY SORRY. IT HAPPENED ALL OF A SUDDEN, JUST LIKE WITH THAT OTHER PATIENT.

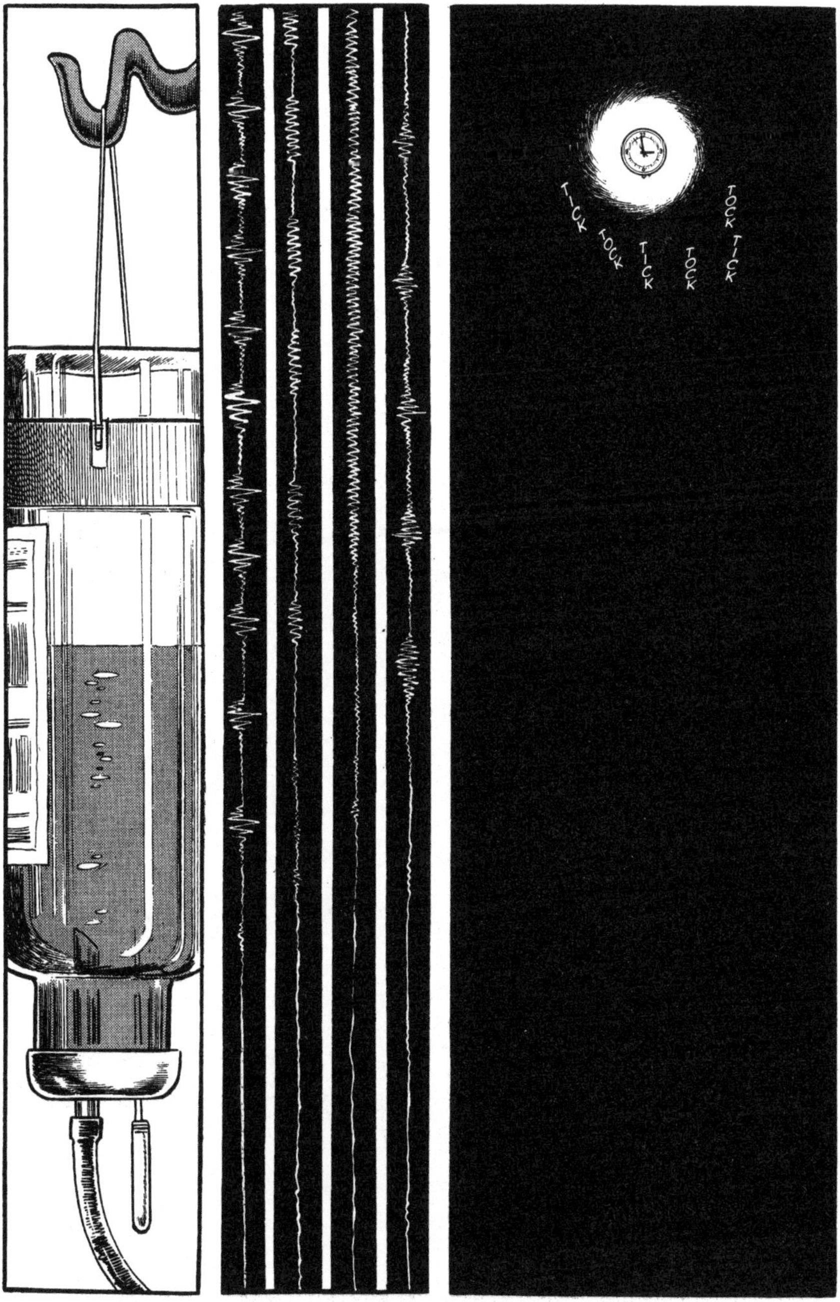
TICK
TOCK
TICK
TOCK
TOCK TICK

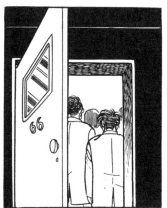

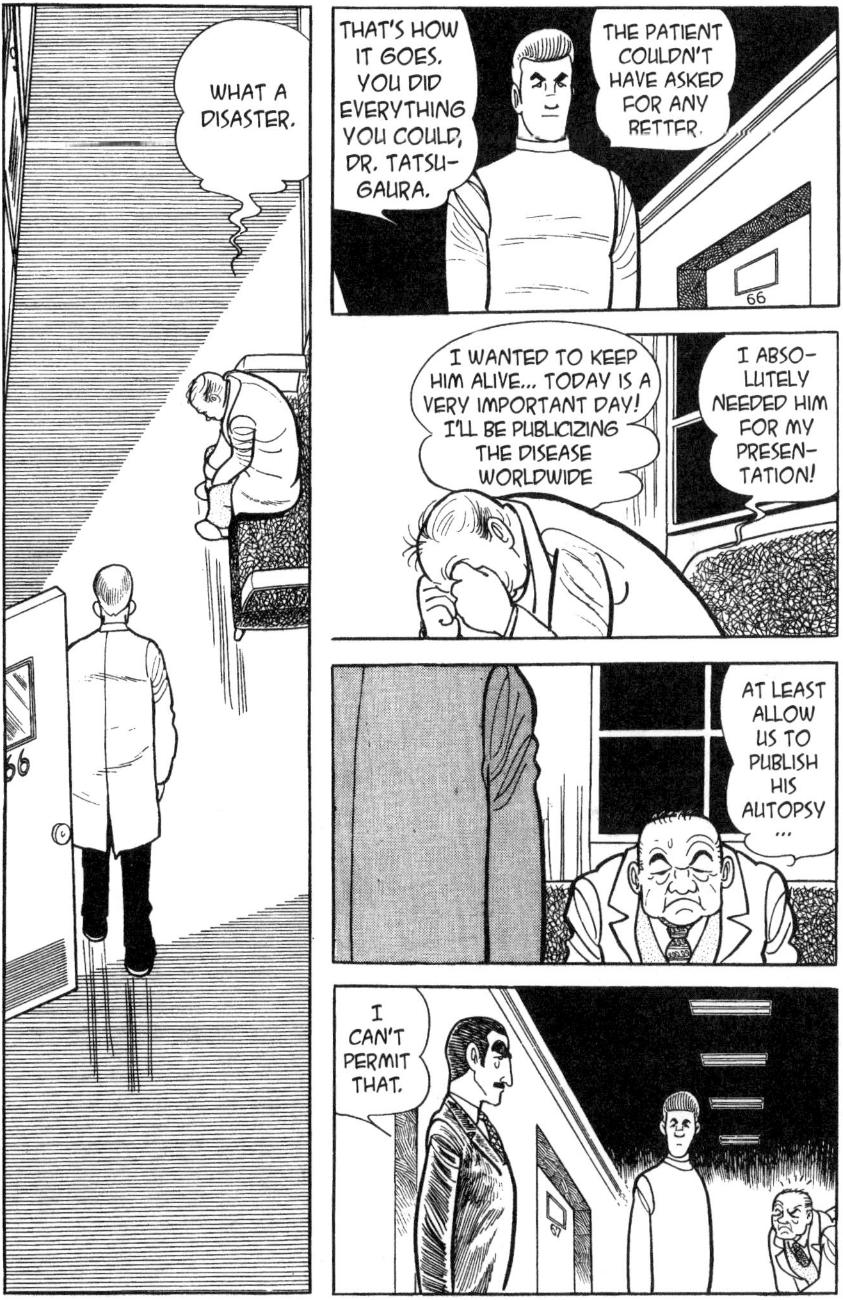
THE PATIENT COULDN'T HAVE ASKED FOR ANY BETTER.
THAT'S HOW IT GOES. YOU DID EVERYTHING YOU COULD, DR. TATSU-GAURA.
WHAT A DISASTER.
I ABSOLUTELY NEEDED HIM FOR MY PRESENTATION!
I WANTED TO KEEP HIM ALIVE... TODAY IS A VERY IMPORTANT DAY! I'LL BE PUBLICIZING THE DISEASE WORLDWIDE
AT LEAST ALLOW US TO PUBLISH HIS AUTOPSY ...
I CAN'T PERMIT THAT.
66
66
67

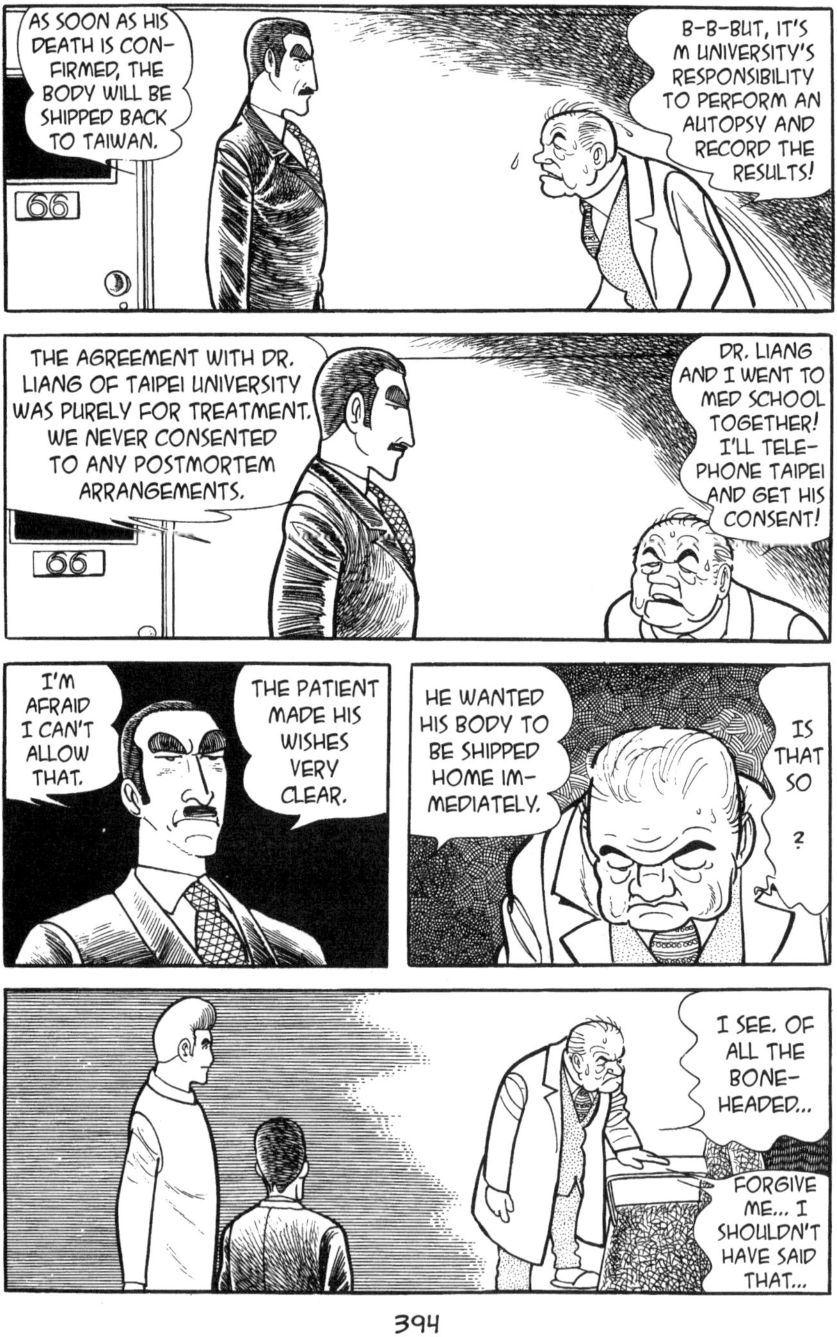

AS SOON AS HIS DEATH IS CONFIRMED, THE BODY WILL BE SHIPPED BACK TO TAIWAN.
B-B-BUT, IT'S M UNIVERSITY'S RESPONSIBILITY TO PERFORM AN AUTOPSY AND RECORD THE RESULTS!
66
THE AGREEMENT WITH DR. LIANG OF TAIPEI UNIVERSITY WAS PURELY FOR TREATMENT. WE NEVER CONSENTED TO ANY POSTMORTEM ARRANGEMENTS.
DR. LIANG AND I WENT TO MED SCHOOL TOGETHER! I'LL TELEPHONE TAIPEI AND GET HIS CONSENT!
66
I'M AFRAID I CAN'T ALLOW THAT.
THE PATIENT MADE HIS WISHES VERY CLEAR.
HE WANTED HIS BODY TO BE SHIPPED HOME IMMEDIATELY.
IS THAT SO ?
I SEE. OF ALL THE BONEHEADED...
FORGIVE ME... I SHOULDN'T HAVE SAID THAT...

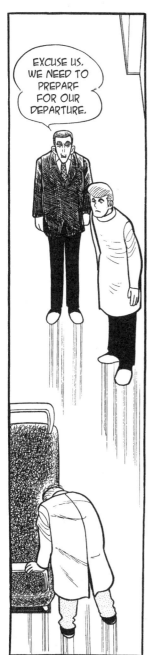

EXCUSE US. WE NEED TO PREPARE FOR OUR DEPARTURE.

CRIPES! MY PRESENTATION TODAY REVOLVES AROUND HAVING A PATIENT TO EXHIBIT! WHAT WILL I DO? WHAT WILL I...

YOSHINAGA? I'M IN A REAL JAM! THE PATIENT IN ROOM 66 IS DEAD! THERE ARE ONLY 9 HOURS LEFT UNTIL MY PRESEN- TATION! IS THERE TIME FOR A REWRITE?

THIS IS TERRIBLE! WHAT A PICKLE! OH, MY...

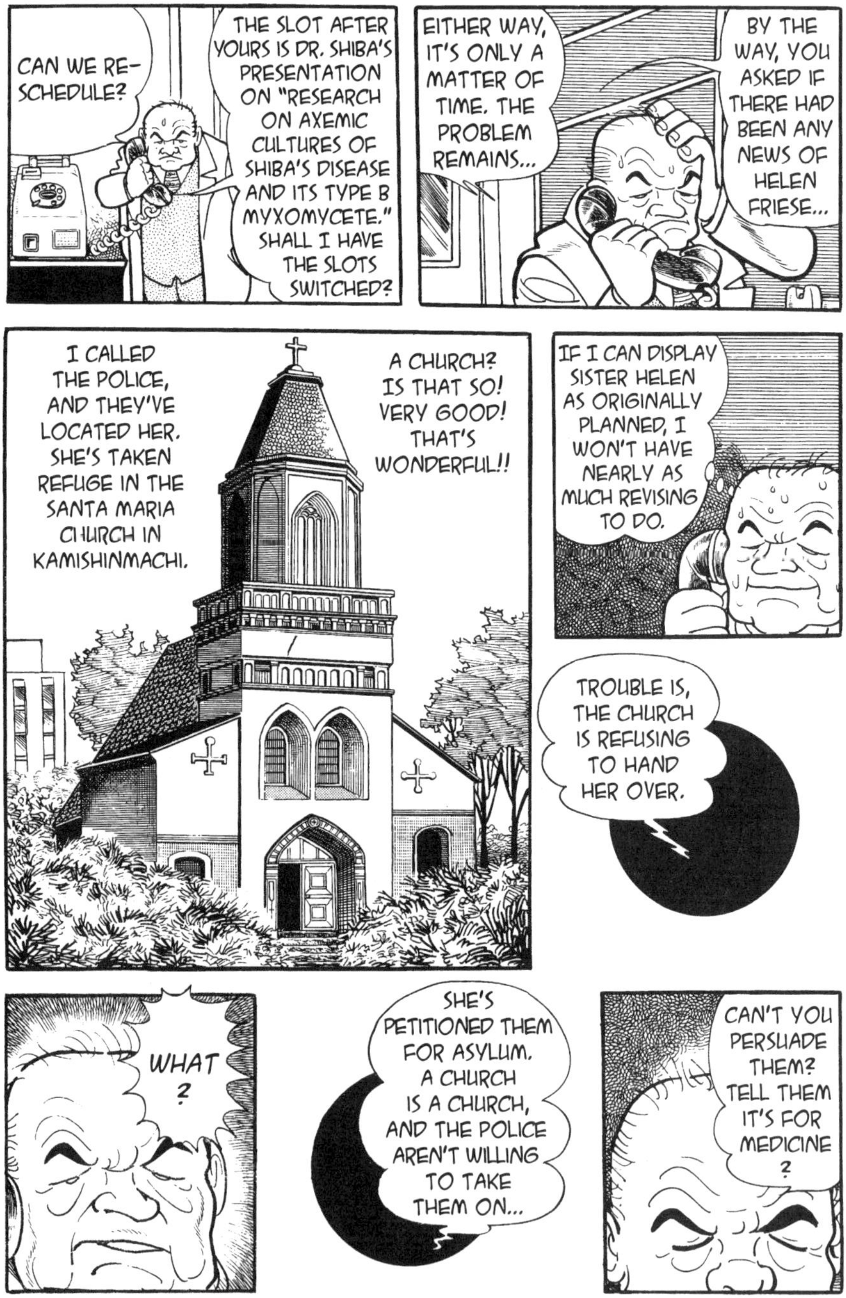
CAN WE RE-SCHEDULE?
THE SLOT AFTER YOURS IS DR. SHIBA'S PRESENTATION ON "RESEARCH ON AXEMIC CULTURES OF SHIBA'S DISEASE AND ITS TYPE B MYXOMYCETE." SHALL I HAVE THE SLOTS SWITCHED?
EITHER WAY, IT'S ONLY A MATTER OF TIME. THE PROBLEM REMAINS...
BY THE WAY, YOU ASKED IF THERE HAD BEEN ANY NEWS OF HELEN FRIESE...
I CALLED THE POLICE, AND THEY'VE LOCATED HER. SHE'S TAKEN REFUGE IN THE SANTA MARIA CHURCH IN KAMISHINMACHI.
A CHURCH? IS THAT SO! VERY GOOD! THAT'S WONDERFUL!!
IF I CAN DISPLAY SISTER HELEN AS ORIGINALLY PLANNED, I WON'T HAVE NEARLY AS MUCH REVISING TO DO.
TROUBLE IS, THE CHURCH IS REFUSING TO HAND HER OVER.
WHAT?
SHE'S PETITIONED THEM FOR ASYLUM. A CHURCH IS A CHURCH, AND THE POLICE AREN'T WILLING TO TAKE THEM ON...
CAN'T YOU PERSUADE THEM? TELL THEM IT'S FOR MEDICINE?

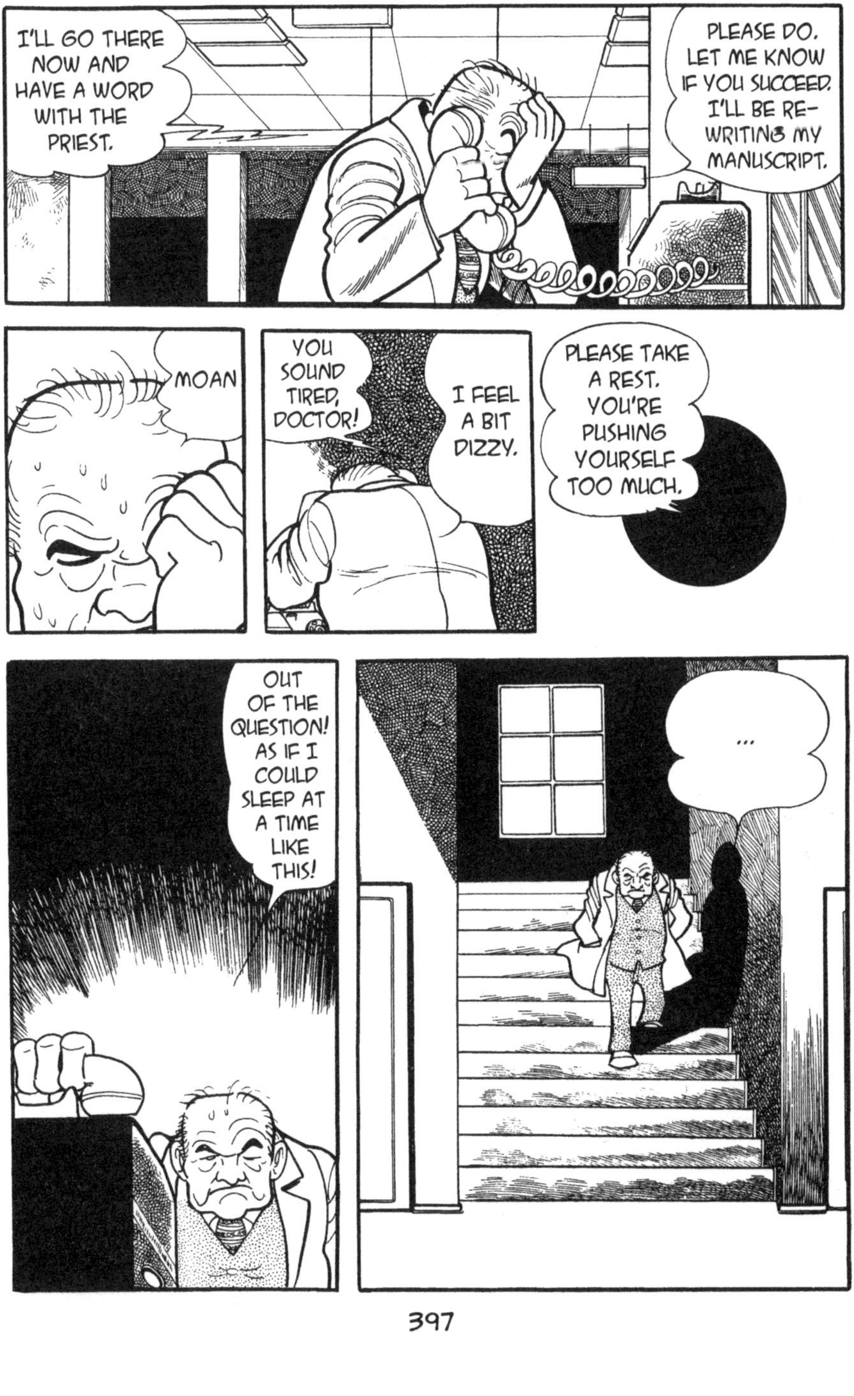
I'LL GO THERE NOW AND HAVE A WORD WITH THE PRIEST.
PLEASE DO. LET ME KNOW IF YOU SUCCEED. I'LL BE RE-WRITING MY MANUSCRIPT.
MOAN
YOU SOUND TIRED, DOCTOR!
I FEEL A BIT DIZZY.
PLEASE TAKE A REST. YOU'RE PUSHING YOURSELF TOO MUCH.
OUT OF THE QUESTION! AS IF I COULD SLEEP AT A TIME LIKE THIS!
...

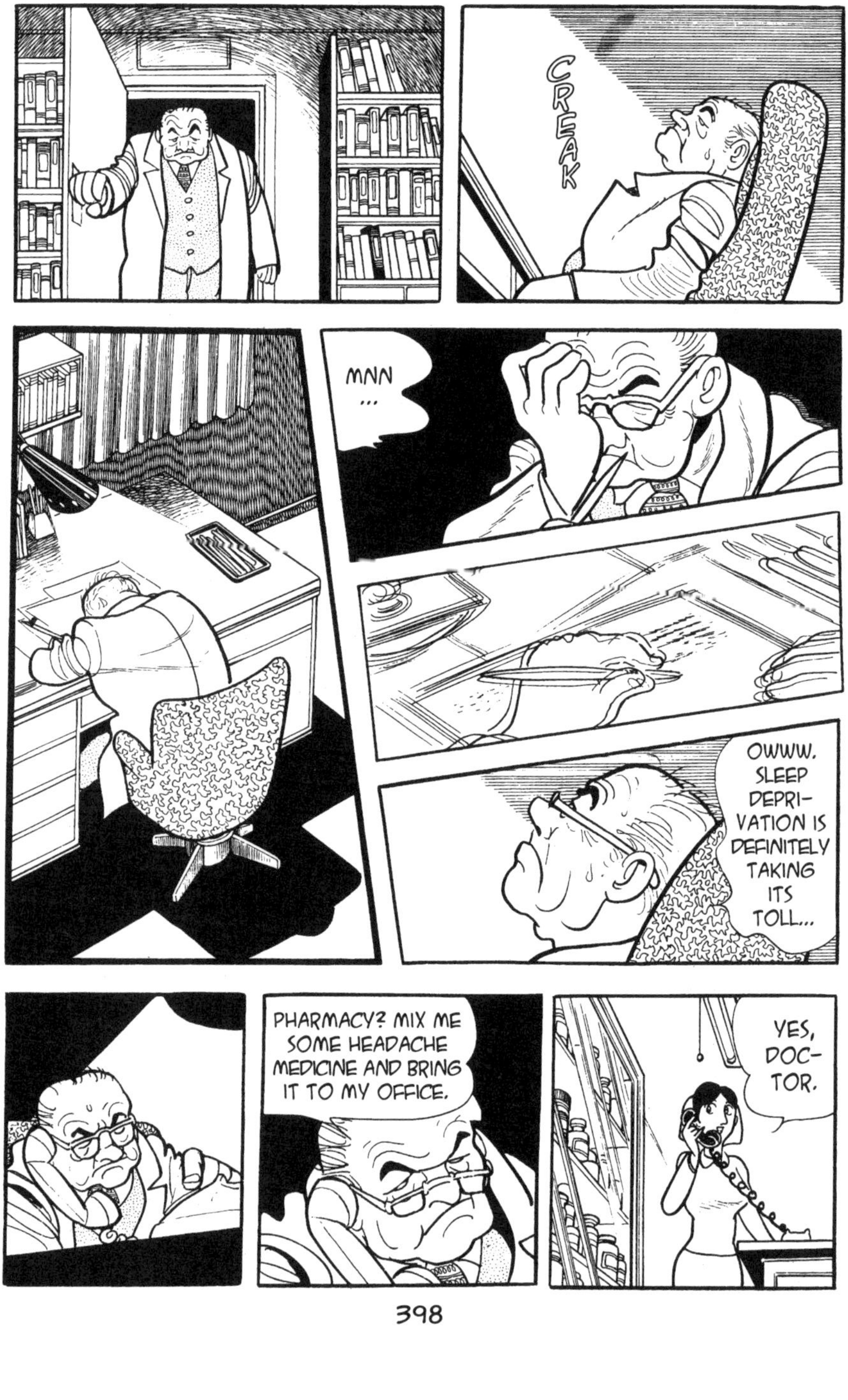
CREAK
MNN ...
OWWW. SLEEP DEPRIVATION IS DEFINITELY TAKING ITS TOLL...
PHARMACY? MIX ME SOME HEADACHE MEDICINE AND BRING IT TO MY OFFICE.
YES, DOCTOR.

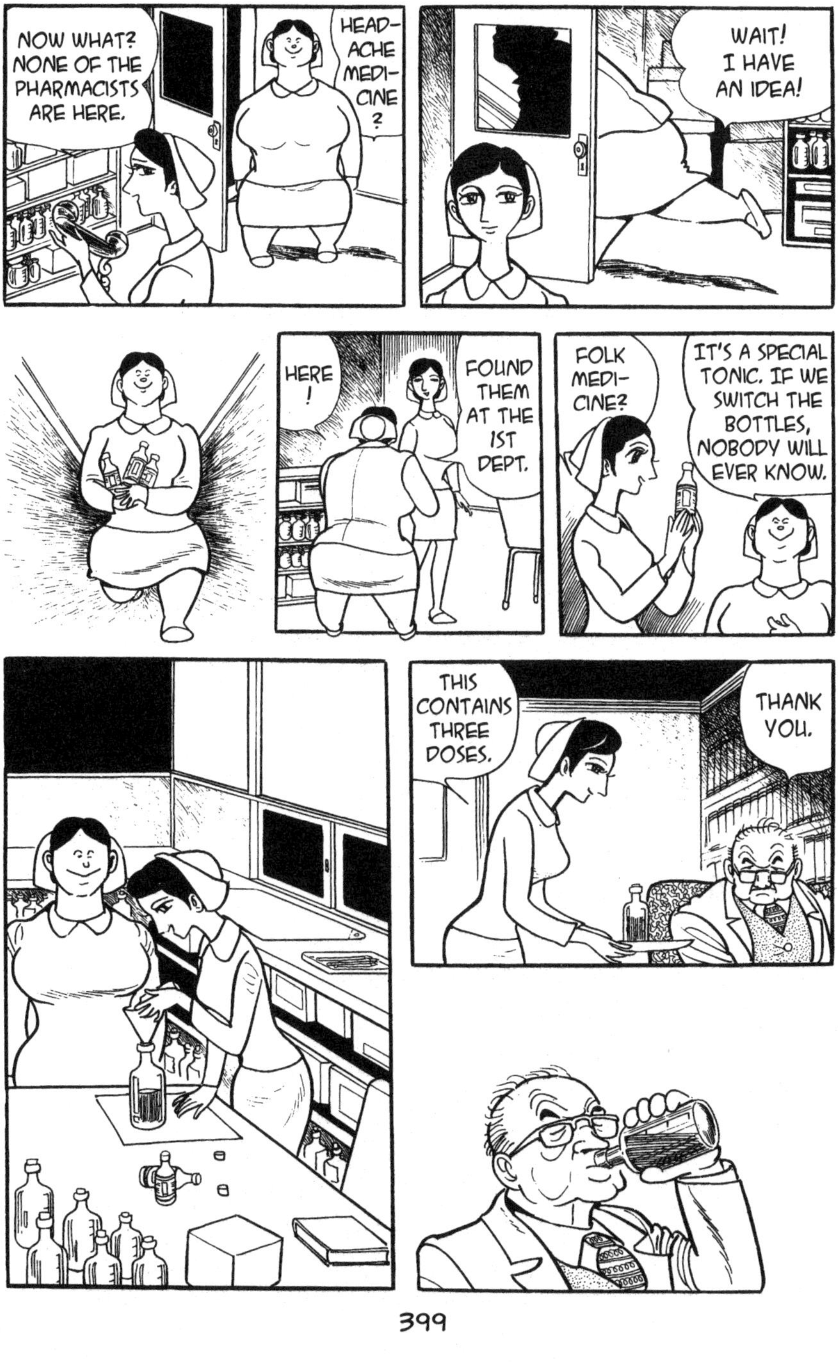
NOW WHAT? NONE OF THE PHARMACISTS ARE HERE.
HEAD-ACHE MEDI-CINE ?
WAIT! I HAVE AN IDEA!
HERE !
FOUND THEM AT THE 1ST DEPT.
FOLK MEDI-CINE?
IT'S A SPECIAL TONIC. IF WE SWITCH THE BOTTLES, NOBODY WILL EVER KNOW.
THIS CONTAINS THREE DOSES.
THANK YOU.

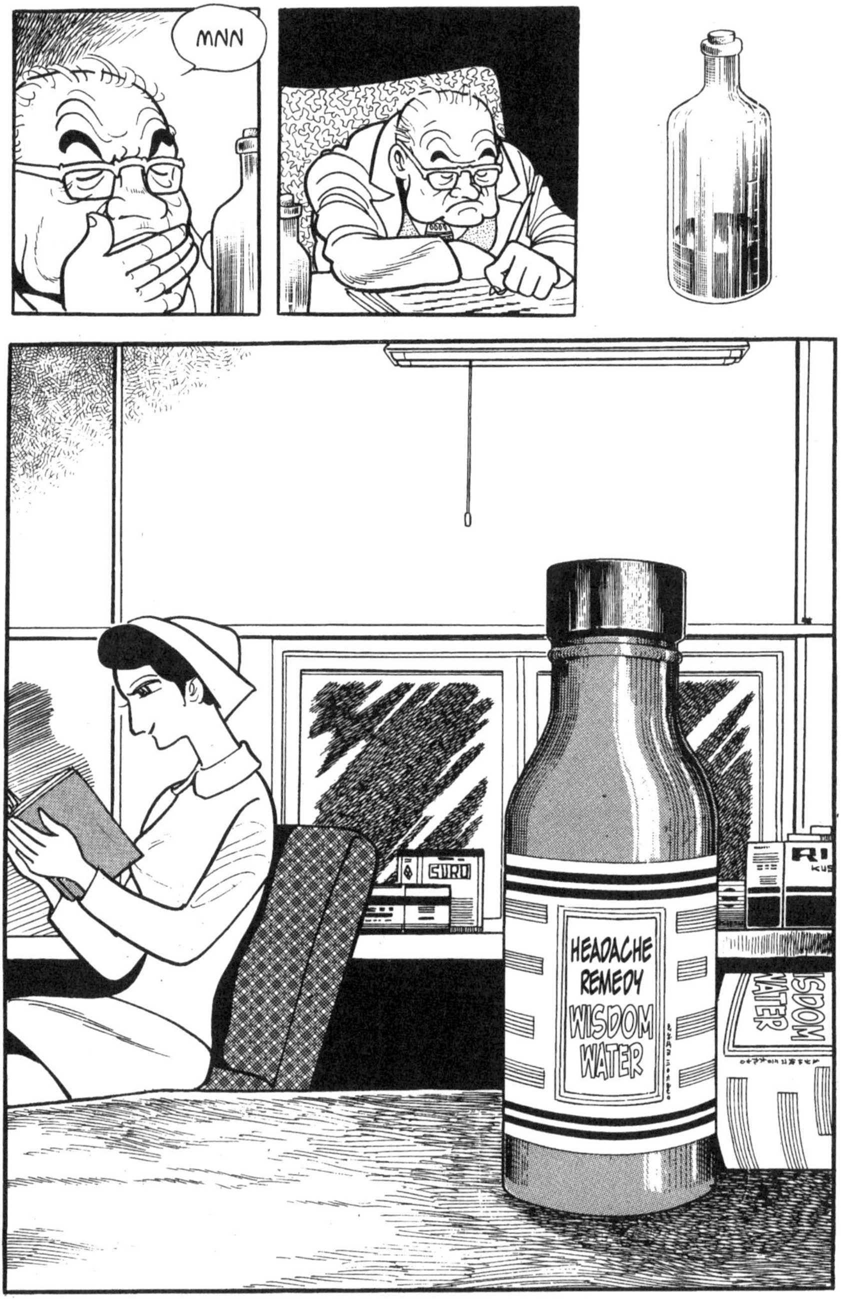
MNN
SURO
HEADACHE REMEDY
WISDOM WATER

CHAPTER 11

HELEN FRIESE

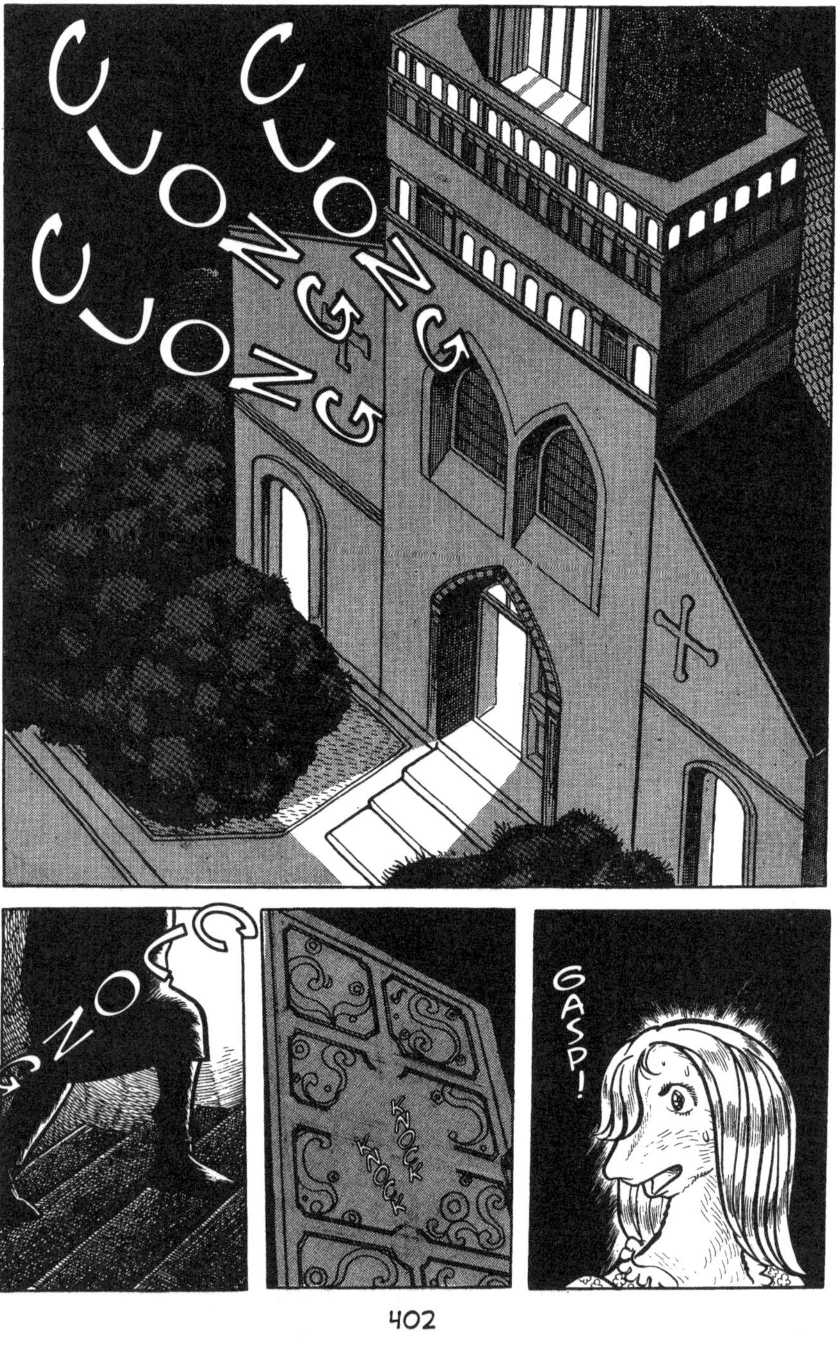
CLONG
CLONG
CLONG
CLONG
KNOCK
KNOCK
GASP!

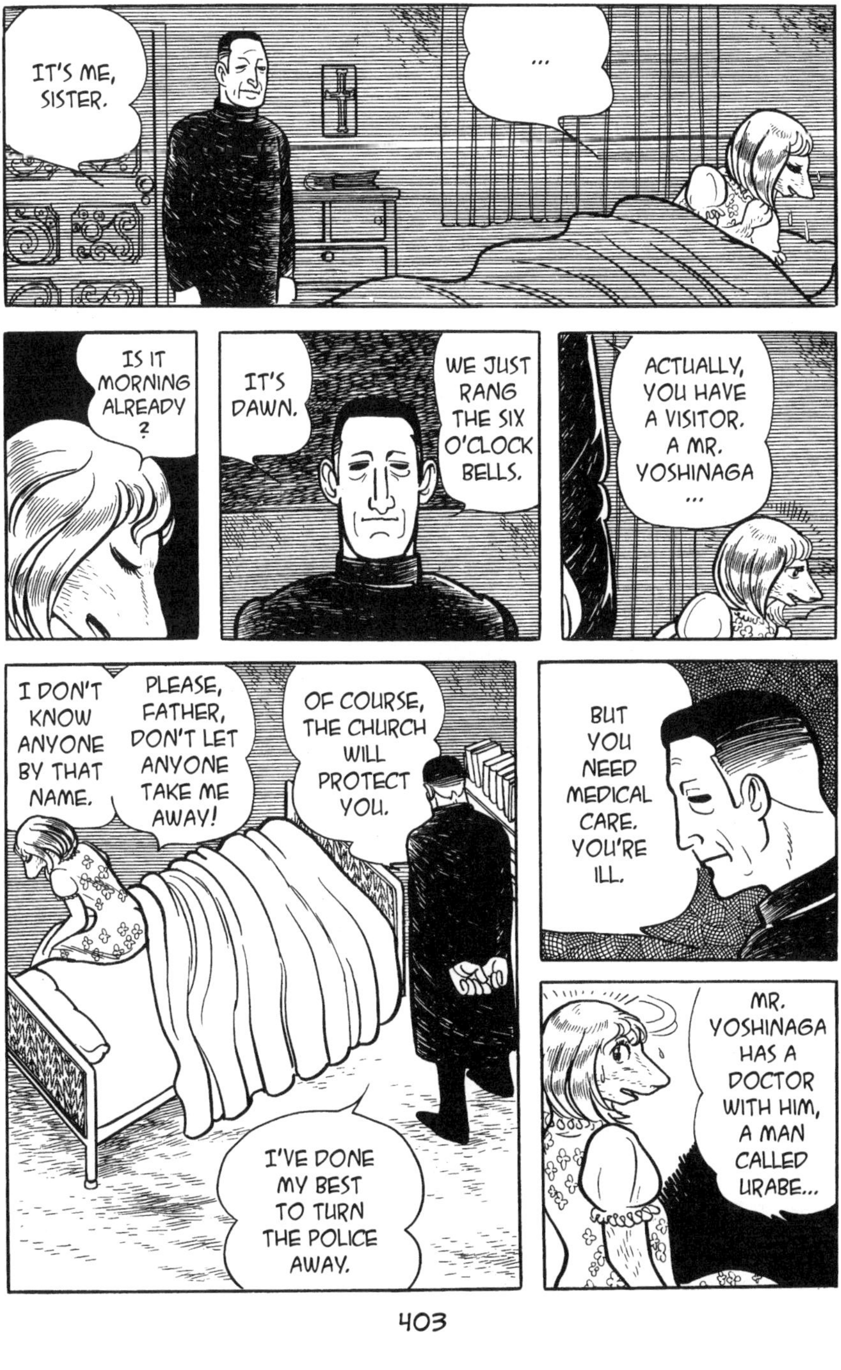
IT'S ME, SISTER.
...
IS IT MORNING ALREADY?
IT'S DAWN.
WE JUST RANG THE SIX O'CLOCK BELLS.
ACTUALLY, YOU HAVE A VISITOR. A MR. YOSHINAGA...
I DON'T KNOW ANYONE BY THAT NAME.
PLEASE, FATHER, DON'T LET ANYONE TAKE ME AWAY!
OF COURSE, THE CHURCH WILL PROTECT YOU.
I'VE DONE MY BEST TO TURN THE POLICE AWAY.
BUT YOU NEED MEDICAL CARE. YOU'RE ILL.
MR. YOSHINAGA HAS A DOCTOR WITH HIM, A MAN CALLED URABE...

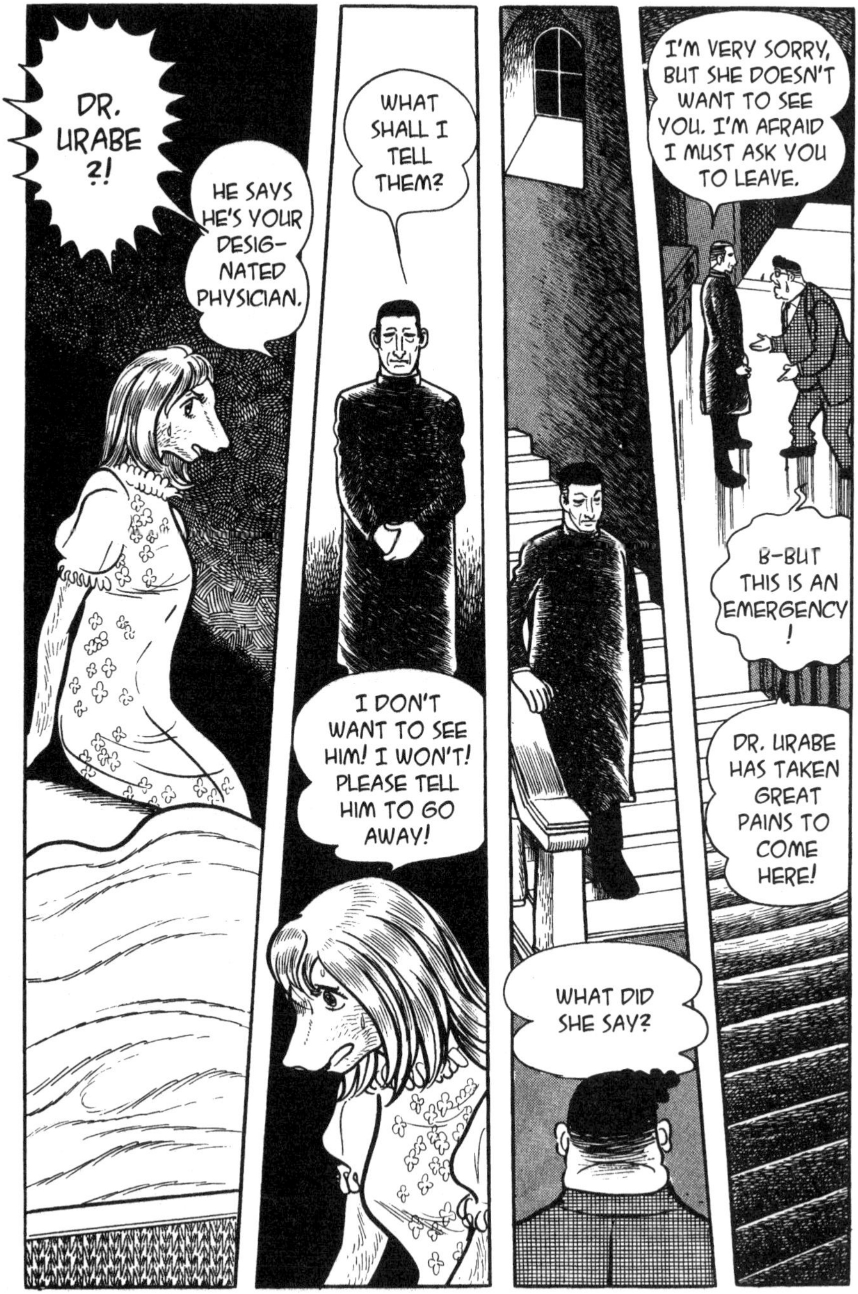
DR. URABE ?!
HE SAYS HE'S YOUR DESIG-NATED PHYSICIAN.
WHAT SHALL I TELL THEM?
I DON'T WANT TO SEE HIM! I WON'T! PLEASE TELL HIM TO GO AWAY!
WHAT DID SHE SAY?
I'M VERY SORRY, BUT SHE DOESN'T WANT TO SEE YOU. I'M AFRAID I MUST ASK YOU TO LEAVE.
B-BUT THIS IS AN EMERGENCY!
DR. URABE HAS TAKEN GREAT PAINS TO COME HERE!

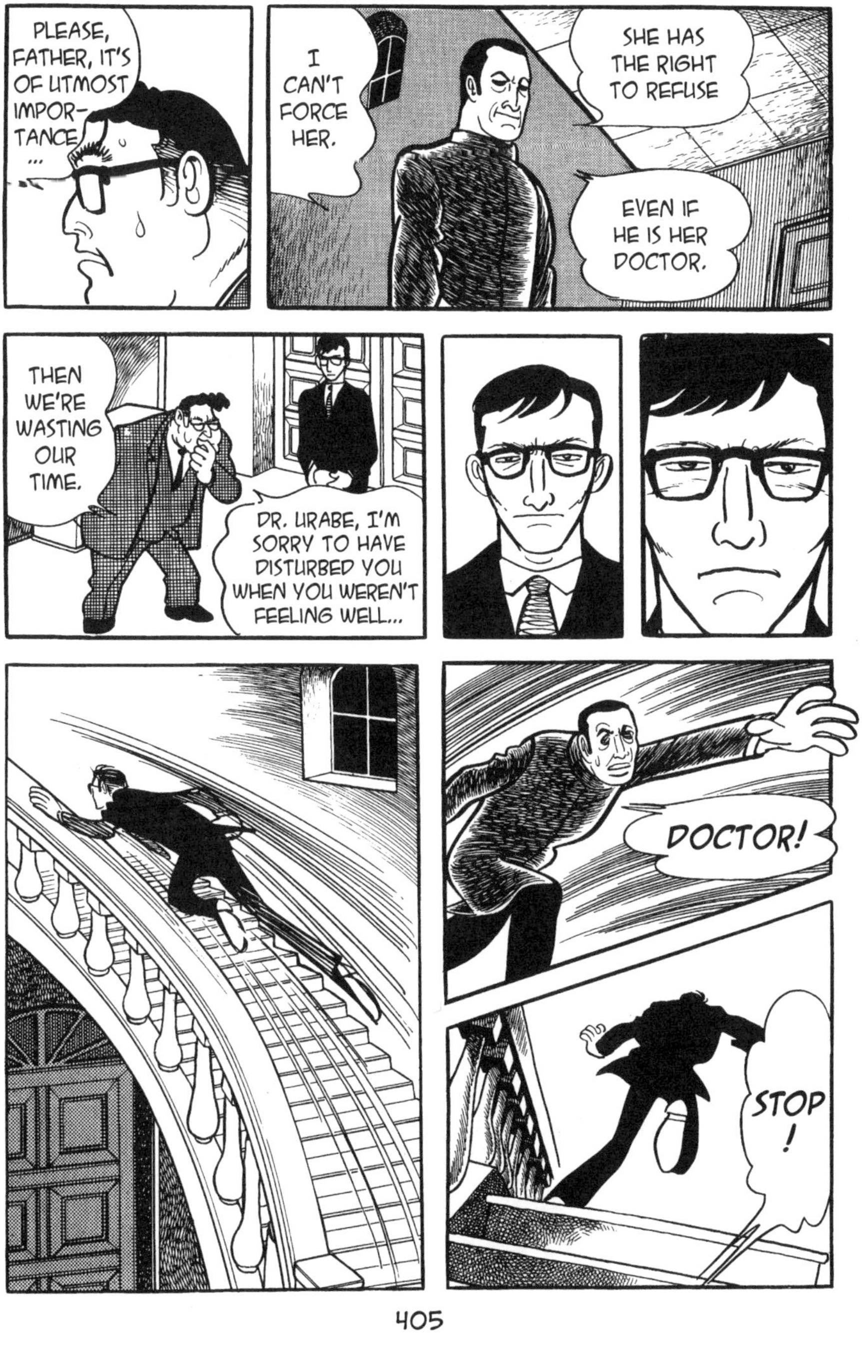
PLEASE, FATHER, IT'S OF UTMOST IMPORTANCE...
I CAN'T FORCE HER.
SHE HAS THE RIGHT TO REFUSE
EVEN IF HE IS HER DOCTOR.
THEN WE'RE WASTING OUR TIME.
DR. URABE, I'M SORRY TO HAVE DISTURBED YOU WHEN YOU WEREN'T FEELING WELL...
DOCTOR!
STOP!

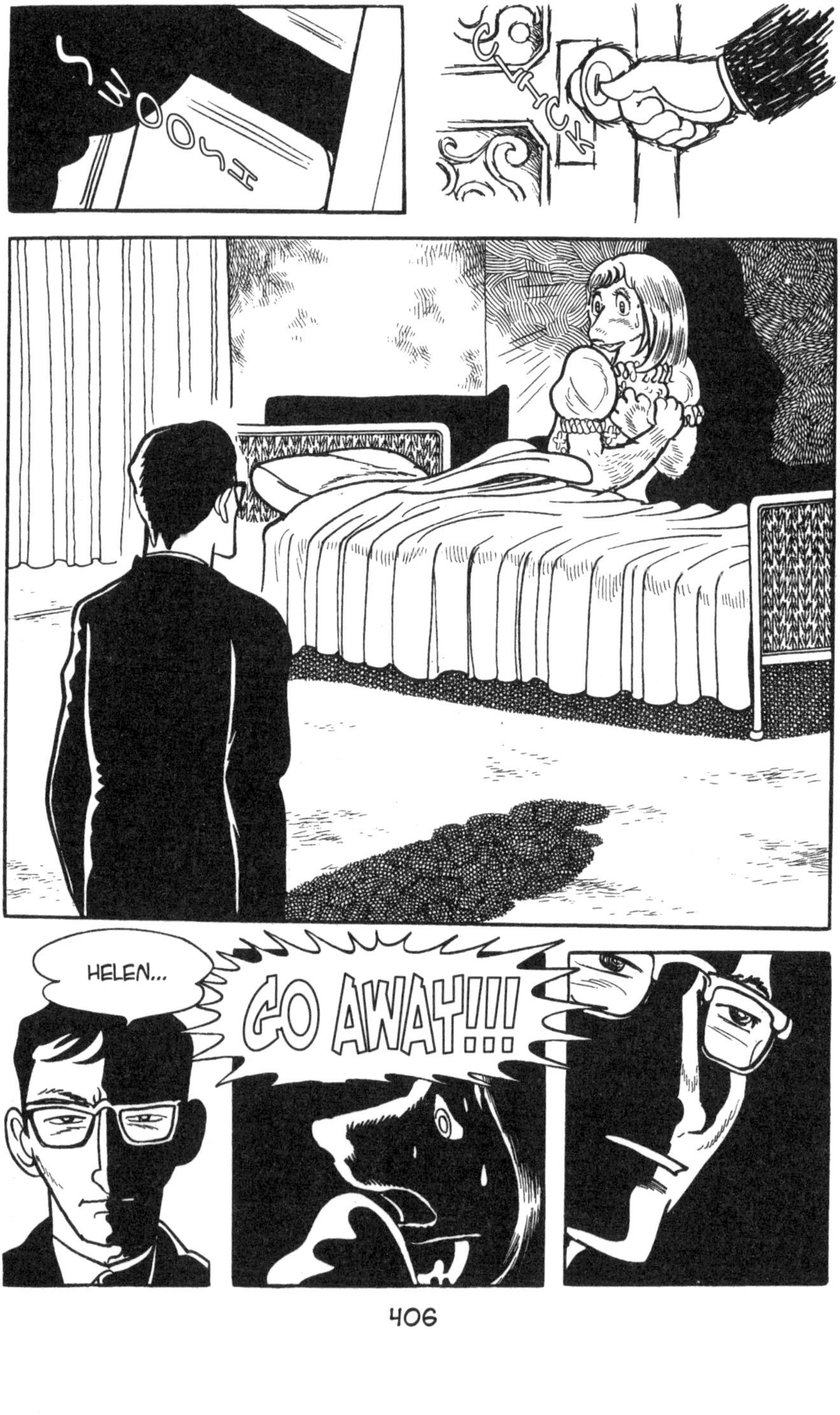
SWOOSH
CLICK
HELEN...
GO AWAY!!!

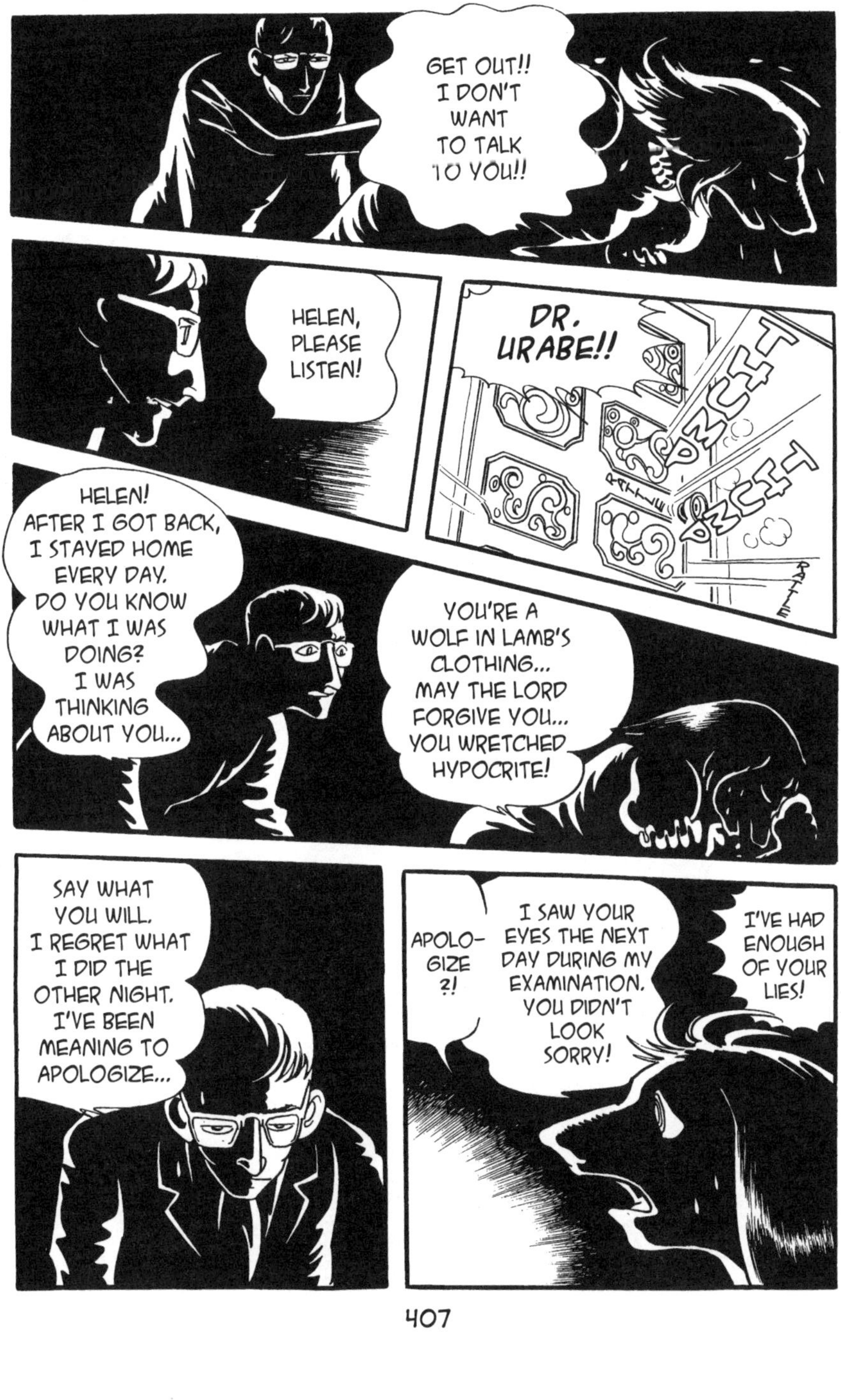
GET OUT!! I DON'T WANT TO TALK TO YOU!!
HELEN, PLEASE LISTEN!
DR. URABE!!
RATTLE
RATTLE
HELEN! AFTER I GOT BACK, I STAYED HOME EVERY DAY. DO YOU KNOW WHAT I WAS DOING? I WAS THINKING ABOUT YOU...
YOU'RE A WOLF IN LAMB'S CLOTHING... MAY THE LORD FORGIVE YOU... YOU WRETCHED HYPOCRITE!
SAY WHAT YOU WILL. I REGRET WHAT I DID THE OTHER NIGHT. I'VE BEEN MEANING TO APOLOGIZE...
APOLO-GIZE ?!
I SAW YOUR EYES THE NEXT DAY DURING MY EXAMINATION. YOU DIDN'T LOOK SORRY!
I'VE HAD ENOUGH OF YOUR LIES!

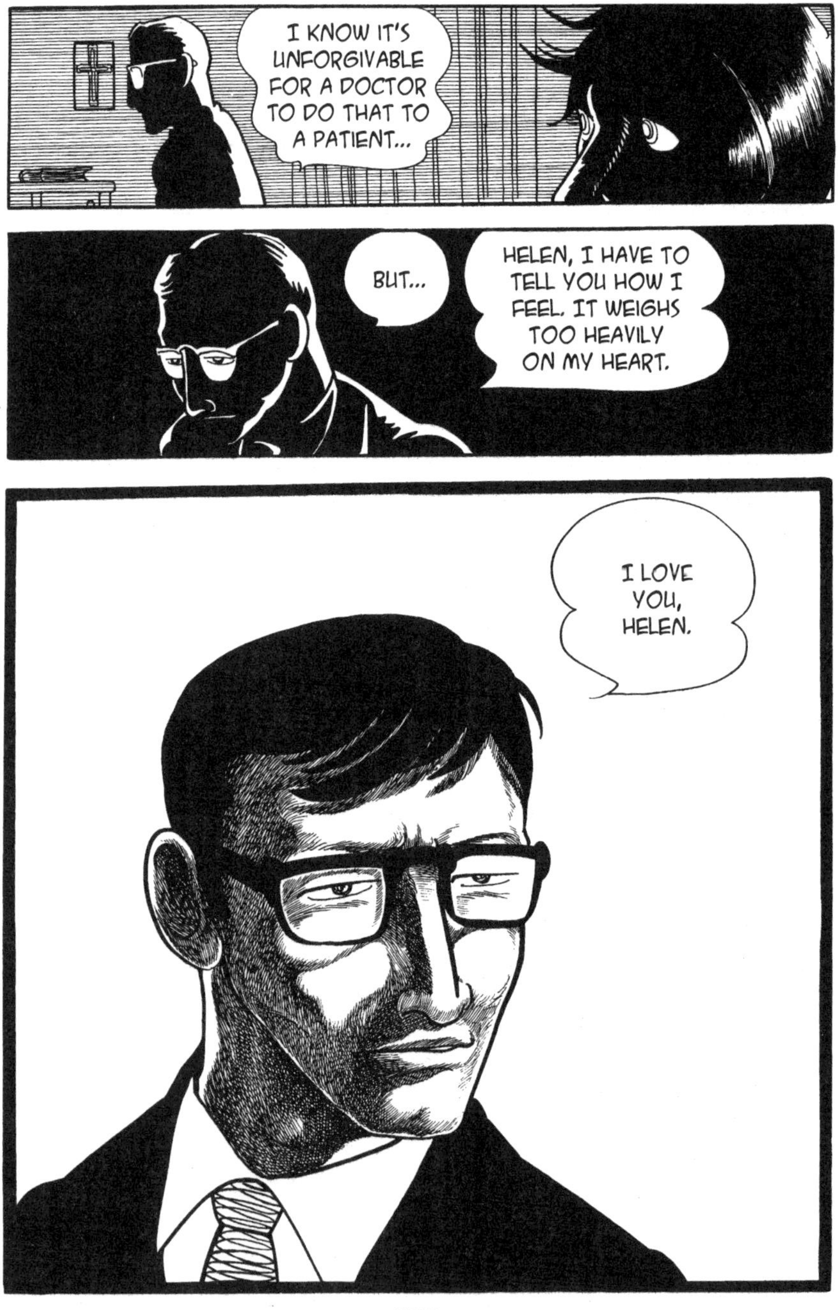
I KNOW IT'S UNFORGIVABLE FOR A DOCTOR TO DO THAT TO A PATIENT...
BUT...
HELEN, I HAVE TO TELL YOU HOW I FEEL. IT WEIGHS TOO HEAVILY ON MY HEART.
I LOVE YOU, HELEN.

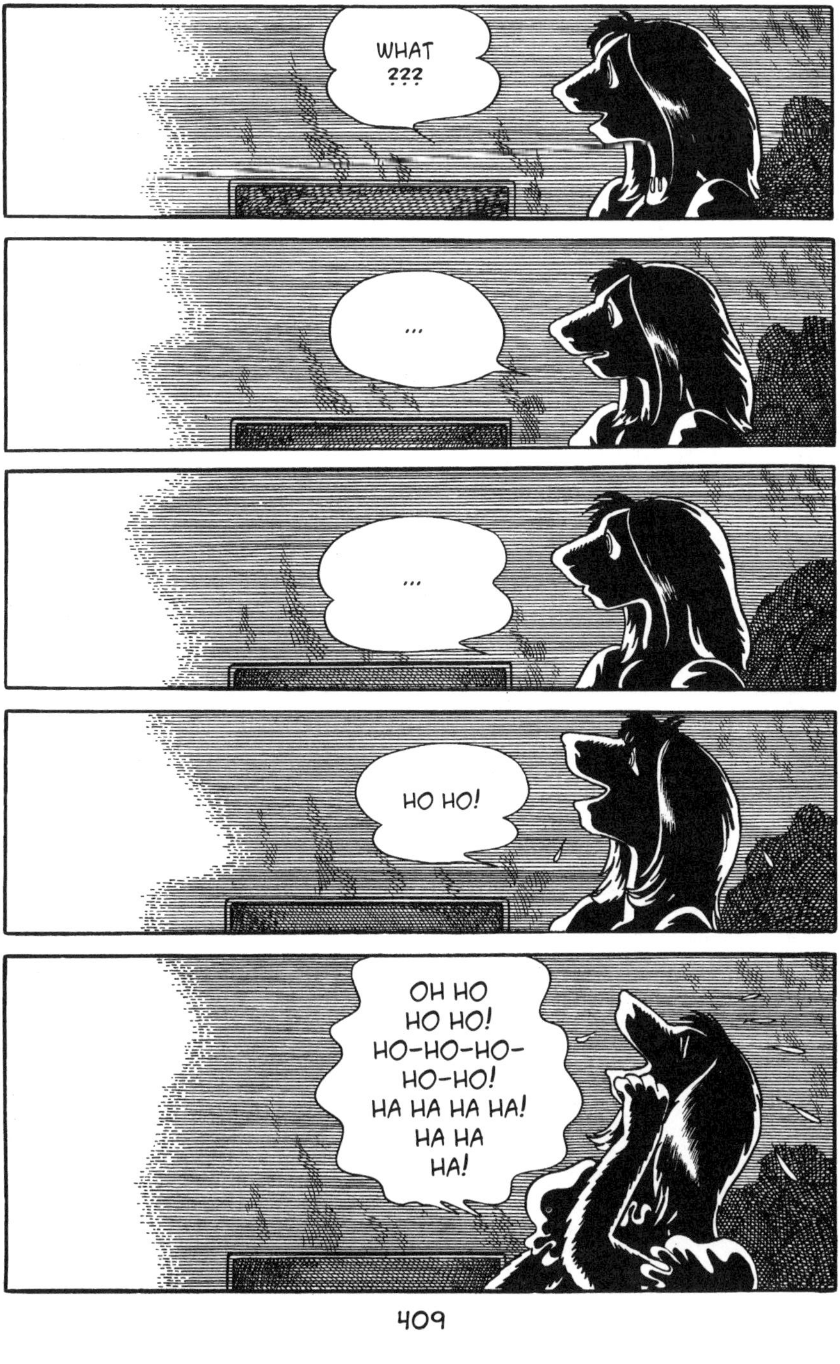
WHAT ???
...
...
HO HO!
OH HO HO HO! HO-HO-HO-HO-HO! HA HA HA HA! HA HA HA!

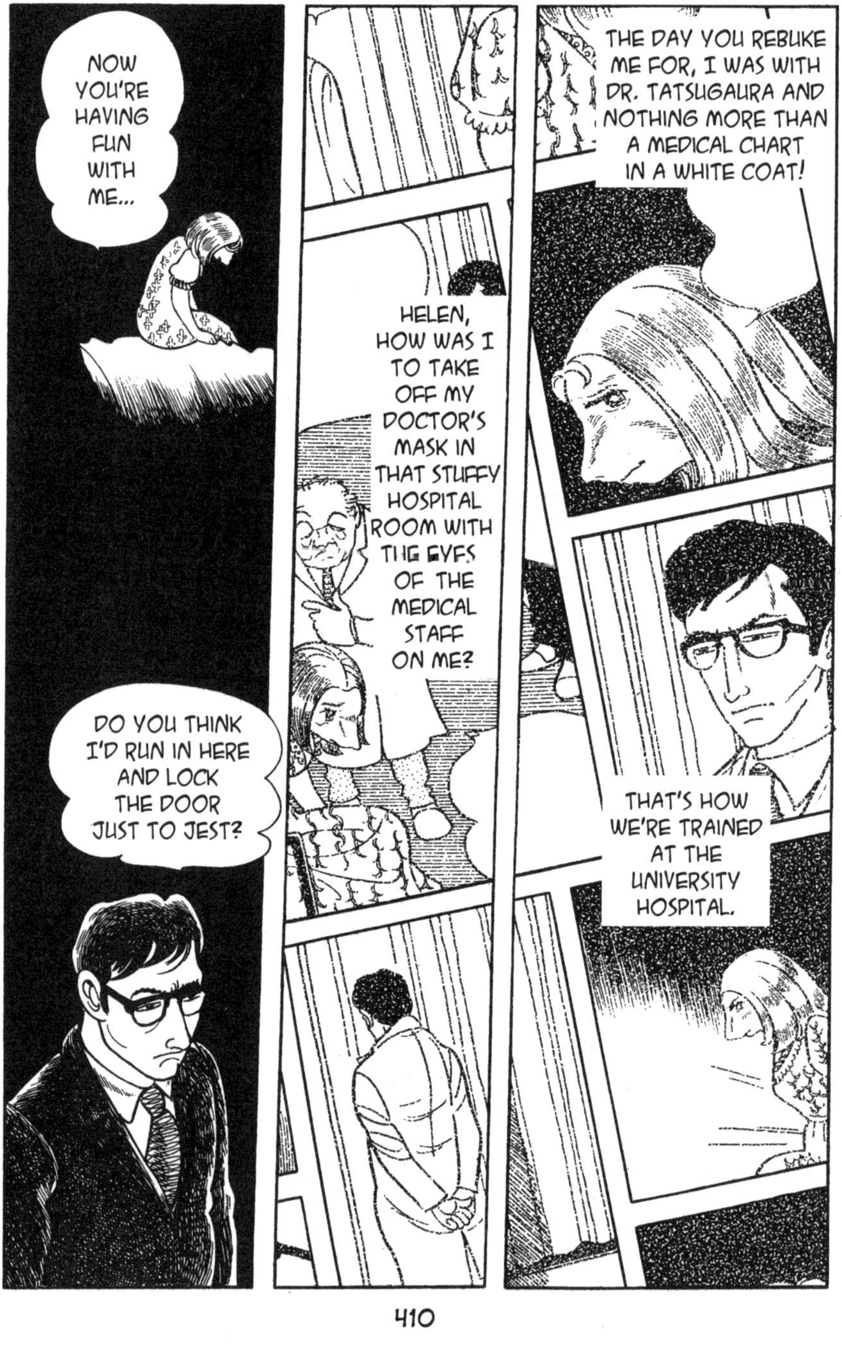
NOW YOU'RE HAVING FUN WITH ME...
DO YOU THINK I'D RUN IN HERE AND LOCK THE DOOR JUST TO JEST?
HELEN, HOW WAS I TO TAKE OFF MY DOCTOR'S MASK IN THAT STUFFY HOSPITAL ROOM WITH THE EYES OF THE MEDICAL STAFF ON ME?
THE DAY YOU REBUKE ME FOR, I WAS WITH DR. TATSUGAURA AND NOTHING MORE THAN A MEDICAL CHART IN A WHITE COAT!
THAT'S HOW WE'RE TRAINED AT THE UNIVERSITY HOSPITAL.

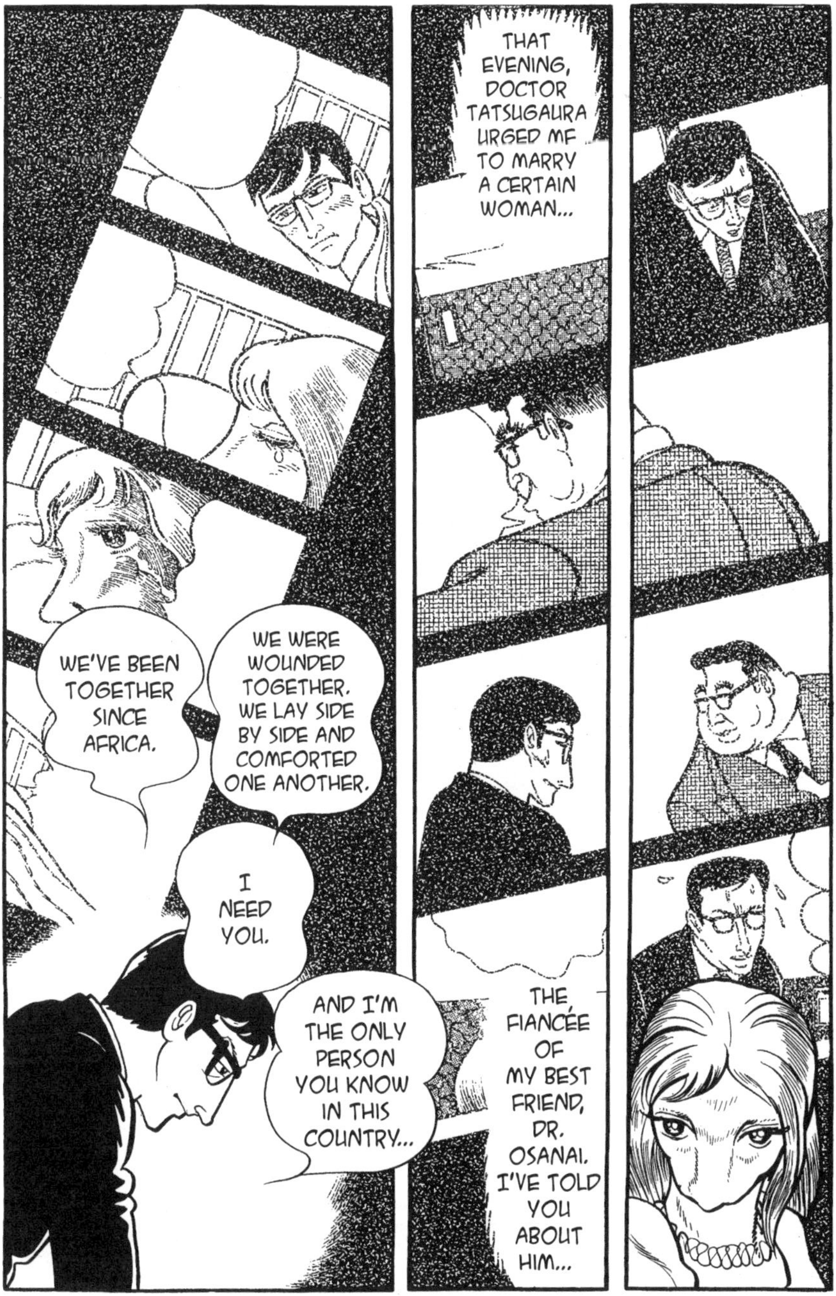

WE'VE BEEN TOGETHER SINCE AFRICA.
WE WERE WOUNDED TOGETHER. WE LAY SIDE BY SIDE AND COMFORTED ONE ANOTHER.
I NEED YOU.
AND I'M THE ONLY PERSON YOU KNOW IN THIS COUNTRY...
THAT EVENING, DOCTOR TATSUGAURA URGED ME TO MARRY A CERTAIN WOMAN...
THE FIANCÉE OF MY BEST FRIEND, DR. OSANAI. I'VE TOLD YOU ABOUT HIM...

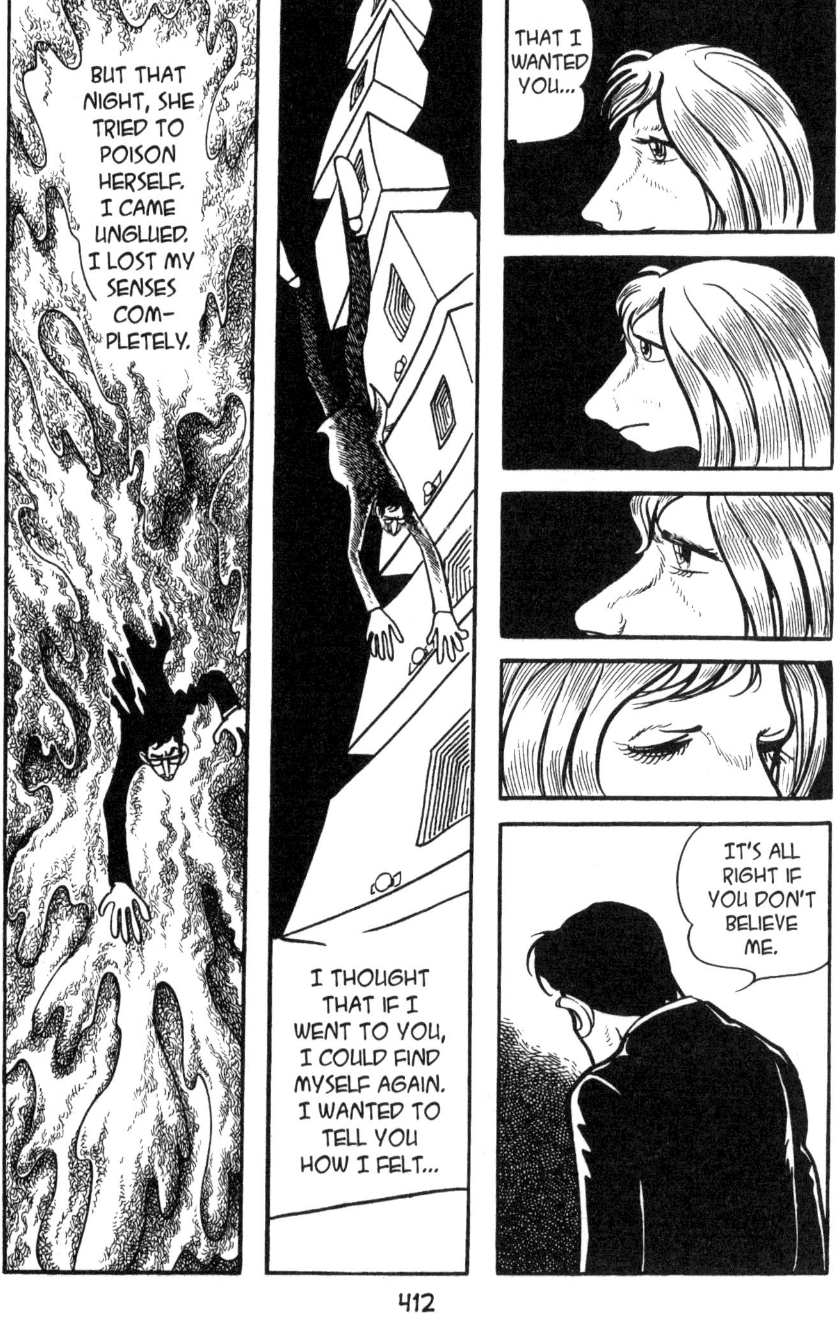
BUT THAT NIGHT, SHE TRIED TO POISON HERSELF. I CAME UNGLUED. I LOST MY SENSES COM-PLETELY.
I THOUGHT THAT IF I WENT TO YOU, I COULD FIND MYSELF AGAIN. I WANTED TO TELL YOU HOW I FELT...
THAT I WANTED YOU...
IT'S ALL RIGHT IF YOU DON'T BELIEVE ME.

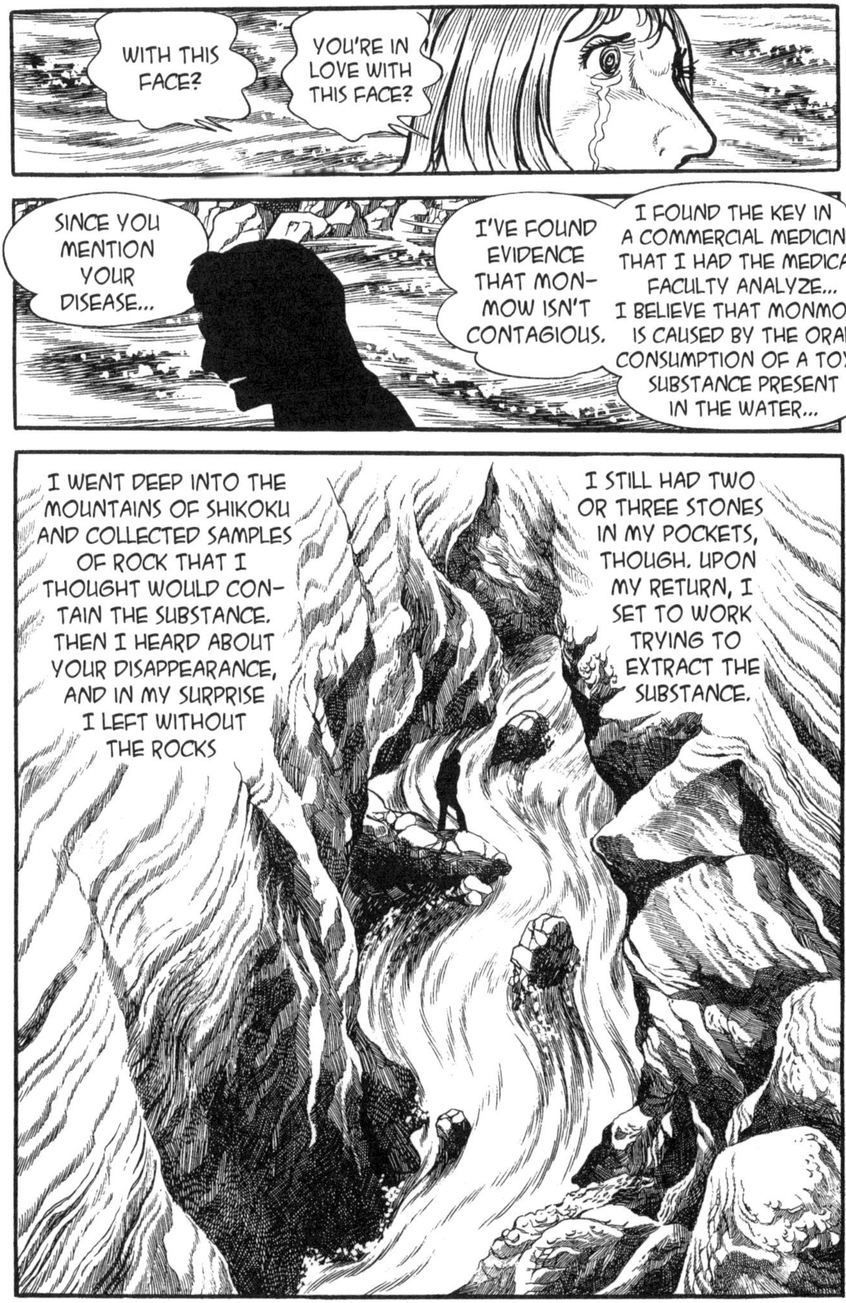
WITH THIS FACE?
YOU'RE IN LOVE WITH THIS FACE?
SINCE YOU MENTION YOUR DISEASE...
I'VE FOUND EVIDENCE THAT MON-MOW ISN'T CONTAGIOUS.
I FOUND THE KEY IN A COMMERCIAL MEDICINE THAT I HAD THE MEDICAL FACULTY ANALYZE... I BELIEVE THAT MONMOW IS CAUSED BY THE ORAL CONSUMPTION OF A TOXIC SUBSTANCE PRESENT IN THE WATER...
I WENT DEEP INTO THE MOUNTAINS OF SHIKOKU AND COLLECTED SAMPLES OF ROCK THAT I THOUGHT WOULD CON-TAIN THE SUBSTANCE. THEN I HEARD ABOUT YOUR DISAPPEARANCE, AND IN MY SURPRISE I LEFT WITHOUT THE ROCKS
I STILL HAD TWO OR THREE STONES IN MY POCKETS, THOUGH. UPON MY RETURN, I SET TO WORK TRYING TO EXTRACT THE SUBSTANCE.

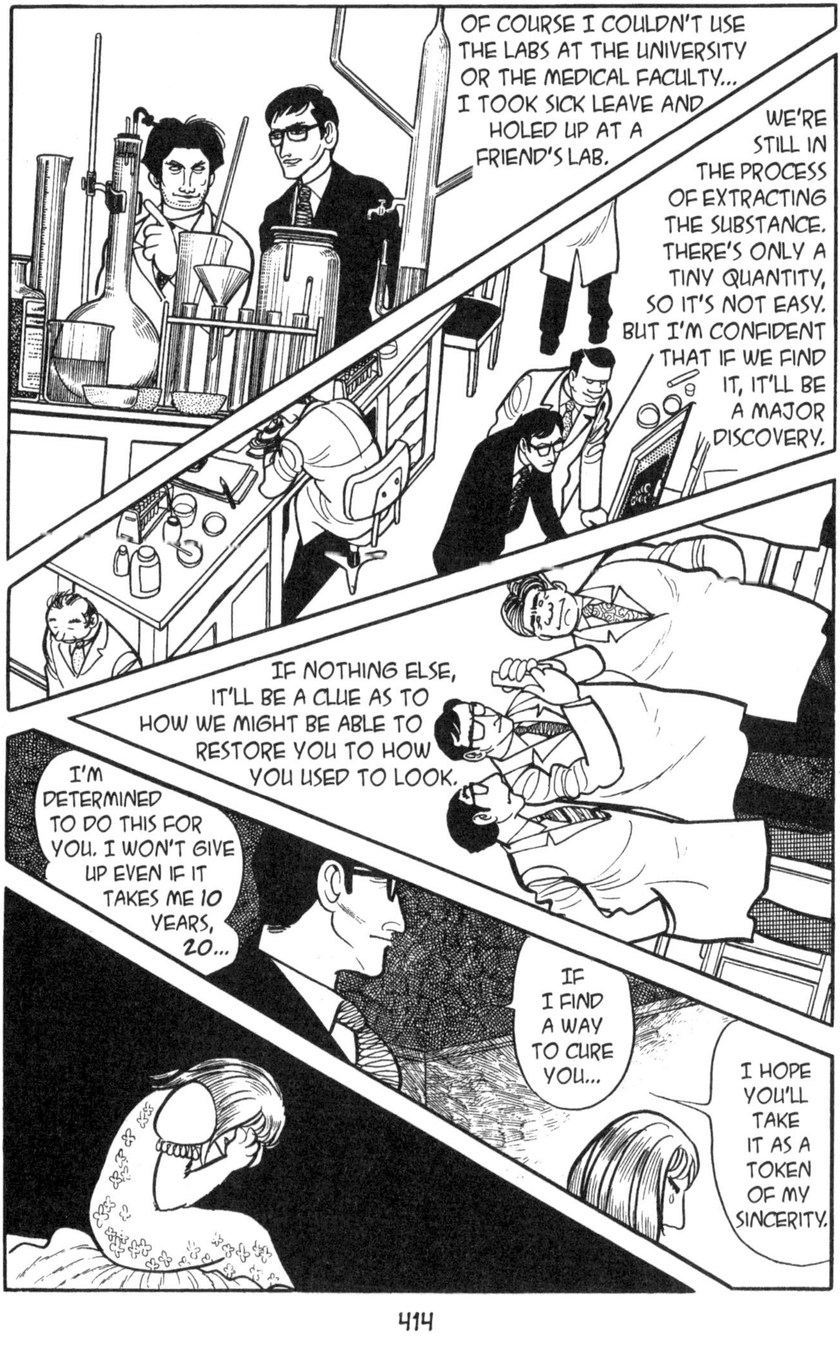
OF COURSE I COULDN'T USE THE LABS AT THE UNIVERSITY OR THE MEDICAL FACULTY... I TOOK SICK LEAVE AND HOLED UP AT A FRIEND'S LAB.
WE'RE STILL IN THE PROCESS OF EXTRACTING THE SUBSTANCE. THERE'S ONLY A TINY QUANTITY, SO IT'S NOT EASY. BUT I'M CONFIDENT THAT IF WE FIND IT, IT'LL BE A MAJOR DISCOVERY.
IF NOTHING ELSE, IT'LL BE A CLUE AS TO HOW WE MIGHT BE ABLE TO RESTORE YOU TO HOW YOU USED TO LOOK.
I'M DETERMINED TO DO THIS FOR YOU. I WON'T GIVE UP EVEN IF IT TAKES ME 10 YEARS, 20...
IF I FIND A WAY TO CURE YOU...
I HOPE YOU'LL TAKE IT AS A TOKEN OF MY SINCERITY.

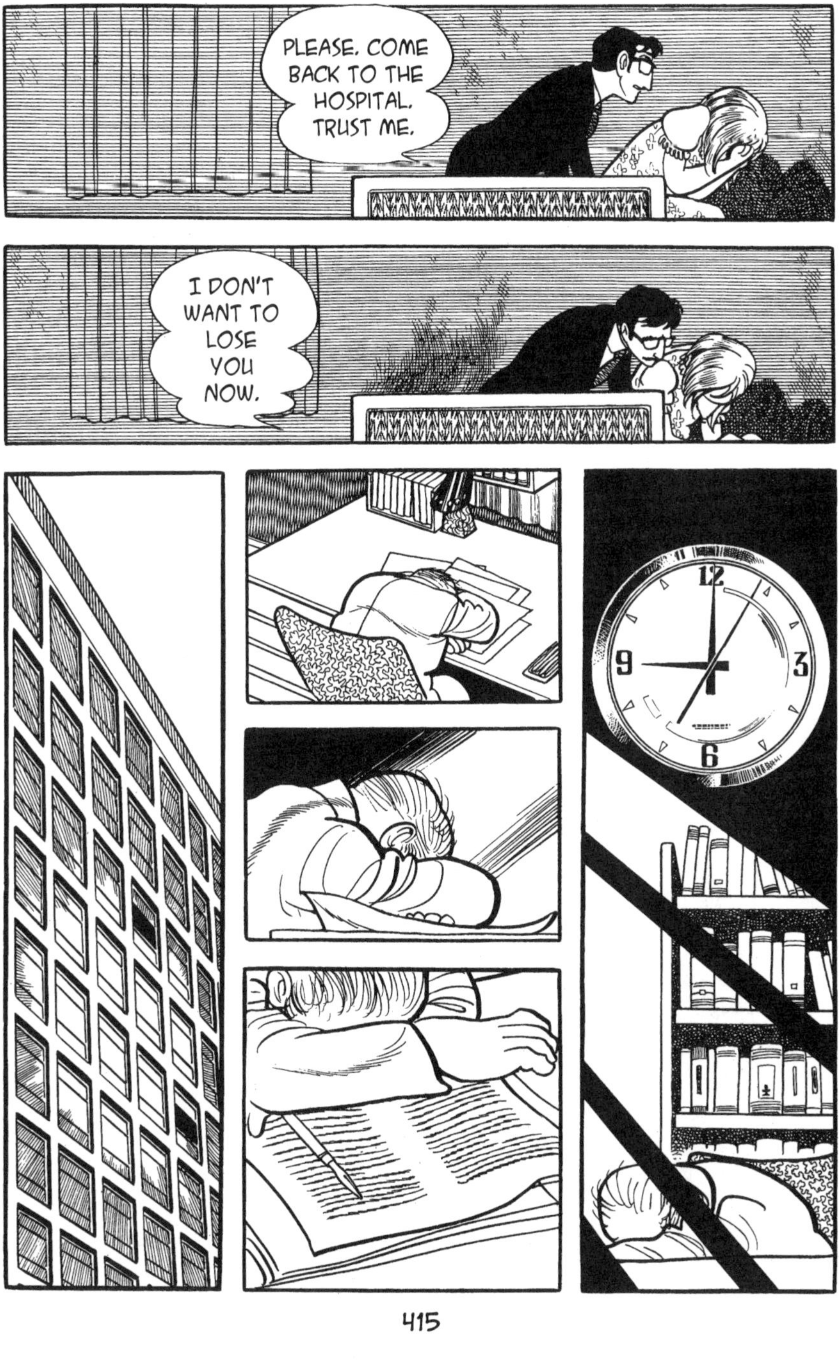
PLEASE. COME BACK TO THE HOSPITAL. TRUST ME.
I DON'T WANT TO LOSE YOU NOW.

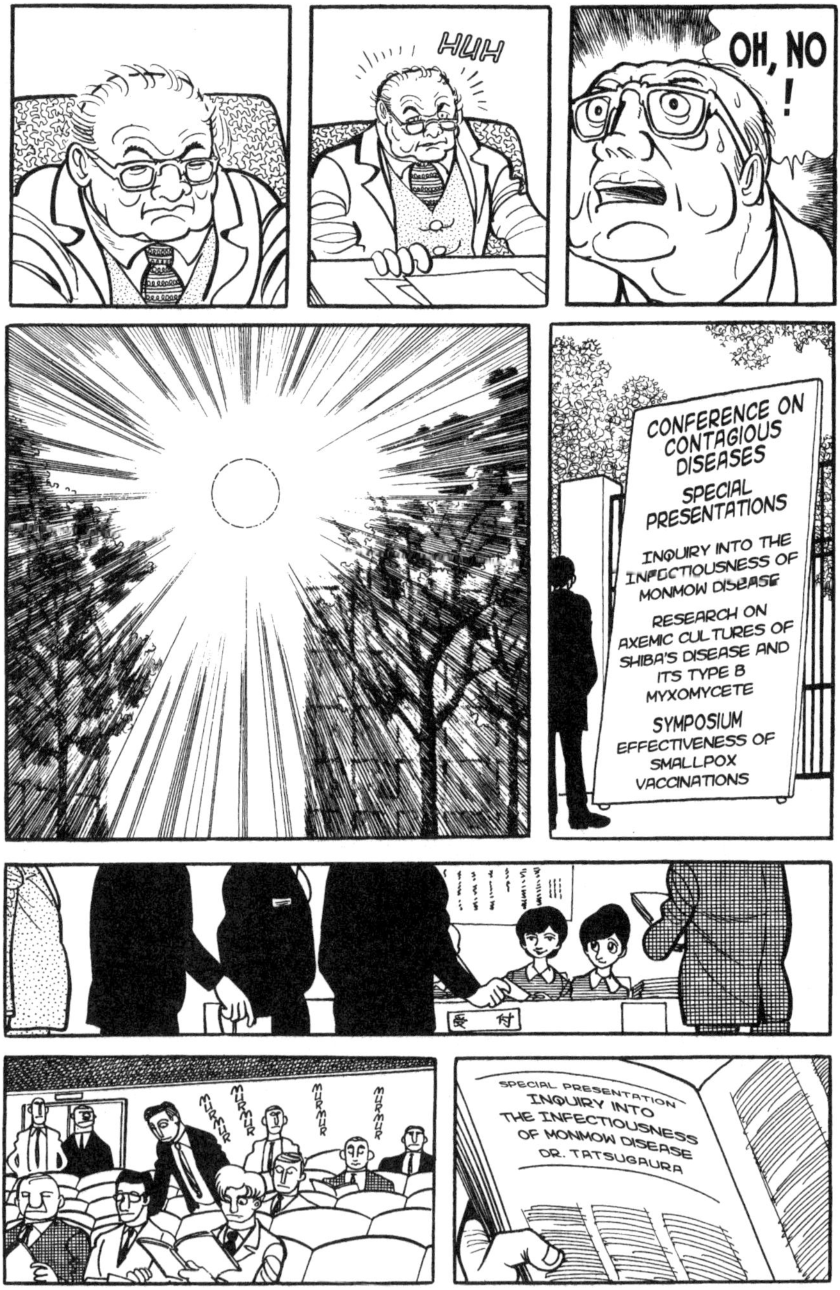
HUH
OH, NO
!
CONFERENCE ON CONTAGIOUS DISEASES
SPECIAL PRESENTATIONS
INQUIRY INTO THE INFECTIOUSNESS OF MONMOW DISEASE
RESEARCH ON AXEMIC CULTURES OF SHIBA'S DISEASE AND ITS TYPE B MYXOMYCETE
SYMPOSIUM
EFFECTIVENESS OF SMALLPOX VACCINATIONS
MURMUR
MURMUR
MURMUR
MURMUR
SPECIAL PRESENTATION
INQUIRY INTO THE INFECTIOUSNESS OF MONMOW DISEASE
DR. TATSUGAURA

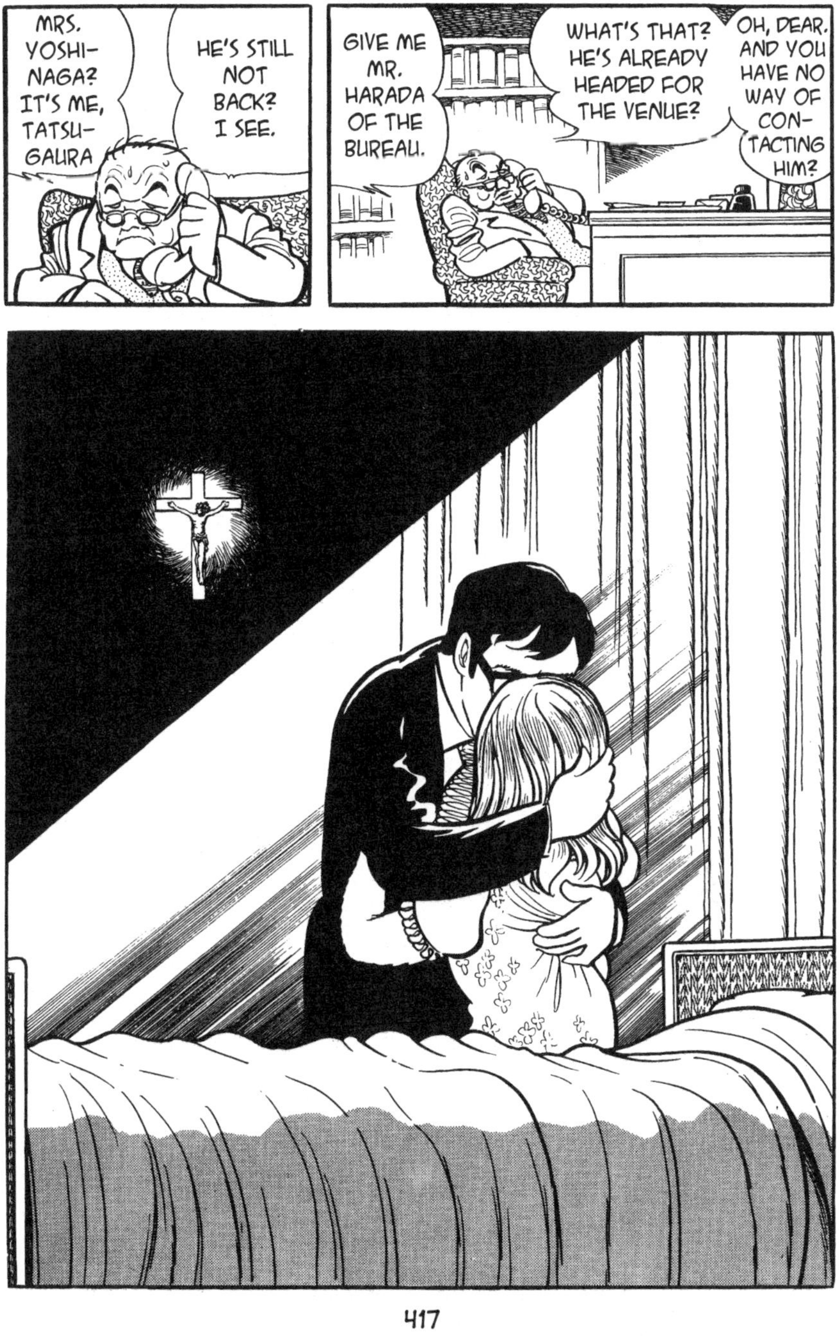
MRS. YOSHINAGA? IT'S ME, TATSUGAURA
HE'S STILL NOT BACK? I SEE.
GIVE ME MR. HARADA OF THE BUREAU.
WHAT'S THAT? HE'S ALREADY HEADED FOR THE VENUE?
OH, DEAR. AND YOU HAVE NO WAY OF CONTACTING HIM?

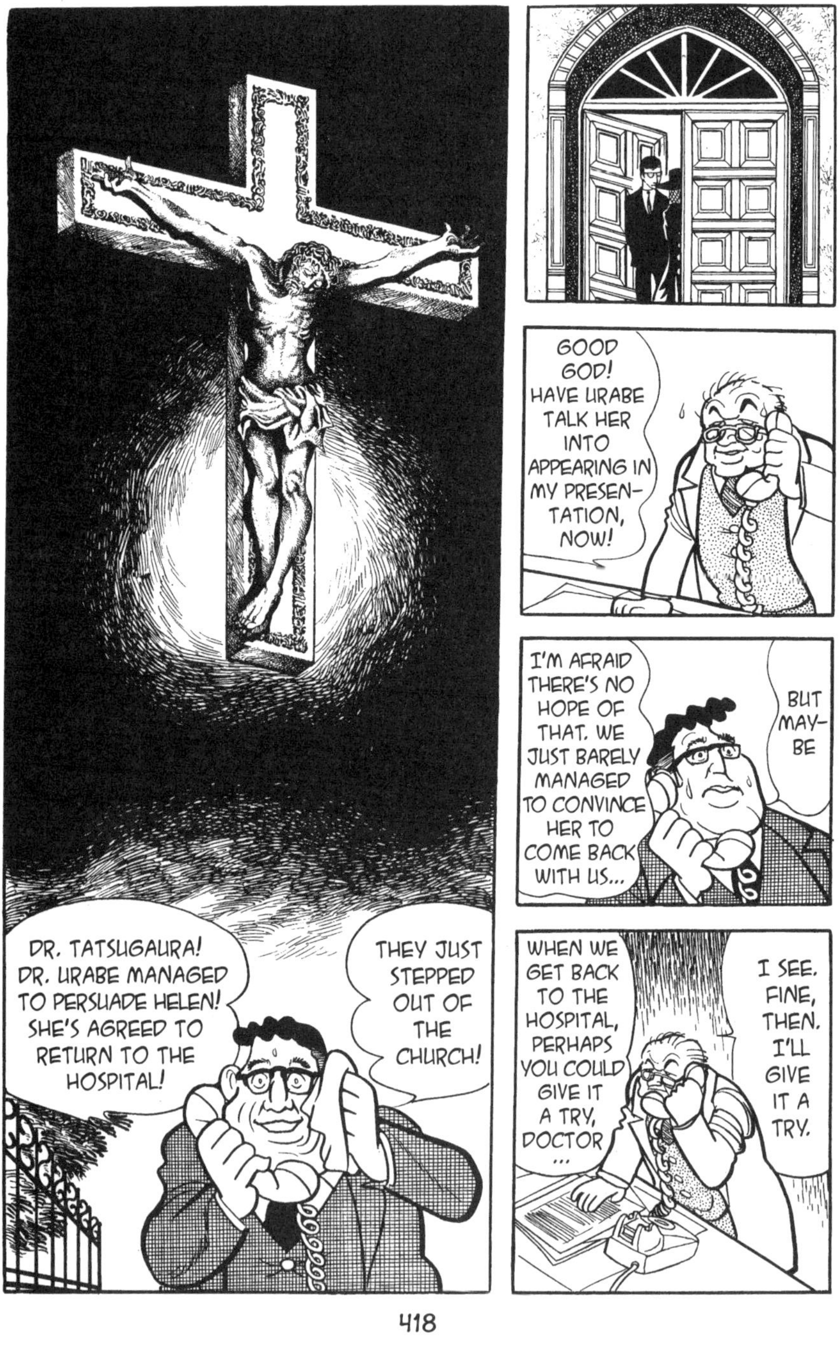
DR. TATSUGAURA! DR. URABE MANAGED TO PERSUADE HELEN! SHE'S AGREED TO RETURN TO THE HOSPITAL!
THEY JUST STEPPED OUT OF THE CHURCH!
GOOD GOD! HAVE URABE TALK HER INTO APPEARING IN MY PRESEN-TATION, NOW!
I'M AFRAID THERE'S NO HOPE OF THAT. WE JUST BARELY MANAGED TO CONVINCE HER TO COME BACK WITH US...
BUT MAY-BE
WHEN WE GET BACK TO THE HOSPITAL, PERHAPS YOU COULD GIVE IT A TRY, DOCTOR ...
I SEE. FINE, THEN. I'LL GIVE IT A TRY.

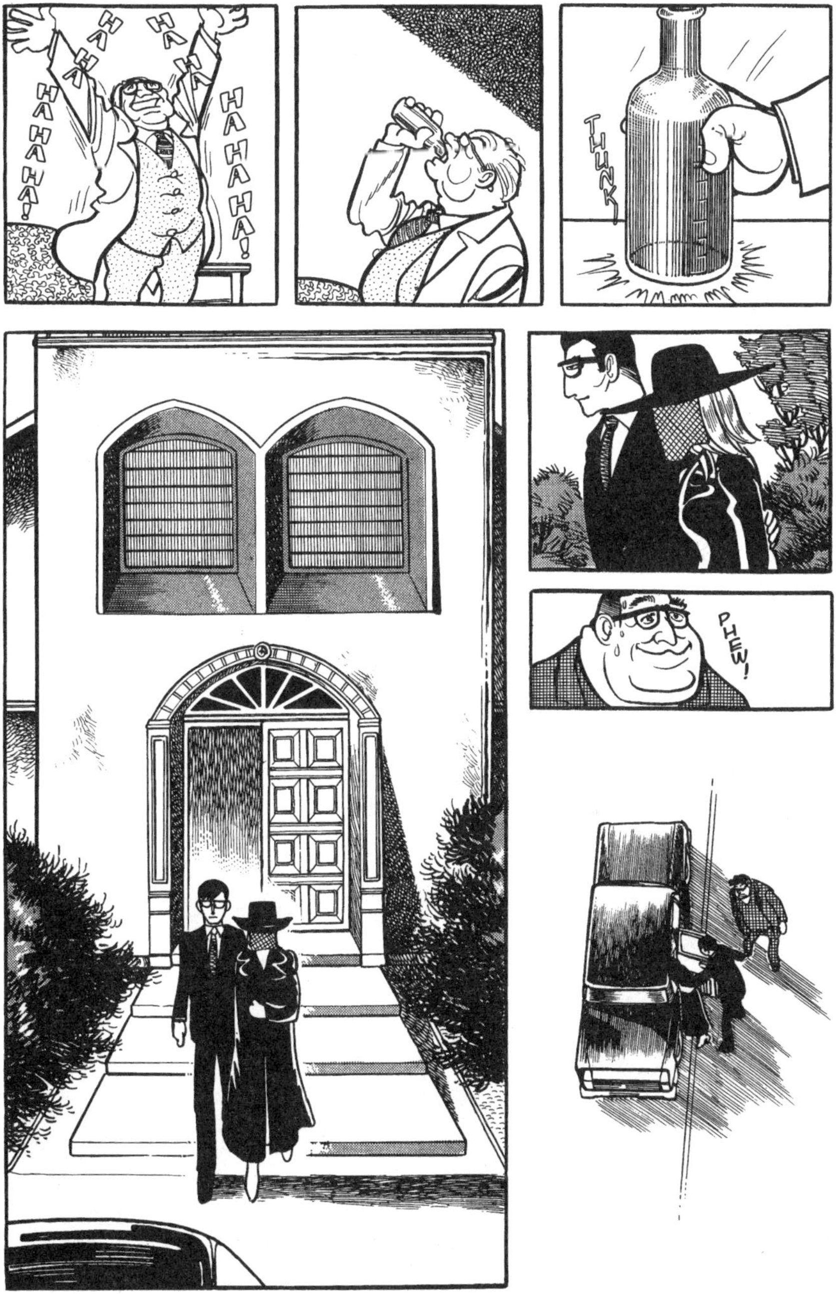
HA HA HA HA HAHAHA!
HAHAHAHA!
THUNK!
PHEW!

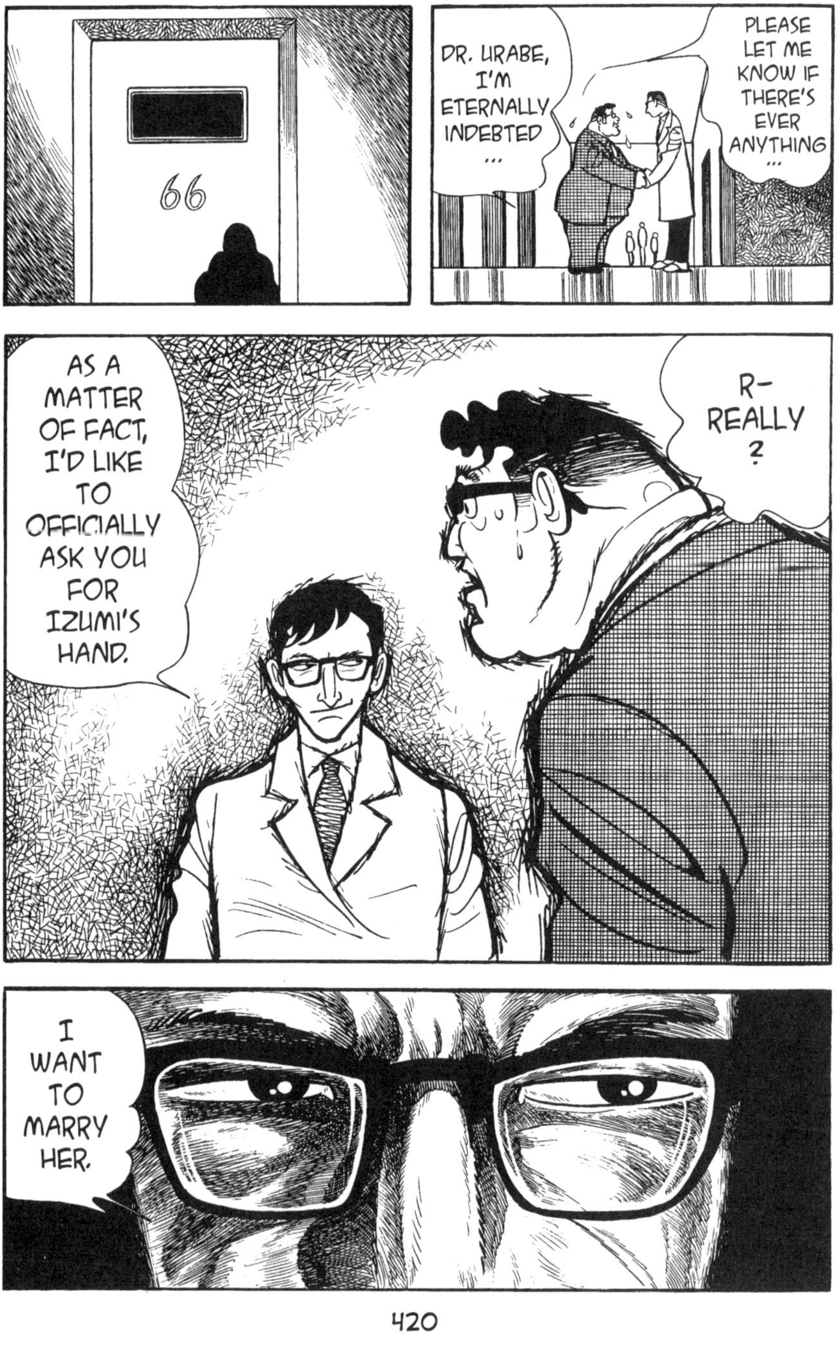
66
DR. URABE, I'M ETERNALLY INDEBTED ...
PLEASE LET ME KNOW IF THERE'S EVER ANYTHING ...
AS A MATTER OF FACT, I'D LIKE TO OFFICIALLY ASK YOU FOR IZUMI'S HAND.
R-REALLY?
I WANT TO MARRY HER.

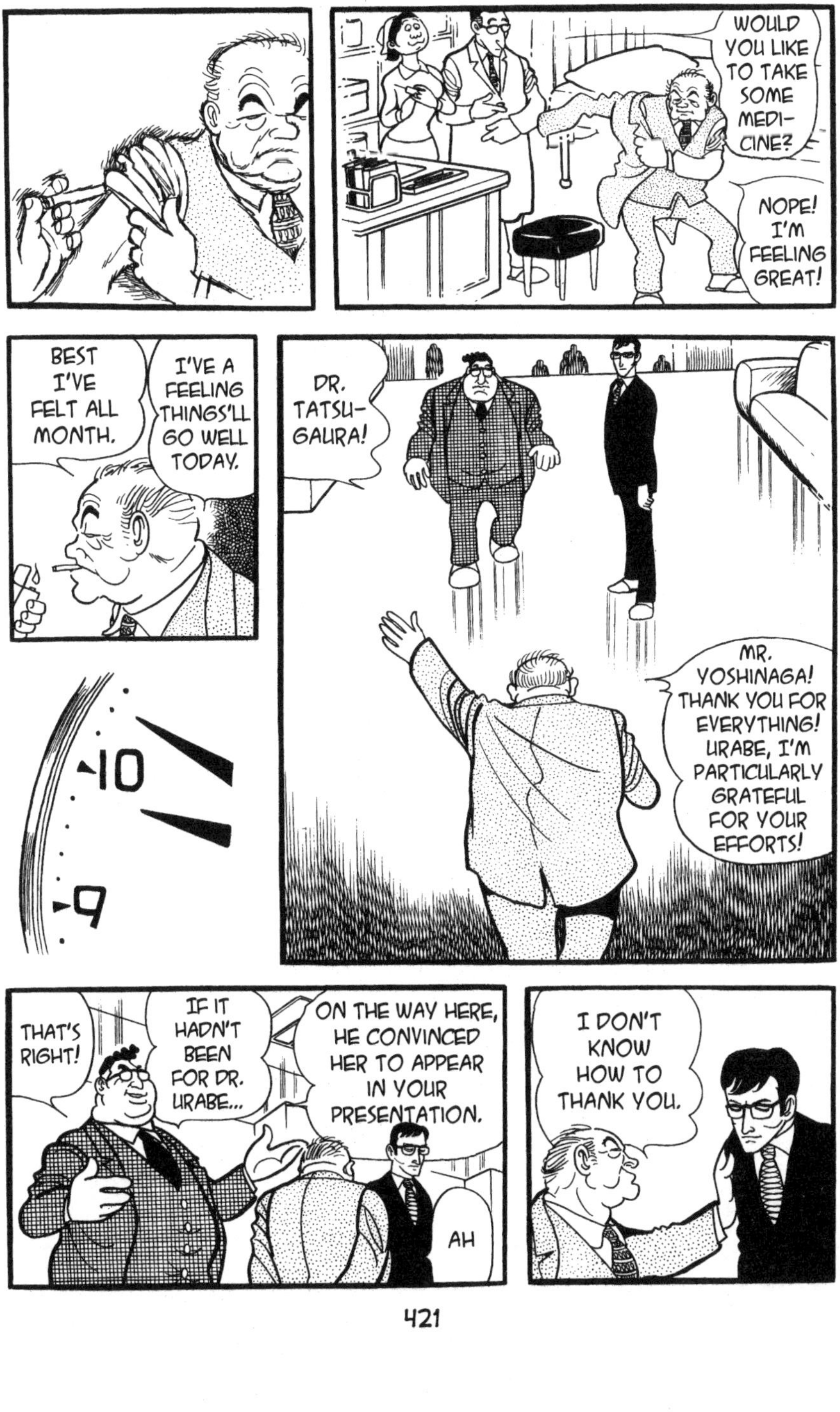
WOULD YOU LIKE TO TAKE SOME MEDI-CINE?
NOPE! I'M FEELING GREAT!
BEST I'VE FELT ALL MONTH.
I'VE A FEELING THINGS'LL GO WELL TODAY.
DR. TATSU-GAURA!
MR. YOSHINAGA! THANK YOU FOR EVERYTHING! URABE, I'M PARTICULARLY GRATEFUL FOR YOUR EFFORTS!
10
9
THAT'S RIGHT!
IF IT HADN'T BEEN FOR DR. URABE...
ON THE WAY HERE, HE CONVINCED HER TO APPEAR IN YOUR PRESENTATION.
AH
I DON'T KNOW HOW TO THANK YOU.

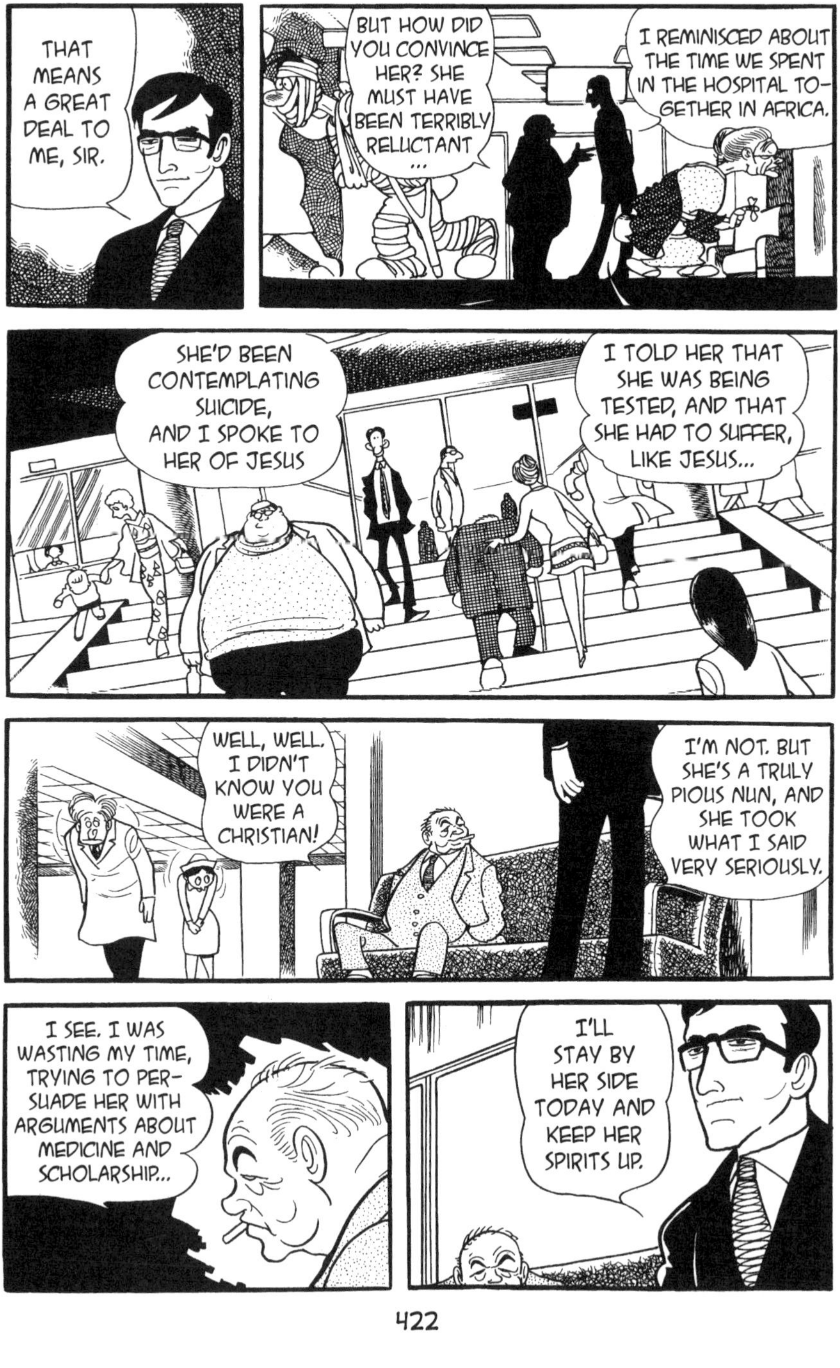
THAT MEANS A GREAT DEAL TO ME, SIR.
BUT HOW DID YOU CONVINCE HER? SHE MUST HAVE BEEN TERRIBLY RELUCTANT ...
I REMINISCED ABOUT THE TIME WE SPENT IN THE HOSPITAL TO-GETHER IN AFRICA.
SHE'D BEEN CONTEMPLATING SUICIDE, AND I SPOKE TO HER OF JESUS
I TOLD HER THAT SHE WAS BEING TESTED, AND THAT SHE HAD TO SUFFER, LIKE JESUS...
WELL, WELL. I DIDN'T KNOW YOU WERE A CHRISTIAN!
I'M NOT. BUT SHE'S A TRULY PIOUS NUN, AND SHE TOOK WHAT I SAID VERY SERIOUSLY.
I SEE. I WAS WASTING MY TIME, TRYING TO PER-SUADE HER WITH ARGUMENTS ABOUT MEDICINE AND SCHOLARSHIP...
I'LL STAY BY HER SIDE TODAY AND KEEP HER SPIRITS UP.

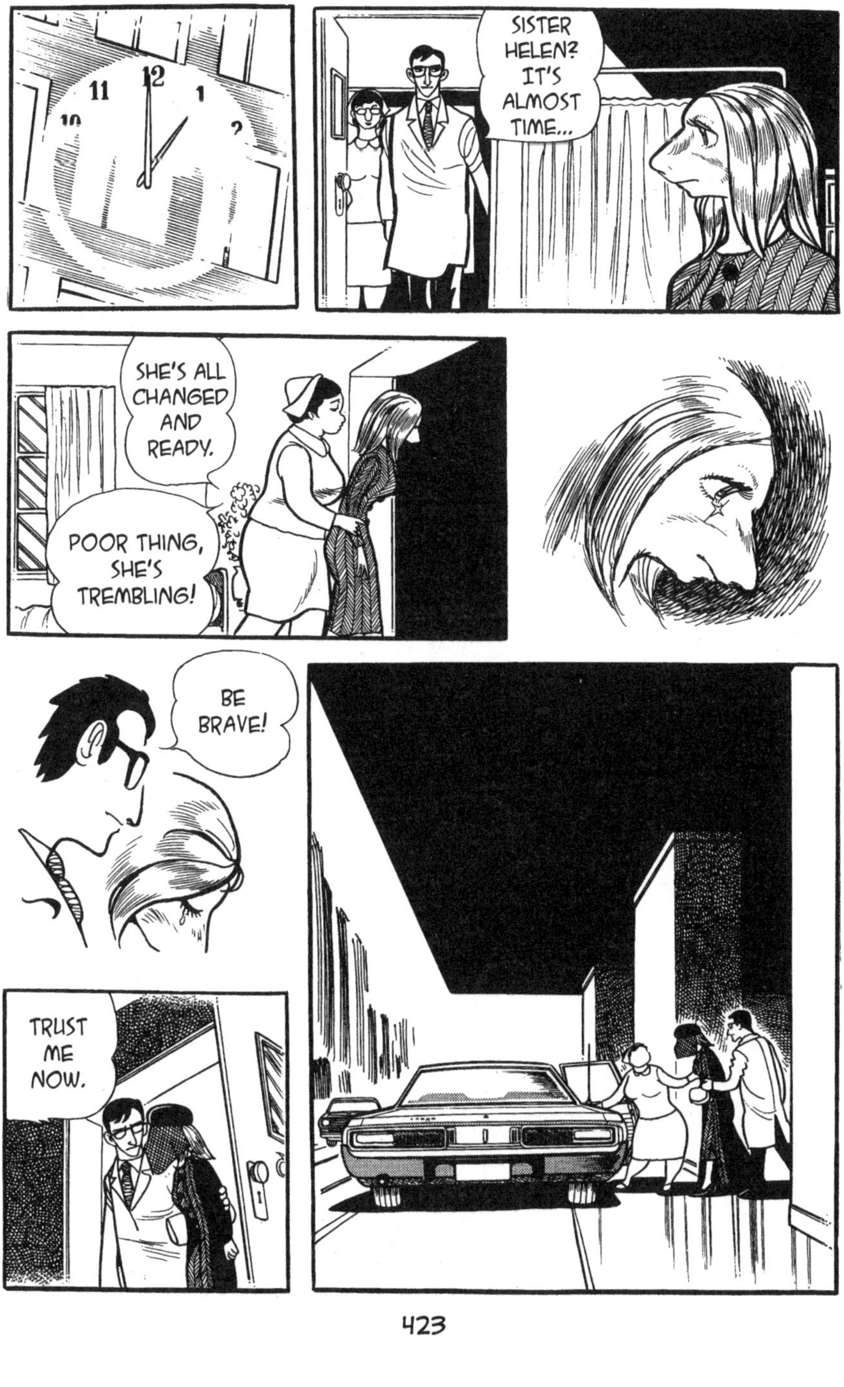
SISTER HELEN? IT'S ALMOST TIME...
SHE'S ALL CHANGED AND READY.
POOR THING, SHE'S TREMBLING!
BE BRAVE!
TRUST ME NOW.

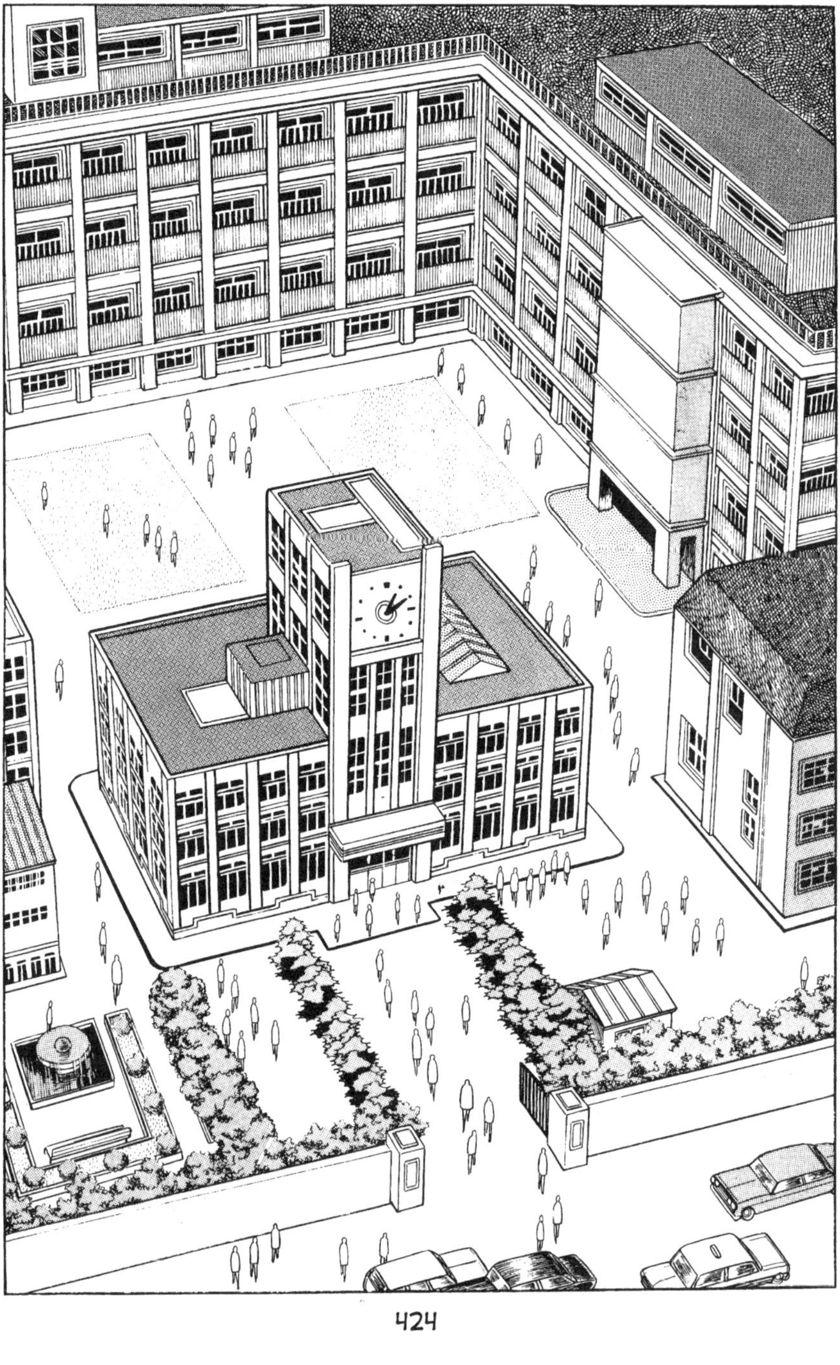

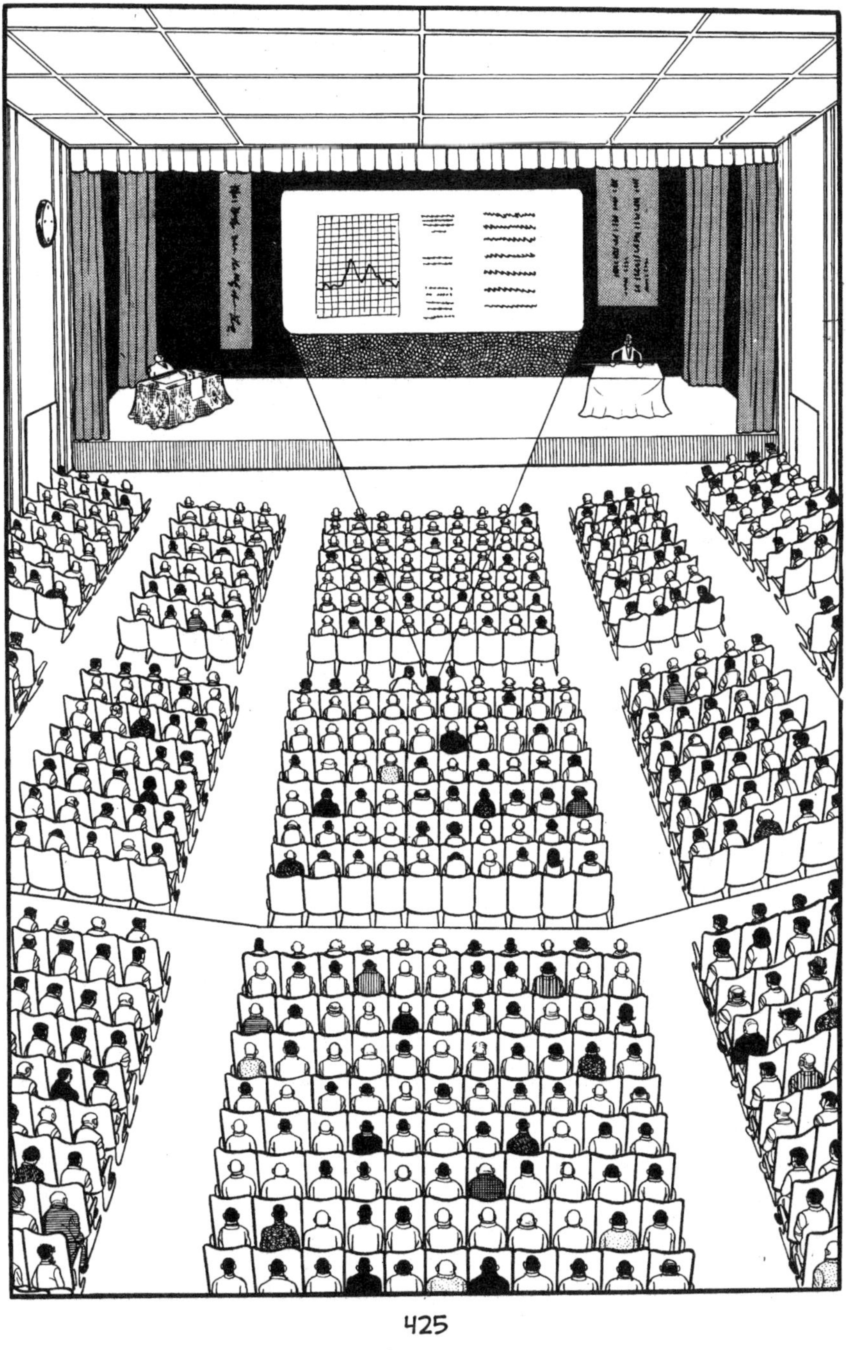

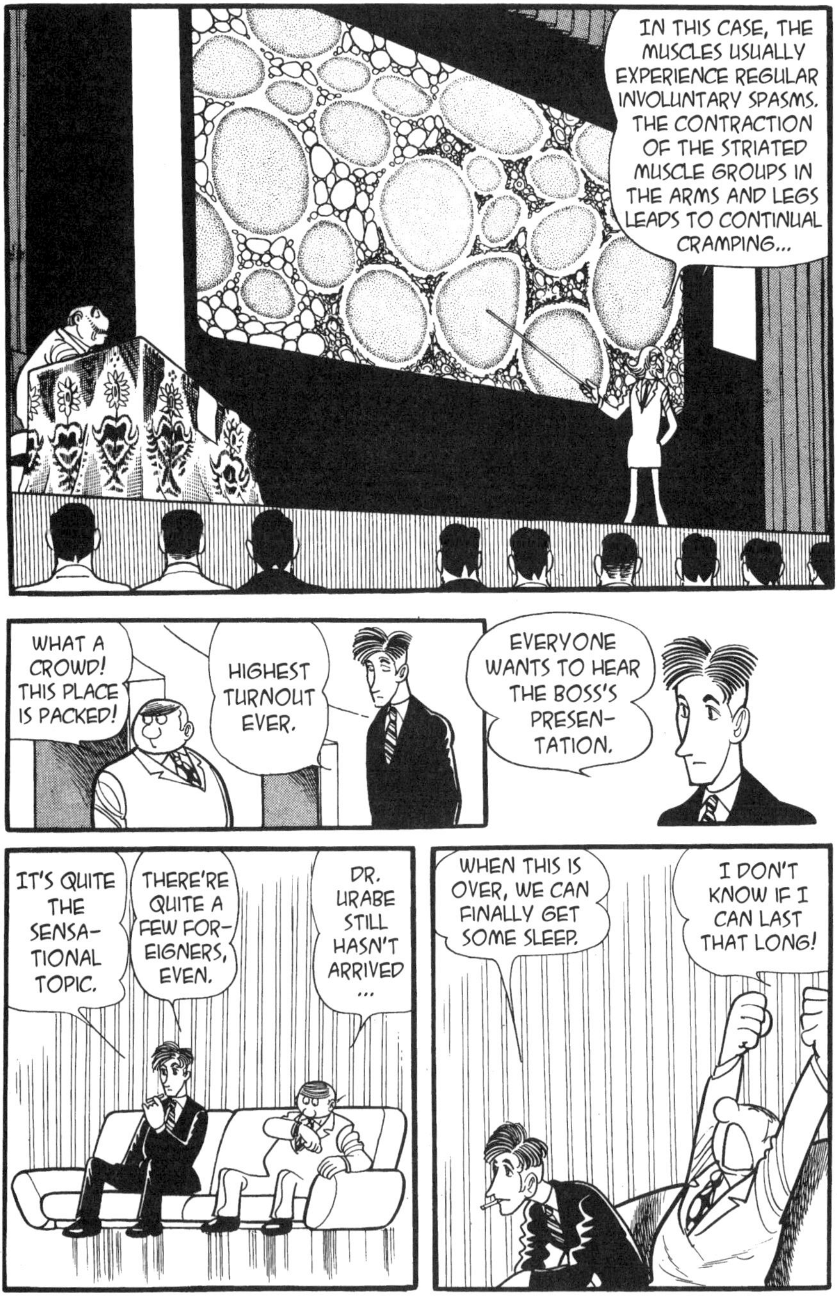
IN THIS CASE, THE MUSCLES USUALLY EXPERIENCE REGULAR INVOLUNTARY SPASMS. THE CONTRACTION OF THE STRIATED MUSCLE GROUPS IN THE ARMS AND LEGS LEADS TO CONTINUAL CRAMPING...
WHAT A CROWD! THIS PLACE IS PACKED!
HIGHEST TURNOUT EVER.
EVERYONE WANTS TO HEAR THE BOSS'S PRESEN-TATION.
IT'S QUITE THE SENSA-TIONAL TOPIC.
THERE'RE QUITE A FEW FOR-EIGNERS, EVEN.
DR. URABE STILL HASN'T ARRIVED ...
WHEN THIS IS OVER, WE CAN FINALLY GET SOME SLEEP.
I DON'T KNOW IF I CAN LAST THAT LONG!

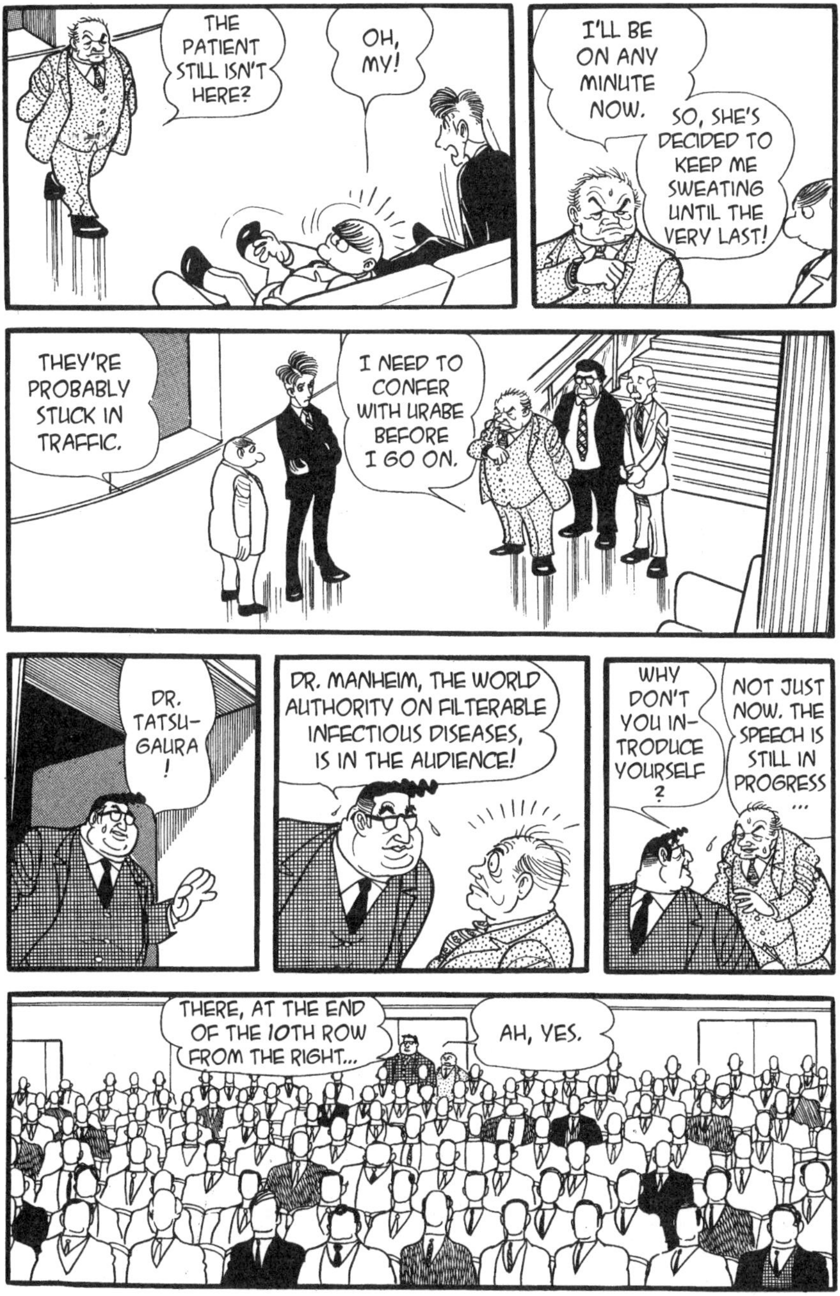
THE PATIENT STILL ISN'T HERE?
OH, MY!
I'LL BE ON ANY MINUTE NOW.
SO, SHE'S DECIDED TO KEEP ME SWEATING UNTIL THE VERY LAST!
THEY'RE PROBABLY STUCK IN TRAFFIC.
I NEED TO CONFER WITH URABE BEFORE I GO ON.
DR. TATSU-GAURA!
DR. MANHEIM, THE WORLD AUTHORITY ON FILTERABLE INFECTIOUS DISEASES, IS IN THE AUDIENCE!
WHY DON'T YOU IN-TRODUCE YOURSELF?
NOT JUST NOW. THE SPEECH IS STILL IN PROGRESS...
THERE, AT THE END OF THE 10TH ROW FROM THE RIGHT...
AH, YES.

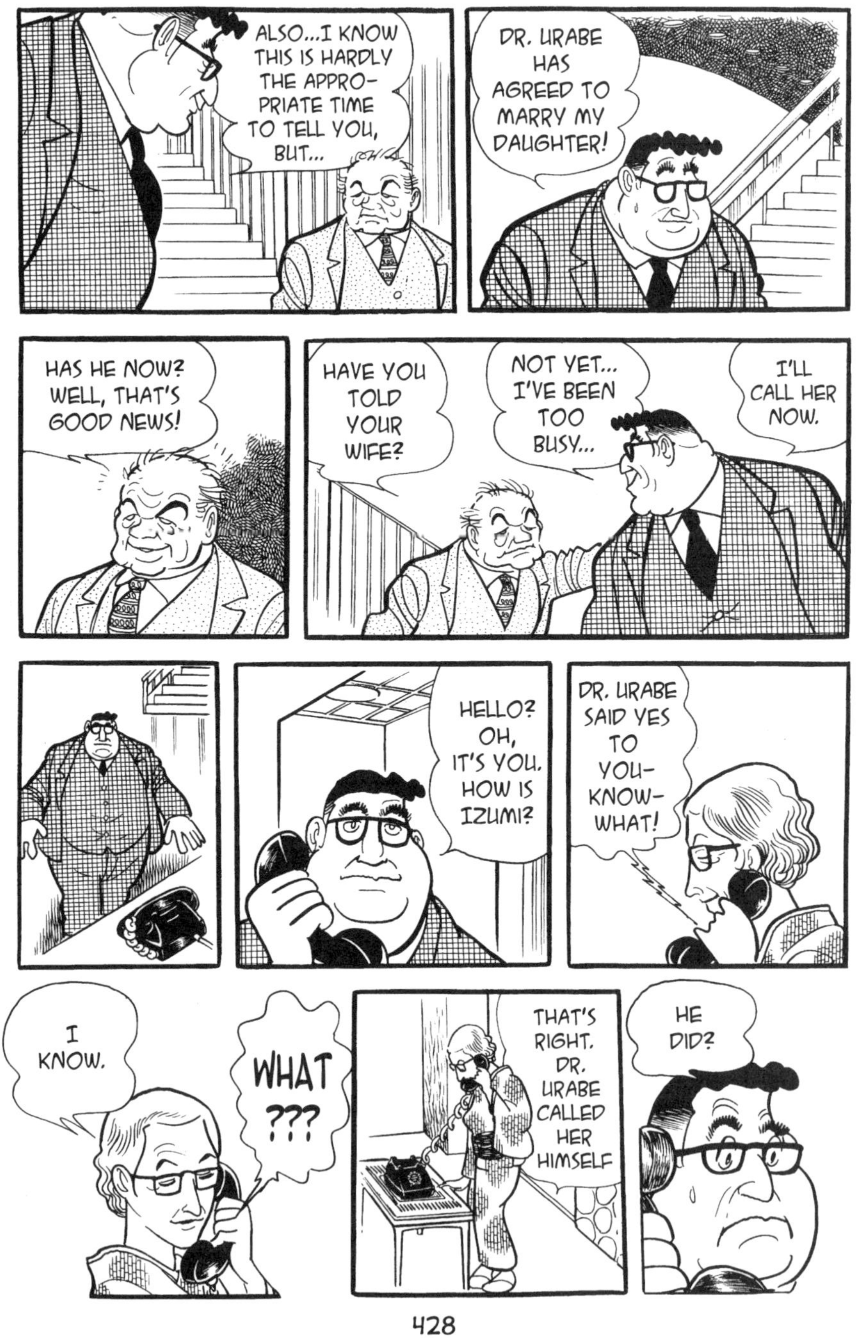
ALSO...I KNOW THIS IS HARDLY THE APPRO-PRIATE TIME TO TELL YOU, BUT...
DR. URABE HAS AGREED TO MARRY MY DAUGHTER!
HAS HE NOW? WELL, THAT'S GOOD NEWS!
HAVE YOU TOLD YOUR WIFE?
NOT YET... I'VE BEEN TOO BUSY...
I'LL CALL HER NOW.
HELLO? OH, IT'S YOU. HOW IS IZUMI?
DR. URABE SAID YES TO YOU-KNOW-WHAT!
I KNOW.
WHAT ???
THAT'S RIGHT. DR. URABE CALLED HER HIMSELF
HE DID?

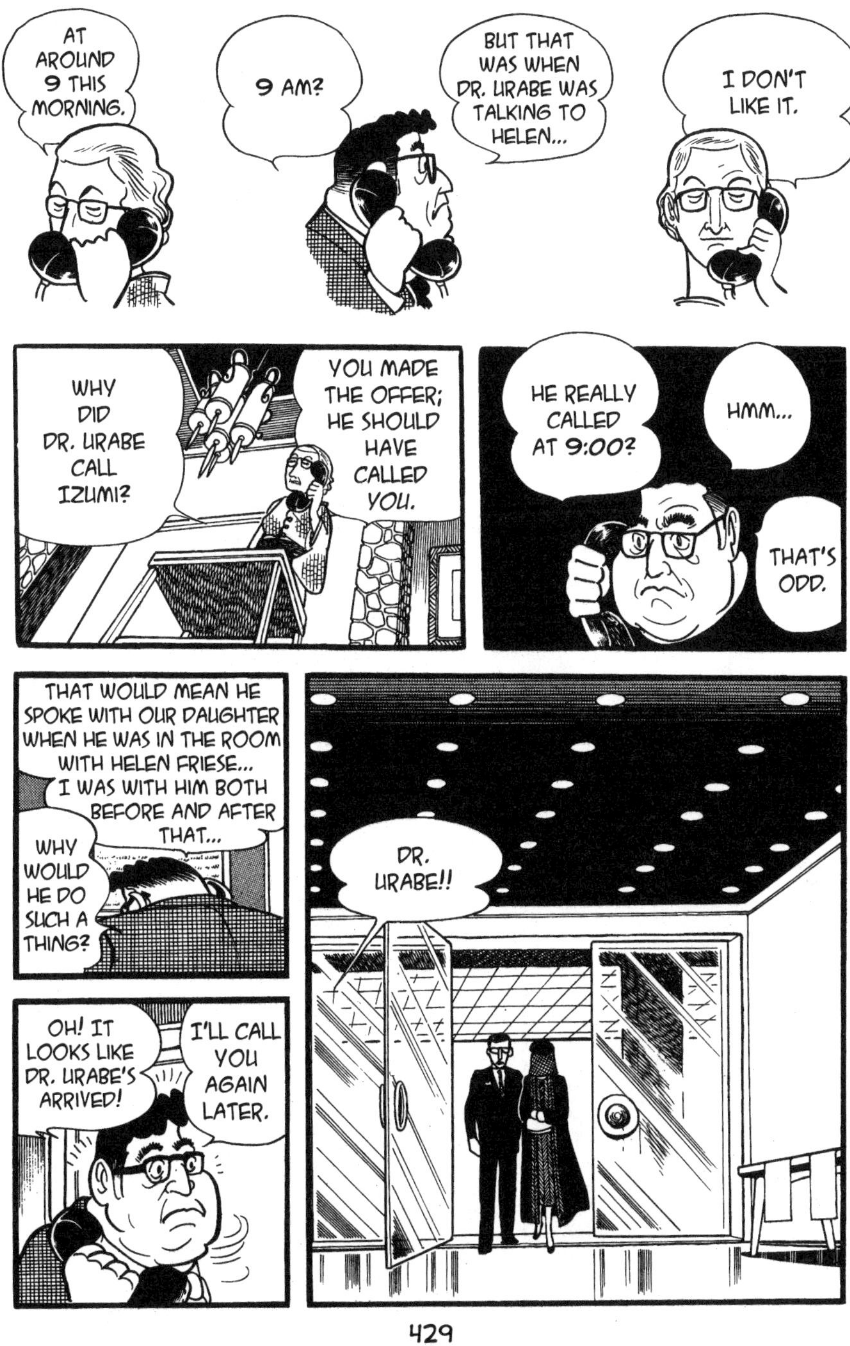
AT AROUND 9 THIS MORNING.
9 AM?
BUT THAT WAS WHEN DR. URABE WAS TALKING TO HELEN...
I DON'T LIKE IT.
WHY DID DR. URABE CALL IZUMI?
YOU MADE THE OFFER; HE SHOULD HAVE CALLED YOU.
HE REALLY CALLED AT 9:00?
HMM...
THAT'S ODD.
THAT WOULD MEAN HE SPOKE WITH OUR DAUGHTER WHEN HE WAS IN THE ROOM WITH HELEN FRIESE... I WAS WITH HIM BOTH BEFORE AND AFTER THAT...
WHY WOULD HE DO SUCH A THING?
DR. URABE!!
OH! IT LOOKS LIKE DR. URABE'S ARRIVED!
I'LL CALL YOU AGAIN LATER.

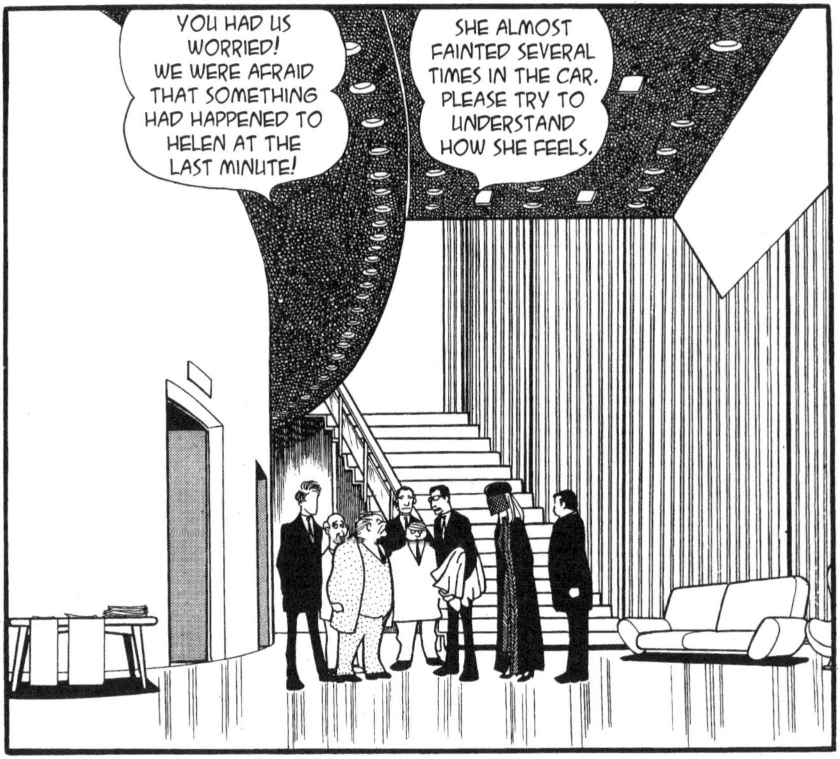
YOU HAD US WORRIED! WE WERE AFRAID THAT SOMETHING HAD HAPPENED TO HELEN AT THE LAST MINUTE!
SHE ALMOST FAINTED SEVERAL TIMES IN THE CAR. PLEASE TRY TO UNDERSTAND HOW SHE FEELS.

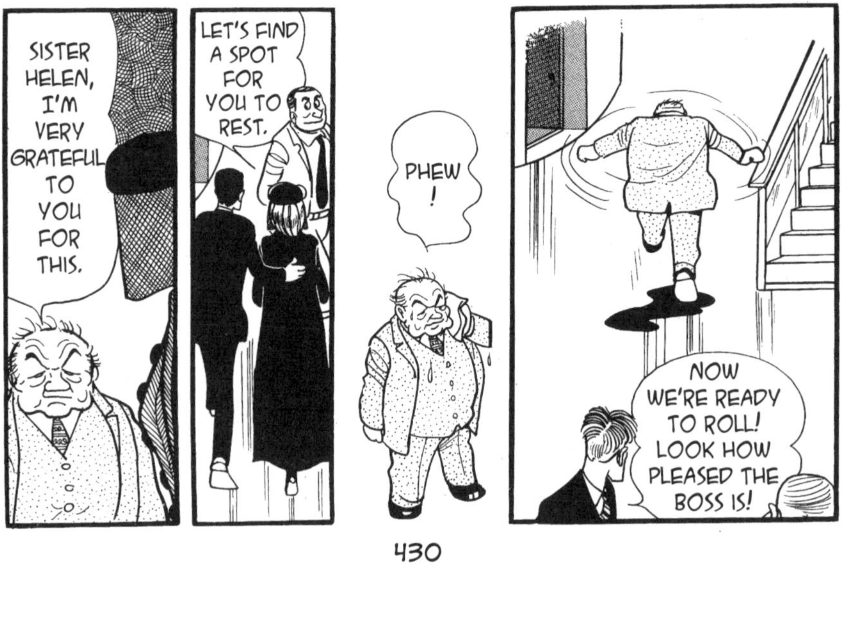
SISTER HELEN, I'M VERY GRATEFUL TO YOU FOR THIS.
LET'S FIND A SPOT FOR YOU TO REST.
PHEW !
NOW WE'RE READY TO ROLL! LOOK HOW PLEASED THE BOSS IS!

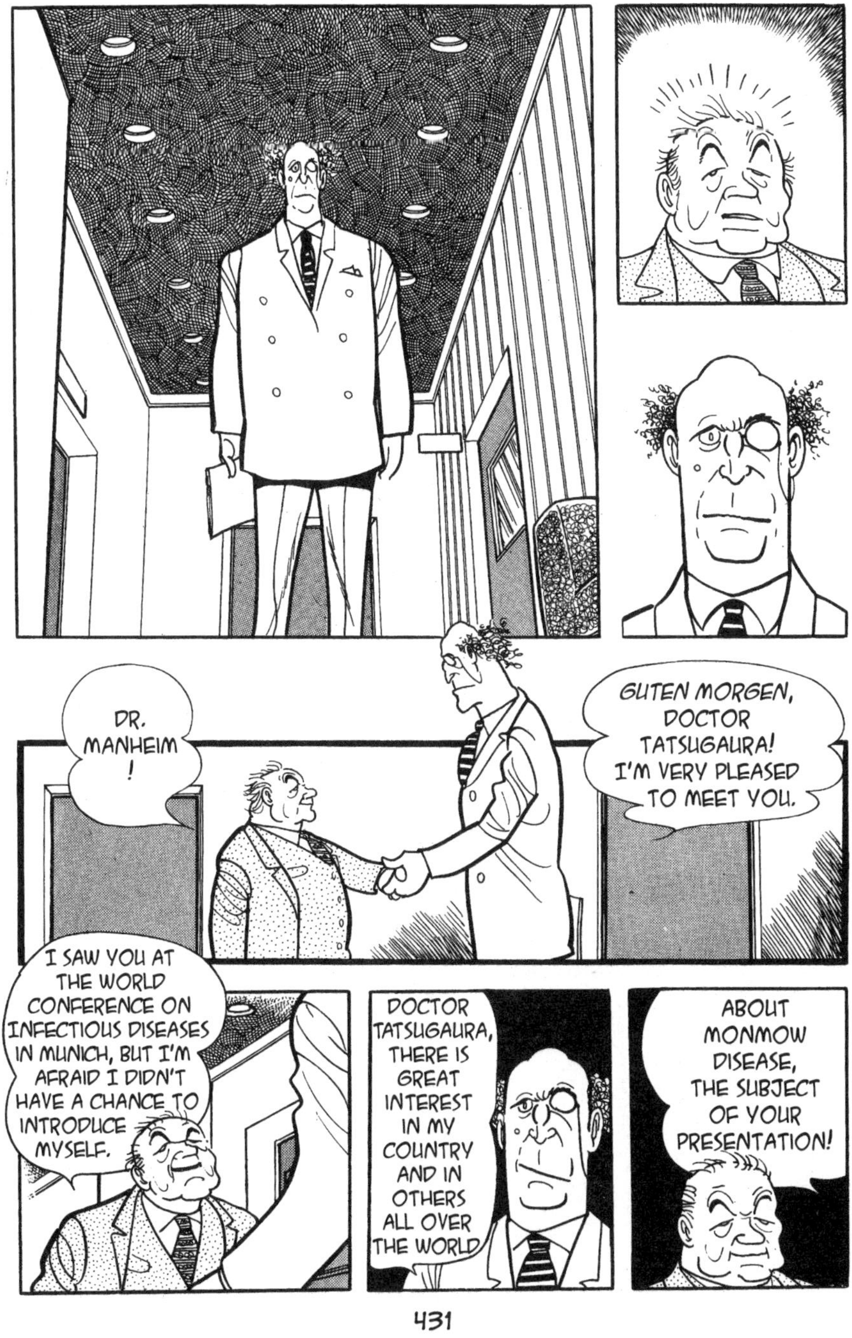
DR. MANHEIM !
GUTEN MORGEN, DOCTOR TATSUGAURA! I'M VERY PLEASED TO MEET YOU.
I SAW YOU AT THE WORLD CONFERENCE ON INFECTIOUS DISEASES IN MUNICH, BUT I'M AFRAID I DIDN'T HAVE A CHANCE TO INTRODUCE MYSELF.
DOCTOR TATSUGAURA, THERE IS GREAT INTEREST IN MY COUNTRY AND IN OTHERS ALL OVER THE WORLD
ABOUT MONMOW DISEASE, THE SUBJECT OF YOUR PRESENTATION!

I FLEW TO AFRICA MYSELF TO INVESTIGATE THE CASES THERE.

IN THE END, I WAS UNABLE TO IDENTIFY THE PATHOGEN OR THE INFECTION ROUTE...

I'M LOOKING FORWARD TO HEARING THE EVIDENCE YOU WILL BE PROVIDING...

DANKE SCHÖN

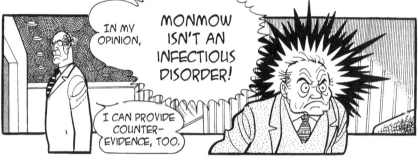

IN MY OPINION, MONMOW ISN'T AN INFECTIOUS DISORDER!

I CAN PROVIDE COUNTER-EVIDENCE, TOO.

DR. TATSUGAURA OF M UNIVERSITY, IT'S TIME FOR YOUR PRESENTATION. DR. TATSU-GAURA!

THIS IS IT, DOCTOR!

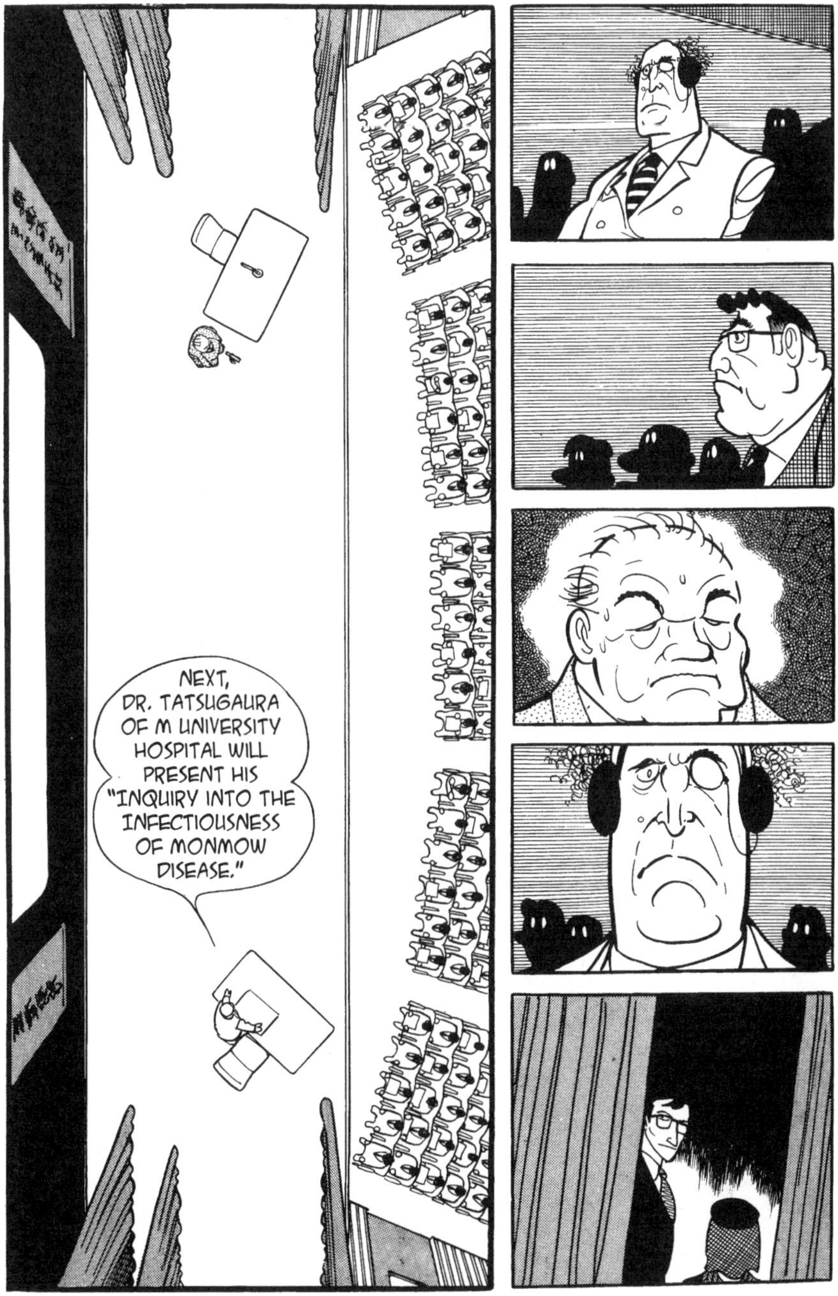
NEXT, DR. TATSUGAURA OF M UNIVERSITY HOSPITAL WILL PRESENT HIS "INQUIRY INTO THE INFECTIOUSNESS OF MONMOW DISEASE."

WE AT M UNIVERSITY HOSPITAL HAVE MAINTAINED CLOSE CONTACT WITH THE VILLAGE OF DOGGODDALE IN ORDER TO STUDY THE DISORDER KNOWN AS MONMOW DISEASE, OF WHICH THERE ARE **223** RECORDED CASES IN THAT REGION OF MIYOSHI COUNTY, TOKUSHIMA PREFECTURE. THE VILLAGE PROMISED TO SEND ANY NEW CASES TO OUR HOSPITAL IMMEDIATELY.

SLIDE...

SEPTEMBER **22** OF LAST YEAR... WHEN PATIENT Y CAME UNDER OUR CARE, HE HAD ALREADY DEVELOPED THESE UNIQUE SYMPTOMS AND IT WAS ALMOST IMPOSSIBLE TO CHECK THE DISEASE'S PROCESS. WE CONTINUED TO TREAT HIS SYMPTOMS BUT HE DIED ON OCTOBER 11. THIS WAS TAKEN APPROXIMATELY 10 DAYS BEFORE HIS DEATH.

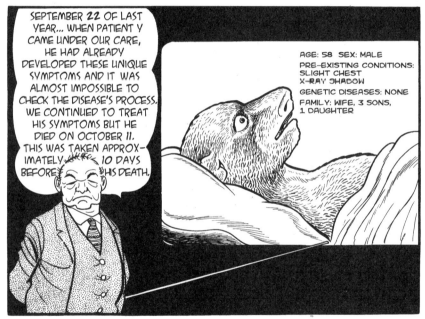

AGE: 58 SEX: MALE
PRE-EXISTING CONDITIONS: SLIGHT CHEST X-RAY SHADOW
GENETIC DISEASES: NONE
FAMILY: WIFE, 3 SONS, 1 DAUGHTER

NEXT SLIDE, PLEASE.

CLICK

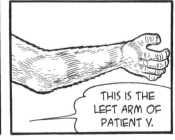

THIS IS THE LEFT ARM OF PATIENT Y.

434

AS YOU CAN SEE, THERE WAS DRASTIC ATROPHY OF THE LONG BONES, AS WELL AS ABNORMAL GROWTH OF BODY HAIR.

"MOAN"

THERE, THERE!

DOC-TOR!

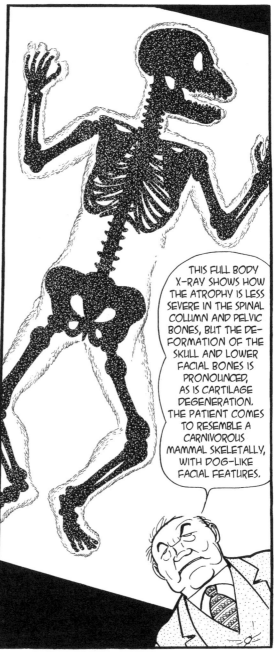

THIS FULL BODY X-RAY SHOWS HOW THE ATROPHY IS LESS SEVERE IN THE SPINAL COLUMN AND PELVIC BONES, BUT THE DE-FORMATION OF THE SKULL AND LOWER FACIAL BONES IS PRONOUNCED, AS IS CARTILAGE DEGENERATION. THE PATIENT COMES TO RESEMBLE A CARNIVOROUS MAMMAL SKELETALLY, WITH DOG-LIKE FACIAL FEATURES.

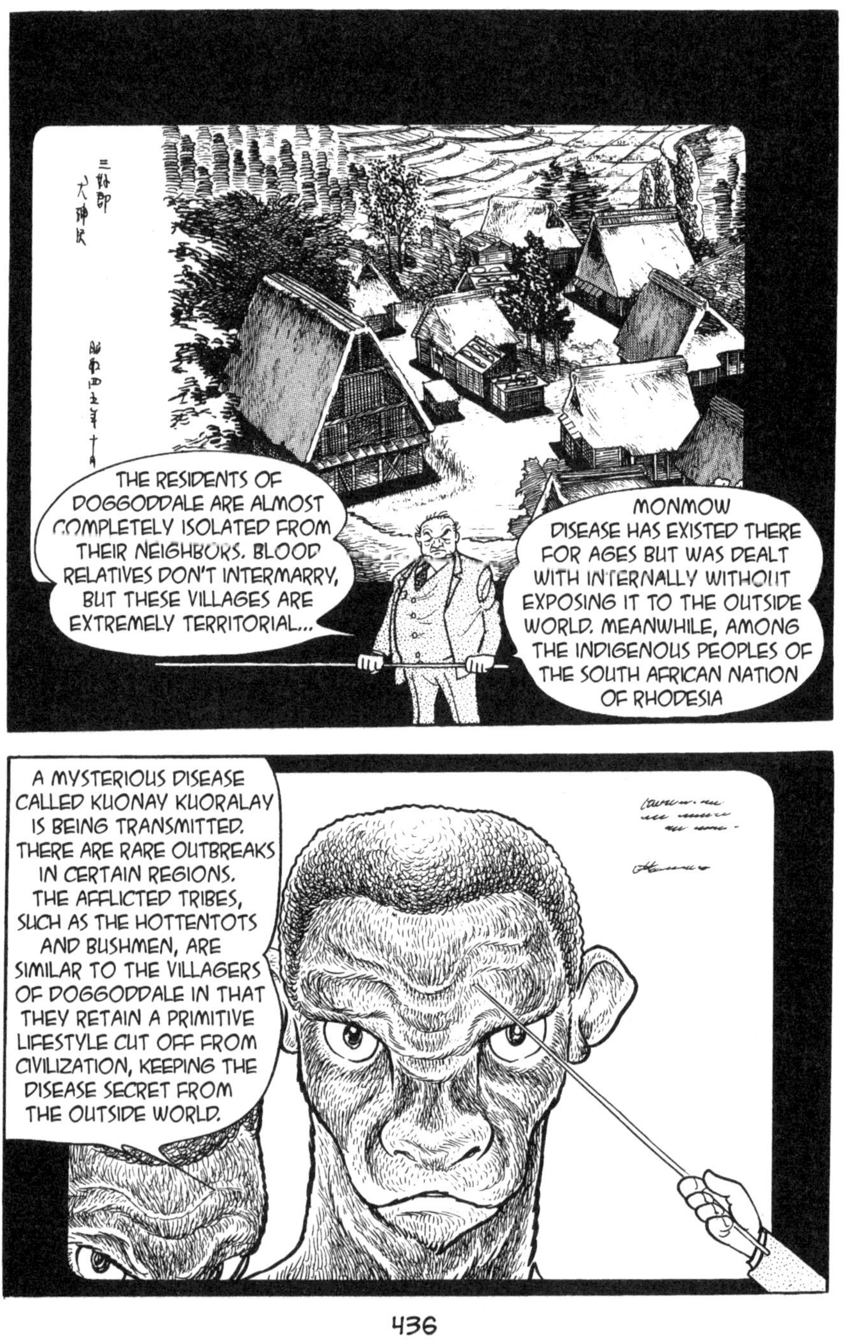

THE RESIDENTS OF DOGGODDALE ARE ALMOST COMPLETELY ISOLATED FROM THEIR NEIGHBORS. BLOOD RELATIVES DON'T INTERMARRY, BUT THESE VILLAGES ARE EXTREMELY TERRITORIAL...
MONMOW DISEASE HAS EXISTED THERE FOR AGES BUT WAS DEALT WITH INTERNALLY WITHOUT EXPOSING IT TO THE OUTSIDE WORLD. MEANWHILE, AMONG THE INDIGENOUS PEOPLES OF THE SOUTH AFRICAN NATION OF RHODESIA
A MYSTERIOUS DISEASE CALLED KUONAY KUORALAY IS BEING TRANSMITTED. THERE ARE RARE OUTBREAKS IN CERTAIN REGIONS. THE AFFLICTED TRIBES, SUCH AS THE HOTTENTOTS AND BUSHMEN, ARE SIMILAR TO THE VILLAGERS OF DOGGODDALE IN THAT THEY RETAIN A PRIMITIVE LIFESTYLE CUT OFF FROM CIVILIZATION, KEEPING THE DISEASE SECRET FROM THE OUTSIDE WORLD.

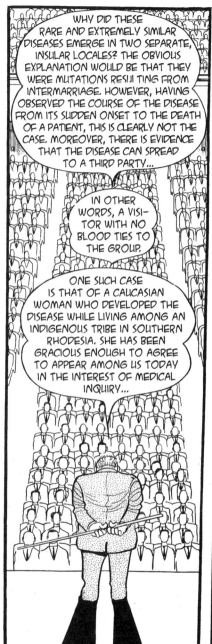

WHY DID THESE RARE AND EXTREMELY SIMILAR DISEASES EMERGE IN TWO SEPARATE, INSULAR LOCALES? THE OBVIOUS EXPLANATION WOULD BE THAT THEY WERE MUTATIONS RESULTING FROM INTERMARRIAGE. HOWEVER, HAVING OBSERVED THE COURSE OF THE DISEASE FROM ITS SUDDEN ONSET TO THE DEATH OF A PATIENT, THIS IS CLEARLY NOT THE CASE. MOREOVER, THERE IS EVIDENCE THAT THE DISEASE CAN SPREAD TO A THIRD PARTY...

IN OTHER WORDS, A VISITOR WITH NO BLOOD TIES TO THE GROUP.

ONE SUCH CASE IS THAT OF A CAUCASIAN WOMAN WHO DEVELOPED THE DISEASE WHILE LIVING AMONG AN INDIGENOUS TRIBE IN SOUTHERN RHODESIA. SHE HAS BEEN GRACIOUS ENOUGH TO AGREE TO APPEAR AMONG US TODAY IN THE INTEREST OF MEDICAL INQUIRY...

NOW, HELEN. GO ON.

NO! NO! NO! I CAN'T!

COME, NOW! BE STRONG!

READ IT NOW, DOCTOR...

THEN THE SOLDIERS STRIPPED HIM, AND PUT ON HIM A SCARLET ROBE. AND WHEN THEY HAD PLATTED A CROWN OF THORNS

THEY PUT IT UPON HIS HEAD, AND A REED IN HIS RIGHT HAND: AND THEY BOWED THE KNEE BEFORE HIM, AND MOCKED HIM, SAYING, HAIL, KING OF THE JEWS! AND THEY SPIT UPON HIM, AND TOOK THE REED, AND SMOTE HIM ON THE HEAD.

AND AFTER THAT THEY HAD MOCKED HIM, THEY TOOK THE ROBE OFF FROM HIM, AND PUT HIS OWN RAIMENT ON HIM, AND LED HIM AWAY TO THE CROSS. AND WHEN THEY WERE COME UNTO A PLACE CALLED GOLGOTHA, THAT IS TO SAY, A PLACE OF A SKULL....

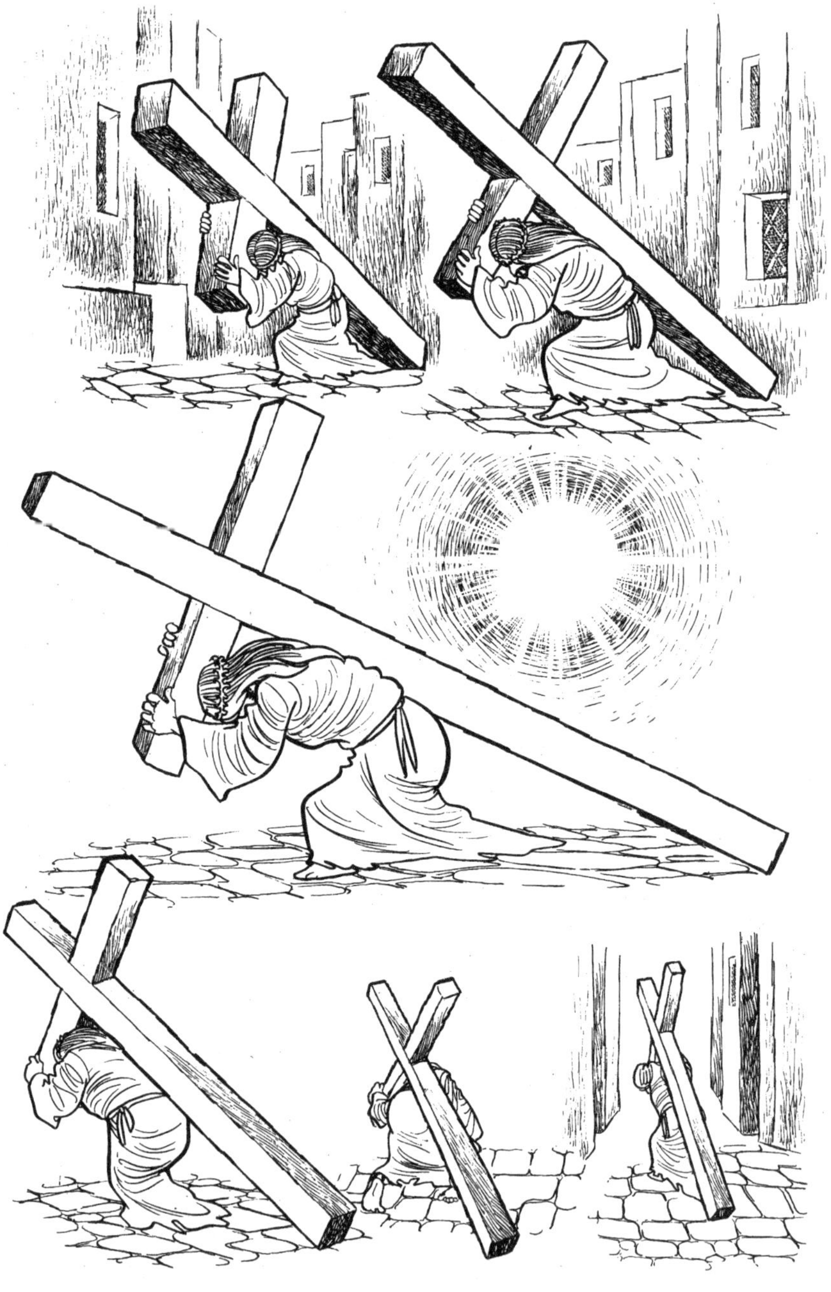

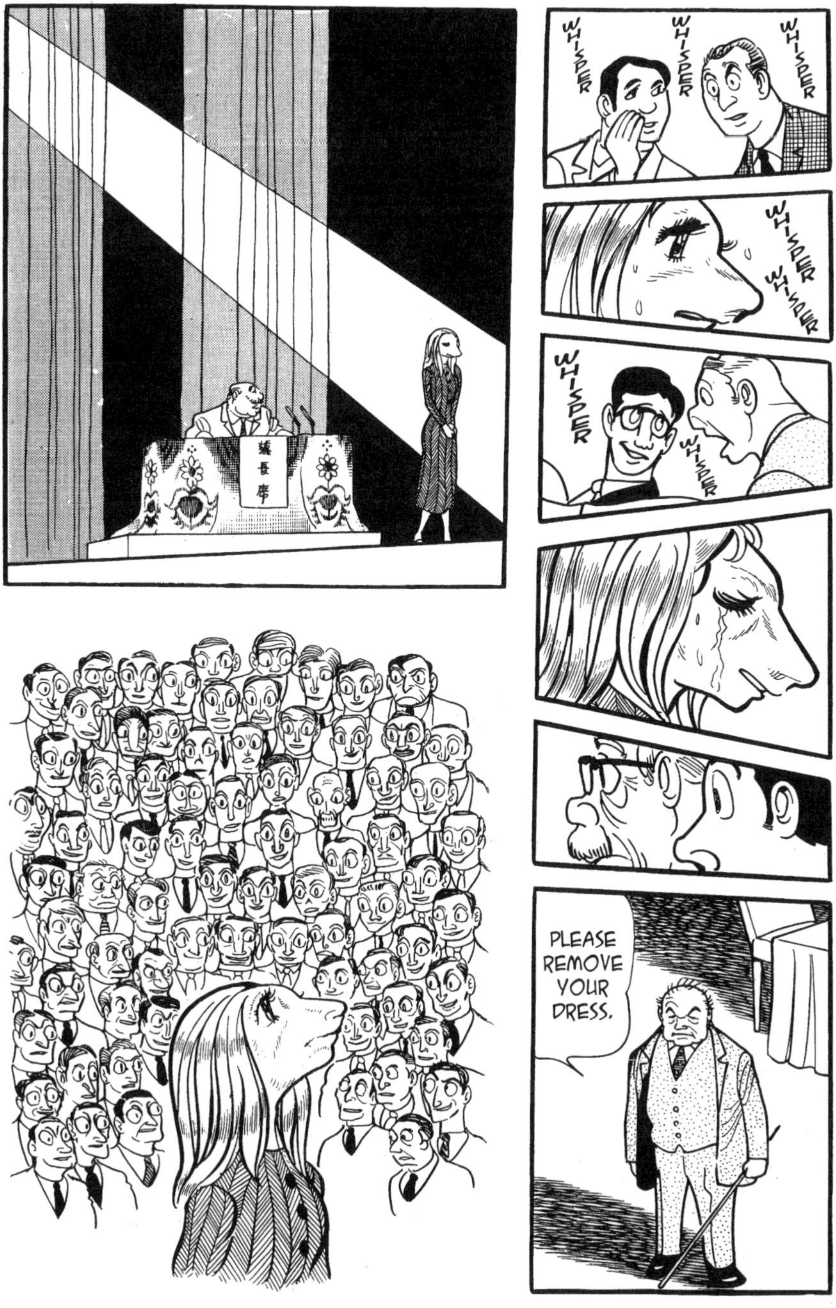
議長席
WHISPER
WHISPER
WHISPER
WHISPER
WHISPER
WHISPER
WHISPER
PLEASE REMOVE YOUR DRESS.

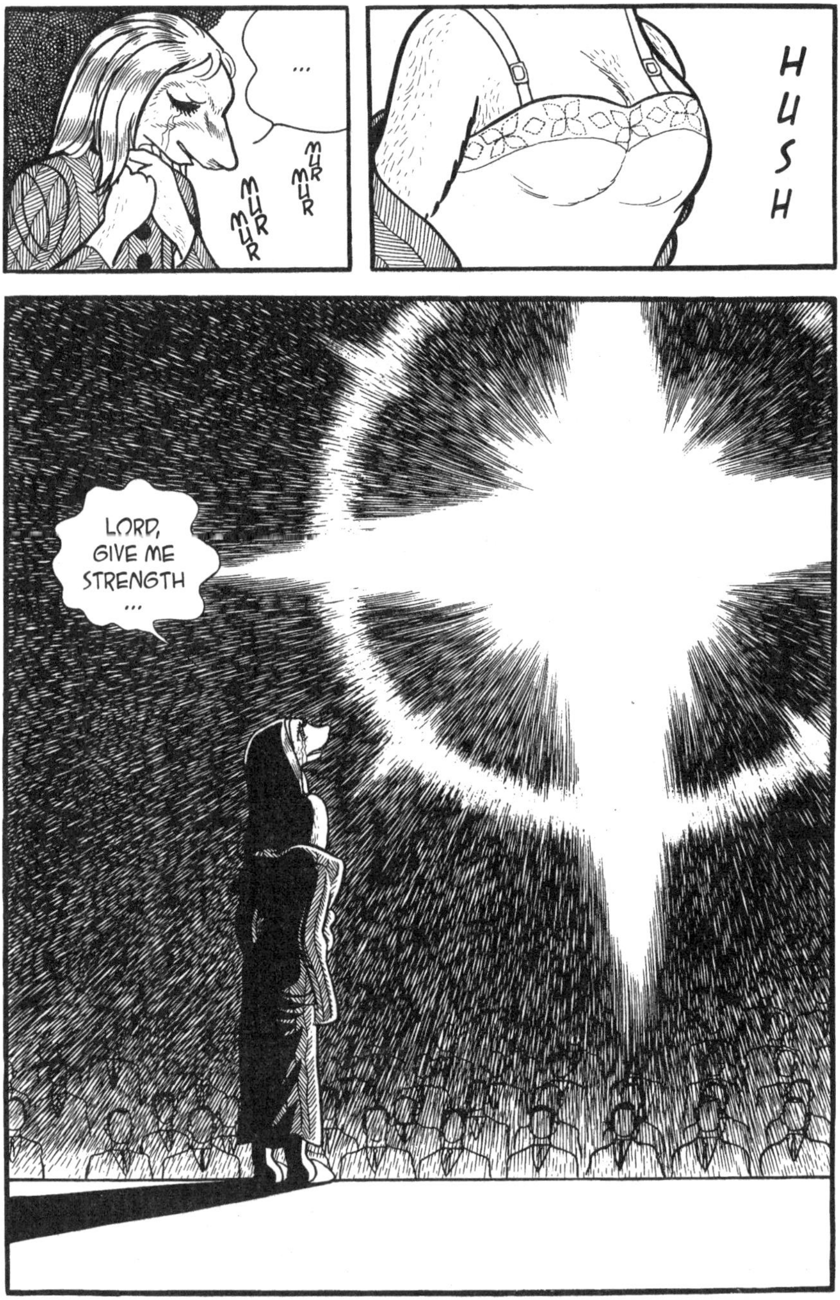
...
MUR MUR
MUR MUR
HUSH
LORD, GIVE ME STRENGTH ...

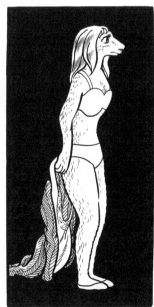

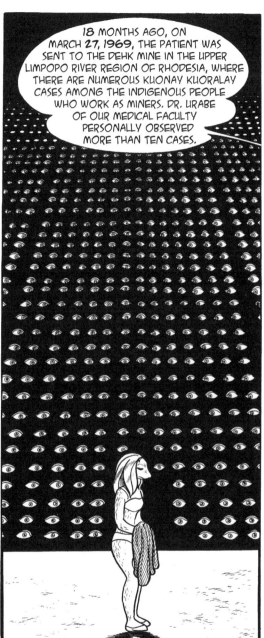

18 MONTHS AGO, ON MARCH 27, 1969, THE PATIENT WAS SENT TO THE DEHK MINE IN THE UPPER LIMPOPO RIVER REGION OF RHODESIA, WHERE THERE ARE NUMEROUS KUONAY KUORALAY CASES AMONG THE INDIGENOUS PEOPLE WHO WORK AS MINERS. DR. URABE OF OUR MEDICAL FACULTY PERSONALLY OBSERVED MORE THAN TEN CASES.

441

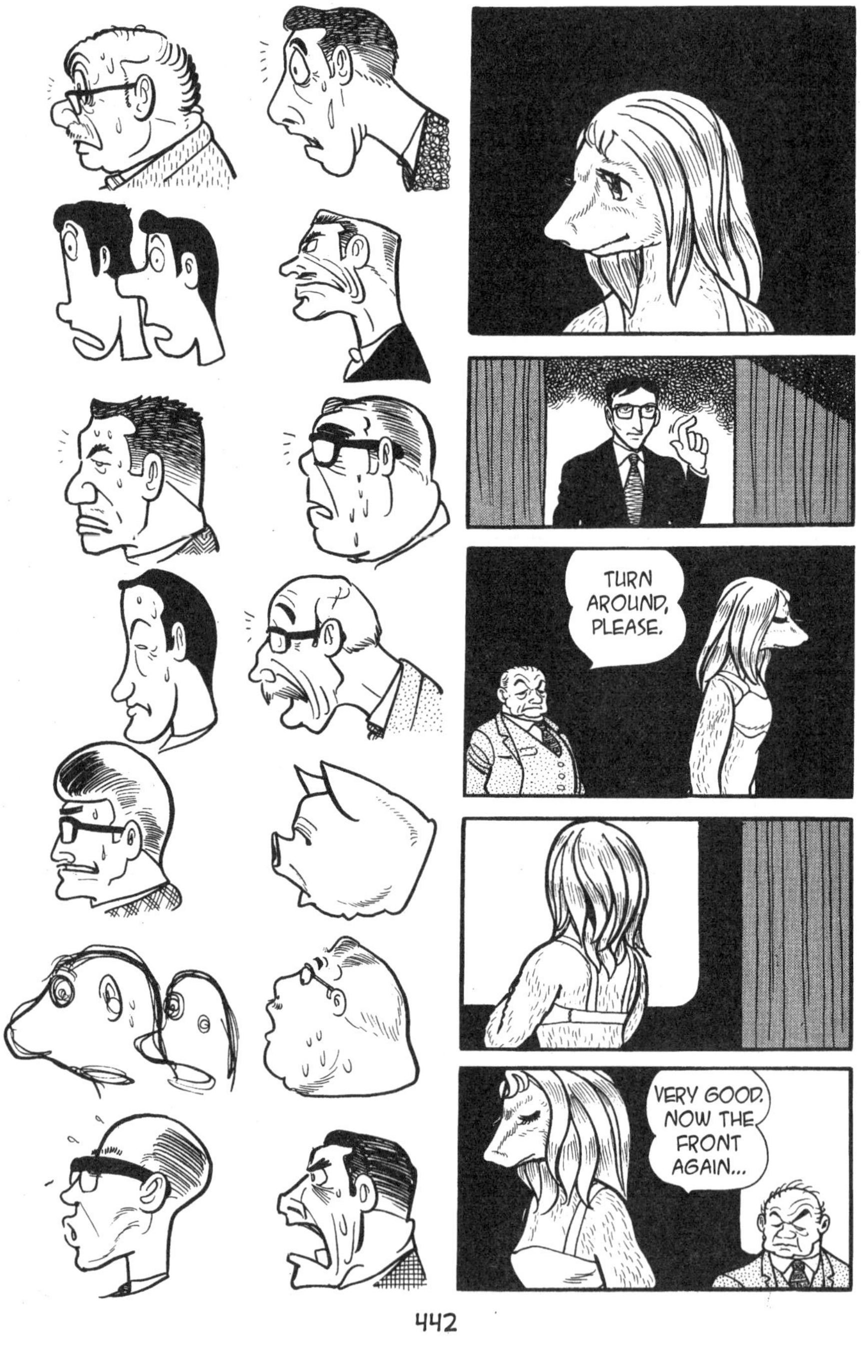
TURN AROUND, PLEASE.
VERY GOOD. NOW THE FRONT AGAIN...

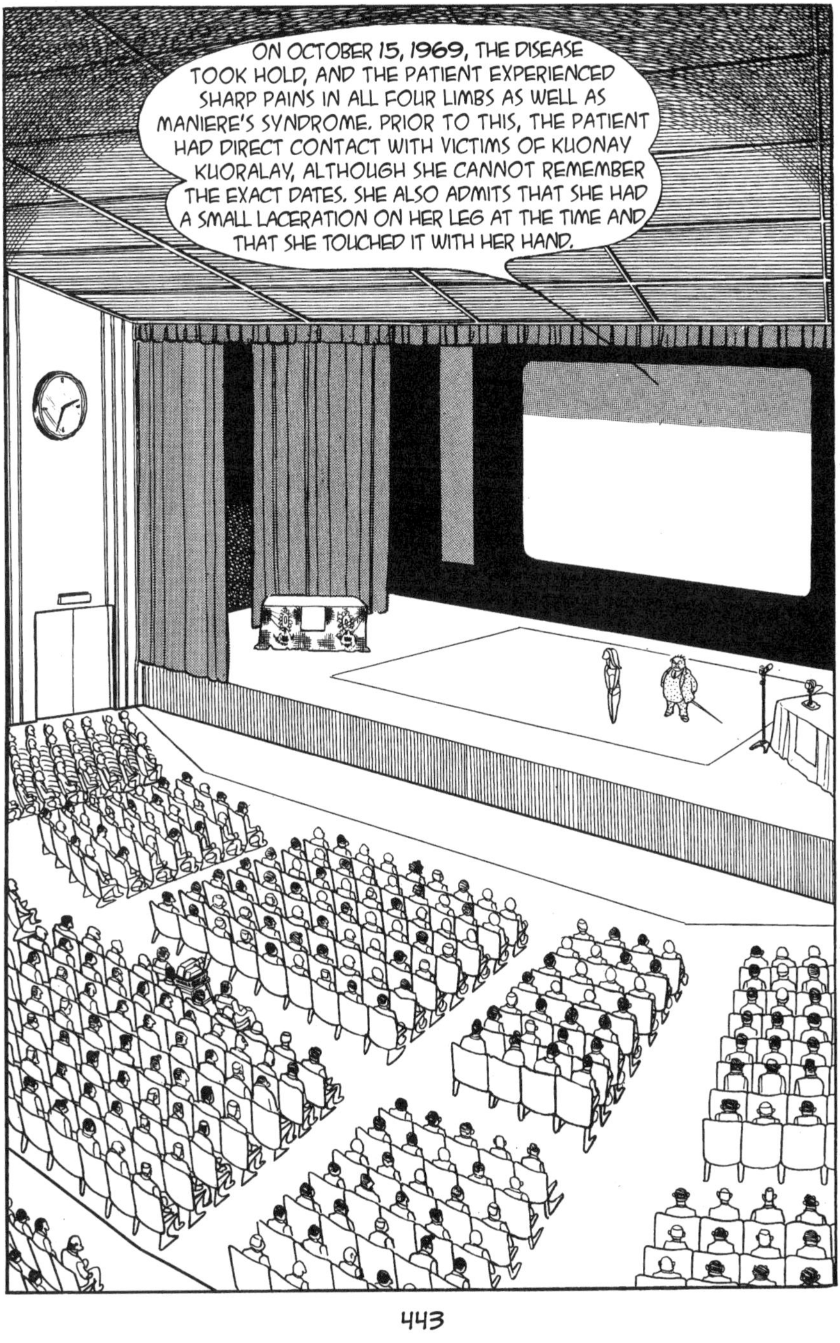
ON OCTOBER 15, 1969, THE DISEASE TOOK HOLD, AND THE PATIENT EXPERIENCED SHARP PAINS IN ALL FOUR LIMBS AS WELL AS MANIERE'S SYNDROME. PRIOR TO THIS, THE PATIENT HAD DIRECT CONTACT WITH VICTIMS OF KUONAY KUORALAY, ALTHOUGH SHE CANNOT REMEMBER THE EXACT DATES. SHE ALSO ADMITS THAT SHE HAD A SMALL LACERATION ON HER LEG AT THE TIME AND THAT SHE TOUCHED IT WITH HER HAND.

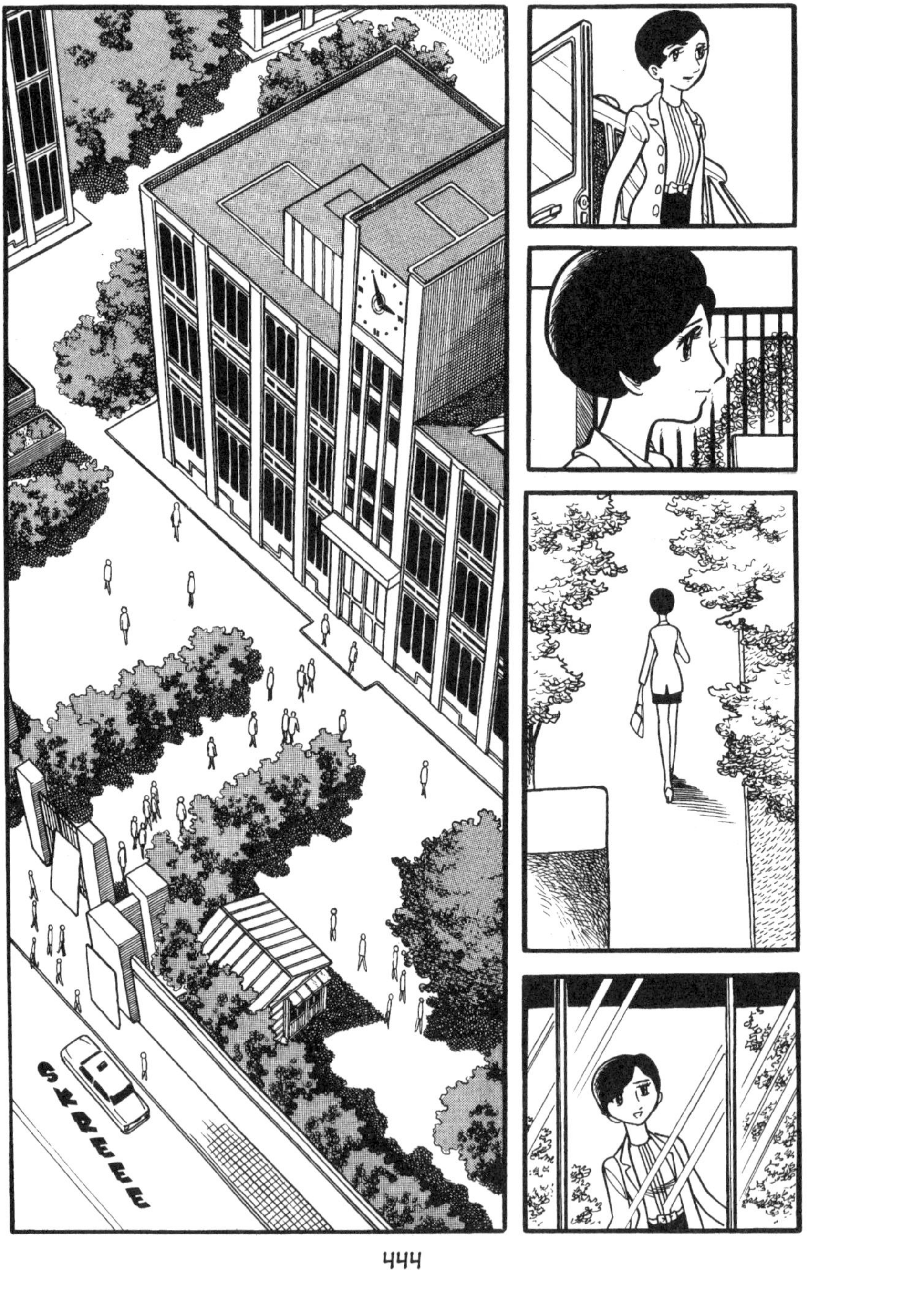
SKREEE

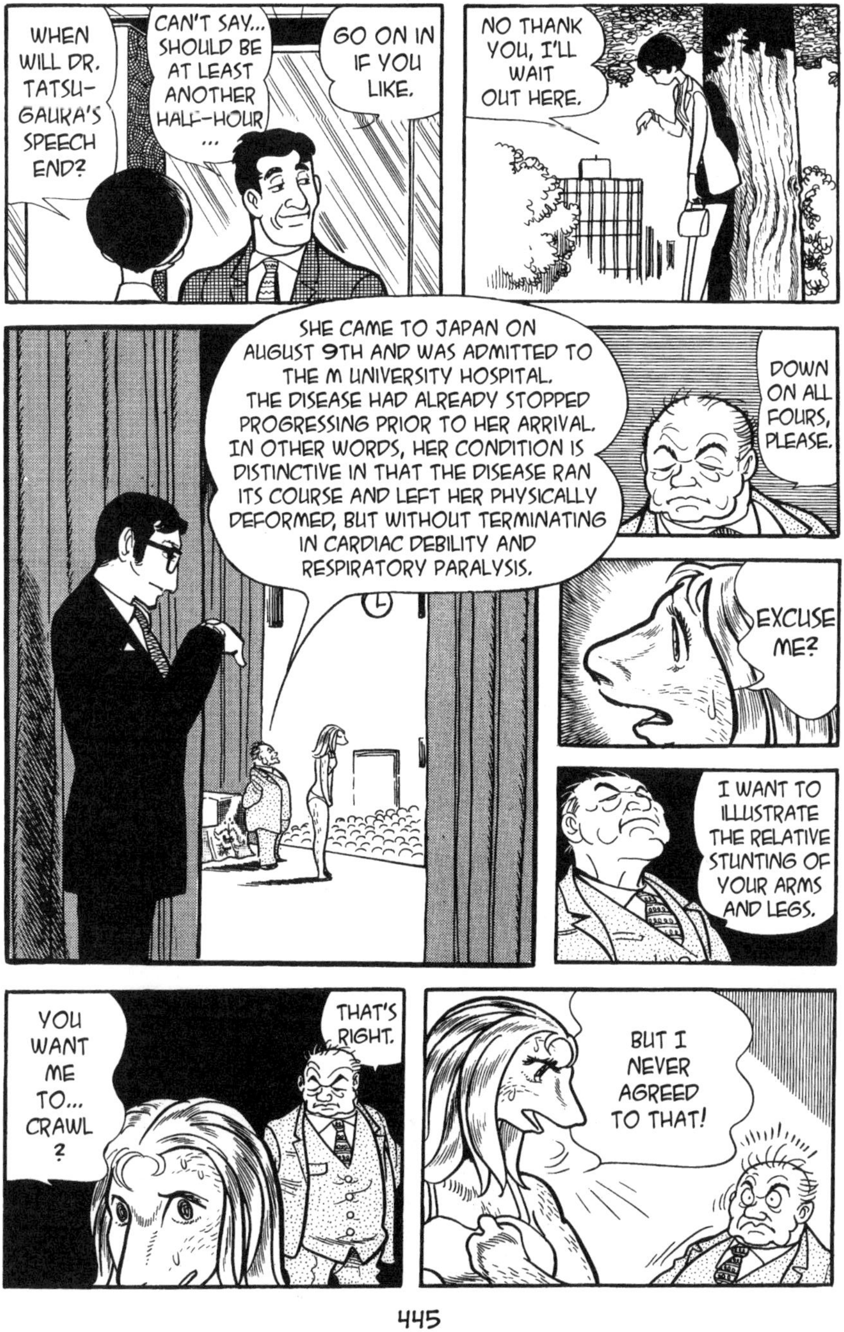
WHEN WILL DR. TATSUGAURA'S SPEECH END?
CAN'T SAY... SHOULD BE AT LEAST ANOTHER HALF-HOUR ...
GO ON IN IF YOU LIKE.
NO THANK YOU, I'LL WAIT OUT HERE.
SHE CAME TO JAPAN ON AUGUST 9TH AND WAS ADMITTED TO THE M UNIVERSITY HOSPITAL. THE DISEASE HAD ALREADY STOPPED PROGRESSING PRIOR TO HER ARRIVAL. IN OTHER WORDS, HER CONDITION IS DISTINCTIVE IN THAT THE DISEASE RAN ITS COURSE AND LEFT HER PHYSICALLY DEFORMED, BUT WITHOUT TERMINATING IN CARDIAC DEBILITY AND RESPIRATORY PARALYSIS.
DOWN ON ALL FOURS, PLEASE.
EXCUSE ME?
I WANT TO ILLUSTRATE THE RELATIVE STUNTING OF YOUR ARMS AND LEGS.
YOU WANT ME TO... CRAWL?
THAT'S RIGHT.
BUT I NEVER AGREED TO THAT!

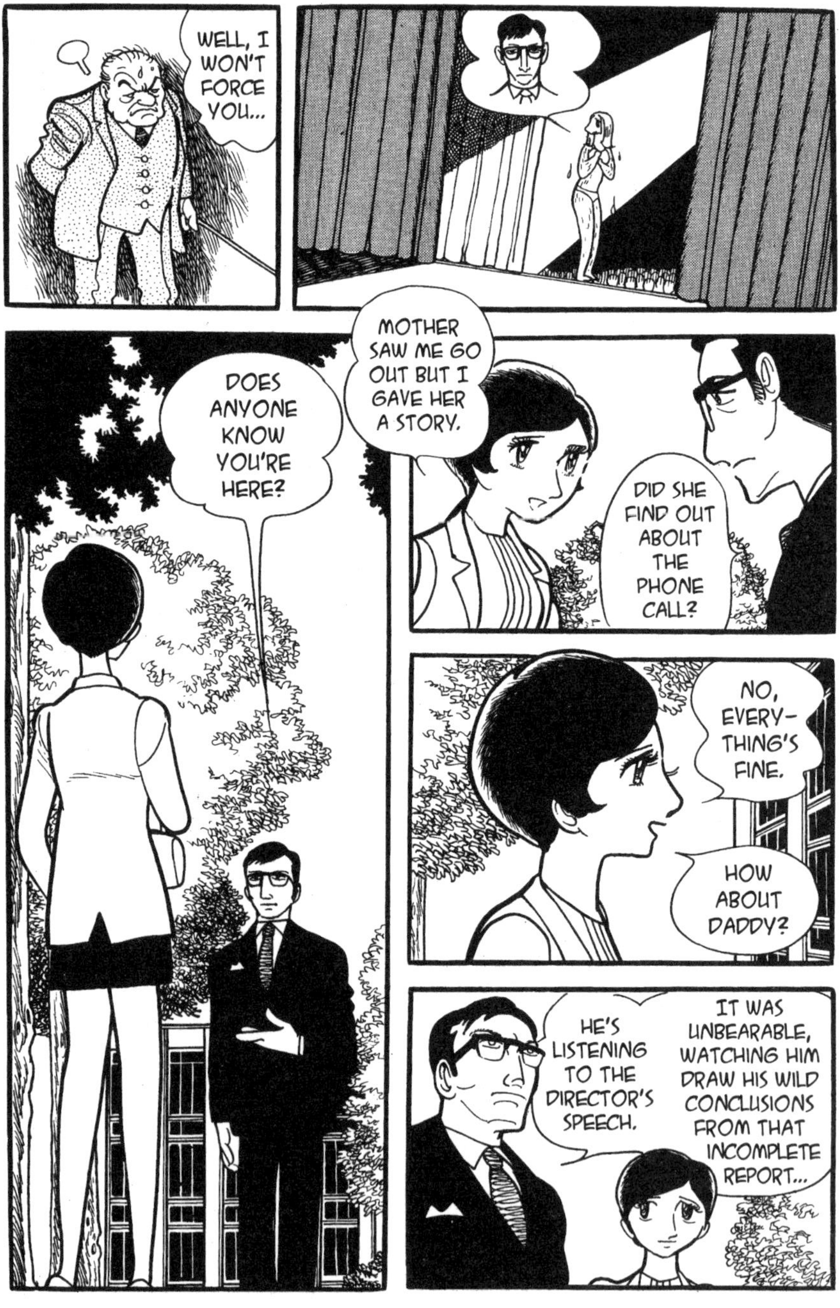

WELL, I WON'T FORCE YOU...
DOES ANYONE KNOW YOU'RE HERE?
MOTHER SAW ME GO OUT BUT I GAVE HER A STORY.
DID SHE FIND OUT ABOUT THE PHONE CALL?
NO, EVERY-THING'S FINE.
HOW ABOUT DADDY?
HE'S LISTENING TO THE DIRECTOR'S SPEECH.
IT WAS UNBEARABLE, WATCHING HIM DRAW HIS WILD CONCLUSIONS FROM THAT INCOMPLETE REPORT...

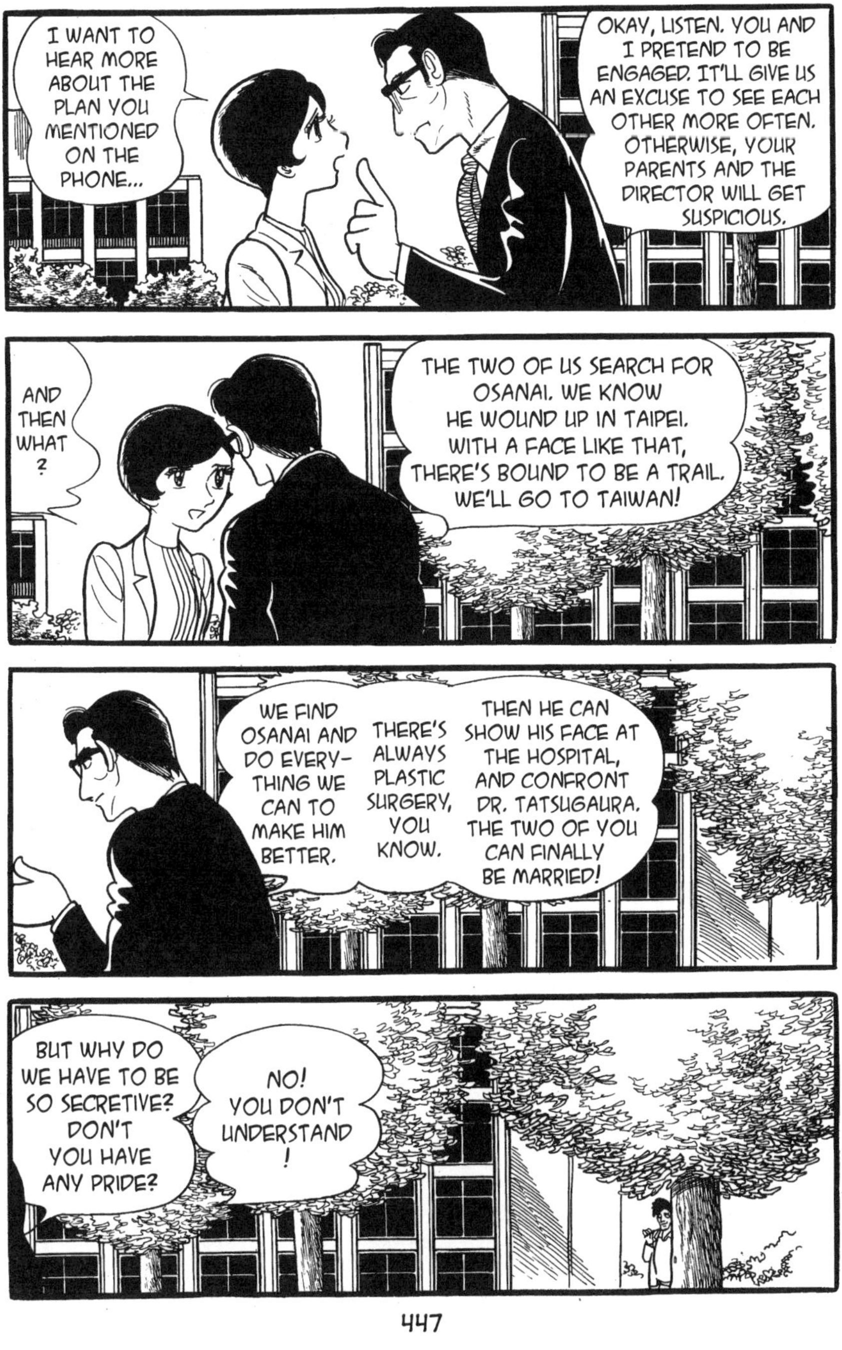
I WANT TO HEAR MORE ABOUT THE PLAN YOU MENTIONED ON THE PHONE...
OKAY, LISTEN. YOU AND I PRETEND TO BE ENGAGED. IT'LL GIVE US AN EXCUSE TO SEE EACH OTHER MORE OFTEN. OTHERWISE, YOUR PARENTS AND THE DIRECTOR WILL GET SUSPICIOUS.
AND THEN WHAT?
THE TWO OF US SEARCH FOR OSANAI. WE KNOW HE WOUND UP IN TAIPEI. WITH A FACE LIKE THAT, THERE'S BOUND TO BE A TRAIL. WE'LL GO TO TAIWAN!
WE FIND OSANAI AND DO EVERY-THING WE CAN TO MAKE HIM BETTER.
THERE'S ALWAYS PLASTIC SURGERY, YOU KNOW.
THEN HE CAN SHOW HIS FACE AT THE HOSPITAL, AND CONFRONT DR. TATSUGAURA. THE TWO OF YOU CAN FINALLY BE MARRIED!
BUT WHY DO WE HAVE TO BE SO SECRETIVE? DON'T YOU HAVE ANY PRIDE?
NO! YOU DON'T UNDERSTAND!

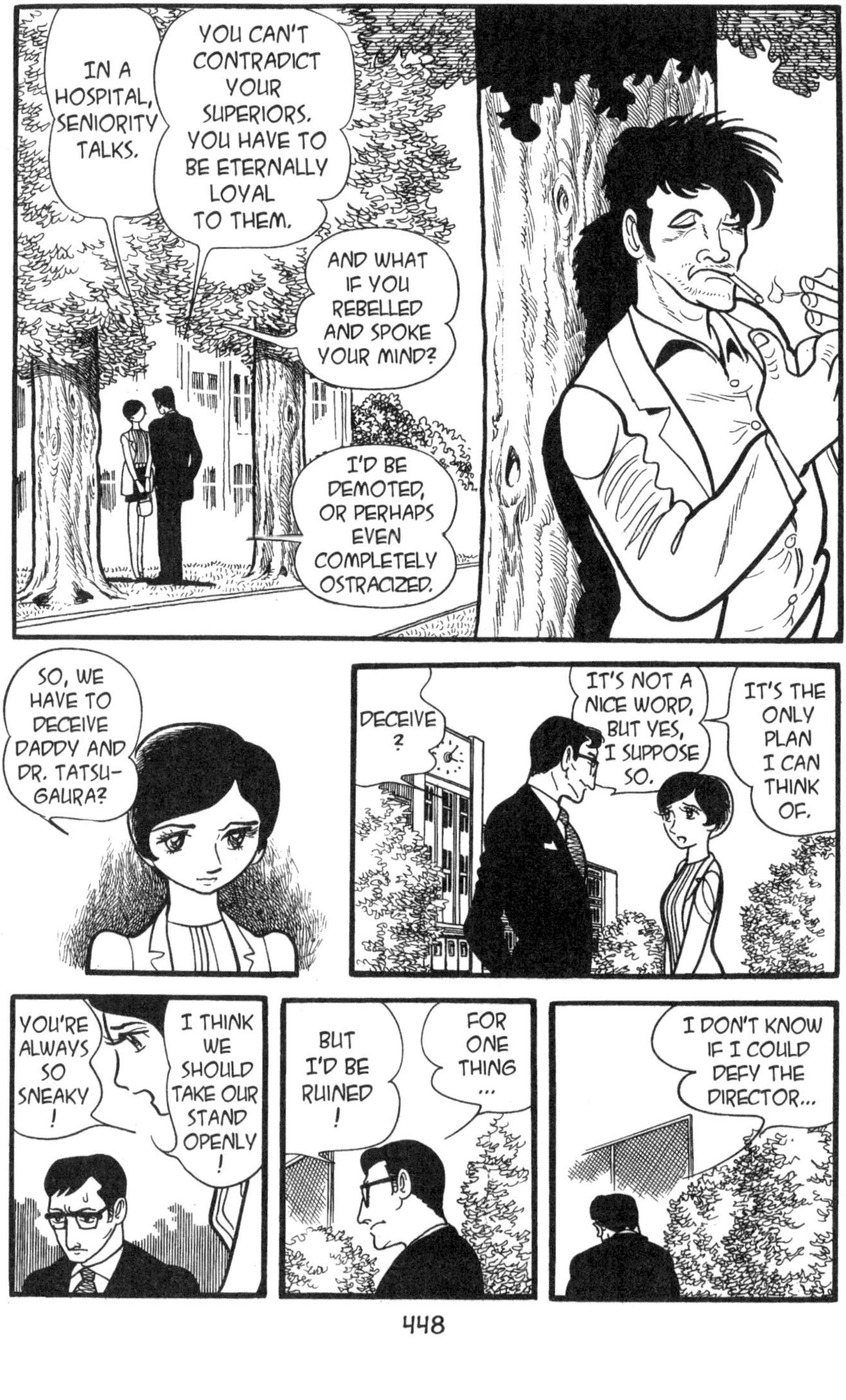
IN A HOSPITAL, SENIORITY TALKS.
YOU CAN'T CONTRADICT YOUR SUPERIORS. YOU HAVE TO BE ETERNALLY LOYAL TO THEM.
AND WHAT IF YOU REBELLED AND SPOKE YOUR MIND?
I'D BE DEMOTED, OR PERHAPS EVEN COMPLETELY OSTRACIZED.
SO, WE HAVE TO DECEIVE DADDY AND DR. TATSU-GAURA?
DECEIVE?
IT'S NOT A NICE WORD, BUT YES, I SUPPOSE SO.
IT'S THE ONLY PLAN I CAN THINK OF.
YOU'RE ALWAYS SO SNEAKY!
I THINK WE SHOULD TAKE OUR STAND OPENLY!
BUT I'D BE RUINED!
FOR ONE THING...
I DON'T KNOW IF I COULD DEFY THE DIRECTOR...

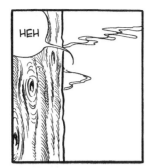

HEH

HEH HEH ...

WHAT HAVE WE HERE ?

THIS URABE DOCTOR, THE RICH YOUNG GIRL, AND THE MISSING DOG-FACED MAN...

I KNEW THAT IF I TAILED THEM, SOMETHING INTERESTING WOULD COME UP.

THERE MAY BE MONEY IN THIS. BIG MONEY.

SO, THEIR ENGAGEMENT IS JUST A RUSE...

BET I COULD SHAKE THINGS UP BY THREATENING TO EXPOSE THEM.

I'M SURE THAT GIRL HAS ACCESS TO PLENTY OF DADDY'S MONEY.

'COURSE, I'LL HAVE TO WATCH OUT FOR THAT OLD CRONE...

449

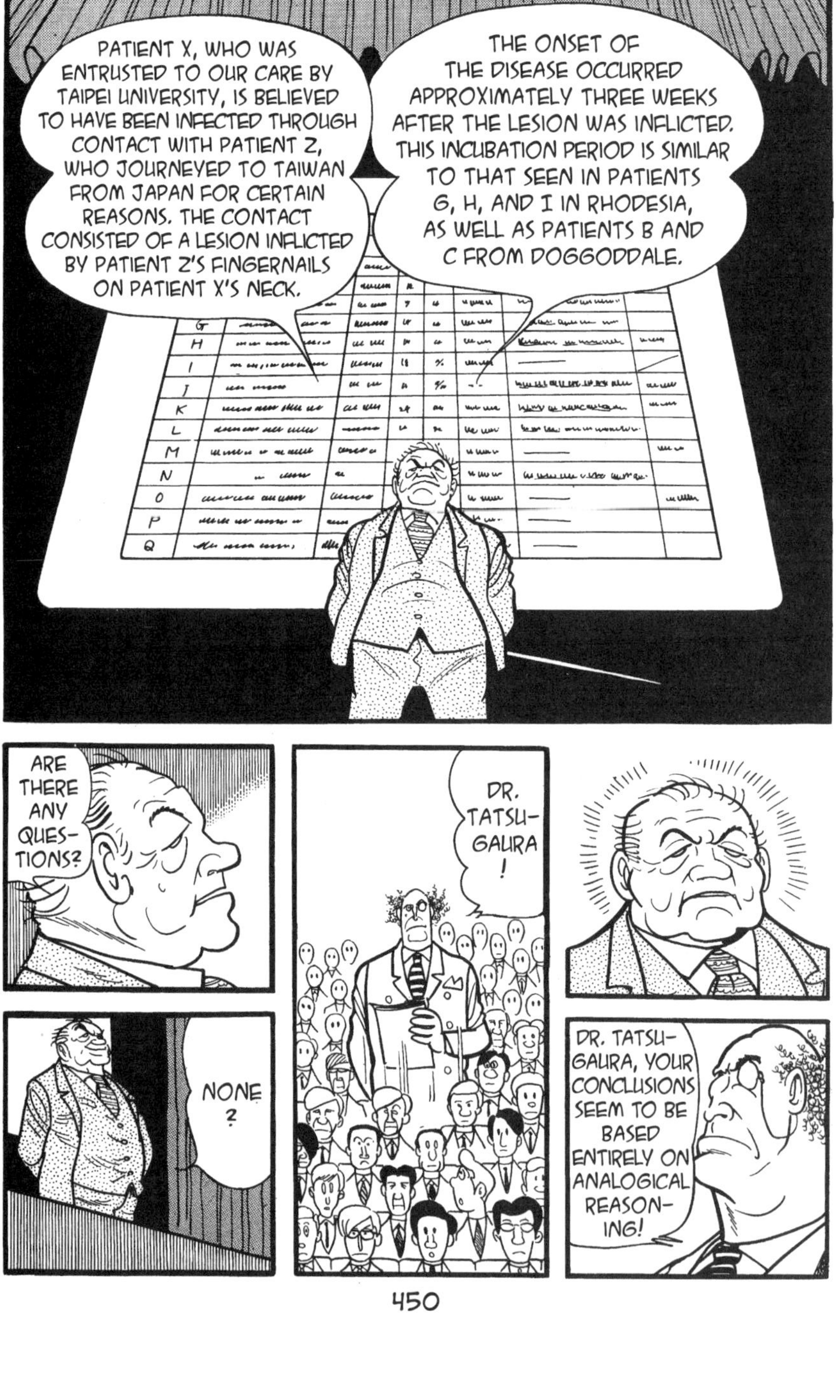
PATIENT X, WHO WAS ENTRUSTED TO OUR CARE BY TAIPEI UNIVERSITY, IS BELIEVED TO HAVE BEEN INFECTED THROUGH CONTACT WITH PATIENT Z, WHO JOURNEYED TO TAIWAN FROM JAPAN FOR CERTAIN REASONS. THE CONTACT CONSISTED OF A LESION INFLICTED BY PATIENT Z'S FINGERNAILS ON PATIENT X'S NECK.
THE ONSET OF THE DISEASE OCCURRED APPROXIMATELY THREE WEEKS AFTER THE LESION WAS INFLICTED. THIS INCUBATION PERIOD IS SIMILAR TO THAT SEEN IN PATIENTS G, H, AND I IN RHODESIA, AS WELL AS PATIENTS B AND C FROM DOGGODDALE.
G
H
I
J
K
L
M
N
O
P
Q
ARE THERE ANY QUESTIONS?
DR. TATSU-GAURA!
NONE?
DR. TATSU-GAURA, YOUR CONCLUSIONS SEEM TO BE BASED ENTIRELY ON ANALOGICAL REASON-ING!

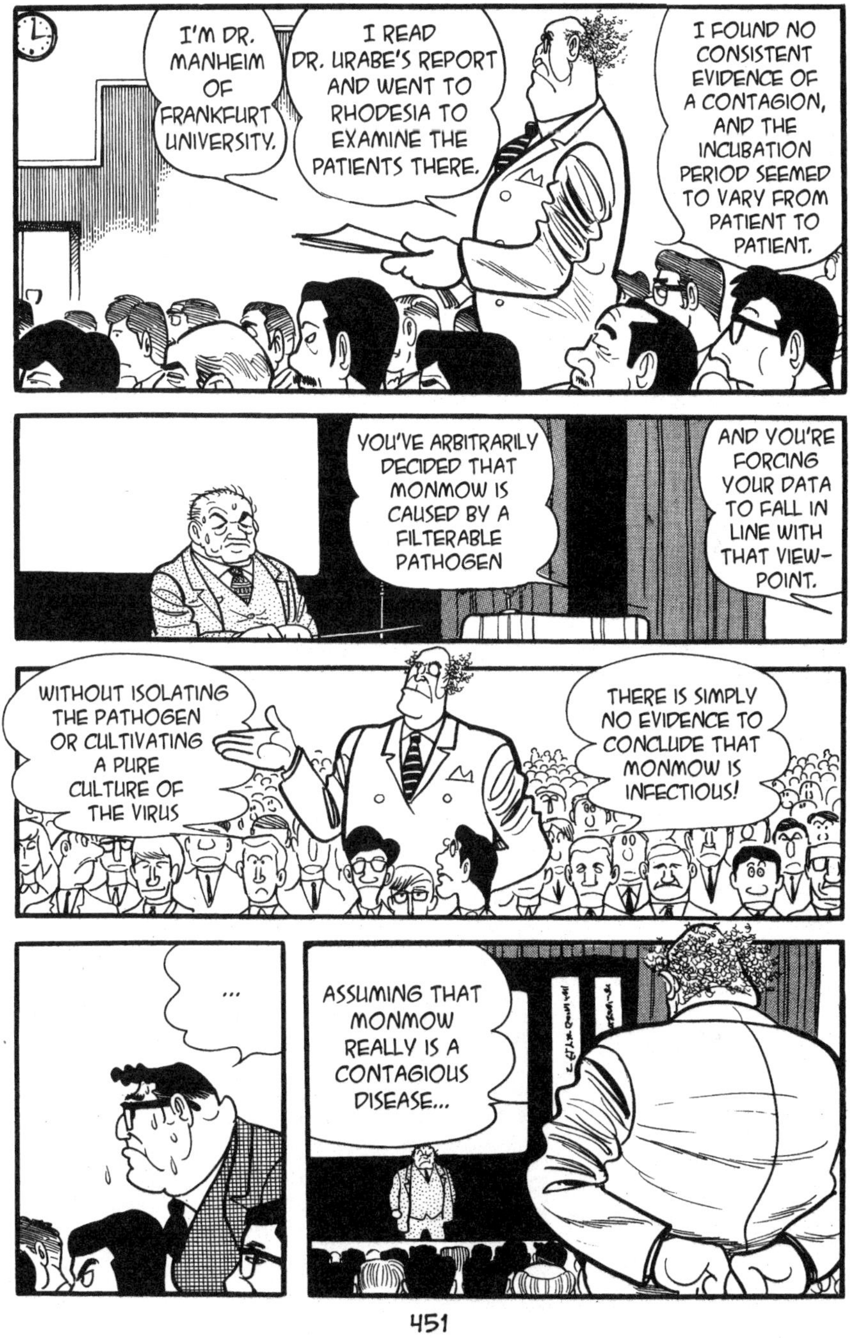
I'M DR. MANHEIM OF FRANKFURT UNIVERSITY.
I READ DR. URABE'S REPORT AND WENT TO RHODESIA TO EXAMINE THE PATIENTS THERE.
I FOUND NO CONSISTENT EVIDENCE OF A CONTAGION, AND THE INCUBATION PERIOD SEEMED TO VARY FROM PATIENT TO PATIENT.
YOU'VE ARBITRARILY DECIDED THAT MONMOW IS CAUSED BY A FILTERABLE PATHOGEN
AND YOU'RE FORCING YOUR DATA TO FALL IN LINE WITH THAT VIEW-POINT.
WITHOUT ISOLATING THE PATHOGEN OR CULTIVATING A PURE CULTURE OF THE VIRUS
THERE IS SIMPLY NO EVIDENCE TO CONCLUDE THAT MONMOW IS INFECTIOUS!
...
ASSUMING THAT MONMOW REALLY IS A CONTAGIOUS DISEASE...

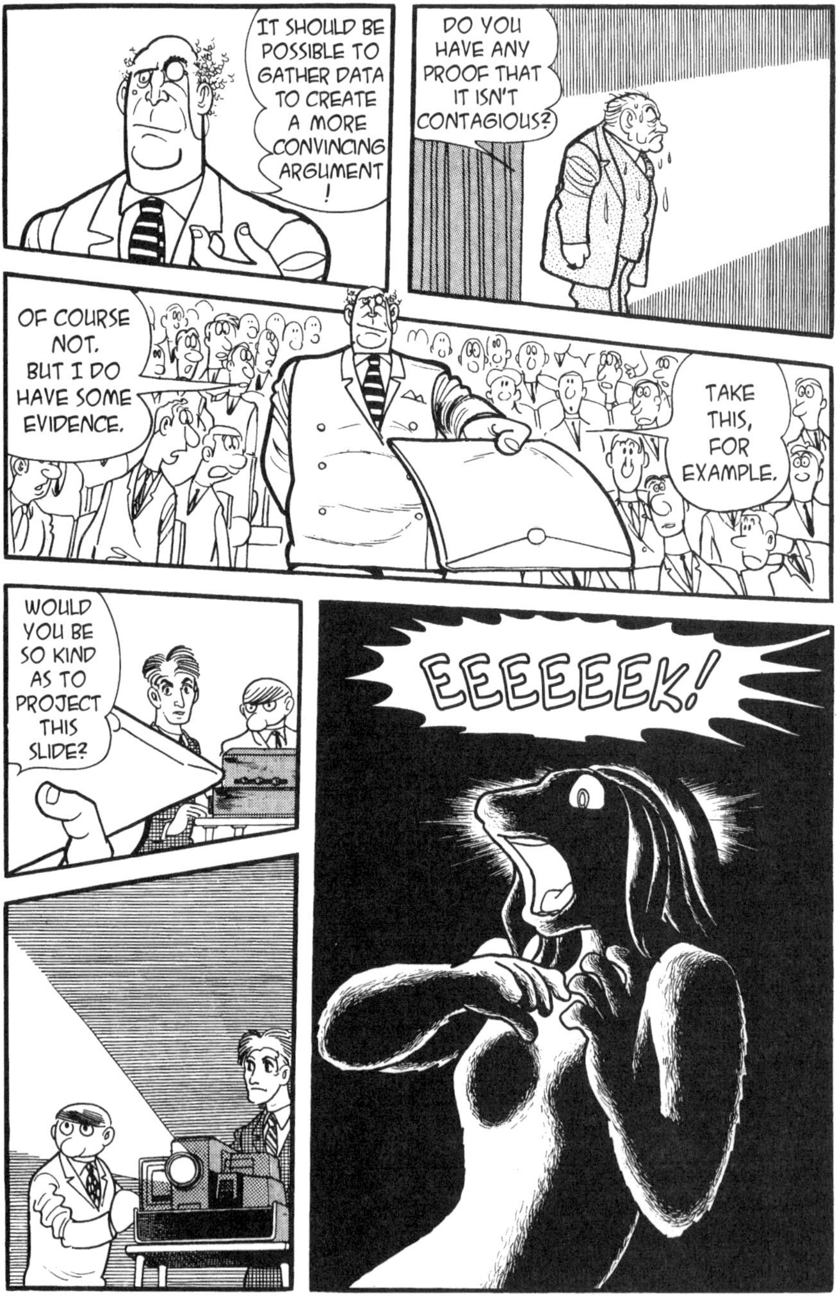
IT SHOULD BE POSSIBLE TO GATHER DATA TO CREATE A MORE CONVINCING ARGUMENT!
DO YOU HAVE ANY PROOF THAT IT ISN'T CONTAGIOUS?
OF COURSE NOT. BUT I DO HAVE SOME EVIDENCE.
TAKE THIS, FOR EXAMPLE.
WOULD YOU BE SO KIND AS TO PROJECT THIS SLIDE?
EEEEEEK!

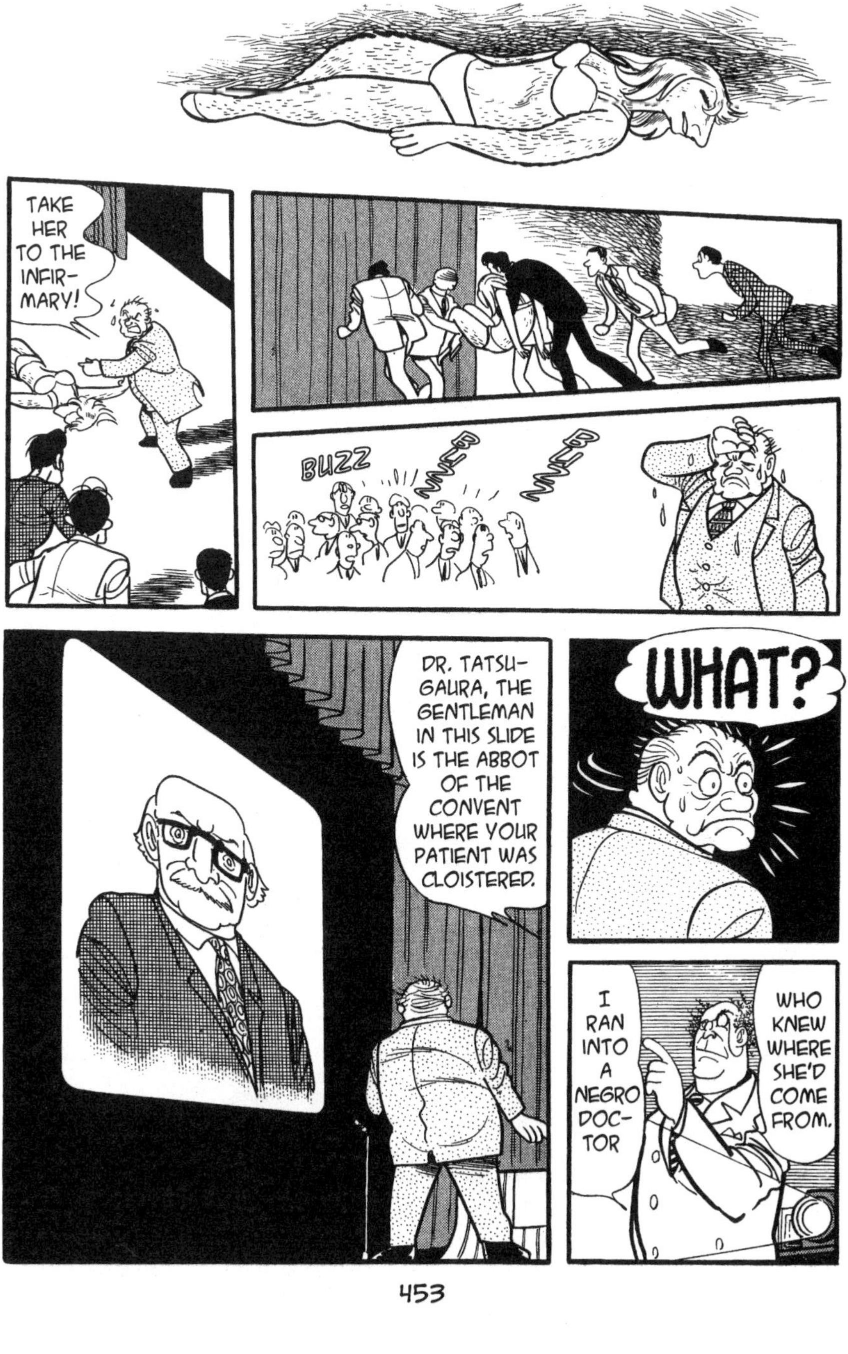
TAKE HER TO THE INFIR-MARY!
BUZZ
BUNNN
BUNNN
DR. TATSU-GAURA, THE GENTLEMAN IN THIS SLIDE IS THE ABBOT OF THE CONVENT WHERE YOUR PATIENT WAS CLOISTERED.
WHAT?
I RAN INTO A NEGRO DOC-TOR
WHO KNEW WHERE SHE'D COME FROM.

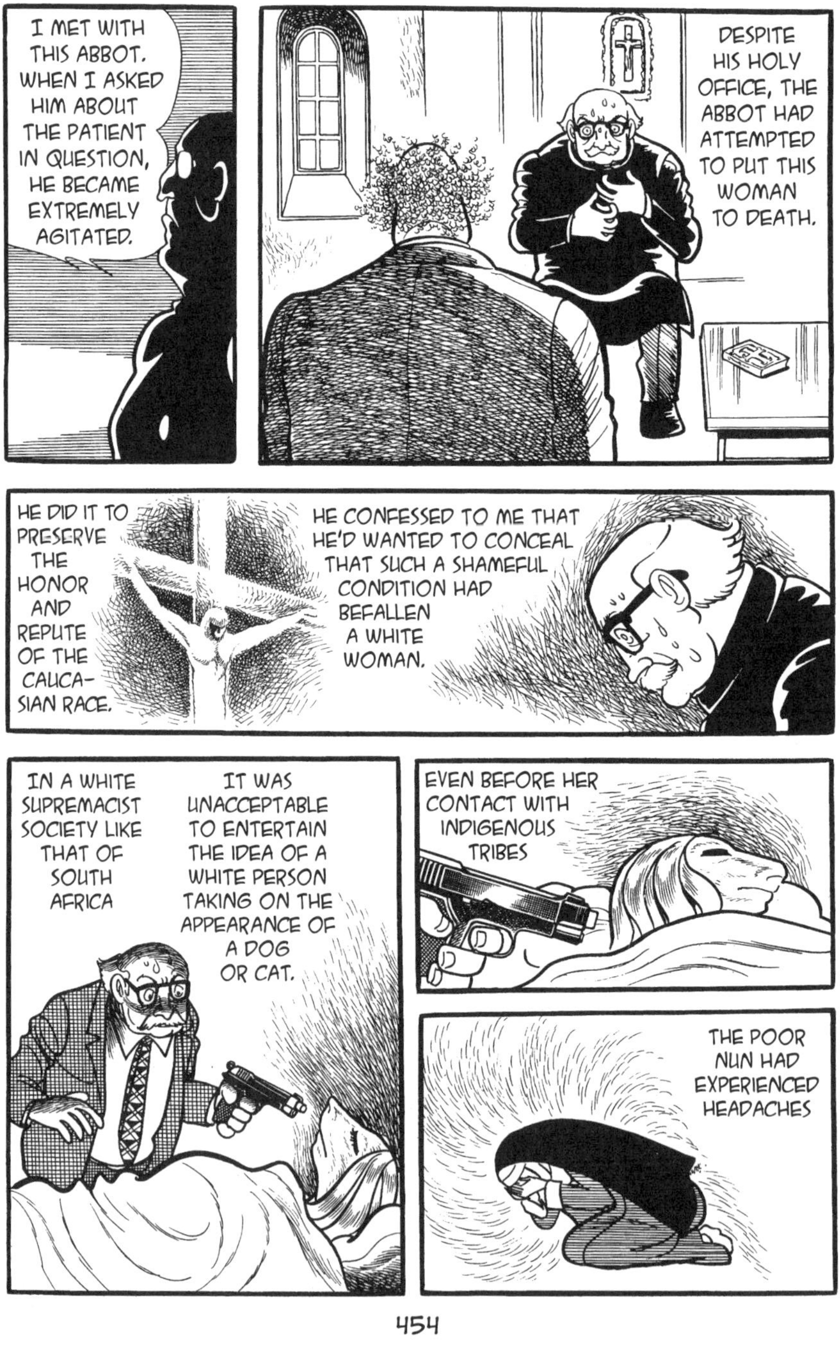

I MET WITH THIS ABBOT. WHEN I ASKED HIM ABOUT THE PATIENT IN QUESTION, HE BECAME EXTREMELY AGITATED.
DESPITE HIS HOLY OFFICE, THE ABBOT HAD ATTEMPTED TO PUT THIS WOMAN TO DEATH.
HE DID IT TO PRESERVE THE HONOR AND REPUTE OF THE CAUCA-SIAN RACE.
HE CONFESSED TO ME THAT HE'D WANTED TO CONCEAL THAT SUCH A SHAMEFUL CONDITION HAD BEFALLEN A WHITE WOMAN.
IN A WHITE SUPREMACIST SOCIETY LIKE THAT OF SOUTH AFRICA
IT WAS UNACCEPTABLE TO ENTERTAIN THE IDEA OF A WHITE PERSON TAKING ON THE APPEARANCE OF A DOG OR CAT.
EVEN BEFORE HER CONTACT WITH INDIGENOUS TRIBES
THE POOR NUN HAD EXPERIENCED HEADACHES

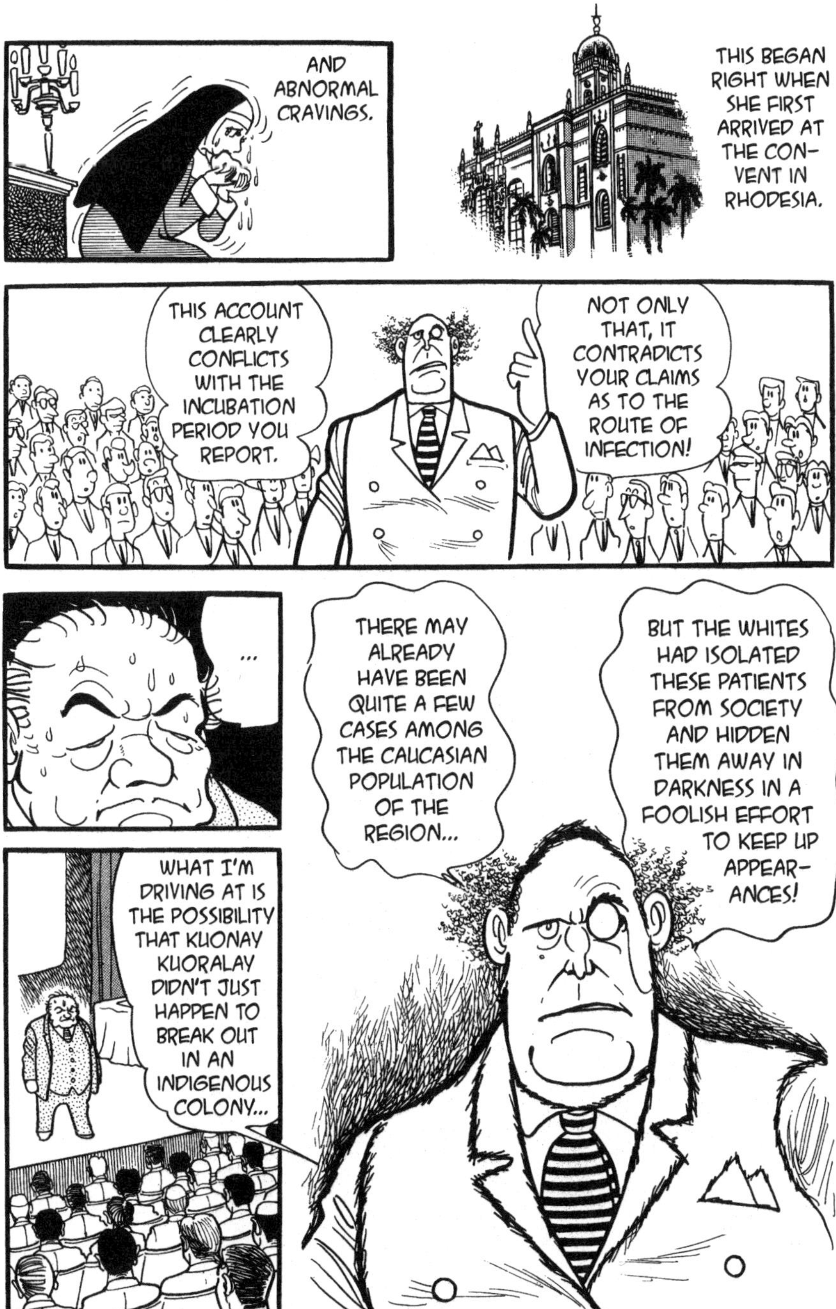

AND ABNORMAL CRAVINGS.
THIS BEGAN RIGHT WHEN SHE FIRST ARRIVED AT THE CONVENT IN RHODESIA.
THIS ACCOUNT CLEARLY CONFLICTS WITH THE INCUBATION PERIOD YOU REPORT.
NOT ONLY THAT, IT CONTRADICTS YOUR CLAIMS AS TO THE ROUTE OF INFECTION!
...
THERE MAY ALREADY HAVE BEEN QUITE A FEW CASES AMONG THE CAUCASIAN POPULATION OF THE REGION...
BUT THE WHITES HAD ISOLATED THESE PATIENTS FROM SOCIETY AND HIDDEN THEM AWAY IN DARKNESS IN A FOOLISH EFFORT TO KEEP UP APPEARANCES!
WHAT I'M DRIVING AT IS THE POSSIBILITY THAT KUONAY KUORALAY DIDN'T JUST HAPPEN TO BREAK OUT IN AN INDIGENOUS COLONY...

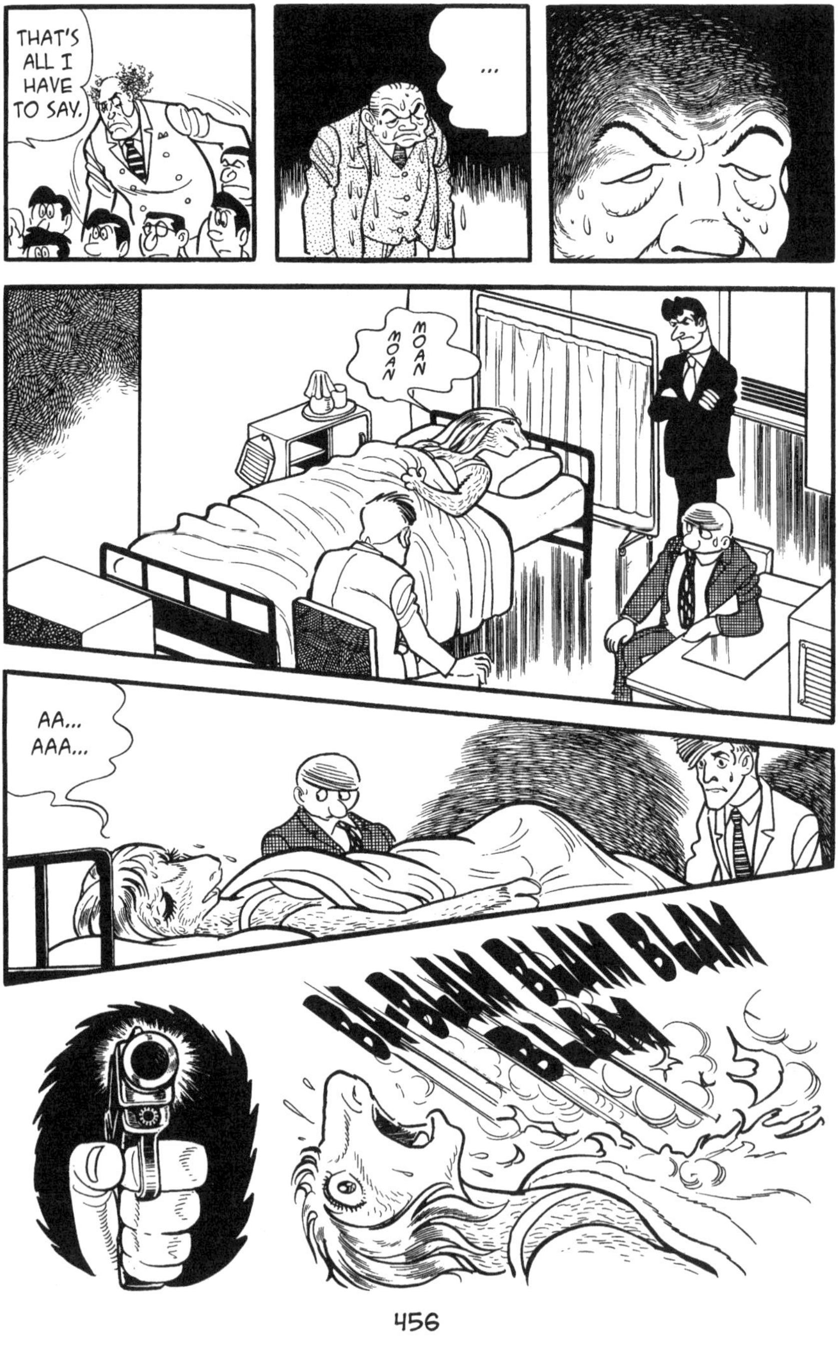
THAT'S ALL I HAVE TO SAY.
...
MOAN MOAN
AA... AAA...
BA-BLAM BLAM BLAM BLAM BLAM

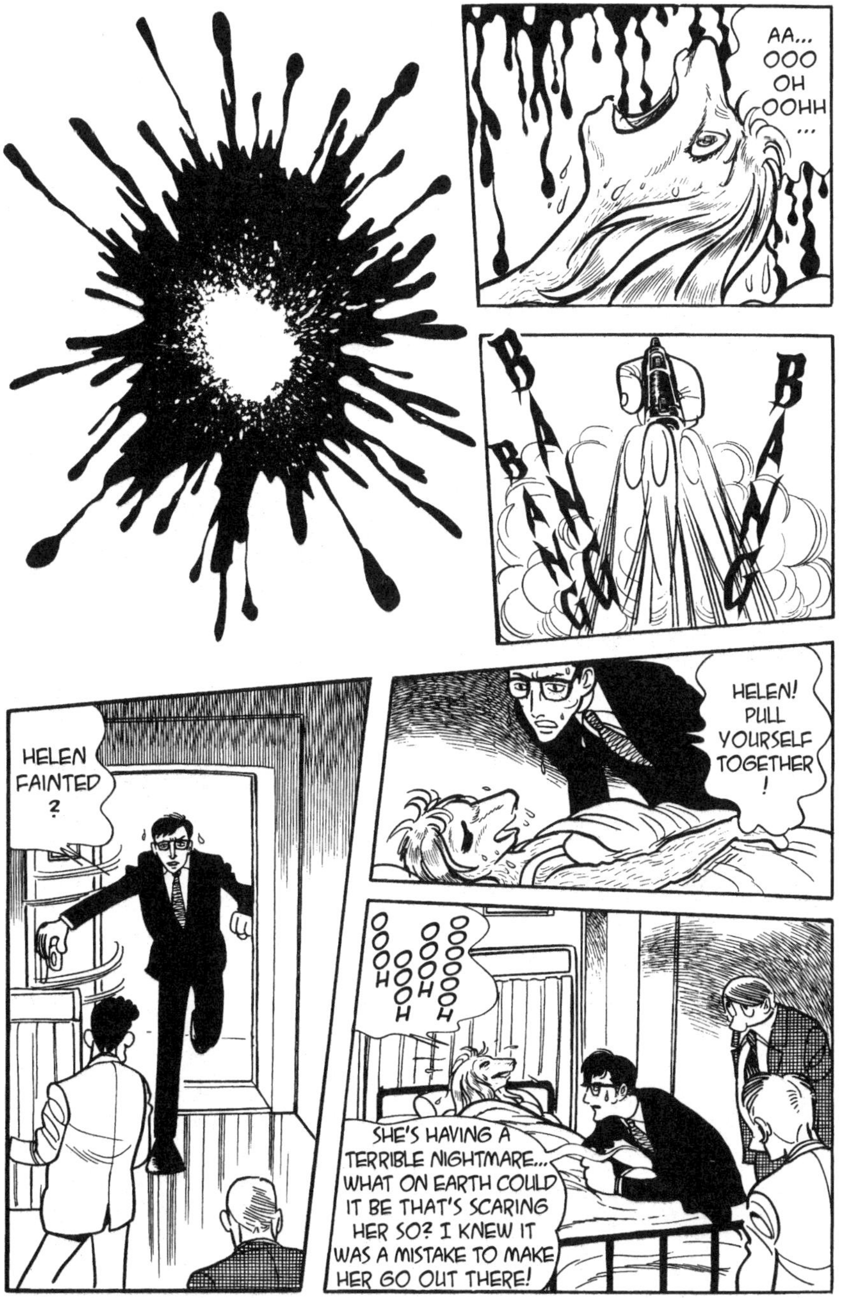
AA... OOO OH OOHH ...
BANG
BANG
HELEN! PULL YOURSELF TOGETHER!
HELEN FAINTED?
OOOOH
OOOOOH
OOOOH
OOOOOOOH
SHE'S HAVING A TERRIBLE NIGHTMARE... WHAT ON EARTH COULD IT BE THAT'S SCARING HER SO? I KNEW IT WAS A MISTAKE TO MAKE HER GO OUT THERE!

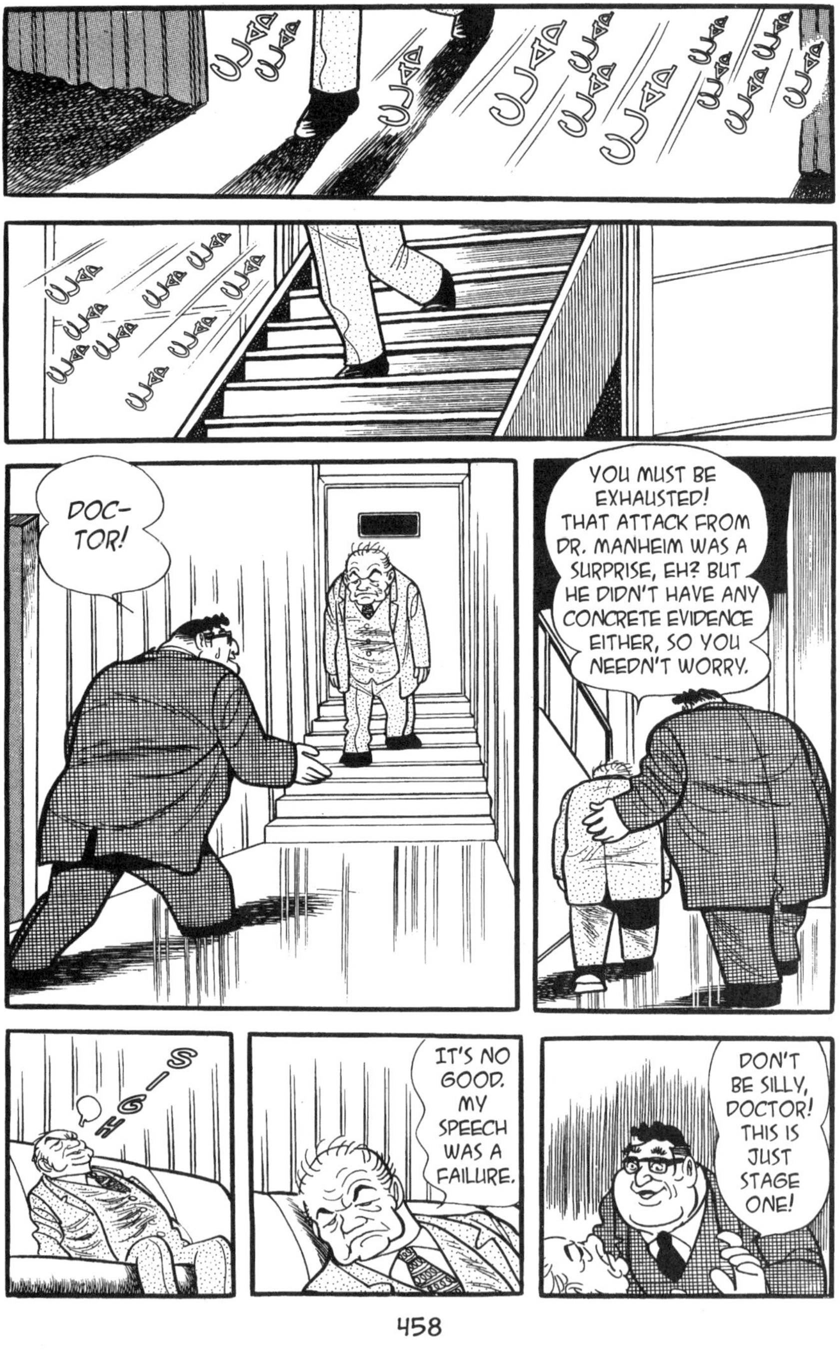
DOC-TOR!
YOU MUST BE EXHAUSTED! THAT ATTACK FROM DR. MANHEIM WAS A SURPRISE, EH? BUT HE DIDN'T HAVE ANY CONCRETE EVIDENCE EITHER, SO YOU NEEDN'T WORRY.
IT'S NO GOOD. MY SPEECH WAS A FAILURE.
DON'T BE SILLY, DOCTOR! THIS IS JUST STAGE ONE!

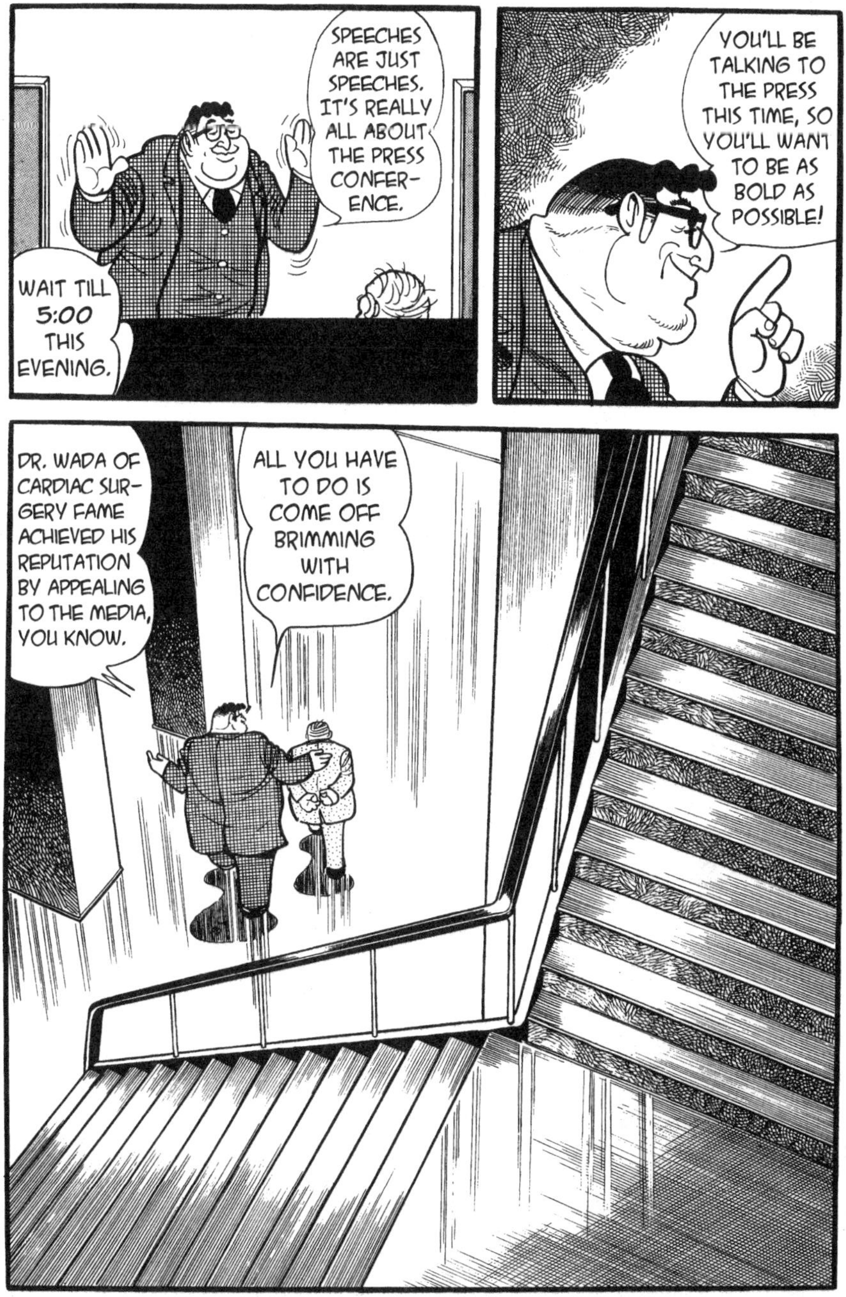
SPEECHES ARE JUST SPEECHES. IT'S REALLY ALL ABOUT THE PRESS CONFERENCE.
WAIT TILL 5:00 THIS EVENING.
YOU'LL BE TALKING TO THE PRESS THIS TIME, SO YOU'LL WANT TO BE AS BOLD AS POSSIBLE!
ALL YOU HAVE TO DO IS COME OFF BRIMMING WITH CONFIDENCE.
DR. WADA OF CARDIAC SURGERY FAME ACHIEVED HIS REPUTATION BY APPEALING TO THE MEDIA, YOU KNOW.

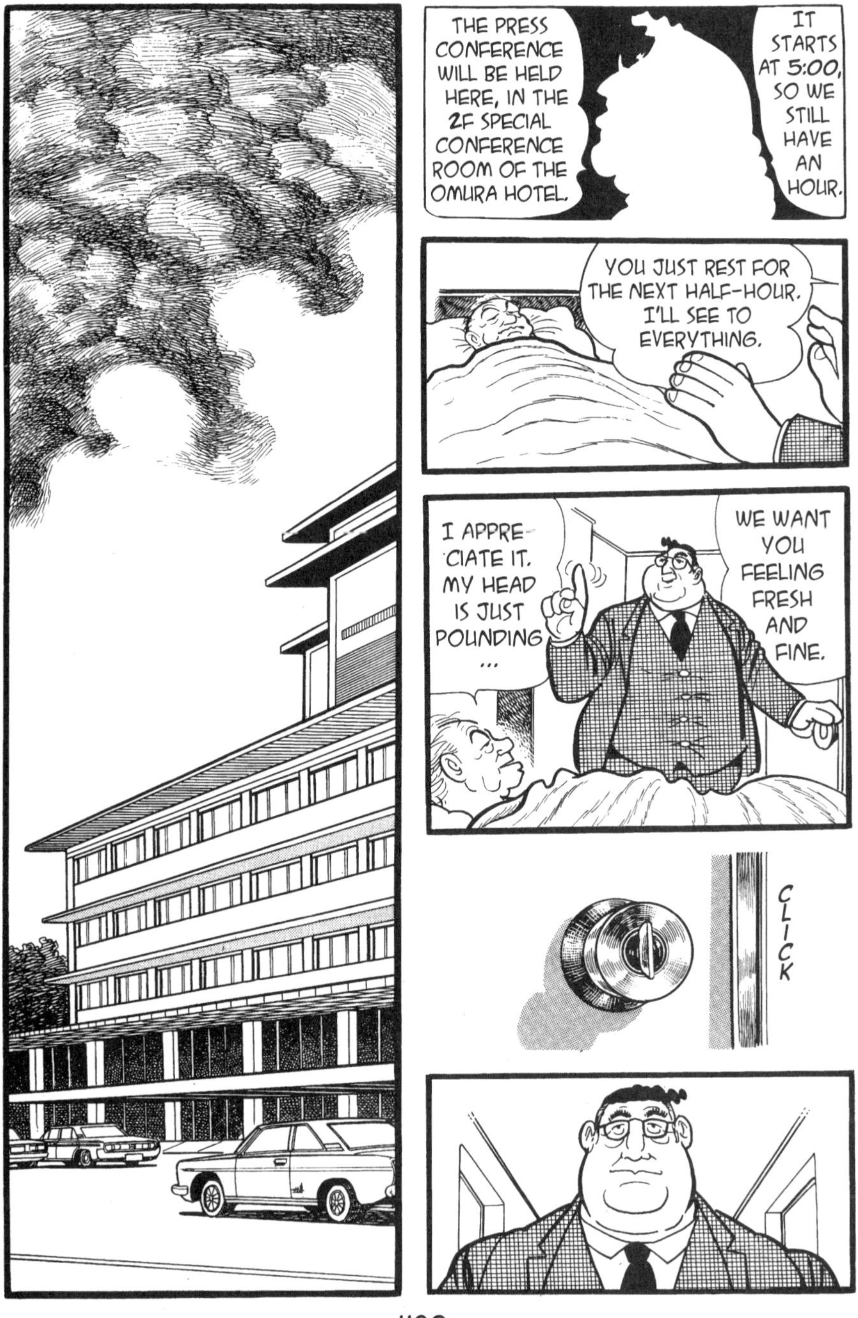
THE PRESS CONFERENCE WILL BE HELD HERE, IN THE 2F SPECIAL CONFERENCE ROOM OF THE OMURA HOTEL.
IT STARTS AT 5:00, SO WE STILL HAVE AN HOUR.
YOU JUST REST FOR THE NEXT HALF-HOUR. I'LL SEE TO EVERYTHING.
I APPRE-CIATE IT. MY HEAD IS JUST POUNDING ...
WE WANT YOU FEELING FRESH AND FINE.
CLICK

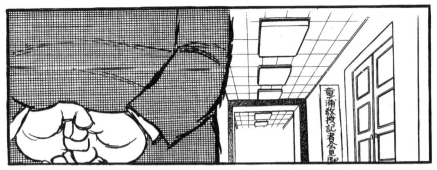

THIS IS WHERE THE REAL BATTLE IS FOUGHT.

LOOKS LIKE THE DOCTOR LOST A LOT OF CONFIDENCE FROM THAT CONFRONTATION WITH DR. MANHEIM. THE NAIL THAT STICKS OUT ALWAYS GETS HAMMERED DOWN...

IN ANY CASE, I'VE HAD A WORD WITH 5 OR 6 VERY INFLUENTIAL REPORTERS WHO HAPPEN TO BE PERSONAL FRIENDS...

SO THERE WON'T BE ANY NASTY QUES- TIONS.

YES ?

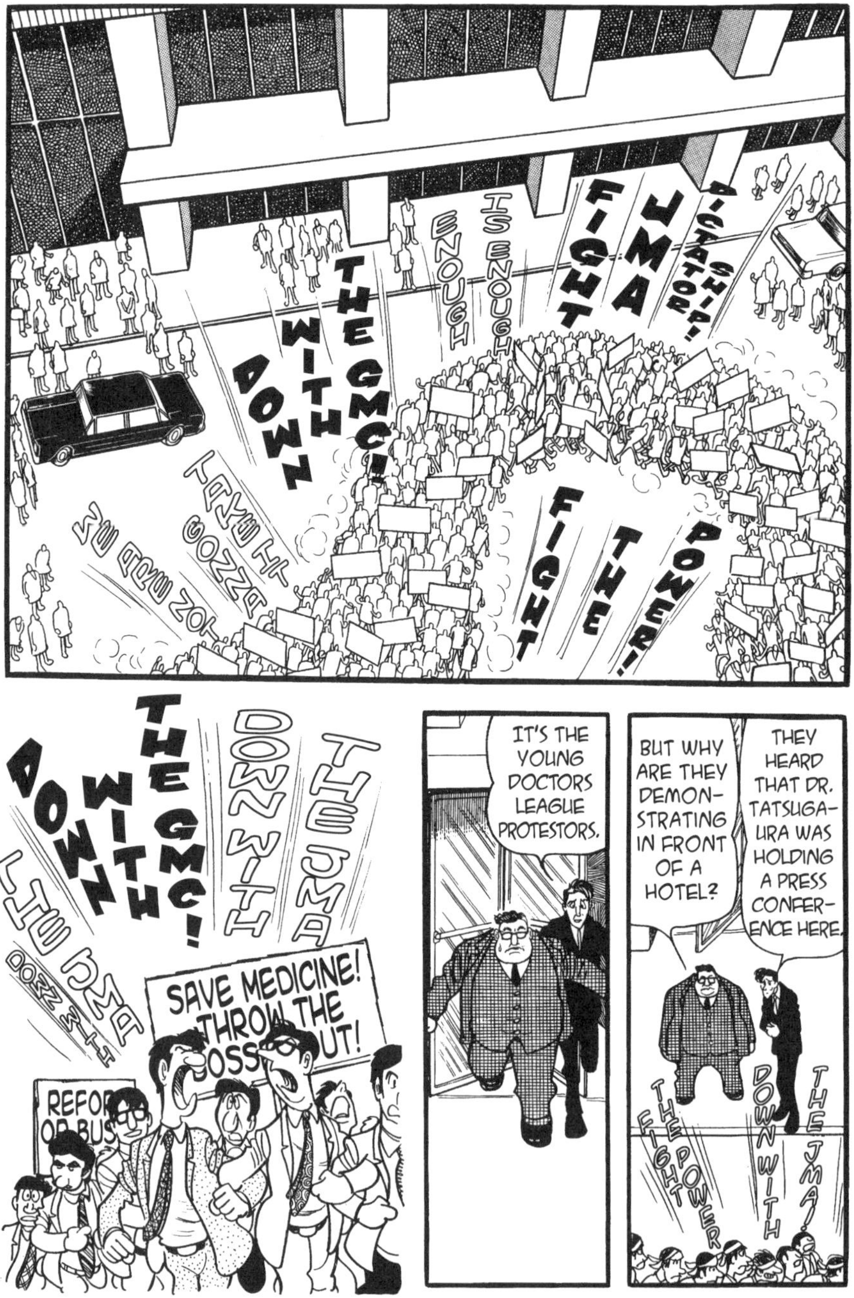

ENOUGH IS ENOUGH
FIGHT JMA DICTATORSHIP!
DOWN WITH THE GMC!!
FIGHT THE POWER!!
DOWN WITH THE GMC!
DOWN WITH THE JMA
SAVE MEDICINE! THROW THE
IT'S THE YOUNG DOCTORS LEAGUE PROTESTORS.
BUT WHY ARE THEY DEMONSTRATING IN FRONT OF A HOTEL?
THEY HEARD THAT DR. TATSUGAURA WAS HOLDING A PRESS CONFERENCE HERE.
FIGHT THE POWER
DOWN WITH THE JMA!

THEY'RE ANTICIPATING DR. TATSUGAURA'S BID FOR CHAIRMANSHIP OF THE JMA AND THEY'RE TRYING TO INTERFERE BY APPEALING TO THE MEDIA.

MORONS! WE'RE IN A PRETTY PICKLE NOW! THE REPORTERS WILL BE HERE ANY MINUTE!

WE'RE HERE ALREADY.

MR. KONISHI OF THE SOCIETY GAZETTE!

SO GLAD YOU COULD MAKE IT TODAY

QUITE A LIVELY EVENT, EH?

I ATTENDED THEIR ANTI-JMA MEETING THE OTHER DAY. THEY VOTED UNANIMOUSLY TO BRING DOWN THE UPCOMING ELECTION. THEY SEEM QUITE DETERMINED. IT SEEMS THEY INTEND TO APPROACH THE VOTERS ONE BY ONE TO ENCOURAGE THEM TO ABSTAIN.

2F	TATSUGAURA PARTY
B2	NAKAMOTO PARTY
B3	NISHIDA PARTY

THE GAZETTE SEEMS FAIRLY SYMPATHETIC TO THEIR CAUSE...

NO, NO, WE'RE STRICTLY NEUTRAL.

I HEARD AN INTERESTING RUMOR FROM ONE OF THEIR MEMBERS ...

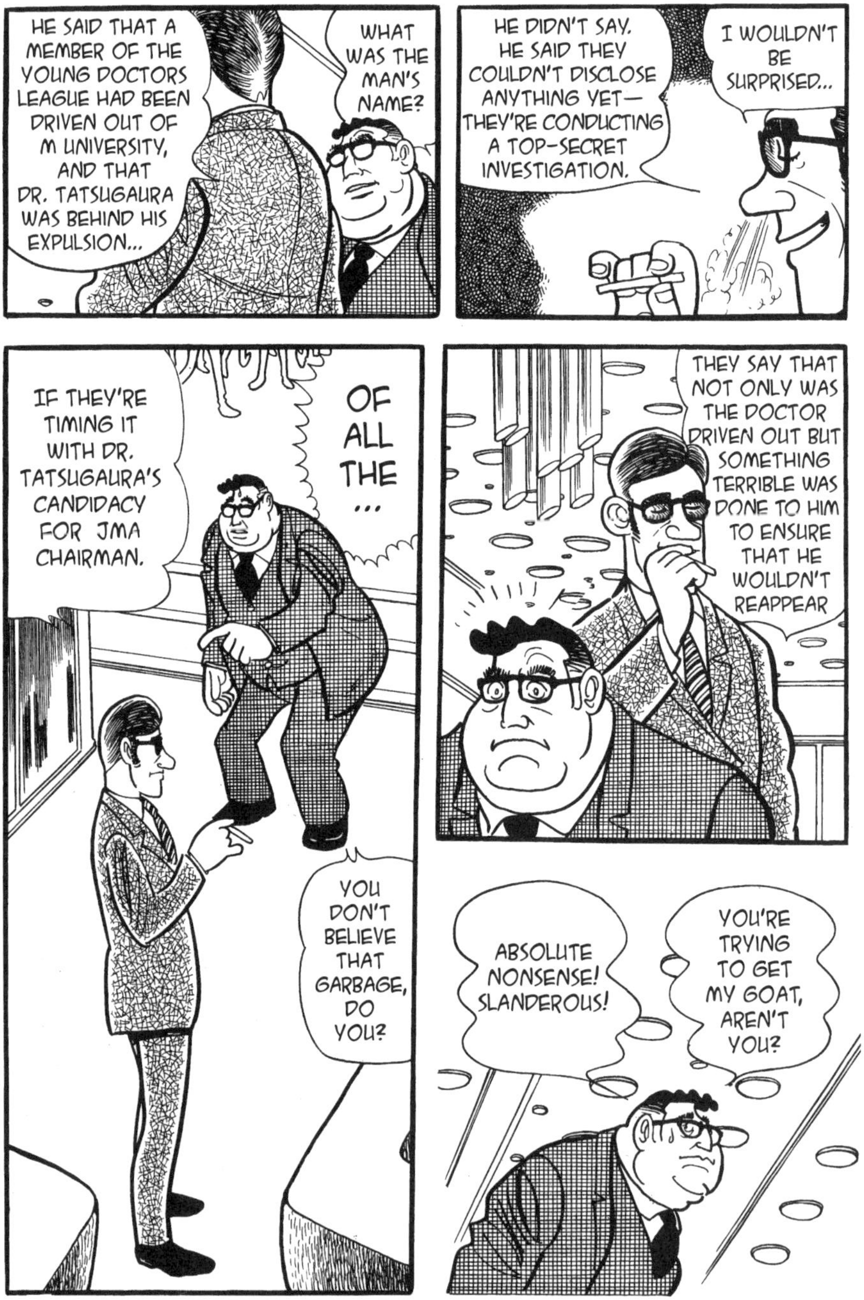
HE SAID THAT A MEMBER OF THE YOUNG DOCTORS LEAGUE HAD BEEN DRIVEN OUT OF M UNIVERSITY, AND THAT DR. TATSUGAURA WAS BEHIND HIS EXPULSION...
WHAT WAS THE MAN'S NAME?
HE DIDN'T SAY. HE SAID THEY COULDN'T DISCLOSE ANYTHING YET— THEY'RE CONDUCTING A TOP-SECRET INVESTIGATION.
I WOULDN'T BE SURPRISED...
IF THEY'RE TIMING IT WITH DR. TATSUGAURA'S CANDIDACY FOR JMA CHAIRMAN.
OF ALL THE ...
THEY SAY THAT NOT ONLY WAS THE DOCTOR DRIVEN OUT BUT SOMETHING TERRIBLE WAS DONE TO HIM TO ENSURE THAT HE WOULDN'T REAPPEAR
YOU DON'T BELIEVE THAT GARBAGE, DO YOU?
ABSOLUTE NONSENSE! SLANDEROUS!
YOU'RE TRYING TO GET MY GOAT, AREN'T YOU?

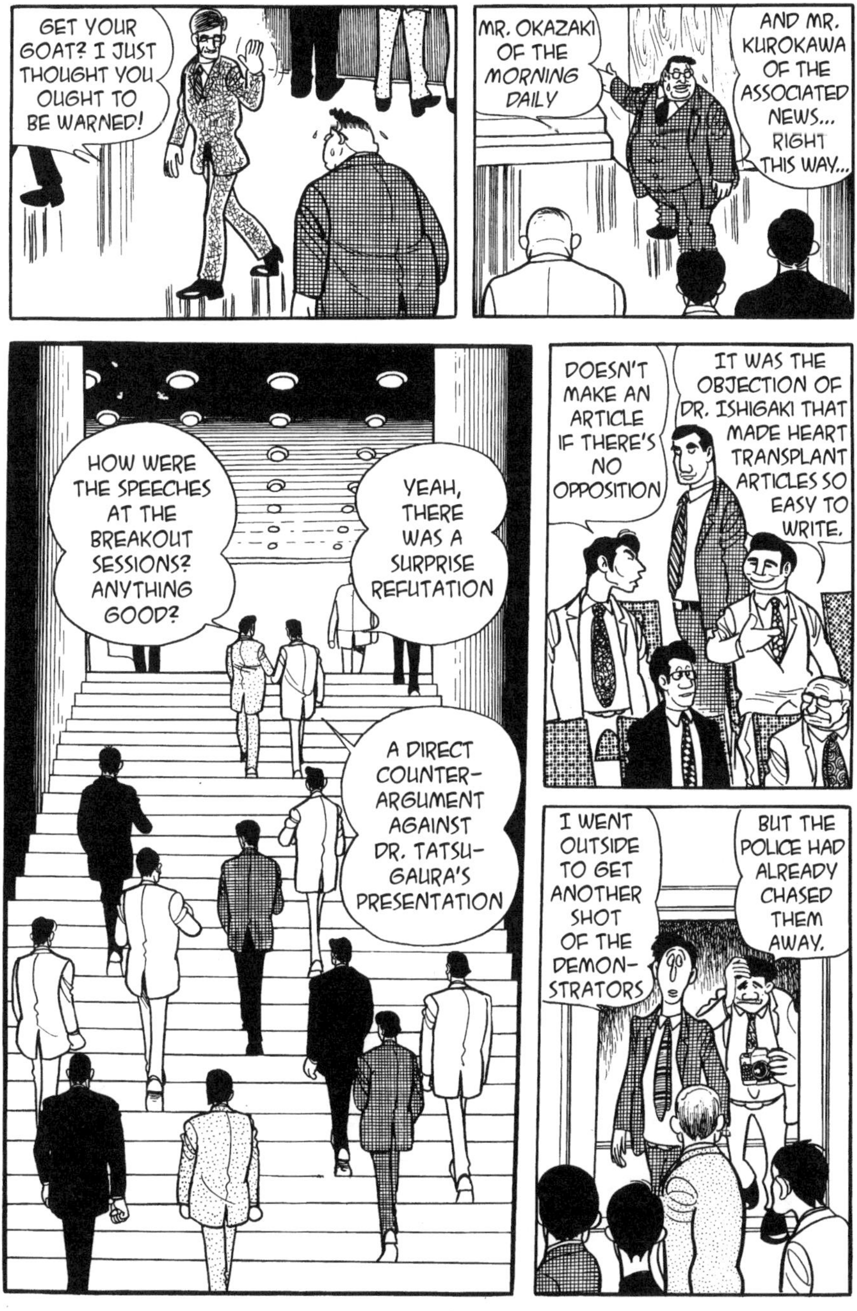
GET YOUR GOAT? I JUST THOUGHT YOU OUGHT TO BE WARNED!
MR. OKAZAKI OF THE MORNING DAILY
AND MR. KUROKAWA OF THE ASSOCIATED NEWS... RIGHT THIS WAY...
HOW WERE THE SPEECHES AT THE BREAKOUT SESSIONS? ANYTHING GOOD?
YEAH, THERE WAS A SURPRISE REFUTATION
A DIRECT COUNTER-ARGUMENT AGAINST DR. TATSU-GAURA'S PRESENTATION
DOESN'T MAKE AN ARTICLE IF THERE'S NO OPPOSITION
IT WAS THE OBJECTION OF DR. ISHIGAKI THAT MADE HEART TRANSPLANT ARTICLES SO EASY TO WRITE.
I WENT OUTSIDE TO GET ANOTHER SHOT OF THE DEMON-STRATORS
BUT THE POLICE HAD ALREADY CHASED THEM AWAY.

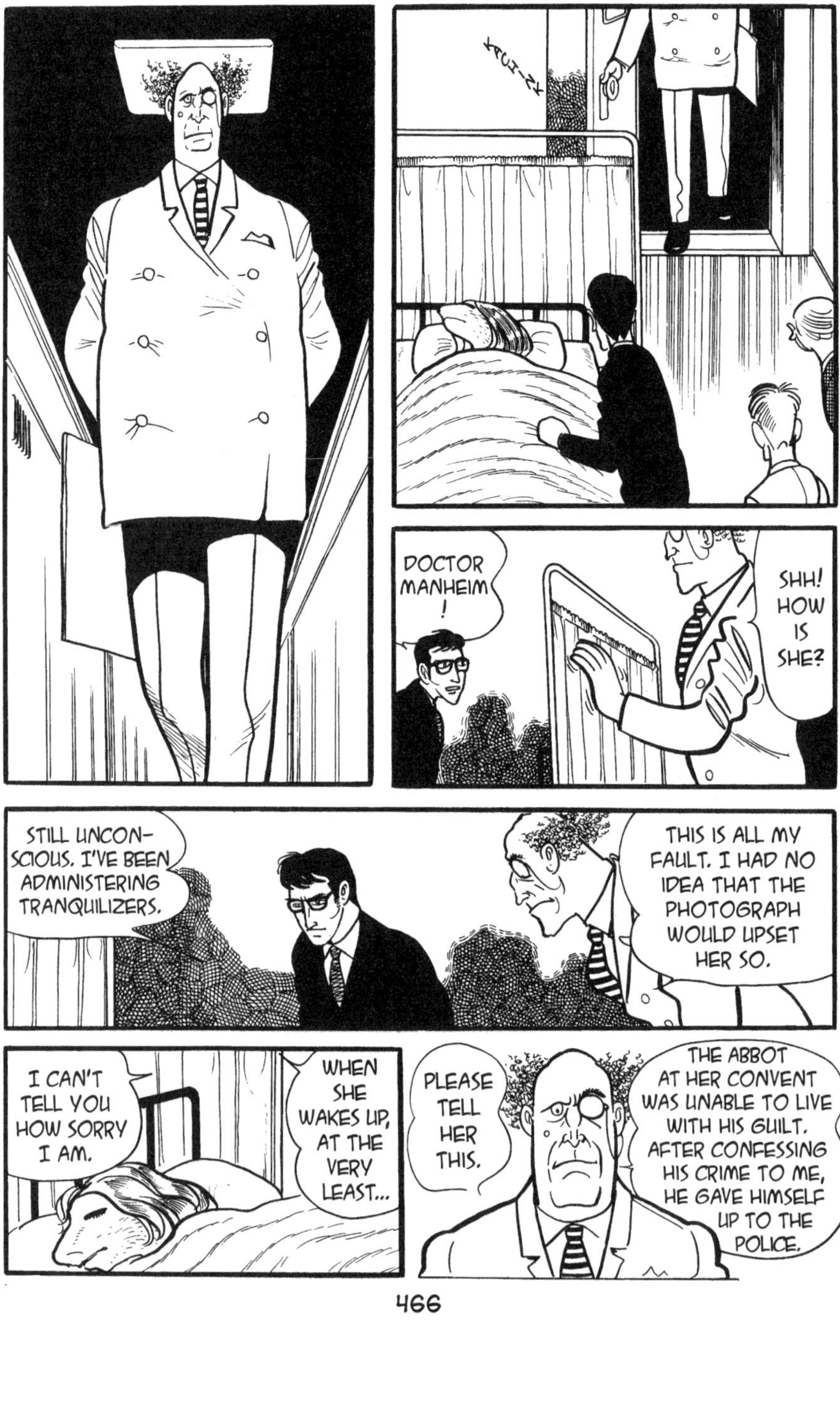
DOCTOR MANHEIM!
SHH! HOW IS SHE?
STILL UNCON-SCIOUS. I'VE BEEN ADMINISTERING TRANQUILIZERS.
THIS IS ALL MY FAULT. I HAD NO IDEA THAT THE PHOTOGRAPH WOULD UPSET HER SO.
I CAN'T TELL YOU HOW SORRY I AM.
WHEN SHE WAKES UP, AT THE VERY LEAST...
PLEASE TELL HER THIS.
THE ABBOT AT HER CONVENT WAS UNABLE TO LIVE WITH HIS GUILT. AFTER CONFESSING HIS CRIME TO ME, HE GAVE HIMSELF UP TO THE POLICE.

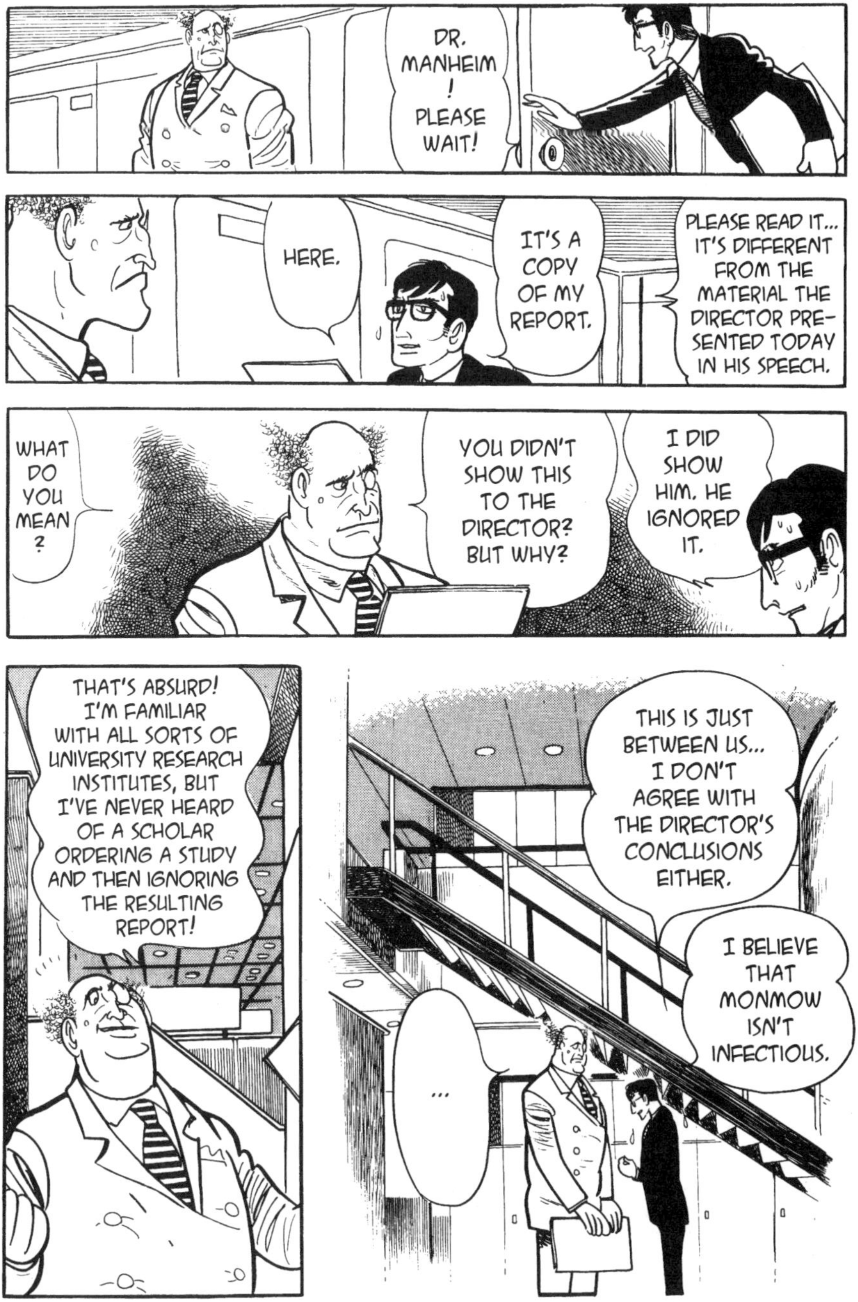

DR. MANHEIM! PLEASE WAIT!
HERE.
IT'S A COPY OF MY REPORT.
PLEASE READ IT... IT'S DIFFERENT FROM THE MATERIAL THE DIRECTOR PRESENTED TODAY IN HIS SPEECH.
WHAT DO YOU MEAN?
YOU DIDN'T SHOW THIS TO THE DIRECTOR? BUT WHY?
I DID SHOW HIM. HE IGNORED IT.
THAT'S ABSURD! I'M FAMILIAR WITH ALL SORTS OF UNIVERSITY RESEARCH INSTITUTES, BUT I'VE NEVER HEARD OF A SCHOLAR ORDERING A STUDY AND THEN IGNORING THE RESULTING REPORT!
THIS IS JUST BETWEEN US... I DON'T AGREE WITH THE DIRECTOR'S CONCLUSIONS EITHER.
I BELIEVE THAT MONMOW ISN'T INFECTIOUS.
...

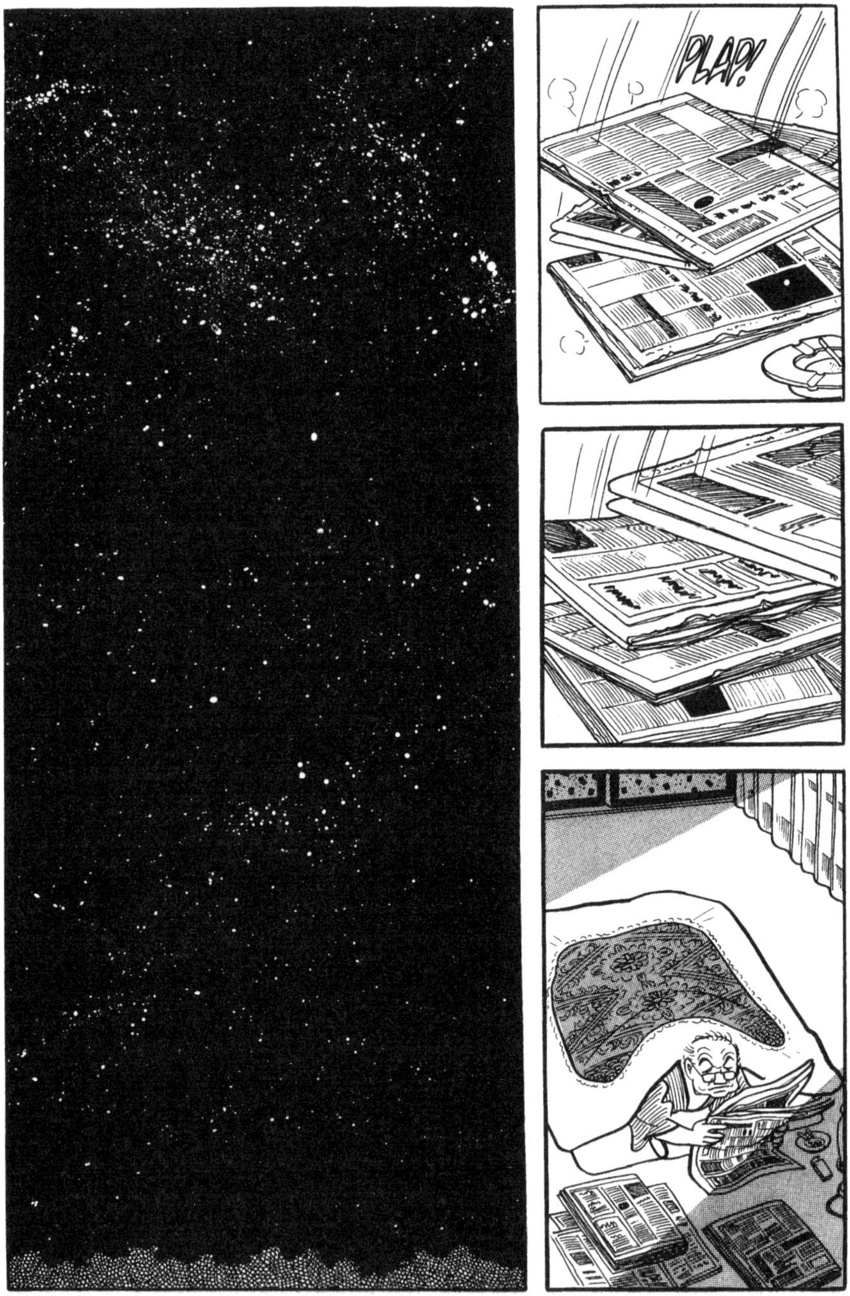

PLAP!

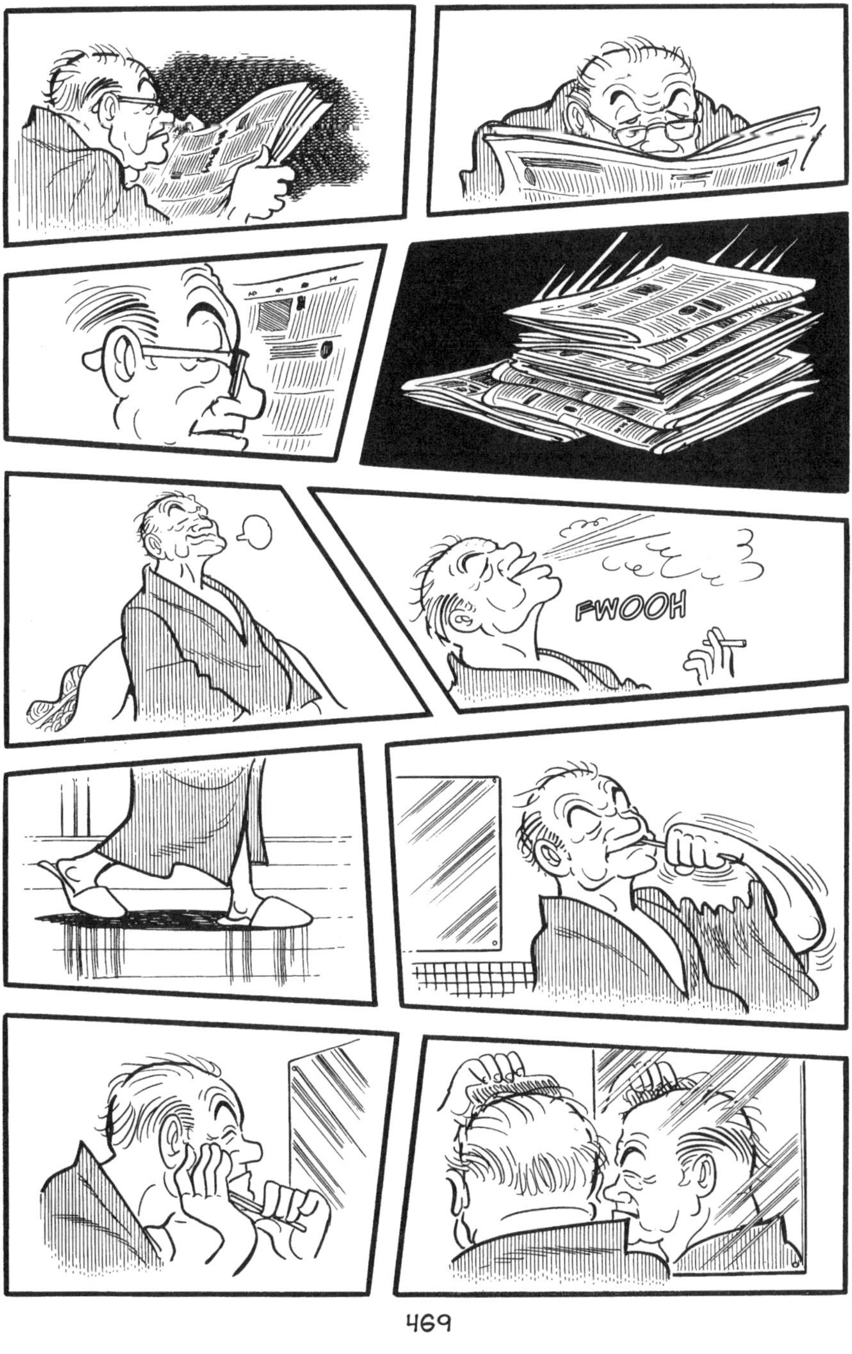
FWOOH

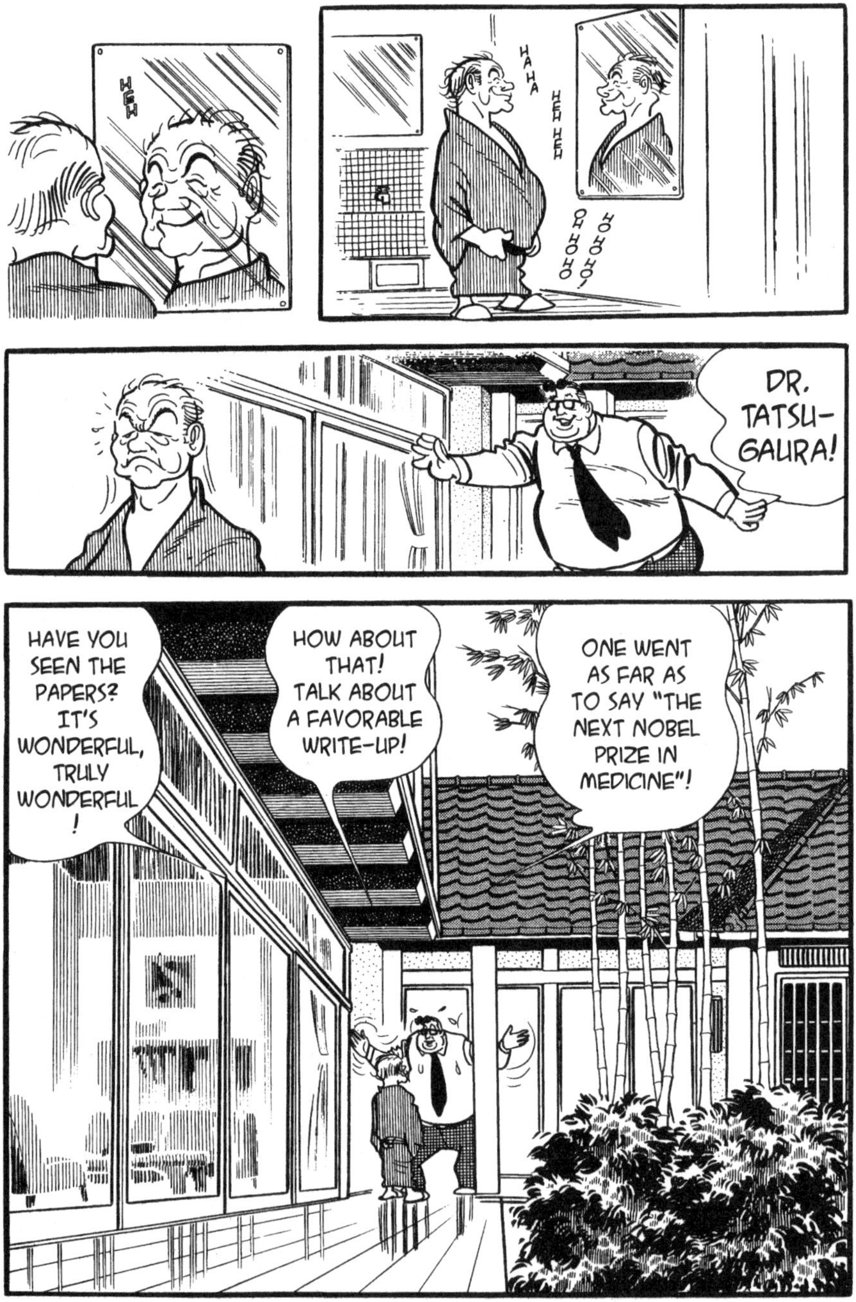
HEH
HA HA
HEH HEH
OH HO HO
HO HO HO!
DR. TATSU-GAURA!
HAVE YOU SEEN THE PAPERS? IT'S WONDERFUL, TRULY WONDERFUL!
HOW ABOUT THAT! TALK ABOUT A FAVORABLE WRITE-UP!
ONE WENT AS FAR AS TO SAY "THE NEXT NOBEL PRIZE IN MEDICINE"!

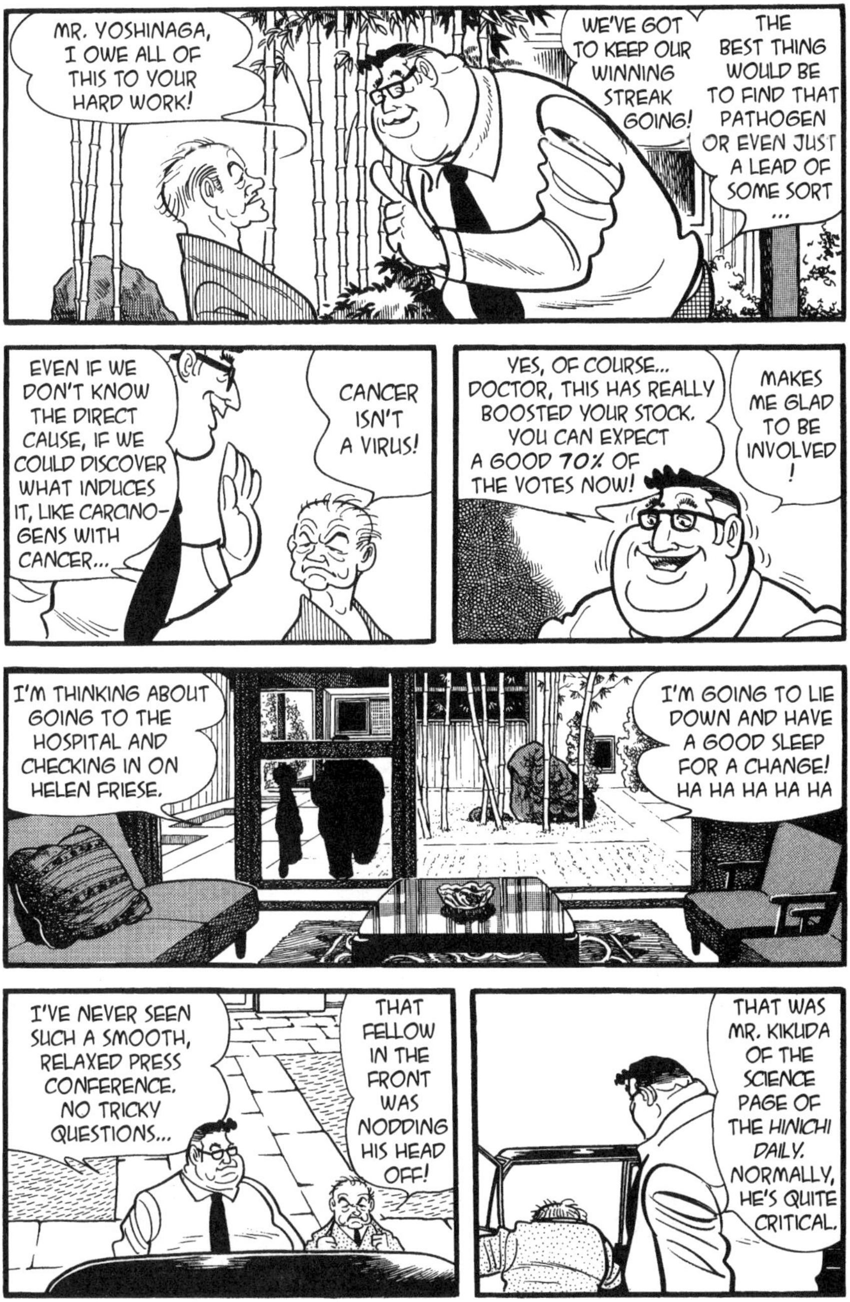
MR. YOSHINAGA, I OWE ALL OF THIS TO YOUR HARD WORK!
WE'VE GOT TO KEEP OUR WINNING STREAK GOING!
THE BEST THING WOULD BE TO FIND THAT PATHOGEN OR EVEN JUST A LEAD OF SOME SORT ...
EVEN IF WE DON'T KNOW THE DIRECT CAUSE, IF WE COULD DISCOVER WHAT INDUCES IT, LIKE CARCINOGENS WITH CANCER...
CANCER ISN'T A VIRUS!
YES, OF COURSE... DOCTOR, THIS HAS REALLY BOOSTED YOUR STOCK. YOU CAN EXPECT A GOOD 70% OF THE VOTES NOW!
MAKES ME GLAD TO BE INVOLVED!
I'M THINKING ABOUT GOING TO THE HOSPITAL AND CHECKING IN ON HELEN FRIESE.
I'M GOING TO LIE DOWN AND HAVE A GOOD SLEEP FOR A CHANGE! HA HA HA HA HA
I'VE NEVER SEEN SUCH A SMOOTH, RELAXED PRESS CONFERENCE. NO TRICKY QUESTIONS...
THAT FELLOW IN THE FRONT WAS NODDING HIS HEAD OFF!
THAT WAS MR. KIKUDA OF THE SCIENCE PAGE OF THE HINICHI DAILY. NORMALLY, HE'S QUITE CRITICAL.

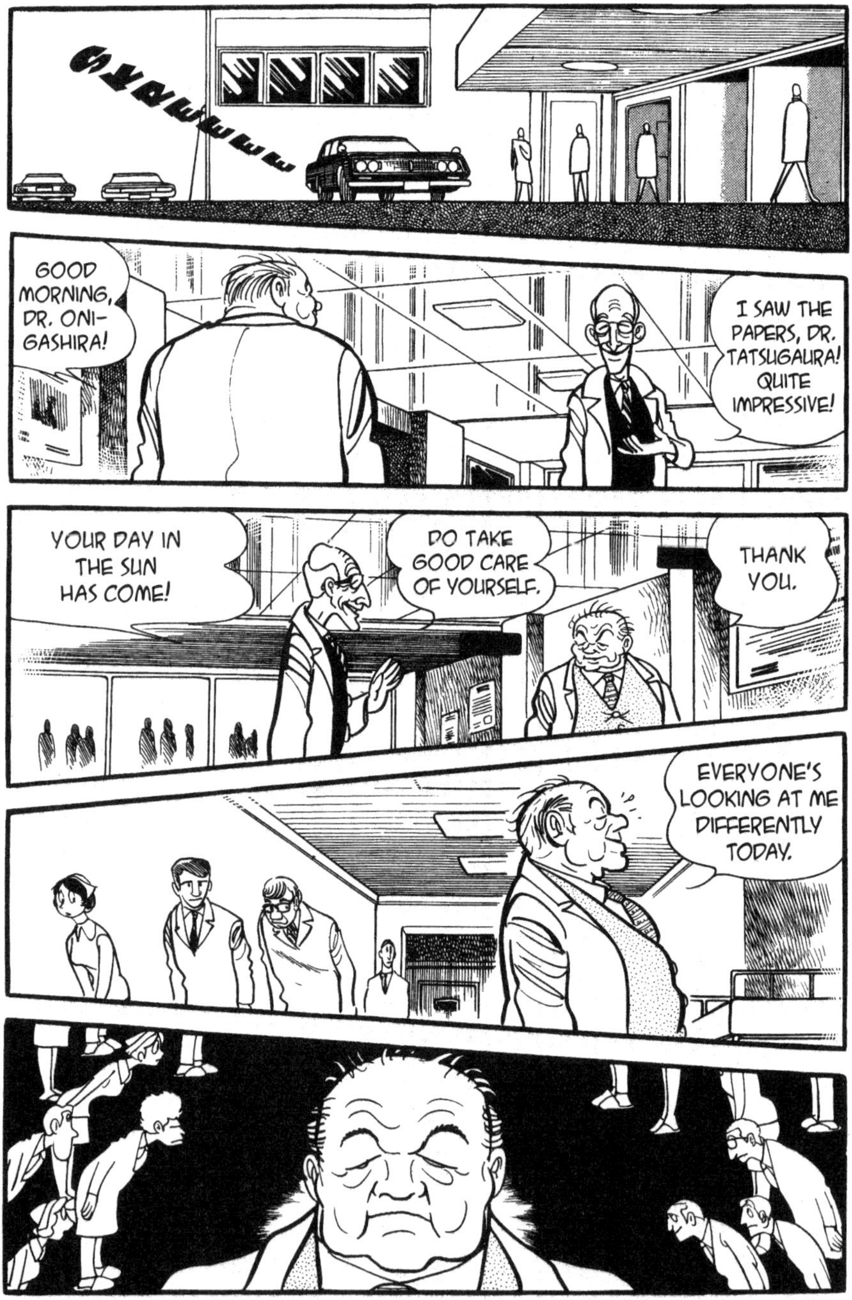
GOOD MORNING, DR. ONI-GASHIRA!
I SAW THE PAPERS, DR. TATSUGAURA! QUITE IMPRESSIVE!
YOUR DAY IN THE SUN HAS COME!
DO TAKE GOOD CARE OF YOURSELF.
THANK YOU.
EVERYONE'S LOOKING AT ME DIFFERENTLY TODAY.

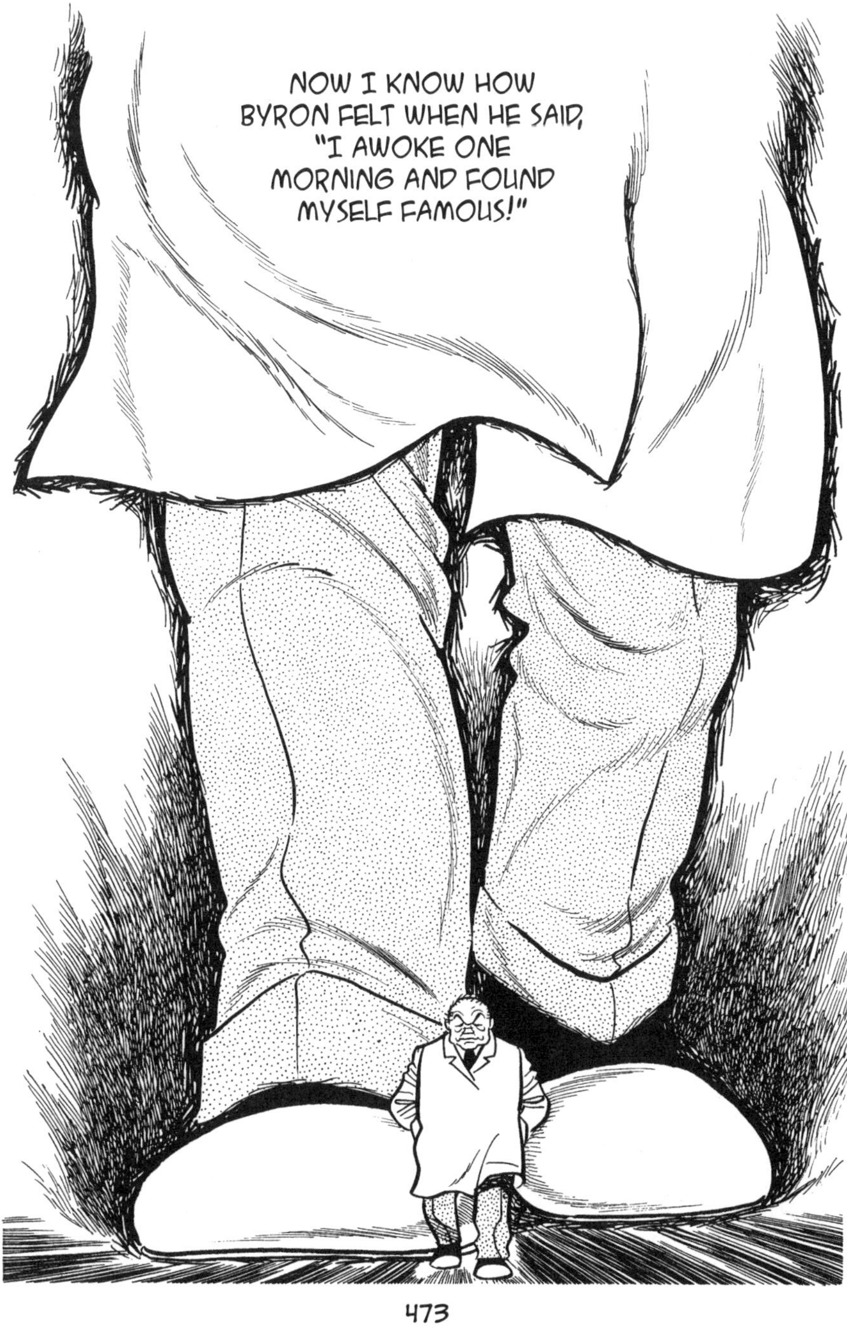
NOW I KNOW HOW BYRON FELT WHEN HE SAID, "I AWOKE ONE MORNING AND FOUND MYSELF FAMOUS!"

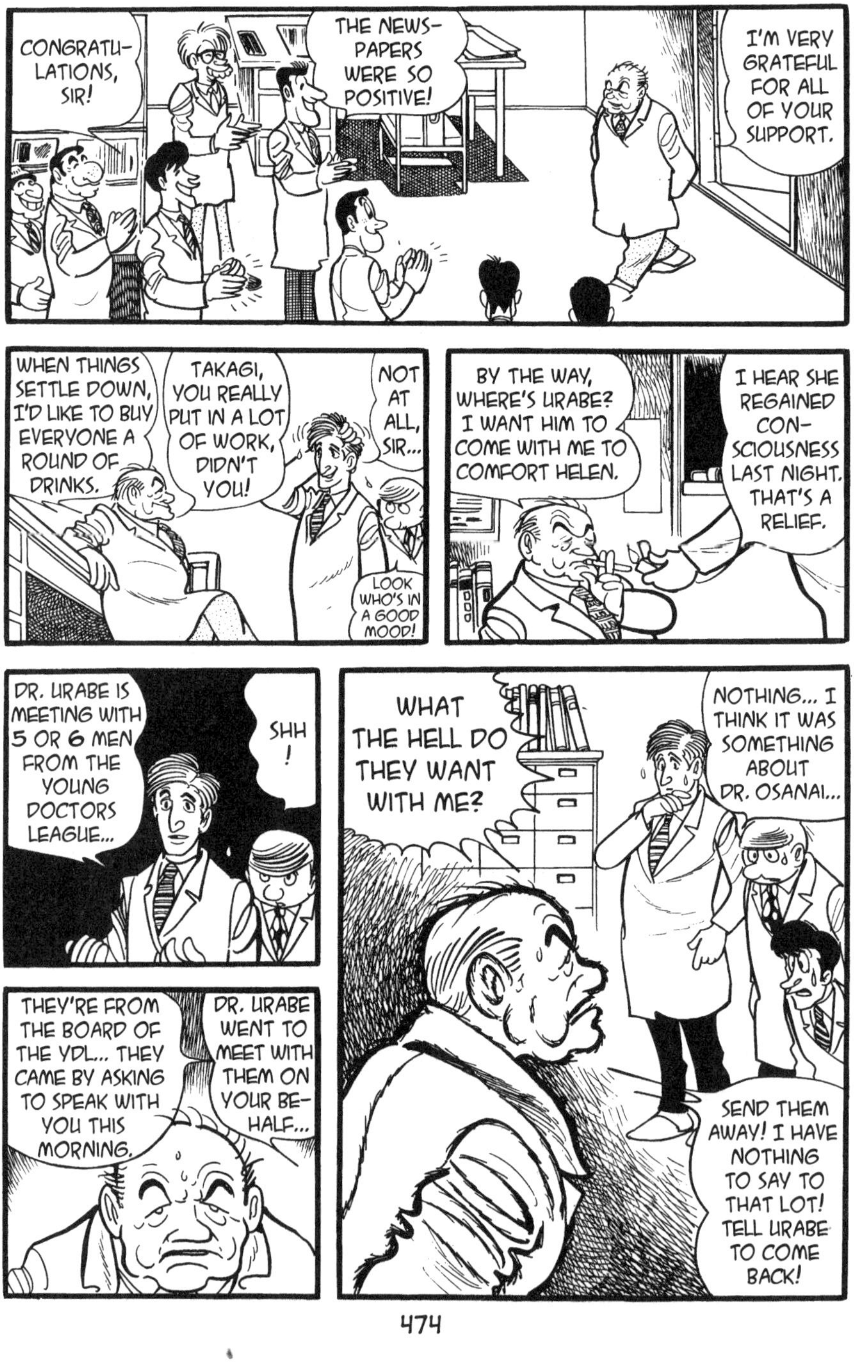

CONGRATULATIONS, SIR!
THE NEWSPAPERS WERE SO POSITIVE!
I'M VERY GRATEFUL FOR ALL OF YOUR SUPPORT.
WHEN THINGS SETTLE DOWN, I'D LIKE TO BUY EVERYONE A ROUND OF DRINKS.
TAKAGI, YOU REALLY PUT IN A LOT OF WORK, DIDN'T YOU!
NOT AT ALL, SIR...
LOOK WHO'S IN A GOOD MOOD!
BY THE WAY, WHERE'S URABE? I WANT HIM TO COME WITH ME TO COMFORT HELEN.
I HEAR SHE REGAINED CONSCIOUSNESS LAST NIGHT. THAT'S A RELIEF.
DR. URABE IS MEETING WITH 5 OR 6 MEN FROM THE YOUNG DOCTORS LEAGUE...
SHH!
THEY'RE FROM THE BOARD OF THE YDL... THEY CAME BY ASKING TO SPEAK WITH YOU THIS MORNING.
DR. URABE WENT TO MEET WITH THEM ON YOUR BEHALF...
WHAT THE HELL DO THEY WANT WITH ME?
NOTHING... I THINK IT WAS SOMETHING ABOUT DR. OSANAI...
SEND THEM AWAY! I HAVE NOTHING TO SAY TO THAT LOT! TELL URABE TO COME BACK!

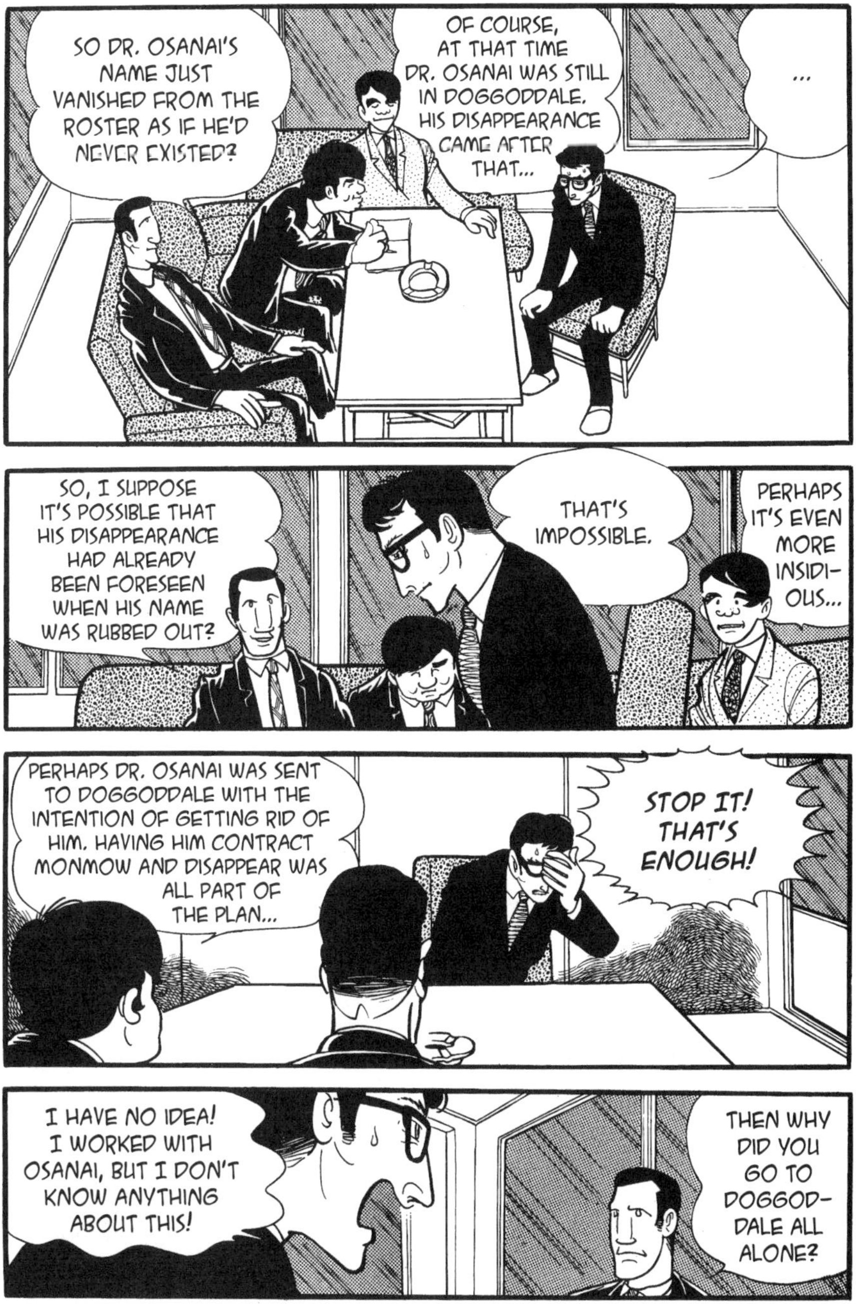
SO DR. OSANAI'S NAME JUST VANISHED FROM THE ROSTER AS IF HE'D NEVER EXISTED?
OF COURSE, AT THAT TIME DR. OSANAI WAS STILL IN DOGGODDALE. HIS DISAPPEARANCE CAME AFTER THAT...
...
SO, I SUPPOSE IT'S POSSIBLE THAT HIS DISAPPEARANCE HAD ALREADY BEEN FORESEEN WHEN HIS NAME WAS RUBBED OUT?
THAT'S IMPOSSIBLE.
PERHAPS IT'S EVEN MORE INSIDI-OUS...
PERHAPS DR. OSANAI WAS SENT TO DOGGODDALE WITH THE INTENTION OF GETTING RID OF HIM. HAVING HIM CONTRACT MONMOW AND DISAPPEAR WAS ALL PART OF THE PLAN...
STOP IT! THAT'S ENOUGH!
I HAVE NO IDEA! I WORKED WITH OSANAI, BUT I DON'T KNOW ANYTHING ABOUT THIS!
THEN WHY DID YOU GO TO DOGGOD-DALE ALL ALONE?

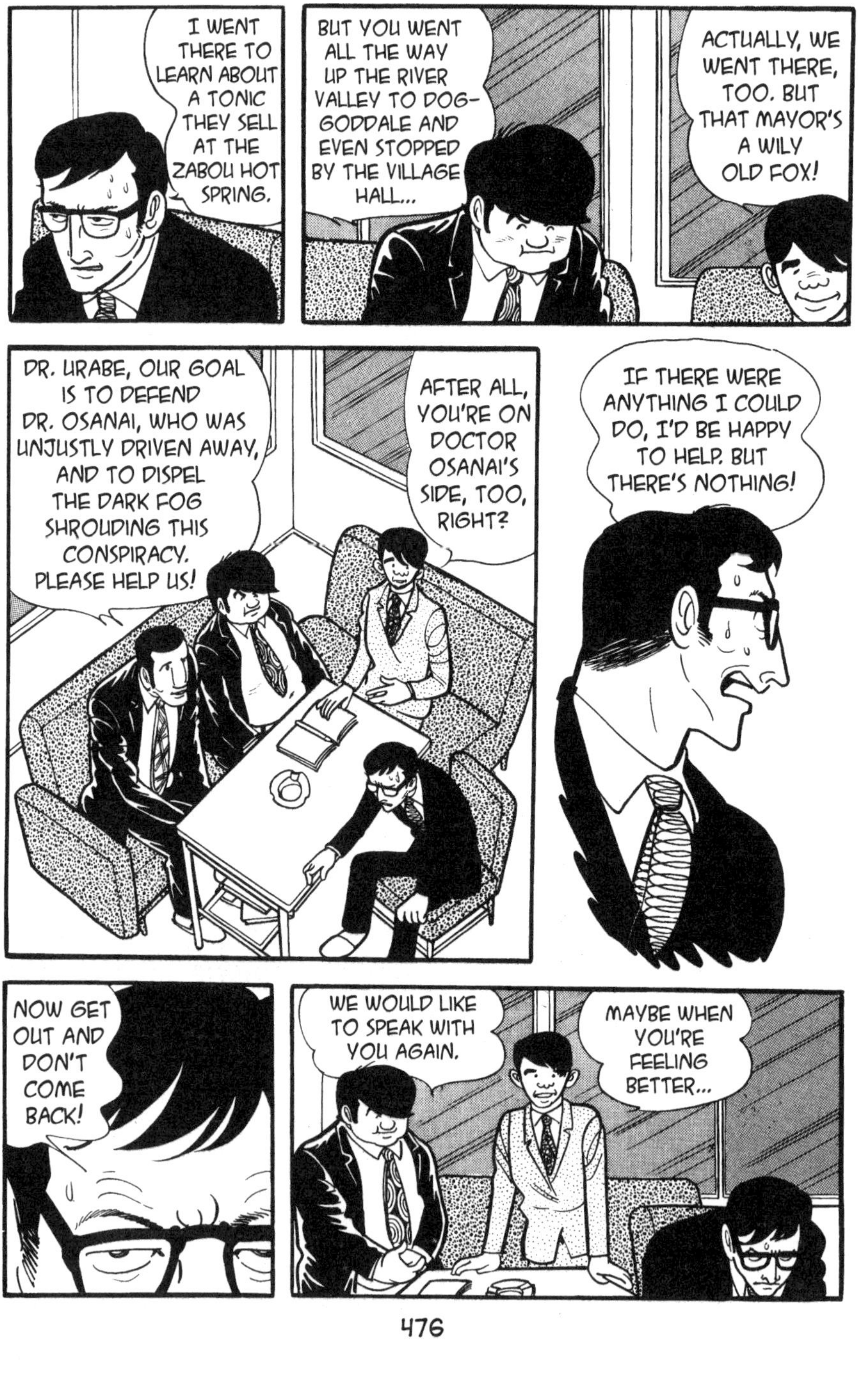
I WENT THERE TO LEARN ABOUT A TONIC THEY SELL AT THE ZABOU HOT SPRING.
BUT YOU WENT ALL THE WAY UP THE RIVER VALLEY TO DOG-GODDALE AND EVEN STOPPED BY THE VILLAGE HALL...
ACTUALLY, WE WENT THERE, TOO. BUT THAT MAYOR'S A WILY OLD FOX!
DR. URABE, OUR GOAL IS TO DEFEND DR. OSANAI, WHO WAS UNJUSTLY DRIVEN AWAY, AND TO DISPEL THE DARK FOG SHROUDING THIS CONSPIRACY. PLEASE HELP US!
AFTER ALL, YOU'RE ON DOCTOR OSANAI'S SIDE, TOO, RIGHT?
IF THERE WERE ANYTHING I COULD DO, I'D BE HAPPY TO HELP. BUT THERE'S NOTHING!
NOW GET OUT AND DON'T COME BACK!
WE WOULD LIKE TO SPEAK WITH YOU AGAIN.
MAYBE WHEN YOU'RE FEELING BETTER...

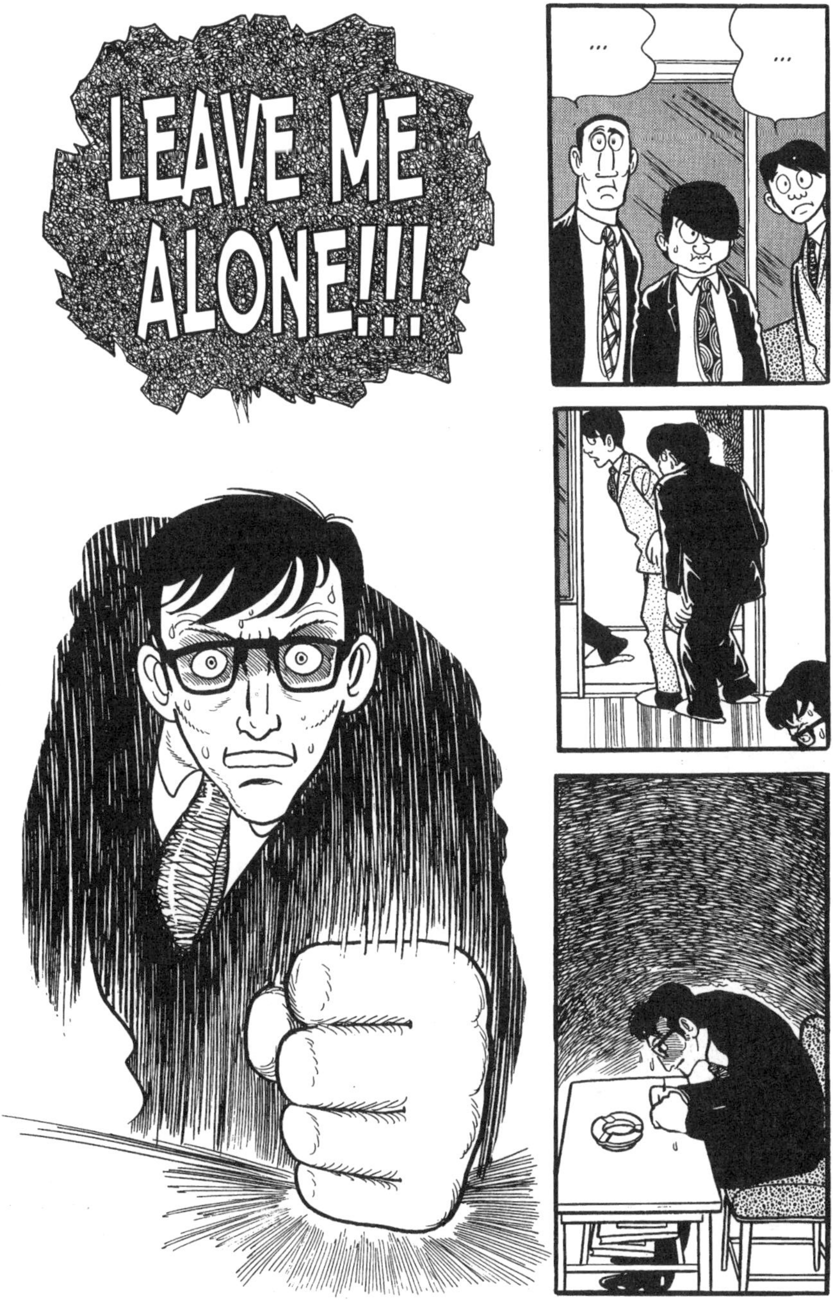
LEAVE ME ALONE!!!
...
...

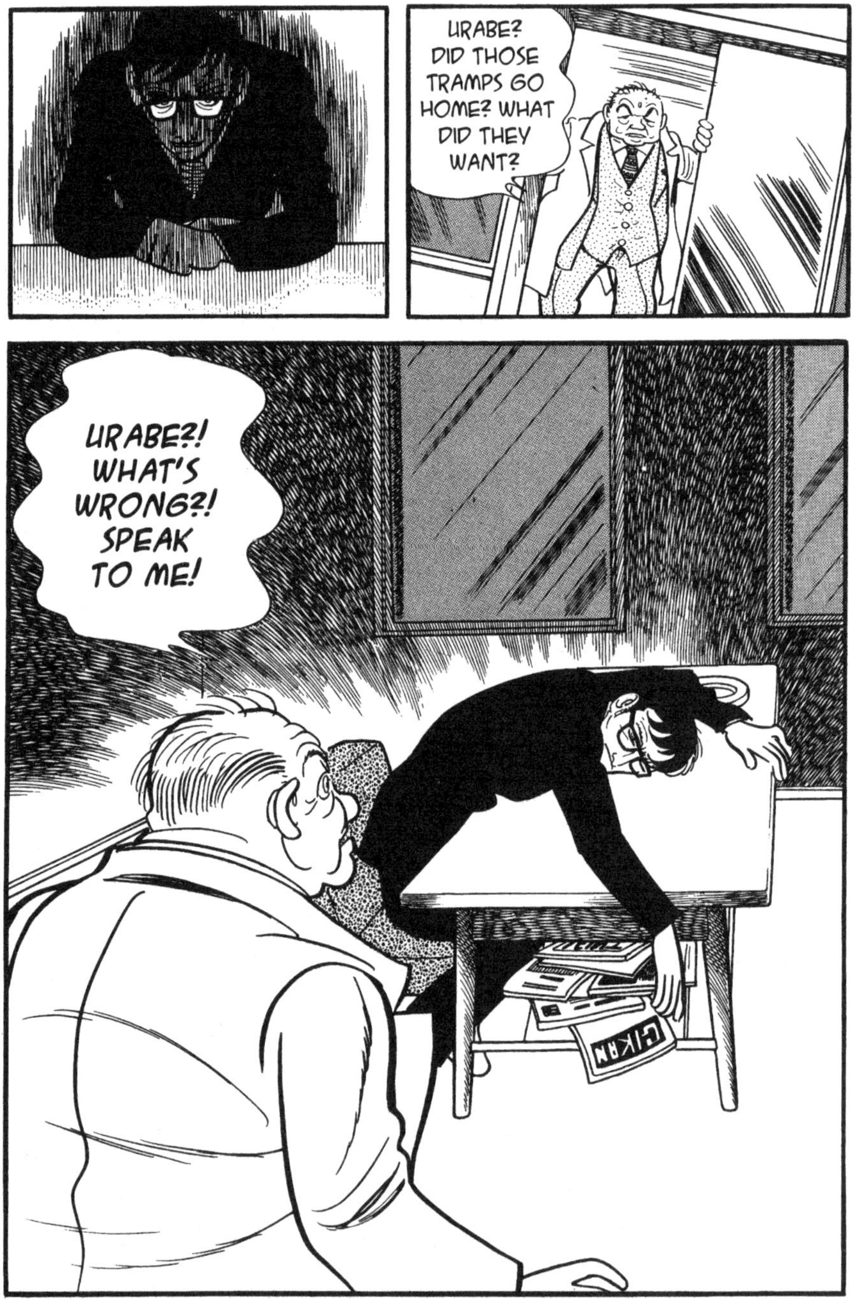
URABE? DID THOSE TRAMPS GO HOME? WHAT DID THEY WANT?
URABE?! WHAT'S WRONG?! SPEAK TO ME!

TO BE CONTINUED
IN
PART TWO

ABOUT THE AUTHOR

Osamu Tezuka (1928-1989) is the godfather of Japanese manga comics. He originally intended to become a doctor and earned his degree before turning to what was still then considered a frivolous medium. With his sweeping vision, deftly intertwined plots, and inde fatigable commitment to human dignity, Tezuka elevated manga to an art form.